PRECISION MEDICINE AND THE REINVENTION OF HUMAN DISEASE

PRECISION MEDICINE AND THE REINVENTION OF HUMAN DISEASE

Jules J. Berman

ELSEVIER

ACADEMIC PRESS
An imprint of Elsevier

Academic Press is an imprint of Elsevier
125 London Wall, London EC2Y 5AS, United Kingdom
525 B Street, Suite 1800, San Diego, CA 92101-4495, United States
50 Hampshire Street, 5th Floor, Cambridge, MA 02139, United States
The Boulevard, Langford Lane, Kidlington, Oxford OX5 1GB, United Kingdom

Notices
Knowledge and best practice in this field are constantly changing. As new research and experience broaden
our understanding, changes in research methods, professional practices, or medical treatment may become necessary.

Practitioners and researchers must always rely on their own experience and knowledge in evaluating and using
any information, methods, compounds, or experiments described herein. In using such information or methods
they should be mindful of their own safety and the safety of others, including parties for whom they have a
professional responsibility.

To the fullest extent of the law, neither the Publisher nor the authors, contributors, or editors, assume any liability
for any injury and/or damage to persons or property as a matter of products liability, negligence or otherwise, or
from any use or operation of any methods, products, instructions, or ideas contained in the material herein.

Library of Congress Cataloging-in-Publication Data
A catalog record for this book is available from the Library of Congress

British Library Cataloguing-in-Publication Data
A catalogue record for this book is available from the British Library

ISBN 978-0-12-814393-3

For information on all Academic Press publications
visit our website at https://www.elsevier.com/books-and-journals

Working together
to grow libraries in
developing countries

www.elsevier.com • www.bookaid.org

Publisher: John Fedor
Acquisition Editor: Rafael Teixeira
Editorial Project Manager: Kathy Padilla
Production Project Manager: Punithavathy Govindaradjane
Cover Designer: Victoria Pearson

Typeset by SPi Global, India

Other Books by Jules J. Berman

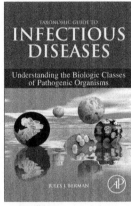

Taxonomic Guide to Infectious Diseases
Understanding the Biologic Classes of
Pathogenic Organisms (2012)
9780124158955

Principles of Big Data
Preparing, Sharing, and Analyzing
Complex Information (2013)
9780124045767

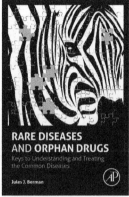

Rare Diseases and Orphan Drugs
Keys to Understanding and Treating
the Common Diseases (2014)
9780124199880

Repurposing Legacy Data
Innovative Case Studies (2015)
9780128028827

Data Simplification
Taming Information with Open
Source Tools (2016)
9780128037812

Principles and Practice of Big Data
Preparing, Sharing, and Analyzing
Complex Information, Second Edition (2018)
9780128156094

Dedication

To Former President Barack Obama, who launched the U.S. Precision Medicine Initiative

Contents

7. Reinventing Diagnosis

8. Precision Data

9. The Alternate Futures of Precision Medicine

About the Author

Jules Berman holds two bachelor of science degrees from MIT (Mathematics, and Earth and Planetary Sciences), a PhD from Temple University, and an MD, from the University of Miami. He was a graduate student researcher in the Fels Cancer Research Institute, at Temple University, and at the American Health Foundation in Valhalla, New York. His postdoctoral studies were completed at the US National Institutes of Health, and his residency was completed at the George Washington University Medical Center in Washington, DC. Dr. Berman served as Chief of Anatomic Pathology, Surgical Pathology, and Cytopathology at the Veterans Administration Medical Center in Baltimore, Maryland, where he held joint appointments at the University of Maryland Medical Center and at the Johns Hopkins Medical Institutions. In 1998, he transferred to the US National Institutes of Health, as a Medical Officer, and as the Program Director for Pathology Informatics in the Cancer Diagnosis Program at the National Cancer Institute. Dr. Berman is a past president of the Association for Pathology Informatics, and the 2011 recipient of the association's Lifetime Achievement Award. He has first-authored over 100 scientific publications and has written more than a dozen books in the areas of data science and disease biology. Several of his most recent titles, published by Elsevier, include:

Taxonomic Guide to Infectious Diseases: Understanding the Biologic Classes of Pathogenic Organisms (2012)

Principles of Big Data: Preparing, Sharing, and Analyzing Complex Information (2013)

Rare Diseases and Orphan Drugs: Keys to Understanding and Treating the Common Diseases (2014)

Repurposing Legacy Data: Innovative Case Studies (2015)

Data Simplification: Taming Information with Open Source Tools (2016)

Principles and Practice of Big Data: Preparing, Sharing, and Analyzing Complex Information, Second Edition (2018)

Preface

When you get to a fork in the road, take it.
Yogi Berra

The past few decades have produced dozens of new terms that may have no meaning 20 years from now: translational medicine, bench-to-bedside research, postgenomics medicine, theragnostics, personalized medicine, pharmacogenomics, next-generation sequencing, metagenomics, drugome, metabolome, big data, deep analytics, actionable pathologic targets, intelligent informatics [1–6].

Is Precision Medicine just another soon-to-be-forgotten anecdote in the trail of abandoned medical nomenclature? Undoubtedly so. The name "Precision Medicine" drips with arrogance, implying that every other medical discipline is imprecise and shabby. Regardless, the exactness promised by this new brand of medicine is exhilarating.

No matter what you call it, something has happened in the past two decades that has changed the way that modern biomedical scientist thinks about diseases. Because the changes in our perceptions have happened slowly, few of us have really taken notice of what it all means. The purpose of this book is to show how advances in the field of Precision Medicine will forever change the way we understand and treat disease. Specifically, these advances are:

– Diseases develop in steps. Modern methodology has enabled us to dissect the biological events and metabolic pathways that ultimately lead to the expression of disease. We can no longer think in terms of the "cause" of a disease, because most diseases have multiple contributory causes, that act over time. [Glossary Pathway]

– Because disease development requires the successful completion of multiple, sequential steps, and because we can now observe some of these steps, Precision Medicine has given us multiple targets that we can attack, with the expectation of preventing diseases from developing, delaying the development of disease, or treating diseases that are driven by identifiable pathways.

– Because different paths of development may lead to the same set of clinical findings, diseases can be subtyped into classes according to the specific pathways that drive their biology. Hence, treatment can be precisely targeted to subtypes of diseases that were formerly indistinguishable from one another.

– Because diseases that appear to be unrelated might share biological pathways that can be successfully targeted by new classes of drugs, we can now prevent or treat a variety of diseases, using a drug that was specifically developed for one rare subtype of disease.

Precision Medicine and the Reinvention of Human Disease explains how we have come to believe that these four advances in Precision Medicine are true, and how these advances are impacting the practice of medicine. Aside from this, there is one

xiii

additional goal that this book attempts to fulfill. This relates to dispelling the myth that we are entering a new era of medicine in which each individual will receive unique treatment, determined by the sequence of his or her genome. This widely promulgated notion is simply ridiculous. There is no practical way to develop a treatment, test the treatment for safety, and titrate the correct dose, for one person. The terms "Precision Medicine" and "Personalized Medicine" have given us the false impression that medical science is moving away from off-the-rack remedies and is seeking treatments tailored to the individual. In actuality, science has always been about seeking generalization. When Isaac Newton watched an apple drop, he was not working on a new Law of Falling Apples. He was trying to understand the general laws of gravity and motion that applied to every object in the universe. When Charles Darwin spent 8 years studying barnacles, he was not trying to build a display collection of handsome barnacles for the national museum. He was developing a general theory of evolution that would apply to every living organism on earth. Likewise, when we study a specific pathway that is operative in a small percentage of cases of a rare tumor, accounting for perhaps a dozen patients worldwide, we expect that our findings will have general application to a wide variety of conditions. Using many examples, appearing through every chapter of this book, we will see how Precision Medicine is providing us with opportunities to find general treatments that will be effective against multiple diseases whose relationships to one another were heretofore unsuspected. [Glossary Genome, Science, Generalization, Cause, Relationship]

Who should read this book? Anyone wishing to prepare for the coming revolution in medicine should give this book a try. Please do not be overwhelmed by the arcane terms encountered through the text. No one is expected to be familiar with the rare diseases and obscure details revealed in these chapters. The only purpose of including descriptions of diseases, and genes, and techniques is to validate the truth and relevance of a relatively small set of concepts that are introduced in the early chapters, and re-examined in later chapters. If you concentrate on the concepts that animate each section of the book, you will understand that the specific examples are merely illustrative, and need not be committed to memory.

Lastly, readers need to know that this book is a single-author literary work. Please take a moment and ask yourself to name some of the books that shaped your own intellectual development. Were these books compilations of chapters written by dozens or even hundreds of contributors? Or were these books written by solitary authors? It is nearly impossible for a multiauthor textbook to forge an intimate connection with the reader. Contrariwise, a thoughtfully written single author book connects the mind of the author to the mind of the reader, much like a Vulcan mind-meld. Of course, no book written by a single author can hope to match the level of authority provided by a multiauthor textbook. Perhaps readers will overlook the limitations of the author, and will appreciate the pleasures of reading a serious literary work, on a subject of great scientific interest.

Glossary

Cause The event or the condition that is responsible for a specific result. The argument is made in this book that diseases develop in a sequence of biological steps, over time, involving multiple cellular pathways. Hence, there are many opportunities to contribute to the disease process, and there is no special reason to think in terms of "the cause" of a disease.

Generalization Generalization is the process of extending relationships from individual objects to classes of objects. For example, Darwin's observations on specific animals could be generalized to yield the theory of evolution, thus explaining the development of all terrestrial organisms. Science would be of little value if observed relationships among individual objects could not be generalized to classes of objects.

Genome The collected assortment of an organism's hereditary information, encoded as DNA. For humans, this would mean the set of chromosomes found in a somatic cell, plus the DNA from one of the cell's mitochondria. In practice, when an organism's genome is sequenced, a haploid set of chromosomes is examined, and the mitochondrial DNA is omitted.

Pathway According to traditional thinking, a pathway is a sequence of biochemical reactions, involving a specific set of enzymes and substrates that produce a chemical product. The classic pathway was the Krebs cycle. It was common for students to be required to calculate the output of the cycle (in moles of ATP) based on stoichiometric equations employing known amounts of substrate. As we have learned more and more about cellular biology, the term "pathway" has acquired a broader and more complex meaning. It can apply to activities (not just chemical products). One pathway may intersect or subsume other pathways. Furthermore, a pathway may not be constrained to an anatomically sequestered area of the cell, and the activity of a pathway may change from cell type to cell type or may change within one cell depending on the cell's physiologic status. Still, the term "pathway" is a convenient conceptual device to organize classes of molecules that interact with a generally defined set of partner molecules to produce a somewhat consistent range of biological actions. Throughout this book, the term pathway will apply to cellular actions produced by groups of interacting molecules. In most cases, the pathways are not named; the existence of the pathway is inferred whenever a complex cellular activity occurs (e.g., replication of DNA, posttranslational modifications of a protein, synthesis of a molecule, DNA repair, apoptosis).

Relationship Two objects are related to one another when there is some fundamental or defining principle that applies to both objects and which, ideally, helps us to better understand the nature of the both objects. For example, when we say that force is mass times acceleration, we are describing a relationship between force and an accelerating mass. The equivalence does not tell us exactly what force is, and it does not tell us exactly what an accelerating mass is, but it describes how they relate to one another, and it brings us a little closer to an understanding of their fundamental natures. Scientists often confuse the concepts of "relationship" and "similarity." To better understand how these terms differ, consider the following. When you look up at the clouds, and you begin to see the shape of a lion. The cloud has a tail, like a lion's tail, and a fluffy head, like a lion's mane. With a little imagination, the mouth of the lion seems to roar down from the sky. You have succeeded in finding similarities between the cloud and a lion. When you look at a cloud and you imagine a tea kettle producing a head of steam, and you recognize that the physical forces that create a cloud from the ocean's water vapor and the physical forces that produce steam from the water in a heated kettle are the same, then you have found a relationship. Finding relationships is really what science is all about; it's how we make some sense of reality. Finding similarities is an esthetic joy, but it is not science.

Science Of course, there are many different definitions of science, and inquisitive students should be encouraged to find a conceptualization of science that suits their own intellectual development. For me, science is all about finding general relationships among objects. In the so-called physical sciences, the most important relationships are expressed as mathematical equations (e.g., the relationship between force, mass and acceleration; the relationship between voltage, current, and resistance). In the so-called natural sciences, relationships are often expressed through classifications (e.g., the classification of living organisms). Scientific advancement is the discovery of new relationships or the discovery of a generalization that applies to objects hitherto confined within disparate scientific realms (e.g., evolutionary theory arising from observations of organisms and geologic strata).

References

[1] Manolio TA, Fowler DM, Starita LM, Haendel MA, MacArthur DG, Biesecker LG, et al. Bedside back to bench: building bridges between basic and clinical genomic research. Cell 2017;169:6–12.

[2] Pene F, Courtine E, Cariou A, Mira JP. Toward theragnostics. Crit Care Med 2009;37:S50–58.

[3] Gong F, Pan YH, Huang X, Zhu HY, Jiang DL. From bench to bedside: therapeutic potential of interleukin-9 in the treatment of asthma. Exp Ther Med 2017;13:389–94.

[4] Chang HT, Akutsu T, Ray O, Draghici S, Pai TW. Intelligent informatics in translational medicine 2016. Biomed Res Int 2017;2017:1572730.

[5] Manyika J, Chui M, Brown B, Bughin J, Dobbs R, Roxburgh C, et al. Big data: the next frontier for innovation, competition, and productivity. McKinsey Global Institute; 2011. June.

[6] Wanjala J, Taylor BS, Chapinski C, et al. Identifying actionable targets through integrative analyses of GEM model and human prostate cancer genomic profiling. Mol Cancer Ther 2015;14:278–88.

Introduction: Seriously, What is Precision Medicine?

I want to thank you for making this day necessary.
Yogi Berra

It's important, from the outset of this book, to discuss the definition of Precision Medicine. Or, more accurately, the definitions of Precision Medicine, as everyone you talk to seems to have a different opinion on the subject. From the US National Institutes of Health comes the following: "Precision Medicine is an emerging approach for disease prevention and treatment that takes into account people's individual variations in genes, environment, and lifestyle. The Precision Medicine Initiative will generate the scientific evidence needed to move the concept of Precision Medicine into clinical practice" [1,2]. An Advisory Committee to the NIH Director would include, under the mantle of Precision Medicine, "providing individual side-effect profiles of drugs, and preventative health care check-ups that include specific recommendations developed from interpreting an individual's genetic risk profile" [3].

Spin-off definitions seem to accept, as a simple fact, that physicians can account for the individual variability in genes, environment, and lifestyle for all their patients [4]. From the Engineering and Medicine group of the National Academies of Sciences came the following: "Every patient is unique, and the evolving field of Precision Medicine aims to ensure the delivery of the right treatment to the right patient at the right time" [5]. This is an uninformative and bombastic definition, implying that without Precision Medicine, doctors have provided the wrong medications at the wrong times, to the wrong patients.

Precision Medicine and the Reinvention of Human Disease
https://doi.org/10.1016/B978-0-12-814393-3.00001-9

Between the millions of interindividual variations in our genomes, the highly personalized lifestyle choices, and the differences in our environments, there seems to be plenty of uniqueness to spread around. It is easy to forget that our uniqueness as individuals often has much less to do with our diseases than does our sameness as members of the same species. Our sameness goes a long way toward explaining why humans seem to suffer from the same list of textbook diseases, regardless of their individualized genes and geography. Someone had to put the brakes on this epidemic of uniqueness. Much to their credit, the National Research Council of the US National Academies tacked on the following caveat to the definition of Precision Medicine: "It does not literally mean the creation of drugs or medical devices that are unique to a patient, but rather the ability to classify individuals into subpopulations that differ in their susceptibility to a particular disease, in the biology and/or prognosis of those diseases they may develop, or in their response to a specific treatment" [6]. The Research Council wisely distinguished Personalized Medicine from Precision Medicine, by adding, "Although the term 'Personalized Medicine' is also used to convey this meaning, that term is sometimes misinterpreted as implying that unique treatments can be designed for each individual. For this reason, the Committee thinks that the term 'Precision Medicine' is preferable to 'Personalized Medicine'" [6]. [Glossary Prognosis, Susceptibility, Uniqueness]

The National Research Council pointed out what should have been obvious from the start. We cannot provide individualized treatments, because treatments must be tested for safety and efficacy on groups of people. The best we can ever do is to assign patients to a group that has been fitted to a preapproved treatment. So where does this leave us?

Before we tackle a definition of Precision Medicine, let's stop a moment and consider our definition of disease. In earlier times, a disease was defined by its cause (e.g., influenza virus) and its pathological or clinical symptoms (e.g., fever, aches, chills). In the last few decades, there has been a profound change in the way we think about diseases. We recognize that every disease, even diseases whose root cause can be assigned to a single factor, such as a genetic mutation or an invasive microorganism, must develop in a sequence of steps, over time, before the disease is fully expressed. Advances in genetic analysis and molecular biology have permitted us to dissect some of those steps, in some diseases. What we are finding is that we can target specific events and pathways that lead to the development of disease, or that drive the clinical and pathological properties of a disease (it's so-called phenotype). [Glossary Phenotype, Root cause]

We can define Precision Medicine as an approach to the prevention, diagnosis, and treatment of disease that is based on a deep understanding of the sequence of biological events that lead to disease. With this approach we are learning: (1) that we can develop new drugs that target specific steps in the development of disease; (2) that drugs developed to interfere with a cellular event or pathway may serve as effective treatments for those individuals whose disease is driven by the pathway; and (3) that a treatment effective for a subtype of one disease may also be effective against other diseases that happen to be driven by the same pathway.

This approach, based on learning the steps that precede the development of disease, shifts the emphasis of Precision Medicine from finding unique treatments for unique individuals to finding general treatments that are effective against precisely identified biological processes, in whichever diseases those processes may occur. In the era of Precision Medicine, every disease has a biological history, and every event in the history of the disease is a possible target for prevention, diagnosis, or treatment. At this point, we can begin to see the thread of a story that will unfold throughout this book. We will need to explore our basic assumptions about disease development, and we will need to demonstrate how our approach to Precision Medicine is leading to a reduction in disease-related morbidity and mortality of diseases; otherwise, Precision Medicine would be just a waste of the time and money lavished on a scientific fad. Finally, the title of this book is *Precision Medicine and the Reinvention of Human Disease*. Somewhere in this narrative, we will need to demonstrate that our concepts of human disease are fundamentally changing, under the aegis of Precision Medicine. Our work is cut out for us, but the task may be somewhat simplified if we break it down into specific questions, as follows:

– **How can one be certain that diseases develop in steps?**

This issue of the stepwise development of disease is a hard sell, perhaps because we often become aware of diseases suddenly, as though we first notice a disease at the moment of its inception. Even when we know that a period of time must pass between the cause of a biological condition and its eventual emergence, we tend to think in terms of a condition that begins fully formed, but too small to notice, until it has had a chance to grow into a clinically detectable result.

As an example, consider the growth and development of a zygote, in the womb. No so long ago, most everyone believed that at the moment of conception, a fully formed human was created—the so-called homunculus. During the nine months of pregnancy, the homunculus grew larger, without needing to change its shape or modify any of its internal organs, until it was ready to emerge through the birth canal. Of course, we now know that gestation is characterized by strict, sequential steps of development, through different biological stages and forms: zygote, blastula, blastocyst, embryo, and fetus. At each stage, certain crucial biological processes must occur for development to proceed.

Generations of medical students have been taught that cancer results from a mutation that confers the property of unregulated growth on the cell bearing the mutation. As the cell divides, it produces more cells, with the same cancer-causing mutation. Over time, the original mutated cell has produced a clonal population of sufficient size to be palpable, and to do damage to the host organism. We now know that this is not true. Although mutations are involved in the development of cancer, the first mutation occurs in a cell that does not suddenly acquire the morphological or biological properties of a cancer cell. In fact, a succession of cellular events, occurring in the descendants of the original mutated cell, must precede the fully developed cancer [7–12].

Biological functions develop as a sequence of events. This rule applies equally to complex processes, such as cell division and growth, and to simpler processes, such as blood coagulation and photoreception. In Section 2.2, "Why We Are Confident that Diseases Develop in Steps" we assemble the arguments that lead us to believe that diseases, like other biological processes, develop over time. [Glossary Host, Results]

– **Precision Medicine assumes that the steps leading to the development of diseases can be dissected and studied. What do we actually know about disease pathways, and why do we believe that we can learn all of the disease pathways for every disease that occurs in humans?**

There are many questions that need answering here. What are these mysterious events and pathways that lead to disease? For that matter, what exactly is a pathway? How do we find disease pathways? Do disease pathways include the normal pathways responsible for cell maintenance? Can we inhibit these pathways without causing cell death? How can we develop drugs that specifically target individual disease pathways? Precision Medicine directs us to deconstruct diseases into sets of pathways, but how do we actually do this?

It turns out that we know a lot about the cellular pathways that lead to the disease, and that we have the tools to learn a lot more. Much of our knowledge on this subject comes from the study of rare, monogenic diseases, covered in Chapter 5. We will see that the rare monogenic diseases provide us with an opportunity to observe the effects of single-pathway disruptions. Furthermore, new treatments developed for the rare diseases are teaching us the general principles of pathway-directed therapeutics. [Glossary Rare disease, Pathway-driven disease, Druggable driver]

– **Precision Medicine assumes that the biological steps leading to any disease are characteristic of the disease (i.e., will lead to the diagnosis of the disease), crucial for the development of the disease (i.e., will result in the prevention of the disease, if the step is eliminated), and responsible for driving the expression of the developed disease (i.e., will result in the successful treatment of the disease, if targeted after the disease has expressed itself clinically).**

How do we know that this is true? Before the advent of Precision Medicine, therapeutics was geared toward counteracting the symptoms of the patient's disease. Every healthcare worker of a certain age is familiar with the following clinical maxims.

– If the patient has constipation, prescribe a laxative
– If the patient has diarrhea, prescribe a drug that decreases gut motility
– If the patient has a fever, prescribe an antipyretic
– If the patient has insomnia, prescribe a CNS suppressant

Countless dermatologists have, knowingly or not, followed the all-embracing adage, "If the lesion is dry, make it wet. If the lesion is wet, make it dry." Of course, nothing simplifies medicine better than the surgeon's motto, "When in doubt, cut it out!"

The past 50 years have witnessed a sophisticated change in the way that drugs are designed and developed. Most of the drugs that have reached the market in the past few decades have been small molecule drugs that were designed to specifically inhibit a critical enzyme in a disease-related biochemical pathway. This holds true for antihypertensive medications (e.g., angiotensin-converting enzyme inhibitors), atherosclerosis (3-hydroxy-3-methylglutaryl-coenzyme (HMG-CoA) reductase inhibitors, also known as statins), type 2 diabetes (dipeptidyl peptidase-4 inhibitors, targeting an enzyme active in postprandial blood glucose regulation), and chronic myelogenous leukemia (imatinib, targeting bcr/abl kinase). We will be discussing many other agents that target the steps in the development of disease, leaving no doubt that Precision Medicine is providing us with new targets for drugs that can prevent or cure diseases that were formerly treated symptomatically (i.e., treating the symptoms of disease without improving the underlying causes). [Glossary Leukemia, Underlying cause]

– **Precision Medicine tells us that finding a treatment for one subtype of one disease, driven by a particular pathway, will serve as an effective treatment for other diseases that happen to be driven by the same pathway.**

Is this really true? If so, how do we know which diseases will respond to the same pathway-based treatment? Although there are a seemingly infinite number of factors that contribute to the development of diseases, there seems to be a limited number of pathways by which diseases develop. Some of the key pathways in rare diseases play significant roles in the development of seemingly unrelated diseases. Furthermore, we now know a great deal about diseases that converge to common pathways. The phenomenon of disease convergence will be discussed in detail in Chapter 4. [Glossary Convergence]

We see many examples where related disease can be treated effectively with the same drug, vindicating the point that a drug that is effective in one disease will show some effectiveness in every disease of the same biological class. This value of class-based treatments will be discussed in Chapters 4, 5, and 9, when we are shown how advances in Precision Medicine are producing radical changes in the design of clinical trials. Of course, science cannot be expected to move forward without taking a few steps backward from time to time. We have already encountered instances wherein two diseases with the same pathways respond discordantly to drugs targeted to their common pathway [13]. The fluid manner in which pathways adapt to their cellular milieu is a confounding factor that will be described in Section 3.4, "Why a Gene-based Disease Classification Is a Bad Idea." [Glossary Clinical trial, Instance, Class]

As we learn more about the pathways of disease development, we will need to have a new classification of diseases, based on disease development. Diseases that share developmental steps will be assigned to the same class or to closely related classes, regardless of their anatomic location or clinical symptoms. We can expect that, in the future, the task of creating a new classification of diseases will preoccupy generations of clinical researchers, much as the classification of living organisms has absorbed the attention of zoologists, for more than two millennia. The principles of classification, and how they can be applied to the field of Precision Medicine, will be described in Chapter 7.

- **In what ways has Precision Medicine actually changed our approach to disease research?**

Aside from the new emphasis on studying the stepwise development of diseases, Precision Medicine's most transformative role has less to do with biology and more to do with the complexity of precision data. Precision Medicine takes us away from symptoms and the relatively simple morphologic expressions of disease and pushes us into a world where hospitals collect terabytes of data every few hours; and where every patient becomes a complex database, with genome sequences that are billions of nucleotides in length, and protein profiles for every type of cell in the body, and complex test results in the form of images and sounds and waveforms, all collected on multiple occasions, under different clinical circumstances. [Glossary Database]

Many of the challenges of Precision Medicine relate to collecting, organizing, annotating, sharing, analyzing, and reanalyzing data. At this point, you need to accept, as a matter of faith, that the standard practices of handling data, that worked quite well throughout the 20th century, must be abandoned and replaced with newer methods. The news gets worse. Off-the-shelf programs such as spreadsheets and statistical packages, that we came to rely on just a few years ago, will not solve our problems today. We can no longer collect our data into a neat package that can be delivered into the hands of a capable statistician. In fact, simple data analysis is dying and is being supplanted by a seemingly endless process of verification, validation, and repeated reanalyses of updated data. [Glossary Validation, Verification]

Just when bioinformatics was coming to maturity, the world of medical research stands perilously close to self-destruction. It seems as though many of the most highly funded and touted works performed in the past decade have yielded irreproducible results [14–29]. A field cannot advance if the conclusions drawn by its researchers cannot be validated. It seems as though the world of Precision Medicine has reached a level of complexity that defies our comprehension and evades objective analysis. At this point, we must remind ourselves that the ultimate purpose of all science is to generalize observations and to simplify our perception of the world around us [30]. In Chapter 8, we will learn the principles of data simplification that will help us to analyze large and complex collections of data, and to prepare our work in a manner that permits other scientists to validate our results and repurpose our data. [Glossary Science]

— **How does Precision Medicine bring about the reinvention of human disease?**

You really cannot grasp the importance of Precision Medicine until you abandon old notions of the cause of a disease. Diseases do not have a cause, any mores than a mouse has a cause, or a tree has a cause. If we accept that diseases develop by sequential, incremental steps, over time, then our old notions of disease causality must be tossed aside forever. The concept of disease etiology must be replaced with the idea of a causality chain. Words written by our predecessors, such as spontaneous disease, sporadic disease, multifactorial, heterogeneous causation, primary disease, secondary disease, acquired disease, disease gene, and randomly occurring disease, barely make any sense today, and will probably be abandoned as we codify the principles of Precision Medicine. [Glossary Primary disease, Secondary disease, Primary disease versus secondary disease, Tertiary disease, Sporadic, Etiology, Acquired disease, Epistasis]

Where we formerly listed diseases based by their site of anatomic occurrence, or based on their most prominent symptoms, we now must grapple with the problem of understanding diseases based on pathogenesis (i.e., the process of disease development). Words like taxonomy, ontology, systemics, superclass, subclass, and class inheritance must be learned and incorporated into our new professional gestalt. [Glossary Inheritance, Taxonomy, Pathogenesis, Subclass, Ontology, Superclass]

Is it all worth the effort? Does Precision Medicine offer us anything that we couldn't otherwise achieve [31]? Let's end the chapter with a life lesson. The past half century has seen incredible advances in the field of brain imaging, including the introduction of computed tomography and nuclear magnetic resonance imaging. Scientists can now determine the brain areas that are selectively activated for specific physiologic functions. These imaging techniques include: positron emission tomography, functional magnetic resonance imaging, multichannel electroencephalography, magnetoencephalography, near-infrared spectroscopic imaging, and single photon emission computed tomography. With all of these available technologies, you would naturally expect that neuroscientists would be in a position to make remarkable progress in the field of psychiatric illnesses. Indeed, the brain research literature has seen hundreds, if not thousands, of early studies purporting to find associations that link brain anatomy to psychiatric diseases. Alas, none of these early findings have been validated. Excluding degenerative and traumatic brain conditions (e.g., Alzheimer disease, Parkinson disease, chronic traumatic encephalopathy), there is, at present, no known psychiatric condition that can be consistently associated with a specific functional brain deficit or anatomic abnormality [32]. The lack of validation for what seemed to be a highly promising field of research, pursued by an army of top scientists, is a bitter disappointment for Precision Medicine. [Glossary Association]

What thwarts the ambitions of this promising young field? The problem seems to be that we have no biological classification for any of the psychiatric diseases. Historically, diagnoses are rendered based on grouping diseases that have similar symptoms, without any knowledge of the underlying biological mechanism that cause the symptoms to appear.

In 2013, a new version of the Diagnostic and Statistical Manual of Mental Disorders (DSM) was released. The DSM is the standard classification of psychiatric disorders, and is used by psychiatrists and other healthcare professionals worldwide. The new version was long in coming, following its previous version by 20 years. Spoiling the fanfare for the much-anticipated update was a chorus of loud detractors, who included among their ranks a host of influential and respected neuroscientists. They complained that the DSM classifies diagnostic entities based on collections of symptoms, not on biological principles. For every diagnostic entity in the DSM, all persons who share the same collection of symptoms will, in most cases, be assigned the same diagnosis, without taking into account the biological events leading to those symptoms [33]. [Glossary Rank]

For example, Rett syndrome is a highly complex neurodevelopmental disorder often accompanied by a variety of neurologic and somatic dysfunctions [34]. Repetitive hand movements and the absence of verbal skills are commonly noted. In early versions of the DSM, Rett syndrome was classified as a pervasive developmental disorder, in the same class of diseases as autism. Subsequently, we have learned a great deal about the pathogenesis of Rett syndrome. Most cases are associated with a mutation of the MECP2 gene located on the X chromosome, and virtually all cases occur in females. Medical researchers are carefully studying the developmental processes affected in Rett syndrome, but the early DSM, wrongfully classifying Rett syndrome with autism, did not serve to advance research in either disease. The latest version of the DSM removes Rett syndrome entirely from the classification, conceding that Rett syndrome is not a mental disorder.

When individuals with unrelated diseases are studied together, simply because they have some symptoms in common, the results of the study are unlikely to have any validity [6]. Dr. Thomas Insel, a former Director of the National Institute of Mental Health, was quoted as saying, "As long as the research community takes the DSM to be a bible, we'll never make progress." When the very first version of the DSM was introduced to the world, in the 1952, its creators were hailed as heroes [35]. Today, with little progress in the field, and with diseases still grouped by symptoms, the DSM is vilified by some of the most active and influential members of the field [35]. The lesson learned here is that Precision Medicine forces us to reinvent our concepts of disease, so that we classify based on biological relationships, not on clinical similarities; a concept revisited in later chapters.

Glossary

Acquired disease Everything is acquired, even inherited germline mutations. In common parlance, an "acquired disease" results from conditions occurring in the environment or as the result of events, processes, or behaviors that happened after birth. Some so-called acquired diseases are genetic conditions that were not clinically expressed at birth (i.e., not congenital). For example, the condition known as focal epilepsy with speech disorder is referred to as an acquired disease because children reported to have this disease are typically born without clinical signs of the condition. Recent analysis indicates that some cases of focal epilepsy are caused by a germ-line mutation and do not fit the definition of an acquired disease [36]. Contrariwise, diseases that are thought to be genetic may prove to be acquired (i.e., not accountable by genetic mutation or variation). A possible example is lactase deficiency. Lactase is an enzyme that is required for the digestion of lactose, a major ingredient of milk. Without lactase, ingested lactose is not absorbed from the gut and is instead metabolized by gut flora to yield gases, thus producing flatulence. Since infants normally ingest milk as the sole or primary component of their diets, all healthy babies are born with the genetic wherewithal to generate intestinal lactase. After weaning, generally around year two, intestinal lactase levels diminish to the point where many adults acquire a deficiency that is not based on a genetic mutation in the lactase gene. As another example, consider infectious diseases. It seems obvious that all infectious diseases are acquired. Nonetheless, there is great variation in susceptibility to infectious diseases, and genetics plays a role in determining who acquires an infection and who does not. The term "acquired" is applied throughout medical literature in such an inconsistent manner that it scarcely retains any biological meaning.

Association In the context of diseases, an association is anything that happens to occur more frequently in the presence of a disease than it occurs in the absence of the disease. Even when we know that one thing is associated with another thing, it can be very difficult to express the association in a manner that is mechanistically useful. For example, in 2000, a Concorde supersonic transport jet, crashed on take-off from Charles de Gaulle Airport, Paris. Debris left on the runway, possibly a wrench, flipped up and tore the underside of the hull. All passengers were killed in the subsequent few seconds as the plane exploded and crashed. What is the association here? Is it, "debris associated with jet crash," or do we need to be more specific, "wrench associated with jet crash?" Do jets need to be afraid of wrenches in general, or only with wrenches that are left out on the runway? If the association contains an implied mechanism that ties an object with a result, wouldn't we need to confine the association to wrenches that are actually run over by the jet, because if the jet tires miss the wrench, the wrench would not flip up and tear the underside of the plane. This would make the assertion: "wrenches that are run over by a tire and flip upwards are associated with jet crashes." It can be very difficult to develop a sensible way to describes associations. The problem is magnified when we are dealing with gene polymorphisms (i.e., gene variants found in a population) associated with diseases that have various causes, poorly understood pathogeneses, and complex phenotypes. Like so many scientific observations, associations serve as clues, not answers.

Class A class is a group of items that are all related to one another. In a classification, a class can have any number of direct subclasses (sometimes called child classes) and may have one direct superclass (sometimes called parent class).

Clinical trial Before a drug can be approved for use, it must undergo and pass three phases of a clinical trial. Phase 1 is the safety phase; the drug must be safe for humans. Phase 2 is the effectiveness phase; the drug must have some desired biological effect. Phase 3 is the large, expensive trial wherein individuals are tested against a control group treated with a placebo or with the standard-of-care medication. Phase 3 trials are very expensive to conduct, and many trials are negative (i.e., fail to indicate that the drug is effective in a phase 3 trial) or demonstrate only incremental success. Of the successful phase 3 trials, a significant number of drugs will eventually be withdrawn, because their effectiveness in clinical practice could not meet the earlier expectations observed in the phase 3 trial results [37]. Clinical trials are experiments, and like any other experiment, they must be repeated over and over in various settings before they can be trusted.

Convergence In zoology, convergence occurs when two species independently acquire an identical or similar trait through adaptation; not through inheritance from a shared ancestor. Examples are: the wing of a bat and the wing of a bird; the opposable thumb of opossums and of primates; the beak of a platypus and the beak of a bird. As applied to diseases, convergence occurs when different genes, cellular events, exposures, and pathogenetic mechanisms all lead to the same clinical phenotype. Convergence is a phenomenon that is observed in virtually every common disease. In the case of systemic responses to injury, convergence seems to have evolutionary origins. The organism evolves to respond in an orchestrated way to a variety of pathologic stimuli (e.g., systemic inflammatory response syndrome [38]). Convergence is also observed in rare diseases that have genetic heterogeneity (e.g., multiple causes for epidermolysis bullosa, retinitis pigmentosa, long QT syndrome). It would seem that for any disrupted pathway, the variety of pathologic responses is limited.

Database A software application designed specifically to create and retrieve large numbers of data records (e.g., millions or billions). The data records of a database are persistent, meaning that the application can be turned off, then on, and all the collected data will be available to the user.

Druggable driver A driver pathway that seems suitable as a therapeutic molecular target. The ideal druggable driver may have the following properties: (1) The target pathway is necessary for the expression of disease, but is not necessary for the survival of normal cells (i.e., you can eliminate the pathway without killing normal cells); (2) The pathway contains a protein that is necessary for the activity of the pathway (i.e., can't be replaced by an alternate protein); (3) the protein is chemically suitable as a target for a drug; and (4) the protein target is itself not necessary for the survival of normal cells (i.e., the protein target does not have important functions in addition to its role in the driver pathway).

Epistasis The condition under which the effect of a gene is influenced by another gene. For example, a gene may be active only when a particular allele of one or more additional genes is also active. Because dependencies among genes are built into cellular systems, the role of epistasis in the penetrance of disease genes and the pathogenesis of disease phenotypes is presumed to be profound. For example, there are at least 27 epistatic interactions among genes associated with Alzheimer disease [39]. Epistatic interactions can be synergistic or antagonistic [40].

Etiology The cause of a disease. One of the themes of this book is that diseases do not have an etiology; diseases have a pathogenesis. Still, it is convenient to assign one cause to a disease, if for no reason other than abbreviating explanations. If the word "etiology" is to be used at all, it should probably refer to whatever is generally believed to be the root cause of the disease.

Host The organism in which an infectious agent resides.

Inheritance In object-oriented languages, data objects (i.e., classes and object instances of a class) inherit the methods (e.g., functions and subroutines) created for the ancestral classes in their lineage.

Instance An instance is a specific example of an object that is not itself a class or group of objects. For example, Tony the Tiger is an instance of the tiger species. Tony the Tiger is a unique animal and is not itself a group of animals or a class of animals. The terms instance, instance object, and object are sometimes used interchangeably, but the special value of the "instance" concept, in a system wherein everything is an object, is that it distinguishes members of classes (i.e., the instances) from the classes to which they belong.

Leukemia Neoplasms that arise from the blood-forming cells.

Ontology An ontology, like a classification, is a class-based organization of objects in a domain of knowledge; the primary difference being that classes in an ontology may have more than one parent class (i.e., multiclass inheritance is permitted) [41]. Hence, all classifications are ontologies, but not all ontologies are classifications.

Pathogenesis The biologic events that lead to the expression of a disease. The term "carcinogenesis" is synonymous with "pathogenesis of cancer." Full understanding of a disease process involves learning its pathogenesis and learning its pathways, the latter being the cellular consequences of the events that occur as pathogenesis proceeds. Together, this knowledge, embodied in the term "Precision Medicine," should allow us to prevent, diagnose, and treat every human disease.

Pathway-driven disease Diseases with similar clinical phenotypes can often be grouped together according to shared pathways. Examples would include the channelopathies, ciliopathies, and lipid receptor mutations. At this point, our ability to sensibly assign diseases to pathways is limited because the effects of a mutation in a single gene may indirectly affect many different pathways, and those pathways may vary from cell type to cell type. Syndromes involving multiple pathways and multiple tissues occur frequently when the mutation involves a regulatory element, such as a transcription factor [42]. One transcription factor may regulate pathways in a variety of cell types with differing functions and embryologic origins. Nonetheless, whenever one pathway has a dominant role in the pathogenesis of a group of diseases, we can begin to ask how we might develop diagnostic tests and treatments that apply to the rare members and the common members of the group.

Phenotype The set of observable traits and features of a biological object. For example, we can describe a dog as best as we can, and that description would be our assessment of its phenotype. If we describe a lot of dogs of a certain breed, we might come up with some consensus on the phenotype of the breed. A "disease phenotype" is the set of observable traits and features that characterize a disease. For example, the term "cancer phenotype" refers to the minimal properties of growth, persistence, invasion, and metastasis that characterize virtually all cancers. You can think of the phenotype as the full description, minus the genotype.

Primary disease The term "primary disease," usually refers to an inherited form of a disease. The acquired, noninherited form of the disease is usually referred to as the "secondary disease." For example, primary ciliary dyskinesia is an inherited disease of cilia in which the normal movements of ciliated epithelia are impeded, leading to the accumulation of cellular debris and mucous, and thus producing chronic otitis, chronic sinusitis, chronic bronchitis, and pneumonias. Secondary ciliary dyskinesia is caused by a toxin (e.g., cigarette smoke) or respiratory infection that impairs ciliary activity, producing the same clinical sequelae as are observed for primary ciliary dyskinesia. It happens that cilia come in two categories: primary and motile. Primary ciliary dyskinesia affects the motile, nonprimary cilia. Hence, the term "primary ciliary dyskinesia" excludes all diseases of primary cilia, of which there are many. All of the recognized diseases of primary cilia are inherited conditions, and thus are "primary diseases of primary cilia," and the class of these conditions excludes "primary ciliary dyskinesia," which is a condition of nonprimary cilia. **It's all very confusing, but it gets much worse.** The term "primary" may refer to a disease that is limited to one organ or that arises from a disease process that is not secondary to any other disease process. Hence, we must endure two terms that seem to contradict one another: "primary cardiac amyloidosis" and "systemic primary amyloidosis." The first term refers to amyloidosis that occurs exclusively in the heart. The second term, "systemic primary amyloidosis," refers to amyloidosis that does not occur secondary to any other condition, but which will be found everywhere in the body [43]. We also see "primary" occurring as the adverb, "primarily" in which case it may have the layman's meaning of "mostly," or it may have the medical meaning, "as a primary condition." The sentence "Diseases occurring in adults are primarily secondary diseases," happens to be true, but it would be best if it were never uttered.

Primary disease versus secondary disease The term "Secondary disease" like the term "Primary disease" is used in so many different ways that it has lost most of its meaning and should probably be abandoned. You'll find people referring to a set of conditions that result from a primary disease as secondary diseases. For example, when finger clubbing (hypertrophic osteoarthropathy) occurs in the setting of underlying diseases of the cardiovascular and pulmonary systems, we call this "secondary" (hypertrophic osteoarthropathy), indicating that the finger clubbing arises secondary to some other disease. When hypertrophic osteoarthropathy occurs as an inherited, familial syndrome, we refer to it as primary hypertrophic osteoarthropathy, indicating that it does not occur secondary to some predisposing concurrent disease. In many other cases, the term "secondary" is used synonymously with "acquired," to indicate that the disease is not inherited and was caused by some acquired event. You'll notice that there are two forms of "secondary" in common usage. One form of secondary refers to a disease caused by some other condition. Another form of "secondary" refers to noninherited form of a disease [44]. Having two definitions for "secondary" is confusing, but troubles deepen when the inherited and secondary forms of a disease are biologically unrelated. We see this in some forms of primary and secondary erythromelalgia. Primary erythromelalgia is a rare genetic channelopathy whose root cause is a mutation in a sodium channel gene (SCN9A), producing neuropathic pain and redness of the extremities. When burning and redness of the extremities occurs due to microthrombi occurring in small arterioles, we call this secondary erythromelalgia. Secondary erythromelalgia has a totally different pathogenesis than primary erythromelalgia [45], and there is no reason to expect a secondary erythromelalgia of the microthrombotic type to respond to a treatment developed for primary erythromelalgia resulting from an inherited mutation in a sodium channel gene. As a final comment, the terms "primary" and "secondary" mean something quite different to oncologists than they do to other healthcare professionals. Within the cancer field, the term "primary" refers to the first site of growth of a cancer. For example, an adenocarcinoma primary in lung refers to a cancer that arose from cells present in the lung. For oncologists, a "secondary" tumor is a second tumor that arises after a primary tumor, and sometimes as the result of treatment of the primary tumor. For example, a sarcoma arising inside the field of radiation of a retinoblastoma, would be considered a secondary cancer. You can see that an oncologist might speak of the primary site of a secondary cancer.

Prognosis The likelihood that a patient will recover. Prognostic markers are used to produce a quantitative estimate of the likelihood of recovery. The term "prognostic test" is sometimes used interchangeably with the term "predictive test," but the two terms are not equivalent.

Rank Synonymous with Taxonomic order. In hierarchical biological nomenclatures, classes are given ranks. In early versions of the classification of living organisms, it was sufficient to divide the classification into a neat handful of divisions: Kingdom, Phylum, class, Order, Family, Genus, Species. Today, the list of divisions has nearly quadrupled. For example, Phylum has been split into the following divisions: Superphylum, Phylum, Subphylum, Infraphylum, and Microphylum. The other divisions are likewise split. The subdivisions often have a legitimate scientific purpose. Nonetheless, current taxonomic order is simply too detailed for readers to memorize. Taxonomists referring to a class of any rank will sometimes use the word "taxon." Is this growing nomenclature for ranking ancestral classes really necessary? Not at all. Taxonomic complexity can be easily averted by dropping named ranks and simply referring to every class as "Class." Modern specifications for class hierarchies encapsulate into each class the name of its superclass. When every object contains its class and superclass, it is possible to trace any object's class lineage. For example, in the classification of living organisms, if you know the name of the parent for each class (i.e., its superclass), you can write a simple software program that generates the complete ancestral lineage for every class and species within the classification, without resorting to a specialized nomenclature [46]. Furthermore, the complex taxonomic ranking system for living organisms does not carry over to the ranking systems that might be used for other scientific domains (e.g., classification of diseases, classification of genes, etc.) and creates an impediment for software developers who wish to write programs that traverse the hierarchy of multiple classifications, in search of relationships among data objects. Hence, the venerable ranking nomenclature, which has served generations of biologists, may need to be abandoned in the current era, wherein computationally driven research prevails.

Rare disease As written in Public Law 107-280, the Rare Diseases Act of 2002, "Rare diseases and disorders are those which affect small patient populations, typically populations smaller than 200,000 individuals in the United States" [47]. Since the population of the United States is about 314 million, in 2013, this comes to a prevalence of about 1 case for every 1570 persons. This is not too far from the definition recommended by the European Commission on Public Health, a prevalence <1 in 2000 people.

Results The term "results" is often confused with the term "conclusions." Interchanging the two concepts is a source of misunderstanding among data scientists. In the strictest sense, "results" consist of the full set of experimental data collected by measurements. In practice, "results" are provided as a small subset of data distilled from the raw, original data. In a typical journal article, selected data subsets are packaged as a chart or graph that emphasizes some point of interest. Hence, the term "results" may refer, erroneously, to subsets of the original data, or to visual graphics intended to summarize the original data. Conclusions are the inferences drawn from the results. Results are verified; conclusions are validated.

Root cause The earliest event or condition that is known to set in motion a chain of additional events that can result in some specified result. The term "root cause" is preferable to another term "underlying cause" that is often applied to the same concept. In this book, "underlying cause" is denigrated because any of the events that precede a result could be construed as underlying causes. The term "root cause" conveys the idea of a first or earliest event in a multievent process. Of course, we can never be certain what the earliest event is in any process. For example, when a smoker dies of lung cancer, is the root cause of death "adenocarcinoma of lung" or "smoking" or "tobacco addiction" or "Unrestricted sales of cigarettes to minors" or "Invention of Cigarettes"? Where do we stop? In the case of an inherited genetic disease, the customary starting point (i.e., the root cause) is the introduction of a genetic error into the germ line of the affected individual. The idea here is that the pathogenesis of a genetic disease begins with the acquisition of the abnormal gene. If you think about it, we don't really know that this is the case. We know of many examples where an individual may carry a disease gene without developing the expected disease. In these cases, some condition required for disease development was not met. Was the condition some environmental factor that influenced the father's sperm or the mother's oocyte prior to fertilization? If so, might this condition, which preceded the acquisition of the genetic mutation, be the "root" cause? Again, even in the simplest of cases, it is difficult to assign a root cause with any certainty. We never know if we've looked backwards far enough. Still, we do the best that we can, and we apply the term "root cause" in this book with the understanding that we may need to modify our thinking, if evidence of an earlier event comes to light.

Science Of course, there are many different definitions of science, and inquisitive students should be encouraged to find a conceptualization of science that suits their own intellectual development. For me, science is all about finding general relationships among objects. In the so-called physical sciences, the most important relationships are expressed as mathematical equations (e.g., the relationship between force, mass and acceleration; the relationship between voltage, current, and resistance). In the so-called natural sciences, relationships are often expressed through classifications (e.g., the classification of living organisms). Scientific advancement is the discovery of new relationships or the discovery of a generalization that applies to objects hitherto confined within disparate scientific realms (e.g., evolutionary theory arising from observations of organisms and geologic strata).

Secondary disease A disease that results from having a primary disease. For example, an individual with diabetes is prone to develop conditions related to vascular insufficiency, such as ischemic necrosis of toes or feet. Diabetes is the primary disease and vascular insufficiency is the secondary disease. It seems like a simple concept, but type 2 diabetes may arise secondary to obesity. This would put obesity as the primary disease, diabetes as the secondary disease, and vascular insufficiency as the tertiary disease. Individuals with vascular insufficiency have reduced ambulation, and may lead sedentary lives, leading to obesity. In such case, the causal rankings produce circularity, with obesity → diabetes → vascular insufficiency → obesity. When the circle is complete, who can say which disease is primary or secondary or tertiary or quaternary? You may as well just spin the wheel.

Sporadic Describes a disease or a specific case occurrence of a disease with no known cause, and without any discernible pattern of occurrence (e.g., genetic, environmental). Thus, diseases that have a familial pattern of inheritance are always considered nonsporadic, even when the root genetic cause is unknown. Likewise, diseases that occur as an epidemic or endemic pattern are always considered nonsporadic, even when the precise environmental cause is unknown. Rare diseases are seldom sporadic, as they typically exhibit some pattern of inheritance. Common diseases are often sporadic, but may contain subsets of disease occurrences that are nonsporadic. An example is schizophrenia. Schizophrenia is a common disease with a prevalence of about 1.1%. This translates to about 51 million individuals, worldwide, who suffer from this mental disorder. Many cases of schizophrenia occur in families and such cases are considered to be inherited and, thus, nonsporadic. Other cases seem to have no familial association and are considered sporadic. Are these sporadic cases caused by environmental factors, or are they caused by de novo mutations that arose in the affected individuals? Recent evidence would suggest that many of the so-called sporadic cases arise from new mutations in affected individuals [48]. When an association is made between a disease and some demographic factor, the distinction between sporadic and nonsporadic may be arbitrary. For example, if a disease occurs predominantly in women, can it be called sporadic? The cause may be completely unknown, but it has a definite pattern. It should be mentioned that the term "sporadic" is fraught with scientific ambiguity and should probably be abandoned altogether. To label a disease "sporadic" seems to legitimize and perpetuate the dubious notion that diseases can occur without cause (i.e., by chance). Many of the diseases that were considered to be sporadic, decades ago, are now known to have specific causes. Would it not be more accurate to use the phrase "not as yet determined" in place of "sporadic," for occurrences of a disease whose cause is currently unknown?

Subclass A class in which every member descends from some higher class (i.e., a superclass) within the class hierarchy. Members of a subclass have properties specific to the subclass. As every member of a subclass is also a member of the superclass, the members of a subclass inherit the properties and methods of the ancestral classes. For example, all mammals have mammary glands because mammary glands are a defining property of the mammal class. In addition, all mammals have vertebrae because the class of mammals is a subclass of the class of vertebrates. A subclass is the immediate child class of its parent class.

Superclass An ancestral class. For example, in the classification of living organisms, the class of craniates is a superclass of the class of mammals. The immediate superclass of a class is its parent class. In common parlance, when we speak of the superclass of a class, we are referring to its parent class.

Susceptibility Refers to a state of increased risk of harm. The frequently encountered term "susceptibility gene" would imply that individuals with the gene have an increased susceptibility to a particular disease. From the point of view of understanding pathogenesis, "susceptibility" is not a helpful concept, in that it doesn't signify a biological process. Is "susceptibility" an event, or is it a pathway, or is it simply a constitutive condition of the individual that heightens risk? "Susceptibility" is an outmoded term that provides no mechanistic insight and should be avoided, when possible.

Taxonomy When we write of "taxonomy" as an area of study, we refer to the methods and concepts related to the science of classification, derived from the ancient Greek taxis, "arrangement," and nomia, "method." When we write of "a taxonomy," as a construction within a classification, we are referring to the collection of named instances (class members) in the classification. To appreciate the difference between a taxonomy and a classification, it helps to think of taxonomy as the scientific field that determines how different members of a classification are named. Classification is the scientific field that determines how related members are assigned to classes, and how the different classes are related to one another. A taxonomy is similar to a nomenclature; the difference is that in a taxonomy, every named instance must have an assigned class.

Tertiary disease A term that is never used, though you might expect it to be, if the terms "primary disease" and "secondary disease" made any logical sense. When the term "secondary disease" is used to describe conditions arising from some other existing disease (i.e., the primary disease), we would expect to see tertiary diseases that arise from secondary diseases. Employing proof by induction, there must be a quaternary disease and a quinary disease and so on. The lack of any such terms in medical terminology indicates our inability to think much beyond the simplest sequences of disease development. One of the important conceptual advances of Precision Medicine lies in its implicit inclusion of successive stages of disease, some of which may have their own clinical phenotypes. The absence of usage of "tertiary disease" and the misapplication of terms such as "primary disease" and "secondary disease" will justify the elimination of these archaic terms as Precision Medicine gradually fills in the missing details of disease development.

Underlying cause The condition that initiated a succession of clinical events that led to some final consequence. Death certificates require physicians to specify an underlying cause of death. The World Health Organization, aware of the difficulties in choosing an underlying cause of death, and assigning a sequential list of the ensuing clinical consequences, has issued reporting guidelines [49]. Instructions notwithstanding, death certificate data is notoriously inconsistent, giving rise to divergent methods of reporting the diseases that cause death [50–52]. In this book, the term "underlying cause" is denigrated in favor of the term "root cause."

Uniqueness Uniqueness is the quality of being separable from every other thing in the universe. For data scientists, uniqueness is achieved when data is bound to a unique identifier (i.e., a randomly chosen string of alphanumeric characters) that has not, and will never be, assigned to any data. The binding of data to a permanent and inseparable identifier constitutes the minimal set of ingredients for a data object. Uniqueness can apply to two or more indistinguishable objects, if they are assigned unique identifiers (e.g., unique product numbers stamped into identical auto parts).

Validation The process whereby a conclusion drawn from results is shown to be repeatable.

Verification The process by which data is checked to determine whether the data was obtained properly (i.e., according to approved protocols), and that the data accurately measured what it was intended to measure, on the correct specimens. Data verification is not easy [53]. In one celebrated case, involving a microarray study, two statisticians devoted 2000 hours to the job [24]. Two thousand hours is just about one full man-year of effort. It is important to remember the difference between verification and validation. Verification is a process performed on data. Validation is a process performed on the conclusions drawn from the data.

References

[1] Precision Medicine Initiative Cohort Program. U.S. National Institutes of Health; January 10, 2016. Available from: http://www.nih.gov/precision-medicine-initiative-cohort-program [Accessed 19 March 2017].

[2] The Precision Medicine Initiative Cohort Program—Building a Research Foundation for 21st Century Medicine. Precision medicine initiative working group Report to the Advisory Committee to the Director, NIH; September 17, 2015.

[3] Unique scientific opportunities for the precision medicine initiative: a workshop of the precision medicine initiative working group of the Advisory Committee to the NIH Director, April 28–29, Bethesda, MD; 2015.

[4] HIMSS Analytics 2016, Essentials Brief: Precision Medicine Study; August, 2016. Available from: http://www.himssanalytics.org/research/essentials-brief-2016-precision-medicine-study [Accessed 29 September 2016].

[5] National Academies of Sciences, Engineering, and Medicine. Biomarker tests for molecularly targeted therapies: key to unlocking precision medicine. Washington, DC: The National Academies Press; 2016.

[6] Committee on A Framework for Developing a New Taxonomy of Disease, Board on Life Sciences, Division on Earth and Life Studies, National Research Council of the National Academies. Toward Precision Medicine: Building a Knowledge Network for Biomedical Research and a New Taxonomy of Disease. Washington, DC: The National Academies Press; 2011.

[7] Berman JJ, Albores-Saavedra J, Bostwick D, Delellis R, Eble J, Hamilton SR, et al. Precancer: a conceptual working definition—results of a Consensus Conference. Cancer Detect Prev 2006;30(5):387–94.

[8] Berman JJ. Neoplasms: principles of development and diversity. Sudbury, MA: Jones and Bartlett; 2009.

[9] Berman JJ. Precancer: the beginning and the end of cancer. Sudbury, MA: Jones and Bartlett; 2010.

[10] Foulds L. Neoplastic development. New York: Academic Press; 1969.

[11] O'Shaughnessy JA, Kelloff GJ, Gordon GB, Dannenberg AJ, Hong WK, Fabian CJ, et al. Recommendations of the American Association for Cancer Research Task Force on the Treatment and Prevention of Intraepithelial Neoplasia. Treatment and prevention of intraepithelial neoplasia: an important target for accelerated new agent development. Clin Cancer Res 2002;8:314–46.

[12] Henson DE, AlboresSaavedra J, Berman JJ, Chung D, Czerniak B, Franklin WA, et al. Available from: http://www3.cancer.gov/prevention/cbrg/molclass.html; February 1–2, 2001.

[13] Carlson RH. Precision medicine is more than genomic sequencing. www.medscape.com; October 24, 2016. Available from: http://www.medscape.com/viewarticle/870723_print [Accessed 11 March 2017].

[14] Unreliable research: trouble at the lab. De Economist; October 19, 2013.

[15] Kolata G. Cancer fight: unclear tests for new drug. The New York Times; April 19, 2010.

[16] Baker M. Reproducibility crisis: blame it on the antibodies. Nature 2015;521:274–6.

[17] Ioannidis JP. Is molecular profiling ready for use in clinical decision making? Oncologist 2007;12:301–11.

[18] Ioannidis JP. Why most published research findings are false. PLoS Med 2005;2:e124.

[19] Ioannidis JP. Some main problems eroding the credibility and relevance of randomized trials. Bull NYU Hosp Jt Dis 2008;66:135–9.

[20] Ioannidis JP. Microarrays and molecular research: noise discovery? Lancet 2005;365:454–5.

[21] Ioannidis JP, Panagiotou OA. Comparison of effect sizes associated with biomarkers reported in highly cited individual articles and in subsequent meta-analyses. JAMA 2011;305:2200–10.

[22] Ioannidis JP. Excess significance bias in the literature on brain volume abnormalities. Arch Gen Psychiatry 2011;68:773–80.

[23] Pocock SJ, Collier TJ, Dandreo KJ, deStavola BL, Goldman MB, Kalish LA, et al. Issues in the reporting of epidemiological studies: a survey of recent practice. BMJ 2004;329:883.

[24] Misconduct in science: an array of errors. The Economist; September 10, 2011.

[25] Begley S. In cancer science, many 'discoveries' don't hold up. Reuters; March 28, 2012.

[26] Abu-Asab MS, Chaouchi M, Alesci S, Galli S, Laassri M, Cheema AK, et al. Biomarkers in the age of omics: time for a systems biology approach. OMICS 2011;15:105–12.

[27] Moyer VA, On behalf of the U.S. Preventive Services Task Force. Screening for prostate cancer: U.S. Preventive Services Task Force recommendation statement. Ann Intern Med 2011;156:880–91.

[28] How science goes wrong. The Economist; October 19, 2013.

[29] Kirchner L. Traces of crime: how New York's DNA techniques became tainted. The New York Times; September 4, 2017.ew.

[30] Berman JJ. Principles of Big data: preparing, sharing, and analyzing complex information. Waltham, MA: Morgan Kaufmann; 2013.

[31] Interlandi J. The paradox of precision medicine: early attempts to tailor disease treatment to individuals based on their DNA have met with equivocal success, raising concerns about a push to scale up such efforts. Scientific American; April 1, 2016.

[32] Borgwardt S, Radua J, Mechelli A, Fusar-Poli P. Why are psychiatric imaging methods clinically unreliable? Conclusions and practical guidelines for authors, editors and reviewers. Behav Brain Funct 2012;8:46.

[33] Berman JJ. Data simplification: taming information with open source tools. Waltham, MA: Morgan Kaufmann; 2016.

[34] Chahrour M, Zoghbi HY. The story of Rett syndrome: from clinic to neurobiology. Neuron 2007;56:422–37.

[35] Belluck P, Carey B. Psychiatry's guide is out of touch with science, Experts Say. The New York Times; May 6, 2013.

[36] Lesca G, Rudolf G, Bruneau N, Lozovaya N, Labalme A, Boutry-Kryza N, et al. GRIN2A mutations in acquired epileptic aphasia and related childhood focal epilepsies and encephalopathies with speech and language dysfunction. Nat Genet 2013;45:1061–6.

[37] Leaf C. Do clinical trials work? The New York Times; July 13, 2013.

[38] Seok J, Warren HS, Cuenca AG, Mindrinos MN, Baker HV, Xu W, et al. Genomic responses in mouse models poorly mimic human inflammatory diseases. Proc Natl Acad Sci U S A 2013;110:3507–12.

[39] Combarros O, Cortina-Borja M, Smith AD, Lehmann DJ. Epistasis in sporadic Alzheimer's disease. Neurobiol Aging 2009;30:1333–49.

[40] Lobo I. Epistasis: gene interaction and the phenotypic expression of complex diseases like Alzheimer's. Nat Educ 2008;1:180.

[41] Berman JJ. Ruby programming for medicine and biology. Sudbury, MA: Jones and Bartlett; 2008.

[42] Seidman JG, Seidman C. Transcription factor haploinsufficiency: when half a loaf is not enough. J Clin Invest 2002;109:451–5.

[43] Thomashow AI, Angle WD, Morrione TG. Primary cardiac amyloidosis. Am Heart J 1953;46:895–905.

[44] Oliveira AM, Perez-Atayde AR, Inwards CY, Medeiros F, Derr V, Hsi BL, et al. USP6 and CDH11 oncogenes identify the neoplastic cell in primary aneurysmal bone cysts and are absent in so-called secondary aneurysmal bone cysts. Am J Pathol 2004;165:1773–80.

[45] Tang Z, Chen Z, Tang B, Jiang H. Primary erythromelalgia: a review. Orphanet J Rare Dis 2015;10:127.

[46] Berman JJ. Methods in Medical Informatics: Fundamentals of Healthcare Programming in Perl, Python, and Ruby. Boca Raton, FL: Chapman and Hall; 2010.

[47] Rare Diseases Act of 2002, Public Law 107-280, 107th U.S. Congress; November 6, 2002.

[48] Xu B, Roos JL, Dexheimer P, Boone B, Plummer B, Levy S, et al. Exome sequencing supports a de novo mutational paradigm for schizophrenia. Nat Genet 2011;43:864–8.

[49] U.S. Vital Statistics System: major activities and developments, 1950–95. Centers for Disease Control and Prevention, National Center for Health Statistics; 1997.

[50] Ashworth TG. Inadequacy of death certification: proposal for change. J Clin Pathol 1991;44:265.

[51] Kircher T, Anderson RE. Cause of death: proper completion of the death certificate. JAMA 1987;258:349–52.

[52] Berman JJ. Rare diseases and orphan drugs: keys to understanding and treating common diseases. Cambridge, MA: Academic Press; 2014.

[53] Committee on Mathematical Foundations of Verification, Validation, and Uncertainty Quantification, Board on Mathematical Sciences and Their Applications, Division on Engineering and Physical Sciences, National Research Council. Assessing the reliability of complex models: mathematical and statistical foundations of verification, validation, and uncertainty quantification. Washington, DC: National Academy Press; 2012. Available from: http://www.nap.edu/catalog.php?record_id=13395.

Redefining Disease Causality

SECTION 2.1 CAUSALITY AND ITS PARADOXES

That all science is description and not explanation, that the mystery of change in the inorganic world is just as great and just as omnipresent as in the organic world, are statements which will appear platitudes to the next generation.
Karl Pearson, in 1899 [1]

This chapter deals with the subject of disease causality, a subject of paramount importance to the field of Precision Medicine. We can assume that all humans, throughout the history of our species, have searched for a cause, whenever bad things happen. When a child became sick, the mother would naturally look for the cause. Was it that mushroom that the child snatched on his walk through the woods? Do those red marks on the child's arm indicate the site where a venomous snake sank his fangs? If the cause were found, the mother may have had a chance of saving her child. Everyone in the village had a stake in knowing what made the child sick. If the cause were known, it could be eliminated, or avoided, thus sparing the other members of the village from sickness. The imperative to find cause permeates every aspect of society.

Because the concept of "cause" is hard-wired into the human psyche, it is shocking to learn that "cause" does not apply to the field of Precision Medicine, which is based on the notion that diseases develop in steps, over time. For most diseases, what we think of as the cause of the disease is most likely an early event that initiated a series of biological processes that culminated in the expression of disease. In order for the disease to develop, some undetermined number of required conditions may have set the stage for the "cause" to have any biological consequence. Furthermore, some additional number of events may have been necessary, after the initial event, and before the disease developed. Most importantly, there may have been many opportunities, in the interim, to delay, or arrest the processes by which the disease developed. All of the aforementioned conditions and events may have played out in a variety of ways, depending on the individual involved, and a host of unknown environmental variables. [Glossary Variable]

At this point, you may be thinking that this kind of analysis ignores the obvious fact that we can often determine the single cause of disease, and doing so has fueled the advance of medicine from time immemorial. We can identify the mushrooms that destroy our livers, and we know the operative biochemical pathway. We can identify the bacteria that cause the sore throat, and we can isolate the toxins that the bacteria produce, and we even know how the toxin kills cells. Understanding the cause of disease has been one of the greatest achievements of modern medicine. The metaphysical issues raised by multistep causality have had little or no practical significance in the healthcare industry.

Here's the dilemma. It is important to think about causality in a new way, if we want to take advantage of the advances brought by Precision Medicine. At the same time, we have good reason to hold onto the old notion that every disease has a cause. What should we think?

Let's look at a few examples of diseases and other natural catastrophes to see how we might properly think about causation [2]. Consider what may happen when the cause of a disease is unknown and an army of geneticists is called to solve the mystery. The following discussion concerns the mythical kingdom of Smokovia where the only crop is tobacco, and everyone in the country smokes cigarettes or cigars. Mothers pass out cigarettes to the whole family, after lunch and dinner. Students are encouraged to smoke in the classroom. Every hospital corridor is filled with smoke emanating from patients and staff.

In Smokovia, there is a very high rate of lung cancer. One out of 5 Smokovians dies of the disease. Nobody has a clue why this might be. Because there is no subpopulation of Smokovians who do not smoke, there is no indication that the risk of lung cancer might be reduced in nonsmokers. [Glossary Lung cancer]

The Smokovian scientists decide that there must be some defect in the gene pool that predisposes some Smokovians to cancer. They have compared the genomes of Smokovians who develop lung cancer from those Smokovians who have lived a full life, without developing lung cancer. Every patient with lung cancer had a characteristic gene variation that was lacking in the cancer-free population. The scientists developed a method for detecting the cancer-prone gene variant from a simple blood test. They suggested that, as a stop-gap measure, Smokovians carrying the lung cancer gene ought not procreate. In the meantime, Smokovian scientists experimented with a spanking-new technology that would repair the cancer-prone gene in affected embryos.

While this work proceeded, Smokovian farmers were hit by a terrible tobacco blight. In a matter of weeks, the entire crop of tobacco was destroyed. It would take scientists years and years to develop a blight-resistant tobacco. Because tobacco was the most important crop in Smokovia, all scientists were inducted into the service of the tobacco industry.

Decades passed. As a nation, Smokovians endured the agony of cigarette withdrawal. Economic times were bad, but the farmers eventually switched to alternate crops. Smokovia was slowly recovering, and people noticed that the rate of lung cancer was dropping and dropping. After about 50 years, lung cancer had become a rare disease. At first, people thought that their eugenics effort had paid off. But a genetic census of Smokovians showed that lung cancer had vanished even in the subpopulation of Smokovians who had the cancer-prone gene. Nobody could understand what had happened.

Fifty years after the cigarette famine, Smokovian scientists found a blight-resistant tobacco plant. Once more, tobacco was planted, cigarettes were produced, and Smokovians resumed their national past-time. High lung cancer rates returned. Again, tumors occurred in the subpopulation of Smokovians with the cancer-prone gene.

The Smokovian scientists were preoccupied by "cause" when they should have been thinking in terms of the processes of pathogenesis. When everyone smoked, there was little hope of pinning the blame on tobacco. Their search for a causal gene was short-sighted. Their plan to breed out cancer-prone individuals was neither helpful nor fair. Had they studied the temporal changes in bronchi that led to the development of cancer, they may have had a better chance to infer that toxic and mutagenic alterations in bronchial epithelial cells were caused by an environmental agent. Their biggest mistake was simply a failure to imagine that diseases occur in steps, and that their simple notion of causation did not serve them well, in this instance. [Glossary Mutagen, Epithelial cell]

Historic debates over the causal link between smoking and lung cancer now serve as object lessons in the finer points of causality. In 1957, there was intense public debate over the role of smoking in the causation of lung cancer. Some of the arguments from the defenders of the tobacco industry played upon causality paradoxes, and they are worth reviewing here. At the time, a prominent statistician, who was of the opinion that cigarettes did not cause lung cancer, raised an interesting point [3]. If we can associate A with B, then we need to be aware that A might be the cause of B, or B might be the cause of A, or some other factor, such as C, may be the cause of A or B, or neither A nor B may be causally related. In particular, this imaginative statistician suggested that lung cancer may be the cause of smoking, and not vice versa. He suggested that as lung cancer develops, it irritates the lungs, thus motivating people to seek a remedy, such as the smooth taste of cigarette smoke, known to calm the bronchi and the tumor therein. As the tumor grew, and the lung irritation worsened, you might expect affected individuals to increase their rate of smoking, thus explaining the dose/effect relationship between cigarettes and cancer.

Not lacking in imagination, the same statistician suggested that a genetic condition may predispose individuals to an inclination to smoke and, independently, to a predisposition to cancer. Hence, smoking may not cause cancer, and cancer may not cause smoking, but both may be caused by an accident of genetics. The statistician testified that the causal link between smoking and lung cancer was mere speculation. We now know something about the temporal sequence of events that occur after individuals begin to smoke cigarettes. Specifically, the bronchial mucosa becomes inflamed and the normal mucosal epithelium is slowly replaced by squamous cells, a cell type that is not present in normal lung. As smoking continues, and time passes, the squamous cells lining the inflamed mucosa begin to display the morphologic features of nuclear atypia, the hallmark of precancerous change. Nuclear atypia worsens over time. These changes are, as a rule, not observed in nonsmokers. Eventually, a cancer may arise from this background of atypical squamous cells. In this particular case, a series of morphologic changes occur, in a temporal sequence that culminates in the appearance of lung cancer. Observations of the progressive changes occurring in the lung biopsies of smokers provide very strong evidence that smoking has a role in the development of lung cancer. Many factors may contribute to the development of lung cancer, after smoking has started, and many factors may help sustain the growth of lung cancer. These issues notwithstanding, simple observations of the steps in disease development inform us that smoking contributes to the development of lung cancer. [Glossary Malignant process, Premalignancy, Precancer, Cell type, Mucosa]

Confusion over the concepts of association and causation confronts us whenever we fail to study the steps of disease development. In a 1994 paper appearing in the *New England Journal of Medicine*, a group of epidemiologists had noticed a significant association between the occurrence of diabetes and pancreatic cancer. In this case, the association prompted speculation that a common factor, perhaps a pancreatic toxin, may have increased the risk of two different diseases in the pancreas: diabetes and ductal carcinoma of the pancreas. The investigators were not to be misled by a statistical association. They noticed that in many of the cases wherein pancreatic cancer and diabetes coexisted in the same individual, the two diseases were often diagnosed at about the same time. When the diabetes was longstanding (i.e., present for many years before the occurrence of cancer), the statistical association between diabetes and cancer disappeared, suggesting that the diabetes could not have caused the cancer. The authors concluded that pancreatic cancer, a disease that insinuates throughout the pancreas, destroying normal pancreatic cells in the process, had wiped out the population of pancreatic islet cells, resulting in diabetes. Again, knowledge of the temporal sequence of events played a crucial role in resolving the biological basis of a causal association.

In many cases, stubborn reliance on the concept of "cause" serves only to diminish our understanding of disease. Let's consider a simple disease whose cause is understood by laypersons and clinicians alike. The common gastric ulcer is an erosion of the stomach wall caused by excess acid eating through the stomach lining. This definition, or something much like it, appears throughout the medical literature [4]. The definition takes a plausible cause and juxtaposes it against an immediate result; acid eats through stomach lining causing ulcer. Enough said. The problem here is that this explanation ignores the biological steps that lead from acid production to ulcer formation, thereby eliminating any chance of rationally preventing, treating, or even understanding the pathogenesis of gastric ulcers (Fig. 2.1).

Here is how ulcers of the stomach, or ulcers of just about any mucosal lining, are created. Under normal conditions, the cells that line the uppermost layer of all mucosal linings regularly die and slough off the mucosa. In the case of gut, the superficial cells slough into the gut lumen and are excreted in the feces. The sloughed cells are replaced by cells regenerated from dividing cells located at the bottom layer of the mucosa. When the mucosal surface is exposed to a toxic chemical agent (such as stomach acid), cells on the surface die and slough at a higher rate than normal. When this happens, the regenerative cells divide more frequently, achieving a new steady state in which the acid-exposed superficial cells are replaced at a higher rate than normal. This condition can continue for a very long time; damaged superficial cells are replaced by overworked regenerative cells, with no net erosion of the mucosal lining. If the

FIG. 2.1 Gross specimen of inner surface of stomach. In the upper left quadrant of the image, there is a large, round ulcer. The margins of the ulcer are well demarcated, and deep, as if pressed by a cookie cutter. The specimen has been washed and fixed in formalin, removing blood, and hardening the tissue. *Reproduced from MacCallum WG. A text-book of pathology. 2nd ed. Philadelphia, London: WB Saunders Company; 1921.*

toxic exposure increases to a level beyond regenerative capacity, then the lining of the mucosa thins. At some point, the lining erodes completely, exposing the submucosa to the direct effects of acid. This usually results in inflammation. Eventually, an ulcer may erode into a large vessel or through a tissue wall, creating a surgical emergency.

When cause is separated from effect by an intervening series of biological steps, we begin to understand the different factors that might influence development of a gastric ulcer. Basically, a gastric ulcer is the final event in a typically long process in which bottom layer regenerative cells balance top layer cell losses, until such time as they yield to exhaustion. If an individual were nutritionally deficient, his ability to regenerate sloughed mucosal cells might be diminished. Likewise, if the individual were taking a drug that inhibited cell division, then the ability to compensate for cell losses would be diminished. Either condition might hasten the development of an ulcer. If an individual had an atrophic (i.e., thinned) lining of the mucosal surface, there might be diminished ability to compensate for any cell loss. In the case of gastric ulcers, this might occur in a low-acid environment. Chronic conditions that exacerbate the turnover of lining cells, such as chronic bacterial infection, might also lead to ulcer production.

Understanding the steps that lead to ulcer formation will help us find alternative approaches to preventing and treating ulcers. In the case of gastric ulcers, knowing the underlying cause is not as helpful as understanding the pathogenesis.

Sometimes, we simply cannot assign a specific cause to a particular disease, without seriously misleading ourselves. For example, what is the cause of rheumatic fever? Rheumatic fever is a an autoimmune process that targets the heart. Rheumatic fever occurs in people who have been infected with a Group A strain of Streptococcus pyogenes. The infection, which usually presents as a pharyngitis, elicits an immune response against a bacterial antigen. The antibodies species that target the bacterial antigen happen to crossreact with proteins in normal heart and vessels. These crossreacting antibodies damage the heart and vessels to produce rheumatic fever. Rheumatic fever is one of the most thoroughly studied and best understood diseases known to medicine. Knowing all that we know about the pathogenesis, pathology, and clinical features of rheumatic fever, it should be easy to specify the cause of the disease. Alas, this is not the case. For example, we cannot assert that rheumatic fever is caused by Streptococcus pyogenes because not all cases of infection will lead to rheumatic fever, and because the clinical features of the disease are not actually caused by the infection. Likewise, we cannot assert that rheumatic fever is an autoimmune disease because it does not result from a defect in the autoimmune system. Basically, rheumatic fever involves a immune response to a foreign antigen (i.e., a protein of Streptococcus pyogenes bacteria) that happens to crossreact with heart proteins. Furthermore, we cannot claim that rheumatic fever is caused by a heart defect; the heart is an innocent bystander in a process that evolved over time, in tissues other than the heart (i.e., the pharynx and other tissues in which immunocytes reside). Despite everything we know about rheumatic fever, it is difficult to specify its cause.

Another example of a "causal" dilemma comes when we consider the dose-related effects of toxins on the influence of genetic variations within exposed populations. When toxic agents are delivered at a very high dose, the effects of genetic variation are typically negligible. Obviously, if everyone becomes ill, then genetic variations in the population have no bearing on the results. At the very lowest exposures, only rare individuals in the population become ill, and gene variation in this group may account for 100% of the observed illnesses. We see this effect whenever we apply low doses of a toxin to a large population. In the rare low-dose cases, we tend to assign the cause of illness to genes, and we consider the toxin to be a noncausal agent that triggers the expression of an otherwise dormant genetic disease.

Let's look at a few real-life examples of what it means to assign cause based on dosage. When humans are exposed to low doses of radiation, it is easy to find differences in individual sensitivity. Some of the differences in sensitivity are due to interindividual variation in DNA repair capacity [5,6]. Individuals with DNA repair disorders are particularly prone to radiation toxicity [7]. Hence, at very low doses of radiation, toxicity is usually considered a genetic disorder. When we move to high doses, in the range of 4 Sieverts, every exposed person would be expected to develop acute radiation sickness. Whole-body exposure to doses exceeding 8 Sieverts is uniformly fatal. There is simply no cellular mechanism that can cope with the radiation damage inflicted on cells at these levels of exposure. Thus, at 8 Sieverts, radiation toxicity is considered an environmental disease, not a genetic disease. [Glossary DNA repair]

Does the low-dose/high-dose effect apply to infections? Specifically, if a population were exposed to a very low dose of a pathogenic microorganism, would we expect to see large variations in the severity of the resulting infections, depending on genetically determined susceptibilities? Furthermore, if we infected individuals in a population with very high doses of a pathogenic organism, would we find that everyone would become severely ill from the overwhelming dose of infectious organisms?

This is the kind of hypothetical question that physicians should never be permitted to test, as doing so would entail purposefully exposing individuals to a pathogenic organism, with no real way of predicting the severity of the ensuing infections. Nonetheless, a tragic incident occurring in 1929, in Lubeck, Germany, has provided us with some indication of how we might answer our question. The incident, now known as the Lubeck disaster, involved 251 neonates who were administered BCG (Bacille Calmette-Guerin), a tuberculosis vaccine produced from an low-virulence strain of bovine tuberculosis (i.e., Mycobacterium bovis). It happens that the batches of BCG delivered to the neonates was contaminated with fully virulent human Mycobacterium tuberculosis. Of the 251 exposed neonates, 171 developed signs of tuberculosis, and 72 died from the disease [8].

The availability of the contaminated batches of BCG permitted investigators to determine which neonates received high doses of human mycobacterium, and which neonates received lower doses. At the low doses, there was wide variation in the severity of the illnesses that developed, with many of the babies suffering no ill effects. At the highest dose, most of the babies developed serious infections, indicating that dose overwhelmed genetically determined resistance to disease. Furthermore, it was noticed that among the babies who received the lowest doses, the two babies who died of TB both had a rapid downhill course. This would indicate tat at low doses, genetic differences greatly influenced the outcome [8].

In either case, low dose or high dose, genes and toxins have a role to play. Nevertheless, we attribute the cause of high-dose illnesses to toxicity, and we attribute the cause of low-dose illnesses to genes. Does this make any sense at all? Wouldn't it be better to avoid putting the blame on either toxins or genes, in favor of examining the process by which toxin and genes contribute to disease?

Pathogenesis is the sequence of events leading to the development of disease. Before the advent of Precision Medicine, medical scientists studied pathogenesis by examining cells under a microscope. For example, the presence of a bacteria or a fungus or a protozoan in a lesion would lead the pathologist to suspect that the visualized organism caused the disease. Neutrophils in the lesion suggested an acute inflammatory process. The presence of small nodules composed of fibroblasts and macrophages might suggest a chronic granulomatous reaction. The presence of necrotic epithelium would suggest that the process was killing cells, and the pathologist might next try to determine whether the death of cells had an ischemic basis (i.e., caused by diminished blood supply) or a toxic basis (i.e., caused by a poison excreted by the infecting organism). Morphologic observations led to tentative guesses about the events that preceded the disease. This method of pathologic analysis worked well for nearly two centuries. [Glossary Lesion, Neutrophils, Protozoa, Pathologist]

Morphologic evaluation remains a useful method for understanding the pathogenesis of disease. Nonetheless, today we have new methods that can supplement, and even replace, morphologic examination. For example, we now know how to find many of the gene mutations that are considered the causes of inherited diseases. Let's look at one such example. Genetic analysis indicates that Acrokeratosis verruciformis of Hopf is caused by a mutation of the ATP2A2 gene, which codes for the sarcoplasmic reticulum Ca2 ATPase2 pump in muscle cells [9]. It so happens that Acrokeratosis verruciformis of Hopf is an inherited skin disease, characterized by multiple, keratotic lesions that occur on the palms of the hands; soles of the feet; and on knees, elbows, and forearms. The lesions are usually evident soon after birth, but seldom produce any serious health consequences. Do you see anything odd about this? How can a mutation of a muscle protein cause a skin disease? Furthermore, the muscle cells of patients harboring the ATP2A2 mutation suffer no ill-effects whatsoever. There seems to be a discordance between genotype and phenotype (i.e., the genetic cause and the pathological consequence). [Glossary Mutation types]

Of course, there is a logical explanation. It seems that myocytes, which are totally reliant on the efficiency of their ATPase pumps for their well-being, are endowed with backup systems that compensate for reductions in the activity of the sarcoplasmic reticulum Ca2 ATPase2 pump. Hence, muscle cells are relatively unaffected by the mutation of the ATP2A2 gene. Keratinocytes, like muscles cells, use the Ca2 ATPase2 pump, but for a purpose unrelated to muscular contraction. In keratinocytes, the pump is involved in cell-to-cell adhesion and keratinocyte maturation [9]. Without the benefit of back-up pathways, keratinocytes are adversely affected by a drop in activity of the Ca2 ATPase2 pump.

Is the mystery solved? Not quite. It seems that Darier disease, another genetically inherited skin disease, is also caused by loss-of-function mutations in the ATP2A2 gene. Darier disease presents as crusty patches on skin, first appearing in young adults. Dermatologists can distinguish between the two diseases by clinical presentation and pathologists can distinguish the two diseases by histologic examination. Here is the next dilemma. How can one genetic abnormality be responsible for two different genetic diseases? [Glossary Histology]

Once again, we are faced with a dilemma of our own creation. We have come to expect a simple causal relation between gene and disease. The truth is that a genetic mutation does not, by itself, cause a disease. A variety of events and conditions must apply before the disease develops. When we stop thinking in terms of the cause of a disease, and begin to think in terms of the steps in development of a disease, we can easily imagine that Darier disease develops through a different set of steps than Acrodermatitis verruciformis of Hopf. Because both diseases seem to conform to a specific familial pattern (i.e., families with Darier disease do not develop Acrodermatitis verruciformis of Hopf, and vice versa) it seems plausible that a set of familial genes modifies the development of each disease.

Luckily, neither Darier disease nor Acrokeratosis verruciformis of Hopf are life-threatening conditions. Nonetheless, precise knowledge of pathogenesis provides us with a metabolic pathway that can serve as a drug target. It has been shown that by inhibiting cyclooxygenase-2 in keratinocytes, the downregulation of ATP2A2 can be reversed, suggesting a novel therapeutic approach to the treatment for both diseases [10].

Just as it is difficult to justify the concept of "cause," it is likewise difficult to provide a scientific definition for its etymologic opposite: the "sporadic" disease. A sporadic disease occurs with no known cause, and without any discernible pattern of occurrence (e.g., neither inherited nor caused by the environment). Thus, diseases that have a familial pattern of inheritance are always considered nonsporadic, even when the root genetic cause is unknown. Likewise, diseases that occur as an epidemic or endemic pattern are always considered nonsporadic, even when the precise environmental cause is unknown. Rare diseases are seldom sporadic, as they typically exhibit some discernible pattern of inheritance.

Common diseases are often sporadic, but may contain subsets of occurrences that are nonsporadic. An example is schizophrenia. Schizophrenia is a common disease with a prevalence of about 1.1%. This translates to over 50 million individuals, worldwide, who suffer from this mental disorder. Many cases of schizophrenia occur in families and such cases are considered to be inherited and, thus, nonsporadic. Other cases seem to have no familial association and are considered sporadic. Are these sporadic cases caused by environmental factors, or are they caused by de novo mutations that arose in the affected individuals? Recent evidence would suggest that many of the so-called sporadic cases arise from de novo mutations equivalent to those seen in the familial (i.e., nonsporadic) cases [11]. Hence, among the sporadic cases of schizophrenia is a subset of nonsporadic cases. Do not dwell on this; it makes no sense. [Glossary De novo mutation disease, Prevalence]

It is not unusual to find a subset of a common disease that is characterized by the same genetic mutation that is found in a rare inherited disease. For example, inherited mutations in the SDBS gene are the root cause Shwachman-Diamond syndrome, a rare congenital disorder characterized by pancreatic insufficiency, bone marrow failure, and short stature. Mutations of the same SDBS gene are found in about 3% of cases of acquired aplastic anemia, indicating that a mutation that causes a rare congenital disease may account for a small subset of occurrences of a more frequently occurring disease [12]. Likewise, in a study of patients with hypertension, a common disease that occurs sporadically, about 6% were shown to have the clinical features of Liddle syndrome, a rare monogenic form of hypertension. Such observations would suggest that common "sporadic" diseases contain subsets of rare genetic diseases. [13,14]. [Glossary Syndrome versus disease, Congenital disorder, Aplastic anemia]

When an association is made between a disease and some demographic factor, the distinction between sporadic and nonsporadic may be arbitrary. For example, if a disease occurs predominantly in women, can it be called sporadic? The cause may be completely unknown, but it has a definite pattern, characterized by gender dominance.

We must conclude that the term "sporadic" is fraught with scientific ambiguity and should probably be abandoned altogether. To label a disease "sporadic" legitimizes and perpetuates the dubious notion that diseases can occur without cause (i.e., by chance). In point of fact, most of the diseases that were, at one time, considered sporadic, have been shown to have known "causes" (i.e., identifiable factors that play important roles in the pathogenesis of disease). The term "sporadic" should probably be replaced with the term "of undetermined pathogenesis." [Glossary Chance occurrence]

Can we simply discard the notion that every disease has a cause? As a practical concession, we will preserve the term "root cause" to indicate the earliest known event that sets in motion a sequence of events that may lead to the development of disease. In the case of inherited genetic diseases, the germline mutation is equivalent to the "root cause" of the disease. In later chapters of this book, we will see that "root causes" are neither necessary nor sufficient to produce disease. For now, suffice it to say that the pursuit of Precision Medicine requires us to deeply examine everything that we think we know about human disease. [Glossary Germline, Germline mutation]

SECTION 2.2 WHY WE ARE CONFIDENT THAT DISEASES DEVELOP IN STEPS

Life can only be understood backwards; but it must be lived forwards.
Soren Kierkegaard

Imagine a planet populated by creatures who look like party balloons. As you might expect, each balloon person has a pull-string. When two balloon people decide to marry, they literally tie the knot connecting their cords. For the balloon people, life was a endless party, until the giant needle came to town. One touch from the needle, and … POP! The party was over. The balloon people, horrified by the existential threat posed by the giant needle, mobilized their best scientific minds. In short order, they wrapped the needle's tip in a thick knot of rubbery balloon material, incapacitating their foe. And so the balloon people were saved, and the endless party resumed.

In our fictional planet, balloon people popped in a simple, one-step process. Does the same one-step process apply here on planet earth? Humans are conditioned to think in terms of simple cause and effect. When a crime is committed, we look to find the person responsible for the crime. When an airplane crashes, we look for the one error that we led to the catastrophe. When we die, we look for the cause of death. In the prior section, we suggested that diseases are complex processes that develop in a sequential fashion, over time. In this section, we will present all of the available evidence that supports this assertion. [Glossary Cause of death]

Why must we devote an entire section of this book to proving that diseases are multistep processes? Much of the "precision" in precision is devoted to learning the steps involved in pathogenesis. This research effort will yield new ways to prevent, diagnose, classify, and treat human diseases in a manner that would be inconceivable to prior generations of researchers. Success depends on knowing that diseases are multistep processes, and so we need to be certain that our knowledge is based on fact. [Glossary Multistep process]

As an intellectual exercise, and as an introduction to concepts that will be developed in later chapters, let's look at the observations and arguments that tell us that diseases develop in precise, sequential steps.

– Biological systems, in general, operate as sequential, multistep processes.

Most biological systems are stepwise processes, and the stepwise nature applies at the molecular level (e.g., molecular pathways) and the organismal level (e.g., physiologic activities). For example, protein synthesis proceeds from DNA transcription to RNA, RNA translation to the synthesis of an amino acid sequence, and posttranslational modifications of the amino acid sequence to produce a simple folded protein, or a complex protein multimer. The regulation and the mechanics of the process involve a dizzying number of steps that must occur in sequence, and on schedule. No serious biochemist would dare to think in terms of "the cause" of protein synthesis. [Glossary Posttranslational protein modification, Ubiquitination]

On the level of the whole organism, we witness the coordinated development of holometabolous (i.e., metamorphosing) insects that mature from one state to another, until the adult form emerges. Larva, pupa, and adult all share the same genome, but each stage is anatomically distinct and composed of cell types specific for its stage of development. No self-respecting zoologist searches for "the cause" of an insect.

It seems unlikely that human disease should be exempted from the multistep processes that govern all other aspects of biological life. Why do medical researchers persist in looking for "the cause" of a disease?

– A multitude of different effects may follow a single cause.

In one-step processes, we expect every cause to produce an effect. For example, if we perform an experiment in which we repeatedly drop a hammer, we can expect it to fall every time, without exception. In a one-step process, when we supply the cause, we expect the effect. Repeatability validates our assumption that a cause directly produces an effect. Contrariwise, the unpredictability of effect following cause leaves us suspecting that something more than a one-step process is occurring.

It is easy to find examples wherein a specific cause may produce any of several different effects. As we have already seen, inherited deficiencies of the Ca2 ATPase2 pump may result in either Darier disease or Acrodermatisis verruciformis of Hopf, never both in the same patient [9]. As another example, asbestos exposure may produce fibrous plaques on the pleural surfaces of some people and mesothelioma in others. It is hard to explain one cause leading to multiple results, in the absence of intervening conditions and events that determine which path is chosen. Likewise, BRAF T1799A(V600E) mutations, implicated in the cause of malignant melanoma, are also found in over 80% of benign nevi, a type of melanocytic growth, with virtually no propensity for malignant transformation [15,16]. Clearly, some additional biological steps, in addition to a putative oncogene mutation, must participate in the process of carcinogenesis [17]. [Glossary Benign tumor, Malignant, Activated oncogene, Carcinogen, Oncogene, Malignant melanoma, Carcinogenesis]

Some of the inherited tumor syndromes are characterized by an inherited genetic mutation that produces a wide variety of physical abnormalities plus various types of neoplasms (e.g., neurofibromatosis [18–20], tuberous sclerosis complex [21,22], Von Hippel Lindau syndrome [23]). Inherited physical abnormalities often arise as congenital malformations, or as conditions that first appear in childhood or adolescence. The various cancers associated with the inherited cancer syndromes generally arise in early adulthood. These observations suggest that each type of lesion associated with the inherited disease gene must proceed along its own biological path, at its own pace. [Glossary Cancer-causing syndrome, Neurofibromatosis, Malformation, Neoplasm]

It was hoped that some of the variability between cause (inherited mutation) and effect (disease syndromes in offspring) could be reduced by employing inbred mice subjected to single gene knockouts. Under the simplest experimental model (i.e., knockouts of one specific gene), and under the most controlled circumstances (i.e., inbred mice), the results have shown wildly diverse sets of fetal anomalies among the mice having the same germline mutation [24]. It would seem that even under these uniform genetic and environmental conditions, intervening biological events must have intruded between the root genetic error and the diverse pathologic outcomes. [Glossary Genetically engineered mouse, Knockout mice]

Just as a known cause of disease may produce any of several effects, we also observe that a known cause, believed to be sufficient to produce disease, may produce no effect whatsoever. In genetics, the term "penetrance" is applied to inherited genes that produce disease in some individuals, but not in others. A genetic disorder with high penetrance is one that will affect most of the individuals who carry the gene. In a low-penetrance genetic disorder, disease will be observed in only a small portion of individuals who carry the gene. Why does an inherited disorder affect some individuals and not others? Presumably, conditions in the individuals from whom disease does not occur have genetic traits or acquired attributes that block one or more steps in the development of the disease. [Glossary Penetrance]

With the advent of fast and economical DNA sequencing, and with the availability of sequence data for large numbers of individuals, we are finding a range of disease mutations in apparently healthy individuals. There is a growing literature devoted to gene variants, previously thought to be the direct cause of human diseases, that occur with surprisingly high prevalence in sample populations [25–32]. It would seem that the presumed tight relationship between genetic cause and genetic effect is much less tight than one might suppose.

As a general rule, humans react to infections with a range of physiological responses [33–37]. For example, Mycobacterium tuberculosis can infect an individual and produce an aggressive pulmonary infection that disseminates through the body, killing the individual in months. The same organism can produce a small, limited pathologic reaction in the lung, and remain in the body in a quiescent state for the life of the individual. The variety of possible clinical phenotypes that can arise from an infection is inconsistent with a simple cause/effect model of disease.

Let's turn our attention to cancers and ask ourselves whether it seems likely that cancers result from a single cellular event. Imagine having a mouse model of cancer in which every mouse is born with an oncogene. If oncogenes cause cancer, wouldn't you expect to see cancer arising in every mouse born with the active oncogene in its germline? Might we not also expect to see a tumor developing in 100% of the cells considered to be target population of the oncogene? For example, if an oncogene is known to cause liver cancer (hepatoma), and if every cell of the body inherits the active oncogene in its germline, then shouldn't we expect to see liver cancer arising from every liver cell of the body? The notion of creating strains of oncogene-carrying mice is not new. There is a thriving area of research devoted to the study of mice genetically engineered to carry specific activated oncogenes in their germlines. A large collection of literature describes the types of cancers occurring in mouse strains bred to carry oncogenes or depleted of tumor suppressor genes [38–40]. In none of these models do we observe a 100% incidence of tumors. In all these models, we see cancers developing in some of the mice, but not others. The cancers arise from rare cells within the affected organs, not from every cell that carries the oncogene. Furthermore, the cancers that develop typically develop in adult mice, and are not found in fetal tissues or in newborn mice. The observations that oncogene-inherited tumors do not occur until adulthood is highly suggestive that a sequence of events must occur, over time, before a tumor emerges. The observation that most oncogene-carrying mice do not develop tumors would suggest that the full sequence of events, following the insertion of the oncogene into the germline, does not often occur. [Glossary Incidence, Tumor suppressor gene, Hepatoma]

The mouse system closely models the human counterpart in which a child inherits a gene associated with certain types of cancer. For example, women who inherit the BRCA gene are predisposed to develop cancer of the breast or ovaries or peritoneal surface. The lifetime risk of developing cancer in one of these tissues is high, exceeding 50%, but many women who carry the BRCA oncogene will never develop cancer, and very few of the women who carry the BRCA gene will develop multiple cancers and almost none of the BRCA gene carriers will develop a cancer before they reach adulthood [41]. These observations tell us that having the BRCA gene is not sufficient to cause cancer. Some other conditions or events must occur before cancer develops. [Glossary Association versus cause, BRCA, Carrier]

Are there any examples for which the acquisition of an active oncogene will, as a rule, lead to the development of cancer in the affected individual. Let's consider chronic myelogenous leukemia (CML) and the bcr/abl fusion gene. Almost every case of CML is associated with the bcr/abl fusion gene. The bcr/abl fusion gene codes for a protein that activates several pathways involved in cell proliferation and the acquisition of properties associated with the malignant phenotype. A one-step mechanism has been proposed in which the bcr/abl fusion gene promotes clonal proliferation of white blood cells, leading directly to the development of CML [42]. The drawback to this hypothetical scenario is that the bcr/abl fusion gene is found in a random screening of healthy individuals, a finding that has been confirmed in multiple laboratories [29–31]. In addition, blood cells sampled from healthy individuals have been found to harbor a range of oncogenes known to specifically characterize other types of leukemias and lymphomas [28,32,43]. These observations indicate that for multiple types of cancer, the presence of a putative causal oncogene is not alone sufficient to cause a cancer. Other conditions must be met, or other events in the pathogenesis of cancer must occur for cancer to develop. [Glossary Philadelphia chromosome, Malignant phenotype, Lymphoma]

The divergence of biological destinies, following the same initiating event, cannot be reconciled with a direct cause-and-event scenario.

– **Every disease has its own latency.**

The time interval that begins with exposure to a toxin or infectious agent, and ends with the clinical expression of disease is usually referred to as the latency of disease, or, in the case of infections, the incubation period of disease. Latency periods vary greatly among diseases. Furthermore, the latency period of any particular disease may vary depending on its host (e.g., a partially resistant host may have a longer latency than a highly susceptible host). [Glossary Dormancy, Latency versus dormancy]

For example, very long latencies follow the exposure of a person to a carcinogen, and the emergence of a cancer. In the case of asbestos-induced mesotheliomas, there are reported cases of navy shipyard workers, and the members of their families, who were exposed to asbestos for a very brief time, during World War II, only to develop cancers 20–40 years later. Postradiation tissue injuries may also have long latency periods, extending over years or decades.

Latencies for infections may be short, as seen with Pasteurella multocida, which can cause cellulitis on its first day of infection, or long, as with rabies, which can take several months or in excess of a year to produce encephalitis. Some organisms may lie dormant for years or decades, before emerging as disease-causing organisms (e.g., herpes viruses 1 and 2, varicella).

It is worthwhile reviewing here the issue of dose-dependent latency periods. We have suggested that after an organism is exposed to a toxic injury, there ensues a series of biological events that eventually lead to the expression of disease. It this were the case, the latency period would be unaffected by the original dose of the toxin. All of the events leading to the expression of disease are expected to unfold according to their own schedule, regardless of the size of the original injury. If we were wrong, and the original toxic injury were the only causal event, then we might expect the latency to be shortened when we increased the dose of the toxin.

To illustrate, consider the carnival sledge hammer striker. If the contestant slams the hammer with a great force, the ball will zoom to the top of the post and ring the bell. The interval between the sledge hammer strike and the bell ring will be very short. If the contestant hits the striker with somewhat less force, that is just able to lift the ball to the bell, then the bell will ring, but with a longer latency period between the strike and the ring. In this example of one-step causation, dose determines latency.

If the carnival striker were a many-step process, then the latency might be dose independent. For example, if the sledge hammer's strike activated a measuring device that recorded the magnitude of the generated impulse, and if the carnival barker were required to print out the measured data, and if the magnitude of the measured data were compared with the previously collected data, held in a reference table, and if a committee were convened to determine whether the measurement exceeded a certain level deemed "bell-worthy" and if, at the end of these deliberations, a messenger were sent to ascend to the top of the striker post and manually ring the bell, then you can see that the original strength of the striker (i.e., the dosage) might not correlate with the latency period (i.e., the time between the strike and the ring of the bell).

Empirical evidence suggests that diseases develop with a characteristic latency, regardless of the size of the initial dose of the toxin. In the case of cancer, a high initial dose of a carcinogen often yields more cancers in the exposed population than a small initial dose. But the latency stays about the same, in either case [44]. Likewise, when you're infected with a cold virus, you might develop sniffles and a mild fever a week later. The infectious load (i.e., the number of viruses to which you have been exposed) may alter the likelihood that you will become ill, but you'll still need to wait a week before seeing symptoms. These findings are consistent with a multistep disease process.

It can be argued that, in the case of infections with pathogenic organisms, the symptoms of disease correlate closely to the growth of the infection. As the number of organisms in the body increases, the damage done by the organism also increases. In this sense, infections are actually one-step diseases and the latency is simply a reflection of the time required for the organism to increase to a population size where its presence becomes clinically detectable. We know that this argument is not valid. During the latency period of an infection, the patient does not have increasing symptoms, as the infection grows in the body. Put simply, if the latency of a cold virus is 6 days, the patient does not have half the symptoms of a cold at day three, and two-thirds the symptoms of a cold at day four. The patient is symptomless until the latency period has ended. As it happens, we know a great deal about the biological events that transpire during the latency periods of infectious organisms, and we will be elaborating upon this topic in Chapter 6.

> - **The cells exposed to a toxin are not always the cells that give rise to the resultant disease.**

In the case of a direct cause-and-effect phenomenon, we would expect that the cell that is acted upon by the cause will be the cell that exhibits the effect. In many cases, this simple relationship between injured cell and diseased cell holds true. When we ingest a poison known to be metabolized to an active state by liver cells, we should expect to see liver cell necrosis. We would not expect to find bone marrow necrosis or kidney cell necrosis. When we overexpose ourselves to ultraviolet rays, known to penetrate no further than the dermis, we might expect to see the toxic effect of cells throughout the epidermis, but we would not expect to see toxicity in the lungs or the liver.

It happens that there are instances wherein a toxic agent exerts an effect on cells that did not exist at the time that the toxin was administered. As a general rule, when embryos are exposed to carcinogens, they do not develop tumors composed of the primitive embryonic cells that are present at the moment of exposure (i.e., transplacental exposures to carcinogenes rarely, if ever, produce teratomas, nephroblastomas, yolk sac tumors, and other tumors of embryonic stem cell origin). Instead, the exposed embryos that survive to birth typically do not develop tumors until they reach adulthood, at which time they may develop adult-type tumors, such as lung cancers and colon cancers. [Glossary Stem cell, Multipotent stem cell, Pluripotent stem cell, Totipotent stem cell]

Rainbow trout eggs are exquisitely sensitive to carcinogens. The tumors that develop, following a single exposure to a low dose of aflatoxin, are hepatocellular carcinomas or mixed hepatocellular/cholangiocarcinomas arising much later, in adult trout. These tumors, known to occur naturally in adult trout, are derived from liver cells and bile duct cells, neither of which were present in the embryo at the time of exposure to the carcinogen.

The authors of a landmark paper, published in 1971, reported an increase in the number of young women who developed an extremely rare cancer: clear-cell adenocarcinoma of the cervix or of the vagina [45]. The mothers of most of these young women had ingested a nonsteroidal synthetic estrogen (diethylstilbestrol, DES) during their pregnancies. In utero exposure to this drug caused a specific rare tumor to occur in the female offspring. This tumor, arising in adolescent women and young adults, is derived from differentiated cell types that were not present in the embryo at the time of exposure [46]. How is this even possible? Presumably, the cells in the embryo that are exposed to diethylstilbestrol fulfill their normal course of development, producing fetal cells and fetal organs, and eventually serving as the progenitors for the fully differentiated cells of the adult human organism. Meanwhile, the steps of carcinogenesis (i.e., the pathogenesis of cancer) continue, until a developed cancer arises from the differentiated tissues of the adult daughter.

We do not need to look to animal models of disease or to rare instances of human cancer to make our point. Lung cancer is the most common cause of cancer deaths in humans. About a quarter of lung cancers are squamous cell carcinomas of the lung. Surprisingly, the squamous cell is not a type of lung cell. To be precise, the normal lung contains zero squamous cells. If a carcinogen such as cigarette smoke exerted its effect directly, by transforming a normal lung cell into a cancer cell, then we would expect never to encounter a squamous cell carcinoma of lung. Because we commonly encounter squamous cell carcinomas in the lung, we can surmise that multiple events intervened after nonsquamous lung cells were exposed to a carcinogen.

- **We observe phases of disease that follow a strict temporal sequence.**

The temporal sequence of disease is best demonstrated in cancers, which often develop over years or decades. By looking backwards, we find convincing evidence that every cancer lesion is preceded by precancer stages, and that the precancer stages occur in strict sequence. In the case of multiple myeloma, we only know of one precancerous condition, known as monoclonal gammopathy of undetermined significance, MGUS for short. MGUS consists of a clonal expansion of plasma cells that can be diagnosed by the presence of a spike in the synthesis of a single species of immunoglobulin molecule produced by the clonal plasma cells and detected by serum electrophoresis. MGUS is a benign condition, but it carries the risk of progression to multiple myeloma, a cancer derived from plasma cells. By examining blood samples of individuals with multiple myeloma, a retrospective study demonstrated that every case of multiple myeloma is preceded by MGUS, indicating that the pathogenesis of multiple myeloma requires at least one intermediary lesion [47]. [Glossary Precancerous condition, Multiple myeloma, MGUS]

Lesions such as MGUS are categorized as precancers. These are the morphologically identifiable nonmalignant lesions that precede the emergence of invasive cancers. After a time, invasive cancers develop from the precancer. If we knew nothing about the biological events that precede the development of precancers, we could nonetheless infer that carcinogenesis is a multistep process, because it passes through a precancerous stage [48–51].

If every invasive cancer of humans is preceded by a well-characterized precancerous condition, then we can infer that every precancer must occur in individuals at a younger age than the age at which the cancer occurs. What applies to an individual must also apply to populations of individuals. The average population age at which a cancer develops must be older than the average population age at which the precancer lesions developed. This inference may seem obvious, but it frees us to follow the progression of disease in population data. Using publicly available cancer data, we can determine whether precancers fit into a timeline of events that lead to cancer.

For example ductal breast cancer, the most common cause of breast cancer in women, is thought to develop through a series of morphologically distinct precursors, specifically: intraductal hyperplasia precedes atypical intraductal hyperplasia, which precedes ductal carcinoma in situ, which precedes invasive breast carcinoma. The published average ages of occurrence for these different lesions seem to bear out the hypothesized chronological precedence for precancers (Fig. 2.2). [Glossary Hyperplasia, In situ]

- The median age of women with intraductal hyperplasia is 45 years [52].
- The median age of women with atypical intraductal hyperplasia is 50 years [52].
- The median age of women with ductal carcinoma in situ is 60 years [53].
- The median age of women with invasive breast cancer is 61 years [54]

Similar observations have been noted for the age of occurrence of uterine cervical cancers [55]. In the following listing, the average age of diagnosis is followed by the name of the lesion. Each successive lesion represents a step in the development of cervical cancer, beginning with a noninvasive precursor lesion (i.e., carcinoma in situ), and ending with a fully invasive cancer (Fig. 2.3).

- 34 years, carcinoma in situ
- 35 years, large cell squamous cell carcinoma in situ
- 37 years, keratinizing squamous cell carcinoma in situ
- 41 years, microinvasive squamous cell carcinoma
- 49–51 years, fully invasive cancer

The observed timeline provides a sequence of lesions that precedes the development of invasive cancer. Without going into the clinical details, the earliest identifiable precancers occur in the youngest population. The interval between the average age of diagnosis of in situ carcinoma of the cervix, and the average age of diagnosis of the cancer from which it develops, is 15 years.

Why is this important? It tells us that cancer is not a disease that simply "happens" at unexpected moments in our lives. Cancer proceeds through biologically distinct lesions, each of which may be susceptible to specific treatment or prevention strategies. By treating precancers in early-aged individuals, we can eliminate the cancers that would otherwise develop.

- **We observe lesions that are stuck in a phase of development**

Many infections have a carrier state. Most healthy persons are reservoirs for hundreds of species of pathogenic organisms that never bother to cause disease, so long as the individual

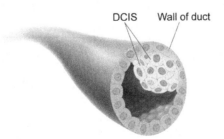

DCIS   Wall of duct

FIG. 2.2 Graphic depicting a breast duct, within which are a clump of proliferating atypical (i.e., not normal) cells. Features of atypia include variation in cellular size and shape from cell to cell, variation in the size and shape of nuclei from cell to cell, and the presence of clumped chromatin (i.e., chromosomal material) in the nuclei. These atypical cells represent a focus of ductal carcinoma in situ, a precancerous lesion that may develop, over time, into invasive breast cancer. *Reproduced from US National Cancer Institute.*

FIG. 2.3 Histologic preparation of one focus of in situ carcinoma of the cervix. Normal appearing glands in connective tissue are present, along with one focus of atypical, crowded squamous cells in the middle-left of the image. The nuclei in these cells are irregularly shaped (i.e., not smooth and oval), and each nucleus has a different shape and size compared with its neighbor. The atypical cells fill all the layers of the mucosal surface, but do not penetrate into the underlying connective tissue. *Reproduced from Wikipedia, donated to the public domain by its author, Haymanj.* [Glossary Connective tissue, Nucleus]

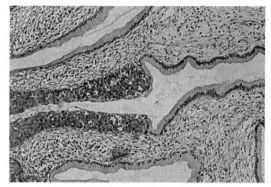

enjoys a healthy immune system [37]. In these extremely common cases, the infection is arrested during pathogenesis, before any real damage occurs. [Glossary Immune system]

Cancer is another disease that can be stuck in an intermediate phase of development. In animal models, carcinogenic protocols tend to produce multiple precancers. Over time, some of these precancers develop into cancers [49,56,57]. Most do not. The occurrence of multiple precancers is also seen in humans. Actinic keratosis is a skin lesion that is the precancer for squamous cell carcinoma of the skin. Actinic keratoses occur almost exclusively on sun-exposed areas of the skin (e.g., face, neck, arms, and back). Their occurrence increases with age. Most individuals with fair complexions who live in tropical climates will eventually develop one or more actinic keratoses. The chance of any particular actinic keratosis progressing to squamous carcinoma of the skin is quite small. An individual who has hundreds of actinic keratoses is likely to have a small number of these lesions, perhaps zero, progressing to squamous cell carcinoma. The so-called dysplastic nevus (also called atypical nevus) is a precancer of malignant melanoma. An individual with hundreds of normal appearing nevi may have a much smaller number of the so-called dysplastic nevi. A small percentage of the dysplastic nevi will progress to melanoma [58]. Likewise, adenomas of the colon are considered to be precursors for adenocarcinoma of colon. Adenomas of the colon are quite common, but adenocarcinoma of the colon is much less common. In each instance, the high number of observable precancers, compared with the relatively low number of cancers arising from these lesions, indicates that the stepwise development of cancers can be blocked at an early step in disease development. [Glossary Nevus, Dysplasia]

The incertitude of disease progression seems to be a general phenomenon that applies to inherited conditions as well as conditions acquired by exposures to environmental agents (e.g., radiation, chemicals, infections). For example, acquired somatic mutations of the CBL gene may play a role in the development of some myeloproliferative disorders, particularly acute myeloid leukemia [59]. An inherited syndrome caused by a germline mutation of CBL is characterized by children with dysmorphic facial development, developmental delay, and several other abnormalities. This inherited disorder is also associated with an increased risk of juvenile myelomonocytic leukemia. Surprisingly, a large percentage of affected children develop an early myeloproliferative disorder that regresses spontaneously, after a time [60]. The occasional spontaneous regression of a leukemia precancer, in an inherited disorder, indicates that the steps leading to leukemia are not inevitable, even in the case when every cell in the body carries the putative disease gene. [Glossary Spontaneous versus sporadic, Regression, Neoplastic regression, Precancer regression, Noninherited genetic disease, Revertant mutation, Somatic mutation, Myeloproliferative disorder]

If the steps leading to disease become blocked, producing the spontaneous regression or the permanent persistence of precursor stages, then why can't we achieve the same results through human intervention? In fact, we can. This topic will be discussed in greater detail in later chapters.

– With the exception of some infectious diseases, there is scarcely any overlap among the diseases that occur in children and the diseases that occur in adults

Children are fundamentally no different from adults. The genes, cells, and tissues of the child and the adult are about the same. In the case of nondividing tissues such as liver cells and neurons, the adult has many of the same cells that persisted in the soma, from childhood. Because adults are basically the same as children, from a cellular perspective, we would expect that a cellular event that causes a disease in a child would cause the same disease in an adult. This is not the case.

We will see in Section 5.1, "The Biological Differences Between Rare Diseases and Common Diseases," that there is almost no overlap in the types of diseases that occur in children and the types of diseases that occur in adults (with the exception of some infectious diseases). It is as though children and adults were two unrelated types of organisms.

As it happens, most diseases of adults take a very long time to time to develop, and that is why they do not occur in children. Most diseases that occur in children have a strong genetic influence and develop over a relatively short time period, producing clinical disease confined to children and adolescents. Even in such cases, where the development of a disease is short-ened, it is rare to find a disease that is present ab initio, in the fetus preceding birth. If diseases happened "all at once" there would simply be no adult-specific diseases, and every genetic disease would express itself clinically in the embryo. [Glossary Ab initio]

– Disease mutations that occur in somatic cells infrequently lead to disease

DNA mutations occur commonly in our cells. When we take into account the many cells that compose a human body, we expect that trillions of mutations occur every few seconds [5]. Luckily, we have very efficient DNA repair mechanisms, but even so, our bodies accumulate lots of mutations, over time. Thanks to whole genome sequencing, we can now compare the sequences of cells collected from various tissues in a single individual, and get some idea of the our accumulated mutation load. In a study wherein samples of chronically sun-exposed eyelid skin were examined for oncogene mutations, the re-searchers found that about a quarter of the skin cells had acquired cancer-causing mutations [61]. We shouldn't be surprised by these findings. It has been estimated that by the time we reach the age of 60 years, every nucleotide in our genome has been mutated in at least one cell of the body [62]. Presumably, every known disease-causing mutation will eventually occur in some of our cells.

Thankfully, most of us get through our lives without developing cancers of the eyelid skin, despite the frequent occurrence of activating oncogene mutations in these tissues. The reason for the discrepancy between oncogene frequency and cancer frequency is that an activated oncogene, by itself, does not cause cancer. Cancer develops as a sequence of events, and none of these events are preordained.

– There are several thousand species of tumors

Tumors, like organisms, occur as species (i.e., distinct types that can be confidently identified and distinguished from all other types of tumors). In fact, there are thousands of well-described species of tumors. Pathologists devote the greater part of their training to distinguishing one species of tumor from another, committing all of these distinctive varieties of tumor to memory. Based on a wealth of past experiences, the collection of classified tumors seems to be stable. Regardless of the chemical carcinogen, or the type of radiation, or the endless combinations of toxic pollutants that we encounter, it is a safe bet that the resulting types of tumors will fall into a preexisting, well-characterized diagnostic category. How is it possible that a seemingly infinite variety of carcinogenic reactions induce a large but strictly finite list of well-characterized tumors?

Whereas there are thousands of species of tumors, there are only a couple hundred different cell types in the human body. Hence, the great variety of tumors cannot be accounted for by the smaller variety of cell types that give rise to tumors.

When we look at individual tumors, we find that each instance of a tumor is genetically unique, suggesting that every cancer that has ever occurred is a unique biological entity. This finding causes us to ask ourselves the following: "If every cancer is genetically unique, then why does every cancer fit into one, and only one, distinct tumor species?" Furthermore, we know that cancers are genetically unstable; their genomes are constantly changing. This being the case, we would expect tumors to constantly change from one tumor type to another, as their genome changes. This does not happen. Hepatomas do not morph into squamous carcinomas. Leukemias do not morph into adenocarcinomas.

We can think of tumor speciation much like we have come to think of animal speciation. Every animal on earth is genetically distinct from every other animal of the same species (with the exception of monozygotic siblings and parthenogenetic offspring) and from every animal of all other species. Despite these genetic differences, every unique individual belongs to one and only one species of animal. How is it possible to achieve uniformity and individuality, together?

Life is a process. Every animal develops through a process that begins with a zygote and a unique set of genes, but develops through a coordinated series of steps that produces an animal that looks and behaves much like every other animal of the same species. Likewise, and in the absence of any better explanation, we are tempted to infer that every cancer arises from the cells of a unique organism, but develops through a coordinated sequence of events that produces a tumor that looks much like every other tumor of the same diagnostic type. The sequence of biological events that account for tumor speciation remains one of the principal mysteries of Precision Medicine. [Glossary Species]

– We see no decline in the incidence of the most common diseases

This is the last, and probably the least, of the arguments presented in this section that support a multistep development of disease. It is included here because it provokes us to think about how common diseases may fundamentally differ from rare diseases. We can observe that the diseases that are most likely to kill us (i.e., aging, cardiovascular disorders, cancer, and infections) have been around for a long time. If a life-threatening common disease were to arise from a direct cause → effect response, then wouldn't we expect to see large drops in mortality from the common diseases, as the causal disease genes are eliminated from our gene pool, through natural selection? Over time, all the common diseases would become rare diseases. We see no evidence of any great decline in the common diseases of humans. [Glossary Natural selection]

We can pretty much rule out a simple genetic cause for any of the common diseases, including aging. We never encounter mutant animals who live forever because their "aging" gene has mutated. For that matter, heritability does not seem to play an important role in the common diseases. There seems to be very little concordance in the rates of occurrence of common diseases among close relatives, even among monozygotic twins [63,64].

If genetic defects are not the direct cause of common diseases, then should we assume that environmental agents are at fault? If this were the case, we might expect huge geographic variations in the rates of occurrence of the common diseases. To an extent, this is the case. The types of cancers that occur at high frequency in industrialized countries are different from the types of cancers occurring in less-industrialized countries. But cancer is a common cause of death worldwide, and there are no common cancers of industrialized countries that are not also observed in less-industrialized countries and vice versa. There are no areas of the world where individuals live to be 1000 years old. There are no areas of the world where infectious diseases are not common. The common diseases of mankind tend to stay common over centuries. [Glossary Infectious disease]

If the common diseases had an isolated cause leading directly to the occurrence of a disease, without any intervening steps to delay and complicate the process, we would expect to observe a very different landscape of disease than we have endured since the dawn of man.

SECTION 2.3 CAUSE OF DEATH

All interest in disease and death is only another expression of interest in life.
Thomas Mann

On July 2, 1881, President James A. Garfield (1831–81) was shot by Charles J. Guiteau, a disgruntled office seeker, at the Baltimore and Potomac Railroad Station in Washington, DC. After eleven weeks of solicitous care, President Garfield died. An autopsy was performed by Dr. D.S. Lamb. The shocking autopsy results were published in the *New York Times* on November 28, 1881 and are publicly available for anyone to review today [65]. In short, a bullet entered President Garfield's back, near the spine, and lodged in soft tissues near the pancreas. During its trajectory, it managed to avoid severing any important structures. All indications were that the bullet would have laid harmlessly where it stopped, coated in fibrous tissue, had it simply been ignored.

In the 11 weeks following the assassination attempt, a steady stream of physicians paraded though the President's bedchamber. Each physician deemed it necessary to fish about for the bullet by sticking a finger or a mechanical probe deep into the entry wound. These manipulations, coupled with remedies of doubtful merit, combined to produce a massive infection from which the President could not recover. When the autopsy report was released, it was evident that the President had survived the attempt at assassination, but had succumbed to the attempt at treatment.

At his trial, Guiteau argued that if anyone should be found guilty of murdering the president, it should be the doctors who attended his bedside. Guiteau's defense was biologically valid, but legally moot. The gunshot wound was the "but-for" cause of the patient's death (i.e., but-for the gunshot wound, the subsequent events leading to the President's death would not have happened). To no one's surprise, but Guiteau's, he was found guilty of murder and hung for the crime. This story illustrates that determining the cause of death is not always a straightforward process. [Glossary But-for]

Let's stop a moment and consider how we have come to think about sequences of causal events that culminate in catastrophe. Everyone has heard the ageless proverb that follows:

For want of a nail the shoe was lost.
For want of a shoe the horse was lost.
For want of a horse the rider was lost.
For want of a rider the message was lost.
For want of a message the battle was lost.
For want of a battle the kingdom was lost.
And all for the want of a horseshoe nail.

The moral of the story is that small errors may produce great catastrophes. We can describe the chain of events using terminology borrowed from medicine and from law. [Glossary Terminology]

The first line, "For want of a nail the shoe was lost," is the "but-for" event. But-for the loss of the nail, the subsequent events, leading to the fall of the kingdom, would not have happened. At the time that the nail was lost, nobody could reasonably foresee the ultimate consequence.

The second line, "For want of a shoe the horse was lost," might be called the underlying cause. We know that a war horse must be properly shod. We cannot foresee how a missing shoe led to the ultimate outcome, but we know enough to say that warhorses are needed in battle.

The third line, "For want of a horse the rider was lost," is an intermediate cause. We still cannot foresee how a missing horseman led to a bad outcome, but we know enough to say that something bad is developing.

The fourth line, "For want of a rider the message was lost," is what we might call the proximate cause. The proximate cause is the first event where we might reasonably expect to foresee the final outcome. We know that battlefield messages can play a crucial role in the outcome of a battle. When you can't convey messages on the field of battle, a bad outcome is not certain, but it is certainly foreseeable. [Glossary Proximate cause]

The sixth and seventh lines, "For want of a message the battle is lost. For want of a battle the kingdom was lost," are the immediate causes of the final outcome. We can say with a high degree of certainty that if the battle is lost, the kingdom will immediately fall.

The sequence of causal events leading to the fall of the kingdom can be schematized as follows:

The but-for cause →
    underlying cause(s) →
        intermediate cause(s) →
            proximate cause →
                immediate cause →
                    final result

Physicians who write death certificates are required to list the diseases and conditions as a chain of cause-related events. In the United States, death certificate data is collected by the Vital Statistics Program of the National Center for Health Statistics. Death certificates are rendered on >99% of individuals who die in the United States [66]. The public has access to an enormous repository of death certificates, collected since 1935 (Fig. 2.4).

The words used to describe the sequence of events will change, slightly, from state to state and country to country, but every jurisdiction recommends a nomenclature similar to that used to describe the demise of our mythical kingdom. Two sample "cause of death" entries, published by the Centers for Communicable Diseases, are listed here [67]:

Case 1

1. Atherosclerotic coronary artery disease (diagnosed 7 years prior to death, the underlying cause)
2. Coronary artery thrombosis (diagnosed 5 years prior to death, an intermediate cause)
3. Acute myocardial infarction (diagnosed 6 days prior to death, the proximate cause)
4. Rupture of myocardium (diagnosed minutes before death, the immediate cause)

Case 2

1. Diabetes mellitus, noninsulin dependent (diagnosed 15 years prior to death, the underlying cause)
2. Hyperosmolar nonketotic coma (diagnosed 8 weeks prior to death, the proximate cause)
3. Acute renal failure (diagnosed 5 days prior to death, the immediate cause)

A voluminous literature is devoted to instructing physicians how to write the "cause of death" section on death certificates [67–71]. With minor variations, these instructions fall along the lines shown in the aforementioned schema. Specifically, a death certificate should contain a list that includes the underlying cause of death, followed by the conditions that occurred as a result of the underlying cause of death, followed by the proximate cause of death (i.e., the condition that led directly to the death of the patient) and the cause immediately preceding the death. A separate listing may include clinically significant conditions that did not directly lead to the death of the patient. If the patient had several underlying conditions that would be expected to lead to death, then the physician should apply a "but-for" test to choose which of the underlying causes of death was indispensable to the final outcome.

Despite hundreds of years of medical tradition, and despite the millions of patients for whom death reports have been written, the quality of death certificates remains abysmal. Numerous studies conducted in many different nations all show that cause of death records are riddled with errors and inconsistencies [66,69,72–77]. Here is one example, recently reported in a *New York Times* expose entitled, "Thousands of deaths from hospital superbugs are going unreported, research shows" [77]. A 72-year-old woman was admitted to a Florida hospital for a bleeding stomach ulcer, requiring surgery. Within hours of leaving the operating room,

TYPE/PRINT IN PERMANENT BLACK INK

FOR INSTRUCTIONS SEE OTHER SIDE AND HANDBOOK

U.S. STANDARD CERTIFICATE OF DEATH

LOCAL FILE NUMBER

STATE FILE NUMBER

DECEDENT

1. DECEDENT'S NAME (First, Middle, Last)
2. SEX
3. DATE OF DEATH (Month, Day, Year)

4. SOCIAL SECURITY NUMBER
5a. AGE—Last Birthday (Years)
5b. UNDER 1 YEAR — Months / Days
5c. UNDER 1 DAY — Hours / Minutes
6. DATE OF BIRTH (Month, Day, Year)
7. BIRTHPLACE (City and State or Foreign Country)

8. WAS DECEDENT EVER IN U.S. ARMED FORCES? (Yes or no)
9a. PLACE OF DEATH (Check only one; see instructions on other side)
HOSPITAL: ☐ Inpatient ☐ ER/Outpatient ☐ DOA
OTHER: ☐ Nursing Home ☐ Residence ☐ Other (Specify)

9b. FACILITY NAME (If not institution, give street and number)
9c. CITY, TOWN, OR LOCATION OF DEATH
9d. COUNTY OF DEATH

10. MARITAL STATUS — Married, Never Married, Widowed, Divorced (Specify)
11. SURVIVING SPOUSE (If wife, give maiden name)
12a. DECEDENT'S USUAL OCCUPATION (Give kind of work done during most of working life. Do not use retired.)
12b. KIND OF BUSINESS/INDUSTRY

13a. RESIDENCE — STATE
13b. COUNTY
13c. CITY, TOWN, OR LOCATION
13d. STREET AND NUMBER

13e. INSIDE CITY LIMITS? (Yes or no)
13f. ZIP CODE
14. WAS DECEDENT OF HISPANIC ORIGIN? (Specify No or Yes — If yes, specify Cuban, Mexican, Puerto Rican, etc.) ☐ No ☐ Yes Specify:
15. RACE — American Indian, Black, White, etc. (Specify)
16. DECEDENT'S EDUCATION (Specify only highest grade completed) Elementary/Secondary (0–12) College (1–4 or 5+)

PARENTS

17. FATHER'S NAME (First, Middle, Last)
18. MOTHER'S NAME (First, Middle, Maiden Surname)

INFORMANT

19a. INFORMANT'S NAME (Type/Print)
19b. MAILING ADDRESS (Street and Number or Rural Route Number, City or Town, State, Zip Code)

DISPOSITION

20a. METHOD OF DISPOSITION
☐ Burial ☐ Cremation ☐ Removal from State
☐ Donation ☐ Other (Specify)
20b. PLACE OF DISPOSITION (Name of cemetery, crematory, or other place)
20c. LOCATION — City or Town, State

21a. SIGNATURE OF FUNERAL SERVICE LICENSEE OR PERSON ACTING AS SUCH
21b. LICENSE NUMBER (of Licensee)
22. NAME AND ADDRESS OF FACILITY

PRONOUNCING PHYSICIAN ONLY

Complete items 23a–c only when certifying physician is not available at time of death to certify cause of death.

23a. To the best of my knowledge, death occurred at the time, date, and place stated.
Signature and Title ▶
23b. LICENSE NUMBER
23c. DATE SIGNED (Month, Day, Year)

ITEMS 24–26 MUST BE COMPLETED BY PERSON WHO PRONOUNCES DEATH

24. TIME OF DEATH M
25. DATE PRONOUNCED DEAD (Month, Day, Year)
26. WAS CASE REFERRED TO MEDICAL EXAMINER/CORONER? (Yes or no)

CAUSE OF DEATH

27. PART I. Enter the diseases, injuries, or complications that caused the death. Do not enter the mode of dying, such as cardiac or respiratory arrest, shock, or heart failure. List only one cause on each line.

Approximate Interval Between Onset and Death

IMMEDIATE CAUSE (Final disease or condition resulting in death) →
a. _____ DUE TO (OR AS A CONSEQUENCE OF):

Sequentially list conditions, if any, leading to immediate cause. Enter UNDERLYING CAUSE (Disease or injury that initiated events resulting in death) LAST
b. _____ DUE TO (OR AS A CONSEQUENCE OF):
c. _____ DUE TO (OR AS A CONSEQUENCE OF):
d.

PART II. Other significant conditions contributing to death but not resulting in the underlying cause given in Part I.

28a. WAS AN AUTOPSY PERFORMED? (Yes or no)
28b. WERE AUTOPSY FINDINGS AVAILABLE PRIOR TO COMPLETION OF CAUSE OF DEATH? (Yes or no)

29. MANNER OF DEATH
☐ Natural ☐ Pending Investigation
☐ Accident
☐ Suicide ☐ Could not be Determined
☐ Homicide
30a. DATE OF INJURY (Month, Day, Year)
30b. TIME OF INJURY M
30c. INJURY AT WORK? (Yes or no)
30d. DESCRIBE HOW INJURY OCCURRED
30e. PLACE OF INJURY — At home, farm, street, factory, office building, etc. (Specify)
30f. LOCATION (Street and Number or Rural Route Number, City or Town, State)

CERTIFIER

31a. CERTIFIER (Check only one)
☐ CERTIFYING PHYSICIAN (Physician certifying cause of death when another physician has pronounced death and completed Item 23) To the best of my knowledge, death occurred due to the cause(s) and manner as stated.
☐ PRONOUNCING AND CERTIFYING PHYSICIAN (Physician both pronouncing death and certifying to cause of death) To the best of my knowledge, death occurred at the time, date, and place, and due to the cause(s) and manner as stated.
☐ MEDICAL EXAMINER/CORONER On the basis of examination and/or investigation, in my opinion, death occurred at the time, date, and place, and due to the cause(s) and manner as stated.

31b. SIGNATURE AND TITLE OF CERTIFIER ▶
31c. LICENSE NUMBER
31d. DATE SIGNED (Month, Day, Year)

32. NAME AND ADDRESS OF PERSON WHO COMPLETED CAUSE OF DEATH (ITEM 27) (Type/Print)

REGISTRAR

33. REGISTRAR'S SIGNATURE ▶
34. DATE FILED (Month, Day, Year)

PHS-T-003

(Left margin, vertical) NAME OF DECEDENT: For use by physician or institution — SEE INSTRUCTIONS ON OTHER SIDE — SEE DEFINITION ON OTHER SIDE — SEE INSTRUCTIONS ON OTHER SIDE — SEE DEFINITION ON OTHER SIDE

DEPARTMENT OF HEALTH AND HUMAN SERVICES — PUBLIC HEALTH SERVICE — NATIONAL CENTER FOR HEALTH STATISTICS — 1989 REVISION

FIG. 2.4 Prototypical death certificate. Item 27 collects the causes of death, Part 1, and other significant conditions, Part 2. *Reproduced from US Government; Documentation for the mortality public use data set, 1999. Mortality Statistics Branch, Division of Vital Statistics, National Center for Health Statistics; 1999.*

pneumonia developed due to infection with Carbapenem-resistant Klebsiella pneumoniae. After 5 weeks in the hospital, the patient expired. On the death certificate, her physician indicated that the patient had died from respiratory failure and septic shock caused by her ulcer. No mention was made of the patient's antibiotic-resistant bacterial pneumonia. Was the omission intentional? In 2013, the CDC published a report indicating that 48.6% of resident physicians in New York City had knowingly reported inaccurate causes of death. According to the surveyed physicians, administrators exerted pressure to under-report causes of death that might reflect poorly on conditions at the hospital [78]. Delving into the deficiencies of death certificate records is a fascinating but ultimately discouraging exercise [75]. Suffice it to say that death certificates do not provide us with reliable temporal sequences of diseases that account for the death of patients.

Death certificate data is our single most important gauge of public health. With this information, we can determine the causes of death in the population, changes in the frequency of occurrences of the different causes of death, and the effect of interventions intended to increase overall life expectancy. In theory, we should be able to examine databases of death certificates and determine the most common pathways of medical events that precede death. For example, if disease X occurs as an event that directly precedes death, then what is the most likely disease to precede disease X? How often is disease X directly preceded by disease Y? How often does disease Q appear among the list of diseases known to precede the proximate causes of death? There are an endless number of questions whose answers may tell us something about the sequence of events leading to death in various categories of patients. We could use this information to intervene in the process or to raise our guard against particularly dangerous sequences or subsequences of events. Alas, we cannot perform these analyses because physicians, as a group, are inept at writing complete and thoughtful death certificates.

The death certificate is a metaphor for disease pathogenesis. Whether we are attempting to determine the cause of a patient's death, or the cause of a patient's disease, we are pursuing the same goal. Deaths and diseases result from sequences of events. We cannot effectively intervene to prevent deaths or diseases unless we understand the processes through which these conditions develop. The psychological sticking point centers on the word "cause." Perhaps, in the new era of Precision Medicine, we can stop thinking in terms of cause, and begin to think in terms of sequences of events that invite our intervention.

SECTION 2.4 WHAT IS A DISEASE PATHWAY?

The physician must be able to tell the antecedents, know the present, and foretell the future.
Hippocrates

According to traditional thinking, a pathway is a sequence of biochemical reactions involving a specific set of enzymes and substrates that produce a chemical product. The classic pathway is the Krebs cycle. The Krebs cycle was so thoroughly understood that it was commonplace to require undergraduates to calculate the output of the cycle (in moles of

ATP) based on stoichiometric equations employing known amounts of substrate. Some pathways operated inside the cell, like the Krebs cycle and the Embden-Meyerhof-Parnas pathway, and some worked outside the cell, such as the blood coagulation pathway, but they all worked in their own lock-step fashion, with every enzyme doing its specified job.

To see why our former concept of "pathway" is so confusing in the era of Precision Medicine, let's take a step back and think a moment about systems engineering. When an engineer designs a machine, from parts, she can assign names to the components of the system, and these named components can be relied upon to behave in a manner that is characteristic of its type. A capacitor will behave like a capacitor, and a resistor will behave like a resistor. The engineer need not worry that the capacitor will behave like a semiconductor or an integrated circuit. The engineer knows that the function of each component in the system will never change. The biologist operates in a world wherein components change their functions, from organism to organism, cell to cell, and moment to moment. As one example, medical researchers discovered an important protein that plays a role in the development of cancer. This protein, p53, was formerly considered to be the primary cellular driver for human malignancy. When p53 mutated, normal cellular regulation was disrupted, and cells proceeded down a slippery path leading to cancer. In the past few decades, as more information was obtained, cancer researchers have learned that p53 is just one of many proteins that play some role in carcinogenesis, and that the role played by p53 changes depending on the species, tissue type, cellular microenvironment, genetic background, and many other factors. Under one set of circumstances, p53 may modify DNA repair; under another set of circumstances, p53 may cause cells to arrest the growth cycle [79,80]. It is difficult to predict a biological outcome when pathways change their primary functionality based on cellular context. Various mutations in the gene coding for p53 have been linked to 11 clinically distinguishable cancer-related disorders, and there is little reason to assume that the same biological role is played in all of these 11 disorders [81].

When you think about it, we should have known that proteins are versatile actors, playing many cellular roles. If this were not the case, pathways would never evolve. Imagine a pathway that uses 10 enzymes, working in tandem. How would such a pathway evolve? As each of the 10 enzymes mutates into existence, does it just wait around for a few million years until all of the other pathway enzymes show up? Of course not. Natural selection does not conserve sequences that code for proteins that have no useful function [82]. We can safely infer that every protein in a pathway must have served some alternate purpose, while the pathway was evolving. We can likewise infer that after a pathway is established, its constituent proteins may have multiple functions in the cell. To a limited extent, cells have ways to compartmentalize specific activities, by creating protein scaffolds and lipid membranes that enclose or otherwise demarcate cellular regions (e.g., nucleoli, Golgi bodies, smooth endoplasmic reticulum, rough endoplasmic reticulum, lysosomes, peroxisomes, nuclear membrane). Nonetheless, cells tend to exercise their biochemical options; otherwise, life would be boring.

It is best to think of enzymes as the impromptu comics of the biological sciences. A quick-witted comedian can find multiple uses for any randomly chosen object. A cardboard shoebox can serve as a hat, or a sleeve, or a house for gerbils. Much the same way, the nucleolar protein dyskerin serves to modify specific uridine residues of ribosomal RNA by converting them to pseudouridine. Dyskerin also serves as a component of the telomerase complex [83].

The adaptability of enzymes to serve different functions promotes evolution. Hemoglobin began its career as an oxygen trapper to protect anaerobic bacteria from the toxic effects of oxygen in the atmosphere [84]. As earth's oxygen levels increased and organisms evolved to use oxygen to their advantage, the hemoglobin molecule evolved into a triple functioning trapper/transporter/releaser of oxygen. The facility by which multimeric proteins, such as hemoglobin, express functionally distinct isoforms of themselves, during different stages of fetal development, reminds us that one protein may serve different pathways, at different times [85].

When we think about how enzymes function, we see that pathways may differ among individuals of the same species. From our high-school biochemistry classes, we remember that an enzyme is a molecule whose function is to hold a substrate molecule, thus facilitating interactions between the substrates. The enzyme itself is a catalyst for the reaction of substrates and is not consumed by the reaction. Because there are minor variations in the genes that code for enzymes (i.e., population polymorphisms), you might expect that one individual's enzyme might fit differently with its substrate than some other individual's equivalent enzyme. In fact, one enzyme might fit a different substrate molecule, in two individuals, depending on very minor variations in their respective gene sequences. This would mean that a pathway in one individual might be different from the pathway in another individual, even when the enzymes in the pathway all have the same names. As an example, a polymorphism found in the MDR1 gene changes the substrate specificity of its enzyme product, thus changing the pathway followed by individuals with different polymorphisms of the same enzyme [86]. [Glossary Polymorphism]

Biological systems often have more redundancy than humanly designed systems, and the activities of a pathway can be pushed aside by competing pathways designed to perform a similar function [5] For example, there are at least seven different DNA repair pathways, each specializing in a particular type of damage repair (e.g., direct reversal repair, mismatch repair, nucleotide excision repair, homologous recombination, base excision repair, single-strand break repair, nonhomologous end joining, and Fanconi Anemia DNA crosslink repair). Some types of DNA lesions are substrates for more than one pathway, and the ways in which these pathways interact are complex [87]. Of course, any of these pathways, when perturbed, can lead to the development of various disorders.

The engineer who builds a device from component parts can depend on the system, as a whole, remaining constant. A cellphone with 50 components, on Monday, will have the same 50 components on Tuesday. Not so in biological systems, which are constantly in flux and subject to major shakeups in composition. For example, the c-Myc gene is believed to regulate the expression of 15% of all genes [88]. This large retinue of genes regulated by c-Myc includes genes involved in transcription (i.e., the machinery for making proteins) and chromatin remodeling (i.e., the basic structure of the genome itself). Hence, alterations in c-Myc gene can fundamentally change the entire system in which c-Myc and everything else functions, thus re-engineering virtually every pathway in the cell.

Our ability to sensibly assign a gene to a pathway is limited because the effects of a mutation in a single gene may indirectly affect many different pathways. Furthermore, pathways, and their regulators, may vary from cell type to cell type. Syndromes involving multiple pathways and multiple tissues occur frequently when a deleterious mutation hits a regulatory element, such as a transcription factor [89,90]. In addition, one gene's role may be influenced by other genes, a phenomenon called epistasis. Likewise, the role of a gene is influenced by the temporal expression of the gene (e.g., at precise moments in the development of an organism), and by its sequential activation (e.g., preceding or succeeding sequential steps in multiple pathways). The activity of a protein encoded by a gene can be influenced by subtle variations in amino acid sequence, by three-dimensional structure, by chemical modifications of the protein, by the quantity of the protein, by location of the protein molecules in cells, and by the type of cell in which the protein is expressed. Attempts to predict the functional effect of single or multiple gene variations are typically futile [91,92]. [Glossary Homeobox, Transcription factor]

At best, the term "pathway" is a convenient conceptual device to organize molecules that interact with a generally defined set of partner molecules to produce a somewhat consistent range of biological actions. About this time, you might be wondering why nature permits pathways to be loosely coupled. Wouldn't we expect natural selection to produce well-defined pathways that interact with other pathways in a predetermined manner? Maybe not. In complex systems, errors are more likely to arise in the way that subsystems interoperate, than from breakdowns in individual components. Loosely coupled (or even decoupled) pathways limit the ability of a disturbance in one subsystem to affect the other parts [93].

If pathways are complex, how can we hope to understand how different pathways interact with one another, in health and in disease, at any one moment? Maybe we can't [94]. When complex systems are perturbed from their normal, steady-state activities, the rules that govern the system's behavior become unpredictable [95]. This being the case, is there anything that we can do to draw useful information from a system that is ultimately unknowable?

Of course, every long-lived complex system is fundamentally stable; otherwise, the system would soon disintegrate under the weight of its own chaotic behavior. There are always simple ways to monitor complex systems, and, within some practical limits, to predict its behavior. Imagine, for a moment, that you are an engineer assigned to monitor a massive steam engine. If a problem arises, your job is to push the panic button. Every hour, you look at the pressure gauge located on one of the steam pipes leaving the engine. The gauge has a needle that sweeps through a range of pressures, and is marked by red zones indicating pressure readings that are too high or too low. On most days, the needle points midway between the red zones, indicating a normal pressure. The gauge has a second meter for temperature; it too reads normal. You notice that the pressure gauge needle is jiggling slightly, at a very fast pace. The fast jiggle tells you that all the pistons in the steam engine are moving, and with about the same pressure kick. If some of the pistons in the engine were failing, the jiggle of the needle would be erratic. A seasoned engineer can determine whether pistons are misfiring, just by looking at the jiggle in the gauge. One day, as you make your customary inspections, you notice that the pressure gauge needle has risen into the red zone. You know that if the pressure continues to rise, pipes will break and delicate parts in the engine will fail. You open a valve that vents steam into the air, and the pressure returns to normal. You immediately call an engine specialist, who tells you to maintain a normal system pressure by continuing to vent steam. He indicates that he will arrive in a few moments. When he arrives, you anxiously ask him what could have gone wrong. He answers, grimly, that it could be almost anything and that he will need to run a complete diagnostic review of all the subsystems.

Readers who have worked in medical wards undoubtedly recognize that the preceding steamy story was a parable for the medical procedure known as "taking vitals." At regular intervals, the vital signs of every patient in a hospital ward are measured and recorded: respirations, temperature, pulse, and blood pressure. If these four measurements fall within normal limits, it is a safe bet that the patient is medically stable. When an abnormal measurement is taken, a physician must be called to work up the problem in the hopes of finding a correctable cause. Fever is not a disease; respiration is not a disease, and high blood pressure is not a disease; they are quantitative indicators that something is amiss. Likewise, the tools of molecular biology provide us with the opportunity to associate phenotypic patterns of disease (e.g., altered genes, dysfunctional pathways, precursor lesions) with the steps leading to the expression of disease.

SECTION 2.5 DOES SINGLE-EVENT PATHOGENESIS EVER HAPPEN?

If I didn't believe it, I would never have seen it.
Anon

Throughout this book, you'll encounter the recurring theme that every disease has a pathogenesis: a multievent process, occurring over time, that eventually leads to the emergence of a clinical phenotype. One of the goals of Precision Medicine is to determine what those steps might be, for any given disease, so that we can find targets, along the path to disease development, by which we can effectively prevent, diagnose, and treat disease. [Glossary Multievent process]

Before proceeding further, though, shouldn't we be asking if our assumptions about disease development are necessarily true, in every case? Might there be diseases that develop in a single step? If so, how would we identify such diseases, and what might we learn from them? The kinds of clues that would indicate that a disease has a short, single-event pathogenesis would be any of the following:

- Diseases that arise very soon after exposure to a physical or biological agent or a precipitating event
- Diseases that can be switched on or off
- Diseases that can be reversed

Let's examine each of these topics in some depth.

- **Diseases that arise very soon after exposure to a physical or biological agent or a precipitating event**

We know of many biological processes that can be quickly disrupted. For example, cyanide inhibits cytochrome c oxidase, thus blocking mitochondrial respiration, and causing the rapid death of brain cells [96]. We can learn a great deal about cellular physiology by studying the effects of rapid acting toxins, but poisonings are not generally counted among the naturally occurring diseases of human beings. They fit more closely with vehicular crashes, explosions, fatal gunshot wounds, and drownings, as unfortunate events that incapacitate or kill through mechanisms unrelated to disease processes. [Glossary Mitochondria]

Among naturally occurring diseases, cancer is usually discussed as a prototypical example of a disease with a long pathogenesis, sometimes extending over decades. There are, however, instances when the carcinogenic process can be abbreviated, raising the question of whether the steps leading to the development of cancer are always necessary.

It is not uncommon to see cancer developing in immunosuppressed patients, sometimes within weeks or months following the initiation of immunosuppressive therapy. The tumors that may arise rapidly following immunosuppression are [Glossary Initiation]:

- Kaposi sarcoma (a type of angiosarcoma)
- Primary central nervous system lymphoma
- Cervical and anal squamous carcinoma
- Squamous carcinoma of skin [97]
- Squamous carcinoma of the mouth
- Keratoacanthoma (of skin) [98,99] [Glossary Keratoacanthoma]
- Dermatofibroma (of skin) [100,101]
- Verrucae (common warts) [102]
- Primary effusion lymphoma [103]

Common warts and several types of squamous cell neoplasms that arise in recently immunosuppressed patients all seem to be caused by oncogenic human papillomaviruses. Human herpesvirus type 8 (HHV8) is a DNA-transforming virus that can cause Kaposi sarcoma, primary effusion lymphoma, and some forms of Castleman disease in immunosuppressed patients. Interestingly, if immunosuppression is halted, the Kaposi sarcoma may regress [104]. Primary central nervous system lymphoma is associated with Epstein-Barr virus, as are Burkitt lymphoma, Hodgkin lymphoma, Posttransplant lymphoproliferative disease, and Nasopharyngeal carcinoma. Human papillomaviruses are found in some cases of keratoacanthoma, and it is speculated that these viruses account for the appearance of eruptive keratoacanthomas occurring in immunosuppressed individuals. The eruption of multiple benign fibrous lesions of the skin, known as dermatofibromas, in immunosuppressed patients, is a rare event. No specific virus has been associated with dermatofibromas. [Glossary Castleman disease, Lymphoproliferative lesions, Hodgkin lymphoma, Eponymous disease]

In all these cases, the recovered viruses are endogenous. That is to say, the viruses persist in human cells for long periods of time, without causing disease. The presumed events that precede the emergence of tumors are:

1. An individual is infected by one or more of the aforementioned oncogenic viruses.
2. The infectious virus takes up long-term residence in target cells.
3. The proliferation of the virus is slowed or held in check by normal immunologic control mechanisms.
4. Immunosuppression (e.g., through drugs intended to impede the rejection of a transplanted organ, or through lymphocyte depletion as happens in individuals in the advanced stages of AIDS infections) releases the viruses from immunologic control.
5. The proliferation of viruses initiates a sequence of events, over a relatively short period (i.e., months), leading to the emergence of benign or malignant neoplasms.

Two points should be noted here. First, the primary infection of cells by tumor viruses may have occurred many years prior to the immunosuppressive episode, and there is no way of telling whether, in this time period, cells have been progressing through the steps leading toward cancer. Second, subsequent to immunosuppression, cells pass through more than one stage of pathogenesis before producing tumors. We infer this because the appearance of tumors takes some time, usually several months. Furthermore, the lesions that appear are not necessarily endowed with all the phenotypic properties of cancer (e.g., Kaposi sarcoma often regresses when a normal immune status is restored, indicating that the tumor had not achieved autonomous growth typical of developed cancers). [Glossary Autonomous growth]

Suffice it to say that carcinogenic viruses dwell within us. Whenever we see tumors developing soon after immunosuppression, particularly when they occur in multiples in the same person, we should strongly suspect a viral origin.

Most of the retroviruses that induce cancer in man and animals do not contain viral oncogenes. Such retroviruses may produce cancer by inserting themselves randomly into host DNA. Sometimes, the inserted viral gene occurs near one of the host's cellular oncogenes. The provirus alters the level of expression of the host cell's oncogene. Following cellular oncogene activation, the infected cells pass through a latency phase and a precancer phase, just as they would in the usual, multistep process leading to cancer. [Glossary Retrovirus]

In a tragic miscarriage of the Law of unintended consequences, the field of gene therapy was dealt a stunning setback that has had repercussions within the field of cancer research. One of the few instances in which gene transfer experiments have yielded positive results has been in the correction of X-linked severe combined immunodeficiency (SCID). The second most common root cause of this disease is an inherited deficiency of adenosine deaminase, producing a profound immunodeficiency. As treatment, a retrovirus is used to carry the missing gene into the genome of autologous lymphocytes of children who have SCID. In some children who received gene transfer therapy, about three years following therapy, a peculiar clonal proliferative process of T-cell lymphocytes developed. Examination of the proliferating T lymphocytes showed that the retrovirus happened to integrate in proximity to the LMO2 proto-oncogene promoter, leading to overexpression of LMO2 [105]. The overexpressed LMO2 resulted in the uncontrolled growth of cells, which eventually manifested as a T-cell lymphoma. This is another example of the peculiar property of hematopoietic cells that sustained hyperproliferation, in the absence of any additional acquired phenotypic properties, is sufficient to produce a leukemia or a lymphoma [105–107]. [Glossary Proto-oncogene, Promoter]

Sometimes, we encounter tumors that appear to arise almost immediately after viral infection. It is as though the virus enters a cell, transforms the cell it enters (i.e., confers malignant properties to the cell), causing the cell to proliferate as a tumor. Infection leads to cancer, with no requirement for additional molecular events to occur, with no precancer stage, and no period of latency. These cases arise after infection with oncogene-containing acutely transforming retroviruses. The Rous sarcoma virus is a transmissible agent that produces sarcomas in chickens. The acutely transforming variant of RSV contains a mutated version of the src oncogene (v-src), which it must have captured from an animal host genome at some time in the past. When the virus is injected into chicks, the v-src gene incorporates into host DNA of connective tissue cells and transforms the infected cells. Within a few days, multiple tumors emerge, killing the chick [108]. So powerful is the integrated src oncogene that injection of DNA extracted from Rous sarcoma virus is sufficient to produce sarcomas in chicks [109].

This phenomenon would suggest that, at least for the Rous sarcoma virus in chickens, when the oncogene is fully activated and expressed, the cancer phenotype is achieved almost immediately. We cannot say with certainty that acutely transforming retroviruses achieve one-step carcinogenesis, but we can at least say that they follow a deadly shortcut.

– Diseases that can be switched on or off

If you can turn a disease on and off, with a simple intervention, then it's reasonable to infer that the transition from the normal state (i.e., the state preceding the clinical phenotype) to a disease state (i.e., the state in which deleterious cellular events occur), or its reverse, must be a 1-step process (i.e., like the flip of a switch).

Transcription of the human genome is controlled, in part, by polypeptide complexes that attach to chromatin, remodeling its structure, and modulating gene expression. One such complex is SWI/SNF, and the gene coding for the complex is Snf5. In a mouse model that reversibly inactivates Snf5, the authors induced lymphomas or rhabdoid tumors in 100% of mice, with a median time for tumor onset of only 11 weeks [110,111]. This suggests modifications to the Snf5 gene can produce malignant cells almost immediately, as though the cancer cells were suddenly switched on. [Glossary Rhabdoid tumor]

In another remarkable paper, from a different laboratory, a malignant tumor was abruptly cured, by inactivating its principal oncogene [112]. The authors used a transgenic mouse that conditionally overexpresses the MYC proto-oncogene in liver cells. All mice that overexpressed MYC in liver cells developed liver tumors in about 12 weeks. The tumors had features of hepatocellular carcinoma or of hepatoblastoma. The tumors were locally invasive, metastatic, and transplantable. In the transgenic mice used, overexpression of MYC can be interrupted when the MYC gene promoter is inactivated by doxycycline. When transgenic mice carrying liver cancers were treated with doxycycline, overexpression of MYC ceased, and the liver tumors regressed soon thereafter. In fact, every liver tumor in every mouse regressed, even in mice who were moribund from their tumor burdens. Furthermore, the liver underwent a restorative process, recruiting normal hepatocytes and bile duct cells from the formerly cancerous cell population. Even nontransgenic mice, carrying transplanted liver tumors from the transgenic strain, enjoyed complete, sustained tumor regressions following doxycycline treatment.

Do these observations in mice indicate that human cancers can be switched on and off, like a light bulb? Probably not. Comparative genomic hybridization is a technique that detects DNA copy number anomalies (for example, amplifications, losses and duplications of DNA sequences). In the mouse MYC-driven liver cancer model, comparative genomic hybridization was performed to compare normal hepatocytes with tumor cells. With the exception of the amplification of c-MYC in tumor cells, the gene copy numbers appeared similar in normal cells, tumor cells and tumor transplants. This suggests that genetic instability, a near-universal feature of human cancers, was not a feature of the transgenic liver tumor model. In mouse tumor models that exhibit multiple genomic mutations, such as are seen in nearly all human cancers, tumors cannot be experimentally "switched off" [113]. [Glossary Copy number, Genetic surplus disorder, Loss of heterozygosity, Aneuploidy]

Together, these observations would suggest that there are some pathways that, by themselves, may account for a disease phenotype (i.e., MYC activation producing liver cancer in mice). If such a pathway were blocked, then cells might revert to a normal phenotype. If there are multiple pathways that contribute to a disease phenotype, then blocking a single pathway, even an important pathway, is less likely to switch off a disease. In the case of human cancer, there is abundant evidence that multiple pathways and multiple genomic and epigenomic changes are involved in cancer development [107]. Hence, Precision Medicine research in the realm of oncology is currently focused on targeting the most important pathways, among many, that drive malignant phenotypes. [Glossary Epigenome, Oncology]

– **Diseases that can be reversed.**

Strictly speaking, diseases are never reversible. What we see as reversal of a disease is actually a multistep process involving:

– Death of diseased cells
– Removal of diseased cells
– Replacement of dead cells with live cells of the same type or of some substitute cell type intended to provide some alternate function (e.g., metaplastic cells), or to at least provide some structural support (e.g., fibrosis).

The reason that diseases do not reverse is that, with the exception of DNA repair, mammalian evolution has developed the strategy of removing and replacing cells, rather than expending the effort to repair damaged cells. It's a throwaway society in which we, and all of our cells, live. There is at least one well-studied process by which cells self-destruct, when damaged, known variously as programmed cell death, cell suicide, or apoptosis. The apoptosis pathway is tightly coupled to the innate immune system, but is also active in normal cells that have fully differentiated and ceased to divide, the so-called postmitotic cell populations. For example, postmitotic keratinocytes, as they are pushed upward into higher and higher levels of the epidermis, undergo apoptosis with complete dissolution of their nuclei and flattening of the cytoplasm. By the time these dead cells have reached to top layer of the epidermis, they have become anucleate husks, consisting largely of keratin, and waiting for the moment when they can simply slough off the skin, and float away in a puff of air. [Glossary Innate immunity, Mitosis, Postmitotic, Apoptosis, Mitotic]

Reversal, for the most part, occurs only with some metabolic drugs and toxins that may reversibly attach to or inhibit some receptor enzymes or some cellular components. If the drug's action does not initiate apoptosis, then it may diffuse out of the cell, or it may undergo metabolization within the cell, leaving its target molecules intact. In such instances, conditions reverse back to normal, without killing cells. Otherwise, disease reversal never occurs. The observation that diseases do not reverse is just one more indication that pathogenesis is a complex and multistep process.

Glossary

Ab initio Latin term meaning from the beginning. In disease biology, it refers to a process that ends much the same way that it began, without changing over time. A recurring lesson taught in this book is that, in the natural world, nothing develops ab initio. Living things, including living diseases, develop through stages and are constantly changing over time. The term "ab initio" should not be confused with the term "de novo," which means beginning with something that is new.

Activated oncogene Oncogenes, the genes that help drive the neoplastic phenotype, are present in animal cells as normal genes that contribute to the normal phenotype of cells. Oncogenes need to be activated before they exert a carcinogenic influence. Activation may involve gain-of-function mutation of the oncogene; amplification (i.e., increasing the number of copies of the oncogene in the genome) or by increasing the function of the oncogene through any mechanism that causes overexpression, including translocation to a highly expressed region of the genome, or heightened local transcription, or by fusion with another gene that enhances the activity of the oncogene. Oncogenes that have not been activated are called proto-oncogenes.

Aneuploidy The presence of an abnormal number of chromosomes (for the species) in a cell. Most cancers contain aneuploid cells. Aneuploidy is seen less often in benign tumors. Aneuploidy is also found in epithelial precancers and other growing lesions that can sometimes regress spontaneously (e.g., keratoacanthomas). These observations have prompted speculation that chromosomal instability, and the acquisition of aneuploidy is an underlying cause of the cancer phenotype (i.e., tumor growth, invasion into surrounding tissues, and metastases). Such causal associations invite skepticism, particularly in the realm of cancer biology, as virtually every cellular process and constituent of cancer cells has been shown to deviate from the norm. Nonetheless, there is good reason to suspect that aneuploidy is at least a factor in tumor development, as mutations that cause aneuploidy are associated with a heightened increased risk of cancer (e.g., BRCA1 gene mutations [114], and mutations of mitotic checkpoint genes [115]). Other researchers have warned that aneuploidy, by itself, may not cause cancer [116]. Aneuploidy may need to be accompanied by other factors associated with genetic instability, such as the accumulation of DNA damage, cytogenetic abnormalities, and reduced cell death [116]. As usual, a rare disease helps to clarify the role of aneuploidy in carcinogenesis. Mosaic variegated aneuploidy syndrome-1 (MVA1) is caused by a homozygous or compound heterozygous mutation in the BUB1B gene, which encodes a key protein in the mitotic spindle checkpoint. This disease is characterized by widespread aneuploidy in more than 25% of the cells of the body, and a heightened risk of developing childhood cancers (e.g., rhabdomyosarcoma, Wilms tumor, and leukemia). Because the underlying cause of mosaic variegated aneuploidy syndrome-1 is a gene that produces aneuploidy, and because such aneuploidy is an early event (i.e., congenital) that precedes the development of cancer and that is found in the developed cancer cells, then it is reasonable to infer that aneuploidy is closely associated with events that lead to cancer.

Aplastic anemia A profound reduction in circulating blood cells, resulting from the loss of bone marrow stem cells. Severe or prolonged cases of aplastic anemia have a high mortality rate. A reduction of all blood cell lineages (whether profound or mild) is called pancytopenia. When an isolated lineage is reduced, the anemia is named after the cell type involved: reticulocytopenia, red cells decline; neutropenia, neutrophils decline; thrombocytopenia, platelets decline; lymphopenia, decline in lymphocytes.

Apoptosis Apoptosis is a coordinated cellular activity leading to cell death. Alternate terms are cell suicide, and programmed senescence. During apoptosis, chromosomal DNA is broken into small fragments, the nucleus shrinks (i.e., karyopyknosis), and the cytoplasmic membrane protrudes outward, as blebs.

Association versus cause We say that A causes B if we are fairly certain that A initiates a series of events that result in the occurrence of B. If we say that A is associated with B, then we are merely indicating that A and B tend to occur together.

Autonomous growth The growth of normal cells is highly controlled in most adult animals, so that every tissue contains about the same number of cells, from day to day. Such controlled growth is referred to as nonautonomous, because each dividing cell is restricted from growing continuously or in a manner that is not somehow matched against a nearly constant tissue-specific number. Cancer cells, which increase in number every day, are said to grow autonomously, and free of the restraining influences of humoral or other external factors. Of course, no cell growth is truly autonomous. Cells in a tumor require a vascular blood supply. Some tumors are hormone-responsive, and when the hormone is withdrawn or blocked, the tumor may stop growing, or may shrink. Such tumors exhibit nonautonomous growth. Some gastric maltomas (i.e., a type of lymphoma arising from mucosa-associated lymphoid tissue) will regress completely after the patient is treated for Helicobactor pylori infection, the presumed cause of the maltoma. These regressed maltomas would be considered nonautonomous [117].

BRCA BRCA1 and BRCA2 are Breast Cancer tumor suppressor genes that code for proteins that play a role in DNA repair. Mutations in BRCA genes are inherited in a small percentage of women who develop breast cancer. In addition, BRCA1 and BRCA2 mutations are found in other tumors, particularly ovarian and prostate cancer [118]. People born with a germline inactivating BRCA2 mutation have a variant type of Fanconi Anemia, and a germline mutation characterized by a large BRCA1 intragenic deletion has been associated with a variant type of Li-Fraumeni syndrome [119–121].

Benign tumor With a few exceptions, benign tumors are tumors that grow continuously, without invading or metastasizing. As a general rule, benign tumors are often diploid. Some benign tumors are stable-aneuploid. This means that they vary from the normal chromosome number, but the variation is stable (i.e., they do not become more aneuploid over time). There are rare examples of benign tumors that are genetically unstable [122].

But-for From the field of law, the "but-for" test attempts to determine whether a sequence of actions leading to an event could have happened without the occurrence of a particular underlying action or condition. In the realm of death certification, the underlying cause of death satisfies the "but-for" test (i.e., but for the condition, the sequence of events leading to the individual's death would not have occurred).

Cancer-causing syndrome There are many inherited conditions that are associated with susceptibility to multiple types of cancers. Cancers that arise in these syndromes often occur in children or at an age earlier than the average age of occurrence of their sporadic equivalents. A few examples of cancer syndromes are: Bloom syndrome, Carney syndrome, Cowden syndrome, Fanconi anemia, Li-fraumeni syndrome, Lynch cancer family syndrome, Muir-torre syndrome, Von Hippel-Lindau syndrome.

Carcinogen The term "carcinogen" is used differently by different people. Confusion arises because carcinogenesis is a multistep process that can be modified at many different biological stages. Some people use the term "carcinogen" to mean a chemical, biological, or physical agent that, when exposed to normal cells, will result in the eventual development of cancers, without the participation of other biological processes. Sometimes, the term "complete carcinogen" is used to emphasize the self-sufficiency of the agent as the primary underlying cause of a cancer. Others in the field use the term "carcinogen" to mean anything that will increase the likelihood of tumor development. An agent that causes an increase in the number of tumors that are produced by a complete carcinogen, or an agent that must be followed or preceded with another agent for tumors to occur, or a process that increases the number of cancers occurring in a population known to be at high risk of cancer due to an inherited condition, would all be considered carcinogens under this alternate definition.

Carcinogenesis The cellular events leading to cancer. Equivalent to the pathogenesis of cancer. Carcinogenesis in adults is a long process that involves the accumulation of genetic and epigenetic alterations that confer the malignant phenotype on a clone of cells. The envisioned sequence of events that comprise carcinogenesis begins with initiation, wherein a carcinogen damages the DNA of a cell, producing a mutant clonal founder cell that yields a group of cells that have one or more subtle (i.e., morphologically invisible) differences from the surrounding cells (e.g., less likely to senesce and die, more likely divide, less genetically stable, better able to survive in an hypoxic environment). After a time, which could easily extend into years, subclones of the original clone emerge that have additional properties that are conducive to the emergence of the malignant phenotype (e.g., new mutations that confer growth or survival advantage, greater ability to grow in hypoxic conditions). The process of continual subclonal selection continues, usually for a period of years, until a morphologically distinguishable group of cells appear: the precancer. Subclonal cells from the precancer eventually emerge, having the full malignant phenotype (i.e., the ability to invade surrounding tissues and metastasize to distant sites). The entire process can take decades.

Carrier In the field of genetics, a carrier is an individual who has a disease-causing gene that does not happen to cause disease in the individual. For example, individuals with one sickle cell gene are typically not affected by sickle cell disease, which usually requires homozygosity (i.e., both alleles having the sickle cell gene mutation) for disease expression. When two carriers mate, they pass the homozygous state to offspring with a likelihood of 25%. As another example, carriers may also have a low-penetrance disease gene. In such cases, offspring having the same gene defect as the carrier may develop disease. In the field of infectious diseases, a carrier is an individual who harbors an infectious organism, but who suffers no observable clinical consequences. If the carrier state is prolonged, and if infectious organisms cross to other individuals, a single carrier can produce and epidemic.

Castleman disease Synonyms include giant lymph node hyperplasi and angiofollicular lymph node hyperplasia. A type of lymphoproliferative disorder characterized by lymph node enlargement and loss of some normal lymph node features (e.g., regression of the germinal centers). Two forms of the disease are recognized: a relatively benign unicentric form that involves a single lymph node and a multicentric form involving multiple lymph nodes. The multicentric form is associated with activation of the body's inflammatory mechanisms, mediated primarily through cytokine activation. Systemic symptoms may be severe and can include POEMS syndrome (Polyneuropathy, Organomegaly, Endocrinopathy, Monoclonal gammopathy, and Skin changes). It is suspected that many cases of multicentric Castleman disease result from infections with human herpesvirus-8. Patients with Castleman disease are at an increased risk for developing neoplasms associated with herpesvirus-8 (i.e., lymphoma and Kaposi sarcoma) [123].

Cause of death In the case of a natural death (i.e., not homicidal and not accidental), assigning the cause of death involves selecting one item from a standard list of medical conditions known to produce death in humans [72].

Cell type The number of different kinds of cells in an organism varies based on how you choose to categorize and count them, but most would agree that there are at least 200 different cell types in the adult body. The number of cell types that appear for a short period during in utero development, then disappear before birth, is not included in the count. It can be difficult to assign a cell type to a fetal cell whose precise function cannot be specified. Nonetheless, we know that every cell type in the body has the same genome as every other cell; the differences between one cell type and another are determined by the epigenome. Because differentiated cells, under normal conditions, do not change their cell type (e.g., a hepatocyte does not transform into a neuron under physiologic conditions), and because cell types of a given lineage produce more cells of the same lineage (e.g., a dividing hepatocyte produces two hepatocytes), we can infer that the epigenome is heritable among somatic cell types.

Chance occurrence Biomedical scientists speak glibly about biological phenomena that occur "by chance" or "at random," but there is no credible evidence to support the intuitively inviting hypothesis that events occur randomly in nature. In point of fact, we know that there are underlying causes for many observed biological processes. For those biological processes for which a specific root cause is unknown (e.g., sporadically occurring diseases), the most we can say is that we do not know what is happening in such instances. We cannot justifiably chalk up such unexplained occurrences to chance, or to randomness, or to bad luck. It is worth noting that randomness is a mathematical abstraction. There are no biological processes that can produce an output that stand up to rigorous tests of randomness. When we say that a biological process is random, or occurs by chance, what we are actually saying is that the outcome of a biological process can be reasonably modeled as a probabilistic construct. For example, when we flip a coin or throw dice, we can expect the outcomes to approximate a probabilistic event, even though we know that the outcomes are actually determined by physical forces (i.e., not probabilistic). Likewise, when an individual develops a disease due to a de novo germline mutation, it may seem that the disease occurred by chance, but we should not kid ourselves into believing that the disease was caused by bad luck. It is best to admit that we simply do not know the underlying cause of the disease.

Congenital disorder Applies to congenital anomalies (i.e., structural or anatomic deformities) plus metabolic diseases, genetic or acquired, that are present at birth.

Connective tissue Tissues whose primary role is connecting one tissue with another, keeping tissues from falling apart, and providing a firm, physical structure to the body. The connective tissues include bone, cartilage, and fibrous tissue.

Copy number It is possible to produce a rare genetic disease without actually producing a mutation in a gene; simply changing the number of genes can be sufficient [124]. Charcot-Marie-Tooth disease is an inherited neuropathy. About 75% of cases are caused by duplication of a 1.5-megabase segment on chromosome 17.

DNA repair With only one exception, damaged cellular molecules need not be repaired. They are simply replaced with newly synthesized molecules. Because DNA is the template for its own replication, damage to the DNA sequence cannot be simply replaced; the damage must be repaired if the organisms is to continue replicating. Repairing DNA is of such great importance to cellular life that mammals have at least seven different DNA repair pathways, each specializing in a particular type of damage repair (e.g., direct reversal repair, mismatch repair, nucleotide excision repair, homologous recombination, base excision repair, single-strand break repair, nonhomologous end joining, and Fanconi Anemia DNA crosslink repair). Some types of DNA lesions are substrates for more than one pathway, and the ways in which these pathways interact are complex [87].

De novo mutation disease A genetic disease that is caused by a new mutation that occurs in the sperm cell that fertilizes the mother's ovum, or occurs in the mother's ovum, or occurs during the fertilization process when the sperm and ovum combine, or in the fertilized zygote, or in any postzygotic cell of the offspring (i.e., morula cell, blastula cell, embryonic cell, fetal cell, or cell of the developed organism).

Dormancy In cancer biology, dormancy is the interval from the time that a primary tumor has appeared, leading up to the appearance of clinically observable metastases. In this interval, nothing seems to be happening, and the tumor is said to be dormant. Dormancy has a variable length, varying from days to decades. We know very little about the pathways that control dormancy. Most people who die from cancer succumb to their metastatic lesions; the primary cancer seldom kills. If we had a method that prolonged the dormancy of metastatic foci, it would have enormous medical benefit to individuals with cancer.

Dysplasia The term means abnormal growth, and it is used in different ways in different biomedical specialties. Developmental biologists and pediatricians use the term "dysplasia" to refer to organs or parts of organs that have not grown properly. Stunted growth of an organ, or morphologically abnormal tissues within an organism would be types of developmental dysplasia. Oncologists (i.e., cancer specialists) use the term "dysplasia" to mean cellular atypia characteristic of neoplastic cells. Cellular dysplasia is found in precancers, cancers, and benign tumors.

Epigenome The genome consists of the 3 billion nucleotide bases that account for the genetic identity of the organism. The epigenome is the set of chemical adducts and modifiers of the genome that accounts for the identity of the cell types within the organism. There are over 200 specialized types of cells in the human body, and each of these 200 types of cells is morphologically and functionally distinct from the others.

Epithelial cell Epithelial cells are polyhedral units that fit tightly together, connected by specialized junctions. Epithelial cells form the mucosal lining of ducts, glands, and most pavemented surfaces. Tumors of the epithelial lining cells account for well over 90% of the cancers that occur in humans.

Eponymous disease From epi, about, and onoma, a name, refers to diseases named for a person. In the past, it was considered proper to specify eponymous diseases using the possessive form (e.g., Hodgkin's lymphoma, Parkinson's disease). More recently, the fashion has been to use the nonpossessive surname, the reason being that "The possessive use of an eponym should be discontinued, since the author neither had nor owned the disorder" [125]. The nonpossessive form of eponymous tumors is used consistently in this book.

Genetic surplus disorder Mutations that expand the genome or that produce an increased dosage of one or more genes, or of portions of a chromosome [126]. Examples are: Charcot-Marie-Tooth disease, an inherited neuropathy, some cases of which are caused by a duplication of a segment of chromosome 17 [124]; and Down syndrome, caused by an extra chromosome 21.

Genetically engineered mouse (GEM) Mice whose genomes contain inserted sequences of DNA that provide a new gene function or that produce the loss of function of a gene. New gene functions are achieved by inserting a gene into a fertilized mouse egg, along with a promoter that drives the expression of the gene. When the promoter is organ specific, the functionality of the new gene can be observed in a single organ. Loss-of-function GEMs are usually created by culturing embryonic stem cells from a mouse, introducing a nonfunctional variant of a gene into the nucleus of a cultured embryonic stem cell using an electroporation, and hoping that the foreign DNA will replace its closely related native DNA sequence through homologous recombination. A marker gene is used to determine if the recombination was successful. At this point, the embryonic stem cell can be inserted into a mouse blastocyst. If the altered embryonic stem cell differentiates into a germ cell, and if the germ cell contributes to a next-generation conceptus, the offspring will have the altered genotype.

Germline The germline consists of the cells that derive from the fertilized egg of an organism. All of the somatic cells (i.e., the cells composing the body), as well as the germ cells of the body (oocyte and spermatozoa) arise from the same germline. The extraembryonic cells (e.g., placental cells) have the same germline as the somatic cells. An inherited condition can be described as being in the germline, as it is present in every cell that derives from the fertilized egg. The word "germline" has confused many students, who use the term "germline cell" interchangeably with "germ cell." The confusion is exacerbated by the usual sequence whereby a mutation enters the organism's germline via an inherited mutation present in a parental "germ cell." It is best to think of a germline mutation by its functional definition, a mutation passed to every cell in an organism, and not by the process through which the mutation came to occur (i.e., passed from a parental germ cell).

Germline mutation A germline mutation is a mutation found in every cell of the body. The word "germline" was perhaps a poor choice of words. "Germline" is used to indicate that the mutation must have been present in the earliest conceptus (i.e., the zygote). It should not be confused with the germinal or germ cell lineage that gives rise to mature germ cells (i.e., sperm cells in males and oocytes in females).

Hepatoma Cancer of hepatocytes, the cells that constitute the functioning units of the liver. Same as hepatocellular carcinoma. The unqualified term, "liver cancer," generally refers to hepatocellular carcinoma.

Histology Histology is the study of cells in tissues. The primary tools of the histologist are the microscope and glass slides. Thin slices of tissues are stained and mounted on glass slides, and the glass slides are examined under a microscope.

Hodgkin lymphoma A common type of lymphoma that departs, in many ways, from the behavior observed in all other lymphomas. Hodgkin lymphoma has a bimodal age distribution, peaking in young adults, and again in much older adults. Unlike most other lymphomas, Hodgkin lymphoma can be successfully treated in the majority of cases, with reported cure rates as high as 90%. Most lymphomas have a characteristic tumor cell that accounts for most of the cells observed in the tumor. Such is not the case for Hodgkin lymphoma, which is characterized by large, atypical, sometimes multinucleated tumor cells sparsely scattered in a population of nonneoplastic lymphocytes and eosinophils, sometimes crisscrossed by bands of connective tissue. Hodgkin lymphoma often has a gradual stepwise anatomic spread of tumor from its primary site of origin, whereas most other lymphomas are widely disseminated from an early phase of disease. We understand very little about the pathogenesis of Hodgkin lymphoma.

Homeobox Genes that code for transcription factors involved in anatomic development in animals, fungi, and plants. Hox genes are homeobox genes found in animals that determine the axial relationship of organs. Mutations of homeobox genes are associated with remarkably specific, often isolated, anatomic alterations. Examples are: MSX2 homeobox gene mutation, which produces enlarged parietal foramina; PITX1 homeobox gene mutation, which produces Rieger syndrome (hypodontia and malformation of the anterior chamber of the eye including microcornea and muscular dystrophy); PITX3 homeobox gene mutation, which produces anterior segment dysgenesis of the eye, cataracts, and anterior segment mesenchymal dysgenesis; NKX2.5 homeobox gene, which produces atrial septal defect and atrioventricular conduction defects; SHOX homeobox (short stature homeobox) gene mutation causes Leri-Weill dyschondrosteosis (deformity of distal radius, ulna, and proximal carpal bones as well as mesomelic dwarfism). The reason why homeobox mutations tend to produce diseases in isolated anatomic locations or involving some specific function probably results from the coordinated regulatory activity of the individual homeobox genes. For example, one gene might regulate the synthesis of a group of proteins exclusively involved in growth of particular skull bones; another homeobox gene might regulate proteins involved in insulin production. Disorders involving alterations in homeobox genes include: aniridia, Axenfeld-Rieger syndrome, branchiootorenal syndrome, coloboma, combined pituitary hormone deficiency, congenital central hypoventilation syndrome, congenital fibrosis of the extraocular muscles, congenital hypothyroidism, craniofacial-deafness-hand syndrome, enlarged parietal foramina, hand-foot-genital syndrome, Langer mesomelic dysplasia, Leri-Weill dyschondrosteosis, microphthalmia, Mowat-Wilson syndrome, nail-patella syndrome, forms of nonsyndromic deafness, nonsyndromic holoprosencephaly, Partington syndrome, Potocki-Shaffer syndrome, renal coloboma syndrome, septo-optic dysplasia, Turner syndrome, Waardenburg syndrome, Wilms tumor aniridia genitourinary anomalies and mental retardation syndrome, Wolf-Hirschhorn syndrome, X-linked infantile spasm syndrome, and X-linked lissencephaly.

Hyperplasia An overgrowth of tissue. Hyperplasia can be diffuse or focal. When hyperplasia is diffuse, the entire involved tissue becomes larger. The basic pathogenesis of diffuse hyperplasia involves a physiologic hyperplasia of all the normal cells in a tissue in response to an inappropriate growth stimulus. An example of diffuse hyperplasia is Menetrier disease, in which the folds of the stomach enlarge and the gastric mucosa thickens. Focal hyperplasia involves a subset of growing cells within a tissue that yield clonal growths that stand out from the surrounding normal tissue. Focal hyperplasias sometimes give rise to neoplastic cells and, unlike diffuse hyperplasias, can be easily confused with benign neoplasms [56].

Immune system In humans, there are three known host defense systems that recognize and destroy foreign organisms: intrinsic, innate, and adaptive.

In situ Latin for "in its place." When referring to a cancer, in situ implies that the cancer has not invaded surrounding tissues and has not metastasized to lymph nodes or to distant organs. The term "in situ epithelial neoplasm" (i.e., neoplasms arising from mucosal surfaces, epidermis, or glandular tissues) is virtually synonymous with the alternate terms "intraepithelial neoplasm" or "epithelial precancer."

Incidence The number of new cases of a disease occurring in a chosen time interval (e.g., 1 year), expressed as a fraction of a predetermined population size (e.g., 100,000 people). For example, if there were 10 new cases of a rare disease occurring in a period of 1 year, in a population of 50,000 people, then the incidence would be 20 cases per 100,000 persons per year.

Infectious disease A disease caused by an organism that enters the human body. The term "infectious disease" is sometimes used in a way that excludes diseases caused by parasites. In this book, the parasitic diseases of humans are included among the infectious disease. The term "infectious disease" is often used interchangeably with "infection," but the two terms are quite different. It is quite possible to be infected with an organism, even a pathogenic organism, without developing a disease. In point of fact, the typical human carries many, perhaps dozens of, endogenous pathogenic organisms that lie dormant under most circumstances. Examples are Pneumocystis jiroveci (the fungus that causes Pneumonia in immunodeficient individuals), Varicella (the virus that may, when the opportunity arises, erupt as shingles), Aspergillus species (which not uncommonly colonize the respiratory tract, producing pneumonia in a minority of infected individuals), Candida (a ubiquitous fungus that lives on skin and in mucosal linings and that produces diseases of varying severity in a minority of infected individuals).

Initiation In the field of cancer, the term "initiation" refers to the inferred changes in cells following exposure to a carcinogen, that may eventually lead to the emergence of a cancer in the cell's descendants. Though we know much about the many possible changes that can occur in cells exposed to carcinogens, the essential and defining changes that begin the process of carcinogenesis are still unknown. The process that begins with initiation and extends to the emergence of a cancer is called carcinogenesis. In molecular biology, the term "initiation" has a distinctly different meaning, referring instead to the necessary molecular events that allow a process (e.g., replication, transcription, or translation) to begin.

Innate immunity An ancient and somewhat nonspecific immune and inflammatory response system found in plants, fungi, insects [127], and most multicellular organisms. This system recruits immune cells to sites of infection, using cytokines (chemical mediators). Innate immunity includes the complement system, which acts to clear microbes and dead cells. It also includes the macrophage system, also called the reticuloendothelial system, which engulfs and removes foreign materials. Crohn disease is the first of the common, genetically complex diseases that were shown to be associated with a germline polymorphism of a gene known to be a component of the innate immune system, specifically, the NF-kappa-B pathway [128,129]. Drugs that inhibit TNF (tumor necrosis factor), a participant in the cytokine pathway recruited by the innate immune system, are active against Crohn disease [130]. Examples of rare genetic disorders of the innate immune system include: Familial Mediterranean fever; TNF receptor-associated periodic syndrome; Hyperimmunoglobulin D syndrome; Familial cold autoinflammatory syndrome; Muckle-Wells syndrome; Neonatal-onset multisystem inflammatory disease, also known as chronic infantile neurologic, cutaneous, and arthritis syndrome; Pyogenic arthritis, pyoderma gangrenosum, and acne; Blau syndrome; Early-onset sarcoidosis, and Majeed syndrome [131,132].

Keratoacanthoma Small skin tumors that grow to produce a characteristic lipped crater of keratin. Keratoacanthomas are unusual neoplasms because they appear suddenly, growing extremely rapidly until they reach their maximal size, after which time they typically regress, leaving that keratin core that eventually sloughs. The entire process may last just a few months. The atypical squamous cells in the rapidly growing lesion are morphologically indistinguishable from the cells in a squamous carcinoma [133].

Knockout mice Strains of laboratory mice in which a specific gene has been knocked out or replaced. Every mouse in the strain has the identical gene deletion in every cell of its body. The primary purpose of producing knockout mouse strains is to show us how the organism behaves in the absence of the gene, thus providing some insight to the normal regulation and system-wide function of the gene. Knockout mice have been used in the study of cancer, obesity, heart disease, diabetes, arthritis, substance abuse, anxiety, aging, and Parkinson disease. About 15% of gene knockouts are developmentally lethal, which means that the genetically altered embryos cannot grow into adult mice and that no knockout mouse strain can be created in these cases. As a rule, highly conserved genes play some important role during the development of the organism or the reproductive life of the organism; otherwise, the genes would not be conserved. Hence, we would expect that the highly conserved genes would not serve well when trying to produce new strains of knockout mice. As it happens, all of the oncogenes are highly conserved. When experimental geneticists try to create a knockout mouse strain with an oncogene or knock-in a dysfunctional oncogene, we would expect, and we sometimes see, lethality in the embryo [134].

Latency versus dormancy Latency refers to the period in the development of a disease when there are no observable clinical or morphologic changes. Dormancy refers to the time after a disease has developed when there are no observable progressive changes.

Lesion Any tissue visibly affected by a disease process. For example, tuberous sclerosis is a complex genetic disease. One of the characteristic lesions produced by the disease process is the shagreen patch, a dimpled and pigmented area of skin. In this case, a dermatologist can biopsy the skin lesions associated with tuberous sclerosis complex, but cannot biopsy the disease itself. Sometimes, the name of the disease is equivalent to the lesion produced by the disease, as we observe in tumors. A dermatologist can excise a basal cell carcinoma; the disease and the lesion produced by the disease are the same thing.

Loss of heterozygosity Most genes come in two copies, the copy produced from the maternally derived chromosome and the copy produced by the paternally derived chromosome. These copies are called alleles, and in many cases, the two alleles are subtly different from one another. In this case, the gene is heterozygous. If one of the two alleles is inactivated or lost within a somatic cell or a germline cell, only one of the alleles will be expressed, and this is referred to as loss of heterozygosity. An apparent loss of heterozygosity may also occur with uniparental disomy (i.e., when a zygote receives two copies of a chromosome, or of part of a chromosome, from one parent and no copy from the other parent), producing two identical alleles, or when a somatic error replaces one allele with its alternate, producing two identical alleles, as is sometimes observed in cancer cells.

Lung cancer A generic name for any of the dozens of different types of malignant tumors that arise from lung tissue. As commonly used, the term "lung cancer" refers to malignant tumors that arise from the bronchial epithelium (i.e., bronchogenic carcinomas).

Lymphoma Neoplasms composed of neoplastic lymphocytes. By convention, all lymphomas are considered malignant (i.e., there are no generally accepted forms of benign lymphoma and there are no generally accepted names for lymphoid precancers). By putting all lymphomas into the same category (malignant lymphoma), tumors of lymphoid origin display a wide variety of perplexing biological diversity (including spontaneous regression, unexpected indolence, phenotypic transformation) that should properly be assigned to defined stages of development or subtypes of tumors (e.g., lymphoid precancers, benign lymphoproliferative diseases) [135].

Lymphoproliferative lesions Though some people include lymphomas in the class of lymphoproliferative lesions, as used herein, the term is restricted to sustained hyperplasias of lymphoid cells, lacking some of the features that would be expected in a fully developed lymphoid malignancy. The lymphoproliferative lesions are the lymphoid equivalent of myeloproliferative lesions. Though there is no agreement over which conditions should be included in this category, a list of lymphoproliferative lesions might include: angioimmunoblastic lymphadenopathy with or without dysproteinemia, hairy cell leukemia, post-transplant lymphoproliferative disease, Helicobacter-responsive maltomas, X-linked lymphoproliferative disease, Epstein-Barr virus associated lymphoproliferative disease, and the histiocytoses of childhood.

MGUS MGUS (Monoclonal Gammopathy of Undetermined Significance) is a monoclonal increase in plasma cells with a resultant spike in circulating levels of the specific antibody synthesized by the clonal plasma cells. MGUS is actually a common condition found in the elderly and may occur in about 1% of the population over 70 years of age. Progression of MGUS to multiple myeloma is infrequent, with a conversion of about 1%–2% per year [136]. Because MGUS occurs in an elderly population, the chance of MGUS progressing to myeloma within the lifespan of the patient is quite low. Virtually every case of multiple myeloma is preceded by MGUS, qualifying MGUS as the precancer of multiple myeloma [47].

Malformation A malformation is a disorder of normal growth or development that usually occurs in utero or during childhood. As a general term, "malformation" technically applies to growth abnormalities that may occur in adults (such as small angiomas and vascular anomalies that can occur in the skin and intestines of older adults). In common parlance, "malformation" is reserved for congenital conditions.

Malignant When applied to neoplasms, the word "malignant" indicates that the natural biological course of the neoplasm would eventually lead to the death of the patient.

Malignant melanoma Synonymous with melanoma, a cancer of the pigment-producing cells of the skin (i.e., melanocytes). In the special case of melanoma, there is no lesion that takes the name "benign melanoma." A benign neoplasm of melanocytic origin is called a nevus or a mole.

Malignant phenotype The term "malignant phenotype" refers to the biological properties of sustained growth, invasiveness, and the ability to metastasize that characterize all cancers. The term "malignant phenotype" may also include the morphological changes to cells that are almost always seen in cancers. These would include nuclear atypia, histologic disorganization, cellular crowding, loss of normal differentiation (i.e., loss of some of the cytologic features expected to be found in the type of cell from which the tumor arises), high rates of mitosis, and high numbers of degenerate or dead cells.

Malignant process Any life-threatening medical condition. Should not be confused with malignancy, a term that is, by convention, only applied to cancers.

Mitochondria Self-replicating organelles wherein respiration, the production of cellular energy from oxygen, occurs. As far as anyone knows, the very first eukaryote came fully equipped with a nucleus, one or more undulipodium, and one or more mitochondria. Similarities between mitochondria and eubacteria of Class Rickettsia suggest that the eukaryotic mitochondrium was derived from an ancestor of a modern rickettsia. All existing eukaryotic organisms, even the so-called amitochondriate classes (i.e., organisms without mitochondria), contain vestigial forms of mitochondria (i.e., hydrogenosomes and mitosomes) [137–140]. A single eukaryotic cell may contain thousands of mitochondria, as is the case for human liver cells, or no mitochondria, as is the case for human red blood cells. The control of mitochondrial number is determined within the nucleus, not within the mitochondrion itself. The mitochondria in a human body are descended from mitochondria contained in the maternal oocyte; hence, mitochondria have a purely maternal lineage.

Mitosis The phase in the cell cycle of somatic cells (i.e., not germ cells) wherein the replicated chromosomes condense and separate to form two daughter cells.

Mitotic Relating to mitosis (i.e., cell division).

Mucosa Refers to the surface layer of epithelial cells, the basement membrane upon which the epithelial cells sit, and the thin layer of connective tissue between the basement membrane and an underlying thin muscle layer (the muscularis mucosa).

Multievent process Same as multistep process.

Multistep process All of life can be described as a multistep process, wherein all cellular events are directly preceded by some other cellular event. If every preceding event has its own preceding event, then you can see that every cellular event that occurs in any organism can be iteratively traced backwards through history, to the first cellular event that occurred on the planet, some 4 billion years ago. For practical reasons, determining the root cause of a disease requires us to choose an arbitrary cutpoint where we say that pathogenesis begins.

Multiple myeloma A tumor composed of neoplastic plasma cells, most often arising in the bone marrow. Plasma cells secrete immunoglobulins, and multiple myelomas are typically characterized by a single immunoglobulin produced by all of the tumor cells and producing a sharp immunoglobulin peak on serum protein electrophoresis. The production of a unique immunoglobulin molecule by every cell in a tumor indicates that the tumor is clonal and that the tumor is differentiated (not a collection of stem cells).

Multipotent stem cell A cell that can produce differentiated cells of more than one cell type. Synonymous with pluripotent stem cell. Must be distinguished from totipotent stem cell, a cell that can produce differentiated cells of any germ cell layer and of extraembryonic origin (e.g., trophoblasts).

Mutagen A chemical that produces alterations in the genetic sequence of DNA molecules. With few exceptions, carcinogens (i.e., chemicals that cause cancer) are mutagens. There are some mutagens that have not been shown to be carcinogens, and these chemicals tend to be so highly reactive with cellular molecules (e.g., lipids, proteins, RNA, etc.) that they cannot effectively reach nuclear DNA, the target molecule, or they kill cells rather than inflicting heritable damage.

Mutation types Some of the mutations that account for genetic diseases are: deletions (e.g., Duchenne muscular dystrophy), Frame-shift mutations (e.g., factor VIII and IX deficiencies), fusions (e.g., chronic myelogenous leukemia, hemoglobin variants), initiation and termination codon mutations (e.g., alpha thalassemia), inversions (a type of beta thalassemia), nonsense mutations (familial hypercholesterolemia), point mutations (e.g., sickle-cell disease, glucose-6-phosphate dehydrogenase deficiency), promoter mutations (a type of thalassemia), RNA processing mutations, including splice mutations (e.g., Phenylketonuria) [141].

Myeloproliferative disorder A blood disorder characterized by a clonal expansion of a hematopoietic cell population. When cells of lymphoid lineage proliferate in the blood, the analogous term, lymphoproliferative disorder, is applied. Most of these disorders have characteristic mutations, which may represent the somatic mutation that accounts, in part, for the growth stimulus: BCR-ABL in chronic myelogenous leukemia; JAK2 mutations in polycythemia vera, essential thrombocythemia and primary myelofibrosis; c-KIT mutation in systemic mastocytosis; rearrangements of PDGFRB in chronic eosinophlic leukemia and chronic myelomonocytic leukemia; and RAS/PTPN11/NF1 mutations in juvenile myelomonocytic leukemia [142].

Natural selection A tendency for favorable heritable traits to become more common over successive generations. The traits are selected from existing genetic variations among individuals in the population. The genetic variations may take the form of genetic sequence variations (e.g., SNPs) or genetic structural variations.

Neoplasm Neoplasm means "new growth," and is a near-synonym for "tumor." Neoplasms can be benign or malignant. Leukemias, which grow as a population of circulating blood cells, and which do not generally produce a visible mass (i.e., do not produce a tumor), are included under the general term "neoplasm." Hamartomas, benign overgrowths of tissue, are generally included among the neoplasms, as are the precancers, which are often small and scarcely visible.

Neoplastic regression See Regression.

Neurofibromatosis Any of several inborn conditions associated with neurofibromas (a benign neoplasm of Schwann cells). Common usage assigns "neurofibromatosis" to type 1 neurofibromatosis, or Von Recklinghausen Disease, which is associated with multiple cafe au lait spots (large epidermal nevi) plus neurofibromas. The so-called central form of neurofibromatosis, now called neurofibromatosis type 2, is characterized by bilateral acoustic schwannomas, and meningiomas. Skin neurofibromas, as seen in neurofibromatosis type 1, are not a prominent feature of neurofibromatosis type 2. Juvenile subcapsular cataracts are often found in neurofibromatosis type 2.

Neutrophils Circulating white blood cells include lymphocytes, platelets, monocytes, and granulocytes (i.e., neutrophils, eosinophils, and basophils). The granulated cells can be distinguished by the dyes that can be absorbed by the different types of granules. Eosinophils retain a pink dye. Basophils retain a blue dye. And neutrophils do not retain dyes of either color.

Nevus A common, benign growth of melanocytic cells, usually a mixture of epidermal melanocytes and dermal melanocytes, the latter often called nevocellular cells. Almost all nevi occur in the skin, the normal site of melanocytic growth. Nevi can be identified as small (usually several millimeters across), slightly raised brown spots. Nevi can be found at birth (congenital nevi) or they can develop at any time of life.

Noninherited genetic disease A significant but unquantified portion of genetic diseases is noninherited, occurring from de novo (new) mutations in the germ cells of the affected individuals. In humans, point mutations (i.e., mutations that occur in a single nucleotide base within the genome) occur with a frequency of about 1–3×10^{-8} per base [143,144]. There are many types of mutational alterations other than point mutations (e.g., mutations in microsatellites) [145]. Our knowledge of the likelihood of occurrence of mutations other than point mutations is limited. In many cases, de novo mutations cause lethal genetic diseases that occur in children, through the action of a dominant gene (i.e., one gene copy that produces the disease). Such diseases are seldom inherited because the mutation responsible for the disease cannot be conserved in the population; those with the gene die early in life, without passing the mutation to progeny. De novo mutations account for a significant number of cases that would otherwise result from inherited dominant mutations. Neurofibromatosis is an example of a disease that occurs through autosomal dominant inheritance in about half of the cases. The other half of occurrences are de novo mutations incurring in the affected individual. In general, de novo mutations are often suspected as the cause of diseases that occur in early childhood for which no other cause (e.g., no evidence of familial or parental inheritance, infectious etiology, or environmental influences) can be determined (e.g., autism) [146].

Nucleus The membrane-bound organelle that contains the genome and the apparatus necessary for transcribing DNA into RNA, and for translating the RNA into protein molecules, and for replicating the DNA in preparation for cell division. Eukaryotes consist of all the organisms whose cells contain nuclei. The prokaryotes, loosely known as bacteria, are organisms that do not contain a nucleus. Every organism on earth is either a eukaryote or a prokaryote. The nucleus, though necessary for cell division, is not necessary for moment-to-moment cell survival. Mature red blood cells have no nucleus, but they manage to live for about 120 days.

Oncogene Normal genes or parts of genes that, when altered to a more active form, or overexpressed, contribute toward a neoplastic phenotype in a particular range of cell types. The constitutive form of the oncogene is called the proto-oncogene. The altered, more active form of the gene, is called the activated oncogene. Activation usually involves mutation, or amplification (i.e., an increase in gene copy number), translocation, or fusion with an actively transcribed gene, or some sequence of events that increases the expression of the gene product. Some retroviruses contain activated oncogenes and can cause tumors by inserting their oncogene into the host genome.

Oncology The medical specialty devoted to treating cancer. Oncologists are practitioners of oncology.

Pathologist Pathology is the study of disease. Broadly speaking, pathologists are individuals whose careers are devoted to the study of disease. In a sense, pathology is all of medicine minus the hands-on patient care. In the past 150 years, the field of pathology has become specialized. Medical pathologists are physicians who perform diagnostic tests on tissue sample (e.g., biopsies and excised tissues), or cells (e.g., exfoliated cells in urine, scraped cells from cervix, aspirated cells from fine needle samplings of tissues) or on blood and other body fluids. Within the specialty of medical pathology, there are numerous subspecialties (e.g., molecular diagnostics, clinical pathology, surgical pathology, cytopathology. dermatopathology, forensic pathology). Research pathologists are scientists who study diseases in laboratories.

Penetrance An individual may have inherited a disease gene without ever developing its associated disease. In medical genetics, the penetrance is the proportion of individuals with the mutation who develop the disease. There are several reasons why the penetrance of a disease-causing gene may be significantly lower than 100%. Some diseases, particularly the common diseases, are polygenic. It may take many genes to produce the disease phenotype. Epistasis may also modify penetrance; one gene may be influenced by a particular allele of another gene. Environmental and epigenetic factors can also influence gene function. An inherited mutation may require environmental triggers (e.g., excessive sunlight exposure in porphyria cutanea tarda) or conditional physiological circumstances (e.g., fatigue or starvation preceding the hyperbilirubinemia associated with Gilbert syndrome) to fully express the clinical trait. Such factors may influence the penetrance of the gene, or the age of the individual when the disease emerges, or the severity of the disease, or the clinical phenotype of the disease (i.e., which clinical features will develop). The concept of disease penetrance serves as a reminder that diseases develop over time, through a sequence of events. It is inaccurate to think of an inherited mutation as the "cause" of a disease.

Philadelphia chromosome Almost all patients with chronic myelogenous leukemia have a characteristic cytogenetic marker produced by a translocation of parts of chromosomes 9 and 22, which produces a fusion gene composed of a part of the BCR (breakpoint cluster region) gene and a part of the ABL (Abelson Leukemia) gene. The fused gene creates a protein product with several functions, including tyrosine kinase activity. The Philadelphia chromosome appears in a hematopoietic stem cell that can give rise to several white blood cell types. The Philadelphia chromosome is found in the vast majority of chronic myelocytic leukemias, which is a leukemia of neutrophils. The Philadelphia chromosome may also be found in about 25% of cases of acute lymphoblastic leukemia occurring in adults and in about 5% of cases of acute lymphoblastic leukemia occurring in children and in some cases of acute myelogenous leukemia.

Pluripotent stem cell The ability to yield, after cell divisions, differentiated cell types from any of the three embryonic layers (i.e., endoderm, ectoderm, and mesoderm.) Pluripotent stem cells differ from totipotent stem cells as they do not yield cells of extraembryonic type (e.g., trophoblasts). It is now possible to induce the formation of human pluripotent stem cells from cultured fibroblasts treated with a cocktail of transcription factors [147,148].

Polymorphism The term "polymorphism" can have several somewhat different meanings in various fields of biology. In this book, polymorphism refers to genetic polymorphism, indicating that variants of a gene occur in the general population. A polymorphism is usually restricted to variants that occur with an occurrence frequency of 1% or higher. If a variant occurs at a frequency of <1%, it is considered to be sufficiently uncommon that it is probably not steadily maintained within the general population. All commonly occurring polymorphisms are assumed to be benign or, at worst, of low pathogenicity, the reasoning being that natural selection would eliminate frequently occurring polymorphisms that reduced the fitness of individuals within the population. Nonetheless, different polymorphisms may code for proteins with at least some differences in functionality.

Postmitotic Refers to fully differentiated cells that have lost the ability to divide. For example, the epidermis of the skin has a basal layer of cells that are capable of dividing to produce a postmitotic cell and another basal cell. The postmitotic cells sit atop the basal cells to flatten out and lose their nucleus as the cells rise through the epidermal layers. The top layer of the epidermis sloughs off the body and is replaced by postmitotic epidermal cells in the next lower layer. This cycle of cell renewal from the bottom and cell sloughing from the top is typical of most epithelial surfaces of the body (e.g., epidermis of skin, gastrointestinal tract, and glandular organs). Aside from epithelial surfaces, postmitotic cells arise from populations of mitotic cells that have exhausted their regenerative potential. One theory of aging holds that certain cell types of the body (e.g., fibroblasts) have a limited number of mitotic cell cycles. When a determined number of cell cycles have elapsed, cells cannot divide further, becoming postmitotic.

Posttranslational protein modification Much happens between the moment when the amino acid sequence of a protein is translated from an RNA template, and the moment when the fully modified protein, in its optimal conformation, arrives at its assigned station. Errors in the post-translational process, including timing errors (i.e., the proper sequence of events that lead to the finished product) can have negative consequences. An example of a rare disease caused by a defect in a posttranslational process is congenital disorder of glycosylation type IIe, caused by homozygous mutation in a gene that encodes a component of a Golgi body protein that is involved in post-translational protein glycosylation, the COG7 gene [149]. This rare disease produces a complex disease phenotype in infants, with multiple disturbances in organs and systems plus various anatomic abnormalities. In the few reported cases, death results in a few months.

Precancer Lesions preceding the development of a cancer, and from which the cancer ultimately arises. Precancers, generally, are neither invasive nor metastatic, and can be cured by excision. Because all cancers seem to be preceded by an identifiable precancer stage, a successful strategy to eliminate all precancers would prevent the occurrence of all cancers [51,107].

Precancer regression It is not unusual for a precancer to stop growing, or to shrink and disappear entirely [51,150]. Cancers, unlike precancers, rarely regress on their own. The common occurrence of regression in precancers provides Precision Medicine researchers with another opportunity to interfere with the process of carcinogenesis by enhancing precancer regression.

Precancerous condition A condition or event that predisposes a person to the development of a precancer and to the eventual development of a cancer. For example, patients with cirrhosis have a high risk of eventually developing cancer. Over time, the cirrhotic liver becomes nodular, and precancerous lesions develop from the nodules. In some cases, the precancerous nodules develop into cancer (i.e., hepatocellular carcinoma). Cirrhosis is a precancerous condition, but it is not a precancer. Cirrhosis simply sets the stage for precancers to develop [51].

Premalignancy Equivalent to precancer.

Prevalence A measure of the number of individuals in a population who have a disease, at a particular time. Prevalence differs from incidence, the latter indicating the rate of new cases of a disease that occur in a population. Chronic diseases, especially those that persist through the patient's normal lifespan, may have a high prevalence and a low incidence. Diseases that have a short clinical span, such as influenza or the common headache, will have a lower prevalence than incidence.

Promoter The DNA site that binds RNA polymerase plus transcription factors, thus initiating RNA transcription. Examples of promoter mutations causing disease include beta-thalassemia, Bernard-Soulier syndrome, pyruvate kinase deficiency, familial hypercholesterolemia, and hemophilia [151]. Monogenic promoter mutations generally cause disease by reducing the quantity of a normal protein, not by producing altered protein and not by reducing the quantity of multiple proteins. Because the drop in protein production may be small, promoter diseases may be hard to detect.

Proto-oncogene An oncogene in an inactive form.

Protozoa Microbiologic nomenclature has many terms that have persisted long after they have outlived their usefulness; "protozoa" is a perfect example. A commonly found definition for protozoa is "one-celled animal," but this is an oxymoron, as all animals are multicellular. Still, it is reasonable to assume that multicelled animals must have evolved from unicellular organisms, and these one-celled prototypical animals could be called protozoans. If we adhered to this line of logic, Class Choanozoa could lay claim as a "protozoan," as the choanozoans are one-celled members of Class Opisthokonta, to which Class Animalia belongs. Most other so-called protozoans have no ancestral relationship to animals. Today, having no formal inclusion in the classification of living organisms, the term "protozoa" is a layperson's term indicating any type of one-celled eukaryotic organism [152].

Proximate cause The proximate cause is the closest action that can be held to be the cause of the event. For example, the rupture of a blood vessel in the lung may be the proximate cause of death, while an invasive lung cancer may have been the underlying cause of death. The immediate cause of death, in this instance, may have been asphyxiation due to massive, acute hemothorax. The erosion of a vessel by tumor cells was one of a sequence of events leading from the underlying cause of death to the proximate cause of death. The underlying cause of death satisfies the "but-for" condition. But for the lung cancer, the vessel would not have eroded, and blood would not have flooded the lung tissue. The proximate cause of death need not be a necessary condition resulting from the underlying cause of death. Had the vessel not ruptured, the individual may have died from an alternate proximate cause (e.g., metastasis, pneumonia).

Regression The act of going back to a previous state. "Regression" is an example of a Janus term, a term that can have opposite meanings, depending on its context. When "regression" is applied to cancer growth, it means that the tumor is shrinking (i.e., returning the patient to an earlier state, when the cancer was smaller). A cancer that has completely regressed is a cancer that can no longer be observed. For oncologists and their patients, regression is a very good thing. In the field of pediatrics, the term "regression" usually applies to children who are losing ground to their disease, and this may take the form of losing the ability to understand spoken language or losing the ability to walk. Thus, the regressing child is returning to a more dependent and more infantile state. Thus, in pediatrics, regression is a very bad thing. Janus terms teach us that we must be aware of the clinical context of words. It's easy to see that this kind of awareness would be difficult to program into a computer that is instructed to look for spontaneously regressing diseases. Another medical Janus word is "divide." When you divide doses, you reduce the size of each dose, while maintaining the equivalent total dosage. When a cell divides, it doubles itself to become two cells. Saying that a cell has divided is the same as saying that the cell has multiplied. Janus expressions are confusing. As an aside, Janus words are not restricted to medical lexicography. If you say, "The stars are out tonight," you probably mean that the stars are visible. If you say, "Put the light out," you're indicating that the light should be made invisible.

Retrovirus An RNA virus that replicates through a DNA intermediate. The DNA intermediate becomes integrated into the host DNA, from which viral RNA is transcribed. When integration of the virus occurs in germ cells, the viral DNA can be inherited. The human genome carries a legacy of retroviral DNA, accounting for about 8% of the human genome [153].

Revertant mutation Mutation occurs frequently in somatic cells, and it is always possible that cells affected by a point mutation disease can undergo a mutation that reverts a point mutation back to its normal sequence [154]. When a restorative mutation occurs in the embryo, the result may be mosaicism in the adult, with some cells having the disease gene, and other cells being normal. Depending on the disease, mosaicism may be either ameliorative or curative or without much effect [155]. If the mutation occurs in an adult cell, only the small subpopulation of cells that descend from the revertant normal cell will be likely to benefit. Depending on the disease, this might be observed as a patch of skin or a focal area of an organ that is not affected by the disease. Not much is known about revertant mutations, and spontaneous recovery from genetic diseases is exceedingly rare.

Rhabdoid tumor A very rare tumor that occurs in children and develops from either neuroectoderm or mesoderm. Rhabdoid tumors are characterized by biallelic loss of the INI1 tumor suppressor gene.

Somatic mutation A mutation occurring in the soma (i.e., the body, specifically, the nongerm cells of the body) and not present in the germline cells that give rise to the cells of the soma. Some diseases associated with acquired somatic mutations include aplastic anemia [156], myeloproliferative disorders [59], paroxysmal nocturnal hemoglobinemia [157], and virtually all cancers occurring in adults.

Species Species is the bottom-most class of any classification or ontology. The term always refers to the plurality of members and this is the reason that only the plural form is used (i.e., species, never specie). Because the species class contains the individual objects of the classification, it is the only class, which is not abstract. The special significance of the species class is best exemplified in the classification of living organisms. Every species of organism contains individuals that share a common ancestral relationship. When we look at a group of squirrels, we know that each squirrel in the group has its own unique personality, its own unique genes (i.e., genotype), and its own unique set of physical features (i.e., phenotype). Moreover, although the DNA sequences of individual squirrels are unique, we assume that there is a commonality to the genome of squirrels that distinguishes it from the genome of every other species. If we use the modern definition of species as an evolving gene pool, we see that the species can be thought of as a biological life form, with substance (a population of propagating genes), and a function (evolving to produce new species) [158–160]. Put simply, species speciate; individuals do not. As a corollary, species evolve; individuals simply propagate. Hence, the species class is a separable biological unit with form and function. We, as individuals, are focused on the lives of individual things, and we must be reminded of the role of species in biological and nonbiological classifications.

Spontaneous versus sporadic The two terms "spontaneous" and "sporadic" are used to describe events that occur without a known cause. The difference between the two words is that "spontaneous" indicates that the event occurs suddenly, and without external cause. The term "sporadic" implies that the occurrence has a usual cause that we do not yet understand.

Stem cell A cell that is capable of employing a strategy for cell division that produces two different types of cells: another stem cell plus a cell that is more differentiated than the original stem cell. According to the stem cell theory of development, all of the differentiated cells of the body derive from stem cells, and all of the stem cells derive from more primitive ancestral stem cells.

Syndrome versus disease A disease is a pathological condition in which all the instances of the condition arise from a common pathogenesis. A syndrome is a constellation of physical findings that can occur together. The symptoms of a syndrome may or may not all have the same pathogenesis, and, hence, may or may not constitute a disease. When infected with a common cold virus, you may get a syndromic pattern of headache, sniffles, cough, and malaise. All these conditions arose after a viral infection and shared the same pathogenesis, up to a point. So a cold is a disease with a syndromic clinical presentation. Multiple expressions of physical disorder, occurring in multiple body systems are more likely to be syndromes than diseases, when the different conditions are inconsistently present or separated by intervals of time. Contrariwise, a localized pathological condition that is restricted to a particular set of cells is almost always a disease, not a syndrome. There are exceptions. It is possible to imagine some highly unlikely syndromes that are restricted to one cell type. Clinorchis sinensis is a species of trematode that causes biliary tract disease when the fluke takes up permanent residence therein [161]. Localized reaction to the fluke infection results in chronic cholangitis (i.e., inflammation of the cells lining the bile ducts). In some cases, cholangiocarcinoma (i.e., cancer of the bile duct) develops. Cholangitis and cholangiocarcinoma arise through different biological pathways, despite having the same root cause (i.e., clinorchiasis). This being the case, it seems reasonable to count cholangitis and cholangiocarcinoma following Clinorchis sinensis infection as a syndrome, not as a disease, thus breaking the general rule that a localized pathologic condition is not a syndrome. There are no hard or fast rules, but the distinction between a disease and a syndrome has therapeutic and diagnostic consequences. A true disease has one pathogenesis, despite its multiorgan manifestations and can be potentially prevented, diagnosed, or treated by targeting events and pathways involved in the development of the disease. A syndrome is a confluence of clinical findings that may or may not be pathogenetically related, and which may not be amenable to any single therapeutic or diagnostic approach.

Terminology The collection of words and terms used in some particular discipline, field, or knowledge domain. Nearly synonymous with vocabulary and with nomenclature. Vocabularies, unlike terminologies, are not be confined to the terms used in a particular field. Nomenclatures, unlike terminologies, usually aggregate equivalent terms under a canonical synonym.

Totipotent stem cell A stem cell that can produce, after cell divisions, differentiated cells of any type. This would include cells of any of the three embryonic layers (ectoderm, endoderm, and mesoderm), germ cells, and cells of the extraembryonic tissue (e.g., trophoblasts). A totipotent stem cell is different from a pluripotent stem cell, which cannot produce extraembryonic cells and cannot produce germ cells.

Transcription factor A protein that binds to specific DNA sequences to control the transcription of DNA to RNA. Some of the most phenotypically complex rare disease syndromes are caused by single gene mutations that code for transcription factors and other regulatory elements [90]. Examples include: mutation in the gene encoding transcription factor TBX5 producing Holt-Oram syndrome consisting of hand malformations, heart defects, and other malformations. As another example, a mutation in the gene encoding microphthalmia-associated transcription factor, MITF, produces Waardenburg syndrome 2A, characterized by lateral displacement of the inner canthus of both eyes, pigmentary disturbances of hair and iris, white eyelashes, leukoderma, and cochlear deafness.

Tumor suppressor gene A gene that arrests, delays, or makes less likely, one or more of the cellular events involved in the pathogenesis of cancer. As you might guess, our genome has not evolved to produce genes whose only purpose is to wait for an opportunity to intervene whenever some tumor begins to develop. All tumor suppressor genes play a role in normal cell function, such as participating in DNA repair or regulating cell division or cell death.

Ubiquitination Ubiquitin is a protein found "ubiquitously" in eukaryotic cells. Ubiquitination is a process involving the ubiquitin protein in which proteins that need to be broken down are tagged for removal.

Variable In algebra, a variable is a quantity that can change; as opposed to a constant, that cannot change.

References

[1] Pearson K. The grammar of science. London: Adam and Black; 1900.

[2] Rose G. Sick individuals and sick populations. Int J Epidemiol 1985;14:32–8.

[3] Stolley PD. When genius errs: RA Fisher and the lung cancer controversy. Am J Epidemiol 1991;133:416–25.

[4] Ajeigbe KO, Olaleye SB, Oladejo EO, Olayanju AO. Effect of folic acid supplementation on oxidative gastric mucosa damage and acid secretory response in the rat. Indian J Pharm 2011;43:578–81.

[5] Nagel ZD, Chaim IA, Samson LD. Inter-individual variation in DNA repair capacity: a need for multi-pathway functional assays to promote translational DNA repair research. DNA Repair (Amst) 2014;19:199–213.

[6] Alapetite C, Thirion P, de la Rochefordiere A, Cosset JM, Moustacchi E. Analysis by alkaline comet assay of cancer patients with severe reactions to radiotherapy: defective rejoining of radioinduced DNA strand breaks in lymphocytes of breast cancer patients. Int J Cancer 1999;83:83–90.

[7] Pollard JM, Gatti RA. Clinical radiation sensitivity with DNA repair disorders: an overview. Int J Radiat Oncol Biol Phys 2009;74:1323–31.

[8] Fox GJ, Orlova M, Schurr E. Tuberculosis in newborns: the lessons of the "Lubeck Disaster" (1929-1933). PLoS Pathog 2016;12:e1005271.

[9] Dhitavat J, Macfarlane S, Dode L, Leslie N, Sakuntabhai A, MacSween R, et al. Acrokeratosis verruciformis of Hopf is caused by mutation in ATP2A2: evidence that it is allelic to Darier's disease. J Invest Dermatol 2003; 120(2):229–32.

[10] Kamijo M, Nishiyama C, Takagi A, Nakano N, Hara M, Ikeda S, et al. Cyclooxygenase-2 inhibition restores ultraviolet B-induced downregulation of ATP2A2/SERCA2 in keratinocytes: possible therapeutic approach of cyclooxygenase-2 inhibition for treatment of Darier disease. Br J Dermatol 2012;166:1017–22.

[11] Xu B, Roos JL, Dexheimer P, Boone B, Plummer B, Levy S, et al. Exome sequencing supports a de novo mutational paradigm for schizophrenia. Nat Genet 2011;43:864–8.

[12] Calado RT, Graf SA, Wilkerson KL, Kajigaya S, Ancliff PJ, Dror Y, et al. Mutations in the SBDS gene in acquired aplastic anemia. Blood 2007;110:1141–6.

[13] Tapolyai M, Uysal A, Dossabhoy NR, Zsom L, Szarvas T, Lengvarszky Z, et al. High prevalence of liddle syndrome phenotype among hypertensive US Veterans in Northwest Louisiana. J Clin Hypertens 2010;12:856–60.

[14] Hanukoglu I, Hanukoglu A. Epithelial sodium channel (ENaC) family: phylogeny, structure-function, tissue distribution, and associated inherited diseases. Gene 2016;579:95–132.

[15] Wu J, Rosenbaum E, Begum S, Westra WH. Distribution of BRAF T1799A(V600E) mutations across various types of benign nevi: implications for melanocytic tumorigenesis. Am J Dermatopathol 2007;29:534–7.

[16] Pollock PM, Harper UL, Hansen KS, Yudt LM, Stark M, Robbins CM, et al. High frequency of BRAF mutations in nevi. Nat Genet 2003;33:19–20.

[17] Kato S, Lippman SM, Flaherty KT, Kurzrock R. The conundrum of genetic "drivers" in benign conditions. J Natl Cancer Inst 2016;108.

[18] DeAngelis LM, Kelleher MB, Post KD, Fetell MR. Multiple paragangliomas in neurofibromatosis: a new neuroendocrine neoplasia. Neurology 1987;37:129–33.

[19] Ferrari A, Bisogno G, Macaluso A, Casanova M, D'Angelo P, Pierani P, et al. Soft-tissue sarcomas in children and adolescents with neurofibromatosis type 1. Cancer 2007;109:1406–12.

[20] Plotkin SR, Merker VL, Halpin C, Jennings D, McKenna MJ, Harris GJ, et al. Bevacizumab for progressive vestibular schwannoma in neurofibromatosis type 2: a retrospective review of 31 patients. Otol Neurotol 2012;33:1046–52.

[21] Mak BC, Yeung RS. The tuberous sclerosis complex genes in tumor development. Cancer Invest 2004;22:588–603.

[22] van Slegtenhorst M, Nellist M, Nagelkerken B, Cheadle J, Snell R, van den Ouweland A, et al. Interaction between hamartin and tuberin, the TSC1 and TSC2 gene products. Hum Mol Genet 1998;7:1053–7.

[23] Nordstrom-O'Brien M, van der Luijt RB, van Rooijen E, van den Ouweland AM, Majoor-Krakauer DF, Lolkema MP, et al. Genetic analysis of von Hippel-Lindau disease. Hum Mutat 2010;31:521–37.

[24] Wilson R, Geyer SH, Reissig L, Rose J, Szumska D, Hardman E, et al. Highly variable penetrance of abnormal phenotypes in embryonic lethal knockout mice. Wellcome Open Res 2017;1:1.

[25] Flannick J, Beer NL, Bick AG, Agarwala V, Molnes J, Gupta N, et al. Assessing the phenotypic effects in the general population of rare variants in genes for a dominant Mendelian form of diabetes. Nat Genet 2013;45:1380–5.

[26] Bell CJ, Dinwiddie DL, Miller NA, Hateley SL, Ganusova EE, Mudge J, et al. Carrier testing for severe childhood recessive diseases by next-generation sequencing. Sci Transl Med 2011;3:65ra4.

[27] Xue Y, Chen Y, Ayub Q, Huang N, Ball EV, Mort M, et al. Deleterious- and disease-allele prevalence in healthy individuals: insights from current predictions, mutation databases, and population-scale resequencing. Am J Hum Genet 2012;91:1022–32.

[28] Brassesco MS. Leukemia/lymphoma-associated gene fusions in normal individuals. Genet Mol Res 2008;7:782–90.

[29] Bayraktar S, Goodman M. Detection of BCR-ABL positive cells in an asymptomatic patient: a case report and literature review. Case Rep Med 2010;2010:939706. Available from: https://www.hindawi.com/journals/crim/2010/939706/.

[30] Bose S, Deininger M, Gora-Tybor J, Goldman JM, Melo JV. The presence of typical and atypical BCR-ABL fusion genes in leukocytes of normal individuals: biologic significance and implications for the assessment of minimal residual disease. Blood 1998;92:3362–7.

[31] Biernaux C, Loos M, Sels A, Huez G, Stryckmans P. Detection of major bcr-abl gene expression at a very low level in blood cells of some healthy individuals. Blood 1995;86:3118–22.

[32] Sidon P, El Housni H, Dessars B, Heimann P. The JAK2V617F mutation is detectable at very low level in peripheral blood of healthy donors. Leukemia 2006;20:1622.

[33] Kwiatkowski DP. How malaria has affected the human genome and what human genetics can teach us about malaria. Am J Hum Genet 2005;77:171–92.

[34] Yazdani SS, Shakri AR, Mukherjee P, Baniwal SK, Chitnis CE. Evaluation of immune responses elicited in mice against a recombinant malaria vaccine based on Plasmodium vivax Duffy binding protein. Vaccine 2004;22:3727–37.

[35] Hill AVS. Evolution, revolution and heresy in the genetics of infectious disease susceptibility. Philos Trans R Soc Lond Ser B Biol Sci 2012;367:840–9.

[36] Warren HS, Fitting C, Hoff E, Adib-Conquy M, Beasley-Topliffe L, Tesini B, et al. Resilience to bacterial infection: difference between species could be due to proteins in serum. J Infect Dis 2010;201:223–32.

[37] Banuls A, Thomas F, Renaud F. Of parasites and men. Infect Genet Evol 2013;20:61–70.

[38] Cardiff RD, Munn RJ, Galvez JJ. The tumor pathology of genetically engineered mice: a new approach to molecular pathology. In: Fox JG, Davisson MT, Quimby FW, Barthold SW, Newcomer CE, Smith AL, eds. The mouse in biomedical research: experimental biology and oncology 2nd ed. New York: Elsevier, Inc, pp 581-622, 2006.

[39] Cardiff RD, Anver MR, Boivin GP, Bosenberg MW, Maronpot RR, Molinolo AA, et al. Precancer in mice: animal models used to understand, prevent, and treat human precancers. Toxicol Pathol 2006;34:699–707.

[40] Lozano G. Mouse models of p53 functions. Cold Spring Harb Perspect Biol 2010;2:a001115.

[41] Leonarczyk TJ, Mawn BE. Cancer risk management decision making for BRCA+ women. West J Nurs Res 2015;37:66–84.

[42] Salesse S, Verfaillie CM. BCR/ABL: from molecular mechanisms of leukemia induction to treatment of chronic myelogenous leukemia. Oncogene 2002;21:8547–59.

[43] Basecke J, Griesinger F, Trumper L, Brittinger G. Leukemia- and lymphoma-associated genetic aberrations in healthy individuals. Ann Hematol 2002;81:64–75.

[44] Guess HA, Hoel DG. The effect of dose on cancer latency period. J Environ Pathol Toxicol 1977;1:279–86.

[45] Herbst AL, Ulfelder H, Poskanzer DC. Association of maternal stilbestrol therapy and tumor appearance in young women. New Engl J Med 1971;284:878–81.

[46] Herbst AL, Scully RE, Robboy SJ. The significance of adenosis and clear-cell adenocarcinoma of the genital tract in young females. J Reprod Med 1975;15:5–11.

[47] Landgren O, Kyle RA, Pfeiffer RM. Monoclonal gammopathy of undetermined significance (MGUS) consistently precedes multiple myeloma: a prospective study. Blood 2009;113:5412–7.

[48] Hanahan D, Weinberg RA. The hallmarks of cancer. Cell 2000;100:57–70.

[49] Foulds L. Neoplastic development. New York: Academic Press; 1969.

[50] Berman JJ, Albores-Saavedra J, Bostwick D, Delellis R, Eble J, Hamilton SR, et al. Precancer: a conceptual working definition—results of a consensus conference. Cancer Detect Prev 2006;30(5):387–94.

[51] Berman JJ. Precancer: the beginning and the end of cancer. Sudbury, MA: Jones and Bartlett; 2010.

[52] Tavassoli FA, Norris HJ. A comparison of the results of long-term follow-up for atypical intraductal hyperplasia and intraductal hyperplasia of the breast. Cancer 1990;65:518–29.

[53] Westbrook KC, Gallagher HS. Intraductal carcinoma of the breast. A comparative study. Am J Surg 1975;130:667–70.

[54] Seer Cancer Stat Fact Sheets. Cancer of the breast. Available from: http://seer.cancer.gov/statfacts/html/breast.html.

[55] Mortality, total U.S. (1969-2005). Surveillance, Epidemiology, and End Results (SEER) Program (www.seer.cancer.gov). National Cancer Institute, DCCPS, Surveillance Research Program, Cancer Statistics Branch; released April 2008. Underlying mortality data provided by NCHS (www.cdc.gov/nchs).

[56] Solt D, Medline A, Farber E. Rapid emergence of carcinogen-induced initiated hepatocytes in liver carcinogenesis. Am J Pathol 1977;88:595–618.

[57] McDonnell TJ, Korsmeyer SJ. Progression from lymphoid hyperplasia to high-grade malignant lymphoma in mice transgenic for the t(14;18). Nature 1991;349:254–6.

[58] Brash DE, Ponten J. Skin precancer. Cancer Surv 1998;32:69–113.

[59] Naramura M, Nadeau S, Mohapatra B, Ahmad G, Mukhopadhyay C, Sattler M, et al. Mutant Cbl proteins as oncogenic drivers in myeloproliferative disorders. Oncotarget 2011;2:245–50.

[60] Niemeyer CM, Kang MW, Shin DH, Furlan I, Erlacher M, Bunin NJ, et al. Germline CBL mutations cause developmental abnormalities and predispose to juvenile myelomonocytic leukemia. Nat Genet 2010;42:794–800.

[61] Martincorena I, Roshan A, Gerstung M, et al. High burden and pervasive positive selection of somatic mutations in normal human skin. Science 2015;348:880–6.

[62] Lynch M. Rate, molecular spectrum, and consequences of human mutation. Proc Natl Acad Sci U S A 2010;107:961–8.

[63] Chatterjee A, Morison IM. Monozygotic twins: genes are not the destiny? Bioinformation 2011;7:369–70.

[64] Wong AHC, Gottesman II, Petronis A. Phenotypic differences in genetically identical organisms: the epigenetic perspective. Hum Mol Genet 2005;14:R11–8.

[65] The Garfield Autopsy. Dr. Lamb relates the manner in which the bullet was found. The New York Times; November 28, 1881.

[66] Frey CM, McMillen MM, Cowan CD, Horm JW, Kessler LG. Representativeness of the surveillance, epidemiology, and end results program data: recent trends in cancer mortality rate. J Natl Cancer Inst 1992;84:872.

[67] Instructions for completing the cause-of-death section of the death certificate. U.S. Department of Health and Human services, Centers for Disease Control and Prevention National Center for Health Statistics; August, 2004.

[68] Ong P, Gambatese M, Begier E, Zimmerman R, Soto A, Madsen A. Effect of cause-of-death training on agreement between hospital discharge diagnoses and cause of death reported, inpatient hospital deaths, New York City, 2008-2010. Prev Chronic Dis 2015;12:e04.

[69] Ashworth TG. Inadequacy of death certification: proposal for change. J Clin Pathol 1991;44:265.

[70] Instructions for classifying the underlying cause of death, 2008. Albany, NY: WHO Publications Center; 2008. Available from: https://www.cdc.gov/nchs/data/dvs/2a2008Final.pdf [Accessed 23 October 2016].

[71] Responsibilities of practicing physicians when the Medical Examiner declines jurisdiction. District 21 Medical Examiner's Office, Florida. Available from: http://www.flame21.com/physicians.htm.death_certificate_rules.pdf [Accessed 23 October 2016].

[72] Documentation for the mortality public use data set, 1999. Mortality Statistics Branch, Division of Vital Statistics, National Center for Health Statistics; 1999.

[73] Kircher T, Anderson RE. Cause of death: proper completion of the death certificate. JAMA 1987;258:349–52.

[74] Walter SD, Birnie SE. Mapping mortality and morbidity patterns: an international comparison. Int J Epidemiol 1991;20:678–89.

[75] Berman JJ. Methods in Medical Informatics: Fundamentals of Healthcare Programming in Perl, Python, and Ruby. Boca Raton, FL: Chapman and Hall; 2010.

[76] Berman JJ. Biomedical informatics. Sudbury, MA: Jones and Bartlett; 2007.

[77] Petersen M. Thousands of deaths from hospital superbugs are going unreported, research shows. LA Times; October 2, 2016.

[78] Wexelman BA, Eden E, Rose KM. Survey of New York City resident physicians on cause-of-death reporting, 2010. Prev Chronic Dis 2013;10:120288.

[79] Madar S, Goldstein I, Rotter V. Did experimental biology die? Lessons from 30 years of p53 research. Cancer Res 2009;69:6378–80.

[80] Zilfou JT, Lowe SW. Tumor suppressive functions of p53. Cold Spring Harb Perspect Biol 2009;1:a001883.

[81] Vogelstein B, Lane D, Levine AJ. Surfing the p53 network. Nature 2000;408:307–10.

[82] Nishikimi M, Yagi K. Molecular basis for the deficiency in humans of gulonolactone oxidase, a key enzyme for ascorbic acid biosynthesis. Am J Clin Nutr 1991;54:S1203–1208.

[83] Mochizuki Y, He J, Kulkarni S, Bessler M, Mason PJ. Mouse dyskerin mutations affect accumulation of telomerase RNA and small nucleolar RNA, telomerase activity, and ribosomal RNA processing. Proc Natl Acad Sci 2004;101:10756–61.

[84] Zimmer C. The continuing evolution of genes. The New York Times; April 28, 2014.

[85] Storz JF. Gene duplication and evolutionary innovations in hemoglobin-oxygen transport. Physiology (Bethesda) 2016;31:223–32.

[86] Kimchi-Sarfaty C, Oh JM, Kim IW, Sauna ZE, Calcagno AM, Ambudkar SV, et al. A "silent" polymorphism in the MDR1 gene changes substrate specificity. Science 2007;315(5811):525–8.

[87] Kothandapani A, Sawant A, Dangeti VS, Sobol RW, Patrick SM. Epistatic role of base excision repair and mismatch repair pathways in mediating cisplatin cytotoxicity. Nucleic Acids Res 2013;41:7332–43.

[88] Gearhart J, Pashos EE, Prasad MK. Pluripotency redux—advances in stem-cell research. New Engl J Med 2007;357:1469–72.

[89] Seidman JG, Seidman C. Transcription factor haploinsufficiency: when half a loaf is not enough. J Clin Invest 2002;109:451–5.

[90] Lee TI, Young RA. Transcriptional regulation and its misregulation in disease. Cell 2013;152:1237–51.

[91] Chi YI. Homeodomain revisited: a lesson from disease-causing mutations. Hum Genet 2005;116:433–44.

[92] Gerke J, Lorenz K, Ramnarine S, Cohen B. Gene environment interactions at nucleotide resolution. PLoS Genet 2010;6:e1001144.

[93] Leveson NG. System safety engineering: back to the future. Self-published ebook; 2002. Available from: http://sunnyday.mit.edu/book2.pdf [Accessed 22 September 2016].

[94] Rog CJ, Chekuri SC, Edgerton ME. Challenges of the information age: the impact of false discovery on pathway identification. BMC Res Notes 2012;5:647.

[95] Rosen JM, Jordan CT. The increasing complexity of the cancer stem cell paradigm. Science 2009;324:1670–3.

[96] Beasley DMG, Glass WI. Cyanide poisoning: pathophysiology and treatment recommendations. Occup Med 1998;48:427–31.

[97] Shamanin V, zur Hausen H, Lavergne D, Proby CM, Leigh IM, Neumann C, et al. Human papillomavirus infections in nonmelanoma skin cancers from renal transplant recipients and nonimmunosuppressed patients. J Natl Cancer Inst 1996;88:802–11.

[98] Dessoukey MW, Omar MF, Abdel-Dayem H. Eruptive keratoacanthomas associated with immunosuppressive therapy in a patient with systemic lupus erythematosus. J Am Acad Dermatol 1997;37(3 Pt 1):478–80.

[99] Guitart J, McGillis ST, Bergfeld WF, Tuthill RJ, Bailin PL, Camisa C. Muir-Torre syndrome associated with alpha 1-antitrypsin deficiency and cutaneous vasculitis. Report of a case with exacerbation of a cutaneous neoplasm during immunosuppressive therapy. J Am Acad Dermatol 1991;24(5 Pt 2):875–7.

[100] Murphy SC, Lowitt MH, Kao GF. Multiple eruptive dermatofibromas in an hiv-positive man. Dermatology 1995;190:309–12.

[101] Cohen PR. Multiple dermatofibromas in patients with autoimmune disorders receiving immunosuppressive therapy. Int J Dermatol 1991;30:507–8.

[102] Jensen JC, Choyke PL, Rosenfeld M, Pass HI, Keiser H, White B, et al. A report of familial carotid body tumors and multiple extra-adrenal pheochromocytomas. J Urol 1991;145:1040–2.

[103] Chen YB, Rahemtullah A, Hochberg E. Primary effusion lymphoma. Oncologist 2007;12:569–76.

[104] Magdi M, Hussein MM, Mooij JM, Roujouleh HM. Regression of post-transplant Kaposi sarcoma after discontinuing cyclosporin and giving mycophenolate mofetil instead. Nephrol Dial Transplant 2000;15:1103–4.

[105] Hacein-Bey-Abina S, Von Kalle C, Schmidt M, McCormack MP, Wulffraat N, Leboulch P, et al. LMO2-associated clonal T cell proliferation in two patients after gene therapy for SCID-X1. Science 2003;302(5644):415–9.

[106] Baum C, Dullmann J, Li Z, Fehse B, Meyer J, Williams DA, et al. Side effects of retroviral gene transfer into hematopoietic stem cells. Blood 2003;101:2099–114.

[107] Berman JJ. Neoplasms: principles of development and diversity. Sudbury, MA: Jones and Bartlett; 2009.

[108] Kufe D, Pollock R, Weichselbaum R, Bast R, Gansler T, Holland J, et al., editors. Holland Frei cancer medicine. Ontario: BC Decker; 2003.

[109] Fung YK, Crittenden LB, Fadly AM, Kung HJ. Tumor induction by direct injection of cloned v-src DNA into chickens. Proc Natl Acad Sci 1983;80:353–7.

[110] Roberts CW, Leroux MM, Fleming MD, Orkin SH. Highly penetrant, rapid tumorigenesis through conditional inversion of the tumor suppressor gene Snf5. Cancer Cell 2002;2:415–25.

[111] Roberts CW, Galusha SA, McMenamin ME, Fletcher CD, Orkin SH. Haploinsufficiency of Snf5 (integrase interactor 1)predisposes to malignant rhabdoid tumors in mice. Proc Natl Acad Sci U S A 2000;97:13796–800.

[112] Shachaf CM, Kopelman AM, Arvanitis C, Karlsson A, Beer S, Mandl S, et al. MYC inactivation uncovers pluripotent differentiation and tumour dormancy in hepatocellular cancer. Nature 2004;431:1112–7.

[113] Giuriato S, Ryeom S, Fan AC, Bachireddy P, Lynch RC, Rioth MJ, et al. Sustained regression of tumors upon MYC inactivation requires p53 or thrombospondin-1 to reverse the angiogenic switch. Proc Natl Acad Sci U S A 2006;103:16266–71.

[114] Xu X, Weaver Z, Linke SP, Li C, Gotay J, Wang XW, et al. Centrosome amplification and a defective G2-M cell cycle checkpoint induce genetic instability in BRCA1 exon 11 isoform-deficient cells. Mol Cell 1999;3:389–95.

[115] Cahill DP, Lengauer C, Yu J, Riggins GJ, Willson JK, Markowitz SD, et al. Mutations of mitotic checkpoint genes in human cancers. Nature 1998;392:300–3.

[116] Weaver BAA, Cleveland DW. The role of aneuploidy in promoting and suppressing tumors. J Cell Biol 2009;185:935–7.

[117] Komoto M, Tominaga K, Nakata B, Takashima T, Inoue T, Hirakawa K. Complete regression of low-grade mucosa-associated lymphoid tissue (MALT) lymphoma in the gastric stump after eradication of Helicobacter pylori. J Exp Clin Cancer Res 2006;25:283–5.

[118] Walsh T, Casadei S, Coats KH, Swisher E, Stray SM, Higgins J, et al. Spectrum of mutations in BRCA1, BRCA2, CHEK2, and TP53 in families at high risk of breast cancer. JAMA 2006;295:1379–88.

[119] D'Andrea AD. Susceptibility pathways in Fanconi's anemia and breast cancer. N Engl J Med 2010; 362(20):1909–19.

[120] Stecklein SR, Jensen RA. Identifying and exploiting defects in the Fanconi anemia/BRCA pathway in oncology. Transl Res 2012;160:178–97.

[121] Silva AG, Ewald IP, Sapienza M, Pinheiro M, Peixoto A, de N brega AF, et al. Li-Fraumeni-like syndrome associated with a large BRCA1 intragenic deletion. BMC Cancer 2012;12:237.

[122] Joensuu H, Klemi PJ. DNA aneuploidy in adenomas of endocrine organs. Am J Pathol 1988;132:145–51.

[123] Menezes BF, Morgan R, Azad M. Multicentric Castleman's disease: a case report. J Med Case Rep 2007;1:78.

[124] Lupski JR, de Oca-Luna RM, Slaugenhaupt S, Pentao L, Guzzetta V, Trask BJ, et al. DNA duplication associated with Charcot-Marie-Tooth disease type 1A. Cell 1991;66:219–32.

[125] Committee report. Classification and nomenclature of morphological defects (Discussion). Lancet 1975;305:513.

[126] Roberts J. Looking at variation in numbers. The Scientist; March 14, 2005.

[127] Vilmos P, Kurucz E. Insect immunity: evolutionary roots of the mammalian innate immune system. Immunol Lett 1998;62:59–66.

[128] Hugot JP, Chamaillard M, Zouali H, Lesage S, Lesage S, Cezard JP, et al. Association of NOD2 leucine-rich repeat variants with susceptibility to Crohn's disease. Nature 2001;411:599–603.

[129] Ogura Y, Bonen DK, Inohara N, Nicolae DL, Chen FF, Ramos R, et al. A frameshift mutation in NOD2 associated with susceptibility to Crohn's disease. Nature 2001;411:603–6.

[130] McGonagle D, McDermott MF. A proposed classification of the immunological diseases. PLoS Med 2006;3:e297.

[131] Glaser RL, Goldbach-Mansky R. The spectrum of monogenic autoinflammatory syndromes: understanding disease mechanisms and use of targeted therapies. Curr Allergy Asthma Rep 2008;8:288–98.

[132] Masters SL, Simon A, Aksentijevich I, Kastner DL. Horror autoinflammaticus: the molecular pathophysiology of autoinflammatory disease. Annu Rev Immunol 2009;27:621–68.

[133] Seidman JD, Berman JJ, Yetter RA, Moore GW. Multiparameter DNA flow cytometry of keratoacanthoma. Anal Quant Cytol Histol 1992;14:113–9.

[134] Mercer K, Giblett S, Green S, Lloyd D, DaRocha Dias S, Plumb M, et al. Expression of endogenous oncogenic V600E B-raf induces proliferation and developmental defects in mice and transformation of primary fibroblasts. Cancer Res 2005;65:11493–500.

[135] Horning SJ, Rosenberg SA. The natural history of initially untreated low-grade non-Hodgkin's lymphomas. N Engl J Med 1984;311:1471–5.

[136] Hillengass J, Weber MA, Kilk K, Listl K, Wagner-Gund B, Hillengass M, et al. Prognostic significance of whole-body MRI in patients with monoclonal gammopathy of undetermined significance. Leukemia 2013;28:174–8.

[137] Stechmann A, Hamblin K, Perez-Brocal V, Gaston D, Richmond GS, van der Giezen M, et al. Organelles in blastocystis that blur the distinction between mitochondria and hydrogenosomes. Curr Biol 2008;18:580–5.

[138] Tovar J, Leon-Avila G, Sanchez LB, Sutak R, Tachezy J, van der Giezen M, et al. Mitochondrial remnant organelles of Giardia function in iron-sulphur protein maturation. Nature 2003;426:172–6.

[139] Tovar J, Fischer A, Clark CG. The mitosome, a novel organelle related to mitochondria in the amitochondrial parasite Entamoeba histolytica. Mol Microbiol 1999;32:1013–21.

[140] Burri L, Williams B, Bursac D, Lithgow T, Keeling P. Microsporidian mitosomes retain elements of the general mitochondrial targeting system. PNAS 2006;103:15916–20.

[141] Weatherall DJ. Molecular pathology of single gene disorders. J Clin Pathol 1987;40:959–70.

[142] Tefferi A, Gilliland DG. Oncogenes in myeloproliferative disorders. Cell Cycle 2007;6:550–66.

[143] Nachman MW, Crowell SL. Estimate of the mutation rate per nucleotide in humans. Genetics 2000;156:297–304.

[144] Roach JC, Glusman G, Smit AF, Huff CD, Hubley R, Shannon PT, et al. Analysis of genetic inheritance in a family quartet by whole-genome sequencing. Science 2010;328:636–9.

[145] Whittaker JC, Harbord RM, Boxall N, Mackay I, Dawson G, Sibly RM. Likelihood-based estimation of microsatellite mutation rates. Genetics 2003;164:781–7.

[146] Veltman JA, Brunner HG. De novo mutations in human genetic disease. Nat Rev Genet 2012;13:565–75.

[147] Takahashi K, Tanabe K, Ohnuki M, Narita M, Ichisaka T, Tomoda K, et al. Induction of pluripotent stem cells from adult human fibroblasts by defined factors. Cell 2007;131:861–72.

[148] Okita K, Ichisaka T, Yamanaka S. Generation of germline-competent induced pluripotent stem cells. Nature 2007;448:313–7.

[149] Ng BG, Kranz C, Hagebeuk EE, Duran M, Abeling NG, Wuyts B, et al. Molecular and clinical characterization of a Moroccan Cog7 deficient patient. Mol Genet Metab 2007;91:201–4.

[150] Beckwith JB, Perrin EV. In situ neuroblastomas: a contribution to the natural history of neural crest tumors. Am J Pathol 1963;43:1089–104.

[151] de Vooght KMK, van Wijk R, van Solingel WE. Management of gene promoter mutations in molecular diagnostics. Clin Chem 2009;55:698–708.

[152] Berman JJ. Taxonomic guide to infectious diseases: understanding the biologic classes of pathogenic organisms. Waltham, MA: Academic Press; 2012.

[153] Emerman M, Malik HS. Paleovirology: modern consequences of ancient viruses. PLoS Biol 2010;8:e1000301.

[154] Jonkman MF. Revertant mosaicism in human genetic disorders. Am J Med Genet 1999;85:361–4.

[155] Wahn V, Stephan V, Hirschhorn R. Reverse mutations—spontaneous amelioration or cure of inherited disorders? Eur J Pediatr 1998;157:613–7.

[156] Solomou EE, Gibellini F, Stewart B, Malide D, Berg M, Visconte V, et al. Perforin gene mutations in patients with acquired aplastic anemia. Blood 2007;109(12):5234–7.

[157] Johnston JJ, Gropman AL, Sapp JC, Teer JK, Martin JM, Liu CF, et al. The phenotype of a germline mutation in PIGA: the gene somatically mutated in paroxysmal nocturnal hemoglobinuria. Am J Hum Genet 2012;90:295–300.

[158] DeQueiroz K. Ernst Mayr and the modern concept of species. PNAS 2005;102(Suppl. 1):6600–7.

[159] DeQueiroz K. Species concepts and species delimitation. Syst Biol 2007;56:879–86.

[160] Mayden RL. Consilience and a hierarchy of species concepts: advances toward closure on the species puzzle. J Nematol 1999;31:95–116.

[161] Choi BI, Han JK, Hong ST, Lee KH. Clonorchiasis and cholangiocarcinoma: etiologic relationship and imaging diagnosis. Clin Microbiol Rev 2004;17:540–52.

Genetics: Clues, Not Answers, to the Mysteries of Precision Medicine

SECTION 3.1 INSCRUTABLE GENES

In most cases, the molecular consequences of disease, or trait-associated variants for human physiology, are not understood.
Teri A. Manolio and co-authors [1]

I guess I should warn you, if I turn out to be particularly clear, you've probably misunderstood what I've said.
Alan Greenspan

The 1960s was a wonderful decade for the field of molecular genetics. Hundreds of inherited metabolic diseases were being studied. Most of these diseases could be characterized by a simple inherited mutation in a disease-causing gene. Back then, we thought we understood genetic diseases. Here's how it all might have worked, if life were simple: one mutation → one gene → one protein → one disease. This lovely genetic parable, from a by-gone generation, seldom applies in the era of Precision Medicine. The purpose of this section is to explain some of the complexities of modern genetics and to lay out the job of the Precision Medicine scientist who must dissect the pathways that lead from gene to disease.

The concepts discussed herein will prepare us for some specific diseases to be explored in later chapters.

Here are the genetic realities that complicate the study of Precision Medicine.

- **One-to-many and many-to-one diseases**

In the prior chapter, we touched on two of the confusing aspects of Precision Medicine: that a single disease may result from one of many distinct molecular defects; and that a single gene may produce many different diseases. These two countervailing phenomena tell us something very important about disease development. The first is that different pathways may converge to the same disease, and that any single gene may perturb a biological system (i.e., a living organism) in different ways.

There are hundreds of examples wherein mutations in one gene may result in more than one disease [2]. In some cases, each of the diseases caused by the altered gene is fundamentally similar (e.g., spherocytosis and elliptocytosis, caused by mutations in the alpha-spectrin gene; Usher syndrome type IIIA and retinitis pigmentosa-61 caused by mutations in the CLRN1 gene). In other case, diseases caused by the same gene may have no obvious relation to one another. For example, the APOE gene encodes apolipoprotein E, which is involved in the synthesis of lipoproteins. One common allele of the APOE locus, e4, increases the risk of Alzheimer disease and of heart disease, two disorders of no obvious clinical similarities [3,4]. [Glossary Allele, Open reading frame]

Let's look at a few other examples where mutations in a single gene play causal roles in the development of diverse diseases. For example, different mutations of the same gene, desmoplakin, cause the following diseases [2]:

- Arrhythmogenic right ventricular dysplasia 8
- Dilated cardiomyopathy with woolly hair and keratoderma
- Lethal acantholytic epidermolysis bullosa [5]
- Keratosis palmoplantaris striata II
- Skin fragility-woolly hair syndrome

How is it possible that errors in the gene coding for desmoplakin, a constituent protein found in intercellular junctions, could account for such apparently unrelated diseases as arrhythmogenic right ventricular dysplasia and lethal acantholytic epidermolysis bullosa? It happens that we know that specialized desmosomes in cardiac cells (i.e., intercalated discs) tightly couple myocytes so that they can function as a coordinated group. Desmosomes are also required to adhese skin epidermal cells to one another and to the underlying basement membrane. In the case of desmoplakin mutations, it is relatively easy to see the pathogenetic relationship among these diseases.

In other sets of diseases that result from an error in one specific gene, the pathogenetic relationship may not be so easily discerned. Some cases of Charcot-Marie-Tooth axonal neuropathy, lipodystrophy, Emery-Dreyfus muscular dystrophy, and premature aging syndromes are all caused by mutation in the LMNA (Lamin A/C) gene. Stickler syndrome type III, Fibrochondrogenesis-2, and a form of nonsyndromic hearing loss are all caused by mutations in the COL11A2 gene. In these cases, how can variations in a single gene cause many different diseases? [Glossary Nonsyndromic disease]

Let's look at just a few of the possibilities:

- One gene can control the synthesis of more than one protein [6].
- A single protein may have multiple functions. For example, nuclear lamina (lamin a/c) has several biological roles: controlling nuclear shape, influencing transcription, and organizing heterochromatin. Mutations in the LMNA gene cause more than 10 different clinical syndromes, including neuromuscular and cardiac disorders, premature aging disorders, and lipodystrophy. Likewise, the polyfunctional TP53 gene has been linked to 11 clinically distinguishable cancer-related disorders [7].
- A single protein with a single function may have different biological effects based on the cell type in which the protein is expressed, the stage of development in which the protein is expressed, and the cellular milieu (e.g., concentrations of substrate or protein inhibitors) for a given cell type, at a particular moment in time.
- Diseases develop through a sequence of biological events occurring over time. A mutation may exert a different biological effect based on where and when, in the sequence of pathogenetic events, it is expressed.

Just as mutational changes in a single gene may be the root cause for any number of different diseases, we see that a single disease may be caused by a variety of single gene mutations, a condition known as genetic heterogeneity. There are two broad categories of genetic heterogeneity [Glossary Genetic heterogeneity]:

- Allelic heterogeneity, in which any of several variants in a gene may cause a disease. For example, more than 2000 distinct allelic variants coding for the cystic fibrosis transmembrane conductance regulator protein may contribute to producing cystic fibrosis [8]. Genetic testing for cystic fibrosis is a continuing challenge, as new pathologic alleles are reported frequently. [Glossary Allelic heterogeneity, Uniparental disomy]
- Locus heterogeneity, in which variants of different genes, at different loci in the genome, cause the same or very similar disease. As a biological phenomenon, locus heterogeneity is much more relevant to this book than is allelic heterogeneity. The very existence of locus heterogeneity confirms that there are multiple biological pathways that lead to a disease, and that we can no longer be certain that any disease is caused exclusively by a single gene. [Glossary Locus heterogeneity]

From the point of view of genetic testing for disease, genetic heterogeneity informs us that we cannot presume that absence of a known disease-associated mutation indicates that there is no risk of developing a disease: the individual may have an untested disease-causing mutation in the same gene (i.e., allelic heterogeneity) or may have a mutation in an altogether different gene that is capable of producing the disease (i.e., locus heterogeneity).

As we look more closely at supposedly well-understood monogenic diseases, we find heterogeneity where none was suspected. Take, for example, Huntington disease. Huntington disease is a progressive neurodegenerative disorder once thought to be caused exclusively by a particular type of genetic aberration (i.e., a trinucleotide repeat) occurring in the HTT gene, resulting in an altered huntingtin protein. We now know that this is not always the case. About one percent of patients with the clinical phenotype of Huntington disease lack the characteristic huntingtin protein alteration [9]. In a study of 285 patients with Huntington Disease, but lacking the characteristic HTT triplet expansion, a diverse set of alternate gene mutations were found [9]. [Glossary Trinucleotide repeat disorder]

Let's look at an extreme example of locus heterogeneity. Severe combined immunodeficiency disease (SCID) has different genetic causes, all producing immunodeficiencies of both arms of the adaptive immune system (i.e., B cells and T cells). The condition arises by any one of a number of different genetic mutations, involving totally different genetic pathways that all lead to a common phenotype, in infants.

- Mutations in the gene encoding the common gamma chain (of interleukin receptors)
- Defective adenosine deaminase, an enzyme involved in the breakdown of purines
- Mutations of the purine nucleoside phosphorylase gene, the protein product of which is a key enzyme in the purine salvage pathway
- Insufficiency of mitochondrial adenylate kinase 2
- Insufficiency of recombination activating gene products, necessary for the manufacture of immunoglobulins
- Loss of expression of major histocompatibility complex proteins
- Janus kinase-3 deficiency
- Mutation in Artemis gene, required for DNA repair and normal immunologic defenses

In SCID, the different pathogeneses are so remarkably diverse that each causal variant could be assigned its own disease subtype, potentially responsive to its own therapeutic strategy.

Let's look, just briefly, at a few instructive examples of monogenic diseases that can be caused by errors in any one of several different genes:

- Tuberous sclerosis is an inherited monogenic rare syndrome that produces multiple benign hamartomas, as well as certain types of cancers. The genetic basis of tuberous sclerosis involves biallelic inactivation of either of two unlinked genes that seem to have equivalent pathogenic roles. The genes are TSC1 (encoding hamartin) and TSC2 (encoding tuberin). In this disease, the hamartin and tuberin genes lock together in a protein complex. A defect in either gene disrupts the same pathway [10]. [Glossary Hamartoma]
- Bardet-Biedl syndrome is characterized by rod-cone dystrophy, obesity, polydactyly, and a variety of organ abnormalities. The various forms of Bardet-Biedl syndrome are accounted for by mutations in one of at least 14 different genes. Although the underlying pathogenesis of Bardet-Biedl syndrome is yet to be clarified, there is evidence to suggest that each of the gene mutations known to cause Bardet-Biedl results in a defect in the basal body of ciliated cells [11]. Such defects produce the pleiotropic (i.e., one gene producing many different perturbations in the organism) phenotype that characterizes Bardet-Biedl syndrome.
- Autosomal dominant cutis laxa can be caused by a mutation of the elastin gene or the fibulin-5 gene.
- Hypotrichosis simplex of the scalp can be caused by mutation in the CDSN gene or the KRT74 gene.

- Oguchi disease can be caused by a mutation in the arrestin gene or the rhodopsin kinase gene.
- An autosomal dominant form of thrombocytopenia can be caused by a mutation in the ANKRD26 gene, or the cytochrome c gene. [Glossary Cytopenia]
- Retinitis pigmentosa is a group of inherited conditions characterized by the progressive loss of photoreceptor cells in the retina. Rhodopsin consists of the protein moiety opsin and a covalently bound cofactor, known as retinal [12]. More than 100 mutations in the rhodopsin gene account for about 25% of cases. About 150 mutations have been reported in the opsin gene. Other mutated genes causing variants of retinitis pigmentosa involve pre-mRNA splicing factors, as well as posttranslational errors in protein folding and other errors of chaperone proteins. Mutations in any one of more than 35 different genes can cause variant forms of retinitis pigmentosa. Retinitis pigmentosa is unusual for being a disease that can be inherited as an autosomal dominant, autosomal recessive, or X-linked disorder. Digenic and mitochondrial forms of retinitis pigmentosa have been described, and the disease can appear as a solitary disorder or as part of a multiorgan syndrome (e.g., NARP syndrome of neuropathy, ataxia, and retinitis pigmentosa caused by a mutation in the mitochondrial DNA gene MT-ATP6). Why there are so many forms of retinitis, with such a large repertoire of disease-causing genes, is somewhat of a mystery. Most of the genes causing various forms of retinitis pigmentosa exclusively affect specialized retinal photoreceptor cells (e.g., rhodopsin). Other genes that cause retinitis pigmentosa are active in many different types of cells (e.g., splicing factors). It happens that photoreceptor rod cells have an extraordinarily high rate of self-renewal, as the cell segments are continuously shed from the tips of cells and replaced by new segments. Small deficiencies in cell synthesis may precipitate the loss of these cells. Hence, any genetic deficiency accounting for a reduction in protein synthesis may theoretically cause retinitis pigmentosa [13–15]. [Glossary Oligogenic inheritance, Combined gene deficiency, Cofactor]
- Epidermolysis bullosa is an inherited disease characterized by blistering of the skin and mucosal membranes (e.g., mouth). It is always caused by a defect causing the epidermis to be poorly anchored to the underlying dermis. Over 300 gene defects can result in epidermolysis bullosa. Depending on the variant form of the disease, any of several different genes may serve as the underlying cause (e.g., COL, PLEC, Desmoplakin genes [5]). There is also an autoimmune form, epidermolysis bullosa acquisita, wherein antibodies target Type VII collagen, a component of the basement membrane glue that helps bind epidermis with dermis. Epidermolysis bullosa will be discussed again, as an example of disease convergence.
- Li-Fraumeni syndrome is an inherited cancer syndrome characterized by an increased risk of developing such common cancers as breast cancer, lung cancer, colon cancer, pancreatic cancer, and prostate cancer. Various types of rare cancers associated with the Li-Fraumeni syndrome include soft-tissue sarcomas, osteosarcomas, brain tumors, acute leukemias, adrenocortical carcinomas, Wilms tumor, and phyllodes tumor of breast. In this syndrome, the occurrence of common cancers along with rare cancers indicates that a rare genetic cause of a

common disease can sometimes occur within the same gene that is known to cause a rare disease. Li-Fraumeni syndrome was originally believed to be associated exclusively by mutations in the TP53-gene-encoding protein p53. TP53 is an example of a tumor suppressor gene. The absence of a tumor suppressor reduces the cell's normal ability to suppress cellular events that increase the susceptibility of cells to cancer. In the case of the p53 gene, loss of activity reduces the ability of cells to undergo apoptosis, a process by which cells commit suicide following DNA damage. By continuing to survive and divide, damaged cells contribute to a subpopulation of cells at risk for progressing through the stages of carcinogenesis. As it turns out, mutations in genes other than TP53 can produce a syndrome similar to, if not indistinguishable from, Li-Fraumeni syndrome. In addition to TP53, the genes that produce forms of Li-Fraumeni syndrome include CHEK2 and BRCA1 [16,17]. All of the genes associated with Li-Fraumeni syndrome have a similar function: controlling whether cells live or die following DNA damage. [Glossary Li-Fraumeni syndrome]

What are the lessons to be drawn from all this perplexing information about the genetic heterogeneity of diseases?

- That despite a diversity of root genetic causes, pathogenesis may converge to a common clinical phenotype (a topic that we will explore in great depth in Section 4.1, "Mechanisms of Convergence")
- That the so-called causal gene for a disease is just one clue, among many clues, that may lead us to understand the true pathogenesis of a disease.

- **Variable expressivity [Glossary Variable expressivity]**

Variable expressivity is a biological phenomenon wherein different individuals who harbor the same gene mutation may express different clinical phenotypes. For example, one individual may have a severe form of the disease; another has a mild form. One individual may express the complete set of physical findings associated with a disease. Another may have just a few of those findings, or none at all. One individual may have one disease and another individual may have a different disease entirely (e.g., Prader Willi syndrome and Angelman disease).

Incomplete penetrance is the name given to the type of variable expressivity in which not all individuals with a disease-causing genetic mutation actually develop disease. A well-known example of incomplete penetrance is observed in women who inherit the BRCA1 gene. These women have an 80% lifetime risk of developing breast cancer. In the remaining 20% of women who carry the BRCA1 gene and who do not develop breast cancer, the gene is nonpenetrant [18]. Other genes, such as the mutated FGFR3 gene associated with achondroplasia, are nearly 100% penetrant (i.e., presence of the mutated gene in the germ line is almost always followed by the development of disease). At this point, we know very little about the biological determinants of penetrance.

Neurofibromatosis type 1 provides an example of a disease that has variable expressivity. This disease, which is associated with a mutation in the NF1 gene, features a variety of lesions including hyperpigmented macules (cafe au lait spots), benign growths (neurofibromas), and an increased risk of some malignancies. The clinical expressivity of this disease is so extreme that one individual may have thousands of neurofibromas, while another close family member, with the identical mutation, may have just a few neurofibromas [18]. It is easy to imagine that modifier genes can influence the time of onset of disease, the severity of disease, and the clinical phenotype of any genetic disease [19]. [Glossary Von Recklinghausen disease]

Another example of variable expressivity is found in inherited Milroy disease, typically characterized by chronic lymphedema of the legs. Individuals with the characteristic FLT4/VEGFR3 mutation may have severe symptoms, mild symptoms, or no symptoms at all [20].

In some cases, two individuals with the same genetic mutation will have two distinctly different diseases. Prader-Willi syndrome is a genetic disease characterized by growth disorders (e.g., low muscle tone, short stature, extreme obesity, and cognitive disabilities). Angelman syndrome is a genetic disease characterized by neurologic disturbances (e.g., seizures, sleep disturbances, hand flapping), and a typifying happy demeanor. Both diseases can occur in either gender and both diseases are caused by the same microdeletion at 15q11-13. When the microdeletion occurs on the paternally derived chromosome, the disease that results is Prader-Willi syndrome. When the microdeletion occurs on the maternally derived chromosome, the disease that results is Angelman syndrome. [Glossary Microdeletion]

In some cases, variation in the sites of mutations in a gene do not produce different diseases, but may account for one disease with different levels of severity. For example, in the case of Wiskott-Aldrich syndrome, mutations that truncate the protein product of the WAS gene will produce severe disease, while mutations that produce changes in single amino acids, without changing the length of the protein, will tend to produce mild disease [21].

In some cases, the gain or loss of methylation at a gene site may produce disorders of nearly opposite clinical features. For example, H19 differentially methylated region is a site on chromosome 11p15.5 in which microdeletions occur in some cases of Beckwith-Wiedemann syndrome and Russell-Silver syndrome. Opposite methylation patterns in the H19 differentially methylated region will cause Beckwith-Wiedemann syndrome, when there is a gain-of-methylation, and Russell-Silver syndrome when there is loss-of-methylation [22]. Beckwith-Wiedemann syndrome is characterized by tissue overgrowth and tumor formation [23]. Russell-Silver syndrome is characterized by dwarfism. [Glossary DNA methylation, Russell-Silver syndrome]

The disease caused by a gene may change depending on whether the gene is expressed as a germline mutation or a somatic mutation. In the case of the MYCN gene, a germline mutation produces MYCN gene haploinsufficiency. This means that the mutated gene is nonfunctional, while the gene on the matching chromosome expresses a normal gene product. Germline haploinsufficiency of the MYCN gene results in Feingold syndrome, a developmental disorder characterized by microcephaly, limb malformations, esophageal and duodenal atresias, and other developmental alterations. The same gene, when amplified in somatic cells, is associated with neuroblastoma formation. [Glossary Somatic]

In a nonconventional sense of the term "variable expressivity," interspecies differences are worthy of note. Although there are many biological differences between humans and mice, their respective genomes are remarkably similar. Nearly all the genes found in humans can also be found in mice. Of the 4000 or so genes that have been carefully studied, fewer than 10 are found in one species but not the other [24]. On average, the protein-coding sequences in mice are 85% identical to the homologous sequences in humans [24]. As far as we can tell, the mouse's genome comes nearly as close to approximating the human genome as does the chimpanzee's genome [25,26]. This being the case, it seems natural to think that a germline mutation in mice that is equivalent to a disease-causing germline mutation in humans will yield a mouse disease that closely models its human counterpart. [Glossary Homolog, Paralog, Ortholog]

As it happens, our experiences with mice have not always met our expectations. There are rare subtypes of type 2 diabetes that have a monogenic origin. These rare types of diabetes become clinically evident in children and have a Mendelian pattern of inheritance. One such monogenic form of diabetes is MODY-8 (Maturity-Onset Diabetes of the Young) caused by a mutation in the carboxyl-ester lipase gene. This mutation was experimentally inserted into the germline of a mouse, producing a transgenic strain of mice carrying the MODY-8 mutation. These mice failed to develop any signs of diabetes, or pancreatic damage, or any dysfunction caused by the mutated gene [27]. Why not? For starters, we must remind ourselves that a gene defect does not cause a disease; it initiates a multistep process that may lead to disease. Perhaps mice do not participate in the same disease process partaken by humans. Beyond that, we should ask ourselves the following question: "If we cannot explain why a pathogenic mutation fails to produce disease in a mouse model, then can we honestly say that we understand how the same mutation leads to disease in humans?

- **Pleiotropia**

Pleiotropia is the condition in which one gene produces an array of apparently unrelated clinical effects. In many cases, pleiotropic diseases are caused by genetic defects in regulatory elements, such as transcription factors. Transcription factors are proteins that bind to specific DNA sequences to control the transcription of DNA to RNA. Because the transcription factor alters the rate of synthesis of many different proteins, we expect to see a diversity in the ways that the disease can express itself in different organs. Furthermore, because each of the genes affected by an altered regulator gene is itself subject to variable expressivity, we can expect that genetic aberrations of transcription factors will produce complex phenotypes with different levels of disease severity. For example, a mutation in the gene-encoding transcription factor TBX5 causes Holt-Oram syndrome, characterized by the variable expression of hand malformations, heart defects, and other malformations.

Not all pleiotropic diseases are caused by alterations of regulatory genes. Consider WHIM syndrome, an acronym for Warts, Hypogammaglobulinemia, Infections, and Myelokathexis (congenital leukopenia and neutropenia). WHIM is a combined immunodeficiency disease caused by an alteration in the chemokine receptor gene CXCR4 [28]. Warts result from a lowered immune repression of papillomaviruses. Likewise, the other phenotypic components of the disease arise from the aberrant chemokine. Though the altered CXCR4 gene produces a syndrome with a complex phenotype, it does so through the action of a nonregulatory protein with one known biological function. [Glossary Chemokine, Pleiotropia]

- **Diseases caused by mutations in noncoding regions of the genome**

For a long time, it was generally assumed that genetic diseases were all caused by mutations involving genes, the protein-encoding segments of the genome. The noncoding regions of the genome were presumably junk DNA, whose mutations would have little or no effect on the organism. This assumption has proven to be almost entirely wrong. It turns out that most of the common diseases are associated with multiple mutations that occur primarily in noncoding regions of the human genome. Only the rare diseases, and not all of them, have gene mutations as their root causes. It happens that there is a logical reason for this counterintuitive finding, but we won't be solving this riddle until we get to Section 5.1, "The Biological Differences Between Rare Diseases and Common Diseases." For now, it suffices to indicate that although nearly all rare diseases involve mutations in genes, there are a few rare diseases known to involve noncoding regions. Examples are:

- A form of frontotemporal dementia with or without amyotrophic lateral sclerosis; involves a heterozygous hexanucleotide repeat expansion (GGGGCC) in a noncoding region of the C9ORF72 gene.
- An inherited form of chronic tubulointerstitial nephropathy; involves a single noncoding nucleotide (adenine) separating the structural genes of 2 tRNAs in mitochondrial DNA.
- Hyperferritinemia-cataract syndrome: involves a heterozygous mutation in the iron-responsive element in the 5-prime noncoding region of the ferritin light chain gene on chromosome 19q13.

- **Susceptibility genes**

The term "susceptibility genes" appears throughout the past and current genetics literature, and will probably persist for a long time to come, because it nicely fills a gap in our popularly held belief that diseases have a cause, and that factors other than the direct cause of a disease must have a name. Genes other than the root cause of a disease are inaccurately named "susceptibility genes." Environmental agents that participate in the development of an inherited disease are callously referred to as "triggers." Conditions that either exacerbate or mitigate clinical symptoms are known by the intentionally evasive term "modifying factors."

In the case of susceptibility genes, we are usually referring to genes that have not been identified as the root genetic cause of a disease, but that are associated with an increased likelihood that the disease will occur. In our minds, these genes often play an abstract, almost magical role, by increasing the probability of an event without involving any identifiable biological process. The pseudoconcept of a susceptibility gene has been hard-wired into our thinking and appears repeatedly in current literature dealing with the genetics of disease [29,30]. Should we allow ourselves to believe that probability genes exist?

Of course, as we emphasize throughout this book, diseases develop through a sequence of biological events, occurring over time. The so-called susceptibility genes are as much a causal event as is any "root cause" inherited genetic defect. It is our job, as researchers and practitioners of Precision Medicine, to understand the causal step filled by "susceptibility genes" in the pathogenesis of disease.

Let's make this discussion a little more practical, with an example. African Americans have a much lower incidence of skin cancer that do Caucasians. The increased pigmentation of African Americans protects against the carcinogenic effect of ultraviolet light. Caucasians are genetically melanin deficient, and we can interpret the extra-high incidence of skin cancer in Caucasians to result from susceptibility genes (i.e., the genes that account for melanin deficiency). Suppose we encounter an African American, who is affected by albinism (i.e., a genetic defect that results in a melanin deficiency). Individuals with albinism have a number of visual impairments and a heightened risk of skin cancer. In these cases, we might think of the genetic defect producing albinism as the root cause of all the attendant clinical conditions, including skin cancer. Ultraviolet light, in this case, is usually interpreted as the environmental trigger. We consider a deficiency of melanin, in Caucasians, to be caused by susceptibility genes. We consider a deficiency of melanin, in albinism, to be the root cause of the disease. It makes no sense to label the same biological condition (i.e., reduction in the skin's protective pigmentation) to be a causal event in one individual and a susceptibility factor in another individual. We find ourselves in these logical conundrums when we forget that all pathogenetic events are causal. The concept of "susceptibility" has no biological meaning and should be recognized as just one of the events that lead to the development of disease. [Glossary Skin cancer]

SECTION 3.2 INSCRUTABLE DISEASES

All I ever wanted to do was to paint sunlight on the side of a house
Edward Hopper

You can observe a lot by watching.
Yogi Berra

A biological interval separates the root cause of any disease from the eventual development of a clinical phenotype. It is within this interval that the secrets of Precision Medicine are hidden. The job of the astute healthcare practitioner and the clever medical researcher is to uncover those secrets and to use them to prevent, diagnose, or treat diseases.

Prior to the advent of Precision Medicine, disease researchers searched for disease genes by using their knowledge of biology to guess which genes were most likely to produce a disease phenotype. They would then examine these genes, in normal and in diseased populations, and in affected and unaffected relatives of diseased individuals, looking for gene variants that segregated with diseased individuals and disease carriers. In the era of Precision Medicine, the task of finding disease genes is relatively simple and straightforward. All the exomes (the expressed sequences of genes) of affected individuals, and family members are sequenced and compared to database entries from the general population, looking for variant sequences that are present in individuals with disease [31–35]. The researcher need no longer depend on biological intuition to find a candidate disease gene. The process is straightforward and data driven. The assumption underlying this strategy is that a variant that occurs in nearly every instance of disease, and in family members of affected individuals, and which is absent, or only rarely observed, in the unaffected population, must be the root cause of the disease. [Glossary Candidate gene approach]

There are actually quite a few pitfalls in this purely data-driven approach to disease gene discovery, not the least of which is referred to as the narrative potential of the human genome. The degree of natural variation in the genome, with an estimated 35 million single nucleotide polymorphisms (i.e., SNPs) distributed through the general population, affords many opportunities to find disease-specific gene variants that have no causal role in disease development (i.e., reading something into the genome narrative that is not biologically relevant). Alternately, exome sequencing may uncover true disease-causing genes that are falsely eliminated from consideration when they are found to be present in the unaffected population. False-negatives should not surprise us. We can expect that some individuals in the general population will have a true disease gene, in the absence of disease. Aside from these considerations, there are many methodological and interpretive limitations to the current approaches to disease gene discovery, and cautionary guides for investigators are readily available [33,34]. Setting aside these concerns, for the moment, what shall we do after we have found a gene that is the putative root cause of a disease? Knowing the name of a disease gene may tell us nothing about the pathogenesis of the ensuing disease. The hard part of Precision Medicine comes when we try to fill in all the steps. [Glossary Single nucleotide polymorphism, Anonymous variation, Silent mutation, Synonymous SNPs, Exome sequencing]

Because our present-day methods for finding disease genes are no longer based on the a priori selection of candidate genes, and because any variation in any sequence of DNA is detectable by modern methodologies, we are finding new disease genes that bear no discernible relation to the resultant clinical phenotype [31]. For example, a mutation in the gene-encoding fumarate hydratase is the underlying cause of Hereditary leiomyomatosis and renal cell carcinoma (HLRCC). A mutation in the gene-encoding magnesium transporter-1 causes XMEN, the acronym for X-linked immunodeficiency with Magnesium defect, Epstein-Barr virus infection, and Neoplasia. What is the pathogenesis that connects these gene defects with their clinical phenotypes? In this section, we'll take a look at some of the diseases wherein a logical connection to its "disease gene" defies simple analysis.

Let's examine a series of diseases whose clinical phenotype could not be explained by its root genetic cause, until further study yielded new information about the pathways involved in the disease process.

– Ligneous conjunctivitis

Consider the example of the rare, inherited disease, ligneous conjunctivitis. The word "ligneous" means hard, like wood, and the term "ligneous conjunctivitis" refers to a thick, hard coating on the conjunctiva of the eye, over the sclera and under the eyelids. In addition to conjunctivitis, affected individuals may also develop middle-ear inflammation, tracheobronchial inflammation (of the lungs), and blockage of the flow of cerebrospinal fluid.

Ligneous conjunctivitis is associated with a deficiency of plasminogen. How does a deficiency of plasminogen lead to conjunctivitis, middle-ear inflammation, trancheobronchitis, and blockages in the cerebrospinal canals? Plasmin, the activated form of plasminogen, breaks down fibrin, a protein produced during coagulation and clot formation. In the absence of plasminogen, fibrin accumulates in various sites, and the accumulating fibrin dries and hardens. On the surface of the eyes, dried fibrin elicits inflammation. Accumulating fibrin in the middle ear and the tracheobronchial mucosa leads to plugging and inflammation at these sites. In the brain, an occlusive hydrocephalus may occur, due to fibrin blocking the normal flow and clearance of cerebrospinal fluid in the brain ventricles. In retrospect, the pathogenesis of ligneous conjunctivitis is simple to understand. Ligneous conjunctivitis is an example of the simplest form of pleiotropism, wherein seemingly unrelated phenotypes result from an alteration in a single expressed protein, and a single functional pathway.

— Severe combined immunodeficiency (SCID)

SCID is an aggregate of diseases with different genetic causes that are all characterized by immunodeficiencies of both arms of the adaptive immune system (i.e., B cells and T cells) in infants. As discussed in the prior section, SCID can arise from any number of seemingly unrelated genetic mutations, all leading to a common immunodeficient phenotype. The second most common form of SCID is associated with defective adenosine deaminase, an enzyme involved in the breakdown of purines. The possible mechanisms whereby a deficiency of adenosine deaminase leads to cellular toxicity and cell death have been the subject of much discussion in the literature, extending over several decades. Without delving into the specifics, there is ample evidence that adenosine deaminase is required for the survival of rapidly dividing cell populations, particularly the immununocytes (B cells and T cells) that are depleted in SCID. This being the case, then why does a deficiency of adenosine deaminase preferentially block the normal fetal development of T and B cells when every cell population in the developing fetus is rapidly dividing? Furthermore, after infancy, why does an inherited deficiency of adenosine deaminase not cause widespread necrosis of all rapidly dividing tissues, including gut epithelium and bone marrow? It doesn't make much sense. [Glossary Aggregate disease]

As is so often the case, a better explanation for the pathogenesis of adenosine deaminase-associated SCID comes from an understanding of the pathogenesis of other forms of SCID. Individuals with deficiencies in any of several proteins that participate in Nonhomologous End Joining (NHEJ) DNA repair account for subtypes of SCID (DNA-PKcs, Artemis, LigIV, NHEJ1/XLF/Cernunnos) [36]. It happens that the process of lymphocyte differentiation involves the enzymatic breakage followed by the enzymatic repair of the so-called V(D)J recombination units that produce the remarkable diversity of recognition sites that characterize the adaptive immune system. Rag1 and Rag2 recombinase enzymes induce double-stranded breaks, in sequences flanking V, D, and J. Following recombination, these breaks are repaired. If repair does not occur, then T and B cells do not differentiate, and this results in variants of SCID that are particularly sensitive to radiation damage (i.e., because the SCID results from a deficiency of DNA repair) [36]. [Glossary Differentiation]

Knowing the relationship between DNA repair deficiencies and immune deficiencies, we may be able to shed some light on the pathogenesis of SCID in adenosine deaminase deficiency. When resting blood lymphocytes are treated with deoxycoformycin, an adenosine deaminase inhibitor, single-strand breaks accumulate [37]. Thus, a relationship between deoxyadenosine deaminase deficiency and DNA repair deficiency is established, suggesting that this form of SCID develops much like the other forms of SCID that result from a DNA repair deficiency.

In this case, our understanding of the pathogenesis of SCID, in genetically heterogeneous forms of the disease, has helped us to hypothesize the pathogenesis of SCID in an enigmatic subtype characterized by a genetic defect that bore no discernible relationship to its clinical phenotype.

— Succinate dehydrogenase mutations in paraganglioma and pheochromocytoma

Mutations in a gene coding for a subunit of succinate dehydrogenase (SDHB) are associated with a familial predisposition to developing pheochromocytoma and paraganglioma [38]. Furthermore, germline mutations in genes that code for three of the subunits of succinate dehydrogenase (SDHB, SDHC, and SDHD) are reported in individuals who have paragangliomas of the head and neck [39,40]. Succinate dehydrogenase is not an oncogene or a tumor suppressor gene. It is a mitochondrial enzyme that participates in both the citric acid cycle and the electron transport chain. Thus, succinate dehydrogenase is vitally important in normal oxidative phosphorylation (i.e., chemical respiration). From a strictly biochemical perspective, knowing that a mutation in succinate dehydrogenase somehow predisposes humans to rare paragangliomas tells us nothing remotely useful about the pathogenesis of these tumors.

Let's take a moment to think about the embryogenesis of paraganglia. Paraganglial cells are cells of neural crest origin that arise in juxtaposition to the ganglial cells of the peripheral nervous system. In the developed human, the paraganglial cells perform a variety of different functions. Paraganglial cells of the adrenal gland give rise to the adrenal medulla, and paraganglial tumors of the adrenal medullary cells are known as pheochromocytomas. Clusters of paraganglial cells can be found in various abdominal organs, and in the head and neck, where they are thought to serve as chemoreceptor cells. Paraganglial clusters in specific locations of large arteries of the head and neck are believed to be oxygen sensors. Paragangliomas that arise from the oxygen-sensing paraganglial cells of the carotid artery are known as chemodectomas. [Glossary Medullary]

For a very long time, pathologists have suspected that chronic hypoxia is a causal factor in the development of carotid artery chemodectomas. This suspicion was based partly on case reports of rare chemodectomas arising in individuals living at high altitudes. More convincing have been veterinary reports indicating that flat-faced dogs are more likely to develop chemodectomas than are dogs with long muzzles. The thinking here is that the flat face of some breeds of dogs limits oxygen exchange and leads to a chronic, subclinical state of hypoxia, which stimulates the carotid body chemoreceptor cells. In a 1978 manuscript, paraganglia were weighed and examined from a series of autopsies. Autopsied individuals who died after long, chronic courses of conditions known to produce chronic hypoxia were shown to have larger paraganglia than were found in nonhypoxic individuals [41]. [Glossary Case report]

Years later, in an ultrastructural study of paragangliomas, it was demonstrated that these tumors are characterized by the cells containing numerous large and structurally abnormal mitochondria, suggesting that mitochondrial dysfunction is a characteristic feature of paragangliomas [42]. [Glossary Mitochondriopathy]

Where do these observations lead us? There seems to be a sequence of biological steps that begins with a genetic root cause (i.e., an inherited mutation in a gene coding for a subunit of succinate dehydrogenase), leading to cellular hypoxia resulting from mitochondrial dysfunction, leading to chemoreceptor cell hyperplasia, leading to mitochondropathic changes in chemoreceptor cells, leading to the emergence of paragangliomas. Of course, at this point, we have nothing that rises to the level of convincing proof. Nonetheless, it's a start, and it shows how we try to connect the dots of pathogenesis.

– Deafness and albinism

For a very long time, careful observers have noticed a relationship between albinism and deafness, a relationship that applies to humans and to other animals. Charles Darwin wrote that cats that were entirely white, with blue eyes, were often deaf. A similar association between albinism and deafness has been noted in dogs and rodents. In humans, the two dominantly inherited hypopigmentation and deafness syndromes are: Waardenburg syndrome type 2A and Tietz syndrome. In every instance wherein albinism and deafness co-occur, the basis of the albinism is due to a reduction in the number of melanocytes (i.e., not in amelanism, the reduction of melanin production by otherwise normal melanocytes, as seen in inherited tyrosinase deficiency). The inference that applies here is that normal hearing, for some obscure reason, requires melanocytes.

Recent studies indicate that cochlear function requires melanocytes in the stria vascularis of the inner ear. In mice, when melanocytes are absent from the stria vascularis, the endocochlear action potential is about zero, indicating no nerve conduction of acoustic signals [43]. In humans with Tietz syndrome mutations are found in the MITF (microphthalmia-associated transcription factor) gene, which regulates melanocyte development from neural crest [44]. The resulting general reduction of melanocytes migrating to the stria vascularis is thought to account for deafness in Tietz syndrome. Waardenburg syndrome type 2A is clinically similar to Tietz syndrome, but skin hair and irides show patchy depigmentation, which typically includes variable degrees of sensorineural hearing loss. Waardenburg syndrome has germline mutations in the MITF gene, allelic to those found in Tietz syndrome. Today, the two clinically and genetically similar syndromes are commonly combined as one: Tietz/Waardenburg type 2A syndrome. [Glossary Allelic to]

– Alpha1-antitrypsin deficiency with cirrhosis and emphysema

Alpha-1 antitrypsin deficiency is an example of an inherited monogenic disease causing disorders of two different organs (lungs and liver) through two different mechanisms. To understand this unusual disease, we should probably start by discussing a third organ, the pancreas.

The pancreas sends digestive enzymes through the pancreatic duct, into the duodenum, where these enzymes aid in the digestion of food. Food contains animal parts, such as organs and muscles and fat; the same stuff that humans are made of. Hence, the pancreatic enzymes are fully capable of digesting human organs, given half a chance. Inevitably, some of the active forms of the digestive enzymes synthesized by the pancreas will make their way into the blood stream. If left unchecked, these enzymes will autodigest internal organs. The pancreas is not the only organ that secretes autodigestive enzymes. Neutrophils are prodigious synthesizers of elastase, another powerful autodigestive enzyme. The liver is the only organ that synthesizes and secretes, into the blood, a protein known as alpha1-antitrypsin, which is a general purpose antiprotease designed to nullify the affects of circulating proteases produced by the pancreas and by white blood cells.

When the circulating levels of alpha1-antitrypsin fall below a certain threshold, somewhere between 15% and 40% of normal, elastase produced by neutrophils will begin to destroy the delicate elastic tissue that invests the scaffold of the lung, producing emphysema. Hence, individuals that cannot manufacture adequate levels of circulating alpha1-antitrypsin will develop emphysema. Adults who smoke and who have relatively low levels of circulating alpha1-antitrypsin are particularly prone to develop emphysema, presumably because cigarette smoke directly deactivates alpha1-antitrypsin. Furthermore, the chronic inflammatory influence of cigarette smoke on the lungs elicits neutrophils to increase their secretion of elastase, thus overwhelming whatever the little alpha1-antitrypsin activity that remains. For these reasons, smoking may be hazardous to individuals who have alpha1-antitrypsin deficiencies, even those individuals who are lucky enough to have clinically benign variants of the disorder.

As noted, the liver is the only organ that synthesizes alpha1-antitrypsin, a protein encoded by the Serpin peptidase inhibitor, clade A, member 1 gene (SERPINA1). Over 75 pathogenic mutations of this gene have been found, but the severe form of the disease, associated with both lung and liver disease, is the PiZZ variant. In this form of the disease, an abnormal alpha1-antitrypsin molecule is produced that is sequestered inside liver cells, leading eventually to liver cell necrosis, cirrhosis and, sometimes, hepatocellular carcinoma [45]. [Glossary Cirrhosis]

Because the liver is the only organ that produces the altered protein, a liver transplant prior to the development of emphysema would be curative. In its most severe form, alpha1-antitrypsin deficiency may affect infants and may require liver transplantation. In many instances, however, affected individuals will have normal lung and liver function well into adulthood. Such cases, if screened and diagnosed early, provide ample opportunities for interrupting the pathogenic events that precede the development of lung disease, cirrhosis, and hepatocellular carcinoma. For example, an autophagy-enhancing drug has been shown to promote the degradation of the altered alpha1-antitrypsin that accumulates in liver cells, thus reducing subsequent hepatic fibrosis [46].

We do not understand the pathogenesis for the great majority of simple, monogenic diseases whose root genetic defect is known. Imagine the challenges we will face when we try to understand the pathogenesis of the common polygenic/environmental diseases. If you would like to exercise your imagination on a few very simple examples, try to imagine the sequence of biological events that connect each of the following inherited diseases to their root genetic cause:

- Mutations in the gene-encoding chromatin-remodeling factor ATRX in the alpha-thalassemia myelodysplasia syndrome [47] [Glossary Thalassemia]
- Mutations in the ELA2 gene-encoding neutrophil elastase leading to cyclic neutropenia and severe congenital neutropenia [48,49]
- Mutations in the gene-encoding oncostatin M receptor-beta and familial primary localized cutaneous amyloidosis-1 [50] [Glossary Amyloidosis]
- Heterozygous mutation in the aryl hydrocarbon receptor-interacting protein and growth hormone-secreting pituitary adenoma-1 [51]
- Homozygous GAA repeat expansion mutation within intron 1 of the FXN gene and Friedreich ataxia [52,53] [Glossary Homozygosity]
- Mutation in the ESCO2 (Establishment of Sister Chromatid Cohesion N-Acetyltransferase 2) gene, inducing premature sister chromatid separation, and Roberts syndrome, characterized by phocomelia [54,55]
- Mutation in the VHL gene, (which codes for a protein that plays a role in an oxygen-sensing pathway, in microtubule stability and orientation, cilia formation, regulation of senescence, cytokine signaling, collagen IV regulation, and the assembly of a normal extracellular fibronectin matrix) and Von Hippel-Lindau syndrome, an inherited familial cancer syndrome predisposing to a variety of malignant and benign neoplasms, including: retinal angiomata, liver hemangiomas, pancreatic

cysts, bilateral papillary cystadenoma of the epididymis, bilateral papillary cystadenomas of the broad ligament, renal angiomyolipoma, renal cell carcinoma, renal cysts, cerebellar hemangioblastoma, spinal cord hemangioblastoma, adrenal hemangioma, polycythemia, pheochromocytoma, paraganglioma and adeoncarcinoma of the ampulla of Vater [56]. [Glossary Von Hippel-Lindau disease, Polycythemia, Renal cell carcinoma]

What have we learned from this section? Even in the case of the monogenic inherited diseases, which have a very simple pathogenesis compared to diseases whose causes involve multiple genes and repeated exposures to multiple environmental agents, the steps leading from mutation to disease may evade simple analysis. To begin to understand any disease, we need to look for patterns of development that recur in diseases that are related to one another (e.g., unanticipated deficiencies in DNA repair pathways that are found in most of the subtypes of severe combined immunodeficiency disease; disorders of neural crest development in combined albinism and deafness; mitochondriopathies in paragangliomas).

SECTION 3.3 RECURSIVE EPIGENOMIC/GENOMIC DISEASES

Reality is merely an illusion, albeit a very persistent one.
Albert Einstein

It is all about the survival of self-replicating instructions for self-replication.
Richard Dawkins p. 392, the greatest show, [57]

The epigenome is a popular subject today. It seems to be called upon to fill every gap in our current understanding of how the genome works. Although the epigenome is a latecomer to the world of molecular biology, a little thought tells us that the existence of an epigenome could have been inferred the moment the genome was discovered. If every nucleated cell in the human body contains the same sequence of DNA as every other cell, then how might we explain the diversity of cell types in the human body? What exactly is the difference, in terms of cellular instructions, that account for one cell being a hepatocyte and another cell being a muscle cell? Furthermore, how does a hepatocyte know that it must produce two identical hepatocytes when it replicates; and not, say, a neuron plus a pancreatic cell? Put simply, how can we account for the heritability of cellular lineages? There must be something that controls the genome. Let's call it the epigenome, a term that appeared as early as 1940, well before the discovery of the chemical structure of DNA and of the genetic code [58].

At a minimum, the epigenome consists of the nonsequence modifications to DNA that control the expression of genes. These modifications include DNA methylations, as well as histone, and nonhistone chromatin complexes and modifications thereof. The most common form of methylation in DNA occurs on Cytosine nucleotides, most often at locations wherein Cytosine is followed by Guanine. These methylations are called CpG sites. CpG islands are concentrations of CpG dinucleotides that have a GC content over 50% and that range from 200 base pairs (bp) to several thousand bp in length. There are about 29,000–50,000 CpG islands in the human genome [59,60]. [Glossary CpG island, Histone]

Beyond this minimalist definition of the epigenome, expanded versions of the definition include noncoding RNAs, microRNAs, RNA splicing factors, nonsequence modifications of RNA that might influence gene expression, pseudogenes, and chromatin remodeling complexes [61,62]. As used herein, the terms "epigenome" and "epigenetics" apply exclusively to nonsequence alterations in chromosomes that are heritable among somatic cell lineages. **A simple way to describe the difference between the genome and the epigenome is that the genome accounts for the identify of the organism; the epigenome accounts for the identity of the cells within the organism**. [Glossary Genomic disease, Spliceosome, Alternative RNA splicing, Pseudogene, MicroRNA]

The epigenome has a role in the pathogenesis of every disease. We know this because all diseases are cell-type specific, and the epigenome is responsible for creating and maintaining all of the different cell types. If the epigenome played no role in disease development, we would expect that every disease would affect every type of cell. Moreover, because the epigenome regulates the genome, we can infer that every genetic disease whose root cause is a monogenic or polygenic loss or gain in the expression of genes, has a potential epigenomic phenocopy [63–65]. Taking this thought one step further, we cannot be certain that an inherited disease has a genetic basis until we exclude alternative mechanisms (i.e., until we identify the root cause genetic mutation). [Glossary Phenocopy disease]

These aforementioned revelations certainly add to the confusion of modern medicine. Where we once had diseases with a simple genetic cause, we now must consider how the epigenome influences the expression of genes, and how the cellular responses to changes in gene expression are controlled by the epigenome. There is a bright side to the epigenome. Because epigenomic diseases do not produce mutations in the genome, and because we know that epigenomic modifications are reversible, we can infer that all purely epigenomic diseases are curable. Furthermore, by modifying the epigenome, we may be able to nullify the expression of pathogenic genes, and thus effectively treat genetic diseases.

How do we know that epigenetic changes are reversible? Our best clue is found early in human development, before the embryo is formed. Erasure is a natural process in which the entire epigenome is stripped off the genome, and the cell is returned to its original, totipotent form. The first of several genomic erasures occurs very early in the life of the organism, soon after the maternal egg and the paternal sperm fuse to form the zygote. The earliest cells of the blastula must be rendered totipotent, so that they may give rise to the embryonic germ layers, and this requires erasure of the epigenomes derived from parental DNA. After erasure, the genome is rendered undifferentiated, totipotent, and able to embark upon the task of building a new organism [66,67]. It stands to reason that if the entire epigenome can be erased, then it should be possible to erase or inactivate parts of the epigenome. [Glossary Dedifferentiation]

As it happens, there is abundant evidence that the epigenome is a highly malleable resource. Nature regularly suppresses entire chromosomes through manipulation of the epigenome. Females are born with two X chromosomes in every nongerm cell, but nature limits each cell to one active X chromosome. In every cell, one of the two X chromosomes is epigenetically inactivated. The inactive chromosome is shrunken, compact, hypermethylated, and usually sticks to the edge of the nucleus (i.e., adjacent to the nuclear envelope). This inactive X-chromosome is called the Barr body. The choice of which X-chromosome is inactivated (i.e., paternal X or maternal X) occurs seemingly randomly in different cells in early development, after the germline is established. Hence, every genetically normal female is a somatic mosaic, composed of patches of cells clonally descended from an embryonic cell that had an active paternally inherited X-chromosomes or an active maternally inherited X-chromosome. [Glossary Somatic mosaicism, X-chromosome]

In general, epigenetic hypermethylation leads to gene suppression. Hypomethylation promotes gene expression. An increase or decrease of methylation can account for clinically opposite disease phenotypes. For example, opposite patterns of methylation in the normal chromosome complementary to a microdeletion region in 11p15.5 account for two clinically near-opposite diseases. Hypermethylation causes Beckwith-Wiedemann syndrome, a syndrome that produces tissue overgrowth. Hypomethylation produces Russell-Silver syndrome, a cause of dwarfism.

Elsewhere, we noted that Prader-Willi syndrome and Angelman syndrome result from the same microdeletion. When the microdeletion occurs on the paternally derived chromosome, the disease that results is Prader-Willi syndrome. When the microdeletion occurs on the maternally derived chromosome, the disease that results is Angelman syndrome. The explanation for this peculiar dichotomy lies in the parental pattern of epigenetic modification. Early in embryogenesis, a small set of genes, probably on the order of 100, are imprinted with either paternal or a maternal methylation profile. Such genes maintain the epigenetic profile of the parental genes, and we say that such genes are "imprinted."

The microdeletion that causes Prader-Will syndrome and Angelman syndrome, at 15q11-13, contains about 4 million base pairs covering many different genes on one chromosome. Let us imagine that the microdeletion is maternally inherited (i.e., lies on the chromosome contributed by the mother). The paired chromosome, contributed by the father, is intact and lacks the 15q11-13 microdeletion. In theory, the paternal chromosome could compensate for the lost genes in the microdeletion area. However, the paternal chromosome has a gender-typical pattern of gene silencing, and certain genes on the undeleted paternal chromosome will be unexpressed, resulting in the absence of expression for such genes in the haploid set of chromosomes. Had the 15q11-13 microdeletion occurred on the paternal chromosome, instead of the maternal chromosome, the mother's gender-typical pattern of gene silencing would result in the lack of expression of a different set of genes. You can see that the gender of the parent who passes the microdeletion to the offspring will determine which genes are unexpressed in the offspring, hence which disease occurs. Diseases whose expression is caused by imprinting do not obey a Mendelian pattern of inheritance. If the 15q11-13 had obeyed Mendelian inheritance, offspring with the microdeletion would all have the same disease traits, regardless of the gender of parent who passed the microdeletion. There are other conditions in which epigenetic imprinting determines the clinical phenotype of a monogenic disease. Pseudopseudohypoparathyroidism provides us with another example wherein epigenomic imprinting produces different diseases depending on whether the mutant gene was maternally and paternally transmitted [68,69]. [Glossary Anticipation, Haplotype, Imprinting, Haploid, Mendelian inheritance]

The epigenome can be easily modified with methylating agents or with hypomethylating agents. Though we cannot predict the changes that result from an epigenetic alteration, we can do a bit of experimentation to see the range of effects that might occur when we alter the methylation patterns in cells. In an often-cited study, the diet of mice during gestation was supplemented with genistein, an agent known to alter DNA methylation patterns, resulting in a shift in coat color of the offspring (from agouti to pseudoagouti) and an associated increased methylation in a regulatory site upstream of the Agouti gene [70,71]. Hence, methylation, via an environmental additive, can produce a heritable epimutation.

- Cancer and the epigenome

Cancer is a disease characterized by changes in just about every organelle, pathway, and molecule in the affected cells [72]. The epigenome is changed drastically in cancer, and epigenetic instability is as much a feature of cancer progression as is genetic instability. A range of genes have been shown to be hypermethylated in cancer; hypermethylation has also been observed the CpG islands in cancer cells. It is tempting to ask whether hypomethylation can reverse some of the malignant phenotype attributed to hypermethylation. This seems to be the case, at least for myelodysplastic syndrome, a preleukemic condition [73]. Two hypomethylating agents, 5-azacytidine and 5-aza-2-deoxycytidine, have already won US FDA approval for the treatment of myelodysplastic syndrome [73,74]. In addition to hypomethylation agents, the histone deactylase inhibitors are being examined as modulators of the cancer epigenome, and as candidate chemotherapeutic agents. [Glossary Genetic instability, Myelodysplastic syndrome, Cancer progression, Epigenetic instability]

Of course, there is an interplay between epigenome and genome in cancers. In acute promyelocytic leukemia, a gene translocation produces the PML/RAR(alpha) fusion protein [75]. Normally, promyelocytes differentiate to become nondividing myelocytes (neutrophils). The PML/RAR(alpha) fusion protein stimulates the promyelocyte to divide, producing more promyelocytes and fewer neutrophils. Eventually, the population of clonal promyelocytes arising from the neoplastic progenitor cell attains a sufficiently large number to be recognized clinically as a promyelocytic leukemia. [Glossary Translocation]

Acute promyelocytic leukemia is one of the few cancers that can achieve clinical remission without treatment with cytotoxic agents. Remission is achieved with all-trans retinoic acid. Treated promyelocytic cancer cells differentiate and become nondividing mature myelocytes [76]. The mechanism by which the neoplastic fusion protein, PML/RAR(alpha), induces a neoplastic phenotype, and the mechanism whereby all-trans retinoic acid reverses the neoplastic phenotype seems to be mediated through the epigenome. It is hypothesized that PML/RAR(alpha) modifies histone deacetylase complexes resulting in the inappropriate transcriptional repression of genes that would normally inhibit promyelocyte proliferation. All-trans retinoic acid is thought to reverse this effect [75]. If this turns out to be the case, promyelocytic leukemia would serve as an example of a gene mutation that employs epigenetic alterations to sustain a neoplastic phenotype.

At present, a few rare hematologic malignancies seem to be responsive to targeted epigenetic therapy. Time will tell whether the same approach will be effective against common cancers.

- Tumor cell atypia is, fundamentally, an epigenomic phenomenon

The term "nuclear atypia" refers to variations from normal nuclear morphology. The term is commonly applied to cancer cells and precancer cells, whose nuclei look different from normal nuclei. Cancerous and precancerous nuclei are larger than normal nuclei, with irregular shape (i.e., not oval or round or smooth), with indentations in the nuclear membrane, coarse chromatin, areas of light and dark within the nucleus, and enlarged, irregularly shaped nucleoli. Traditionally, pathologists were taught that genetic changes accounted for the atypia present in cancer cells. This opinion was based on observations of cytogenetic abnormalities in cancer cells (e.g., increased numbers of chromosomes, missing pieces of chromosomes, duplicated pieces of chromosomes, and translocated pieces of chromosomes). It was simply assumed that these same changes produced the visible alterations in the chromatin known as nuclear atypia.

It turns out that nuclear atypicality, the morphologic hallmark of cancerous cells, is determined by epigenetic, not genetic, factors.

Observations that support an epigenetic cause of nuclear atypia include the following:

- Some cancers have marked atypia with little or no genetic instability and with euploid complement of chromosomes (e.g., rhabdoid tumor [77]);
- Profound changes in nuclear morphology can be produced by alteration in a single protein, as is seen in rare Pelger-Huet anomaly [78], suggesting that multiple and widespread changes in DNA are not necessary to produce misshapen nuclei.
- The common histologic stains with which we assess nuclear atypia bind to the histone and nonhistone proteins of the epigenome, and do not bind to DNA; hence, the morphologic abnormalities of cancer nuclei reflect changes in the nuclear distribution of epigenetic constituents.

Let's look at an example of a tumor whose phenotype seems to be the product of epigenomic dysregulation. Rhabdoid tumors, though rare, are a common malignant tumor of the central nervous system among children below the age of 6 months [79]. These tumors break nearly every generalization about tumor biology. The secret for their dramatic departure from the norms of cancer biology resides within the epigenome.

Here are surprising features of rhabdoid tumors (Fig. 3.1):

- Rhabdoid tumors may arise very early in life, indicating that they simply bypass most of the time-consuming steps observed by most tumors during their development. Fast carcinogenesis of rhabdoid tumors is a phenomenon that is observed in animal models of this tumor [80,81].
- Rhabdoid tumors can arise in the brain (i.e., an embyrologic derivative of neurectoderm), but they can also arise from kidney (i.e., from mesoderm). Virtually all other tumors arise exclusively from one specific embryologic layer. [Glossary Ectoderm, Neurectoderm, Mesoderm]
- All rhabdoid tumors contain a characteristic cell containing a large inclusion composed of whorled intermediate filaments. Intermediate filaments are proteins that contribute to the structure of cells and provide resistance to deformity. Normal cells contain intermediate filaments that are specific for their developmental lineage. Rhabdoid cells contain intermediate filaments specific for several different embryologic layers, all within the cells of one tumor (an embryologic impossibility).
- Rhabdoid cells have been reported as subpopulations of cells arising in tumors of adults including mucinous carcinoma of pancreas [82] and uterine carcinosarcomas [83]. This is equivalent to a colon cancer arising within a lymphoma. It should not happen.

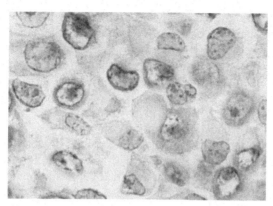

FIG. 3.1   Histopathologic image of a highly malignant rhabdoid tumor. Look closely at all the nuclei. Notice that the nuclei vary in shape and size from one cancer cell to another. The nuclei are mottled, with areas of light and of dark, and the sizes and locations of these light and dark areas vary from nucleus to nucleus. Some nuclei have large nucleoli; the number of nucleoli varies from nucleus to nucleus, ranging from 0 to 3; the nucleoli are not uniform in size or contour, or color. The nuclei are outlined by a highly irregular membrane, with thick, dark borders in some areas, alternating with light borders elsewhere, with no constant pattern from nucleus to nucleus. The nuclei are not consistently round, or oval or bean-shaped. Numerous sharp puckerings are seen on the nuclear border; some nuclei seem to have tails and protrusions; others have focally straight edges. Though you can't judge it from this image, which exclusively shows malignant cells, the nuclei of the rhabdoid tumor cells are larger than the nuclei of normal cells. All of these observations are consistent with nuclear atypia, the morphologic hallmark of cancer. In the past, pathologists assumed that whenever they saw highly abnormal nuclei, the observed abnormalities were an indication of genetic alterations in the nucleus, such as increases or decreases from the normal number (diploid) number of chromosomes (i.e., aneuploidy) and karyotypical abnormalities within chromosomes (e.g., translocations, deletions, duplications), resulting from genetic instability, all hallmarks of cancer. This is not the case in rhabdoid tumors, which are genetically stable and have a normal karyotype (i.e., are diploid, not aneuploid). Though most tumors exhibit genetic abnormalities, the morphologic atypia observed in cancer nuclei is largely caused by changes in the epigenome, not the genome. *Reproduced from Wikipedia, courtesy of US Government Armed Forces Institute of Pathology public domain image.* [Glossary Karyotype]

- The rhabdoid cell has no "normal" histogenetic precursor from which it arises. To illustrate, a squamous cell carcinoma is composed of cells that resemble normal squamous cells biochemically, ultrastructurally, and by light microscopic examination. The rhabdoid cell has no known counterpart in any adult tissue or in any stage of development. Essentially, the rhabdoid tumor arises from a nonexistent cell type. [Glossary Histopathology, Tissue block]
- Most cancers are aneuploid and genetically unstable. Rhabdoid tumors are, as far as anyone can tell, uniformly euploid and genetically stable [77].

How is it possible that rhabdoid tumors manage to disobey almost every general rule of carcinogenesis? The answer seems to be that rhabdoid tumors are the product of an epigenome gone wild. Because the epigenome controls differentiation, the most striking features of rhabdoid tumors all relate to the abandonment of the normal restraints of cellular differentiation. Specifically, the root cause of rhabdoid tumors involves biallelic loss of INI1 (also known as SNF5), a member of the SWI/SNF chromatin remodeling complex. The SWI/SNF complexes in mammals, flies, and plants strongly influence many developmental pathways [84].

Currently, there is no other known genetic mutation that produces a tumor phenotype anything remotely like the association between INI1 and rhabdoid cells. Whereas all other cancers seem to be driven by genes, rhabdoid tumors seem to be the sine qua non of an epigenomic malignancy. [Glossary Transdifferentiation, Undifferentiated tumor]

Let's look at another example of a disease driven by the epigenome. Rett syndrome is an example of an epigenomic disease whose root cause is an inherited defect in a gene. A brief discussion of this disease will help us understand the relationship between the genome and the epigenome. This syndrome occurs almost exclusively in female infants and is characterized clinically by neurologic dysfunction, slow growth of the head, sometimes causing microcephaly, and small hands and feet [85]. Rett syndrome is a prominent cause of mental retardation in female children. In 1999, mutations of the X-linked MECP2 gene, encoding methyl-CpG-binding protein, were found to be the root genetic cause of most cases of Rett syndrome [86]. MECP2 is a chromatin-associated protein that binds to CpG sites, thereby modulating transcription. CpG sites can be methylated, and the pattern of methylation of CpG sites is a factor in determining how the epigenome modulates transcription. Hence, the manner in which the Rett gene modulates transcription (an epigenomic function) is determined by the manner in which the epigenome is chemically methylated and chromatin is structured, at specific gene locations. Apparently, the bulk of the clinical consequences of the mutation of MECP2 comes down to regulation of one imprinted gene, DLX5, which is involved in normal brain development [87,88]. [Glossary Gene regulation, Cis-acting, Trans-acting, Regulatory DNA element, Regulatory RNA element]

It is curious that a disease of the epigenome produces a clinical syndrome that predominantly involves neurologic function. Following the discovery of the root cause gene for Rett syndrome, several other conditions involving inherited defects of the epigenome, specifically defects in methylation and histones, have been discovered, all of which lead to neurologic disorders [89,90]. The close and nearly exclusive relationship between epigenomic diseases and the central nervous system is a mystery, and behooves us to wonder why other organ systems are so little affected by epigenomic alterations.

Several observations reinforce the view that the epigenome, aside from its role in development and in cell type determination, may have relatively little importance in adult organisms. [Glossary Histone]

– Plant cells and totipotent cells in humans have no epigenome, and they do just fine.

Every eukaryotic cell has a genome, but not all eurkaryotic cells have an epigenome. All dividing plant cells are potentially able to differentiate to produce leaves, flowers, seeds, ova, ovules and anthers, and so on. Though plants have some of the same epigenetic resources as are found in mammalian cells, they do not terminally differentiate (i.e., they do not produce fully differentiated cell incapable of further cell division), and they do not rely upon heritable epigenomic modifications to determine their cell fates [91]. Hence, there is some reason to suspect that the primary purpose of the epigenome in adult mammalian organisms is to prohibit differentiated cells from becoming totipotent, a function that would not necessarily enter into the pathogenesis of most diseases.

– Erasure of the epigenome is a nontoxic event.

If you remove the genome from a cell (i.e., the 3 billion nucleotides that compose our genetic material), the cell will die. Red blood cells are an example of a differentiated cell whose genome has been extracted. Though the anucleate red blood cell can circulate for about 120 days, it cannot survive indefinitely, and it obviously cannot replicate. Without a genome, there can be no transcription and translation, and the necessary chores of cellular maintenance must ultimately cease. Contrariwise, when you remove the epigenome from a cell, it survives and becomes a totipotent cell, capable of indefinite replication. This is precisely what happens during erasure. If the epigenome were vital, we would expect its absence to be lethal.

– The epigenome is constantly changing.

Unrepaired DNA damage leads to mutations, cell death, and disease. The genome does everything it can to preserve its ordered chemical structure. There are at least seven distinct DNA repair pathways that specialize in specific types of DNA lesions [36]. Defects in any of these pathways always result in serious diseases. We cannot say the same for the epigenome. The epigenome changes constantly, and there are strong indications that the heritability of epigenomic modifications, from parent cell to daughter cell, is anything but faithful. When the epigenome is damaged or altered, there seems to be no repair mechanisms that come to its rescue. [Glossary Ataxia telangiectasia, Xeroderma pigmentosum]

There is every indication that the longer we live, the greater is the deviation from our neonatal epigenome. Much of our current understanding comes from observations on monozygotic (i.e., identical) twins. It is a common observation that monozygotic twins look alike at birth, often growing into early adulthood as a pair of strikingly similar individuals. As the decades go by, identical twins begin to diverge in appearance.

Monozygotic twins are born with nearly identical epigenetic patterns of DNA methylation and histone acetylation. This near-identity of epigenomes persists in the early years, but in later years, monozygotic twins had widely divergent patterns of DNA methylation and histone acetylation. These divergent patterns are accompanied by discordances in gene expression [92].

As time passes, monozygotic twins seem to age differently. They develop different diseases, with the greatest discordance in the common diseases of adulthood [93,94], an observation you would not expect to see if disease susceptibility was determined by genes. [Glossary Late onset]

– Little toxicity from methylation inhibitors

Because the epigenome is largely composed of methylation markers on nucleotides, we might expect that agents that interfere with methylation would be highly toxic. This is not the case. Hypomethylating agents (i.e., DNA methyltransferase inhibitors such as azacitidine and decitabine) are minimally toxic and have manageable toxicity profiles when used in a medical setting [95].

– Globally reducing microRNAs produce no phenotypic changes in animals

MicroRNAs are noncoding, small RNAs that regulate the expression and the function of genes. As such, microRNAs are another component of the epigenome. An enzyme known as

Dicer plays a key role in the synthesis of microRNAs. Without Dicer, microRNA synthesis stops. In a mouse model, Dicer was eliminated from the proximal tubular cells of the kidney, thus reducing microRNA levels in the kidney. Paradoxically, blocking microRNA synthesis in kidney caused no phenotypic changes in the animal (i.e., caused no disease of kidneys and other organs) and actually increased the resistance of the kidneys to ischemia (enabled the kidneys to withstand low perfusion and anoxia at levels that caused kidney damage in control mice) [96].

Again, if the epigenome is important for cellular maintenance in adult organisms, how is it possible to inhibit its activity without pathologic consequences?

- There are very few primary diseases of the epigenome.

There are many thousands of diseases that occur following small mutations in the genome. Wouldn't you expect to find thousands of diseases that can be attributed to alterations of the epigenome? The paucity of primary epigenomic diseases tells us that there is something that we do not know. Either there are primary epigenomic diseases that we do not recognize as such, or there are control mechanisms in play that dampen the deleterious effects of a damaged epigenome, of which we are unaware.

In summary, it would seem that the epigenome plays an important role in the development of the embryo and fetus, particularly in neurodevelopment. The 200 or so cell types that constitute the variety of cells that are present in the adult organisms have their epigenomic profiles established every early in human development. In adults, the importance of the epigenome in maintaining the viability of cells is less certain.

- **Recursive nature of epigenomic/genomic alterations**

If the genome codes for the proteins that create the epigenome, and the epigenome determines how the genome may function, then we must infer that diseases that affect either the genome or the epigenome will put into motion a recursive set of interactions that, in theory, have no end. Epigenome effects genome, effects epigenome, effects genome, effects epigenome, ad nauseum. As the recursive effects proceed, they become impossible to trace in a stepwise fashion. Nonetheless, we see some of the echoes of epigenomic/genomic recursions in human diseases. For example, inherited mutations of the ATRX gene are the root cause of alpha-thalassemia myelodysplasia syndrome. The ATRX gene (acronym for Alpha-Thalassemia/mental-Retardation-syndrome-X-linked) codes for a chromatin remodeling factor, and, as such, it helps to create the epigenome [47,97]. Hence, a genetic mutation (i.e., ATRX) produces an epigenomic alteration (i.e., chromatin remodeling defect), which produces a change in genetic expression (i.e., globin synthesis), which produces an epigenomic phenocopy of a genetic disease (i.e., alpha-thalassemia).

In fact, we might expect epigenomic/genomic alterations to reverberate through many diseases. When we look at affected cells, from just about any disease that we choose, we should be prepared to see deviations from normal, in just about every subcellular system. As a general rule, in tightly coupled, closed systems, changes in one subsystem will affect all of the other subsystems. Cancer cells have been studied extensively over the past century, and the medical literature has been inundated with ultrastructural and biochemical studies of tumor cells that convincingly demonstrate that every examined aspect of normal cellular physiology and anatomy is altered in cancer [72]. In the case of cancer, a plausible sequence of steps may involve a primary genetic lesion that leads to an epigenomic alteration, which leads to genetic instability, which leads to further changes in the epigenome, which leads to accelerated genetic instability. All the while, the cells careen forward on a reckless course marked by deficits in genetic and epigenetic controls.

When we think about the recursive nature of epigenomic/genomic alterations, we can easily conjure nightmarish scenarios in which the disease process accelerates in an endless, vicious cycle. If the cycle can be interrupted, then the disease can be arrested, but we need to have a much firmer grip on how the epigenome is regulated. Until such time, Precision Medicine will rely on trial and error and will be much less precise than we may claim.

SECTION 3.4 WHY A GENE-BASED DISEASE CLASSIFICATION IS A BAD IDEA

> Make everything as simple as possible, but not simpler.
> *Albert Einstein*

> It is once again the vexing problem of identity within variety; without a solution to this disturbing problem there can be no system, no classification.
> *Roman Jakobson*

For well over 150 years, the diagnosis of lesions has been based on microscopic examination [98]. The fundamental reasoning that underlies the morphologic diagnosis of disease is based on the concept that diseases of the body are caused by diseases of cells in the body, and that diseased cells provide us with morphologic clues to diagnosis. This system has worked fairly well, with some notable limitations. Most significantly, patients having the same diagnosis, based on pathological examination, may respond quite differently to the same treatment. One patient may recover fully. Another patient may die.

As an increasing number of diseases have been examined by advanced molecular techniques, it has become apparent that patients grouped under a single morphological diagnosis may have genetically distinctive diseases. In some cases, response to treatment can be more accurately determined by precise genetic sequences than by somewhat imprecise and subjective morphologic features. In some cases, the genetic findings seem to be both pathognomic (i.e., seen in every case of the disease and not seen in any other diseases or in the normal population) and causal. In this book, we will see many examples where genetic findings have led us to a deeper understand of disease biology that was unobtainable through a morphologic approach.

A growing number of scientists and physicians are drawing the conclusion that morphologic examination of tissue might have run its course, and that new genetic and molecular methods may be the best way to diagnose and to classify diseases. This sentiment was expressed by the Director of the US National Institutes of Health, who convened an ad hoc Committee of the National Research Council to develop a new framework for the classification of human diseases, based on molecular biology [99].

The purpose of this section is to show that despite the advances to medicine brought by molecular techniques, a classification of diseases, based on genetic analyses, is not feasible. Here is a lengthy list of arguments against a gene-based classification of diseases.

– **Many diseases do not have a genetic basis.**

The nongenetic diseases would include the diseases caused by environmental toxins, and the so-called wear and tear degenerative diseases, such as osteoarthritis. It is difficult to create a classification of diseases around a concept that does not apply to all diseases.

– **There are many diseases whose causes and genetic characteristics are unknown.**

These would include the many developmental diseases that are observed at birth (i.e., congenital anomalies). Of the clinically significant congenital anomalies, an estimated 60% are so-called sporadic, meaning that they have no discernible genetic cause or environmental cause. Of the 12%–25% of clinical congenital anomalies that have a genetic cause, the majority of these are characterized by chromosomal anomalies. With few exceptions, chromosomal anomalies cannot be reduced to any particular gene or set of genes. This means that of the congenital anomalies that occur in humans, about 95% would be unclassifiable under a genetic classification of human diseases.

Moreover, quite a few of the gene mutations that are assigned to diseases are, in fact, errors. Whole genome data sets are prone to misinterpretation, due in part to the large number of candidate mutations in any sampled genome. We have learned that many of putative gene-causing mutations are variants found in populations of healthy individuals, prompting new guidelines for identifying the genes that cause diseases [33,34,100,101].

– **Genes are just one factor among many that contribute to the development of diseases.**

A recurring theme in this book is that diseases with genetic components must develop in sequential steps, over time. A favorite adage among disease researchers is that our genes load the gun, and our environment pulls the trigger. It's hard to build a classification that is determined by one component of disease development, while ignoring all the others.

– **The same gene mutations that play an important role in the clinical expression of one particular disease may have a negligible role when found in some other disease.**

For example, malignant melanomas having the BRAF V600E mutation respond well to treatment with vemurafenib, while colorectal carcinomas with the identical mutation do not respond to the same drug [102,103]. The rationale for developing a gene-based classification of diseases is that diseases classified by the same mutation will respond similarly to mutation-targeted therapies. How will we deal with conditions that do not comply with the fundamental rationale underlying a molecular classification of disease? [Glossary Melanoma, Nontoxic cancer chemotherapy]

– **The genetic aberrations found in diseases may involve a large set of mutations that defy classification.**

In the case of cancer, the advanced tumors in adults are nearly always highly unstable genetically, and a single tumor may have thousands of different mutations. Multiple samples, selected from different locations in the same tumor, may yield widely different genetic profiles. Classifying every tumor by a genetic marker is an impossible task [104]. [Glossary Intratissue genetic heterogeneity, Tumor heterogeneity, Sample size]

- **The genes that drive a disease in one stage of development may be absent in later stages.**

For example, BRAF V600E mutations are found more often in dysplastic nevi, the presumed precursors of melanoma, than in melanomas that arise therefrom. Likewise, human epidermal growth factor receptor 2 is more often overexpressed in ductal carcinoma in situ than in invasive breast cancer. Similarly, fibroblast growth factor rector 3 mutations decrease as the bladder tumor grade increases, over time [105]. It is difficult to classify a disease based on a gene mutations that may not be present in the cells of the fully developed disease that is being classified. [Glossary Grading]

- **A single disease, occurring in different individuals, may result from one of many distinct molecular defects.**

For example, breast cancer may result from inherited defects in p53 (as in the Li Fraumeni syndrome), or PTEN (as in Cowden syndrome), or from STK11 (as in Peutz-Jegher syndrome), or from none of the above. MYC amplification may be seen in some neuroblastomas and may even correlate with prognosis, but it is not seen in all neuroblastomas and is seen in tumors other than neuroblastoma. Colon cancer can be associated with any of several distinct molecular classes of tumor suppressor genes, all of which seem to confer increased genetic instability [106]. Angiomyolipomas are associated with von Hippel Lindau syndrome and with tuberous sclerosis, each having a distinct genetic cause. Even in the case of chronic myeloid leukemia, strongly associated with a bcr/abl fusion gene mutation, some cases of clinically typical CML may occur in patients with an alternate fusion gene [107]. We now know that chronic myeloid leukemia may develop without the bcr/abl fusion gene, and that the bcr/abl fusion gene may occur without the development of chronic myeloid leukemia [108–111]. [Glossary Cowden syndrome]

Dilated cardiomyopathy is a serious heart condition that has a heritable pattern of occurrence in about a quarter of cases. The heritable cases have been associated with single gene mutations in any of the following list of genes: LDB3 gene, TNNT2 gene, SCN5A gene, TTN gene, DES gene, EYA4 gene, SGCD gene, CSRP3 gene, ABCC9 gene, PLN gene, ACTC gene, MYH7 gene, PSEN1 gene, PSEN2 gene, gene-encoding metavinculin, gene-encoding fukutin, TPM1 gene, TNNC1 gene, ACTN2 gene, DSG2 gene, NEXN gene, MYH6 gene, TNNI3 gene, SDHA gene, BAG3 gene, CRYAB gene, LAMA4 gene, MYPN gene, PRDM16 gene, MYBPC3 gene, TNNI3 gene, and GATAD1 gene [56]. This being the case, how would we settle on a genetic classifier for dilated cardiomyopathy?

We also see disparities between the putative genetic causes of inherited diseases and the sporadic forms of what we have always assumed to be the same disease. For example, atrial myxomas are rare tumors. Familial atrial myxomas that occur as part of Carney complex tend to have a mutation in the PRKAR1A gene, while atrial myxomas that arise sporadically lack the mutation. We see a similar phenomenon when we compare sporadic and familial pituitary adenomas. The familial pituitary adenomas have a mutation in the aryl hydrocarbon receptor interacting protein gene, a mutation that is seldom seen in the sporadically occurring tumors [51]. Likewise, patients with aplastic anemia associated with Shwachman-Diamond syndrome have mutations in both alleles of the SBDS gene. Patients with acquired aplastic anemia seldom have the SDBS gene mutation; when they do have an SDBS mutation, it is heterozygous [112]. [Glossary Atrial myxoma]

All these observations indicate that we cannot always assign a particular gene to a particular disease, although these observations do no preclude assigning a particular gene to a particular subtype of disease (See Section 7.5, "What is Precision Diagnosis?"). [Glossary Precision diagnosis]

– A single gene may produce many different diseases.

As we have seen earlier in this chapter, it is quite common for an inherited mutation of a gene to produce any of several different diseases. As just one example, consider the Pelger-Huet anomaly and Hydrops-ectopic calcification-"moth-eaten" (HEM). Both conditions are caused by mutations of the gene that codes for the lamin B receptor. Pelger-Huet anomaly is a morphologic aberration of neutrophils wherein the normally multilobed nuclei become coffee bean-shaped, or bilobed, with abnormally clumped chromatin. The condition is called an anomaly, rather than a disease, because despite the physical abnormalities, the affected white cells seem to function adequately. HEM is a congenital chondrodystrophy that is characterized by hydrops fetalis (i.e., accumulations of fluid in the fetus), and skeletal abnormalities. It would be difficult to imagine any two diseases as unrelated as Pelger-Huet anomaly and HEM. How could these disparate diseases be caused by a mutation involving the same gene? As it happens, the lamin B receptor has two separate functions: preserving the structure of chromatin, and serving as a sterol reductase in cholesterol synthesis [113]. These two different and biologically unrelated functions, in one gene product, account for two different and biologically unrelated diseases.

We now know of hundreds of instances wherein various mutations of a single gene are the root causes of multiple phenotypically diverse diseases [2]. Because a single gene may produce many different diseases, it would be difficult to build a simple classification based solely on gene/disease correlations. [Glossary One-gene-to-many-diseases]

– Healthy individuals carry putative disease-causing genes

In the last decade of the 20th century, disease genes were being discovered at a very fast rate, and there was the hope that most of the inherited diseases and most cancers would soon be defined by a set of disease-specific mutations; one of which would be present in every individual with the disease; none of which would be present in individuals without the disease. Such hopes were dashed when rare healthy individuals, without any sign of disease, were shown to carry disease-specific gene mutations.

As previously discussed, one of the earliest surprises came when the bcr/abl fusion gene, thought to be pathognomonic for chronic myelogenous leukemia, was found in healthy individuals, a finding that was confirmed by a number of different laboratories [108–110]. Disease genes involved in the pathogenesis of other hematologic disorders were also found in healthy individuals [111,114,115]. Was the finding of disease genes in healthy individuals an oddity confined to blood disorders? No. Milroy disease patients affected by the FLT4/VEGFR3 fusion gene had family members who were unaffected by disease, but who carried the same mutation [20]. As another example, about 1% of individuals in the long-term

Framingham study carry the gene thought to produce an extremely rare, dominantly inherited form of diabetes known as maturity-onset diabetes of the young-13. The vast majority of these disease-gene carriers remain euglycemic through middle age [35].

Genome testing on large populations confirms the presence of disease genes in the healthy population [100]. Many of the putative disease genes are now recognized as common polymorphisms, indicating the discordance between genotype and phenotype (i.e., between the genetic findings and the clinical findings) [101].

A classification of disease cannot be based on gene markers, if those gene markers are present in unaffected individuals. Furthermore, the finding of disease mutations in healthy individuals has raised a number of questions. The first question we might ask is: "If mutations that were considered diagnostic of disease are cropping up in healthy individuals, then must we abandon current efforts to use genomic analyses to predict the risk of developing genetic diseases?" It would seem that the presence of a disease gene, in the absence of any other confirmatory information, may not be sufficient for diagnosis [101,109]. A second question we might ask is: "If we can identify populations of healthy individuals who carry disease genes, then should we be trying to learn the reason why such people are spared from illness?" In the case of healthy carriers of disease genes, knowing how these people escape disease might lead to new ways to prevent and treat the diseases that would otherwise occur. It happens that a new project, Led by the Icahn Institute for Genomics at Mount Sinai, and dubbed "The Resilience Project," seeks out individuals unaffected by disease gene mutations, in hopes of solving the mystery of their good health [116].

- **There is no way to separate genetic diseases and diseases caused by the environment**

We will see many examples throughout this book of diseases that have genetic and environmental components. As one example, consider a report of a 77-year-old male, and an 81-year-old female, who had what first appeared to be an acquired refractory anemia with ringed sideroblasts. This type of anemia is, as its name implies, is refractory to the usual treatments. The expected clinical course usually involves a progressive worsening anemia, sometimes developing into acute myeloid leukemia. In the two subjects of the aforementioned case report, the anemia rapidly reversed after treatment with vitamin B6 [117]. Furthermore, both patients had germline missense mutations in the erythroid delta-aminolevulinate synthase (ALAS2) gene. Addition of pyridoxal 5′-phosphate in vitro stabilized the mutant enzymes. A reasonable reconstruction of the pathogenesis of this disease posits that both patients had an inherited enzyme deficiency that was compensated throughout most of their lives by adequate dietary intake of vitamin B6. In their advanced years, their intake of vitamin B6 failed to compensate for their enzyme deficiency [117,118]. A sideroblastic anemia ensued that was reversible by increasing the patient's intake of vitamin B6. In these cases, patients were born with a gene that could not cause disease on its own. About 80 years later, an environmental factor precipitated the disease.

It is difficult to classify diseases by a genetic mutation when we know that many so-called genetic diseases are biologically complex processes with multiple genetic and environmental components.

If you recall, this section of the book began by discussing a request, from the Director of the US National Institutes of Health, to the National Research Council, for a new framework for the classification of human diseases, based on molecular biology [99]. How did the NRC respond? After due deliberation, the National Research Council advised that a framework for a new taxonomy of disease should not be limited or constrained to molecular biology [99].

Although a gene-based classification of diseases is probably a bad idea, we must not despair. Genetics will play a pivotal role in the growth of Precision Medicine, and in the development of a new classification of human diseases. We will need to read a few more chapters to learn how.

Glossary

Aggregate disease A condition that includes diseases of various causes that follow a pathway that leads to a common set of clinical parameters. COPD (Chronic Obstructive Pulmonary Disease) has been called an aggregate of many "small COPDs" representing individual diseases that happen to be difficult to distinguish from one another [119]. All the so-called end-stage conditions are types of aggregate disease.

Allele One of a pair of matched genes on paired chromosomes, wherein each of the matched genes may vary in sequence from the other. In most cases one allele comes from the father, the other from the mother (the biological exception being uniparental disomy).

Allelic heterogeneity Occurs when different mutations within the different alleles of a gene can yield the same clinical phenotype. For example, hundreds of different alleles of the cystic fibrosis gene can yield the same phenotype [120]. Additionally, a study of 424 families with members affected by Hemophilia B found 167 different allelic mutations of the disease gene [121]. Allelic heterogeneity should not be confused with two diseases being allelic to one another. When two biologically distinct diseases are caused by different mutations in the same gene, the two diseases are said to be allelic to one another.

Allelic to One genetic disease is allelic to another genetic disease if both are caused by mutations of different alleles of the same gene (i.e., in different inherited forms of the gene). For example, distal myopathy with rimmed vacuoles is allelic to hereditary inclusion body myopathy. Each results from a different loss-of-function mutation in different alleles of the gene-encoding UDP-N-acetylglucosamine 2-epimerase/N-acetylmannosamine kinase [122]. Whenever a gene associated with two or more distinct diseases is mapped to the same physical location in the genome, then the cause of the diseases may be due to allelic variation, or to contiguous gene defects (i.e., defects in several genes located in close proximity to one another).

Alternative RNA splicing A normal mechanism whereby one gene may code for many different proteins [123]. In humans, about 95% of genes that have multiple exons are alternately spliced. It has been estimated that 15% of disease-associated mutations involve splicing [124,125]. Cancer cells are known to contain numerous splicing variants that are not found in normal cells [126,127]. Normal cells eliminate most abnormal splicing variants through a posttranscriptional editing process. Alternative RNA splicing may result from mutations in splice sites or from spliceosome disorders. In hereditary thrombocythemia, characterized by overproduction of platelets, there is a mutation in the gene coding for thrombopoietin. This gene mutation leads to mRNAs with shortened untranslated regions that are more efficiently translated than the transcripts that lack the mutation. This, in turn, causes the overproduction of the thrombopoietin, which induces an increase in platelet production [128].

Amyloidosis A term that includes at least 30 different subtypes of disease, each characterized by the accumulation of misfolded proteins that cannot be digested by proteolytic enzymes, in the extracellular spaces in tissues. There are inherited and acquired forms of the disease, producing dysfunction in the tissues where amyloid deposits.

Anonymous variation A genetic variation for which there is no change in gene function. Today, the bulk of the 3 billion base-pair sequence comprising the human genome cannot be assigned to any particular function; a randomly occurring mutation is likely to be anonymous; hence, it is assumed that most SNPs are anonymous. Other commonly encountered anonymous markers include the microsatellites, for which there occur variations in the length of repeated sequences within the microsatellites, but these variations cannot be assigned to a gene or to a particular function. Mutations that occur in somatic, postmitotic cells (i.e., cells that will never divide) are, for all practical purposes, anonymous and undetectable. A mutation must be passed to a population of progeny cells before it can be do much damage and before it can be detected by current molecular biological techniques. Some types of mutations are difficult to find, even when they occur in large numbers of cells. For example, when a mutation is a duplicated exon, the alteration cannot be detected by methods that find base sequence alterations.

Anticipation The phenomenon by which an offspring develops an inherited disease at a younger age than the age at which the parent developed the disease. In most cases, anticipation is associated with an expansion of the trinucleotide repeat in the inherited gene causing the disease. The expansion of trinucleotide repeats is a common occurrence within the genome and may have any of several consequences: (1) producing disease via a gain-of-function mutation within a gene coding for a protein (e.g., Huntington disease); (2) producing disease via a loss-of-function mutation (e.g., myotonic dystrophy); (3) producing anticipation in a preexisting disease-causing gene, possibly by altering the level of expression; and (4) producing no discernible biological effect. Examples of diseases that may display anticipation include: Behcet disease, Crohn disease, Dyskeratosis congenita, Fragile X syndrome, Friedreich Ataxia (rare cases), Huntington Disease, Myotonic Dystrophy, Spinal cerebellar ataxias (several forms). Why such expansions occur is not well understood.

Ataxia telangiectasia Also known as Louis-Bar syndrome and as Boder-Sedgwick syndrome, and caused by a mutation of the ATM gene, resulting in a defect in DNA repair. Cells of individuals with ataxia telangiectasia are highly vulnerable to radiation toxicity. The clinical phenotype consists of cerebellar ataxia (i.e., a body movement disorder secondary to cerebellar impairment), telangiectases (i.e., small focal vascular malformations), immune deficits predisposing to ear, sinus, and lung infections, and a predisposition to malignancy (e.g., lung, gastric, lymphoid, and breast cancers).

Atrial myxoma A tumor that grows on the internal surface of the atria of the heart. These rare tumors were once thought to be organizing thrombi (i.e., old blood clots, not neoplasms) because they had the histologic appearance of thrombi, occurred in locations where thrombi can appear, and occasionally dislodged, traveling through the arterial system to cause an abrupt ischemic event in an extremity, a biological event sometimes encountered with thrombi. It is now widely recognized that these tumors may occur in families with Carney complex type I, where tumor cells have the PRKAR1A mutation found in Carney syndrome and in some sporadically occurring atrial myxomas [129]. Furthermore, cells from the tumor may demonstrate aneuploidy [130]. All of these features suggest a neoplastic origin of atrial myxomas.

Cancer progression The acquisition of additional properties of the malignant phenotype, over time. Progression is achieved through a variety of mechanisms (e.g., genetic instability [131], epigenetic instability, and aberrant cell death regulation) and results in the eventual emergence of subclones that have growth advantages over other cells in the same tumor. The presence of subclones of distinctive phenotype and genotype, within a single tumor, accounts for tumor heterogeneity [132]. Tumors that grow without accumulating changes in genotype or phenotype tend to be benign (i.e., benign tumors do not progress or their rate of progression is much less than that observed in malignant tumors).

Candidate gene approach One of several methods whereby the gene that causes a disease may be discovered. In the candidate gene approach, the researcher begins with some insight into the disease, and the various pathways and metabolic activities that are affected. The researcher chooses a candidate gene to study, based on knowledge of the function of the gene, and a suspicion that alterations in the gene might play an important role in the pathogenesis of the disease. She studies the sequence of the candidate gene in DNA samples from a set of people with the disease, and compares her findings with the sequence of the gene in DNA samples from a set of people who do not have the disease. Consistent differences between the gene in the disease-carrying individuals and the control subjects would suggest that the gene contributes to the development of the disease. Finding a disease association for a candidate gene does not tell us whether other, unexamined, genes may play an important role in disease development. Conversely, failing to find an association does not rule out the presence of an association that was not detected in the gene sequence (e.g., a defect in any of the processes that regulate the transcription, assembly, or deployment of the final gene product).

Case report The case report, also known as the case study, is a detailed description of a single event or situation, often devoted to an outlier, or a detail, or a unique occurrence of an observation. Case studies highlight the utility of seeking general truths based on observations of rare events. Case reports are common in the biomedical literature, often beginning with a comment regarding the extreme rarity of the featured disease. You can expect to see phrases such as "fewer than a dozen have been reported in the literature" or "the authors have encountered no other cases of this lesion," or such and such a finding makes this lesion particularly uncommon and difficult to diagnose; and so on. The point that the authors are trying to convey is that the case report is worthy of publication specifically because the observation is rare. Too often, case reports serve merely as a cautionary exercise, intended to ward against misdiagnosis. The "beware this lesion" approach to case reporting misses the most important aspect of this type of publication, namely, that science, and most aspects of human understanding, involve generalizing from the specific. Case reports gives us an opportunity to clarify the general way things work, by isolating one specific and rarely observed factor [133,134]. Scientists should understand that rare cases are not exceptions to the general laws of reality; they are the exceptions upon which the general laws of reality are based.

Chemokine A cytokine that stimulates white blood cells to move to a tissue target. An allele of the beta-chemokine receptor 5 (CCR5) gene seems to confer a high level of protection against HIV infection. In a study of over 1200 individuals at-risk for HIV infection, the homozygous allele was always absent from infected individuals. Among the individuals at high-risk of HIV infection who remained infection-free, the homozygous allele was found in 3.6% of the population [135].

Cirrhosis A liver condition in which liver cells die and fibrous tissue proliferates in the liver acini (i.e., the functional units of the liver). This results in a loss of liver functionality that is often progressive and fatal.

Cis-acting A gene regulation function that is exerted by some segment of genetic material on another segment of genetic material. In most instances, a short sequence of DNA regulates the transcriptional activity of a nearby gene that codes for a protein. The cis-acting sequence is typically activated or inactivated by some diffusible molecule that attaches to the cis-acting sequence. Cis-acting processes apply to RNA as well as to DNA. The regulation of alternative splicing of mRNAs employs proteins that bind to cis-acting sites on pre-mRNA.

Cofactor When biochemists use the term "cofactors," they are referring to chemicals that bind to enzymes, to activate the enzyme or to enhance the activity of the enzyme. Some enzymes or enzyme complexes need several cofactors (e.g., the pyruvate dehydrogenase complex, which has five organic cofactors and one metal ion). Vitamins are often cofactors for enzymes.

Combined gene deficiency Occasionally a disease is encountered wherein several genes are affected. Some of these diseases are due to large or small deletions of DNA, wherein multiple genes are deleted as a single chromosomal event. Alternately, a combined deficiency may be caused by one gene that controls the synthesis of several different proteins. In combined factor V and factor VIII clotting factor deficiency, a defect in either the LMAN1 or MCFD2 genes results in diminished transport of both factor V and factor VIII from the endoplasmic reticulum to the Golgi apparatus. Hence, the posttranslational processing of both these factors is incomplete, and a combined deficiency results. The gene products of MCFD2 and LMAN1 form a cargo receptor complex that acts on a set of proteins that includes factor V and factor VIII. Hence, mutations in either gene can produce the same combined deficiency of factor V and factor VIII [136].

Cowden syndrome An inherited disease syndrome characterized by hamartomatous neoplasms of the face, breast, colon, and other organs. The root genetic cause of Cowden syndrome is a loss of function mutation in PTEN, the phosphatase, and tensin homolog gene.

CpG island DNA methylation is a form of epigenetic modification that does not alter the sequence of nucleotides in DNA. The most common form of methylation in DNA occurs on Cytosine nucleotides, most often at locations wherein Cytosine is followed by Guanine. These methylations are called CpG sites. CpG islands are concentrations of CpG dinucleotides that have a GC content over 50% and that range from 200 base pairs (bp) to several thousand bp in length. There are about 29,000–50,000 CpG islands and most of these are associated with a promoter [59]. Various proteins bind specifically to CpG sites. For example, MECP2 is a chromatin-associated protein that modulates transcription. MECP2 binds to CpGs; hence, alterations in CpG methylation patterns can alter the functionality of MECP2. Mutations in MECP2 cause RETT syndrome, a progressive neurologic developmental disorder and a common cause of mental retardation in females. It has been suggested that the MECP2 mutation disables normal protein-epigenome interactions [86].

Cytopenia A reduction in the normal number of cells of a particular type. The term is usually applied to hematopoietic cells (i.e., marrow-derived blood cells). Anemia is a cytopenia of red blood cells. Thrombocytopenia is a cytopenia of platelets (i.e., thrombocytes). Neutropenia is a cytopenia of lymphocytes. A pancytopenia refers to a reduction of all the different types of cells of hematopietic lineage.

DNA methylation DNA methylation is a chemical modification of DNA that does not alter the sequence of nucleotide bases. It is currently believed that DNA methylation plays a major role in cellular differentiation, controlling which genes are turned on and which genes are turned off in a cell, hence determining a cell's "type" (e.g., hepatocyte, thyroid follicular cell, neuron). Because cells of a particular cell lineage divide to produce more cells of the same lineage, DNA methylation patterns must be preserved with each somatic cell generation. The cellular processes by which DNA is modified and controlled without altering the sequence of nucleotide bases is called epigenomics, and the collection of such modifications in DNA comprises the epigenome. About 1% of DNA is methylated in human somatic DNA, and DNA methylation occurs primarily on Cytosine, usually at locations for which Cytosine is followed by Guanine, and designated as "CpG."

Dedifferentiation A cellular condition in which a cell no longer exhibits the biological properties that are characteristic of its cell type (i.e., the features that make one cell type different from another cell type). The term dedifferentiation is often applied to tumor cells that display some, but not all, of the morphologic features that would characterize its histogenetic cell type (i.e., the cell population from which the tumor arose).

Differentiation The human body contains several hundred types of cells endowed with a set of functions and morphologic features that distinguish each cell type from all of the other cell types. The process by which each type of cell becomes different from the other (several hundred) cell types is called differentiation. Because every cell type, regardless of its particular properties, has the same genome as every other cell type, we can infer that some factors other than genome sequence contribute to the process of differentiation. In mammals, differentiation is determined by the epigenome, which controls the levels of expression of genes in a cell, which in turn determines how a gene looks and behaves. Epigenomic modifications are heritable from a cell to its progeny (e.g., when a hepatocyte replicates, it produces hepatocytes and not any other cell types), and this would lead us to expect that when a cell of a given cell type replicates, it will give rise to another cell of the same cell type. This, in fact, is the case. The process by which undifferentiated cells give rise to a lineage of cells with progressively greater levels of differentiation, until a fully differentiated cell type is achieved, is often referred to as stem cell maturation, or lineage maturation.

Ectoderm There are three embryonic layers that eventually develop into the fully developed animal: endoderm, mesoderm, and ectoderm. The ectoderm gives rise to the skin epidermis and the skin appendages (hairs, sebaceous glands, breast glandular tissue).

Epigenetic instability The condition in which the normal epigenetic modifications are progressively changing, within one cell or, from one cell generation to another. Epigenomic instability, like genomic instability, is a near-constant feature of tumor progression. Because cellular differentiation is under epigenetic control, the loss of tumor cell differentiation observed with tumor progression is presumably due to epigenetic instability. Likewise, cancer cells that have an unstable epigenome may inactivate or activate a variety of disease genes in surprising ways. For example, epigenetic instability may produce cancer cells with inactivated Werner syndrome gene, the same gene that causes a premature aging syndrome when it occurs in the germline cells of an organism [64]. In similar fashion, cancer cells may have epigenetic inactivation of the lamin A/C gene, the same gene that, when inactivated in germline cells causes a form of cardiomyopathy [65,137].

Exome sequencing Also known as targeted exome capture, exome sequencing is a relatively new laboratory technique wherein only the exons (the sections of DNA that code for proteins) are sequenced, sparing analysts from dealing with the noncoding regions of DNA [138]. In the human genome, there are only about 180,000 exons, accounting for about 1% of the genome, and about 85% of known disease-causing mutations [138].

Gene regulation Gene expression is influenced by many different regulatory systems, including the epigenome (e.g., chromatin packing, histone modification, base methylation), transcription (e.g., transcription factors, DNA promoter sites, DNA enhancer sites, trans-acting factors), posttranscription (splicing, RNA silencing, RNA polyadenylation, mRNA stabilizers), translation (e.g., translation initiation factors, ribosomal processing), and posttranslational protein modifications. Mutations in any of the genes that control or participate in any of these regulatory mechanisms may contribute to a disease phenotype. Moreover, anything that modifies any regulatory process (e.g., environmental toxins, substrate availability, epistatic genes) can influence gene regulation, hence, can produce a disease phenotype.

Genetic heterogeneity In the context of genetic diseases, the term refers to diseases that can be expressed by any one of multiple allelic variants in a gene (allelic heterogeneity) or by any one of multiple different genes that carry disease-producing alleles (locus heterogeneity). Retinitis pigmentosa is a disease with enormous genetic heterogeneity, and can result from allele heterogeneity or from locus heterogeneity. When a rare disease demonstrates genetic heterogeneity, we are provided with an opportunity to learn how a common pathogenesis develops from different genes. Genetic heterogeneity should be contrasted with the concept of genetic pleiotropism, in which one gene may be responsible for several different functions or disorders. In general, the more common the genetic disease, the more heterogeneous it is. For example, retinitis pigmentosa. This genetic disease is relatively common, with a worldwide prevalence of 1 in 4000 individuals. Retinitis pigmentosa is remarkably heterogeneous and can be caused by at least 4000 different mutations involving any of at least 100 different genes. Retinitis pigmentosa may have autosomal dominant, autosomal recessive, or x-linked inheritance. It can occur in the absence of a family history (i.e., as a de novo mutation). Its clinical phenotype is highly variable, and it can occur by itself, or as part of a syndrome. For example, Usher Syndrome combines retinitis pigmentosa and deafness. Usher syndrome, the most common form of syndromic retinitis pigmentosa, is itself clinically and genetically heterogeneous. Basically, the more genetic heterogeneity in a disease, the more opportunities there will be for the disease to occur, increasing the number of cases of the disease that may occur. As a general rule, diseases with the greatest genetic heterogeneity are the least rare of the genetic diseases.

Genetic instability The process whereby the genome accumulates genetic alterations (e.g., SNPs, GSVs) over time. Low levels of unrepaired DNA damage are an inescapable feature of living cells. The older the cell, the more mutations might be found [139]. Many cancers have a high rate of genetic instability. Mutations that arise in germ cells are sometimes passed onto progeny [140].

Genomic disease Although all genetic diseases are technically genomic diseases, the term "genomic disease" is usually reserved for disorders arising from the loss or gain of portions of the DNA in chromosomes (i.e., not single nucleotide mutations). Disorders in which there is an increase or decrease of portions of DNA that normally occur as multiple copies (i.e., copy number losses and copy number gains) are included in the genomic diseases.

Grading The process of assigning a tumor specimen to a biological category, based on morphologic features that seem to correspond to the biological aggressiveness of the tumor. Often, a tumor's grade is largely determined by the degree of nuclear atypia. A tumor with minimal nuclear atypia might be assigned a "low grade" suggestive of an indolent behavior. A tumor of the same type, but with marked nuclear atypia might be labeled a "high-grade" tumor with an expected aggressive clinical course. Sometimes grading is not based on nuclear atypia. In the case of prostate cancer, grading is based on glandular size, shape, and distribution.

Hamartoma Hamartomas are benign tumors that occupy a peculiar zone lying between neoplasia (i.e., a clonal expansion of an abnormal cell) and hyperplasia (i.e., the localized overgrowth of a tissue). Some hamartomas are composed of tissues derived from several embryonic lineages (e.g., ectodermal tissues mixed with mesenchymal tissue). This is almost never the case in cancers, which are clonally derived neoplasms wherein every cell is derived from a single embryonic lineage. Tuberous sclerosis is an inherited hamartoma syndrome. The pathognomonic lesion in tuberous sclerosis is the brain tuber, from which the syndrome takes its name. Tubers of the brain consist of localized but poorly demarcated malformations of neuronal and glial cells. Like other hamartoma syndromes, the germline mutation in tuberous sclerosis produces benign hamartomas as well as carcinomas, indicating that hamartomas and cancers are biologically related. Hamartomas and cancers associated with tuberous sclerosis include cortical tubers of brain, retinal astrocytoma, cardiac rhabdomyoma, lymphangiomyomatosis (very rarely), facial angiofibroma, white ash leaf-shaped macules, subcutaneous nodules, cafe-au-lait spots, subungual fibromata, myocardial rhabdomyoma, multiple bilateral renal angiomyolipoma, ependymoma, renal carcinoma, subependymal giant cell astrocytoma [56]. Another genetic condition associated with hamartomas is Cowden syndrome, also known as multiple hamartoma syndrome. Cowden syndrome is associated with a loss of function mutation in PTEN, a tumor suppressor gene. Features that may be encountered are macrocephaly, intestinal hamartomatous polyps, benign hamartomatous skin tumors (multiple trichilemmomas, papillomatous papules, and acral keratoses), dysplastic gangliocytoma of the cerebellum, and a predisposition to cancers of the breast, thyroid, and endometrium.

Haploid From Greek haplous, "onefold, single, simple." The chromosome set of a gamete. In humans, this would be 23 chromosomes, one set unpaired autosomes (chromosomes 1 to 22) plus one sex chromosome (X or Y chromosome).

Haplotype A set of DNA polymorphisms that tend to be inherited together, often as a result of their close proximity on a chromosome. It is often used in a restricted sense to refer to a set of SNPs that are statistically associated with one another, on a chromosome. A related term, "haplogroup," refers to a subpopulation of individuals that share a common ancestor and a haplotype.

Histone The major protein in chromatin (i.e., the material composing chromosomes). When histones are deacetylated, they tighten around DNA, reducing normal transcription by blocking transcription factors from attaching to their target sites.

Histopathology Pathologists render diagnoses by examining biopsied specimens. Sampled tissues are fixed in formalin and embedded in paraffin (wax). Thin slices of the paraffin-embedded tissues are mounted on glass slides and stained so that the cellular detail can be visualized under a microscope. A histopathologic diagnosis is based on finding specific cellular alterations that characterize diseases.

Homolog Genes from two different organisms are considered homologous to one another if they both descended from the same gene in a common ancestral organism.

Homozygosity Occurs when only one allele of a gene is expressed in cells. This may occur when both of the inherited alleles of a gene (the maternally derived allele and the paternally derived allele) are identical to each other. It may also result when the expression of one of the inherited alleles is unattained or lost, in which case homozygosity is said to result from loss of heterozygosity.

Imprinting Early in mammalian embryogenesis, the pattern of epigenetic modifications (e.g., methylations) inherited from the paternal and maternal gametes is erased, forcing the embryo to develop its own unique pattern of methylations. This process of epigenome erasure is necessary; otherwise, the embryonic germline would have a differentiated epigenome, and the normal process of gradual epigenetic modifications, applied throughout embryogenesis, could not occur. Erasure is not a totally thorough process. There are about 100 known genes that retain their parental epigenetic patterns. Retention of parental epigenetic patterns is known as imprinting. When imprinted genes contain disease-causing mutations, the disease that develops will express a phenotype that is influenced by paternal lineage. For example, Prader-Willi syndrome a genetic disease characterized by growth disorders (e.g., low muscle tone, short stature, extreme obesity, and cognitive disabilities). Angelman syndrome is genetic disease characterized by neurologic disturbances (e.g., seizures, sleep disturbances, hand flapping), and a typifying happy demeanor. Both diseases can occur in either gender and both diseases are caused by the same microdeletion at 15q11–13. When the microdeletion occurs on the paternally derived chromosome, the disease that results is Prader-Willi syndrome. When the microdeletion occurs on the maternally derived chromosome, the disease that results is Angelman syndrome. Another example is the NOEY2 tumor suppressor gene, which is imprinted in females and which contributes to some cases of breast and ovarian cancers [141].

Intratissue genetic heterogeneity Refers to the expression of different gene variants in different cells within the same organism or lesion (i.e., the cells directly involved in the disease process). The term is most often applied to cancers, wherein subclones of cell emerge, each with a unique genotype and phenotype. The expression of different forms of the same gene in different cells is a type of somatic mosaicism. Hypothetically, somatic mosaicism may play a significant role in the development of polygenic or multifactorial diseases [142].

Karyotype From the Greek root, karyon, meaning nucleus, the karyotype is a standard shorthand describing the chromosomal complement of a cell. The normal karyotype of a human male diploid somatic cell is 46 XY, a somewhat confusing way to express that there are two sets of 23 chromosomes, producing a total complement of 46 chromosomes, which includes one X and one Y sex chromosome. The normal female karyotype is 46 XY. Abnormalities in karyotype are described using The International System for Human Cytogenetic Nomenclature (ISCN).

Late onset Refers to diseases that occur late in life (i.e., middle age or older), or that require more time to develop than one might otherwise expect (e.g., rabies developing clinically one year after infection occurred). Late onset usually tells us that the disease has a nongenetic component. There may be exceptions (e.g., Huntington disease).

Li-Fraumeni syndrome A rare inherited cancer syndrome. Affected individuals are at risk of developing rhabdomyosarcoma, soft-tissue sarcomas, breast cancer, brain tumors, osteosarcoma, leukemia, adrenocortical carcinoma, lymphoma, lung adenocarcinoma, melanoma, gonadal germ cell tumors, prostate carcinoma, and pancreatic carcinoma. The Li-Fraumeni syndrome is associated with a mutation of the p53 tumor suppressor gene.

Locus heterogeneity (LOH) Also known as nonallelic heterogeneity, occurs when mutations in different genes can produce the same disease. For example, mutations in c-KIT or PDGFRalpha can lead to GIST tumors. Mutations in the gene encoding the protein hamartin or the gene encoding the protein tuberin can produce the disease tuberous sclerosis. Carney complex can be caused by mutations in the PRKAR1A gene on chromosome 17q23-q24, or it may be caused by a mutations in chromosome 2p16. Both types of mutations produce the same clinical phenotype, which carries an increased risk of developing several types of tumors, including cardiac myxoma. Locus heterogeneity is a special case of the broader concept of genetic heterogeneity.

Medullary From the Latin, medius, or middle. The term has different medical meanings depending on anatomic context. A medullary tumor of thyroid and a medullary tumor of breast are not the same tumor, occurring in different sites. They are completely unrelated tumors, composed of unrelated cells, the first tumor arising from the thyroid and the second tumor arising from the breast. The marrow of bones is often referred to as the medulla, and histiocytic medullary reticulosis is a lymphoma involving bone marrow. Furthermore, terms that use a suffix derived from "medullo" may have no predictable meaning. A medulloblastoma of the brain is not a tumor composed of medulloblasts nor does it typically arise from the medulla oblongata. A medulloblastoma is a brain tumor that usually appears near the midline of the CNS axis, almost always within the cerebellum.

Melanoma A malignant tumor derived from melanocytes, the pigment-producing cells of skin.

Mendelian inheritance A pattern of inheritance observed for traits that are determined by genes contributed by the mother or the father. The modes of Mendelian inheritance are autosomal dominant, autosomal recessive, sex-linked dominant, and sex-linked recessive. The most comprehensive listing and discussion of the Mendelian diseases has been collected, for many decades, in Mendelian Inheritance in Man, currently available online [56]. Most of the documented rare genetic diseases occurring in humans are Mendelian and are included in Mendelian Inheritance in Man. The number of Mendelian diseases varies depending on how they are counted (e.g., a smaller number if counted by disease phenotype; a larger number if counted by genotypic subtypes), but it is generally accepted that there are at least 7000 documented Mendelian diseases that occur in humans.

Mesoderm The embryonic germ layer that lies between Ectoderm and Endoderm and which gives rise to the mesenchyme, which consists of the connective tissue, muscles and bones of the body.

MicroRNA Small but abundant species of RNA that regulate gene expression by pairing with complementary sequences of mRNA. Such complementation usually causes silencing of the mRNA. It is estimated that humans have more than 1000 different microRNA, also called miRNA species [143]. A form of autosomal dominant hearing loss is caused by mutations in MIRN96 microRNA.

Microdeletion Microdeletions are cytogenetic abnormalities that typically span several megabases of DNA. Microdeletions are too small to be visible with standard cytogenetics, but they can often be detected with FISH (fluorescent in situ hybridization). All of the microdeletion syndromes are rare diseases, and they typically arise as de novo germline aberrations (i.e., not inherited from mother or father, in most instances). Conditions that occur rarely and sporadically to produce a uniform set of phenotypic features in unrelated subjects, may be new cases of microdeletion syndromes [144]. DiGeorge syndrome is a typical microdeletion disease, with a germline 22q11.2 deletion encompassing about 3 million base pairs on one copy of chromosome 22, containing about 45 genes. Neurofibromatosis I sometimes occurs as a microdeletion syndrome involving a region of chromosome 17q11.2 that includes the NF1 gene. Microdeletion disorders are a subtype of contig disorders (i.e., contiguous gene disorder). Examples of microdeletion syndromes include: Cri du Chat, Kallman syndrome, Miller-Dieker syndrome, Prader-Willi/Angelman syndrome, Retinoblastoma, Rubinstein-Taybi syndrome, Smith-Magenis syndrome, Steroid sulfatase deficiency (ichthyosis), Velocardiofacial syndrome (also known as DiGeorge syndrome), Williams-Beuren syndrome, and Wolf-Hirschhorn syndrome.

Mitochondriopathy A disease whose underlying cause is mitochondrial pathology (i.e., dysfunctional mitochondria, or an abnormal number of mitochondria). Mitochondriopathies can be genetic or acquired. Most of the genetic mitochondriopathies are caused by nuclear gene mutations. Though mitochondria have their own genes, the mitochondrial genome codes for only 13 proteins of the respiratory chain. All the other proteins and structural components of the mitochondria are coded in the nucleus. Mitochondriopathies can involve many different organs and physiologic processes. Mitochondrial defects affecting muscles include myopathy (weakness), fatigue, and lactic acidosis. In the peripheral and central nervous systems, disorders include: polyneuropathy, leucoencephalopathy, brain atrophy, epilepsy, upper motor neuron disease, ataxia, and extrapyramidal side-effects. Endocrine manifestations may include hyperhidrosis, diabetes, hyperlipidemia, hypogonadism, amenorrhoea, delayed puberty, and short stature). Heart damage may include conduction abnormalities, heart failure, and cardiomyopathy. Ocular changes may include cataract, glaucoma, pigmentary retinopathy, and optic atrophy. Hearing changes may include deafness, tinnitus, and vertigo. Gastrointestinal disorders may include dysphagia, diarrhea, liver disease, motility disorder, pancreatitis, and pancreatic insufficiency. Renal disease may include renal failure and cyst formation. Blood cells may develop sideroblastic anemia. A mitochondriopathy should be in the differential work-up for any unexplained multisystem disorder, especially those arising in childhood [145].

Myelodysplastic syndrome The myelodysplasias consist of several closely related diseases characterized by pancytopenia, disorders of myeloid maturation, the appearance of blast cells in the circulating blood, chromosomal abnormalities, and the frequent progression to leukemia. Listed by increasing grades of hematologic severity, the myelodysplasias are: refractory anemia, refractory anemia with ringed sideroblasts, refractory anemia with excess blasts, and refractory anemia with excess blasts in transformation. Chronic myelomonocytic leukemia has been included with the myelodysplasias, and with the myeloproliferative disorders. Transitions commonly occur from one level of dysplasia to the next higher grade of dysplasia. The myelodysplasias have a bimodal age distribution.

Most cases occur in the elderly. Rare instances of myelodysplasia occur in children. A secondary type of myelodysplasia occurs following a bout of aplastic anemia or following chemotherapy for some other neoplasm.

Neurectoderm Alternate spelling of neuroectoderm, the embryologic derivative that gives rise to the central nervous system.

Nonsyndromic disease A disease that affects a single organ or function, unaccompanied by abnormalities of other organs or physiologic systems. Congenital deafness and deafness in early childhood usually appears as part of a syndrome, possibly involving facial structures or nerves. A pediatrician may use the term nonsyndromic deafness for emphasis, when deafness occurs without other accompanying pathologies.

Nontoxic cancer chemotherapy Until the last few years, all cancer chemotherapy was designed to be toxic to human cells. The underlying rationale for using toxic drugs is that tumor cells are more sensitive to certain types of toxins than are normal cells. A new generation of nontoxic drugs are aimed at inhibiting pathways in tumor cells that play a key role in the malignant phenotype. Because these new drugs are not intended to kill cells, they are often referred to as nontoxic chemotherapeutic agents. The term "nontoxic" is somewhat misleading because all medications have unintended toxic effects. Still, the new generation of nontoxic chemotherapeutic agents is vastly safer and more tolerable than the preceding generation of cytotoxic agents.

Oligogenic inheritance In the context of genetic diseases, occurs when the expression of several genes (i.e., not one gene, and not many genes) produces a disease phenotype. If two genes are required, the term "digenic disease" applies. Macular degeneration may qualify as a common disease with oligogenic inheritance. A few gene variants present in the general population may account for 70% of the risk of developing age-related macular degeneration [146,147], the third leading cause of blindness worldwide [148]. Other oligogenic rare diseases are Bardet-Biedl syndrome [149], and Williams-Beuren syndrome [150].

One-gene-to-many-diseases Various alterations in a single gene can result in several different diseases. For example, the ALAS2 gene codes for delta-aminolevulinate synthase-2. A gain-of-function mutation in the ALAS2 gene causes X-linked erythropoietic protoporphyria. A deficiency of the enzyme results in insufficient hemoglobin production in red cells and causes X-linked sideroblastic anemia. Several different diseases may result from mutations that causes graded losses in gene activity. For example, Lesch-Nyhan syndrome and Kelley-Seegmiller syndrome both result from mutations in the HGPRT gene. In the Kelley-Seegmiller syndrome, the deficiency of hypoxanthine guanine phosphoribosyltransferase is less than that observed in Lesch-Nyhan syndrome, and the symptoms are milder.

Open reading frame (ORF) A sequence within the genome that codes for a protein and has a start and an end codon.

Ortholog An orthologous gene. Refers to genes from different organisms that evolved from a common ancestor's gene through speciation. Orthologs in different species often have the same or similar functionality.

Paralog A paralogous gene. Refers to genes from different organisms that evolved from a common ancestor's gene through gene duplication. Paralogs permit the organism to get a new functionality from a gene without losing the functionality of the gene that has been duplicated. Paralogy accounts for gene classes that consist of genes with sequence similarity, but each with a somewhat different purpose. A paralog is a type of homolog. All homologs are either orthologs or paralogs.

Phenocopy disease A disease that shares the same phenotype as a genetic disease, but without the genotypic features. We typically think of a phenocopy disease as the nongenetic equivalent of a genetic disease. Examples would include acquired porphyria due to alcohol abuse; acquired Parkinson-type syndrome due to antipsychotic medications. Phenocopy diseases provide important clues to the pathogenesis of rare and common diseases. The drug that produces a phenocopy disease is likely to share the same disease pathways observed in the genetic disease. Pharmacologic treatments for the phenocopy disease may be effective against the genetic form of the disease.

Pleiotropia Refers to an effect wherein one gene influences more than one phenotypic trait. A gene that exhibits pleiotropia is said to be pleiotropic (alternate spelling pleiotrophic). An example of pleiotropia is found in x-linked heterotaxy-1. Heterotaxy is a developmental disorder in which one or more organs are found in abnormal locations. X-linked heterotaxy-1 is characterized by situs inversus, wherein the positions of the major organs are reversed along the body axis. Because normal development requires the customary positioning of organs, X-linked heterotaxy-1 is accompanied by complex cardiac defects, and splenic defects. All these changes are caused by a single alteration, in a single gene: ZIC3.

Polycythemia Polycythemia is an increase in the number of circulating red blood cells. An increase in red blood cells can occur as a response to a physiologic stimulus (e.g., chronic anoxia, high-altitude living). When polycythemia occurs as an intrinsic defect of red blood cells, it is called primary polycythemia. The term polycythemia vera, or "true" polycythemia, is reserved for a clonal disorder of the red blood cell lineage in cells that have a genetic aberration that drives proliferation. The cause of polycythemia vera is a mutation of the JAK2 gene occurring in a single hematopoietic stem cell from which a clonal expansion eventually raises the number of circulating erythrocytes [151]. Mutations in JAK2 are associated with a variety of myeloproliferative conditions, including myelofibrosis, and at least one form of hereditary thrombocythemia [151,152].

Precision diagnosis Involves bringing all of our intellectual resources to produce a specific, clinically relevant, diagnosis from a biologically sensible classification of diseases.

Pseudogene Genes that do not code for proteins. Theories explaining the origin of pseudogenes are many. Some pseudogenes presumably devolved from genes that acquired mutations that rendered the genes nonfunctional. Other pseudogenes may have been reverse-transcribed into DNA via RNA retrotransposons. Pseudogenes are identified from sequence data by computational algorithms that search for stretches of DNA that have some sequence similarities to functional genes, along with sequences that might render the gene nonfunctional (e.g., premature stop codons, frameshift mutations, a Poly-A tail, the lack of promoters). Though pseudogenes do not code for translated proteins, they may play an important role in disease. The RNA transcribed by a pseudogene, and protein molecules translated from the RNA, may have regulatory or modifier functions acting on a variety of cellular processes. At present, pseudogenes are thought to play a role in the dysregulation of cancer cells, and in cell defects found in neurodegenerative disorders [153,154].

Regulatory DNA element Sites in DNA that bind to other molecules (e.g., transcription factors and RNA polymerase) to regulate transcription. Promoters and enhancers are types of regulatory DNA elements. As we learn more and more about how DNA is regulated, it is likely that additional types of DNA regulatory elements will be discovered.

Regulatory RNA element Transcribed RNA can influence the subsequent transcription of other RNA species. The various RNA regulatory elements include: antisense RNA (including cis-natural antisense transcript and transacting siRNA), long noncoding RNA, microRNA, piwi-interacting RNA, repeat-associated siRNA, RNAi, small interfering RNA, and small temporal RNA. Mutations of regulatory RNA elements may cause disease. For example, miR-96 is expressed exclusively in the inner ear and the eye. Mutations in the miR-96 precursor molecule may cause a rare form of autosomal dominant hearing loss [155].

Renal cell carcinoma Technically, the term renal cell carcinoma applies to any cancer arising from the kidney. In common parlance, the term renal cell carcinoma refers to the most common cancers of the kidney, which arise from the renal epithelial tubules, particularly clear-cell carcinoma of kidney.

Russell-Silver syndrome A growth disorder that produces primordial dwarfism, a rare form of proportionate growth reduction. Because affected infants are small, but have an otherwise unremarkable physical appearance, they are often undiagnosed until they are about three years old. Russell-Silver syndrome is an imprinting disorder, produced by hypomethylation of the H19 to IGF2 regions of chromosome 11p15, the same area involved in Beckwith-Wiedemann syndrome [156].

Sample size The number of samples used in a study. Methods are available for calculating the required sample size to rule out the null hypothesis, when an effect is present at a specified significance level, in a population with a known population mean, and a known standard deviation [157].

Silent mutation A mutation that does not alter phenotype. Silent mutations can occur in noncoding regions or in exons. It has been reported that silent mutations may have subtle effects on the tertiary structure of proteins [158].

Single nucleotide polymorphism (SNP) Locations in the genome wherein different individuals are known to have single base differences in DNA sequence. It is currently estimated there are more than 35 million SNPs in the human population, and an SNP occurs about once in every 300 nucleotides [159]. By general acquiescence, the term SNP is reserved for variations that are found in at least 1% of the general population. The term SNV (Single nucleotide variant) is applied to any observed variations among individuals, regardless of its frequency of occurrence in the general population. As DNA samples are sequenced for more and more individuals, the number of single nucleotide variants increases. Presumably, SNVs may occur anywhere along the 3 billion nucleotides that sequentially line the genome. Assuming that there is, at each nucleotide location, one particular nucleotide that dominates in the general population, then there would be three possible nucleotide variants at each location, producing a theoretical limit of 9 billion SNV location/nucleotide pairs. SNPs are just one form of genetic polymorphism that would include alterations in chromosome number, small alterations within a chromosome, deletions of stretches of DNA, insertions of DNA, and a host of subtle complex variations wherein parts of chromosomes are translocated elsewhere within the same chromosomes or to other chromosomes.

Skin cancer Any cancer arising from the epidermis (the multilayered blanket of squamous cells that covers the body), adnexa (e.g., hair, sweat glands, sebaceous glands), or integument (dermis and subcutis). Basal cell carcinoma and squamous carcinoma account for the greatest number of skin tumors. Each year in the United States, squamous carcinoma of skin plus basal cell carcinoma of skin account for more than a million new cancers. This number exceeds the yearly occurrence of all other types of cancer, from all other anatomic sites in the body, combined. Because these tumors are seldom fatal, and because they are so frequent, they are not recorded in cancer registries, and are not included in statistical compilations of cancers affecting the US population. Melanoma is another type of skin cancer, and is potentially lethal, if not treated in an early stage of growth. Though melanoma occurs with a much lower frequency than either squamous cell carcinoma or basal cell carcinoma, it accounts for the greatest number of deaths due to skin tumors.

Somatic From the Greek, meaning body, refers to nongerm cells (i.e., not oocytes, not spermatocytes). The somatic cells, then, consist of the differentiated cells of the body and the stem cells in their lineage. Somatic cells cannot undergo meiosis, and, under natural conditions, cannot pass acquired mutations to progeny. Most cancers are believed to arise after somatic cells acquire mutations that activate oncogenes that, in turn, lead the cell on a path that eventually results in a clonal expansion of cells having a malignant phenotype.

Somatic mosaicism If a new mutation occurs in an embryonic cell after the zygote has split to produce daughter cells, then the new mutation produces somatic mosaicism, meaning that it will only occur in those somatic cells that descended from the embryonic cells in which the mutation occurred. Proteus syndrome is an example of a disease that exhibits somatic mosaicism [160]. Presumably, the gene causing Proteus syndrome, if present in the germline, would have been lethal to the embryo. Somatic mosaicism is a particular type of de novo mutation.

Spliceosome In animals, DNA sequences are not transcribed directly into full-length RNA molecules, ready for translation into a final protein. There is a pretranslational process wherein transcribed sections of DNA, so-called introns, are spliced together, and a single gene can be assembled into alternative spliced products. Alternative splicing is one method whereby more than one protein form can be produced by a single gene [13]. Cellular proteins that coordinate the splicing process are referred to, in aggregate, as the spliceosome. Errors in normal splicing can produce inherited disease, and it estimated that 15% of disease-causing mutations involve splicing [124,125]. Examples of spliceosome diseases are spinal muscular atrophy and some forms of retinitis pigmentosa [13]. In both diseases, pathology is limited to a specific type of cell; retinal cells and their pigment layer in retinitis pigmentosa, and motor neuron cells in the spinal muscular atrophy. One might expect that mutations in spliceosomes would cause deficiencies in diverse cell types, with multiorgan and multisystem disease (e.g., syndromic disease). That this is not the case is somewhat of a mystery, and the catalyst for much speculation. Faustino and Cooper have categorized splicing diseases into different types, including: those that affect a single gene, those that affect multiple genes, those that cause aberrant splicing that result in unnatural mRNAs, and those that cause the inappropriate expression of natural mRNAs [13].

Synonymous SNPs Single nucleotide polymorphisms (SNPs) that have different sequences but which produce an equivalent transcriptional result due to triplet redundancy in the genetic code. For example, guu, guc, gua, gug all code for the amino acid valine and are therefore synonymous with one another.

Thalassemia Alpha thalassemia and beta thalassemia are the most common inherited monogenic disorders worldwide. The disorder is characterized by ineffective red blood cell production due to a reduction in the synthesis of the alpha or beta chains of hemoglobin. As is the case with sickle cell disease, Alpha thalassemia trait seems to confer some protection against malaria [161], and this beneficial effect may explain the conservation of the thalassemia gene in those populations wherein malaria is endemic. Also, as with sickle cell disease, one consequence for mated carriers of the thalassemia trait is the chance of producing offspring with severe homozygous disease.

Tissue block All tissues removed from patients (e.g., by surgeons during operations, by dermatologists who sample small skin lesions) are brought to the pathology department where they are examined grossly (i.e., by the unaided eye) and histologically (i.e., by microscopic examination). Samples of the received tissues are fixed in formalin and then processed to produce a paraffin-infiltrated tissue encased in a block of paraffin. These blocks, sometimes referred to as cassettes (because plastic cassettes hold the paraffin block), are used as the source of thin tissue sections that can be mounted and stained on glass slides. Pathologists reach a diagnosis based on a correlation of clinical, gross, and microscopic features of the observed tissues. Unlike radiologists, who look at visual representations of physical lesions, pathologists look at the actual cells taken from the patient. In most cases, after some of the block has been used to produce tissue sections mounted on glass slides, the majority of the embedded tissue remains in the block and serves as a permanent sample of the biopsied tissue. Some laboratories have paraffin-embedded blocks that have been saved for over a century. Ancient paraffin-embedded tissues are suitable for modern research studies. There are at least 25 million surgical pathology specimens collected each year in the United States.

Trans-acting In molecular biology, a trans-acting agent is usually a regulatory sequence of DNA that acts through an intermediary molecule (i.e., protein or RNA), on some other location of the chromosome or on some other chromosome. A cis-acting agent does not operate through an intermediary molecule.

Transdifferentiation The biological process whereby one cell, of a particular cell type, converts into another cell type. In mammals, transdifferentiation may be a phenomenon that does not occur naturally in living organisms. What may appear to be naturally occurring transdifferentiation in tissues is more easily explained as the replacement of one existing cell type by another existing cell type that happens to be coexisting in the same tissue. For example, in the esophagus, patches of squamous epithelium are sometimes replaced by mucus-secreting cells (a process called metaplasia). It is wrong to say that the squamous cells transdifferentiated into mucus-secreting cells. What actually happens is that mucus stem cells generate mucus-secreting cells that gradually replace the squamous cells. Over the past decade, evidence has mounted indicating that differentiated cells can, under the proper circumstances, dedifferentiate to stem cells, and the stem cells can redifferentiated as some alternate differentiated cell type. Hence, one cell type eventually becomes another cell type, but not through a direct biological process of transdifferentiation. Under naturally occurring situations, there seems to be the requirement of an intermediate cell type: differentiatied cell → undifferentiated stem cell → alternate type of differentiated cell [162,163]. At this point, it is uncertain whether tumor cells can undergo transdifferentiation. Gastric adenocarcinomas have been observed with a component of choriocarcinoma, suggesting that the tumor cells have somehow acquired totipotency [164]. Current evidence indicates that direct transdifferentiation can be induced in cultured cells, with the use of transcription factors. For example, hepatocytes can be induced to become neurons, without dividing, and without reverting to a pluripotent intermediate cell [165]. This would be an example of true transdifferentiation, but until proven so, we cannot assume that transdifferentiation is a natural process that occurs in living tissues.

Translocation Exchanges of sections of a chromosome between two noncomplementary chromosomes (i.e., unpaired chromosomes).

Trinucleotide repeat disorder Rare diseases characterized by trinucleotide repeats in DNA. About half of the studied trinucleotide repeat disorders have repeated CAG sequences. CAG codes for glutamine, so the repeat sequences code for polyglutamine amino acid sequences. Examples of polynucleotide repeat disorders are: dentatorubropallidoluysian atrophy, fragile x syndrome, Friedreich ataxia, Huntington disease, mytotonic dystrophy, some forms of spinocerebellar ataxia, and spinobulbar muscular atrophy.

Tumor heterogeneity During tumor progression, genetic and epigenetic instability results in subclones of the tumor, each having a genome and epigenome that is slightly different from the genome and epigenome of cells in other subclones of the same tumor [132]. In effect, tumor heterogeneity is a condition wherein lots of different tumors, all deriving from the same original cancer cell, exist within the same tumor. The subclones that have the greatest number of cells will be those with that have a growth advantage that can prevail in an enlarging tumor (e.g., enhanced growth under anaerobic conditions, increased invasiveness). Tumors that have progressed to develop a high degree of tumor heterogeneity may be very difficult to treat successfully.

Undifferentiated tumor As the result of tumor progression, cancers cells tend to become more aneuploid, larger, and have fewer of the morphologic features of the cells into which their progenitor would have normally developed. For instance, an advanced, unpigmented melanoma may have few of the morphologic features of a normal melanocyte. The tumor is said to be undifferentiated if it lacks any of the morphologic features of the differentiated cells that are its normal developmental counterparts. If the cells in a tumor lack most (but not all) of these differentiated features, the tumor is said to be poorly differentiated. Likewise, tumors may be called moderately differentiated or well differentiated based on their deviance from normal cells. The term "undifferentiated tumor" is generally meant to confer a poor prognosis because tumors generally become "undifferentiated" as the result of tumor progression. We should remember that "undifferentiation" is a morphologic assessment, and that so-called undifferentiated tumors may employ pathways that are highly conserved for their cell lineage, enhancing the vulnerability of cells to therapeutic agents targeted to lineage-specific pathways. It is also worth noting that some primitive tumors, particularly the primitive tumors of childhood, lack differentiation because they derive from primitive cells, not from differentiated cells. The primitive tumors, such as the primitive neuroectodermal tumors, are ab initio undifferentiated lesions that have never progressed from a differentiated cell type to an undifferentiated cell type. There is no reason to expect primitive, undifferentiated tumors of childhood to behave like undifferentiated tumors in adults.

Uniparental disomy Occurs when the offspring's germline has a chromosome pair derived from one parent, with no contribution from the other parent. Uniparental disomy of a chromosome or of a part of a chromosome can also occur as an acquired feature in somatic (i.e., nongermline) cells and is a frequent alteration found in cancers. There are several mechanisms whereby somatic cell mitosis can lead to an acquired uniparental disomy; these involve faulty chromosome migration with or without accompanying translocations when the chromosomes migrate to daughter cells [166]. The acquired, or somatic form of uniparental disomy does not actually involve the participation of parents (as seen in uniparental disomy of germline cells), and is often referred to by the less mechanistic, but more precise term, "copy neutral loss of heterozygosity." Because only one allele is represented in the uniparental disomic gene, there is loss of heterozygosity. Because cells have the normal number of copies of expressed genes, producing a normal gene expression level, the result is "copy neutral." Uniparental disomy is frequently found in myelodysplastic syndrome and is always found in hydatidiform moles.

Variable expressivity A term that refers to differences in the symptoms and pathologic findings between individuals with the same genetic disease.

Von Hippel-Lindau disease An inherited tumor syndrome characterized by an increased risk for several types of benign or malignant tumors, and the occurrence of cysts in the kidneys, pancreas, and genital tract [167].

Von Recklinghausen disease Eponym for neurofibromatosis type 1. Should not be confused with Von Recklinghausen disease of bone, also known as osteitis fibrosa cystica.

X-chromosome The female sex chromosome. Genetically normal human males have one X chromosome and one Y chromosome. Genetically normal human females have paired X chromosomes, one inherited from the mother, and one from the father. In each somatic cell, one X chromosome is active, and the other X-chromosome is inactive. The inactive cell can often be visualized in cytologic preparations as a small dense clump of heterochromatin hugging the nuclear membrane. Which X chromosome is inactivated will vary from cell to cell; hence, genotypically normal human females are X-chromosome mosaics, composed of cells expressing one of two different X-chromosomes.

Xeroderma pigmentosum An inherited disorder in which affected persons cannot efficiently repair DNA damage produced by UV light. Persons with xeroderma pigmentosum are extremely sensitive to the acute (e.g., sunburn) and chronic (e.g., skin cancer) effects of sunlight.

References

[1] Manolio TA, Collins FS, Cox NJ, Goldstein DB, Hindorff LA, Hunter DJ, et al. Finding the missing heritability of complex diseases. Nature 2009;461:747–53.

[2] Berman JJ. Rare diseases and orphan drugs: keys to understanding and treating common diseases. Cambridge, MA: Academic Press; 2014.

[3] Pritchard JK, Cox NJ. The allelic architecture of human disease genes: common disease-common variant ... or not? Hum Mol Genet 2002;11:2417–23.

[4] Corder EH, Saunders AM, Strittmatter WJ, Schmechel DE, Gaskell PC, Small GW, et al. Gene dose of apolipoprotein E type 4 allele and the risk of Alzheimer's disease in late onset families. Science 1993;261:921–3.

[5] Jonkman MF, Pasmooij AMG, Pasmans SGMA, van den Berg MP, ter Horst HJ, Timmer A, et al. Loss of desmoplakin tail causes lethal acantholytic epidermolysis bullosa. Am J Hum Genet 2005;77:653–60.

[6] Schnabel D, Schroder M, Furst W, Klein A, Hurwitz R, Zenk T, et al. Simultaneous deficiency of sphingolipid activator proteins 1 and 2 is caused by a mutation in the initiation codon of their common gene. J Biol Chem 1992;267:3312–5.

[7] Vogelstein B, Lane D, Levine AJ. Surfing the p53 network. Nature 2000;408:307–10.

[8] Bonadia LC, de Lima Marson FA, Ribeiro JD, Paschoal IA, Pereira MC, Ribeiro AF, et al. CFTR genotype and clinical outcomes of adult patients carried as cystic fibrosis disease. Gene 2014;540:183–90.

[9] Wild EJ, Mudanohwo EE, Sweeney MG, Schneider SA, Beck J, Bhatia KP, et al. Huntington's disease phenocopies are clinically and genetically heterogeneous. Mov Disord 2008;23:716–20.

[10] van Slegtenhorst M, Nellist M, Nagelkerken B, Cheadle J, Snell R, van den Ouweland A, et al. Interaction between hamartin and tuberin, the TSC1 and TSC2 gene products. Hum Mol Genet 1998;7:1053–7.

[11] Ansley SJ, Badano JL, Blacque OE, Hill J, Hoskins BE, Leitch CC, et al. Basal body dysfunction is a likely cause of pleiotropic Bardet-Biedl syndrome. Nature 2003;425:628–33.

[12] Hubbard R, Wald G. The mechanism of rhodopsin synthesis. Proc Natl Acad Sci U S A 1951;37:69–79.

[13] Faustino NA, Cooper TA. Pre-mRNA splicing and human disease. Genes Dev 2003;17:419–37.

[14] Korenbrot JI, Fernald RD. Circadian rhythm and light regulate opsin mRNA in rod photoreceptors. Nature 1989;337:454–7.

[15] Tanackovic G, Ransijn A, Thibault P, Abou Elela S, Klinck R, Berson EL, et al. PRPF mutations are associated with generalized defects in spliceosome formation and pre-mRNA splicing in patients with retinitis pigmentosa. Hum Mol Genet 2011;20:2116–30.

[16] Silva AG, Ewald IP, Sapienza M, Pinheiro M, Peixoto A, de N brega AF, et al. Li-Fraumeni-like syndrome associated with a large BRCA1 intragenic deletion. BMC Cancer 2012;12:237.

[17] Walsh T, Casadei S, Coats KH, Swisher E, Stray SM, Higgins J, et al. Spectrum of mutations in BRCA1, BRCA2, CHEK2, and TP53 in families at high risk of breast cancer. JAMA 2006;295:1379–88.

[18] National Academies of Sciences, Engineering, and Medicine. An evidence framework for genetic testing. Washington, DC: The National Academies Press; 2017.

[19] Nebert DW, Zhang G, Vesell ES. From human genetics and genomics to pharmacogenetics and pharmacogenomics: past lessons, future directions. Drug Metab Rev 2008;40:187–224.

[20] Gordon K, Spiden SL, Connell FC, Brice G, Cottrell S, Short J, et al. Hum Mutat FLT4/VEGFR3 and Milroy disease: novel mutations, a review of published variants and database update. Hum Mutat 2013;34:23–31.

[21] Jin Y, Mazza C, Christie JR, Giliani S, Fiorini M, Mella P, et al. Mutations of the Wiskott-Aldrich Syndrome Protein (WASP): hotspots, effect on transcription, and translation and phenotype/genotype correlation. Blood 2004;104:4010–9.

[22] Soejima H, Higashimoto K. Epigenetic and genetic alterations of the imprinting disorder Beckwith-Wiedemann syndrome and related disorders. J Hum Genet 2013;58:402–9.

[23] Weksberg R, Shuman C, Beckwith JB. Beckwith-Wiedemann syndrome. Eur J Hum Genet 2010;18:8–14.

[24] Why mouse matters. National Human Genome Institute. Available from: https://www.genome.gov/10001345 [Accessed 19 July 2017].

[25] Mural RJ, Adams MD, Myers EW, Smith HO, Miklos GL, Wides R, et al. A comparison of whole-genome shotgun-derived mouse chromosome 16 and the human genome. Science 2002;296:1661–71.

[26] Wetterbom A, Sevov M, Cavelier L, Bergstrom TF. Comparative genomic analysis of human and chimpanzee indicates a key role for indels in primate evolution. J Mol Evol 2006;63:682–90.

[27] Raeder H, Vesterhus M, El Ouaamari A, Paulo JA, McAllister FE, Liew CW, et al. Absence of diabetes and pancreatic exocrine dysfunction in a transgenic model of carboxyl-ester lipase-MODY (maturity-onset diabetes of the young). PLoS One 2013;8:e60229.

[28] Hernandez PA, Gorlin RJ, Lukens JN, Taniuchi S, Bohinjec J, Francois F, et al. Mutations in the chemokine receptor gene CXCR4 are associated with WHIM syndrome, a combined immunodeficiency disease. Nat Genet 2003;34:70–4.

[29] Splawski I, Timothy KW, Tateyama M, Clancy CE, Malhotra A, Beggs AH, et al. Variant of SCN5A sodium channel implicated in risk of cardiac arrhythmia. Science 2002;297(5585):1333–6.

[30] Klupa T, Skupien J, Malecki MT. Monogenic models: what have the single gene disorders taught us? Curr Diab Rep 2012;12:659–66.

[31] Gilissen C, Hoischen A, Brunner HG, Veltman JA. Disease gene identification strategies for exome sequencing. Eur J Hum Genet 2012;20:490–7.

[32] Worthey EA, Mayer AN, Syverson GD, Helbling D, Bonacci BB, Decker B, et al. Making a definitive diagnosis: successful clinical application of whole exome sequencing in a child with intractable inflammatory bowel disease. Genet Med 2011;13:255–62.

[33] MacArthur DG, Manolio TA, Dimmock DP, Rehm HL, Shendure J, Abecasis GR, et al. Guidelines for investigating causality of sequence variants in human disease. Nature 2014;508:469–76.

[34] Wallis Y, Payne S, McAnulty C, Bodmer D, Sistermans E, Robertson K, et al. Practice guidelines for the evaluation of pathogenicity and the reporting of sequence variants in clinical molecular genetics. Association for Clinical Genetic Science; 2013. Available from: http://www.acgs.uk.com/media/774853/evaluation_and_reporting_of_sequence_variants_bpgs_june_2013_-_finalpdf.pdf.

[35] Flannick J, Beer NL, Bick AG, Agarwala V, Molnes J, Gupta N, et al. Assessing the phenotypic effects in the general population of rare variants in genes for a dominant Mendelian form of diabetes. Nat Genet 2013;45:1380–5.

[36] Nagel ZD, Chaim IA, Samson LD. Inter-individual variation in DNA repair capacity: a need for multi-pathway functional assays to promote translational DNA repair research. DNA Repair (Amst) 2014;19:199–213.

[37] Cohen A, Thompson E. DNA repair in nondividing human lymphocytes: inhibition by deoxyadenosine. Cancer Res 1986;46:1585–8.

[38] Astuti D, Latif F, Dallol A, Dahia PLM, Douglas F, George E, et al. Gene mutations in the succinate dehydrogenase subunit SDHB cause susceptibility to familial pheochromocytoma and to familial paraganglioma. Am J Hum Genet 2001;69:49–54.

[39] Baysal BE, Willett-Brozick JE, Lawrence EC, Drovdlic CM, Savul SA, McLeod DR, et al. Prevalence of SDHB, SDHC, and SDHD germline mutations in clinic patients with head and neck paragangliomas. J Med Genet 2002;39:178–83.

[40] Niemann S, Muller U, Engelhardt D, Lohse P. Autosomal dominant malignant and catecholamine-producing paraganglioma caused by a splice donor site mutation in SDHC. Hum Genet 2003;113:92–4.

[41] Lack EE. Hyperplasia of vagal and carotid body paraganglia in patients with chronic hypoxemia. Am J Pathol 1978;91:497–516.

[42] Papadimitriou JC, Drachenberg CB. Giant mitochondria with paracrystalline inclusions in paraganglioma of the urinary bladder: correlation with mitochondrial abnormalities in paragangliomas of other sites. Ultrastruct Pathol 1994;18:559–64.

[43] Cable J, Huszar D, Jaenisch R, Steel KP. Effects of mutations at the W locus (c-kit) on inner ear pigmentation and function in the mouse. Pigment Cell Res 1994;7:17–32.

[44] Grill C, Bergsteinsdottir K, Ogmundsdottir MH, Pogenberg V, Schepsky A, Wilmanns M, et al. MITF mutations associated with pigment deficiency syndromes and melanoma have different effects on protein function. Hum Mol Genet 2013;22:4357–67.

[45] DA R, Perlmutter DH. Alpha-1-antitrypsin deficiency: a new paradigm for hepatocellular carcinoma in genetic liver disease. Hepatology 2005;42:514–21.

[46] Hidvegi T, Ewing M, Hale P, Dippold C, Beckett C, Kemp C, et al. An autophagy-enhancing drug promotes degradation of mutant alpha1-antitrypsin Z and reduces hepatic fibrosis. Science 2010;329:229–32.

[47] Gibbons RJ, Pellagatti A, Garrick D, Wood WG, Malik N, Ayyub H, et al. Identification of acquired somatic mutations in the gene encoding chromatin-remodeling factor ATRX in the alpha-thalassemia myelodysplasia syndrome (ATMDS). Nat Genet 2003;34:446–9.

[48] Horwitz MS, Duan Z, Korkmaz B, Lee HH, Mealiffe ME, Salipante SJ. Neutrophil elastase in cyclic and severe congenital neutropenia. Blood 2007;109:1817–24.

[49] Wiesmeier M, Gautam S, Kirschnek S, Hacker G. Characterisation of neutropenia-associated neutrophil elastase mutations in a murine differentiation model in vitro and in vivo. PLoS One 2016;11:e0168055.

[50] Arita K, South AP, Hans-Filho G, Sakuma TH, Lai-Cheong J, Clements S, et al. Oncostatin M receptor-beta mutations underlie familial primary localized cutaneous amyloidosis. Am J Hum Genet 2008;82:73–80.

[51] Barlier A, Vanbellinghen JF, Daly AF, Silvy M, Jaffrain-Rea ML, Trouillas J, et al. Mutations in the aryl hydrocarbon receptor interacting protein gene are not highly prevalent among subjects with sporadic pituitary adenomas. J Clin Endocrinol Metab 2007;92:1952–5.

[52] Al-Mahdawi S, Pinto RM, Varshney D, Lawrence L, Lowrie MB, Hughes S, et al. GAA repeat expansion mutation mouse models of Friedreich ataxia exhibit oxidative stress leading to progressive neuronal and cardiac pathology. Genomics 2006;88:580–90.

[53] Li L, Matsui M, Corey DR. Activating frataxin expression by repeat-targeted nucleic acids. Nat Commun 2016;7:10606.

[54] Virchow R. Die Phokomelen und das Barenweib. Verh Berl Gesell Anthrop 1898;30:55–61.

[55] Brooker AS, Berkowitz KM. The roles of cohesins in mitosis, meiosis, and human health and disease. Methods Mol Biol 2014;1170:229–66.

[56] Omim. Online Mendelian inheritance in man. Available from: http://omim.org/downloads [Accessed 20 June 2013].

[57] Dawkins R. The greatest show on earth: the evidence for evolution. New York: Free Press; 2009.

[58] Slack JM. Conrad Hal Waddington: the last Renaissance biologist? Nat Rev Genet 2002;3:889–95.

[59] Bogler O, Cavenee WK. Methylation and genomic damage in gliomas. In: Zhang W, Fuller GN, editors. Genomic and molecular neuro-oncology. Sudbury, MA: Jones and Bartlett; 2004. p. 3–16.

[60] Lancaster AK, Masel J. The evolution of reversible switches in the presence of irreversible mimics. Evolution 2009;63:2350–62.

[61] Sadikovic B, Al-Romaih K, Squire J, Zielenska M. Cause and consequences of genetic and epigenetic alterations in human cancer. Curr Genomics 2008;9:394–408.

[62] Jia G, Fu Y, Zhao X, Dai Q, Zheng G, Yang Y, et al. N6-methyladenosine in nuclear RNA is a major substrate of the obesity-associated FTO. Nat Chem Biol 2011;7:885–7.

[63] Martin DIK, Cropley JE, Suter CM. Epigenetics in disease: leader or follower? Epigenetics 2011;6:843–8.

[64] Agrelo R, Cheng WH, Setien F, Ropero S, Espada J, Fraga MF, et al. Epigenetic inactivation of the premature aging Werner syndrome gene in human cancer. Proc Natl Acad Sci U S A 2006;103:8822–7.

[65] Agrelo R, Setien F, Espada J, Artiga MJ, Rodriguez M, P rez-Rosado A, et al. Inactivation of the lamin A/C gene by CpG island promoter hypermethylation in hematologic malignancies, and its association with poor survival in nodal diffuse large B-cell lymphoma. J Clin Oncol 2005;23:3940–7.

[66] Seisenberger S, Peat JR, Hore TA, Santos F, Dean W, Reik W. Reprogramming DNA methylation in the mammalian life cycle: building and breaking epigenetic barriers. Philos Trans R Soc Lond Ser B Biol Sci 2013;368.

[67] Allegrucci C, Thurston A, Lucas E, Young L. Epigenetics and the germline. Reproduction 2005;129:137–49.

[68] Davies SJ, Hughes HE. Imprinting in Albright's hereditary osteodystrophy. J Med Genet 1993;30:101–3.

[69] Wilson LC, Oude Luttikhuis ME, Clayton PT, Fraser WD, Trembath RC. Parental origin of Gs alpha gene mutations in Albright's hereditary osteodystrophy. J Med Genet 1994;31:835–9.

[70] Dolinoy DC, Weidman JR, Waterland RA, Jirtle RL. Maternal genistein alters coat color and protects Avy mouse offspring from obesity by modifying the fetal epigenome. Environ Health Perspect 2006;114:567–72.

[71] Wolff GL, Kodell RL, Moore SR, Cooney CA. Maternal epigenetics and methyl supplements affect agouti gene expression in Avy/a mice. FASEB J 1998;12:949–57.

[72] Berman JJ. Neoplasms: principles of development and diversity. Sudbury, MA: Jones and Bartlett; 2009.

[73] Garcia-Manero G. Modifying the epigenome as a therapeutic strategy in myelodysplasia. Hematology Am Soc Hematol Educ Program 2007;2007:405–11.

[74] Raza A, Cruz R, Latif T, Mukherjee S, Galili N. The biology of myelodysplastic syndromes: unity despite heterogeneity. Hematol Rev 2010;2:e4.

[75] Nouzova M, Holtan N, Oshiro MM, Isett RB, Munoz-Rodriguez JL, List AF, et al. Epigenomic changes during leukemia cell differentiation: analysis of histone acetylation and cytosine methylation using CpG island microarrays. J Pharmacol Exp Ther 2004;311:968–81.

[76] Flynn PJ, Miller WJ, Weisdorf DJ, Arthur DC, Brunning R, Branda RF. Retinoic acid treatment of acute promyelocytic leukemia: in vitro and in vivo observations. Blood 1983;62:1211–7.

[77] McKenna ES, Sansam CG, Cho YJ, Greulich H, Evans JA, Thom CS, et al. Loss of the epigenetic tumor suppressor SNF5 leads to cancer without genomic instability. Mol Cell Biol 2008;28:6223–33.

[78] Wang E, Boswell E, Siddiqi I, CM L, Sebastian S, Rehder C, et al. Pseudo-Pelger-Huet anomaly induced by medications: a clinicopathologic study in comparison with myelodysplastic syndrome-related pseudo-Pelger-Hu t anomaly. Am J Clin Pathol 2011;135:291–303.

[79] Fruhwald MC, Biegel JA, Bourdeaut F, Roberts CWM, Chi SN. Atypical teratoid/rhabdoid tumors-current concepts, advances in biology, and potential future therapies. Neuro-Oncology 2016;18:764–78.

[80] Roberts CW, Galusha SA, McMenamin ME, Fletcher CD, Orkin SH. Haploinsufficiency of Snf5 (integrase interactor 1)predisposes to malignant rhabdoid tumors in mice. Proc Natl Acad Sci U S A 2000;97:13796–800.

[81] Roberts CW, Leroux MM, Fleming MD, Orkin SH. Highly penetrant, rapid tumorigenesis through conditional inversion of the tumor suppressor gene Snf5. Cancer Cell 2002;2:415–25.

[82] Cho YM, Choi J, Lee OJ, Lee HI, Han DJ, Ro JY. SMARCB1/INI1 missense mutation in mucinous carcinoma with rhabdoid features. Pathol Int 2006;56:702–6.

[83] Donner LR, Wainwright LM, Zhang F, Biegel JA. Mutation of the INI1 gene in composite rhabdoid tumor of the endometrium. Hum Pathol 2007;38:935–9.

[84] Kwon CS, Wagner D. Unwinding chromatin for development and growth: a few genes at a time. Trends Genet 2007;23:403–12.

[85] Neul JL, Kaufmann WE, Glaze DG, et al. Rett syndrome: revised diagnostic criteria and nomenclature. Ann Neurol 2010;68:944–50.

[86] Amir RE, Van den Veyver IB, Wan M, Tran CQ, Francke U, Zoghbi HY. Rett syndrome is caused by mutations in X-linked MECP2, encoding methyl-CpG-binding protein 2. Nat Genet 1999;23:185–8.

[87] Preuss P. Solving the mechanism of Rett syndrome: how the first identified epigenetic disease turns on the genes that produce its symptoms. Research News Berkeley Lab; 2004. December 20.

[88] Horike S, Cai S, Miyano M, Chen J, Kohwi-Shigematsu T. Loss of silent chromatin looping and impaired imprinting of DLX5 in Rett syndrome. Nat Genet 2005;32:31–40.

[89] Weissman J, Naidu S, Bjornsson HT. Abnormalities of the DNA methylation mark and its machinery: an emerging cause of neurologic dysfunction. Semin Neurol 2014;34:249–57.

[90] Shen E, Shulha H, Weng Z, Akbarian S. Regulation of histone H3K4 methylation in brain development and disease. Philos Trans R Soc Lond Ser B Biol Sci 2014;369:20130514.

[91] Costa S, Shaw P. 'Open minded' cells: how cells can change fate. Trends Cell Biol 2007;17:101–6.

[92] Fraga MF, Ballestar E, Paz MF, Ropero S, Setien F, Ballestar ML, et al. Epigenetic differences arise during the lifetime of monozygotic twins. Proc Natl Acad Sci U S A 2005;102:10604–9.

[93] Chatterjee A, Morison IM. Monozygotic twins: genes are not the destiny? Bioinformation 2011;7:369–70.

[94] Wong AHC, Gottesman II, Petronis A. Phenotypic differences in genetically identical organisms: the epigenetic perspective. Hum Mol Genet 2005;14:R11–8.

[95] Cruijsen M, Lubbert M, Wijermans P, Huls G. Clinical results of hypomethylating agents in AML treatment. J Clin Med 2015;4(1):1–17.

[96] Wei Q, Bhatt K, He HZ, Mi QS, Haase VH, Dong Z. Targeted deletion of Dicer from proximal tubules protects against renal ischemia-reperfusion injury. J Am Soc Nephrol 2010;21:756–61.

[97] Schenkel LC, Kernohan KD, McBride A, Reina D, Hodge A, Ainsworth PJ, et al. Identification of epigenetic signature associated with alpha thalassemia/mental retardation X-linked syndrome. Epigenetics Chromatin 2017;10:10.

[98] Virchow R. Die Cellularpathologie in ihrer Begrundung auf physiologische und pathologische Gewebelehre. Berlin: August Hirschwald; 1858.

[99] Committee on A Framework for Developing a New Taxonomy of Disease, Board on Life Sciences, Division on Earth and Life Studies, National Research Council of the National Academies. Toward precision medicine: building a knowledge network for biomedical research and a new taxonomy of disease. Washington, DC: The National Academies Press; 2011.

[100] Xue Y, Chen Y, Ayub Q, Huang N, Ball EV, Mort M, et al. Deleterious- and disease-allele prevalence in healthy individuals: insights from current predictions, mutation databases, and population-scale resequencing. Am J Hum Genet 2012;91:1022–32.

[101] Bell CJ, Dinwiddie DL, Miller NA, Hateley SL, Ganusova EE, Mudge J, et al. Carrier testing for severe childhood recessive diseases by next-generation sequencing. Sci Transl Med 2011;3:65ra4.

[102] Yang H, Higgins B, Kolinsky K, Packman K, Go Z, Iyer R, et al. RG7204 (PLX4032), a selective BRAFV600E inhibitor, displays potent antitumor activity in preclinical melanoma models. Cancer Res 2010;70:5518–27.

[103] Carlson RH. Precision medicine is more than genomic sequencing. www.medscape.com; October 24, 2016. Available from: http://www.medscape.com/viewarticle/870723_print [Accessed 11 March 2017].

[104] Gerlinger M, Rowan AJ, Horswell S, Larkin J, Endesfelder D, Gronroos E, et al. Intratumor heterogeneity and branched evolution revealed by multiregion sequencing. N Engl J Med 2012;366:883–92.

[105] Kato S, Lippman SM, Flaherty KT, Kurzrock R. The conundrum of genetic "drivers" in benign conditions. J Natl Cancer Inst 2016;108.

[106] Wang Z, Cummins JM, Shen D, Cahill DP, Jallepalli PV, Wang TL, et al. Three classes of genes mutated in colorectal cancers with chromosomal instability. Cancer Res 2004;64:2998–3001.

[107] Al D, Steer EJ, Heath C, Taylor K, Bentley M, Allen SL, et al. The t(8;22) in chronic myeloid leukemia fuses BCR to FGFR1: transforming activity and specific inhibition of FGFR1 fusion proteins. Blood 2001;98:3778–83.

[108] Bayraktar S, Goodman M. Detection of BCR-ABL positive cells in an asymptomatic patient: a case report and literature review. Case Rep Med 2010;2010:939706. Available from: https://www.hindawi.com/journals/crim/2010/939706/.

[109] Bose S, Deininger M, Gora-Tybor J, Goldman JM, Melo JV. The presence of typical and atypical BCR-ABL fusion genes in leukocytes of normal individuals: biologic significance and implications for the assessment of minimal residual disease. Blood 1998;92:3362–7.

[110] Biernaux C, Loos M, Sels A, Huez G, Stryckmans P. Detection of major bcr-abl gene expression at a very low level in blood cells of some healthy individuals. Blood 1995;86:3118–22.

[111] Basecke J, Griesinger F, Trumper L, Brittinger G. Leukemia- and lymphoma-associated genetic aberrations in healthy individuals. Ann Hematol 2002;81:64–75.

[112] Calado RT, Graf SA, Wilkerson KL, Kajigaya S, Ancliff PJ, Dror Y, et al. Mutations in the SBDS gene in acquired aplastic anemia. Blood 2007;110:1141–6.

[113] Waterham HR, Koster J, Mooyer P, van Noort G, Kelley RI, Wilcox WR, et al. Autosomal recessive HEM/Greenberg skeletal dysplasia is caused by 3-beta-hydroxysterol delta(14)-reductase deficiency due to mutations in the lamin B receptor gene. Am J Hum Genet 2003;72:1013–7.

[114] Sidon P, El Housni H, Dessars B, Heimann P. The JAK2V617F mutation is detectable at very low level in peripheral blood of healthy donors. Leukemia 2006;20:1622.

[115] Brassesco MS. Leukemia/lymphoma-associated gene fusions in normal individuals. Genet Mol Res 2008;7:782–90.

[116] Giller G. Genetic heroes may be key to treating debilitating diseases: the resilience project seeks to find people who are unaffected by genetic mutations that would normally cause severe and fatal disorders. Scientific American; May 30, 2014. Available from: https://www.scientificamerican.com/article/genetic-heroes-may-be-key-to-treating-debilitating-diseases/ [Accessed 12 March 2017].

[117] Cotter PD, May A, Fitzsimons EJ, Houston T, Woodcock BE, Al-Sabah AI, et al. Late-onset X-linked sideroblastic anemia: missense mutations in the erythroid delta-aminolevulinate synthase (ALAS2) gene in two pyridoxine-responsive patients initially diagnosed with acquired refractory anemia and ringed sideroblasts. J Clin Invest 1995;96:2090–6.

[118] Furuyama K, Uno R, Urabe A, Hayashi N, Fujita H, Kondo M, et al. R411C mutation of the ALAS2 gene encodes a pyridoxine-responsive enzyme with low activity. Br J Haematol 1998;103:839–41.

[119] Rennard SI, Vestbo J. The many "small COPDs", COPD should be an orphan disease. Chest 2008;134:623–7.

[120] Estivill X, Bancells C, Ramos C. Geographic distribution and regional origin of 272 cystic fibrosis mutations in European populations. Hum Mutat 1997;10:135–54.

[121] Green PM, Saad S, Lewis CM, Giannelli F. Mutation rates in humans. I. Overall and sex-specific rates obtained from a population study of hemophilia B. Am J Hum Genet 1999;65:1572–9.

[122] Nishino I, Noguchi S, Murayama K, Driss A, Sugie K, Oya Y, et al. Distal myopathy with rimmed vacuoles is allelic to hereditary inclusion body myopathy. Neurology 2002;59:1689–93.

[123] Sorek R, Dror G, Shamir R. Assessing the number of ancestral alternatively spliced exons in the human genome. BMC Genomics 2006;7:273.

[124] Pagani F, Baralle FE. Genomic variants in exons and introns: identifying the splicing spoilers. Nat Rev Genet 2004;5:389–96.

[125] Fraser HB, Xie X. Common polymorphic transcript variation in human disease. Genome Res 2009;19(4):567–75.

[126] Venables JP. Aberrant and alternative splicing in cancer. Cancer Res 2004;64:7647–54.

[127] Srebrow A, Kornblihtt AR. The connection between splicing and cancer. J Cell Sci 2006;119:2635–41.

[128] Wiestner A, Schlemper RJ, van der Maas AP, Skoda RC. An activating splice donor mutation in the thrombopoietin gene causes hereditary thrombocythaemia. Nat Genet 1998;18:49–52.

[129] Mabuchi T, Shimizu M, Ino H, Yamguchi M, Terai H, Fujino N, et al. PRKAR1A gene mutation in patients with cardiac myxoma. Int J Cardiol 2005;102:273–7.

[130] Seidman JD, Berman JJ, Hitchcock CL, Becker Jr RL, Mergner W, Moore GW, et al. DNA analysis of cardiac myxomas: flow cytometry and image analysis. Hum Pathol 1991;22:494–500.

[131] Benvenuti S, Arena S, Bardelli A. Identification of cancer genes by mutational profiling of tumor genomes. FEBS Lett 2005;579:1884–90.

[132] Swanton C. Intratumor heterogeneity: evolution through space and time. Cancer Res 2012;72:4875–82.

[133] Brannon AR, Sawyers CL. N of 1 case reports in the era of whole-genome sequencing. J Clin Invest 2013;123:4568–70.

[134] Subbiah IM, Subbiah V. Exceptional responders: in search of the science behind the miracle cancer cures. Future Oncol 2015;11:1–4.

[135] Huang Y, Paxton WA, Wolinsky SM, Neumann AU, Zhang L, He T, et al. The role of a mutant CCR5 allele in HIV-1 transmission and disease progression. Nat Med 1996;2:1240–3.

[136] Zhang B, McGee B, Yamaoka JS, Guglielmone H, Downes KA, Minoldo S, et al. Combined deficiency of factor V and factor VIII is due to mutations in either LMAN1 or MCFD2. Blood 2006;107:1903–7.

[137] Malhotra R, Mason PK. Lamin A/C deficiency as a cause of familial dilated cardiomyopathy. Curr Opin Cardiol 2009;24:203–8.

[138] Choi M, Scholl UI, Ji W, Liu T, Tikhonova IR, Zumbo P, et al. Genetic diagnosis by whole exome capture and massively parallel DNA sequencing. Proc Natl Acad Sci U S A 2009;106:19096–101.

[139] Dolle MET, Snyder WK, Gossen JA, Lohman PHM, Vijg J. Distinct spectra of somatic mutations accumulated with age in mouse heart and small intestine. PNAS 2000;97:8403–8.

[140] Crow JF. The high spontaneous mutation rate: is it a health risk? Proc Natl Acad Sci U S A 1997;94:8380–6.

[141] Yu Y, Xu F, Peng H, Fang X, Zhao S, Li Y, et al. NOEY2 (ARHI), an imprinted putative tumor suppressor gene in ovarian and breast carcinomas. Proc Natl Acad Sci U S A 1999;96:214–9.

[142] Gottlieb B, Beitel LK, Alvarado C, Trifiro MA. Selection and mutation in the "new" genetics: an emerging hypothesis. Hum Genet 2010;127:491–501.

[143] Bentwich I, Avniel A, Karov Y, Aharonov R, Gilad S, Barad O, et al. Identification of hundreds of conserved and nonconserved human microRNAs. Nat Genet 2005;37:766–70.

[144] Harmon A. The DNA age: searching for similar diagnosis through DNA. The New York Times; December 28, 2007.

[145] Finsterer J. Mitochondriopathies. Eur J Neurol 2004;11:163–86.

[146] Lotery A, Trump D. Progress in defining the molecular biology of age related macular degeneration. Hum Genet 2007;122:219–36.

[147] Maller J, George S, Purcell S, Fagerness J, Altshuler D, Daly MJ, et al. Common variation in three genes, including a noncoding variant in CFH, strongly influences risk of age-related macular degeneration. Nat Genet 2006;38:1055–9.

[148] Katta S, Kaur I, Chakrabarti S. The molecular genetic basis of age-related macular degeneration: an overview. J Genet 2009;88:425–49.

[149] Eichers ER, Lewis RA, Katsanis N, Lupski JR. Triallelic inheritance: a bridge between Mendelian and multifactorial traits. Ann Med 2004;36:262–72.

[150] Pober BR. Williams-Beuren syndrome. N Engl J Med 2010;362:239–52.

[151] Zhang L, Lin X. Some considerations of classification for high dimension low-sample size data. Stat Methods Med Res 2011. Available from: http://smm.sagepub.com/content/early/2011/11/22/0962280211428387.long.

[152] Barosi G, Bergamaschi G, Marchetti M, Vannucchi AM, Guglielmelli P, Antonioli E, et al. JAK2 V617F mutational status predicts progression to large splenomegaly and leukemic transformation in primary myelofibrosis. Blood 2007;110:4030–6.

[153] Poliseno L. Pseudogenes: newly discovered players in human cancer. Sci Signal 2012;5:5.

[154] Costa V, Esposito R, Aprile M, Ciccodicola A. Non-coding RNA and pseudogenes in neurodegenerative diseases: "The (un)Usual Suspects". Front Genet 2012;3:231.

[155] Mencia A, Modamio-Hoybjor S, Redshaw N, Morin M, Mayo-Merino F, Olavarrieta L, et al. Mutations in the seed region of human miR-96 are responsible for nonsyndromic progressive hearing loss. Nat Genet 2009;41:609–13.

[156] Bartholdi D, Krajewska-Walasek M, Ounap K, Gaspar H, Chrzanowska KH, Ilyana H, et al. Epigenetic mutations of the imprinted IGF2-H19 domain in Silver-Russell syndrome (SRS): results from a large cohort of patients with SRS and SRS-like phenotypes. J Med Genet 2009;46:192–7.

[157] How to determine sample size, determining sample size. Available from: http://www.isixsigma.com/tools-templates/sampling-data/how-determine-sample-size-determining-sample-size/ [Accessed 8 July 2015].

[158] Kimchi-Sarfaty C, Oh JM, Kim IW, Sauna ZE, Calcagno AM, Ambudkar SV, et al. A "silent" polymorphism in the MDR1 gene changes substrate specificity. Science 2007;315(5811):525–8.

[159] Genetics home reference. National Library of Medicine; July 1, 2013. Available from: http://ghr.nlm.nih.gov/handbook/genomicresearch/snp [Accessed 6 July 2013].

[160] Lindhurst MJ, Sapp JC, Teer JK, Johnston JJ, Finn EM, Peters K, et al. A mosaic activating mutation in AKT1 associated with the Proteus syndrome. N Engl J Med 2011;365:611–9.

[161] Wambua S, Mwangi TW, Kortok M, Uyoga SM, Macharia AW, Mwacharo JK, et al. The effect of alpha+-thalassaemia on the incidence of malaria and other diseases in children living on the coast of Kenya. PLoS Med 2006;3:e158.

[162] Jopling C, Boue S, Belmonte JCI. Dedifferentiation, transdifferentiation and reprogramming: three routes to regeneration. Nat Rev Mol Cell Biol 2011;12:79–89.

[163] Rishniw M, Xin HB, Deng KY, Kotlikoff MI. Skeletal myogenesis in the mouse esophagus does not occur through transdifferentiation. Genesis 2003;36:81–2.

[164] Liu AY, Chan WY, Ng EK, Zhang X, Li BC, Chow JH, et al. Gastric choriocarcinoma shows characteristics of adenocarcinoma and gestational choriocarcinoma: a comparative genomic hybridization and fluorescence in situ hybridization study. Diagn Mol Pathol 2001;10:161–5.

[165] Marro S, Pang ZP, Yang N, Tsai MC, Qu K, Chang HY, et al. Direct lineage conversion of terminally differentiated hepatocytes to functional neurons. Cell Stem Cell 2011;9:374–82.

[166] Tuna M, Knuutila S, Mills GB. Uniparental disomy in cancer. Trends Mol Med 2009;15:120–8.

[167] Herman JG, Latif F, Weng Y, et al. Silencing of the VHL tumor-suppressor gene by DNA methylation in renal carcinoma. Proc Natl Acad Sci U S A 1994;91:9700–4.

Disease Convergence

SECTION 4.1 MECHANISMS OF CONVERGENCE

Our similarities are different.
Yogi Berra

There are 10,000 diseases and only 200 to 300 symptoms.
Mark L. Graber [1]

Disease convergence is the common process by which diseases of different root causes express the same phenotype. Through many examples, in this chapter, we will see that disease convergence often occurs when a single metabolic pathway accounts for the clinical phenotype of several different diseases. Disease convergence is a relatively new concept, and you're not likely to find it discussed in any of the standard textbooks of disease biology. Nonetheless, we will soon see that if convergence did not occur, advances in the field of Precision Medicine would not appreciably reduce the morbidity or mortality of diseases.

Humans, like automobiles, are highly complex. Nonetheless, there are a limited number of ways that complex systems can respond to malfunctions [1]. Think about all the things that can go wrong with your car. The engine can stop, the fuel system can be interrupted, the battery may die, the brakes may fail, any of the four tires can flatten, the headlights may not work, the electrical system may suffer a circuit shortage, and so on. It seems like a long list, but it is not. Maybe a dozen common problems account for the vast majority of car problems. Add these to a few dozen less likely problems, and you have a listing that would cover 99% of automobile repair issues. Every auto repairman knows that there are a limited number of systems in the car that can go bad. Repairs are relatively easy if the repairman can determine the system or part that is at fault for a vehicle breakdown.

Thanks to the phenomenon of convergence, an uncountable large number of possible defects will lead to a much smaller number of potential repair jobs. Convergence is a phenomenon that we can expect to see in every stable system: mechanical or biological. Convergence tells us that regardless of the complexity of a system, the outcome of a system disturbance is typically finite and repeatable. When we look at the night sky, we know that there are a few dozen types of heavenly bodies (e.g., stars, planets, moons, galaxies, black holes). Somehow, the night sky beyond our solar system looks the same from any direction: twinkling stars and galaxies as far as the eye can see. The galaxies are flat and spinning. The stars and planets are round and spinning. Ho hum. Complex systems, on a large scale, develop as simple, and stable patterns of objects; otherwise, the universe would be chaotic, and we wouldn't be here to philosophize on the subject.

Likewise, biological systems, despite their complexity, behave according to simple rules, and all terrestrial organisms are similar to one another (e.g., DNA, RNA, proteins, a requirement for water, finite life-spans). A perturbation to a highly complex biological system will tend to produce the same response, whenever the perturbation is repeated. We shouldn't be surprised that cellular perturbations, regardless of their causes (e.g., genetic, toxic), converge to a limited set of outcomes.

Let's imagine that disease phenotypes are patterns in a complex system. What might be the simplifying rules that apply to disease convergence?

- **We can expect to find examples wherein monogenic, polygenic, epigenetic, and environmental alterations all converge to the same phenotype.**

Most monogenic diseases are loss-of-function mutations, in which a mutation in the gene that codes for a protein serves as the primary event leading to a clinical phenotype. Secondary events would presumably involve reductions in the activity of the pathway or pathways in which the protein would normally engage. You can imagine that multiple polymorphisms (i.e., minor sequence variants), each mildly reducing the activity of proteins involved in the affected pathways, might yield a net loss of pathway activity that is functionally equivalent to what may occur if one of the pathway genes is lost completely. Reductions or enhancements in the activity of a protein may also result from small variations in noncoding regions that alter the level of expression of a gene, or from small changes in regulatory proteins (e.g., transcription factors) that modify the expression of multiple proteins [2]. Epigenetic changes may also produce a decrease or increase in the expression of a protein [3]. Deficiencies can also be produced by genetic mutations involved in the posttranslational assembly and modification of proteins. Finally, environmental agents can shut down proteins and pathways, and could, in theory, account for a deficiency in any protein. Hence, it is easy to see that there are many mechanisms that can converge to reduce a cellular function. [Glossary Transcription factor, Translation factor]

There are exceptions to this general rule. Gain-of-function mutations, unlike deficiency mutations, are not likely to be reproduced by alternate genetic, epigenetic, or environmental processes. When a gain-of-function mutation occurs, a protein is produced that behaves differently from normal. Nearly all gain-of-function mutations work to the detriment of the organism. Occasionally, a gain-of-function mutation enhances the ability of the organism to survive, and such mutations may sometimes pass into the germline of an organism and the gene pool of a species. Sickle cell anemia is an example of a detrimental gain-of-function mutation that confers a sickle shape on erythrocytes, leading to hemolysis, microthrombi, microinfarctions of bone and spleen, and other clinical sequelae. A unique mutation at the 6th amino acid position of the hemoglobin beta chain, where glutamic acid is replaced by valine, produces Hemoglobin S. No other mutation produces the protein alteration of sickle cell disease, and everyone with sickle cell anemia has the identical mutation. There is no plausible mechanism whereby regulatory, posttranslational, epigenetic, or environmental conditions would produce sickle cell anemia. [Glossary Gain-of-function]

- **For diseases that share a common phenotype, and can be caused by monogenic mutations or by other means, most occurrences of the disease will result from "other means."**

An alternate way of phrasing the same message is that the sporadic version of a disease is nearly always more common than the monogenic version of the same disease. The reason is simple: more options. There is often only one way to produce a monogenic version of a disease, and that involves finding an individual with the disease gene in his or her germline (i.e., a rare event). The sporadic disease can arise from any of the aforementioned alternate mechanisms. In the case of environmentally produced disease, the event can occur almost anytime through the life of the individual.

When we look at de novo or familial diseases that can also occur sporadically, we observe that the sporadic version of the disease is always much more common.

Here are a few examples:

- Breast cancer occurring in women who have inherited the BRCA gene versus sporadic breast cancers. Only about 5% of all breast cancer cases are accounted for by germline mutations in the BRCA1 or BRCA2 genes [4]. Nearly all of the remaining cases are sporadic.
- Colon cancer arising in an individual with an inherited colon cancer syndrome versus sporadic colon cancers. About 15% of colon cancers are characterized by microsatellite instability. One-fifth of these cases are accounted for by individuals with Lynch Syndrome. The remaining four-fifths of cases with microsatellite instability are sporadic [5]. [Glossary Microsatellite, Microsatellite instability, Lynch syndrome]
- Inherited prion disease versus sporadic prion disease. Prion diseases occur in inherited, acquired, and sporadic forms. Approximately 15% are inherited and associated with coding mutations in the PRNP gene. The remaining 85% are acquired or sporadic [6,7]. [Glossary Prion disease]

Examples wherein inherited versions of a disorder occur more often than the sporadic version are probably confined to the not-so-rare inherited diseases, such as retinitis pigmentosa, which occurs in 1 in 4000 individuals. Retinitis pigmentosa is a group of ocular diseases characterized by progressive retinal degeneration due to necrosis of photoreceptor cells. As discussed in Section 3.1, retinitis pigmentosa can be caused by any one of hundreds of documented mutations. Because the high incidence of this disorder results from the aggregate of numerous individual rare disorders, it is understandable that a sporadic version of the same disease might occur less frequently than the inherited form. Still, we might speculate that the sporadic version of retinitis pigmentosa (i.e., the form of the disease not associated with any known gene mutation) might account for more cases of retinitis pigmentosa than any single known genetic cause.

- **Dysfunctions of a single pathway account for much of what we observe in genetically heterogeneous diseases**

Locus heterogeneity refers to instances when any one of several different mutations, occurring in different loci of the genome, all yield the equivalent clinical phenotype. In most instances, the different loci correspond to different genes, coding for different proteins. The phenomenon of locus heterogeneity reminds us that it is short-sighted for us to think in terms of a gene causing a disease. Clearly, when locus heterogeneity applies, it is silly to look for "the cause" of a disease. It's much more realistic to think in terms of genes that participate in the events that may lead to a disease-defining phenotype.

We would expect that phenotypes (i.e., normal phenotypes or disease phenotypes) are achieved by collections of genes that work together. These coworking genes might be part of a single multiprotein complex, or a single organelle, or a single functional subunit of the cell, or a single metabolic pathway. Regardless, it seems obvious that genes cooperate with one another in functional units to produce a cell. Hence, whenever a defined disease phenotype is achieved, we can expect to explain that phenotype by finding observable malfunctions in sets of genes that cooperate functionally. Knowing which specific gene is malfunctioning may be much less important than knowing which functional set of genes is malfunctioning.

When we look for a single protein network or pathway that accounts for a disease phenotype, we can sometimes find what we need. For example, all the known genes that account for the inherited ataxias seem to contribute to a single network of interacting proteins [8]. Similarly, the various mutations involved in Milroy disease (hereditary lymphedema) all seem to be involved in angiogenesis [9,10,11]. [Glossary Angiogenesis]

- **When a disease phenotype is fully accounted for by the function of one pathway, then we can expect that every disease having the same phenotype to have alterations in the same pathway.**

Diseases with the same clinical phenotype tend to exhibit similar aberrant metabolic pathways regardless of any differences in the underlying defects that caused the diseases. Earlier in this chapter, we asserted that "Regardless of the path taken, many pathologic processes will converge to the same pathologic condition." Here, we approach the phenomenon of disease convergence from the opposite direction. Let's ask the following question: "If we have two conditions that have converged to the same clinical phenotype, can we assume that both conditions employ the same cellular pathways?" Probably so, because diseases are manifestations of pathologic conditions in specific types of cells. Cells of a specific type are highly restrained to express a limited set of cell-type-specific pathways.

To illustrate the principle, let's think a moment about the possible steps leading to a flat tire. You can have a nail that penetrates the tire, or you can have a structurally unsound tire that breaks at a weak seam, or an overinflated tire that bursts open, or you can have a misalignment that puts excess stress on one edge of a tire, until it rips apart. If you can fully explain a flat tire by demonstrating a nail penetrating its wall, then you can infer that the process by which a tire suddenly flattens will always converge to an intrinsic or acquired defect in the tire. You need not inspect the engine, or the muffler, to learn why your tire is flat.

Hypertension is an example in which a pathway that fully accounts for one form of the disease happens to be the convergent pathway for every form of the disease. As discussed elsewhere, there are numerous genetic and environmental causes of hypertension. The causes of hypertension may include overactivity of the renin-angiotensin system, or channel defects at various sites of the renal tubule, or arterial wall pathology, or increased salt consumption. Regardless of the underlying cause of hypertension, all inherited and acquired forms of the disease converge onto one physiologic pathway: increased net salt balance leading to increased intravascular volume, leading to augmented cardiac output, leading to elevated blood pressure [12]. Hence, diuretics that reduce the reabsorption of sodium in the kidneys, such as hydrochlorothiazide or furosemide, will almost always lower blood pressure, no matter what the underlying cause of hypertension. [Glossary Channelopathy]

Likewise, it doesn't seem to matter the exact genetic or environmental factors that are the underlying causes of neural tube defects. Folic acid supplementation seems to be effective for most of them, reducing the incidence of several different types of neural tube defects by more than 70% [13].

We see a similar phenomenon with rare and common causes of diabetes. Extremely rare single gene diabetes, including HNF1A MODY, and permanent neonatal diabetes associated with the KCNJ11 and ABCC8 genes are benefited by sulfonylurea, the same drug used to treat common type 2 diabetes. The cause of monogenic diabetes is quite different from the cause of common, type 2 diabetes, but chronic hyperglycemia accounts for the clinical phenotype of diabetes, and all forms of the disease will respond to a treatment that reduces glucose levels [14].

Here is another example. Chondrodysplasia punctata 1 (CDPX1) is caused by mutation in the arylsulfatase E gene. Arylsulfatase is required for the normal growth of bone and cartilage. The disease occurs in male infants and is characterized by failure to thrive, apparent mental retardation, atypical facies with nasal hypoplasia, hypoplasia of the distal phalanges, and punctate calcifications in radiographs of the feet and other sites. Warfarin has been shown to inhibit arylsulfatase activity and is known to produce an embryopathy with striking similarity to CDPX1 in the offspring (male or female) of women exposed to the drug during pregnancy. Findings of fetal warfarin syndrome include nasal hypoplasia, shortened fingers, and stippling of vertebrae or bony epiphyses, occurring in more than 6% of children born to mothers treated with warfarin during the first trimester [15]. The remarkably close clinical correlations between Chondrodysplasia punctata-1 and warfarin embryopathy, and their associations with deficiencies of the same enzyme, provide strong evidence that arylsulfatase deficiency, either inherited or acquired, is the root cause of both diseases.

What can we say about the arylsulfatase-sensitive pathway that is responsible for the phenotype observed in CDPX1 and warfarin embryopathy? Although the particular pathway function of arylsulfatase is unknown, it seems as though the pathway's activity is vitamin

K-dependent. Several other disorders are characterized by some of the same dysmorphisms found in CDPX1, including autosomal recessive vitamin K epoxide reductase deficiency and phenytoin embryopathy. Phenytoin is known to inhibit vitamin K. It is looking as though there is one vitamin K-dependent pathway that plays a key role in every syndrome that expresses a set of dysmorphic features similar to chondrodysplasia punctata 1 [16].

As an important corollary, when a rare disease converges to the same phenotype as one or more common diseases, the rare disease will reveal the key pathway that drives the phenotype of the common disease. We can say this because the rare diseases, being mostly monogenic, are likely to have one driving pathway determined by the root causal disease gene. Once that pathway has been identified for the rare form of the disease, we can assume that every disease with the same phenotype will converge to that pathway.

Let's look at a few examples of convergent forms of diseases.

– Myocardial infarction

Heart attacks exemplify pathological convergence. Many different pathological processes can lead to the blockage of a coronary artery, including: atherosclerotic plaque, hypertrophy of the arterial wall, spasms of the artery, acute infection of the artery, thrombus formation within the artery, arterial tear or dissection, and developmental defects resulting in narrowing. Genes and environment contribute to these processes. In the end, they can all produce one clinical phenotype; the all-too-common heart attack.

– Heart failure

Heart failure is a somewhat generic term, encompassing a multitude of diseases, all characterized by an inability of the heart to pump a sufficient quantity of blood, with sufficient force, to adequately perfuse all the tissues of the body. There is evidence to suggest that all types of heart failure, regardless of pathogenesis, will eventually involve damage to dystrophin. Dystrophin is the same muscle protein that is affected by loss of function mutations in Duchenne muscular dystrophy. In the absence of properly functioning dystrophin, extracellular calcium penetrates through the sarcolemma (i.e., the muscle cell membrane), leading to cellular damage. According to the authors of the study, heart failure from any cause (e.g., inherited mutation in dystrophin, toxic damage to myocardiocytes, dilated cardiomyopathy, heart failure of unknown etiology, acute heart failure or chronic heart failure) will lead to damaged dystrophin [17].

– Ciliopathies

The ciliopathies are a genetically and phenotypically diverse set of diseases that could not have made any biological sense, as a class of related diseases, prior to the advent of Precision Medicine, and its retinue of techniques and data resources. Included in the ciliopathies are: Joubert syndrome, nephronophthisis, Senior-Loken syndrome, orofaciodigital syndrome, Jeune chondrodysplasia syndrome, autosomal dominant polycystic kidney disease, recessive polycystic kidney disease, Leber congenital amaurosis, Meckel-Gruber syndrome, Bardet-Biedl syndrome, Usher syndrome, Alstrom syndrome, McKusick-Kaufman syndrome, Ellis van Creveld syndrome, cranioectodermal dysplasia (Sensenbrenner syndrome), short rib polydactyly, some forms of retinal dystrophy, and heterotaxy (including visceral situs anomalies, asplenia or polysplenia, congenital heart defects, biliary atresia, and midline defects)

[18,19]. There are only a few organs and functional systems of the human body that escape involvement by this strange collection of related rare diseases.

All of these ciliopathies have mutations in one or more of dozens of genes that, until quite recently, had no recognized relationship to one another. The key to the ciliopathies lies in the primary cilium, a mostly unary structure that exists in virtually every cell of the body. The primary cilium escaped attention until recently, standing as it does in the shadow of its more populous, more frenetic relative, the motile cilium. Every school child is taught about the structure, cytology, and function of the motile cilia. These organelles protrude from the apical cell wall of epithelial cells lining the respiratory tract, intestines, and of ducts throughout the body, pushing intraluminal materials along their way up a bronchus or down the intestines or through a duct. Motile cilia have a 9-paired microtubule axoneme, with a central pair of microtubules and outer dynein arms. One cell may have many motile cilia. The primary cilium has the appearance of a deformed motile cilium, lacking, as it does, the central pair of microtubules and outer dynein arms that are essential for normal motility. The primary cilium was first observed by microscopists in the 1950s, but because there was only one primary cilium per cell, and because it didn't seem to serve any function, it was long dismissed as an evolutionary relic, much like the coccygeal bone or the vermiform appendix [20]. Around the 1990s, it was recognized that the primary cilium, which grows out from its tip, has no synthetic machinery within itself to transport growth substrates up through the cilium to the growth zone. Hence, it was presumed that the primary cilium must rely on some hypothetical transport mechanism to achieve its growth. This hypothetical mechanism was dubbed IFT (the abbreviation for IntraFlagellar Transport). Soon thereafter, the genes involved in intraflagellar transport were discovered, and these genes, when knocked out in mice, seemed able to produce heterotaxy (i.e., left-right organ asymmetry), indicating that primary cilia play a regulatory role in embryonic and fetal development [20]. Today, the ciliopathies are a well-defined class of phenotypically diverse inherited diseases. Each ciliopathy, regardless of its phenotype, is associated with the proteins whose functions converge upon the primary cilium [18,21]. Hence, the ciliopathies, despite their phenotypic diversities, involve disorders of the primary cilium. For example, primary ciliary dyskinesia features bronchiectasis, sinusitis, otitis media, infertility, situs defects. Alstrom syndrome features dilated cardiomyopathy, obesity, sensorineural hearing loss, retinitis pigmentosa, endocrine abnormalities, renal and hepatic disease. It is hard to imagine two diseases less similar to one another than primary ciliar dyskinesia and Alstrom syndrome. Nonetheless, both are caused by aberrations affecting the primary cilia. There is hope that treatments developed for any member of the ciliopathies might be of benefit for every type of ciliopathic disease [18,22] (Fig. 4.1).

- Blistering diseases

All blistering diseases result from defects in the mechanism by which the cells of the epidermis are held together or anchored to the underlying dermis. Blisters are formed in locations where the epidermis lifts up from the dermis, usually at sites of friction. For example, epidermolysis bullosa is an inherited disease characterized by blistering of the skin and mucosal membranes (e.g., mouth). Over 300 gene defects can account for variants of epidermolysis bullosa. Depending on the variant form of the disease, any of several different genes may serve as the underlying cause (e.g., COL, PLEC, Desmoplakin genes). There is also an autoimmune form of epidermolysis bullosa acquisita, wherein antibodies target Type VII

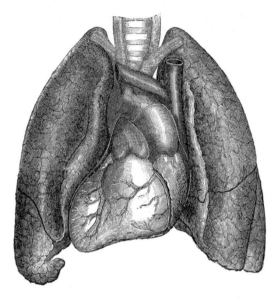

FIG. 4.1 The heart, lungs, and great vessels are switched around to appear the mirror image of normal chest anatomy. The easy giveaway is the normal, posterior location of the trachea, proving that the error is in the anatomy, and not the result of a flipped image. It is hard to imagine that this malformation could result from a defect in cilia, but current evidence indicates that situs inversus is a ciliopathy. *Reproduced from 20th US edition of Gray's Anatomy of the Human Body, originally published in 1918.*

collagen, a component of the basement membrane glue that lies between the epidermis and the dermis. Regardless of the underlying cause, all variants of epidermolysis bullosa converge in a blistering phenotype, and all forms of blistering diseases may benefit from a drug that enhances intercellular adhesion and the adhesion of cells to their underlying basement membrane and dermis.

Before we close this section, you must be warned of pseudoconvergent diseases. Astute healthcare providers must be wary of diseases that have a certain superficial similarity to one another, but which are biologically unrelated and therefore not convergent. A crude example would be amputation of a toe due to a lawn-mowing accident and amputation of a toe due to diabetes-associated small-vessel disease. In either case, the patients are down one toe, but the pathogeneses are totally unrelated, and the two conditions are not convergent.

A much less obvious example of nonconvergent diseases having similar phenotypes is seen in erythromelalgia. Primary erythromelalgia and secondary erythromelalgia are characterized by burning pain and redness of the extremities. Primary erythromelalgia is caused by a mutation in a sodium channel gene (SCN9A) and falls in the general class of diseases known as channelopathies. Primary erythromelalgia is treated with sodium channel blockers [23].

Secondary erythromelalgia is an aggregate of diseases and conditions characterized by burning pain and redness. It includes such common conditions as arterialor venous insufficiency, peripheral neuropathy, frostbite, and gout and can be encountered as a side effect of some common medications, including calcium channel blockers and topical isopropanol [23]. Some cases of secondary erythromelalgia are associated with various myeloproliferative disorders. When the myeloproliferative disorder is treated, the secondary erythromelalgia goes away. Aspirin is useful in cases of secondary erythromelalgia caused by platelet aggregates plugging small arteries.

There is no reason to expect a secondary erythromelalgia of the microthrombotic type to respond to a treatment developed for primary erythromelalgia whose root cause is a mutation in a sodium channel gene. Despite the pain and redness noted in the two disorders, primary and secondary erythromelalgia are nonconvergent when one is a neuropathy and the other is a microthrombotic disorder.

In the remaining sections of this chapter, we'll look at examples of disease convergence that clarify why the unproven assertions listed in this section have had some degree of biological validation.

SECTION 4.2 PHENOCOPY DISEASES: CONVERGENCE WITHOUT MUTATION

Mille viae ducunt homines per saecula Romam (A thousand roads lead men forever to Rome)
Alain de Lille in "Liber Parabolarum", c.1175

A phenocopy is an acquired disease that has the same, or nearly the same, clinical features as a genetic disease. As we saw in Section 3.1, "Inscrutable Genes," knowing the root genetic cause of a disease is a far cry from understanding its pathogenesis. The phenocopy diseases help us to focus on the specific metabolic pathways that drive the disease phenotype. Knowing the operational pathway of a disease provides us with an opportunity to develop new strategies to repair, control, or bypass the metabolic damage caused by a flawed gene. [Glossary Sporadic disease versus phenocopy disease]

Let's start this section with a simple question: "If a phenocopy disease has the same clinical phenotype as its genetic equivalent, then how do we identify a phenocopy when it occurs?" Here are a few of the clues that help us identify phenocopy diseases.

- Not rare (i.e., more common than its rare genetic equivalent)
- Association with an identified causal agent
- Disease cohorts confined to particular occupations or activities (e.g., smokers)
- Absence of disease in family members
- Often produces symptoms in organs known to metabolize or process ingested chemicals (e.g., liver, kidney, lungs)
- Often reversible
- Rapid onset of symptoms
- May develop in a wide range of ages of individuals exposed to the same agent
- May develop in a cluster of unrelated individuals (e.g., as an endemic or an epidemic)
- Lacks any characteristic genetic mutation (obviously)

Most of these aforementioned assertions require no explanation. Because environmental agents always contribute to the cause of phenocopy diseases, and because many environmental agents have a direct action on cellular constituents, we would expect to see rapid onset of symptoms, and clusters of reported cases in high-risk locations. We also note that phenocopy diseases do not generally arise in infants, and tend to increase in frequency in older populations, as the cumulative toxic effects of environmental agents take their tolls. Put simply, genes account for diseases in the young; environment accounts for their phenocopies in the older population. In the case of all of the inherited cancer syndromes, genes account for the cancers that occur in childhood and early adulthood. As age increases, genes account for fewer and fewer of the cancers. By late adulthood, phenocopies dominate [24,25].

In a sense, the aging process itself is one of the great phenocopiers of genetic diseases. Many of the cellular abnormalities that are considered pathognomonic of one or another genetic diseases are found in occasional normal cells, increasing in number as the body ages. These might include Lewy bodies, amyloid plaques, neurofibrillary tangles, psammoma bodies [26], ragged red fibers [27], corpora amylacea [28], and tubular aggregates [29]. Although no one has made a survey of all the cellular abnormalities that arise in rare genetic diseases, it wouldn't be much of a stretch to suggest that most of them are phenocopied in increased numbers in aging cells of normal individuals.

Phenocopy diseases can be rare or common, depending on exposure conditions; while genetic diseases are almost always rare. As we have previously observed for the sporadic diseases, in nearly every situation where we look at the differences in occurrence rates between a specific genetic disease and its phenocopy, the phenocopy is much more common. For example, in cases of colorectal cancer, 20% of cases have an identifiable predisposing gene, while the remaining 80% are presumably phenocopies [5]. For breast cancer, about 5% of cases have a germline BRCA gene mutation. The vast majority of breast cancer cases are nongenetic phenocopies. About 15% of prion diseases occurring in human are thought to be inherited, the remainder being phenocopies [6,7]. Pulmonary alveolar proteinosis occurs in inherited and phenocopy forms. The acquired form of pulmonary alveolar proteinosis is common, accounting for ~90% of cases [30]. Myasthenia gravis may rarely occur as a congenital genetic condition, but the common form of this disease is found in adults, as a phenocopy [31]. Likewise, the autoantibody phenocopy of thrombotic thrombocytopenic purpura is more common than the genetic form of the disease. The alcohol-related phenocopy of cirrhosis is much more common than the genetic form, whose root cause is a mutation in Keratin 18 [32].

There may be a few exceptions to the rule. In 36 unrelated patients with hereditary angioedema, mutations were found in the gene coding for the serpin C1 inhibitor in 34 patients. The remaining two patients had antibodies against the C1 inhibitor [33], indicating that the genetic form of the disease seems to be more prevalent than its phenocopy.

Phenocopies, more so than genetic diseases, are often reversible by the elimination of a causative factor, or the introduction of a vitamin, or the reduction of a dietary constituent [34]. The genetic diseases are characterized by genes that persist in every cell of the organism, through the life of the organism; hence, genetic diseases cannot be easily reversed. There are exceptions, and not all phenocopy diseases are reversible. Cumulative environmental exposures that produce chronic damage, particularly to nondividing cell populations with limited repair capacity are not generally reversible. Examples might include postradiation ischemia, solar elastosis, heavy metal poisoning to nerves and brain, asbestos-induced pulmonary disease, and postinfluenzal encephalopathy.

Inherited diseases follow a common pattern that help distinguish them from their nongenetic phenocopies [35].

- Familial
- Usually progressive and irreversible unless there is medical intervention
- Early age of onset

- Types of organ dysfunctions that are otherwise rare in the general population (tremors, nystagmus, wasting)
- Usually rare (fatal genetic diseases are seldom common; common genetic diseases are seldom fatal)
- Neurocognitive impairment are sometimes present (found in nearly every partial monosomy [35])
- Multiple dysmorphisms and multiple abnormalities are often encountered

Many of the most common diseases are polygenic. This means that multiple genes are involved, with no single gene that can be identified as the root cause of the disease. Many of the polygenic diseases have an acquired component (i.e., some factor or factors from the environment that is involved in pathogenesis), or are triggered by some specific environmental event (e.g., an allergen, dehydration, extreme cold). The polygenic diseases cannot always be distinguished from phenocopies of rare diseases, but the following general features usually apply to polygenic diseases. [Glossary Polygenic disease]

- Nonfamilial
- Very common (the most common killers of humans (heart disease, cancer) are usually polygenic)
- Older population than Mendelian genetic disease
- Often triggered by an environmental factor
- Typically involve mutations in noncoding regions of the genome

These lists are intended as generalizations that might suggest one category of disease over another, and should not be construed as rules. A few noteworthy exceptions to the list entries are worth discussing. For example, the genetic diseases are seldom confined to a geographic cluster, but Tangier disease is a notable exception. Tangier disease is endemic to individuals living on Tangier Island, in the Chesapeake Bay. This disease is characterized by hypercholesterolemia, abnormal deposits of cholesterol in various tissues (producing big yellow tonsils and multiple xanthomas of the skin) and a propensity for heart attacks occurring at an early age. The high rate of occurrences of Tangier disease, on one island, would suggest a dietary cause (e.g., sedentary life and shellfish diet). Not so. Tangier disease is a rare genetic disorder, with an autosomal recessive inheritance pattern, characterized by very low levels of high-density lipoproteins [36]. It occurs in high frequency on Tangier Island because there happens to be a lot of intermarriage among islanders, and recessive mutations are difficult to eliminate from gene pools, in general. A clue to the genetic origin of Tangier disease comes from knowing that cases of Tangier disease are not limited to Tangier Island. Like all genetic diseases, it can occur anywhere on earth, because genetic mutations do not respect geographic boundaries [37].

There are about 7000 known rare genetic diseases, and most of them do not have known phenocopies. Nonetheless, when we look for phenocopies of genetic diseases, we can often find them. Here is a partial listing.

- Acquired conduction defect—inherited conduction defect
- Acquired porphyria cutanea tarda—inherited porphyria cutanea tarda
- Acquired von Willebrand disease—inherited von Willebrand disease

- Aminoglycoside-induced hearing loss—inherited mitochondriopathic deafness
- Antabuse (disulfiram) treatment—inherited alcohol intolerance
- Drug-induced methemoglobinemia—inherited methemoglobinemia
- Fetal exposure to methotrexate—Miller syndrome [38]
- Methylmalonic acidemia caused by severe deficiency of vitamin B12—inherited methylmalonic acidemia
- Osteolathyrism and scurvy—inherited collagenopathies [Glossary Collagenopathy]
- Alcohol-induced sideroblastic anemia—inherited sideroblastic anemia
- B12 deficiency—inherited pernicious anemia
- Cardiomyopathy due to alcohol abuse—inherited dilated cardiomyopathy [39]
- Lead-induced encephalopathy—inherited tau encephalopathy [40]
- Myopathy produced by nucleoside analog reverse transcriptase inhibitors (i.e., HIV drugs)—inherited mitochondrial myopathy
- Pseudo-Pelger-Huet anomaly—inherited Pelger-Huet anomaly [41,42]
- Thalidomide-induced phocomelia—Roberts syndrome and SC pseudothalidomide syndrome [43]
- Warfarin embryopathy—brachytelephalangic chondrodysplasia punctata [44]
- Drug-induced cerebellar ataxia [45] and hereditary spinocerebellar ataxia [46]
- Copper poisoning and Wilson disease
- Chronic iron overload hemochromatosis and inherited hemochromatosis
- Quinacrine-induced ochronosis and inherited ochronosis (i.e., mutation in the HGD gene for the enzyme homogentisate 1,2-dioxygenase) [47]
- Drug-induced Parkinsonism [48,49] and autosomal-dominant inherited Parkinsonism [50]
- Acquired pulmonary hypertension due to hypoxia, thromboembolism, left-sided heart failure, or drugs and inherited pulmonary hypertension [51]
- Amphotericin B toxicity and renal tubular acidosis [52]
- Acquired and hereditary storage pool platelet disease [53]
- Acquired and inherited porphyrias [54,55]
- Acquired iron overload and hemochromatosis and inherited hemochromatosis
- Acquired cirrhosis and genetic cirrhosis (due to mutation in keratin 18) [32]
- Anticoagulant drugs that inhibit thrombus formation and inherited Factor X deficiency (a form of hemophilia)

It is probably safe to infer that in addition to the many known genetic diseases for which there are phenocopies, there must be a large number of cryptic genetic errors whose phenocopies can never be known. Among these cryptic genetic conditions are all of the embryo-lethal mutations that account for the high rate of naturally occurring so-called spontaneous abortions [56]. In addition, through the use of knockout mice, we know that there are many genes whose existence is necessary for embryonic survival (e.g., desmoplakin [57]), and we would presume that aberrations in any of these genes might lead to spontaneous abortions in human embryos and fetuses. Obviously, germline errors in genes that are lethal to embryos cannot be phenocopied, but somatic errors of these same genes can be phenocopied in adult organisms, when the affected cellular pathways are no longer crucial to the survival of the organisms. [Glossary Knockout mice]

We also note that there are many more known phenocopies of rare diseases than there are phenocopies of common diseases. This is largely true due to the fact that there are many more rare diseases than there are common diseases. Aside from that, we know that rare diseases typically result when one mutated gene influences a pathway, leading to a sequence of events that eventually yields a characteristic clinical phenotype. It is easy to imagine that any environmental agent affecting the same pathway would produce a disorder that closely mimics the rare disease.

When we stop and compare the genetic diseases, as a group, with their phenocopies, we learn a great deal about the pathogenesis of both forms of the disease. Here are a few observations that seem to hold for most phenocopies.

- There is usually one dominant pathway that drives the clinical expression of the phenocopy in a limited number of cell types. And this greatly facilitates study of the phenocopy diseases.
- As we would expect, the pathway disrupted in the phenocopy disease is almost always the same pathway that is disrupted in the rare genetic disease. Hence, the phenocopy tells us how the rare disease expresses itself, and this is something that we can seldom infer from our knowledge of the gene mutation associated with the rare disease.
- When the genetic cause of the rare disease is unknown, the careful study of its phenocopy will often yield a set of candidate genes that may operate in the rare disease.
- Pharmacologic treatments for the phenocopy disease may apply to pathways operative in the genetic form of the disease.
- The pathway involved in a phenocopy disease can contribute to the pathogenesis of related common diseases.
- Recognizing the cause of a phenocopy disease may curtail potential environmental catastrophes. The phenocopy diseases help us to focus on the cellular pathways leading to disease. If we exclusively study the genetics of disease, we will likely miss out on such opportunities.
- The phenocopy diseases remind us that we can have a disease without a causal gene, but we cannot have a disease without a causal pathway.
- Phenocopies indicate the ways that heritable and environmental factors can contribute to the converging pathways of related diseases
- The phenocopies remind us that after a genetic root cause of a disease has been discovered, we must not assume that every instance of the disease has a genetic cause.
- Phenocopy diseases should be included in the differential diagnosis of every suspected genetic disease, particularly in those diseases that present themselves in adults.
- An increase in the occurrences of any rare disease, within a population of unrelated individuals, should prompt a thorough search for an acquired phenocopy disease.

- **Epigenomic phenocopies.**

There are many ways in which a phenocopy disease may come to be. Most often, we see examples wherein a specific protein is targeted by a drug or toxin. Alternately, a phenocopy may result when the capacity of a pathway is exhausted. For example, inherited pernicious anemia can be phenocopied by reducing the quantities of substrate available for its key pathway (e.g., by producing a dietary B12 deficiency). Cellular pathways can be simply overwhelmed by adding stressors or competitors or, bluntly, by reducing the population of a functional cell type. For example, most of the blood proteins are synthesized exclusively by the liver. If the population of healthy hepatocytes is reduced or depleted, as in cirrhosis or fulminant hepatitis, then there is a reduction of liver proteins in blood, leading to a clinical phenotype that mimics inherited deficiencies. As one example among dozens, liver is the only source of Protein Z-dependent protease inhibitor, a blood protein that inhibits factors Xa and Xia. A reduction in protein Z-dependent protease inhibitor, due to liver failure, may produce a phenocopy of genetic thrombophilia (i.e., the pathologic tendency to form blood clots). [Glossary End-stage condition]

An overlooked source of phenocopy diseases is the epigenome. In theory, any genetic deficiency can be phenocopied by an epigenomic downregulation of the protein affected in the genetic disease. As an example, defects in the MLH1 (MutL homolog 1) gene are associated with hereditary nonpolyposis colorectal cancer syndrome-2. The MLH1 protein is a component of the DNA mismatch repair pathway. In addition to the characteristic deficiency in mismatch repair pathway observed in colon cancers arising in nonpolyposis colorectal cancer syndrome-2, deficiencies in mismatch repair are also observed in 13% of sporadically occurring cancers. Two individuals with the clinical phenotype of hereditary nonpolyposis colorectal cancer syndrome, including the occurrence of colorectal cancers, without the germline mutations of the MLH1 gene, were shown to have hypermethylation of the gene [58]. Gene hypermethylation is an epigenetic mechanism that blocks expression (i.e., blocks RNA transcription from the gene). The epimutation of the MLH1 gene was present in cells other than tumor cells and seemed to be a germline defect. In these two cases, the evidence suggests that an epigenetic gene-silencing mutations can phenocopy an inherited deficiency disease. [Glossary Hereditary nonpolyposis colorectal cancer syndrome]

SECTION 4.3 THE AUTOANTIBODY PHENOCOPIES

We have met the enemy and he is us.
Walt Kelly's cartoon character, Pogo

An autoantibody phenocopy is a disease in which an antibody targets a specific protein, initiating a sequence of cellular events that culminates in a clinical phenotype that closely mimics the phenotype of a genetic disease. Because the autoantibody phenotype targets a specific protein, the pathogenesis of autoantibody diseases can often be dissected with great precision, and the lessons learned from research on the autoantibody diseases may apply to the genetic form and to the nonimmune acquired forms of the equivalent disease.

In this section, we will be discussing some of the autoantibody phenocopy diseases, but before we do so, let's look at some general rules that apply to all of the autoantibody phenocopies.

- Autoantantibody phenocopies, unlike their genetic equivalents, rarely arise at birth or during childhood.

Our repertoire of antibodies begins after birth and accrues throughout life, as we are exposed to more and more new antigens. Hence, autoantibody diseases do not, as a rule, occur at birth. It would be very rare to encounter an autoantibody disease in a child under the age of five. Consequently, the occurrences of autoantimmune phenocopies increase throughout life. For example, the prevalence of thyroid antibodies increases with age, particularly so for women. By the age of 70, about a third of women will have thyroid antibodies in their blood [59].

The general exception to rule are the inherited monogenic diseases of the immune system, which can produce a wide range of immunologic dysfunctions, beginning in early childhood. Among these would be the inherited defects in thymic development and T-cell tolerance regulation, as well as acquired deficiencies due to almost any condition that reduces the population of regulatory T-cells. In normal development, "self" antigens, particularly the cell surface antigens (e.g., major histocompatibility antigens), are normally spared from eliciting an antibody response, courtesy of a T-cell mediated tolerance mechanism that begins in fetal life, within the thymus gland [60]. IPEX (Immunodysregulation Polyendocrinopathy Enteropathy X-linked) results from a profound dysfunction of the regulatory T cell lineage and is associated with autoimmune disorders. Also, DiGeorge syndrome, also known as 22q11.2 deletion syndrome, produces thymic aplasia and may be associated with autoimmune disorders such as rheumatoid arthritis or Graves disease. [Glossary Autoantibody disease versus autoimmune disease]

There is one autoantibody disease that occurs in utero. Rh incompatibility disease, which involves a congenital antibody response against the infant's RH-factor positive red blood cells. Rh incompatibility disease is not a proper example of a congenital autoantibody disease. In this case, the mother, lacking the RH factor, launches an antibody response against the fetal red blood cells, producing hemolysis and hydrops fetalis. Because the fetus does not synthesize Rh antibodies against itself (they come from the mother), it is probably fair not to count hydrops fetalis as a type of autoantibody disease.

– Autoantibody phenocopy diseases never have Mendelian patterns of inheritance.

Diseases with Mendelian inheritance almost always have peak occurrence in children or young adults. The autoantibody phenocopy diseases occur in adults, increasing in frequency with age, a pattern typical of polygenic (i.e., non-Mendelian) and environmental influences. Empirically, predispositions to the autoantibody phenocopy diseases seem to run in families, but do not follow a Mendelian pattern of inheritance.

– The autoantibody phenocopies are mimics of rare inherited diseases, not common diseases

Mendelian diseases are monogenic, and usually result from a deficiency or impairment of a single protein molecule. Likewise, autoantibody diseases target a single molecule. Most of the non-Mendelian inherited diseases are polygenic, and the non-Mendelian diseases cannot be linked to one genetic defect in one gene. Hence, autoantibody diseases mimic monogenic diseases, not polygenic diseases. [Glossary Non-Mendelian inherited genetic disease]

– When an autoantibody disease phenocopies a common disease, it is almost always the case that only a narrow subpopulation of the common disease is characterized by a deficiency of the protein that is targeted by the autoantibody phenocopy.

As noted (vida supra), the bulk of the instances of a common disease will not be characterized by a deficiency of a single protein. Nonetheless, we sometimes encounter a subpopulation of individuals affected by a common disease who may have a monogenic variant. In this case, the monogenic variant may be deficient in the same protein that is targeted by the autoantibody phenocopy.

– Autoantibody diseases are much more common than the genetic diseases they phenocopy

Autoantibody conditions are common, with over 8.5 million individuals in the United States suffering from one or another of these diseases [61,62]. The common autoantibody diseases are the various autoantibody thyroid diseases (the most common form of autoantibody disease [63]), type 1 diabetes mellitus, pernicious anemia, rheumatoid arthritis, and vitiligo, together accounting for about 93% of individuals with autoantibody disease in the United States. One in 31 Americans has an autoantibody disease.

– The common autoantibody diseases involve one or two organs, seldom more.

The adaptive immune system is designed to produce antigen-specific antibodies. Assuming that the defective pathway is limited to the adaptive immune system, the likelihood that a disorder will yield an antibody that crossreacts with many different tissues is small. In point of fact, most autoantibody diseases are organ-specific. For example, type 1 diabetes targets beta cells of the islets of the pancreas. Goodpasture syndrome involves the production of an antibasement membrane antigen found in lung and the kidney; and the disease is isolated to these two organs.

– The common autoantibody diseases have a polygenic origin.

Though the common autoantibody diseases (i.e., Graves disease, type 1 diabetes mellitus, pernicious anemia, rheumatoid arthritis, and vitiligo) tend to run in families, they seldom display a simple Mendelian inheritance pattern. Inheritance that is non-Mendelian usually has a polygenic origin [62]. There are a few examples of single gene mutations that cause autoimmune diseases, but these are exceedingly rare and have a pathogenesis that is different from the autoantibody diseases occurring n adults [64]. As always, the monogenic forms of autoimmune diseases are instructive, allowing us to delineate individual steps in the pathogenesis of disease [65].

– Autoantibody diseases can be induced by a variety of diseases.

Autoantibody disease can be acquired as a paraneoplastic phenomenon (i.e., a condition caused by a cancer). Cancer cells elicit the adaptive immune system to produce a variety of antibodies. When a cancer elicits antibodies against desmoplakins, a component of normal desmosomes, the immune response can produce an immunologic phenocopy of pemphigus [66]. As discussed previously, desmosomes are found in high concentration in the epidermis, where they hold the various layers of keratinocytes together, and where they bind the epidermis to the underlying dermis. Processes that disrupt desmosomal integrity tend to produce blistering diseases, such as pemphigus. [Glossary Paraneoplastic syndrome, Carcinoid syndrome]

Autoantibody diseases can result from bacterial infections. Following infection with streptococcus pyogenes, an immune response crossreacting with bacterial antigens and normal host proteins (e.g., heart muscle proteins, glomerular basement membranes), may lead to rheumatic fever or to glomerulonephritis.

Bites by the lone-star tick may occasionally elicit antibodies to alpha-gal, and such antibodies, on IgE molecules, can precipitate anaphylaxis when sensitized individuals ingest red meat [67]. Red meat carries the blood group oligosaccharide epitope, galactose-alpha-1,3-galactose (alpha-gal), which crossreacts with the tick antigen. Similar autoantibody crossreactions, following infection by parasites or exposure to blood antigens from animals, have triggered anaphylactic reactions after ingestion of drugs, and of pork [67].

– Physiologic systems influence the development of autoantibody diseases.

Autoantibody diseases can occur in men or women, but most occur disproportionately in women. For all the autoantibody diseases taken together, women are 2.7 times more likely to develop disease than men [61]. This would suggest that the physiological state of the organism, not simply the summation of genetic and environmental conditions, influences the development of autoantibody disease. Of course, there are always exceptions to the rule; Goodpasture syndrome occurs more often in men than in women.

– Autoantibody diseases are almost always more common than the monogenic disease they phenocopy.

Monogenic diseases are almost always rare [64]. Autoantibody diseases, in general, are quite common. Hence any particular autoantibody disease is likely to be more common than any particular genetic disease, an inference that has been shown to be true, empirically [62]. For example, inherited TTP (thrombotic thrombocytopenic purpura) is caused by a deficiency of vWF-cleaving protease and is characterized by platelet microthrombi forming in small blood vessels. The acquired autoantibody disease results from an antibody that inhibits vWF-cleaving protease. It has been reported that there are many more cases of the autoimmune form than the inherited form [68]. Pernicious anemia, associated with autoantibodies to intrinsic factor, is another one of those diseases wherein the phenocopy is much more frequent than the genetic disease. Two previously mentioned examples with an autoimmune phenocopy far more common than the inherited disease are pulmonary alveolar proteinosis [30], and myasthenia gravis [31].

– General disorders of the immune system (in contradistinction to autoantibody diseases characterized by antibodies specific for one antigen) occur in neonates and tend to be monogenic

Autoantibody diseases occur within an otherwise normally functioning immune system. We can think of autoantibody diseases as something that develop as we age, and as our immune system increases the number of its protein targets. Eventually, we can expect to find that some of those targets will crossreact with normal constituents of blood and of cells. Although the terms autoantibody disease and autoimmune disease are often used interchangeably in the medical literature, we should try to reserve the term "autoimmune disease" for primary disorders of the immune system that produce a dysfunctional immune response.

Generalized disorders of the immune system (in contradistinction to autoantibody diseases that target one specific antigen) are extremely rare and occur in neonates [64]. An example of a rare, monogenic immune disorder is C1q deficiency. C1q is a protein involved in the normal fixation of antigen-antibody complexes to complement. A deficiency of C1q leads to the production of multiple autoantibodies and reduces cytotoxicity targeted against infectious organisms. C1q deficiency results in a syndrome much like systemic lupus erythematosus, but with recurrent and chronic infections. Autoimmune lymphoproliferative syndrome is another example of an inherited monogenic autoimmune condition character-ized by lymphocytosis and any of various types of autoimmune diseases, including autoimmune-mediated cytopenias of blood cells: hemolytic anemia, neutropenia, and throm-bocytopenia. The term autoimmune lymphoproliferative syndrome covers a group of related disorders caused by mutations of FAS, FASLG, CASPASE 8, CASPASE 10, and several RAS genes. These genes play a role in apoptosis, a normal pathway that induces cell death. Mu-tations in these genes result in the persistence of once-active lymphocytes that have outlived their usefulness. The persistent lymphocytes elevate the number of lymphoid cells, in circu-lation and in lymph nodes, and raise the likelihood of an inappropriate autoimmune response.

The immune diseases, as a group, are pathogenetically related to one another. Whenever two different diseases occur in the same individual, they are often causally related to one an-other. For example, the co-occurrence of lung cancer and emphysema occurring in an indi-vidual with a 40-year history of smoking cigarettes is no mere coincidence. Likewise, when we observe two or more immune diseases occurring in the same individual, we should be looking for a common link. In particular, a common genetic cause should be suspected when families predisposed to immune disorders demonstrate more than one type of immune disorder among family members [69]. For example, a specific polymorphism in the intracel-lular tyrosine phosphatase gene (PTPN22) seems to predispose to four immune disorders: type 1 diabetes, rheumatoid arthritis, systemic lupus erythematosus, and Hashimoto thyroid-itis [70]. This finding indicates that different autoimmune diseases are sometimes genetically related [65,71]. [Glossary DNA polymorphism]

In addition, it is worth remembering that all immune disorders involve some of the same components of a complex pathway that leads to the development of antibodies. In every autoantibody disease, a plasma cell precursor hypermutates to produce a clonal expansion of cells that produce the specific antibody. By calling these diseases autoantibody diseases, the emphasis is placed on the antibody product, distracting us from seeing that these disor-ders can all be classified as clonal proliferative diseases of plasma cells.

Here are a few examples of autoimmune phenocopies of genetic diseases:

- Autoantibody phenocopy of dystrophic epidermolysis bullosa [72] [Glossary Identification]
- Autoantibody phenocopy of junctional epidermalolysis bullosa [73]
- Autoantibody phenocopy of hemophilia A (factor VIII deficiency) [74]
- Autoantibody phenocopy of hemophilia due to antibodies to factor XI [75]
- Autoantibody phenocopy of hemophilia due to antibodies to factor XIII [76]
- Autoantibody phenocopy of familial hypocalciuric hypercalcemia type i (antibodies reacting with the extracellular domain of the calcium sensing receptor [77,78]
- Autoantibody phenocopy of inherited thrombophilia (i.e., increased risk of thrombosis) due to protein c deficiency [79]
- Autoantibody phenocopy of inherited cutis laxa [80]

- Autoantibody phenocopy of hereditary angioedema (due to autoantibodies to C1 inhibitor) [81]
- Autoantibody phenocopy of congenital adrenal insufficiency [82]
- Autoantibody phenocopy of atransferrinemia [83]
- Autoantibody phenocopy of inherited Bernard-Soulier syndrome [84]
- Autoantibody phenocopy of inherited intrinsic factor deficiency
- Autoantibody phenocopy of inherited Von Willebrand disease
- Autoantibody phenocopy of thrombophilia due to inherited protein C deficiency [85]
- Autoantibody form of hemolytic uremic syndrome. Some children with autoimmune hemolytic uremic syndrome have antibodies to plasma complement factor H [86] The hereditary form is caused by loss of activity of complement pathway proteins [87,88]
- Autoantibody to collagen type II and acquired bilateral progressive sensorineural hearing loss [89]
- Autoantibody phenocopy of rare congenital myasthenia

SECTION 4.4 PATHWAY-DIRECTED TREATMENTS FOR CONVERGENT DISEASES

If you want to make an apple pie from scratch, you must first create the universe.
Carl Sagan

Before the 20th century, how did physicians treat disease? Traditional remedies for disease were based on providing a drug that had the opposite effect on the body as the symptoms of the disease. This strategy was intended to provide some relief from the illness, while the body healed itself. For many diseases, the old ways of treatment were reasonably effective, because the ancient practitioners of medicine found drugs that reversed an important convergent pathway. For example, foxglove, the source of digitalis, increases the contractility of the heart. Hence, digitalis provides some benefit to every cardiac disease that reduces cardiac contractility, and this would include every cardiac disease that converges to a congestive heart failure phenotype and some types of cardiac arrhythmias. Likewise, warfarin, a natural anticoagulant originally found in spoiled sweet clover, was useful for thrombotic diseases. Atropine, from belladonna, the deadly nightshade plant, was a naturally occurring drug that depressed the parasympathetic neurons, and could be used for any disease associated with an overactivity of the parasympathetic system. Of course aspirin, brewed from willow bark, was used since antiquity to soothe any and all inflammatory diseases.

In the era of Precision Medicine, we can do a lot better than treating the symptoms of disease. Precision Medicine focuses on the precise sequence of events that lead to the clinical phenotype of a disease. We can intervene at any of these steps, to prevent diseases from developing. With Precision Medicine, we can diagnose the individual steps that lead to the development of disease, and we can determine which steps are shared by related diseases. Most importantly, we can hope to find treatments that might be effective for every disease that converges to the same pathway.

Here are some examples:

– Diuretics

What is the quantitative measure of hypertension? Definitions vary, but a common cut-off is a systolic blood pressure exceeding 140 mm Hg, or a diastolic pressure exceeding 90 mm Hg. It is estimated that 25% of adults (i.e., over one billion people worldwide) are hypertensive [12,90]. High blood pressure is a quantitative trait, and not a disease. Theory, strengthened by empiric observations, informs us that quantitative traits have multifactorial causes, and that inherited quantitative traits have non-Mendelian polygenic inheritance. The non-Mendelian origin of inherited quantitative traits has been recognized since the early studies of RA Fisher, in 1919 [91–93]. Hence, we would expect that hypertension would not have a monogenic origin. Research scientists searching in vain for the "hypertension gene" could have saved themselves a great deal of effort, if they had they simply recognized that hypertension is a quantitative trait, and not a disease. [Glossary Non-Mendelian inheritance]

As discussed earlier in this chapter, all causes of hypertension lead to an increase in net salt balance; hence, virtually every individual with hypertension will respond to treatment with diuretics (i.e., drugs that reduce the reabsorption of sodium in the kidneys). The mainstay of prevention of hypertension, regardless of its cause, is dietary salt reduction [94]. In the case of hypertension, treating a convergent pathway benefits nearly everyone with a certain clinical phenotype (i.e., high blood pressure), regardless of which pathogenetic route had been followed (Fig. 4.2).

– **Aromatase inhibitors**

Aromatase is an enzyme that synthesizes estrogen. Because breast cancers and some types of ovarian cancer need estrogen to grow, the aromatase inhibitors were developed as a potential treatment for these types of cancers. As it happens, it is relatively easy to block estrogen production in postmenopausal women, using aromatase inhibitors, and in 2005, clinical trials proved that an aromatase inhibitor was effective in the treatment for hormone-sensitive breast cancers in postmenopausal women [95]. Use of aromatase inhibitors to treat breast cancer in premenopausal women is less effective than in postmenopausal women because

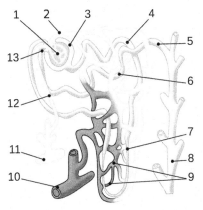

FIG. 4.2   Illustration of a single nephron, demonstrating specific anatomic components targeted by inherited forms of hypertension: (1) Glomerulus; (2) Efferent arteriole; (3) Bowman capsule; (4) Proximal convoluted tubule; (5) Collecting duct, target of Liddle syndrome; (6) Distal convoluted tubule, target of Gitelman syndrome; (7) Loop of Henle, wherein the thick ascending limb is targeted in Bartter syndrome; (8) Bellini duct; (9) Capillaries; (10) Arcuate vein; (11) Arcuate artery; (12) Afferent arteriole; (13) Juxtaglomerular apparatus, effector of the renin-angiotensin-aldosterone system targeted, an active pathway employed in the pathogenesis of various causes of hypertension, including hypertension associated with renal artery dysplasia. *Reproduced from Wikipedia, and released into the public domain.*

aromatase inhibition ultimately upregulates aromatase synthesis and stimulates hormone production by the active hormone-producing cells in the premenopausal ovary.

Fortunately, it seems that all breast cancers pass through a precancerous stage that is sensitive to aromatase inhibitors. Consequently, aromatase cuts the risk of developing breast cancer, in women prone to the disease, by a hefty 65%. This was found to be true regardless of the age of the patient and regardless of the underlying type of genetic risk [96]. In this case, a convergence pathway predated the clinical phenotype of disease, and patients benefited from a drug that interfered with an early step in carcinogensis.

– Losartan as blocker of TGF-beta

Losartan is an angiotensin II receptor antagonist drug used in the treatment of hypertension. More recently, it has been shown that losartan blocks signaling by Transforming Growth Factor-beta (TGF-beta). TGF-beta signaling is involved in fibrogenesis and inflammation, and is a convergent pathway for a variety of diseases that were previously considered unrelated. Consequently, losartan is being developed as a potential treatment for Marfan syndrome [97,98], epilepsy [99], hypertrophic cardiomyopathy, and various other myopathic disorders [100,101].

Losartan is an FDA-approved drug, currently available as an inexpensive generic. Losartan has been used daily, for years, in millions of patients, for the treatment of hypertension. Healthcare professionals have wide experience with losartan's side-effects. Hence, clinicians would be eager to adopt losartan's new uses, based on updated knowledge of the converged pathways targeted by the drug.

– Granulocyte macrophage colony-stimulating factor

Two drugs have been shown to be useful in the treatment of diseases characterized by neutropenia (low white blood cells). These drugs are Granulocyte Colony-Stimulating Factor (G-CSF) and Granulocyte/Macrophage Colony-Stimulating Factor (GM-CSF) [102]. Surprisingly, GM-CSF has been shown to be effective in another group of diseases with highly diverse pathogeneses, known as the pulmonary alveolar proteinoses.

The pulmonary alveolar proteinoses (PAPs) are characterized by an infusion of surfactant and debris in alveoli (i.e., air sacs), thus reducing oxygen and carbon dioxide exchange into and out of the blood. There are inherited, congenital forms of this serious disease, and acquired forms that can arise at any age. As is almost always the case, our greatest insights into the disease process have come from studying the rare, congenital forms of the disease.

Congenital PAPs present clinically as neonatal respiratory distress syndrome. Their root causes are mutations in the genes coding for surfactant proteins, or mutations in the gene coding for GM-CSF receptor. In the cases wherein a defect in surfactant synthesis is found, abnormal lamellar inclusions swell type II pneumocytes, increasing the alveolar content of phospholipoproteinaceous material, and overwhelming the ability of normal macrophages to remove the debris [103]. In the cases wherein there is a deficiency in GM-CSF receptor, macrophages cannot competently remove the surfactant-containing material that normally sloughs into alveoli [104,105].

Autoimmune PAP is caused by the presence of neutralizing autoantibodies against GM-CSF, which prevents the binding of GM-CSF to GM-CSF receptors on alveolar macrophages. Other secondary forms of PAP develop in conditions in which there are reduced numbers of alveolar macrophages or in which there is functional impairment of alveolar macrophages, or in which alveolar debris accumulates with a rapidity that overwhelms the normal capacity of the lung to cleanse itself. This latter form of acquired PAP is associated with inhalation of inorganic dust or toxic fumes. Hematologic malignancies, pharmacologic immunosuppression, and certain types of infection can reduce the functionality of alveolar macrophages. The acquired forms of pulmonary alveolar proteinosis are the most common form, accounting for ~90% of cases [30].

All forms of PAP, inherited or acquired, and regardless of their respective pathogeneses, converge on a pathway wherein proteinaceous material accumulates in the alveoli at a rate exceeding the clearance rate. It appears that every type of PAP, regardless of differences in their respective early steps in pathogenesis, may benefit from treatment with GM-CSF, [104,106,107].

– Botox for muscle spasms

The sudden release of excess amounts of acetylcholine at neuromuscular junctions may cause muscle spasms. Clostridia botulinum toxin A (botox) blocks the nerve from releasing acetylcholine and relaxes the spasm. Hence, we would expect botox to be effective in a variety of conditions whose pathways converge to produce muscle spasms. This would include cerebral palsy, movement disorders characterized by muscle overactivity and spasticity, spasmodic torticollis, strabismus, local dystonias including laryngeal dystonia, blepharospasm (spasmic eye closure or blinking), and hemifacial spasm.

– Angiogenesis inhibitors

Bevacizumab is an angiogenesis inhibitor (i.e., it reduces the formation of new small vessels). All cancers, at some point in their pathogeneses, must vascularize themselves, to deliver oxygen to tumor cells. Hence, an angiogenesis inhibitor, such as bevacizumab, has the potential of serving as a universal anticancer drug, effective against any kind of cancer, regardless of which specific genetic errors drives its proliferation. Bevacizumab is currently employed in the treatment of common cancers, including cancers of the colon, lung, breast, kidney, ovaries, and brain (i.e., glioblastoma). Bevacizumab produces tumor shrinkage in more than half of vestibular schwannomas occurring in Neurofibromatosis 2 [108]. [Glossary Schwannoma]

As you might expect, Bevacizumab has value in treating diseases other than cancer, for which angiogenesis occurs. Two noncancerous diseases of neovascularization (i.e., diseases caused in whole or in part by overgrowth of new vessels), and treated with angiogenesis inhibitors, are hereditary hemorrhagic telangiectasia [109], and various forms of ocular neovascularization, including common age-related macular degeneration [110].

– MTOR pathway inhibitors

Tuberous sclerosis is an inherited disease that is characterized by the early development of hamartomatous growths of varying types, in many different organs, including: brain, kidneys, lungs, heart, skin, eyes, and pancreas. Hamartomas are benign, malformative overgrowths of tissues. The tubers of tuberous sclerosis, from which the disorder takes its name, are focally thickened, pale gyri of the brain cortex. Seizures, intellectual delay, and autism are commonly found in individuals with this disorder.

As discussed previously, root genetic mutation associated with the majority of cases of tuberous sclerosis is a mutation of either the TSC1 gene, coding for the protein hamartin, or in the TSC2 gene, which codes for the protein tuberin. Either of these mutations result in the hyperactivation of the mammalian target of rapamycin (mTOR) signaling pathway. Consequently, inhibitors of the convergent mTOR pathway, such as sirolimus, everolimus and rapamycin, are considered potential drugs for managing the growth of hamartomas and developmental disorders arising from mTOR pathway overactivity in this inherited syndrome [111].

As it happens, the mTOR signaling pathway ties into several other important pathways and the mTOR inhibitors have been proposed as potential drugs in the treatment of various diseases in which mTOR participates, including Alzheimer disease, cancers, and aging-related disorders, and as a preventive measure against transplant rejection [112].

– Unidentified pulmonary hypertension pathway

Pulmonary hypertension can occur as an inherited condition or as an acquired condition following hypoxia, thromboembolism, left-sided heart failure, or drugs and inherited pulmonary hypertension. Regardless of the cause, all forms of pulmonary hypertension seem to be associated with one signaling pathway involving several proteins, including angiopoietin-1, TIE2 (endothelial-specific receptor for angiopoietin-1), BMPR1A (bone morphogenetic protein receptor 1A), and BMPR2 (bone morphogenetic protein receptor 1A) [51]. If this is the case, then any of these proteins would serve as candidate targets for new drugs that may prove to be effective against all forms of pulmonary hypertension.

– CD1a as a therapeutic target in inflammatory skin diseases

The CD1a molecule is expressed abundantly in Langerhans cells, a reticuloendothelial cell that inhabits skin. Some types of inflammatory responses in skin are triggered by CD1a, and these happen to include the response pathway observed in poison ivy allergy (i.e., reaction to the plant-derived lipid urushiol) and in psoriasis. Treatment with antibodies blocking CD1a reduced the inflammatory responses in both diseases [113]. Hence, drugs targeted to CD1a may be potentially useful for any inflammatory diseases wherein the CD1a-initiated inflammatory pathway operates.

– JAK2 inhibitors for myeloproliferative disorders, particularly those with splenomegaly

Janus Kinase genes (e.g., AK1, JAK2, JAK3, TYK2) influence growth and immune response in various types of blood cells, through their effect on cytokines. Mutations of the JAK2 gene are involved in several myeloproliferative conditions, including myelofibrosis, polycythemia vera, and at least one form of hereditary thrombocythemia [114–116]. Inhibitors of JAK genes have been approved for the treatment of a wide range of hematologic disorders characterized by proliferating blood cells, including myeloproliferative disorders and immunologic reactions. For example, Ruxolitinib has been approved, in the United States for use in psoriasis, myelofibrois, and rheumatoid arthritis [117]. A host of JAK pathway inhibitors are either approved or under clinical trials for the treatment of allergic diseases, rheumatoid arthritis, psoriasis, myelofibrosis, myeloproliferative disorders, acute myeloid leukemia, and relapsed lymphoma [118].

The specific JAK2 mutation observed in some, but not all, myeloproliferative neoplasms is JAK2V617F [119,120]. Because the JAK2 inhibitors currently in use cannot discriminate between wild-type and mutant JAK2 enzymes, they exert an effect on all proliferating hematopoietic cells, neoplastic or normal, and relieve the debilitating conditions that accompany myeloproliferative disorders, such as splenomegaly and constitutional symptoms that result from inflammation triggered by blood cells (e.g., fever) [121]. This serves as an example where drugs targeting a pathway (i.e., the JAK2 pathway) and not the specific mutant protein (i.e., JAK2V617F) provide a wide array of benefits to individuals with a range of JAK2-related diseases. [Glossary Wild-type gene]

- Pembrolizumab for any tumor that has microsatellite instability or is mismatch repair deficient

Regardless of type of tumor, if the tumor demonstrates high microsatellite instability or is mismatch repair deficient, then the tumor may respond to treatment with Pembrolizumab [122]. Microsatellite instabilities and mismatch repair deficiencies are commonly found in colorectal, endometrial, and gastrointestinal cancers.

- Cytokine storm inhibitors

Hemophagocytic lymphohistiocytosis is a rare condition characterized by widespread proliferation of lymphocytes and the engorgement of macrophages by red blood cells. This condition is always life threatening and can quickly progress to hyperpyrexia, shock, and multiorgan failure. Hemophagocytic lymphohistiocytosis can occur in genetic form, in infants, or as an acquired condition following infections (e.g., Epstein-Barr virus), or may occur in association with several genetic diseases [123,124]. Every form of hemophagocytic lymphohistiocytosis, regardless of the different pathogeneses, will converge to a pathway that calls into action an inflammatory response characterized by the secretion of large amounts of cytokines, vividly referred to as a cytokine storm. Knowing the converged pathway common to all cases of hemophagocytic lymphohistiocytosis provides us with a therapeutic opportunity. Drug development for the treatment of the convergent cytokine storm pathway is an active area of research [125,126]. [Glossary Familial hemophagocytic lymphohistiocytosis]

- C-KIT inhibitors

Gastrointestinal stromal tumor (GIST) is a soft-tissue tumor that often contains a mutation in the c-KIT gene [127]. As it happens, not all GISTs have the c-KIT mutation [128,129]. An alternate mutation, in the Platelet-Derived Growth Factor Receptor-alpha gene (PDGFR-alpha), was shown to be the root cause of a minority of GIST cases. Mutations in the gene coding for PDGFR-alpha or c-kit proteins lead to phenotypically identical GIST tumors, and cause activation of the same tyrosine kinase pathway. Most importantly, GISTs associated with either gene benefit from imatinib treatments [130].

Imatinib (trade name Gleevec) inhibits tyrosine kinase, an enzyme involved in a pathway that drives the growth of various rare tumors and proliferative diseases (e.g., chronic myelogenous leukemia, gastrointestinal stromal tumor, hypereosinophilic syndrome) [128,131–134]. Pathways with increased tyrosine kinase activity, and pathways whose tyrosine kinase activity are particularly sensitive to the inhibiting action of imatinib would make the best drug targets. Because imatinib is targeted to a key protein in a general pathway that contributes to a proliferative phenotype, it can benefit a variety of different diseases.

– Treat the key pathway, not the mutation

Some of the earliest and most successful Precision Medication drugs have targeted specific mutations occurring in specific subsets of diseases. One such example is ivacaftor, which targets the G551D mutation present in about 4% of individuals with cystic fibrosis [135]. It is seldom wise to argue with success, but it must be mentioned that the cost of developing a new drug is about $5 billion [136]. To provide some perspective, $5 billion exceeds the total gross national product of many countries, including Sierra Leone, Swaziland, Suriname, Guyana, Liberia, and the Central African Republic. Many factors contribute to the development costs, but the most significant is the incredibly high failure rate of candidate drugs. About 95% of the experimental medicines that are studied in humans fail to be both effective and safe. The costs of drug development are reflected in the rising costs of drugs. [Glossary Translational research]

When a new drug is marketed to a very small population of affected individuals, the cost of treating an individual may be astronomical. Americans should not pin their hopes on the belief that one day, the FDA or CMS (which administrates Medicare) will step in and put a stop to the price rises. The Food and Drug Administration can approve or reject drugs, but it does not regulate prices. Likewise, Medicare is not permitted to consider cost when it decides whether a treatment can be covered. Knowing this, some notable pharmaceutical companies have raised the prices of medications far beyond their manufacturing costs [137–139]. In effect, the cost of curing curable diseases may exceed our ability to pay for those cures [139].

It is strongly in the interests of society to develop drugs that have the widest possible user market [140]. Drugs that target a mutation that is specific for a few individuals with a rare disease, or a tiny subpopulation of individuals who have a common disease, are highly problematic.

Our experiences with disease convergence teach us that clinical phenotypes are influenced by the activities of pathways and are seldom restricted to a specific mutation in a specific gene. We know this because rare diseases that exhibit locus heterogeneity affect different genes, but often target the same pathway. Likewise, acquired phenotypes of genetic diseases often involve inhibitors of the same key pathways that drive their genetic counterparts, without involving the protein product of the genetic form of the disease. We also know that the acquired version of most genetic diseases account for the bulk of disease occurrences. Therefore, if we want to develop treatments that benefit the greatest number of individuals affected by a disease, it would be far more practical to find treatments that target the disease-driving pathways than to design drugs that target a specific gene mutation involved in a small subset of affected patients.

Before closing this section, here are a few summary points worth considering:

– As a generalization, any drug that can block a pathway, without producing serious side effects, may serve as a candidate treatment for all of the diseases that are driven by the pathway.

- Individuals in the early stages of common diseases, before multiple disease pathways converge to produce an intractable clinical phenotype, may be particularly amenable to treatments that interfere with the pathways that promote the ensuing steps in pathogenesis.

The topic of clinical trials designed to test drugs targeting convergent disease pathways will be further discussed in Section 9.6, "Fast, Cheap, Precise Clinical Trials."

Glossary

Angiogenesis The formation of new vessels. Angiogenesis in the adult organism always refers to the growth of small vessels, not arteries and veins. The large vessels in the human body develop in utero. Tumor cells must receive oxygen from blood; hence, every invasive and growing solid tumor is capable of inducing angiogenesis. As the tumor grows, so do the vessels feeding the tumor. The vessels arise from nonneoplastic connective tissue and are induced to grow by angiogenesis factors secreted by the tumor cells. Because every solid tumor must develop its own vasculature, angiogenesis is a universal feature of all solid tumors. The so-called liquid tumors (i.e., leukemias and myeloproliferative syndromes) do not grow as solid masses, receiving oxygen directly from the blood in which they circulate. Hence, angiogenesis would not be a constitutive property of leukemias. Because angiogenesis is a necessary biological step in the pathogenesis of all solid tumors, angiogenesis inhibitors (e.g., bevacizumab, sorafenib, sunitinib, pazopanib, and everolimus) are used in the treatment of various cancers. Angiogenesis inhibitors may have some value in treating disorders that are characterized by an overgrowth of new vessels [108–110,141].

Autoantibody disease versus autoimmune disease The two terms are often used interchangeably, but they probably represent to pathogenetically distinct conditions. Autoantibody diseases occur when the adaptive immune system synthesizes antibodies against some normal body constituent. In most cases, as far as anyone can tell, individuals with the common autoantibody diseases have normal functioning immune systems. For some unspecified reason (e.g., an antigen in an infectious organism elicits antibodies that happen to crossreact with a normal cellular protein), a pathological antibody is produced, occasionally having clinical consequences. In autoimmune diseases, there is a primary dysfunction of the immune system, often producing an array of clinical sequelae, including the synthesis of one or more antibodies that react against self antigens [142].

Carcinoid syndrome Carcinoids are tumors of neuroendocrine cells that derive from endoderm (i.e., the embryologic layer that gives rise to the epithelium of the lung and gastrointestinal tract). Carcinoids may secrete serotonin-like hormones, which are normally deactivated in the liver. When carcinoids metastasize to the liver, the normal deactivation of serotonin-like molecules, received through the portal vein, is bypassed. Subsequently, patients may develop a paraneoplastic syndrome produced by hormones synthesized by the tumor: carcinoid syndrome.

Channelopathy Disorders of the electrical systems in humans, all of which depend on the depolarization and repolarization of electrical current (i.e., the flux of charged molecules), across ion channels (e.g., sodium channel, potassium channel, chloride channel, calcium channel). Ion channels are found on the membranes of specialized cells. Disorders of these channels are termed channelopathies, and encompass a wide range of neural, cardiac, and muscular disorders and always play at least a contributing role in common seizures and arrhythmias. Specific rare conditions in which channel disorders play a principal role, in at least some forms of the disease, include: Alternating hemiplegia of childhood, Bartter syndrome, Brugada syndrome, Congenital hyperinsulinism, Cystic fibrosis, Dravet Syndrome (Severe Myoclonic Epilepsy of Infancy), Episodic Ataxia, Erythromelalgia (Mitchell disease), Generalized epilepsy with febrile seizures plus, Familial hemiplegic migraine, Hyperkalemic periodic paralysis, Hypokalemic periodic paralysis, Long QT syndrome, Malignant hyperthermia, Mucolipidosis type IV, Myasthenia Gravis, Myotonia congenita, Neuromyotonia, Nonsyndromic deafness, Paramyotonia congenita, Retinitis pigmentosa, Short QT syndrome, and Timothy syndrome.

Collagenopathy A variety of clinical conditions involving genetic alterations of the various collagen genes or other genes involved in the complex processes of collagen synthesis. Lists of clinical collagenopathies usually include Ehlers-Danlos syndrome, Osteogenesis imperfecta, familial aneurysmal disorders or aortic dissection disorders, Caffey disease (infantile cortical hyperostosis), and Bruck syndrome. Some of the noncollagen genes involved in collagenopathies include the ACTA2 gene (thoracic aortic aneurysms and aortic dissection), PLOD2 gene (procollagen-lysine dioxygenase 2 involved in Bruck syndrome). Collagenopathies may involve mutations in noncollagen genes that influence collagen synthesis, such as those involved in familial aneurysm disorders (e.g., smad3, tgfbr1, tgfbr2, and tgfb2). There are over 17 genes coding for the different species of collagen molecules.

DNA polymorphism The different alleles for a gene occurring among various members of a population (i.e., variants in the species gene pool). DNA polymorphisms usually consist of small differences in nucleotide sequence or to variable numbers of repeated nucleotide units

End-stage condition A set of pathologic features that represent the typical morphologic status of an organ that has suffered a series of events rendering the organ poorly functioning; with no reasonable expectation that the organ will regain normal function. The term "end-stage" evokes the idea that many different diseases will follow pathways that converge to the same pathological outcome for the organ. Every organ has its own brand of "end-stage" condition. For example, an end-stage condition for many different types of heart disease is dilated cardiomyopathy, characterized by cardiac dilation and reduced systolic function. Dilated cardiomyopathy is a common outcome of many different acquired and inherited heart diseases, including myocarditis, coronary artery disease, systemic diseases, and myocardial toxins. Dilated cardiomyopathy can occur in children or adults and is the primary indication for cardiac transplantation [143].

Familial hemophagocytic lymphohistiocytosis A rare disease of early childhood, characterized by lymphocytosis (i.e., increased blood lymphocytes) and rapidly enlarging lymph nodes infiltrated by lymphocytes and histiocytes, many of which are seen engulfing red blood cells (i.e., phagocytosis). The underlying defect in this disease is the absence of functional perforin. Perforin is a cytolytic protein expressed by activated cytotoxic lymphocytes and natural killer cells. Without perforin, lymphocytes and histiocytes cannot adequately destroy organisms. In such cases, lymphocytes and histiocytes accumulate and release cytokines, in an ineffectual response to infection.

Gain-of-function Occurs when a mutation produces a new type of functionality for a gene. It should be noted that the new functionality gained by such mutations are seldom beneficial. They represent a "gain" only in the restricted sense that the mutated gene does something that is different from normal. Most mutations in a gene produce no effect or they reduce the functionality or the expression (e.g., the quantity of expressed protein) of the gene. It is unusual for a mutation to produce a gain in function, and it turns out that most gain-of-function mutations are unique to the disease they cause. For example, everyone with sickle cell disease, caused by a gain-of-function mutation, has precisely the same point mutation causing glutamic acid to be replaced by valine in the sixth position of the beta-globin chain in hemoglobin. Other diseases wherein a particular gain-of-function mutation accounts for most or all affected individuals are hemochromatosis and achondroplasia. Nephrogenic syndrome of inappropriate antidiuresis is an exception to the general rule, being caused by one of two gain-of-function mutations in the same gene.

Hereditary nonpolyposis colorectal cancer syndrome (HNPCC) A hereditary cancer syndrome characterized by an increased risk of colorectal cancer, endometrial cancer, and cancers of the ovary, stomach, small intestine, hepatobiliary tract, upper urinary tract, brain, and skin. The syndrome is associated with mutations that impair DNA mismatch repair.

Identification The process of providing a data object with an identifier, or the process of distinguishing one data object from all other data objects on the basis of its associated identifier.

Knockout mice Strains of laboratory mice in which a specific gene has been knocked out or replaced. Every mouse in the strain has the identical gene deletion in every cell of its body. The primary purpose of producing knockout mouse strains is to show us how the organism behaves in the absence of the gene, thus providing some insight to the normal regulation and system-wide function of the gene. Knockout mice have been used in the study of cancer, obesity, heart disease, diabetes, arthritis, substance abuse, anxiety, aging, and Parkinson disease. About 15% of gene knockouts are developmentally lethal, which means that the genetically altered embryos cannot grow into adult mice. As a rule, highly conserved genes play some important role during the development of the organism or the reproductive life of the organism; otherwise, the genes would not be conserved. Hence, we would expect that the highly conserved genes would not serve well when trying to produce new strains of knockout mice. As it happens, all of the oncogenes are highly conserved. When you try to create a knockout mouse strain with an oncogene or knock-in a dysfunctional oncogene, we would expect, and we sometimes see, lethality in the embryo [144].

Lynch syndrome Eponymous equivalent of hereditary nonpolyposis colorectal cancer syndrome.

Microsatellite Also known as Simple Sequence Repeats (SSRs), microsatellites are DNA sequences consisting of repeating units of 1–4 base pairs. Microsatellites are inherited and polymorphic. Within a population, there may be wide variation in the number of repeats at a chosen microsatellite locus. Friedreich ataxia, a neurodegenerative disease characterized by ataxia and an assortment of neurologic and muscular deficits, is an example of a microsatellite disease. A common molecular abnormality of Friedreich ataxia is a GAA trinucleotide repeat expansion within an intron belonging to the gene encoding frataxin. Normal levels of frataxin are apparently necessary for the health of nerve cells and muscle cells [145].

Microsatellite instability When there is a deficiency of proper mismatch repair (a type of DNA repair), DNA replication is faulty, and novel microsatellites appear in chromosomes. This phenomenon is called microsatellite instability, and it is observed in various types of cancer. It is present in almost every colon cancer occurring in Hereditary Nonpolyposis Colorectal Cancer syndrome.

Non-Mendelian inheritance A term that most commonly refers to inheritance due to a combination of polymorphisms (i.e., gene variants) that are prevalent within a family. In non-Mendelian inheritance, it is possible that neither the mother nor the father will carry the complete set of gene variants that cause inherited disease, but that the combination of disease-causing gene variants will occur in an offspring, through meiotic recombination. Generally, Mendelian inheritance is monogenic; Non-Mendelian inheritance is polygenic. Diseases that have Mendelian patterns of inheritance tend to be less common than diseases with polygenic inheritance.

Non-Mendelian inherited genetic disease Genetic diseases that do not exhibit the ratios of trait inheritance described by Mendel. Specifically, diseases with an autosomal dominant inheritance pattern would be expected in half the offspring of a couple in which one parent was affected. A recessive inheritance pattern would be expected in one-quarter of offspring in which each parent carried one recessive gene. Polygenic diseases (i.e., in which altered variants must occur in multiple genes for the expression of disease) are never Mendelian. In addition, monogenic diseases that might be expected to display a Mendelian inheritance pattern may become non-Mendelian due to a variety of confounding factors not fully discussed herein (e.g., allelic heterogeneity, epistasis, expressivity, genetic heterogeneity, incomplete dominance, lethal genotypes, penetrance, phenocopies, pleiotropy). It is important to keep in mind that the DNA sequence of a gene is not the only determinant of the activity of a gene product. Every step of gene activity is subject to regulation and to individual variation, and this would include splicing, protein folding, protein transport, and compartmentalization of the protein produce [146]. The term "non-Mendelian" inheritance is seldom actually used, because most inherited diseases do not strictly follow Mendel's ratio rules for inheritance. Practical geneticists cut Mendel a little slack.

Paraneoplastic syndrome Clinical disorders attributed to a cancer but not produced by the destructive growth of the tumor (i.e., not due to tumor growth or invasion or metastasis). The majority of paraneoplastic syndromes are caused by humoral factors released by the tumor. Examples of paraneoplastic syndromes include: acanthosis nigricans, Eaton-Lambert syndrome, carcinoid syndrome, hyperthermia of malignancy, hypoglycemia, limbic encephalopathy, night sweats of malignancy, sign of Leser-Trelat, some cases of anemia of malignancy, wasting disease of malignancy, malignancy-associated autoimmune hemolytic anemia, and opsoclonic-myoclonic ataxia.

Polygenic disease A disease whose underlying cause involves alterations in multiple genes. In general, the development of polygenic diseases is highly dependent upon environmental modifiers that trigger bouts of disease, that enhance or reduce susceptibility to disease, or that sometimes serve as the apparent root cause of the disease.

Prion disease Everyone has heard the aphorism: "One bad apple spoils the bunch." This trite adage seems to be the principle underlying the prion diseases. A prion is a misfolded protein that can somehow serve as a template for proteins of the same type to misfold, producing collections of nonfunctioning protein globs that accumulate, causing cells to degenerate. The cells of the body that are most vulnerable to prion-produced disease are the neurons of the brain. The reason for the particular sensitivity of neurons to prion disease relates to the limited ability of neurons to replicate (i.e., to replace damaged neurons with new neurons), reconnect (to replace damaged connections between a neuron and other cells), and to remove degenerated cells and debris. The term prion was introduced in 1982 by Stanley Prusiner [147]. Prions are the only infectious agent that contain neither DNA nor RNA. Though few scientists would consider prions to be organisms, living or otherwise, they are included here to ensure that readers are aware of these biological agents. Prions are not confined to mammals. They have been observed in fungi, where their accumulation does not seem to produce any deleterious effect and may even be advantageous to the organism [148]. There are five known prion diseases of humans, and all of them produce encephalopathies characterized by decreasing cognitive ability and impaired motor coordination. At present, all of the human prion disease are progressive and fatal. Infectious species include: Kuru prion (Kuru); CJD prion (Creutzfeldt-Jakob disease, CJD); nvCJD prion, or vCJD prion, or Bovine Spongiform Encephalopathy prion (New variant Creutzfeldt-Jakob disease, vCJD, nvCJD); GSS prion (Gerstmann-Straussler-Scheinker syndrome, GSS); and FFI prion (Fatal familial insomnia, FFI) [149].

Schwannoma A tumor composed of neoplastic Schwann cells; cells that are normally found wrapped around the axonal extensions of peripheral nervous system neurons. Schwannomas of the acoustic spinal nerves occur in neurofibromatosis type 2.

Sporadic disease versus phenocopy disease A sporadic disease is a disease with no known cause. A phenocopy disease is a nongenetic disease that mimics a genetic disease. Despite the clear-cut difference in the two definitions, it is often impossible to distinguish sporadic diseases from phenocopy diseases, because the distinction often relies upon information that is not available. For example, if a patient presents with the clinical features of a well-described genetic disease, but lacks the genetic biomarker for the disease, we might say that the disease is sporadic (i.e., of no known cause). Nonetheless, we know that diseases do not arise spontaneously. Even sporadic diseases have a causal pathogenesis; and if the pathogenesis is not genetic, it must be acquired. Hence, when a genetic cause is ruled out, we are tempted to say that the sporadic disease is a phenocopy (i.e., a clinical mimic without a root genetic cause). But suppose that further research shows that the presumptive sporadic disease has a root genetic cause that is different from the genetic mutation that had been previously identified in cases of the inherited disease. In this case, the disease is no longer sporadic (i.e., without known cause) and no longer a phenocopy (i.e., without genetic cause). Everything we thought to be true is now false, and it's all because we did not know the full story when we committed our errors. These kinds of misjudgements arise all the time in Precision Medicine. We must always remind ourselves that our conclusions are tentative and must be constantly re-examined.

Transcription factor A protein that binds to specific DNA sequences to control the transcription of DNA to RNA. Some of the most phenotypically complex rare disease syndromes are caused by single gene mutations that code for transcription factors and other regulatory elements [150]. Examples include: mutation in the gene encoding transcription factor TBX5 producing Holt-Oram syndrome consisting of hand malformations, heart defects, and other malformations. As another example, a mutation in the gene encoding microphthalmia-associated transcription factor, MITF, produces Waardenburg syndrome 2A, characterized by lateral displacement of the inner canthus of both eyes, pigmentary disturbances of hair and iris, white eyelashes, leukoderma, and cochlear deafness.

Translation factor Also called initiation factor or, more precisely, translation initiation factor. These factors facilitate the initiation of protein synthesis from mRNA by forming a complex with ribosomal RNA. Mutations in the eukaryotic initiation factor EIF2B gene result in leukoencephalopathy with vanishing white matter. Pathogenic mutations in any one of five genes encoding subunits of EIF2B may occur [151]. Amazingly, these five genes, that contribute to the eventual synthesis of one aggregate protein, are located on five different chromosomes.

Translational research Scientific activities aimed at finding applications for basic research discoveries. The term is roughly equivalent to the older term "Development," as it appears in R&D (Research and Development).

Wild-type gene The functional, nonmutated gene found naturally in a population.

References

[1] Bernstein L. 20 percent of patients with serious conditions are first misdiagnosed, study says. Washington Post; April 4, 2017.

[2] Agarwal S, Moorchung N. Modifier genes and oligogenic disease. J Nippon Med Sch 2005;72:326–34.

[3] Martin DIK, Cropley JE, Suter CM. Epigenetics in disease: leader or follower? Epigenetics 2011;6:843–8.

[4] Van der Groep P, Bouter A, van der Zanden R, Siccama I, Menko FH, Gille JJP, et al. Distinction between hereditary and sporadic breast cancer on the basis of clinicopathological data. J Clin Pathol 2006;59:611–7.

[5] Boland CR. Clinical uses of microsatellite instability testing in colorectal cancer: an ongoing challenge. J Clin Oncol 2007;25:754–6.

[6] Gambetti P, Cali I, Notari S, Kong Q, Zou WQ, Surewicz WK. Molecular biology and pathology of prion strains in sporadic human prion diseases. Acta Neuropathol 2011;121:79–90.

[7] Hill AF, Joiner S, Wadsworth JD, Sidle KC, Bell JE, Budka H, et al. Molecular classification of sporadic Creutzfeldt-Jakob disease. Brain 2003;126:1333–46.

[8] Oti M, Brunner HG. The modular nature of genetic diseases. Clin Genet 2007;71:1–11.

[9] Brice G, Child AH, Evans A, Bell R, Mansour S, Burnand K, et al. Milroy disease and the VEGFR-3 mutation phenotype. J Med Genet 2005;42:98–102.

[10] Gordon K, Spiden SL, Connell FC, Brice G, Cottrell S, Short J, et al. Hum Mutat FLT4/VEGFR3 and Milroy disease: novel mutations, a review of published variants and database update. Hum Mutat 2013;34: 23–31.

[11] Gordon K, Schulte D, Brice G, Simpson MA, Roukens MG, van Impel A, et al. Mutation in vascular endothelial growth factor-C, a ligand for vascular endothelial growth factor receptor-3, is associated with autosomal dominant milroy-like primary lymphedema. Circ Res 2013;112:956–60.

[12] Lifton RP, Gharavi AG, Geller DS. Molecular mechanisms of human hypertension. Cell 2001;104:545–56.

[13] Li K, Wahlqvist ML, Li D. Nutrition, One-carbon metabolism and neural tube defects: a review. Nutrients 2016;8:741.

[14] Klupa T, Skupien J, Malecki MT. Monogenic models: what have the single gene disorders taught us? Curr Diab Rep 2012;12:659–66.

[15] Hou JW. Fetal warfarin syndrome. Chang Gung Med J 2004;27:691–5.

[16] Munroe PB, Olgunturk RO, Fryns JP, Van Maldergem L, Ziereisen F, Yuksel B, et al. Mutations in the gene encoding the human matrix Gla protein cause Keutel syndrome. Nat Genet 1999;21:142–4.

[17] Toyo-Oka T, Kawada T, Nakata J, Xie H, Urabe M, Masui F, et al. Translocation and cleavage of myocardial dystrophin as a common pathway to advanced heart failure: a scheme for the progression of cardiac dysfunction. Proc Natl Acad Sci U S A 2004;101:7381–5.

[18] Novarino G, Akizu N, Gleeson JG. Modeling human disease in humans: the ciliopathies. Cell 2011;147:70–9.

[19] Ware SM, Aygun MG, Hildebrandt F. Spectrum of clinical diseases caused by disorders of primary cilia. Proc Am Thorac Soc 2011;8:444–850.

[20] Satir P. CILIA: before and after. Cilia 2017;6:1.

[21] Jakobsen L, Vanselow K, Skogs M, Toyoda Y, Lundberg E, Poser I, et al. Novel asymmetrically localizing components of human centrosomes identified by complementary proteomics methods. EMBO J 2011;30:1520–35.

[22] Tang Z, Zhu M, Zhong Q. Self-eating to remove cilia roadblock. Autophagy 2014;10:379–81.

[23] Tang Z, Chen Z, Tang B, Jiang H. Primary erythromelalgia: a review. Orphanet J Rare Dis 2015;10:127.

[24] Houlston RS, Collins A, Slack J, Morton NE. Dominant genes for colorectal cancer are not rare. Hum Genet 1992;56:99–103.

[25] Whiffin N, Houlston RS. Architecture of inherited susceptibility to colorectal cancer: a voyage of discovery. Genes (Basel) 2014;5:270–84.

[26] Jovanovic I, Stefanovic N, Antic S, Ugrenovic S, Djindjic B, Vidovic N. Morphological and morphometric characteristics of choroid plexus psammoma bodies during the human aging. Ital J Anat Embryol 2004;109:19–33.

[27] Rifai Z, Welle S, Kamp C, Thornton CA. Ragged red fibers in normal aging and inflammatory myopathy. Ann Neurol 1995;37:24–9.

[28] Loiseau H, Marchal C, Vital A, Vital C, Rougier A, Loiseau P. Polysaccharide bodies: an unusual finding in a case of temporal epilepsy. Review of the literature. Rev Neurol (Paris) 1993;149:192–7.

[29] Chevessier F, Marty I, Paturneau-Jouas M, Hantai D, Verdiere-Sahuque M. Tubular aggregates are from whole sarcoplasmic reticulum origin: alterations in calcium binding protein expression in mouse skeletal muscle during aging. Neuromuscul Disord 2004;14:208–16.

[30] Doerschuk CM. Pulmonary alveolar proteinosis—is host defense awry? N Engl J Med 2007;356:547–9.

[31] Croxen R, Vincent A, Newsom-Davis J, Beeson D. Myasthenia gravis in a woman with congenital AChR deficiency due to epsilon-subunit mutations. Neurology 2002;58:1563–5.

[32] Ku NO, Wright TL, Terrault NA, Gish R, Omary MB. Mutation of human keratin 18 in association with cryptogenic cirrhosis. J Clin Invest 1997;99:19–23.

[33] Verpy E, Biasotto M, Brai M, Misiano G, Meo T, Tosi M. Exhaustive mutation scanning by fluorescence-assisted mismatch analysis discloses new genotype-phenotype correlations in angiodema. Am J Hum Genet 1996;59:308–19.

[34] Dobzhansky T. Genetics of the evolutionary process. New York: Columbia University Press; 1970.

[35] Solomon BD, Muenke M. When to suspect a genetic syndrome. Am Fam Physician 2012;86:826–33.

[36] Hayden MR, Clee SM, Brooks-Wilson A, Genest Jr J, Attie A, Kastelein JJ. Cholesterol efflux regulatory protein, Tangier disease and familial high-density lipoprotein deficiency. Curr Opin Lipidol 2000;11:117–22.

[37] Huang W, Moriyama K, Koga T, Hua H, Ageta M, Kawabata S, et al. Novel mutations in ABCA1 gene in Japanese patients with Tangier disease and familial high density lipoprotein deficiency with coronary heart disease. Biochim Biophys Acta 2001;1537:71–8.

[38] Ng SB, Buckingham KJ, Lee C, Bigham AW, Tabor HK, Dent KM, et al. Exome sequencing identifies the cause of a mendelian disorder. Nat Genet 2010;42:30–5.

[39] Piano MR. Alcoholic cardiomyopathy: incidence, clinical characteristics, and pathophysiology. Chest 2002;121:1638–50.

[40] Zhu H-L, Meng S-R, Fan J-B, Chen J, Liang Y. Fibrillization of human tau is accelerated by exposure to lead via interaction with His-330 and His-362. PLoS One 2011;6:e25020.

[41] Wang E, Boswell E, Siddiqi I, CM L, Sebastian S, Rehder C, et al. Pseudo-Pelger-Huet anomaly induced by medications: a clinicopathologic study in comparison with myelodysplastic syndrome-related pseudo-Pelger-Hu t anomaly. Am J Clin Pathol 2011;135:291–303.

[42] Juneja SK, Matthews JP, Luzinat R, Fan Y, Michael M, Rischin D, et al. Association of acquired Pelger-Huet anomaly with taxoid therapy. Br J Haematol 1996;93:139–41.

[43] Schule B, Oviedo A, Johnston K, Pai S, Francke U. Inactivating mutations in ESCO2 cause SC phocomelia and Roberts syndrome: no phenotype-genotype correlation. Am J Hum Genet 2005;77:1117–28.

[44] Franco B, Meroni G, Parenti G, Levilliers J, Bernard L, Gebbia M, et al. A cluster of sulfatase genes on Xp22.3: mutations in chondrodysplasia punctata (CDPX) and implications for warfarin embryopathy. Cell 1995;81:1–20.

[45] Van Gaalen J, Kerstens FG, Maas RP, Harmark L, van de Warrenburg BP. Drug-induced cerebellar ataxia: a systematic review. CNS Drugs 2014;28:1139–53.

[46] Rossi M, Perez-Lloret S, Doldan L, Cerquetti D, Balej J, Millar Vernetti P, et al. Autosomal dominant cerebellar ataxias: a systematic review of clinical features. Eur J Neurol 2014;21:607–15.

[47] Penneys NS. Ochronosislike pigmentation from hydroquinone bleaching creams. Arch Dermatol 1985;121:1239–40.

[48] Langston JW, Ballard P, Tetrud JW, Irwin I. Chronic parkinsonism in humans due to a product of meperidine-analog synthesis. Science 1983;219:979–80.

[49] Priyadarshi A, Khuder SA, Schaub EA, Shrivastava SA. Meta-analysis of Parkinson's disease and exposure to pesticides. Neurotoxicology 2000;21:435–40.

[50] Zimprich A, Biskup S, Leitner P, Lichtner P, Farrer M, Lincoln S, et al. Mutations in LRRK2 cause autosomal-dominant parkinsonism with pleomorphic pathology. Neuron 2004;44:601–7.

[51] Du L, Sullivan CC, Chu D, Cho AJ, Kido M, Wolf PL, et al. Signaling molecules in nonfamilial pulmonary hypertension. N Engl J Med 2003;348:500–9.

[52] DuBose TD. Experimental models of distal renal tubular acidosis. Semin Nephrol 1990;10:174–80.

[53] Weiss HJ, Rosove MH, Lages BA, Kaplan KL. Acquired storage pool deficiency with increased platelet-associated IgG: report of five cases. Am J Med 1980;69:711–7.

[54] Bleiberg J, Wallen M, Brodkin R, Applebaum I. Industrially acquired porphyria. Arch Dermatol 1964;89:793–7.

[55] Cam C, Nigogosyan G. Acquired toxic porphyria cutanea tarda due to hexachlorobenzene. JAMA 1963;183:88–91.

[56] Hardy K, Hardy PJ. 1st trimester miscarriage: four decades of study. Transl Pediatr 2015;4:189–200.

[57] Gallicano GI, Kouklis P, Bauer C, Yin M, Vasioukhin V, Degenstein L, et al. Desmoplakin is required early in development for assembly of desmosomes and cytoskeletal linkage. J Cell Biol 1998;143:2009–22.

[58] Suter CM, Martin DI, Ward RL. Germline epimutation of MLH1 in individuals with multiple cancers. Nat Genet 2004;36:497–501.

[59] Dayan CM, Daniels GH. Chronic autoimmune thyroiditis. N Engl J Med 1996;335:99–107.

[60] Wing K, Sakaguchi S. Regulatory T cells exert checks and balances on self tolerance and autoimmunity. Nat Immunol 2010;11:7–13.

[61] Jacobson DL, Gange SJ, Rose NR, Graham NM. Epidemiology and estimated population burden of selected autoimmune diseases in the United States. Clin Immunol Immunopathol 1997;84:223–43.

[62] Marson A, Housley WJ, Hafler DA. Genetic basis of autoimmunity. J Clin Invest 2015;125:2234–41.

[63] Vaidya B, Kendall-Taylor P, Pearce SHS. The genetics of autoimmune thyroid disease. J Clin Endocrinol Metab 2002;87:5385–97.

[64] Cheng MH, Anderson MS. Monogenic autoimmunity. Annu Rev Immunol 2012;30:393–427.

[65] Berman JJ. Rare diseases and orphan drugs: keys to understanding and treating common diseases. Cambridge, MA: Academic Press; 2014.

[66] Oursler JR, Labib RS, Ariss-Abdo L, Burke T, O'Keefe EJ, Anhalt GJ. Human autoantibodies against desmoplakins in paraneoplastic pemphigus. J Clin Invest 1992;89:1775–82.

[67] Commins SP, Platts-Mills TAE. Delayed anaphylaxis to red meat in patients with IgE specific for galactose alpha-1,3-galactose (alpha-gal). Curr Allergy Asthma Rep 2013;13:72–7.

[68] Furlan M, Lammle B. Aetiology and pathogenesis of thrombotic thrombocytopenic purpura and haemolytic uraemic syndrome: the role of von Willebrand factor-cleaving protease. Best Pract Res Clin Haematol 2001;14:437–54.

[69] Diaz-Gallo L, Martin J. Common genes in autoimmune diseases: a link between immune-mediated diseases. Expert Rev Clin Immunol 2012;8:107–9.

[70] Criswell LA, Pfeiffer KA, Lum RF, Gonzales B, Novitzke J, Kern M, et al. Analysis of families in the multiple autoimmune disease genetics consortium (madgc) collection: the ptpn22 620w allele associates with multiple autoimmune phenotypes. Am J Hum Genet 2005;76:561–71.

[71] Cotsapas C, Voight BF, Rossin E, Lage K, Neale BM, Wallace C, et al. Pervasive sharing of genetic effects in autoimmune disease. PLoS Genet 2011;7:e1002254.

[72] Lapiere JC, Woodley DT, Parente MG, Iwasaki T, Wynn KC, Christiano AM, et al. Epitope mapping of type VII collagen. Identification of discrete peptide sequences recognized by sera from patients with acquired epidermolysis bullosa. J Clin Invest 1993;92:1831–9.

[73] Domloge-Hultsch N, Gammon WR, Briggaman RA, Gil SG, Carter WG, Yancey KB. Epiligrin, the major human keratinocyte integrin ligand, is a target in both an acquired autoimmune and an inherited subepidermal blistering skin disease. J Clin Invest 1992;90:1628–33.

[74] Sakurai Y, Takeda T. Acquired hemophilia A: a frequently overlooked autoimmune hemorrhagic disorder. J Immunol Res 2014;2014:320674.

[75] Salomon O, Zivelin A, Livnat T, Dardik R, Loewenthal R, Avishai O, et al. Prevalence, causes, and characterization of factor XI inhibitors in patients with inherited factor XI deficiency. Blood 2003;101:4783–8.

[76] Lorand L, Velasco PT, Rinne JR, Amare M, Miller LK, Zucker ML. Autoimmune antibody (IgG Kansas) against the fibrin stabilizing factor (factor XIII) system. Proc Natl Acad Sci U S A 1988;85:232–6.

[77] Li Y, Song YH, Rais N, Connor E, Schatz D, et al. Autoantibodies to the extracellular domain of the calcium sensing receptor in patients with acquired hypoparathyroidism. J Clin Invest 1996;97:910–4.

[78] Pallais JC, Kifor O, Chen YB, Slovik D, Brown EM. Acquired hypocalciuric hypercalcemia due to autoantibodies against the calcium-sensing receptor. N Engl J Med 2004;351:362–9.

[79] Mitchell CA, Rowell JA, Hau L, Young JP, Salem HH. A fatal thrombotic disorder associated with an acquired inhibitor of protein C. N Engl J Med 1987;317:1638–42.

[80] Tsuji T, Imajo Y, Sawabe M, Kuniyuki S, Ishii M, Hamada T, et al. Acquired cutis laxa concomitant with nephrotic syndrome. Arch Dermatol 1987;123:1211–6.

[81] Frigas E. Angioedema with acquired deficiency of the C1 inhibitor: a constellation of syndromes. Mayo Clin Proc 1989;64:1269–75.

[82] Winqvist O, Karlsson FA, Kampe O. 21-Hydroxylase, a major autoantigen in idiopathic Addison's disease. Lancet 1992;339:1559–62.

[83] Larrick JW, Hyman ES. Acquired iron-deficiency anemia caused by an antibody against the transferrin receptor. N Engl J Med 1984;311:214–8.

[84] Stricker RB, Wong D, Saks SR, Corash L, Shuman MA. Acquired Bernard-Soulier syndrome. Evidence for the role of a 210,000-molecular weight protein in the interaction of platelets with von Willebrand factor. J Clin Invest 1985;76:1274–8.

[85] Dahlback B. Advances in understanding pathogenic mechanisms of thrombophilic disorders. Blood 2008;112:19–27.

[86] Dragon-Durey MA, Loirat C, Cloarec S, Macher MA, Blouin J, Nivet H, et al. Anti-factor H autoantibodies associated with atypical hemolytic uremic syndrome. J Am Soc Nephrol 2005;16:555–63.

[87] Stahl AL, Kristoffersson A, Olin AI, Olsson ML, Roodhooft AM, Proesmans W, et al. A novel mutation in the complement regulator clusterin in recurrent hemolytic uremic syndrome. Mol Immunol 2009;46:2236–43.

[88] Roodhooft AM, McLean RH, Elst E, Van Acker KJ. Recurrent haemolytic uraemic syndrome and acquired hypomorphic variant of the third component of complement. Pediatr Nephrol 1990;4:597–9.

[89] Helfgott SM, Mosciscki RA, San Martin J, Lorenzo C, Kieval R, McKenna M, et al. Correlation between antibodies to type II collagen and treatment outcome in bilateral progressive sensorineural hearing loss. Lancet 1991;337:387–9.

[90] International Consortium for Blood Pressure Genome-Wide Association Studies. Genetic variants in novel pathways influence blood pressure and cardiovascular disease risk. Nature 2011;478:103–9.

[91] Fisher RA. The correlation between relatives on the supposition of Mendelian inheritance. Trans R Soc Edinb 1918;52:399–433.

[92] Ward LD, Kellis M. Interpreting noncoding genetic variation in complex traits and human disease. Nat Biotechnol 2012;30:1095–106.

[93] Visscher PM, McEvoy B, Yang J. From Galton to GWAS: quantitative genetics of human height. Genet Res 2010;92:371–9.

[94] Hideaki Nakagawa H, Katsuyuki Miura K. Salt reduction in a population for the prevention of hypertension. Environ Health Prev Med 2004;9:123–9.

[95] Howell A, Cuzick J, Baum M, Buzdar A, Dowsett M, Forbes JF, et al. Results of the ATAC (Arimidex, Tamoxifen, Alone or in Combination) trial after completion of 5 years' adjuvant treatment for breast cancer. Lancet 2005;365:60–2.

[96] Stein R. Some of the best weapons in the precision medicine have a very dull blade. Breast cancer trial hailed as big leap. The Washington Post; June 6, 2011.

[97] Gelb BD. Marfan's syndrome and related disorders—more tightly connected than we thought. N Engl J Med 2006;355:841–4.

[98] Singh MN, Lacro RV. Recent clinical drug trials evidence in Marfan syndrome and clinical implications. Can J Cardiol 2016;32:66–77.

[99] Bar-Klein G, Cacheaux LP, Kamintsky L, Prager O, Weissberg I, Schoknecht K, et al. Losartan prevents acquired epilepsy via TGF-? signaling suppression. Ann Neurol 2014;75:864–75.

[100] Lim DS, Lutucuta S, Bachireddy P, Youker K, Evans A, Entman M, et al. Angiotensin II blockade reverses myocardial fibrosis in a transgenic mouse model of human hypertrophic cardiomyopathy. Circulation 2001;103:789–91.

[101] Cohn RD, van Erp C, Habashi JP, Soleimani AA, Klein EC, Lisi MT, et al. Angiotensin II type 1 receptor blockade attenuates TGF-beta-induced failure of muscle regeneration in multiple myopathic states. Nat Med 2007;13:204–10.

[102] Mehta HM, Malandra M, Corey SJ. G-CSF and GM-CSF in neutropenia. J Immunol 2015;195:1341–9.

[103] Wert SE, Whitsett JA, Nogee LM. Genetic disorders of surfactant dysfunction. Pediatr Dev Pathol 2009;12:253–74.

[104] Patel SM, Sekiguchi H, Reynolds JP, Krowka MJ. Pulmonary alveolar proteinosis. Can Respir J 2012;19:243–5.

[105] Martinez-Moczygemba M, Doan ML, Elidemir O, Fan LL, Cheung SW, Lei JT, et al. Pulmonary alveolar proteinosis caused by deletion of the GM-CSFRalpha gene in the X chromosome pseudoautosomal region 1. J Exp Med 2008;24:2711–6.

[106] Zsengeller ZK, Reed JA, Bachurski CJ, LeVine AM, Forry-Schaudies S, Hirsch R, et al. Adenovirus-mediated granulocyte- macrophage colony-stimulating factor improves lung pathology of pulmonary alveolar proteinosis in granulocyte-macrophage colony stimulating factor-deficient mice. Hum Gene Ther 1998;9:2101–9.

[107] Venkateshiah SB, Yan TD, Bonfield TL, Thomassen MJ, Meziane M, Czich C, et al. An open-label trial of granulocyte macrophage colony stimulating factor therapy for moderate symptomatic pulmonary alveolar proteinosis. Chest 2006;130:227–37.

[108] Plotkin SR, Merker VL, Halpin C, Jennings D, McKenna MJ, Harris GJ, et al. Bevacizumab for progressive vestibular schwannoma in neurofibromatosis type 2: a retrospective review of 31 patients. Otol Neurotol 2012;33:1046–52.

[109] Bose P, Holter JL, Selby GB. Bevacizumab in hereditary hemorrhagic telangiectasia. N Engl J Med 2009;360:2143–4.

[110] Eyetech Study Group. Anti-vascular endothelial growth factor therapy for subfoveal choroidal neovascularization secondary to age-related macular degeneration: phase II study results. Ophthalmology 2003;110:979–86.

[111] Curatolo P, Moavero R. mTOR inhibitors in tuberous sclerosis complex. Curr Neuropharmacol 2012;10:404–15.

[112] Tsang CK, Qi H, Liu LF, Zheng XF. Targeting mammalian target of rapamycin (mTOR) for health and diseases. Drug Discov Today 2007;12:112–24.

[113] Kim JH, Hu Y, Yongqing T, Kim J, Hughes VA, Le Nours J, et al. CD1a on Langerhans cells controls inflammatory skin disease. Nat Immunol 2016;17:1159–66.

[114] Mead AJ, Rugless MJ, Jacobsen SEW, Schuh A. Germline JAK2 mutation in a family with hereditary thrombocytosis. N Engl J Med 2012;366:967–9.

[115] Barosi G, Bergamaschi G, Marchetti M, Vannucchi AM, Guglielmelli P, Antonioli E, et al. JAK2 V617F mutational status predicts progression to large splenomegaly and leukemic transformation in primary myelofibrosis. Blood 2007;110:4030–6.

[116] Zhang L, Lin X. Some considerations of classification for high dimension low-sample size data. Stat Methods Med Res 2011. November 23. Available from: http://smm.sagepub.com/content/early/2011/11/22/0962280211428387.long.

[117] Mesa RA, Yasothan U, Kirkpatrick P. Ruxolitinib. Nat Rev Drug Discov 2012;11:103–4.

[118] Pesu M, Laurence A, Kishore N, Zwillich SH, Chan G, O'Shea JJ. Therapeutic targeting of Janus kinases. Immunol Rev 2008;223:132–42.

[119] McLornan D, Percy M, MF MM. JAK2 V617F: a single mutation in the myeloproliferative group of disorders. Ulster Med J 2006;75:112–9.

[120] Steensma DP, Dewald GW, Lasho TL, Powell HL, McClure RF, Levine RL, et al. The JAK2 V617F activating tyrosine kinase mutation is an infrequent event in both "atypical" myeloproliferative disorders and myelodysplastic syndromes. Blood 2005;106:1207–9.

[121] Verstovsek S. Therapeutic potential of JAK2 inhibitors. Hematology Am Soc Hematol Educ Program 2009;2009:636–42.

[122] FDA grants accelerated approval to pembrolizumab for first tissue/site agnostic indication. U.S. Food and Drug Administration; May 23, 2017.

[123] Dufourcq-Lagelouse R, Pastural E, Barrat FJ, Feldmann J, Le Deist F, Fischer A, et al. Genetic basis of hemophagocytic lymphohistiocytosis syndrome (Review). Int J Mol Med 1999;4:127–33.

[124] Janka G, zur Stadt U. Familial and acquired hemophagocytic lymphohistiocytosis. Hematology Am Soc Hematol Educ Program 2005;2005:82–8.

[125] D'Elia RV, Harrison K, Oyston PC, Lukaszewski RA, Clark GC. Targeting the cytokine storm for therapeutic benefit. Clin Vaccine Immunol 2013;20:319–27.

[126] Lee DW, Gardner R, Porter DL, Louis CU, Ahmed N, Jensen M, et al. Current concepts in the diagnosis and management of cytokine release syndrome. Blood 2014;124:188–95.

[127] Fletcher CD, Berman JJ, Corless C, Gorstein F, Lasota J, Longley BJ, et al. Diagnosis of gastrointestinal stromal tumors: a consensus approach. Int J Surg Pathol 2002;10:81–9.

[128] Berman J, O'Leary TJ. Gastrointestinal stromal tumor workshop. Hum Pathol 2001 Jun;32(6):578–82.

[129] O'leary T, Berman JJ. Gastrointestinal stromal tumors: answers and questions. Hum Pathol 2002;33:456–8.

[130] Burger H, den Bakker MA, Kros JM, van Tol H, de Bruin AM, Oosterhuis W, et al. Activating mutations in c-KIT and PDGFRalpha are exclusively found in gastrointestinal stromal tumors and not in other tumors overexpressing these imatinib mesylate target genes. Cancer Biol Ther 2005;4:1270–4.

[131] Heinrich MC, Joensuu H, Demetri GD, Corless CL, Apperley J, Fletcher JA, et al. Phase II, open-label study evaluating the activity of imatinib in treating life-threatening malignancies known to be associated with imatinib-sensitive tyrosine kinases. Clin Cancer Res 2008;14:2717–25.

[132] Heinrich MC, Corless CL, Demetri GD, Blanke CD, von Mehren M, Joensuu H, et al. Kinase mutations and imatinib response in patients with metastatic gastrointestinal stromal tumor. J Clin Oncol 2003;21:4342–9.

[133] Selvi N, Kaymaz BT, Sahin HH, Pehlivan M, Aktan C, Dalmizrak A, et al. Two cases with hypereosinophilic syndrome shown with real-time PCR and responding well to imatinib treatment. Mol Biol Rep 2013;40:1591–7.

[134] Cools J, DeAngelo DJ, Gotlib J, Stover EH, Legare RD, Cortes J, et al. A tyrosine kinase created by fusion of the PDGFRA and FIP1L1 genes as a therapeutic target of imatinib in idiopathic hypereosinophilic syndrome. N Engl J Med 2003;348:1201–14.

[135] Kotha K, Clancy JP. Ivacaftor treatment of cystic fibrosis patients with the G551D mutation: a review of the evidence. Ther Adv Respir Dis 2013;7:288–96.

[136] Herper M. The cost of creating a new drug now $5 billion, pushing big pharma to change. Forbes Magazine; August 11, 2013.

[137] Goldberg P. An Old drug's 21st century makeover begins with 84-fold price increase. Cancer Lett May 13, 2005.

[138] Berenson AA. Cancer drug's big price rise is cause for concern. New York Times; March 12, 2006.

[139] Vanchieri C. When will the U.S. flinch at cancer drug prices? J Natl Cancer Inst 2005;97:624–6.

[140] Hurley D. Why are so few blockbuster drugs invented today? The New York Times; November 13, 2014.

[141] Leung E, Landa G. Update on current and future novel therapies for dry age-related macular degeneration. Expert Rev Clin Pharmacol 2013;6:565–79.

[142] Lleo A, Invernizzi P, Gao B, Podda M, Gershwin ME. Definition of human autoimmunity—autoantibodies versus autoimmune disease. Autoimmun Rev 2010;9:A259–266.

[143] Olson TM, Keating MT. Mapping a cardiomyopathy locus to chromosome 3p22-p25. J Clin Invest 1996;97:528–32.

[144] Mercer K, Giblett S, Green S, Lloyd D, DaRocha Dias S, Plumb M, et al. Expression of endogenous oncogenic V600E B-raf induces proliferation and developmental defects in mice and transformation of primary fibroblasts. Cancer Res 2005;65:11493–500.

[145] Al-Mahdawi S, Pinto RM, Varshney D, Lawrence L, Lowrie MB, Hughes S, et al. GAA repeat expansion mutation mouse models of Friedreich ataxia exhibit oxidative stress leading to progressive neuronal and cardiac pathology. Genomics 2006;88:580–90.

[146] Van Heyningen V, Yeyati PL. Mechanisms of non-Mendelian inheritance in genetic disease. Hum Mol Genet 2004;13:R225–33.

[147] Prusiner SB. Novel proteinaceous infectious particles cause scrapie. Science 1982;216:136–44.

[148] Michelitsch MD, Weissman JS. A census of glutamine/asparagine-rich regions: Implications for their conserved function and the prediction of novel prions. PNAS 2000;97:11910–5.

[149] Berman JJ. Taxonomic guide to infectious diseases: understanding the biologic classes of pathogenic organisms. Waltham: Academic Press; 2012.

[150] Lee TI, Young RA. Transcriptional regulation and its misregulation in disease. Cell 2013;152:1237–51.

[151] Pavitt GD. EIF2B, a mediator of general and gene-specific translational control. Biochem Soc Trans 2005;33:1487–92.

The Precision of the Rare Diseases

SECTION 5.1 THE BIOLOGICAL DIFFERENCES BETWEEN RARE DISEASES AND COMMON DISEASES

History doesn't repeat itself, but it rhymes.
Attributed variously to Mark Twain and to Joseph Anthony Wittreich

As well as providing new approaches to carrier detection, prenatal diagnosis, and treatment of single gene disorders, these advances promise to provide important information about the pathophysiology of many common polygenic diseases.
Sir David Weatherall [1]

If you were asked to state the fundamental difference between a rare disease and a common disease, you would probably indicate that the difference is totally numeric. Rare diseases are infrequently encountered, and common diseases are commonly encountered. No mystery there. When we delve more deeply into the question, we see that numeric differences must have some underlying biological explanation. In this section, we will see that rare diseases comprise a distinctive group of disorders with a defining set of biological properties.

Moreover, these defining properties render the rare diseases particularly amenable to prevention, diagnosis, and treatment. Most importantly, the lessons learned from rare diseases are directly applicable to the common diseases, if we master the fundamentals of Precision Medicine.

For legal purposes, rare diseases are defined with numbers. In the United States, as written in Public Law 107-280, the Rare Diseases Act of 2002, "Rare diseases and disorders are those which affect small patient populations, typically populations smaller than 200,000 individuals in the United States." [2]. Since the population of the United States was about 314 million, in 2013, this comes to about 1 case for every 1570 persons. This is not too far from the definition recommended by the European Commission on Public Health; fewer than 1 in 2000 people. It is important to have numeric criteria for the rare diseases, because regulatory incentives apply, in the United States and in Europe, to stimulate research and drug development for qualifying "rare" diseases. It is difficult to know, with any certainty, the specific prevalence or incidence of any disease, as a certain percentage of the cases will go unreported, or undiagnosed, or misdiagnosed. Nevertheless, the US National Institutes of Health has estimated that rare diseases affect, in aggregate, 25–30 million Americans [3].

There seems to be a growing consensus that there are about 7000 rare diseases [4]. Depending on how you choose to count diseases, this may be a gross underestimate. There are several thousand inherited conditions with a Mendelian inheritance pattern, nearly all of which are rare [5]. To these, we must add the different types of cancer. Every cancer other than the top five or ten most common cancers occurs with an incidence much lower than 200,000 and would qualify as rare diseases. There are more than 3000 named types of cancer, and many of these cancers have well-defined subtypes, with their own morphologic, clinical, or genetic characteristics. Including defined subtypes, there are well over 6000 rare types of cancer [6–9]. Regarding the infectious diseases, over 1400 different infectious organisms have been reported in the literature [10]. A single infectious organism may manifest as several different named conditions, each with its own distinctive clinical features. For example, Leishmaniasis, an infectious disease that is common in Asia, South America, and Africa, but rare in Europe, may present in one of 4 different forms (cutaneous, visceral, diffuse cutaneous, and mucocutaneous). When we add in the many rare nutritional, toxic, and degenerative diseases that occur in humans, the consensus estimate of the number of rare diseases seems woefully inadequate. Nonetheless, the low-ball "7000" number tells us that there are many rare diseases, way too many for any individual to fully comprehend.

The rare diseases are sometimes referred to as orphan diseases. The term is apt for several reasons. First, the term "orphan" applies to children, and it happens that neonates, infants, and children are at highest risk for the most devastating rare diseases. Secondly, the concept of an "orphan disease" implies a lack of stewardship. For far too long, the rare diseases were neglected by clinicians, medical researchers, the pharmaceutical industry, and society in general. In recent times, a confluence of political, social, and scientific enlightenments have led to stunning advances in the field of rare diseases, and these advances have shaped the field of Precision Medicine.

Aside from numerics, there are a number of biological differences that distinguish rare diseases from common diseases. Here is a table that lists the differences.

Rare Diseases	Common Diseases
Occur predominantly in children	Occur predominantly in middle-aged and older adults
Some rare diseases affect only a few dozen individuals	Some common diseases affect billions of individuals
Strong genetic influence	Strong environmental/lifestyle influence
Single root cause	Many different root causes
In genetic disease, a monogenic root cause	In genetic disease, a polygenic cause [11]
Potentially correctable by gene therapy in some cases	Not correctable by gene therapy
Not reversible without gene-based therapy	Sometimes reversible without gene-based therapy
Medically manageable with one targeted drug	Unlikely to be managed by a single targeted drug
One drug gets similar response from all patients	One drug unlikely to get equivalent responses from all patients
Root causal mutation in a protein-coding gene	Mutations in noncoding regions of genome
Epigenome plays no known role, generally	Strong epigenomic influence
Limited number of potential causes	Many different potential causes
Seldom preventable	Often preventable
Simple pathogenesis	Complex pathogenesis
Phenotype accountable by one pathway	Phenotype accountable by many pathways
Includes all the developmental disorders	Excludes all the developmental disorders
Uniform population with similar phenotype	Aggregate of different diseases with range of phenotypes

Of course, there are exceptions to every line on the list, but the generalizations are sufficiently accurate to tell us that the differences between rare diseases and common diseases are biologically valid. A thorough analysis of this list would be a diversion, but let's look at a few of the points that have particular relevance to Precision Medicine.

– **Age of occurrence**

Rare diseases typically occur in a young population. Common diseases typically occur in adults, increasing in frequency with age. This observation presents us with something of a mystery. Every child is biologically very similar to the adult he becomes. The genome of the child is identical to the genome of the adult. Many of the same cells found in the child will persist into adulthood and throughout the span of life. These include hepatocytes, neurons, osteocytes, and chondrocytes. The oocytes of the baby girl are the same cells as the oocytes of the woman. The biological differences between child and adult are negligible. This being the case, why do children suffer from a different set of diseases than are found in the adult population?

The differences between the diseases that occur in children and the diseases that occur in late adulthood have remarkably little overlap. There are many instances of childhood diseases that never occur in adults; and diseases of adults that never occur in children. As a general class of diseases with no overlap between the age groups, cancers provide a prime example [12]. Cancers of children are all rare, and none of them occur in adults. In addition, we can subdivide cancers of children into congenital tumors, tumors occurring in young children, tumors of adolescents, and tumors of young adults, and we would see very little overlap in tumor types among these narrowly separated groups [13]. Rare cancers occurring in infants, in descending order of incidence, are: neuroblastoma, leukemias, central nervous system cancers, germ cell cancers, and soft-tissue tumors. The rare cancers of adolescents, 15–19 years of age, in descending order of incidence, are: Hodgkin lymphoma, germ cell tumors, CNS tumors, non-Hodgkin's lymphoma, and thyroid cancer [13]. [Glossary Germ cell]

The glib explanation for the differences in the types of diseases in children, compared with adults, is that rare diseases occurring in children are genetic; whereas the common diseases are nongenetic, acquired following many years of repeated exposures to detrimental environmental agents (e.g., toxins in air, water, and food), and lifestyle indiscretions (e.g., poor diet, cigarette smoking, alcohol consumption). Crudely put, the rare diseases are given to us, while the common diseases are earned. It's easy to see why a germline mutation will produce disease in younger individuals than a disease resulting from lifestyle choices, but how would this explain the difference in the types of diseases that occur?

At a simplistic level, the rare diseases, most of which result from germline mutations, account for all of the developmental disorders. Obviously, there is no biological opportunity to acquire a dysmorphism, or a congenital abnormality, or an inborn error of metabolism, after the organism has achieved adulthood. On a deeper level, we can return to our definition of pathogenesis: an ordered sequence of biological events that lead to the development of a clinical phenotype. Because the events leading to a clinical phenotype occur as an ordered sequence, we can infer that the timing of events will influence the clinical outcome.

Let's consider PTEN mutations. PTEN is a tumor suppressor gene, and mutational inactivation of this gene is found in glioblastoma, endometrial cancer, and prostate cancer in adults. In Cowden syndrome, there is a germline mutation of PTEN. Cowden syndrome is associated with dysplastic gangliocytoma of the cerebellum (also known as Lhermitte-Duclos syndrome); multiple hamartomas of skin, mucous membranes, thyroid gland, and breast; and a predisposition to develop breast carcinoma, follicular carcinoma of the thyroid, and endometrial carcinoma. Dysplastic gangliocytoma of the cerebellum is a rare cancer, whose root cause is a PTEN mutation, that never occurs in middle aged and older individuals. Glioblastoma is a central nervous system cancer that is commonly associated with PTEN mutations and which virtually never occurs in young children. We can safely infer that there is something about the timing of the events that influences the cancer phenotype. [Glossary Bannayan-Riley-Ruvalcaba syndrome, Lhermitte-Duclos syndrome]

When we see a cancer that can occur in young individuals or older individuals, we can often find obvious biological differences in clinical behavior, suggesting that the tumors may share a morphological resemblance, but that the diseases are biologically separable. We see this phenomenon in chordomas, seminomas, Hodgkin lymphoma, and myelodysplastic syndrome. Myelodysplastic syndrome peaks in two age groups (very young and very old). The myelodysplasias occurring in children often show a chromosomal aberration of chromosome 7 that is not often encountered in the myelodysplasias occurring later in life [14]. Likewise, acute myeloid leukemias have two age peaks (young and old). The acute myeloid leukemias seen in children often lack multilineage hematopoietic dysplasia and often have a good outcome with cytotoxic chemotherapy [15]. The acute myeloid leukemias occurring in elderly individuals often have a mutator phenotype, multilineage hematopoietic dysplasia, and poor outcome with cytotoxic chemotherapy [15]. [Glossary Seminoma, Mutator phenotype]

As a general rule, the rare cancers occurring in children respond better to chemotherapy than the common cancers of adulthood. Early successes in cancer treatment trials in children, in the 1970s, raised our hopes that equivalent trials would result in cures for cancers occurring in adults. Such was not the case. We've never achieved the kinds of astounding success in the common tumors of adults that we enjoyed for the rare tumors of childhood.

– Pattern of inheritance

Rare diseases usually occur with a Mendelian pattern of inheritance. Common diseases, with just a few exceptions (e.g., glucose-6-phosphate dehydrogenase deficiency affecting 400 million people worldwide), have an environmental cause, or a polygenic cause, or both. In any cases, common diseases almost never have a Mendelian pattern of inheritance.

A polygenic disease is caused by variations in numerous genes that work in concert to produce a disease. Imagine that a common disease is caused by a set of 10 variant genes that, together, confer susceptibility to an environmental toxin. How would you predict that an individual will develop the disease? You'd need to know which variants of each of the 10 contributing genes were present in the patient, and you'd need to know exactly how every combination of these variants will behave, as a group. It turns out that that diseases cannot be predicted for polygenic diseases; the problem is simply too complex to solve. In a well-controlled experiment, in a simple yeast cell system, the authors tried to predict outcome for a set of four gene variants known to influence a specific yeast phenotype, in this case, yeast sporulation efficiency [16]. As expected, genotype could not predict phenotype; four genes made the system too complex to predetermine sporulation efficiency in progeny.

What is the absolute minimum number of mutated genes needed to produce a non-Mendelian pattern of inheritance? Just two may do. A team of scientists developed a digenic model of type 2 diabetes in mice. Like the common disease in humans, diabetes arose in mouse offspring in an age-dependent manner, and the pattern of inheritance was non-Mendelian [17]. [Glossary Digenic disease]

There is at least one instance of a 3-gene disease that has a non-Mendelian pattern of inheritance in humans. The rare disease Bardet-Biedl syndrome is characterized by obesity in infancy, retinal dystrophy, polydactyly, and abnormalities of multiple organs. In most cases, Bardet-Biedl syndrome is a monogenic rare disease with an autosomal recessive pattern of inheritance. In a small percentage of cases Bardet-Biedl syndrome is polygenic, and does not exhibit the usual Mendelian pattern of inheritance. These non-Mendelian cases of Bardet-Biedel are accounted for by three mutations occurring at two loci [18].

What is it about the polygenic diseases that makes them common? Darwinian selection keeps the incidence of life-threatening monogenic diseases low; individuals with serious childhood diseases will be less likely to procreate and to pass disease genes onto others. In the case of the polygenic diseases, there is no natural process of selection that would cull disease genes from the general population. If a disease occurs late in adulthood, as is often the case for polygenic diseases, natural selection may not even apply. Affected individuals are likely to be healthy when they procreate, and that's all that matters to the survival of the species. More importantly, though, natural selection cannot operate efficiently on a set of polygenic disease genes. If the variant genes that cause a polygenic disease are conserved common polymorphisms (i.e., conserved gene variants), then we can assume that each variant has value, in some subset of cells, or under certain sets of conditions. Otherwise, the polymorphism would not have been conserved in the gene pool. When dealing with a polygenic disease, selecting against any of the disease gene variants may have unpredictable adverse consequences.

– Environmental factors

The common diseases are often caused by well-studied environmental or lifestyle conditions. The connections between diet and atherosclerosis, obesity and metabolic syndrome, sodium intake and stroke, cigarette use and emphysema, alcohol abuse and cirrhosis, are seldom contested. [Glossary Metabolic syndrome]

For the common cancers that occur in adults, environmental factors are absolutely required for their pathogenesis. Just three cancers account for the majority of neoplasms occurring in adult humans: basal-cell carcinoma of skin, squamous-cell carcinoma of skin, and lung cancer. Ultraviolet light exposure is the most prominent cause of the common skin cancers. Smoking causes about 90% of lung cancers. Hence, most of the occurrences of cancers in humans have an identified environmental cause. [Glossary Basal-cell carcinoma]

As a generalization, common diseases arise from the cells that line the outer or inner surfaces of the body (i.e., the skin and the alimentary tract, and the lungs). These same body sites are directly exposed to chemical, physical, or biological agents delivered by food, water, and air. These same sites yield the highest number of cancers (e.g., cancers of skin, lungs, and colon, stomach, esophagus), and some of the most common diseases of adults (e.g., chronic obstructive pulmonary disease, gastroenteritis, dermatitis). Tissues of the body that are not directly exposed to outside agents (e.g., muscle, connective tissues) are the sites at which common cancers do not develop.

Heart disease and stroke are an exception to the rule that common diseases arise from the outer and inner surfaces of the body, as vessels and muscle are derived from mesoderm. Nonetheless, the root causes of both diseases seem to be gut-derived, through a lifetime of nutritional indiscretions (i.e., caloric excess leading to atherosclerosis, salt excess leading to hypertension and stroke).

– Rare diseases involve genes. Common diseases involve noncoding regions of the genome.

Genes are the DNA sequences that code for proteins. Nearly every rare disease whose root cause is known, is associated with a gene. With just a few exceptions, none of the common diseases are associated with an identifiable root cause gene. Genome-wide association studies, conducted over the past decade, seem to indicate that the common diseases are associated with multiple gene polymorphisms, nearly all of which are located in noncoding regions of the genome. Furthermore, these multiple polymorphisms in noncoding regions seem to account for only a small fraction of the heritability of the diseases [11,19–21]. [Glossary Genome-Wide Association Study]

Mutations in noncoding regions are almost always less deleterious than mutations in coding regions (i.e., genes). Gene mutations often cause the loss of functional protein from the affected allele. Mutations in noncoding regions usually modify the amount of expression of coding genes, without actually eliminating the normal gene project. Each mutation in a noncoding sequence is unlikely to do much damage and may do some good. We might expect that it would require multiple mutations in noncoding regions to produce a disease phenotype that is equivalent to the phenotype produced by a loss-of-function mutation in one gene.

– Causal relationships between the rare and the common diseases

We have seen that common diseases are complex. This means that they are likely to have several or many potential root causes, plus any number of contributing causes and conditions, and are likely to develop over time, through multiple biological steps. In general, agents that are considered to be the root causes of common diseases will tend to affect multiple molecular targets and multiple pathways, adding to the biological complexity that characterizes almost all common diseases. Some of these altered pathways, aside from any role they may play in the development of a common disease, are likely to be involved in the pathogenesis of one or more rare diseases. [Glossary Complex disease]

As it happens, examples abound of agents, known to cause both common and rare diseases. For example, consider alcohol, the cause of liver cirrhosis, a common and often fatal disease. Alcohol is also a cause of pancreatitis, another common and sometimes fatal disease. Alcohol also produces Marchiafava-Bignami disease, a rare disease characterized by demyelination of the corpus callosum. Alcohol is a contributing cause of Wernicke-Korsakoff syndrome, a rare disease characterized by vision changes, ataxia, and impaired memory resulting from brain atrophy involving the maxillary bodies, thalamus, periaqueductal gray, third and fourth ventricles, and the cerebellum. In addition to its role as a cause of rare neurologic diseases in adults, alcohol ingestion during pregnancy can produce fetal alcohol syndrome in offspring. Fetal alcohol syndrome is associated with various abnormalities that may include short height, low body weight, small head size, poor coordination, low intelligence, behavior problems, problems with hearing or seeing, and a host of alcohol-related neurodevelopmental disorders and birth defects [22]. Alcoholism also triggers or aggravates various metabolic diseases (e.g., gout, gall stones) and is thought to increase the incidence of several types of cancers (e.g., esophageal cancer, liver cancer, oral cancer). It would be hard to imagine how a disturbance of a single metabolic pathway could result in both common diseases (cirrhosis, pancreatitis) and in rare neurological diseases (Marchiafava-Bignami and Wernicke-Korsakoff). It is easier to imagine that alcohol is a chemical that affects multiple pathways, at once.

Cigarette smoke also seems to be an all-purpose toxin, producing common diseases and rare diseases. Common diseases caused by smoking include bronchogenic lung cancer, emphysema, and chronic obstructive pulmonary disease. Buerger disease is a rare consequence of smoking. Also known as thromboangiitis obliterans, Buerger disease is a progressive vasculopathy involving small and medium arteries and veins. Smokers are at increased risk of developing Warthin tumor, an uncommon benign salivary gland tumor characterized by a proliferation of ductal cells swollen by thousands of mitochondria (so-called oncocytes) [23]. How cigarette smoke produces biologically diverse, rare diseases, such as Buerger disease and Warthin tumor, is anyone's guess. [Glossary Warthin tumor]

In the following sections of this chapter, we will see how we can take advantage of the fundamental differences between rare diseases and common diseases to advance Precision Medicine.

SECTION 5.2 PRECISION MEDICINE'S FIRST BENEFIT: CURES FOR RARE DISEASES

The study of rare diseases offers a way of implementing the tools and procedures that will later be used in more widespread applications of genomic medicine.
From Institute of Medicine workshop summary [24]

As previously noted, most rare genetic diseases are monogenic, meaning that one gene is considered to be the root cause of the disease. At present, more than 2000 genes have been identified as the root causes of about 2000 rare diseases [5,25]. Virtually every gene known to cause a rare disease was discovered within the past half century.

Progress in the genetic diseases greatly accelerated in the 1960s, and the earliest advances came to the group of diseases known as inborn errors of metabolism [26]. Treatments were aimed to compensate for or cope with the metabolic defects (e.g., avoidance of phenylalanine in newborns with phenylketonuria, supplements of thyroid hormone in congenital hypothyroidism, avoidance of galactose in newborns with galactosemia, supplementation with biotin in newborns with biotinidase deficiency, specially formulated low protein diets for newborns with maple syrup urine disease, and so on).

Some of the ground-breaking advances in rare disease research include the 1956 discovery of the specific molecular alteration in hemoglobin that causes sickle cell disease [27,28], and the identification of the cystic fibrosis gene in 1989 [29]. In 2007, Leber congenital amaurosis, a form of inherited blindness, was the first disease to be treated with genetic engineering technology. The mutated RPE65 gene was replaced with a functioning gene [30]. Partial vision was obtained, in individuals who were previously blind. It remains to be seen whether genetic engineering will ever restore adequate and long-term vision to individuals with Leber congenital amaurosis [31]. In August 2017, a gene therapy for the treatment of children and young adults with rare B-cell acute lymphoblastic leukemia was approved by the US Food and Drug Administration [32]. It is worthy to note that, at this point in time, every disease successfully treated with new genetic engineering technology has been a rare disease.

Currently, drug development for the rare diseases is far exceeding anything seen in the common diseases. Since 1983, more than 350 drugs have been approved to treat rare diseases [33]. In 2011, the US Food and Drug Administration has designated over 2,300 medicines as orphan drugs. That same year, 460 drugs were in development to treat or prevent rare diseases [33]. Meanwhile, in Europe, 20% of the innovative products with marketing authorization were developed for rare diseases [25]. [Glossary Orphan drug]

Because rare diseases often have a specific genetic root cause, or a specific environmental cause, their pathogeneses can be studied relatively easily. At present, we know much more about the rare diseases, in terms of pathogenesis and treatment, than we know about the common diseases. At this point, there is every expectation that the greatest breakthroughs in understanding the general mechanisms of diseases processes will come from research on the rare diseases [34,35].

Consider cancer. Nearly every cancer that is curable while in an advanced stage of growth (e.g., with extensive regional spread and invasiveness or with distant metastases) is a rare disease. Common cancers, when diagnosed in an advanced stage, are, with few exceptions, incurable.

The list of cancers that are routinely cured in an advanced stage of growth are exclusively rare cancers [35,36]

- Choriocarcinoma
- Acute lymphocytic leukemia of childhood
- Burkitt lymphoma
- Hodgkin lymphoma
- Acute promyelocytic leukemia
- Large follicular center cell (diffuse histiocytic) lymphoma
- Embryonal carcinoma of testis
- Hairy cell leukemia
- Seminoma

The newest drugs that target specific cancer pathways, by in large, offer their greatest benefits to rare cancers (e.g., gastrointestinal stromal tumors, chronic myelogenous leukemia). Today, owing to the remarkable effectiveness of imatinib and other tyrosine kinase inhibitors, individuals with chronic myelocytic leukemia, a disease that was nearly always fatal a half century ago, can look forward to a nearly normal life expectancy [37].

The decline in mortality from childhood cancers, all of which are rare, has been one of the greatest achievements in the field of cancer research [13]. Between 1975 and 1995, the overall mortality of childhood cancer has declined 40%. The declines ranged from 2.0% to 3.2% per year over this period [13]. While the death rates declined, the overall incidence of childhood cancers increased 0.8% per year. There were 2275 cancer deaths among children in 1995, representing less than a half-percent of all cancer deaths [13].

In August 2017, a gene therapy for the treatment of children and young adults with B-cell acute lymphoblastic leukemia was approved by the US Food and Drug Administration [32]. The therapy is centered on several stunning refinements of an old and nearly defunct approach, using a patient's own immune system to destroy cancer cells. The successful methodology that was developed is known as CAR-T (Chimeric Antigen Receptor for T cells). Here are the steps involved in employing CAR-T [38]:

1. Choose some antigen in the disease-causing cells that is present in high concentration in those cells or that is unique to those cells. It is best if the antigen lies on the cell surface, where it can easily bind to T-cell receptors. In cancers, the target cells for this procedure will be the cancer cells themselves. In the case of CAR-T therapy for B-cell acute lymphoblastic leukemia, the target antigen is CD-19, a B-cell surface antigen. Researchers are hoping that this technique can be applied to diseases other than cancer [39]. Perhaps, in the future, the target cells may be the chief effector cells within many different types of lesions (e.g., parasitic infections).
2. Create the chimeric receptor to the antigen. This is the step that awaited several advances in genetic engineering [40]. Basically, the different units of a receptor designed to provide the greatest possible biological response, when bound to an antigen, are combined with a unique antigen-recognizing subunit. The final product is an artificial receptor molecule capable of arming T cells.
3. Determine the gene sequence that encodes the artificial receptor and synthesize it in vast number.

4. Enclose copies of the synthesized gene in an appropriate vector (e.g., lentivirus).
5. Extract a sample of T cells from the patient.
6. Transfect those T cells with the vector.
7. Grow the transfected T cells, now expressing the chimeric receptor, in culture.
8. Deplete the patient of his or her own T cell population, to "make room" for the cultured T cells that it will soon receive.
9. Transfuse the cultured and transfected T cells into the patient.
10. Wait as the transfused T cell recognize and destroy the patient's cancer cells.
11. Watch to see if the patient develops any adverse events, and treat complications aggressively [41].

In the case of B-cell acute lymploblastic leukemia, a rare form of cancer, the results have been nothing short of miraculous. In early trials, complete and lasting remissions have been achieved in more than two-thirds of treated patients [39]. As is so often the case, early successes come to the rare diseases. The common diseases come later, if at all. At present, CAR-T therapy is not particularly effective against common solid tumors, possibly due to the enormous phenotypic heterogeneity of epithelial tumors, and the emergence of cells that lack the target antigen, following an initial response to treatment [39].

Rare diseases have a great advantage over common diseases when clinical trials are designed. Most individuals with a rare genetic disease will have a biologically equivalent genetic aberration (e.g., a mutation in the same gene, or a mutation affecting the same key pathway), with a similar clinical phenotype, often limited to a similar age group. Under these conditions, clinical trials tend to yield clear-cut outcomes, with relatively uniform responses among the test subjects. Results for clinical trials on the rare diseases tend to be more definitive than the results for common diseases, and can be conducted on smaller populations. In some cases, under exigent circumstances, clinical trials are conducted on a single individual (to be discussed in Section 9.6, "Fast, Cheap, Precise Clinical Trials).

As a society, we devote the majority of our research funds to the most imprecisely understood diseases: obesity, hypertension, mental illnesses, diabetes, lower back pain. Have we been missing something? Why are there so many startling new cures for the rare diseases, and such meager progress against the common diseases? As discussed, the pathogenesis of a rare disease is almost always simpler than the pathogenesis of a common disease. Because the steps leading to the development of rare diseases are yielding to the tools of Precision Medicine, arriving at effective cures for the rare diseases has become relatively straightforward.

SECTION 5.3 WHAT THE RARE DISEASES TELL US ABOUT THE COMMON DISEASES

Most result from a dysfunction of a single pathway due to a defective gene. Understanding the impact of a single defect may therefore yield insights into the more complex pathways involved in common diseases which are generally multifactorial. [Glossary Multifactorial cause]
Segolene Ayme and Virginie Hivert, from Orphanet [25]

Nature is nowhere accustomed more openly to display her secret mysteries than in cases where she shows tracings of her workings apart from the beaten paths; nor is there any better way to advance the proper practice of medicine than to give our minds to the discovery of the usual law of nature, by careful investigation of cases of rarer forms of disease.
William Harvey (1657)

An objective review of the genetics of common diseases yields only bad news. Without exceptions, the common diseases are pathogenetically complex. Attempts at predicting the behavior of common diseases, based on detailed, yet incomplete, knowledge of their complex genetic attributes, have led to failure after failure [42–44].

Not to be discouraged, data analysts believe that with the right algorithm, and the right supercomputer, the complexities of common diseases can be predicted. Physicians have bought into this fantasy. When a sampling of physicians was asked to rank the areas in which they needed additional genetics training, their number one choice was the "genetics of common disease" [45,46]. [Glossary Algorithm]

Rare diseases are not exceptions to the general rules of disease biology; they are the exceptions upon which the general rules are based. All biological systems must follow the same rules. If a rare disease is the basis for a general assertion about the biology of disease, then the rule must apply to the common diseases. The rare diseases provide us with an opportunity to study how general phenomena express themselves in isolation, thus providing insight to those processes that occur concurrently with many other processes, in the common diseases. Because we have not seriously accepted this simple and self-evident truth, progress in the medical sciences suffered severe stagnation in the last few decades of the twentieth century.

Excluding genes causing rare cancers (of which there are thousands), more than 2000 genes have been linked to 7000 rare genetic diseases [5,25]. In most cases, these links are presumed to be causal (i.e., mutations in the gene lead to the development of the disease). Virtually every gene known to cause a rare disease was discovered within the past half century. The diseases whose underlying causes were known, prior to about 1960, numbered in the hundreds, and the majority of these well-understood diseases were caused by infectious organisms. At this point, there is every expectation that the greatest breakthroughs in understanding the general mechanisms of diseases processes will come from research on the rare diseases [34].

- **Much of what we know about dysfunctional disease pathways come from studying the rare diseases**

Every rare disease tells us something about the normal functions of organisms. When we study a rare hemoglobinopathy, we learn something about the consequences that befall when the normal hemoglobin is replaced with an abnormal hemoglobin. This information leads us to a deeper understanding of the normal role of hemoglobin. Likewise, rare urea cycle disorders, coagulation disorders, metabolic disorders, and endocrine disorders have taught us how these functional pathways operate under normal conditions [34].

Complex physiological pathways that are unique to humans (e.g., coagulation pathways, immune pathways, neural pathways, metabolism pathways) can only be understood by studying rare diseases affecting steps in the pathway. Researchers have had great success collecting cases of rare deficiencies, and then piecing together a plausible and testable complex pathway.

Here is a sampling of classes of genetic diseases and the normal cellular pathways they helped elucidate [35]:

- Immune deficiencies →normal immune mechanisms
- Collagenopathies →collagen synthesis
- Sarcoglycanopathies →sarcoglycan complex synthesis [47]
- Hemophilias →blood clotting cascade
- Inherited conduction disorders →cardiac conduction system
- Glucose-6-phosphate dehydrogenase deficiency →hexose monophosphate shunt
- Congenital disorders of glycosylation →posttranslational modifications of proteins [48] [Glossary Congenital disorders of glycosylation]
- Leukocyte adhesion deficiencies →integrin pathway, by which circulating blood cells modulate their affinity for endothelial ligands, thus promoting the extravasation of immune-response cells into sites of infection [49]
- Mitochondriopathies →cellular respiration
- Inborn errors of metabolism →pathways of cellular metabolism
- Inherited dyslipidemias (e.g., Tangier disease [50]) →lipid metabolism
- Peroxisome biogenesis disorders →assembly and function of peroxisomes [51].
- Inherited disorders of DNA repair deficiencies →DNA repair mechanisms
- Inherited conditions that have phenocopy diseases →toxicologic mechanisms of disease
- Vesicular trafficking disorders →mechanisms for transporting proteins to their appropriate locations [52]. [Glossary Vesicular trafficking disorders]

For every common disease, there is a monogenic disease that is its clinical mimic, as shown:

Common Disease	Rare Disease Subset
Diabetes	MODY (Maturity-Onset Diabetes of the Young) [53]
Atherosclerosis	Familial hypercholesterolemia
Emphysema	Alpha-1-antitrypsin deficiency
Lung cancer	NUT-1 Gene
Cirrhosis	Alpha-1-antitrypsin, Hemochromatosis
Hypertension	Early-onset, autosomal dominant, hypertension with severe exacerbation in pregnancy
Gastric ulcer	Zollinger-Ellison syndrome
Colon cancer	Lynch syndrome
Breast cancer/Ovarian cancer	BRCA gene

Common Disease	Rare Disease Subset
Basal-cell carcinoma	Gorlin syndrome
Infectious diseases	IRAK4 or NEMO gene mutations and sensitivity to pneumococcal disease [54]
Parkinson disease	Parkinson disease associated with LRRK2 gene mutation [55]
Alzheimer disease	Early-onset familial Alzheimer disease

Uncommon presentations of common diseases are sometimes rare diseases, camouflaged by a common clinical phenotype. Common diseases tend to occur with a characteristic clinical phenotype and a characteristic history (e.g., risk factors, underlying causes). Deviations from the normal phenotype and history are occasionally diagnostically significant. Rare diseases may produce a disease that approximates the common disease; the differences lie within subtle findings revealed to the most astute observers. [Glossary Forme fruste, Phenotypic heterogeneity]

For example, mutations of the JAK2 gene are involved in several myeloproliferative conditions, including myelofibrosis, polycythemia vera, and at least one form of hereditary thrombocythemia (i.e., increased blood platelets) [56–58]. Surprisingly, somatic blood cells with JAK2 mutations are found in 10% of apparently healthy individuals [59]. The high incidence of JAK2 mutations in the general population, and the known propensity for JAK2 mutations to cause thrombocythemia and thromboses should alert physicians to the possibility that some cases of idiopathic thrombosis may be caused by a platelet disorder caused by undiagnosed JAK2 mutation of blood cells. As it happens, it has been shown that a JAK2 mutation can be found in 41% of patients who present with idiopathic chronic portal, splenic, and mesenteric venous thrombosis [60]. Such thrombotic events are uncommon in otherwise-healthy patients. The search for a zebra, in this case a cryptic myeloproliferative disorder caused by a JAK2 mutation, paid off.

As noted in Section 2.1, Liddle syndrome is an ultrarare disease caused by a dysfunction of an epithelial sodium channel [61]. It is characterized by hypertension, metabolic alkalosis, and low blood potassium, arising in young individuals. Fewer than 30 cases had been reported as of 2008 [62]. Nonetheless, in a study of US veterans living in Louisiana, 6% were found to have laboratory values consistent with Liddle syndrome [63]. Furthermore, in a study of young Chinese with hypertension, 1.5% were found to have a mutation in genes encoding subunits of the epithelial sodium channel. These findings suggest that variants of the inherited genetic defect in extremely rare diseases may account for a significant proportion of individuals who have an extremely common disease, such as hypertension, that affects about one-third of the adult population, worldwide [19].

– Rare diseases are the sentinel lesions for the common diseases

When a toxic agent produces a small rise in the incidence of a common disease, the increase cannot usually be distinguished from statistical noise, and the hazard goes undetected. To illustrate, imagine a disease that affects 500 million people. An environmental agent that produces 5 million new cases will produce a negligible 1% increase in the affected population. If the same agent increases the incidence of a rare disease, sometimes by as few as a half-dozen cases, the rise in incidence will be noticed, and the agent can be identified. Imagine that some external toxin produces two diseases: one rare, one common. Increases in the rare disease will draw attention to the problem.

It is easy to find examples of rare diseases that have served as sentinels for environmental hazards. Here are a few examples [35]:

- Angiosarcoma of liver as a sentinel for cancer-causing plastics (polyvinyl chloride) [64]

In 1974, healthcare workers noticed a handful of new cases of liver angiosarcomas, an extremely rare cancer. It was soon discovered that all of the cases of hepatic angiosarcoma occurred in individuals who were employed by the rubber and tire manufacturing industries [65]. Furthermore, all these individuals had worked at the site of vinyl chloride polymerization reactor vessels. Aerosolized polyvinyl chloride was known to cause tumors in rats. Here was proof enough that the agent also caused cancer in humans. Soon thereafter, measures were taken to reduce the hazardous effects of polyvinyl chloride in populations at-risk [65].

- Aplastic anemia as a sentinel for environmental bone marrow toxins (e.g., benzene and chloramphenicol)

Aplastic anemia is a condition in which there is profound reduction of hematopoietic bone marrow cells. Previously healthy, red, marrow is replaced by adipocytes and fibrous tissue. Aplastic anemia may be the only example of a disease characterized by the physical disappearance of a normal tissue. Blood cell blasts (i.e., the stem cells that give rise to the differentiated cells that circulate in blood) are reduced in number, to such a degree that the peripheral blood is nearly depleted of red cells, white cells, and platelets. Acute aplastic anemia is a medical emergency, requiring replacement blood products. Those who survive aplastic anemia, regardless of its etiology, are at increased risk of developing blood dyscrasias of clonal origin (e.g., acute leukemia, myelodysplastic syndrome) later in life.

In the late 1960s, and continuing into the 1970s, epidemiologic studies of leukemia in Istanbul linked increased cases of these rare tumors to benzene exposure among shoe industry workers [66]. In many cases, leukemias followed bouts of aplastic anemia. Benzene is a known toxin of hematopoietic tissue, and it is reasonable to assume that bone marrow toxicity secondary to occupational benzene exposure commonly preceded the development of leukemia. A reduction in benzene exposure was followed by a striking drop in the incidence of leukemia in shoe industry workers [66].

- Cancer of the scrotum as a sentinel for cancers caused by common air pollutants

Carcinoma of the scrotum is essentially a nonexistent tumor today, but it was a common tumor of chimney sweeps back in 1775 [67]. Percivall Pott, the first cancer epidemiologist, linked hot soot rising up the pant legs of chimney sweeps to the occurrence of squamous carcinoma of the scrotum [68]. His studies helped eradicate a rare disease confined to a small occupational group. Even more importantly, Pott raised awareness to the potential dangers of air pollutants and launched the scientific field of cancer prevention.

- Cholangiocarcinoma as a sentinel for cancers caused by radiological reagents

In the early days of X-ray technology, radiologists searched for radio-opaque agents that could be swallowed or injected to provide a contrast material that outlined anatomic abnormalities. In the 1930s, when the dangers of persistent low-dose radioactive agents were still unknown, radiologists seized upon thorotrast, a colloidal suspension of radioactive thorium dioxide, as their ideal contrast agent [69]. Some of the ingested thorotrast avoided excretion through the bowels and traveled to the reticuloendothelial cells lining the liver sinusoids (i.e., the liver's Kupffer cells). The Kupffer cells engulfed the thorotrast, storing it permanently. From its location within Kupffer cells, the lingering thorotrast emitted alpha particles, for years. Alpha particles do not travel very far in tissues. In this case, the cells most likely to be damaged are the Kupffer cells carrying the thorotrast and the cells immediately adjacent to these cells (i.e., heptocytes and bile duct cells). As we might expect the cancers caused by exposure to radiological thorotrast were hepatocellular carcinoma, cholangiocarcinoma, and hepatic angiosarcoma. Hepatocellular carcinoma is a common tumor, but cholangiocarcinoma is rare, as is angiosarcoma of the liver. Increases in these two rare tumors warned workers in the fledgling field of nuclear medicine that thorotrast was a public menace [35].

- Clear-cell adenocarcinoma of cervix or vagina in young women as a sentinel for carcinogens delivered transplacentally

In 1971 physicians noticed that they were encountering more and more cases of young women with an extremely rare cancer: clear-cell adenocarcinoma of the cervix or of the vagina [70]. The mothers of the affected women had all ingested a nonsteroidal synthetic estrogen (diethylsilbestrol, DES) during their pregnancies. A short, in utero exposure to a medication resulted in the occurrence of rare tumors several decades later, in the female offspring. In the original study, tumors occurred in an age range of 7 years to 27 years; 91% were in young women over the age of 14 [70,71]. Exposed males were not at risk of cancer [72]. At the time, there were no known examples of transplacental carcinogenesis occurring in humans. If the tumors caused by in utero exposure to DES had been common cancers, such as breast carcinoma or colon carcinoma, the link connecting the drug to cancer would have been impossible to discover. Just as thorotrast kindled interest in the relatively new field of radiation-induced cancers, DES helped create the field of transplacental carcinogenesis. [Glossary Transplacental carcinogenesis]

- Mesothelioma as a sentinel for cancers induced by airborne minerals

Asbestos is an insulating material that was used extensively in the mid-20th century. Asbestos inhalation is associated with an increased risk of bronchogenic lung cancer, the number one cause of cancer deaths in the United States. [73]. In most cases of asbestos-related lung cancer, patients have a history of smoking. If asbestos caused bronchogenic lung cancer exclusively, we probably would have no idea of its carcinogenicity, because its effect among the many smoking-related lung cancers would be negligible.

In 1960, a link was established between occupational asbestos exposure in miners and mesotheliomas of the pleura and peritoneum, the tissues lining the lung cavity and the abdominal cavity, respectively [74]. The news came too late to help individuals who were exposed to asbestos in its heyday, during the booming construction years of World War II. In those days, naval shipworkers, eager to protect vessels from fire, lavished pipes and ceiling with asbestos insulation. In so doing, they exposed themselves to asbestos dust. Their family members, who washed their dusty uniforms, were also exposed. Single exposures to the dust seemed to be all that was required to produce a mesothelioma. Some of these shipyard-associated mesotheliomas occurred 20–40 years following exposure.

Today, we treat asbestos as a serious occupational and environmental hazard. At enormous cost, we have abated our exposures to asbestos found in attic and pipe insulation, brake liners, and cigarette filters. Once again, occurrences of a rare cancer warned us to take measures to reduce exposure to a hazardous substance. Asbestos carcinogenicity also taught us a new lesson: that solid and nonreactive agents could cause cancer.

– Mad Hatter disease as a sentinel for occupational exposure to heavy metals

Beginning in the 17th century, European hatters used mercury in the preparation of felt from animal fur. Mercury vapors induced tremors in the hatters, and the disease came to be known, callously, as mad hatter disease. Occurrences of the disease among hatters continued for at least two more centuries. By the mid-19th century, the link between mercury exposure and tremors was a scientific certainty. England passed laws to protect hatters from mercury exposure, and the incidence of disease declined. Though a rarity, new cases of mad hatter disease have occurred in the twentieth century. Today, mercury is used in gold extraction. As a result, mercury contamination has increased in gold mining areas, and new cases of occupational tremors are occurring among gold workers [35,75].

– Phocomelia as a sentinel for teratogens

Thalidomide was first marketed in 1957 as a treatment for morning sickness of pregnancy. Thalidomide was used in many countries, but not in the United States, where it was denied FDA approval. Extreme cases of phocomelia characterized by congenital absences of one or more limbs, were reported for the first time in Germany. Soon thereafter large numbers of congenital limb malformations were reported throughout Europe. The occurrences of limb malformations were traced to a common exposure: thalidomide. The drug was removed from the European market in 1961. By that time, over 10,000 children were affected worldwide [76]. Current theory holds that thalidomide kills fetal cells that are needed for limb development [76]. The thalidomide tragedy sparked scientific interest in the field of transplacental teratogenesis.

– Phossy jaw as a sentinel for occupational exposure to bone toxins

From the mid-19th century until the first decade of the 20th century, phosphorus was used as an ingredient in so-called easy-strike matches. Many workers in this industry developed mutilating necrotic oral lesions extending from gingiva into underlying bone (i.e., mandible or maxilla). It took nearly a half-century to associate the jaw condition (eventually called "phossy jaw") with phosphorus exposure, and to eliminate phosphorus in the manufacture of matches [77].

Today, bisphosphonates are drugs that retard the normal process of bone resorption. Bisphosphonates are used to treat osteoporosis. In high doses, bisphosphonates are sometimes used to treat bone that has been eroded by metastatic tumor deposits. When used at high doses, bisphosphonates can produce a condition indistinguishable from phossy jaw. It is presumed that phosphorus exposure creates chemical intermediates that are similar to the chemical structure of today's bisphosphonates, and that both toxins produce the same jaw conditions via the same biological pathway [78]. The 21st century lesion is sometimes called "bisphossy jaw" [78]. Historical experiences with an extinct and rare condition, phossy jaw, have sensitized us to a variety of toxic agents that can cause osteonecrosis of the jaw (e.g., radium, heavy elements, bisphosphonates).

- Thyroid carcinoma in children as a sentinel for radiation leakage from nuclear power plants

In the wake of the 1986 Chernobyl nuclear accident, there was an increase in the incidence of an uncommon form of cancer: childhood thyroid cancer. In the case of Chernobyl, the children most likely to develop thyroid cancer were between 0 and 4 years of age at the time of the exposure [79]. An increase in thyroid cancers was not observed among exposed adults. The increase in thyroid cancers was first detected 3–4 years after the accident [79]. Some cancers take decades to develop. When cancers occur in just a few years after exposure to a carcinogen, it indicates that the exposure was large, or that the carcinogen was very potent. In this case, the majority of thyroid cancers occurred in Gomel, Belarus, the region exposed to the greatest concentrations of iodine-131, the chief radioactive component of the fallout, and a chemical known to concentrate in the thyroid after absorption [79].

It is worth remembering that when we drop our guard, a rare disease can become a common disease. In 1963, there were only 17 reported cases of malaria in Sri Lanka. Five years later, after mosquito control measures were relaxed, 440,000 cases were reported [80]. When we do not take adequate measures to limit our exposure to agents that cause rare diseases (e.g., asbestos, benzene, silicates, radiation), we can expect the incidence of the rare diseases to rise, sometimes to the point of becoming common diseases. Before smoking became a national pastime, bronchogenic carcinoma was a rare tumor. If smoking had been curtailed when cigarettes were a novelty, the current worldwide epidemic of lung cancer would have been prevented. The role of Precision Medicine in public health will be discussed in Section 9.4. [Glossary Bronchogenic carcinoma]

SECTION 5.4 TREATMENTS FOR RARE DISEASES ARE EFFECTIVE AGAINST THE COMMON DISEASES

> Breakthrough discoveries among the rare diseases are now viewed as opportunities to understand and treat the common diseases. Hence, there is an increasing emphasis, coming from government, academia, and private research organizations, to increase funding for rare diseases research and orphan drug development.
> *Stephen G. Groft, Director of the NIH Office of Rare Diseases Research, retired [35]*

In this section, we'll consider the assertion that every common disease will benefit from treatments that were developed for one or more of the rare diseases. Here are the steps that lead us to this assertion:

1. Every cellular pathway serves a useful function in the organism, under some circumstances. Otherwise, the pathway would be eliminated by natural selection.
2. Rare diseases, unlike common diseases, are typically monogenic, with a single altered gene product initiating an abbreviated sequence of events that leads to the dysfunction of one pathway that is the major driver of the clinical phenotype.

3. The aggregate collection of rare diseases accounts for dysfunctions of every cellular pathway. We know this because pathways are built from proteins, and every protein is subject to mutation, and such mutations act as underlying causes of the 7000+ known rare genetic diseases.

4. Every common disease is produced by a combination of dysfunctional cellular pathways. If every cellular pathway were functioning normally, there would be no disease.

5. The dysfunctional pathways in common diseases are the same dysfunctional pathways that produce rare diseases. See point 3.

6. In the new era of Precision Medicine, wherein treatments are targeted to dysfunctional disease pathways, the aggregate of rare diseases will provide us with a comprehensive assortment of treatments for every individual disease pathway.

7. Hence, from the available selection of treatments for the rare diseases, combinations of drugs can be selected, which will target the key driver pathways of every common disease. [Glossary Driver pathway]

Of course, it's great fun to play with biological hypotheses, but is there any real merit to these logical sophistries? As it happens, there are many instances in which treatments for a specific rare disease, or biological insights, gained by studying a rare disease, have benefited the treatment of one or more common diseases. Here are a few examples.

– Gorlin syndrome and basal-cell carcinoma

Gorlin syndrome, alternatively known as nevoid basal-cell carcinoma syndrome is a rare inherited condition that produces facial dysmorphism and a predisposition to several types of skin tumors, particularly basal-cell carcinomas and odontogenic keratocysts [81]. Individuals with Gorlin syndrome inherit a mutation in the PTCH (Patched) gene, and this mutation leads to derepression of Smoothened, a multifunctional protein involved in several signaling pathways [82,83]. Without delving into the details, it suffices to say that research into Gorlin syndrome had led to an understanding of a key pathway involved in the pathogenesis of commonly occurring basal-cell carcinoma, the most frequently occurring cancer in humans. [Glossary Odontogenic keratocyst]

Smoothened inhibitors such as vismodegib, itraconazole, and cyclopamine, all result in partial resolution of basal-cell carcinoma, in animal models [84]. When treatments with the various smoothened inhibitors are combined, the growth of ultraviolet-induced basal-cell carcinomas is inhibited 90% [84]. Although simple surgical excision is usually curative for commonly occurring basal-cell carcinomas, a drug discovered for a rare basal-cell carcinoma syndrome may one day be used to prevent or reduce the frequencies of occurrences of basal-cell carcinomas, or to treat the occasional occurrences of surgically unresectable basal-cell carcinomas.

– Osteoporosis and osteoporosis-pseudoglioma syndrome

Osteoporosis-pseudoglioma syndrome is a rare disease characterized clinically by multiple bone fractures and various eye and neurologic abnormalities. It is caused by loss-of-function mutations in the low-density lipoprotein receptor-related protein-5 (LRP5). LRP5, under normal conditions, reduces the production of serotonin in the gut. Based on rare disease research directed toward understanding the role of LRP5, agents that compensate for the reduction in LRP5 by reducing gut serotonin are candidate drugs for the treatment of both rare osteoporosis-pseudoglioma syndrome, and common osteoporosis [4,85,86].

- **Blepharospasm and wrinkles**

As previously mentioned, botox (Botulinum toxin type A) was originally developed, tested, and approved to treat several rare diseases characterized by uncontrolled blinking. Soon thereafter, botox was found to be extremely effective for rare spasmodic conditions, including spasmodic torticollis (i.e., wry neck). Eventually, it was observed that botox could temporarily erase wrinkles. Aside from its cosmetic applications, botox has been used in the treatment of chronic migraines, overactive bladder, and benign prostatic hyperplasia.

- Rare genetic form of Parkinson disease and sporadic form of Parkinson disease

Parkinson disease is a disorder of the central nervous system that affects the motor system. It affects over 6 million people worldwide. Most cases arise sporadically, without family history, and without any associated inherited genetic mutation. A rare subset of Parkinson disease is familial, and such cases are associated with mutations in the LRRK2 gene encoding leucine-rich repeat kinase 2 [55,87]. Currently, LRRK2 inhibitors have emerged as a strategy for treating both rare and common forms of Parkinson disease [88]. Clinical testing is currently in an early stage, but the LRRK2 protein kinase is just one of many kinases, mutated in rare diseases, for which selective drug inhibitors are being designed and tested.

- Familial hypercholesterolism and atherosclerosis

The Framingham Heart Study is often given credit for establishing the connection between high cholesterol levels and heart disease, back in 1961. Although the Framingham Heart Study provided important statistical evidence, based on a careful study of a large number of individuals, it is historical fact that physicians were well aware of the association between cholesterol and heart attacks, decades prior to 1961. Rather early in the 20th century, the common blood chemistry tests that we use today were established, and these tests were clinically interpreted much like they are interpreted today. An association between high cholesterol levels and arteriosclerosis was recognized by 1921 [89]. Twenty-five years later, a form or familial hypercholesterolemia was observed in families with familial hypercholesterolemia, revealing two distinct forms of the disease. A homozygous form affected infants at birth, produced blood cholesterol levels of about 800 mg/dL, and resulted in heart attacks in children as young as 5 years of age. A heterozygous form, occurring in the same families, produced lower levels of cholesterol, 300–400 mg/dL, and produced heart attacks at the age of 35–60 years [90].

Observations that heart attacks occurred in inherited hypercholesterolemias inspired a search for cholesterol-lowering drugs. In the 1970s, Akiron Endo found that several species of fungi extrude defensive compounds that inhibit the synthesis of cholesterol in fungal pathogens. Endo studied 6000 fungal compounds, eventually finding mevastatin, the first effective inhibitor of human HMG-CoA reductase, the rate-limiting enzyme in the cholesterol biosynthetic pathway [91]. Regardless of the cause of elevated cholesterol (i.e., a familial form of hypercholesterolemia, dietary cholesterol, or a physiologic disposition to oversynthesize cholesterol), statins can effectively lower blood cholesterol and reduce the associated morbidities.

– Rare dyslipidemia and diabetes

A subfield of internal medicine is devoted to the dyslipidemias. Without going into detail, various types of lipoproteins in the blood transport cholesterol and other lipids to tissues [92]. Dyslipidemias can be monogenic, polygenic, or acquired. Regardless of their cause, most of the dyslipidemias are treated with statins. Some monogenic rare diseases can be effectively treated with replacement therapy, restoring the deficient protein. For example, some cases of inherited lipodystrophy are caused by a deficiency of leptin. Twice daily leptin injections improve the lipodystrophy, but this treatment has also been found to counter insulin resistance and improve fasting glucose and triglyceride levels [93]. Hence, leptin, a drug that shows some effectiveness in a rare lipodystrophy, may have a role in the treatment of a common disease characterized by insulin resistance: diabetes [94].

We learn how to treat common diseases by studying the rare diseases. We can also learn how to treat common diseases by studying rare individuals who are impervious to disease. Individuals with a rare resistance to HIV infection have a specific deletion in the gene that codes for the CCR5 coreceptor. The gene plays a role in the entry of HIV into cells; no entry, no infection. Knowledge of the role of CCR5 in HIV infection has inspired the development of a new class of HIV drugs targeted against entry receptors [95]. As it happens, both HIV virus and smallpox virus enhance their infectivity by exploiting a receptor, CCR5, on the surface of white blood cells. This shared mode of infection may contribute to the cross-protection against HIV that seems to come from smallpox vaccination. It has been suggested, but not proven, that the emergence of HIV in the 1980s may have resulted, in part, from the cessation of smallpox vaccinations in the late 1970s [96].

In a similar anecdote, individuals with genetic absence of Duffy antigen receptor for chemokines (i.e., DARC, formerly known as Duffy blood group antigen) are protected from malaria caused by Plasmodium vivax. It turns out that entry of the parasite requires participation by DARC [97,98]. A new vaccine candidate for P. vivax malaria, targeted against the Duffy binding protein was developed based on observations of naturally occurring resistance in a small set of individuals lacking DARC [97,99].

When we encounter a common disease, we look to see which pathways are dysfunctional, and we develop a rational approach for prevention, diagnosis, and treatment based on experiences drawn from the rare diseases that are driven by those same dysfunctional pathways. It's easy to see why a good portion of the research effort in the field of Precision Medicine will be devoted to finding general uses for drugs that were designed to be effective for any of the 7000 + rare diseases. Now, whenever a new treatment for a rare disease is announced, clinicians should refrain from asking, "Why was all that research money spent on a disease that affects none of the patients in my practice?" and instead ask themselves, "What common diseases can benefit from this treatment?" Because the number of new treatments for the rare diseases is growing at a fast pace, it is easy to see that much of the research in the field of Precision Medicine will be devoted to finding the most general possible applications for rare disease drugs.

Glossary

Algorithm An algorithm is a logical sequence of steps that lead to a desired computational result. Algorithms serve the same function in the computer world as production processes serve in the manufacturing world and as pathways serve in the world of biology. Fundamental algorithms can be linked to one another, to create new algorithms (just as biological pathways can be linked). Algorithms are the most important intellectual capital in computer science.

Bannayan-Riley-Ruvalcaba syndrome A variant of Cowden syndrome.

Basal-cell carcinoma Basal-cell carcinoma is the most common cancer, with about 600,000 new cases occurring each year in the United States. They occur as small, smooth, patches on sun-exposed skin (e.g., face, arms, neck). Basal-cell carcinoma seldom, if ever, metastasizes from its primary site of growth. Along with squamous carcinoma of skin, occurrences of these two conditions exceed the number of all other cancers, combined. Neither basal-cell carcinoma of skin or squamous-cell carcinoma of skin account for many human deaths. Neither of these extremely common tumors are recorded in hospital-based cancer registries, and when statistics are compiled on the incidences of cancers, these tumors are usually excluded. This common practice of omitting basal-cell carcinomas and squamous-cell carcinomas of skin yields an under-representation, by about 50%, of the true biological burden of cancer in the human population.

Bronchogenic carcinoma Cancers arising from the pulmonary bronchus and its branches, rather than from the alveoli (oxygen-exchanging sacs). Most of the common cancers of the lung are bronchogenic. The nonbronchogenic tumors account for under 10% of lung cancers and can be considered rare cancers. The bronchogenic cancers are adenocarcinoma, squamous carcinoma, small-cell carcinoma, and their various undifferentiated and mixed variants. About 90% of cases of bronchogenic carcinoma arise in smokers. It is safe to presume that some additional percentage of individuals with bronchogenic carcinoma who are nonsmokers may have been exposed to second-hand smoke in the workplace or at home (i.e., more than 90% of bronchogenic carcinoma is linked to cigarette smoking or to secondary inhalation of cigarette smoke). Bronchoalveolar carcinoma, alternately known as bronchioloalveolar carcinoma or as alveolar carcinoma, is a nonbronchogenic lung cancer arising from cells in or near the alveolar sacs [100].

Complex disease A somewhat vague term often indicating that the pathogenesis of a disease cannot be understood. The presumption is that our lack of understanding is not based on our failure to discover the underlying cause of the disease; our lack of understanding is based on our discovery that there are so many different factors to consider that it is impossible to understand the pathogenesis in a way that we can fully grasp. When the development of a disease involves numerous environmental factors, some known and others assumed, as well as multiple genetic and epigenetic influences, we have no way of fully understanding how all of these factors interact with one another, and we have no way of fully describing the biological steps that lead to the clinical expression of disease. Likewise, we have no way of predicting how different individuals with a complex disease will respond to treatment. In this book, we use the term "common disease" interchangeably with "complex disease." Without exception, all of the common diseases of humans are complex.

Congenital disorders of glycosylation A group of congenital, multiorgan syndromes caused by posttranslational defects in protein glycosylation [48]. The steps in posttranslational glycosylation are complex, and may involve systems that move nascent proteins from the endoplasmic reticulum to other sites (e.g., Golgi apparatus). In such cases, there may be overlap between the congenital disorders of glycosylation and the vesicular trafficking disorders. Many different disorders of glycosylation have been identified, involving N-glycosylation, O-glycosylation, or both. Because there are many different inherited glycosylation disorders, and because these disorders tend to produce neurologic symptoms and multiorgan impairments, physicians should always include congenital disorders of glycosylation in the differential diagnosis when evaluating infants with otherwise-unexplained multiorgan involvement or neurologic abnormalities [48].

Digenic disease Digenic diseases require mutations in two genes to produce the complete clinical phenotype. There are several rare diseases that are known or suspected to be digenic. Several different forms of Usher disease, combined retinitis pigmentosa, and hearing loss, are digenic. A digenic cause of several forms of Long QT syndrome, a type of heart arrhythmia, has also been reported [101]. Kallman syndrome, a form of hypogonadotrophic hypogonadism, is suspected to be digenic [101]. Digenic diseases often have a variable clinical phenotype, even among family members with the disease. Mice with digenic diabetes have a non-Mendelian pattern of inheritance, typical of a polygenic familial disease [17]. As a group of disorders, the inherited digenic disease occupies an intermediate niche, between monogenic diseases and polygenic diseases.

Driver pathway A pathway that develops during the pathogenesis of disease and that persists to play a necessary role in the clinical expression of the disease. A "driver pathway" is distinguished from a "passenger pathway," the latter being a pathway that plays a role in the development of the disease, but does not play a necessary role after the disease has developed. The distinction between driver pathways and passenger pathways may have therapeutic importance. A driver pathway, even if it is present in a small portion of people affected with a disease, is likely to be a valid therapeutic target in the subset of patients who are shown to have the driver pathway. A passenger pathway, even if it operates at one time or another in 100% of individuals with the disease, is unlikely to be a useful therapeutic target, once the disease has developed.

Forme fruste From the French, crude, or unfinished form; plural formes frustes. A term used by diagnosticians and applied to difficult cases wherein a patient presents with some of the features of a recognized disease or syndrome, but who does not quite fit the accepted diagnostic criteria. The clinical presentation is said to be the forme fruste (i.e., wrong, incomplete, or unfinished form) of the disease. In the context of a rare disease, the forme fruste may present as a near-syndrome, lacking one or more of the definitive features of a set of inherited abnormalities. In many, if not all, cases, studying the forme fruste will help us to understand the classic form of a disease. For example, geneticists reported a child who presented with renal angiomyolipoma, a rare tumor sometimes found in patients with tuberous sclerosis. Several years later, the same patient developed cystic disease in the contralateral kidney, a condition often associated with polycystic kidney disease. Genetic analysis demonstrated a contiguous gene deletion involving both the TSC2 gene for tuberous sclerosis and the PKD1 gene for polycystic kidney disease. The patient's phenotype was the forme fruste of two rare diseases, but genetic analysis proved that the presentation fit a contiguous gene syndrome [102].

Genome-Wide Association Study (GWAS) A method to find common SNPs (single nucleotide polymorphisms) that are statistically associated with a polygenic disease. The methodology involves hybridizing DNA from individuals with disease, as well as individuals from a control group, against a DNA array of immoblilized fragments of DNA known to contain commonly occurring SNPs (i.e., allele-specific oligonucleotides). The SNPs that hybridize against the DNA extracted from individuals with disease (i.e., the SNPs matching the case samples) are compared with the SNPs that hybridize against the controls. SNPs that show a statistical difference between case samples and control samples are said to be associated with the disease. Of course, there are many weaknesses to this approach; one being that differences in SNPs do not necessarily imply any functional variance in the gene product [103]. In addition, differences in SNPs may lead to statistically valid results that nonetheless have no relevance to the pathogenesis of disease [104]. Aside from false-positive GWAS associations, the methodology is virtually guaranteed to miss valid SNP associations, simply because SNP arrays are not exhaustive (i.e., do not contain all 50 million SNPs) and are limited to a selected set of commonly occurring polymorphisms. For example, a rare variant of the APOE gene has been shown to be strongly correlated with longevity [105]. This variant, because it is not included among the common APOE variants included in SNP arrays, would have been missed by a GWAS study. True associations are those that can be found repeatedly from laboratory to laboratory, and that can be shown to have pathogenetic relevance. To date, very few disease-associated SNPs found in GWAS studies have met these criteria. It has been suggested that the GWAS studies, in toto, have had little scientific merit and have been misleading [106]. A sympathetic evaluation of GWAS studies is that they help us to see recurrent sets of pathway genes involved in diseases. Knowing that a related set of genes seems to implicate a pathway in the development or expression of a common disease has great value [4]. By focusing attention on a pathway, scientists can start to dissect the important events in the pathogenesis of a disease. If the pathway is known to be disrupted in a monogenic disease, particularly when the monogenic disease replicates the phenotype of a common disease, then an effective new treatment, aimed at the pathway, may be feasible. The best mathematical methods for the proper analysis of GWAS studies have been the subject of review [107].

Germ cell Same as gamete (i.e., an ova in females and a sperm cell in males).

Lhermitte-Duclos syndrome A variant of Cowden syndrome characterized by a hamartomatous overgrowth of enlarged ganglion cells, which replace the granular cell layer and Purkinje cells of the cerebellum. This results in global hypertrophy of the cerebellum, with enlarged, coarse gyri.

Metabolic syndrome The combination of obesity plus hypertriglyceridemia plus low levels of HDL cholesterol plus hypertension plus hyperglycemia (i.e., prediabetes or diabetes). Metabolic syndrome occurs in nearly 1 in 4 adults in the United States and carries an increased risk of death from a variety of common causes, including heart attacks [108].

Multifactorial cause The term "multifactorial cause" is denigrated because it has almost no meaning; and the little meaning it has is wrong. Does it mean that multiple factors must act together to cause a disease, or does it mean that a disease can be produced by any one of many possible factors, or does it mean that the development of the disease is complex and occurs over time, as many different factors contribute to the disease phenotype, or does it mean that no single factor can rationally account for the occurrence of the disease? The primary thesis developed in this book promotes the idea that diseases emerge from a series of cellular events that alter cellular pathways, that lead to the development of a clinical phenotype, over time. Although it is possible to conceive this process as a culmination of factors, term "multifactorial cause" serves only to obfuscate reality.

Mutator phenotype One of the hallmarks of cancer is genetic instability. The common cancers typically have thousands of genetic mutations, and these mutations perturb virtually every aspect of cellular physiology. It is hypothesized that during carcinogenesis, cells acquire a mutator phenotype that increases the rate at which genetic aberrations occur in cells, thus raising the likelihood that a clone of cells will emerge with an oncogenic mutation that confers a malignant phenotype [109].

Odontogenic keratocyst A neoplasm arising within jaws, near the teeth, and composed of a cystic structure lined by squamous cells that can invade into bone. This lesion occurs sporadically or as part of Gorlin syndrome (multiple basal-cell carcinoma syndrome).

Orphan drug A drug that is helpful to a small number of people, usually indicating a drug developed for individuals who have a rare disease. In the past, the term "orphan drug" was applied to existing drugs that were not marketed due to their perceived unprofitability.

Phenotypic heterogeneity Occurs when one genotype produces different phenotypes. In the context of disease, it occurs when a specific gene mutation may produce any of several different clinical disorders, in different individuals.

Seminoma A tumor of male germ cells, almost always arising in the testis. The female equivalent of the seminoma (i.e., a tumor arising from female germ cells) is the ovarian dysgerminoma.

Transplacental carcinogenesis The induction of a cancer in offspring via exposure of the mother to a carcinogen during her pregnancy. The most notorious examples of transplacental carcinogenesis were reported after women were exposed to DES (diethystilbestrol) during their pregnancies. Their female offspring suffered a high incidence of malformations and tumors of the genital tract [70,71]. From a scientific standpoint, the three most perplexing features of transplacental tumors produced by in utero DES exposure were (1) the tumors did not occur until the children were in their teens or were in early adulthood; (2) the tumors that arose were tumors of adult-type tissues, not primitive embryonic tissues; (3) the cell types of the tumors, being of differentiated cells, were not present in the embryos and fetuses at the time of DES exposure; hence, the tumor arose from a type of cell that was not exposed to the carcinogen. Similar findings have been reported in transplacental carcinogenesis studies in animals [110]. Taken together, these findings clearly indicate that tumors arise through biological steps occurring over years and decades, during which fetal cells involved in the carcinogenic process may mature as different cell types, and that the type of cell observed in the developed tumor may be different from the type of cell in which the carcinogenic process originated.

Vesicular trafficking disorders Alternately known as protein trafficking disorder, cargo disorder, and vesicular transport disorder. After a protein molecule is translated from mRNA, a complex set of posttranslational events must occur for the protein to serve its intended purpose. The protein must be modified (e.g., glycosylated), shaped (e.g., folded), transported from the endoplasmic reticulum into a series of subcellular locations (e.g., Golgi apparatus and cargo vesicle), and delivered to its ultimate location. Such posttranslational steps are often divided into disorders of posttranslational modification (e.g., congenital disorders of glycosylation) and protein transport disorders. Much of the progress in this field was based on examining transport gene mutants in yeast cells, as well as inherited transport disorders in humans [111]. Examples of such disorders in humans include: Congenital disorder of glycosylation type IIe, Combined Factor V and Factor VIII coagulation factor deficiency; Hermansky-Pudlak syndrome; Chediak-Higashi syndrome; Cranio-lenticulo-sutural dysplasia; Choroideremia; Warburg Micro syndrome and Martsolf syndrome; Bardet-Biedl syndrome-3; Griscelli syndrome types I, II, III; Charcot-Marie-Tooth disease 2a,2b; Hereditary spastic paraplegia SPG10, SPG4; Troyer syndrome; Spinocerebellar ataxia 5; Lowe oculocerebrorenal syndrome; Usher syndrome type IB; Slow-progressing amyotrophic lateral sclerosis-8; CEDNIK syndrome; Familial hemophagocytic lymphohistiocytosis; Limb girdle muscular dystrophy; and Miyoshi myopathy [52].

Warthin tumor Also known as papillary cystadenoma lymphomatosum. Warthin tumor is a benign tumor of salivary glands that most often arises in the parotid gland. The cell of origin of the Warthin tumor is a ductal cell (i.e., a cell lining the salivary gland ducts) in which there is a proliferation of mitochondria, producing the so-called oncocyte (i.e., a cell in which the cytoplasm is filled with proliferating mitochondria, appearing as an enlarged cell stuffed with foamy cytoplasm).

References

[1] Weatherall DJ. Molecular pathology of single gene disorders. J Clin Pathol 1987;40:959–70.
[2] Rare Diseases Act of 2002, Public Law 107-280, 107th U.S. Congress; November 6, 2002.
[3] FAQ about rare diseases. National Center for Advancing Translational Sciences. National Institutes of Health. http://www.ncats.nih.gov/about/faq/rare/rare-faq.html [Accessed 24 October 2013].
[4] Field MJ, Boat T. Rare diseases and orphan products: accelerating research and development. Institute of Medicine (US) Committee on Accelerating Rare Diseases Research and Orphan Product Development, Washington, DC: The National Academics Press; 2010. Available from: http://www.ncbi.nlm.nih.gov/books/NBK56189/.
[5] Omim. Online Mendelian Inheritance in Man. Available from: http://omim.org/downloads [Accessed 20 June 2013].
[6] Berman JJ. Modern classification of neoplasms: reconciling differences between morphologic and molecular approaches. BMC Cancer 2005;5:100.
[7] Berman JJ. Tumor taxonomy for the developmental lineage classification of neoplasms. BMC Cancer 2004;4:88.
[8] Berman JJ. Tumor classification: molecular analysis meets Aristotle. BMC Cancer 2004;4:10.
[9] Berman JJ. Neoplasms: principles of development and diversity. Sudbury, MA: Jones and Bartlett; 2009.
[10] Berman JJ. Taxonomic guide to infectious diseases: understanding the biologic classes of pathogenic organisms. Waltham: Academic Press; 2012.
[11] Manolio TA, Collins FS, Cox NJ, Goldstein DB, Hindorff LA, Hunter DJ, et al. Finding the missing heritability of complex diseases. Nature 2009;461:747–53.
[12] Moore SW, Satge D, Sasco AJ, Zimmermann A, Plaschkes J. The epidemiology of neonatal tumours: report of an international working group. Pediatr Surg Int 2003;19:509–19.
[13] Ries LAG, Smith MA, Gurney JG, Linet M, Tamra T, Young JL, et al. Cancer Incidence and Survival among Children and Adolescents: United States SEER Program 1975-1995. Bethesda, MD: National Cancer Institute, SEER Program; 1999. NIH Pub. No. 99-4649.
[14] Lizcova L, Zemanova Z, Malinova E, Jarosova M, Mejstrikova E, Smisek P, et al. A novel recurrent chromosomal aberration involving chromosome 7 in childhood myelodysplastic syndrome. Cancer Genet Cytogenet 2010;201:52–6.
[15] Head DR. Revised classification of acute myeloid leukemia. Leukemia 1996;10:1826–31.
[16] Gerke J, Lorenz K, Ramnarine S, Cohen B. Gene environment interactions at nucleotide resolution. PLoS Genet 2010;6:e1001144.
[17] Bruning JC, Winnay J, Bonner-Weir S, Taylor SI, Accili D, Kahn CR. Development of a novel polygenic model of NIDDM in mice heterozygous for IR and IRS-1 null alleles. Cell 1997;88:561–72.
[18] Eichers ER, Lewis RA, Katsanis N, Lupski JR. Triallelic inheritance: a bridge between Mendelian and multifactorial traits. Ann Med 2004;36:262–72.
[19] Pritchard JK. Are rare variants responsible for susceptibility to complex diseases? Am J Hum Genet 2001;69:124–37.
[20] The Precision Medicine Initiative Cohort Program—Building a Research Foundation for 21st Century Medicine. Precision Medicine Initiative Working Group Report to the Advisory Committee to the Director, NIH; September 17, 2015.
[21] Pritchard JK, Cox NJ. The allelic architecture of human disease genes: common disease-common variant ... or not? Hum Mol Genet 2002;11:2417–23.
[22] Riley EP, Infante MA, Warren KR. Fetal alcohol spectrum disorders: an overview. Neuropsychol Rev 2011;21:73–80.
[23] Pinkston JA, Cole P. Cigarette smoking and Warthin's tumor. Am J Epidemiol 1996;144:183–7.

[24] Olson S, Beachy SH, Giammaria CF, Berger AC. Integrating large-scale genomic information into clinical practice: workshop summary. Washington, DC: The National Academies Press; 2012.

[25] Ayme S, Hivert V, editors. Report on rare disease research, its determinants in Europe and the way forward. INSERM; 2011. May. Available from: http://asso.orpha.net/RDPlatform/upload/file/RDPlatform_final_report.pdf.

[26] Garrod AE, Harris H. Inborn errors of metabolism. London: Henry Frowde, Hodder, and Stoughton; 1909.

[27] Pauling L, Itano HA, Singer SJ, Wells IC. Sickle cell anemia, a molecular disease. Science 1949;110:543–8.

[28] Ingram VM. A specific chemical difference between globins of normal and sickle-cell anemia hemoglobins. Nature 1956;178:792–4.

[29] Riordan JR, Rommens JM, Kerem B, Alon N, Rozmahel R, Grzelczak Z, et al. Identification of the cystic fibrosis gene: cloning and characterization of complementary DNA. Science 1989;245:1066–73.

[30] Hauswirth WW, Aleman TS, Kaushal S, Cideciyan AV, Schwartz SB, Wang L, et al. Treatment of leber congenital amaurosis due to RPE65 mutations by ocular subretinal injection of adeno-associated virus gene vector: short-term results of a phase I trial. Hum Gene Ther 2008;19:979–90.

[31] Cideciyan AV, Jacobson SG, Beltran WA, Sumaroka A, Swider M, Iwabe S, et al. Human retinal gene therapy for Leber congenital amaurosis shows advancing retinal degeneration despite enduring visual improvement. Proc Natl Acad Sci U S A 2013;110:e517–525.

[32] FDA approval brings first gene therapy to the United States: CAR T-cell therapy approved to treat certain children and young adults with B-cell acute lymphoblastic leukemia. U.S. Food and Drug Administration; August 30, 2017.

[33] Orphan drugs in development for rare diseases; 2011 Report. America's Biopharmaceutical Research Companies. Available from: http://www.phrma.org/sites/default/files/pdf/rarediseases2011.pdf [Accessed 14 July 2013].

[34] Wizemann T, Robinson S, Giffin R. Breakthrough Business Models: Drug Development for Rare and Neglected Diseases and Individualized Therapies Workshop Summary. Institute of Medicine (US) Forum on Drug Discovery, Development, and Translation. Washington, DC: National Academies Press; 2009.

[35] Berman JJ. Rare diseases and orphan drugs: keys to understanding and treating common diseases. Cambridge, MA: Academic Press; 2014.

[36] Kufe D, Pollock R, Weichselbaum R, Bast R, Gansler T, Holland J, et al., editors. Holland Frei cancer medicine. Ontario: BC Decker; 2003.

[37] Bower H, Bjorkholm M, Dickman PW, Hoglund M, Lambert PC, Andersson TM. Life expectancy of patients with chronic myeloid leukemia approaches the life expectancy of the general population. J Clin Oncol 2016;34:2851–7.

[38] Ren J, Zhang X, Liu X, Fang C, Jiang S, June CH, et al. A versatile system for rapid multiplex genome-edited CAR T cell generation. Oncotarget 2017;8:17002–11.

[39] Chmielewski M, Abken H. TRUCKs: the fourth generation of CARs. Expert Opin Biol Ther 2015;15:1145–54.

[40] Zhang C, Liu J, Zhong JF, Zhang X. Engineering CAR-T cells. Biomark Res 2017;5:22.

[41] Morgan RA, Yang JC, Kitano M, Dudley ME, Laurencot CM, Rosenberg SA. Case report of a serious adverse event following the administration of T cells transduced with a chimeric antigen receptor recognizing ERBB2. Mol Ther 2010;18:843–51.

[42] Cecile A, Janssens JW, vanDuijn CM. Genome-based prediction of common diseases: advances and prospects. Hum Mol Genet 2008;17:166–73.

[43] Ioannidis JP. Is molecular profiling ready for use in clinical decision making? Oncologist 2007;12:301–11.

[44] Venet D, Dumont JE, Detours V. Most random gene expression signatures are significantly associated with breast cancer outcome. PLoS Comput Biol 2011;7:e1002240.

[45] Calefato JM, Nippert I, Harris HJ, Kristoffersson U, Schmidtke J, Ten Kate LP, et al. Assessing educational priorities in genetics for general practitioners and specialists in five countries: factor structure of the Genetic-Educational Priorities (Gen-EP) scale. Genet Med 2008;10:99–106.

[46] Julian-Reynier C, Nippert I, Calefato JM, Harris H, Kristoffersson U, Schmidtke J, et al. Genetics in clinical practice: general practitioners' educational priorities in European countries. Genet Med 2008;10:107–13.

[47] Duggan DJ, Hoffman EP. Autosomal recessive muscular dystrophy and mutations of the sarcoglycan complex. Neuromuscul Disord 1996;6:475–82.

[48] Lefeber DJ, Morava E, Jaeken J. How to find and diagnose a CDG due to defective N-glycosylation. J Inherit Metab Dis 2011;34:849–52.

[49] Bunting M, Harris ES, McIntyre TM, Prescott SM, Zimmerman GA. Leukocyte adhesion deficiency syndromes: adhesion and tethering defects involving beta 2 integrins and selectin ligands. Curr Opin Hematol 2002;9:30–5.

[50] Hayden MR, Clee SM, Brooks-Wilson A, Genest Jr J, Attie A, Kastelein JJ. Cholesterol efflux regulatory protein, Tangier disease and familial high-density lipoprotein deficiency. Curr Opin Lipidol 2000;11:117–22.

[51] Weller S, Cajigas I, Morrell J, Obie C, Steel G, Gould SJ, et al. Alternative splicing suggests extended function of PEX26 in peroxisome biogenesis. Am J Hum Genet 2005;76(6):987–1007.

[52] Gissen P, Maher ER. Cargos and genes: insights into vesicular transport from inherited human disease. J Med Genet 2007;44:545–55.

[53] Tallapragada DSP, Bhaskar S, Chandak GR. New insights from monogenic diabetes for common type 2 diabetes. Front Genet 2015;6:251.

[54] Ku CL, Picard C, Erd SM, Jeurissen A, Bustamante J, Puel A, et al. IRAK4 and NEMO mutations in otherwise healthy children with recurrent invasive pneumococcal disease. J Med Genet 2007;44:16–23.

[55] Zimprich A, Biskup S, Leitner P, Lichtner P, Farrer M, Lincoln S, et al. Mutations in LRRK2 cause autosomal-dominant parkinsonism with pleomorphic pathology. Neuron 2004;44:601–7.

[56] Mead AJ, Rugless MJ, Jacobsen SEW, Schuh A. Germline JAK2 mutation in a family with hereditary thrombocytosis. N Engl J Med 2012;366:967–9.

[57] Barosi G, Bergamaschi G, Marchetti M, Vannucchi AM, Guglielmelli P, Antonioli E, et al. JAK2 V617F mutational status predicts progression to large splenomegaly and leukemic transformation in primary myelofibrosis. Blood 2007;110:4030–6.

[58] Zhang L, Lin X. Some considerations of classification for high dimension low-sample size data. Stat Methods Med Res 2013;22:537–50. Available from: http://smm.sagepub.com/content/early/2011/11/22/0962280211428387.long.

[59] Sidon P, El Housni H, Dessars B, Heimann P. The JAK2V617F mutation is detectable at very low level in peripheral blood of healthy donors. Leukemia 2006;20:1622.

[60] Orr DW, Patel RK, Lea NC, Westbrook RH, O'Grady JG, Heaton ND, et al. The prevalence of the activating JAK2 tyrosine kinase mutation in chronic porto-splenomesenteric venous thrombosis. Aliment Pharmacol Ther 2010;31:1330–6.

[61] Hanukoglu I, Hanukoglu A. Epithelial sodium channel (ENaC) family: phylogeny, structure-function, tissue distribution, and associated inherited diseases. Gene 2016;579:95–132.

[62] Rossier BC, Schild L. Epithelial sodium channel: mendelian versus essential hypertension. Hypertension 2008;52:595–600.

[63] Tapolyai M, Uysal A, Dossabhoy NR, Zsom L, Szarvas T, Lengvarszky Z, et al. High prevalence of liddle syndrome phenotype among hypertensive US Veterans in Northwest Louisiana. J Clin Hypertens 2010;12:856–60.

[64] Falk H, Creech Jr JL, Heath Jr CW, Johnson MN, Key MM. Hepatic disease among workers at a vinyl chloride polymerization plant. JAMA 1974;230:59–68.

[65] Wagoner JK. Toxicity of vinyl chloride and poly(vinyl chloride): a critical review. Environ Health Perspect 1983;52:61–6.

[66] Aksoy M. Hematotoxicity and carcinogenicity of benzene. Environ Health Perspect 1989;82:193–7.

[67] Gerber C, von Hochstetter AR, Schuler G, Hofmann V, Rosenthal C. Penis carcinoma in a young chimney sweep. Case report 200 years following the description of the first occupational disease. Schweiz Med Wochenschr 1995;125:1201–5.

[68] Brown JR, Thornton JL. Percivall Pott (1714-1788) and chimney sweepers' cancer of the scrotum. Br J Ind Med 1957;14:68–70.

[69] Sharp GB. The relationship between internally deposited alpha-particle radiation and subsite-specific liver cancer and liver cirrhosis: an analysis of published data. J Radiat Res 2002;43:371–80.

[70] Herbst AL, Ulfelder H, Poskanzer DC. Association of maternal stilbestrol therapy and tumor appearance in young women. N Engl J Med 1971;284:878–81.

[71] Herbst AL, Scully RE, Robboy SJ. The significance of adenosis and clear-cell adenocarcinoma of the genital tract in young females. J Reprod Med 1975;15:5–11.

[72] Strohsnitter WC, Noller KL, Hoover RN, Robboy SJ, Palmer JR, et al. Cancer risk in men exposed in utero to diethylstilbestrol. J Natl Cancer Inst 2001;93:545–51.

[73] Kamp DW. Asbestos-induced lung diseases: an update. Transl Res 2009;153:143–521.

[74] Wagner JC, Sleggs CA, Marchand P. Diffuse pleural mesothelioma and asbestos exposure in the North Western Cape Province. Br J Ind Med 1960;17:260–71.

[75] Eisler R. Mercury hazards from gold mining to humans, plants, and animals. Rev Environ Contam Toxicol 2004;181:139–98.

[76] Knobloch J, Ruther U. Shedding light on an old mystery: thalidomide suppresses survival pathways to induce limb defects. Cell Cycle 2008;7:1121–7.

[77] Marx RE. Uncovering the cause of "phossy jaw" Circa 1858 to 1906: oral and maxillofacial surgery closed case files—case closed. J Oral Maxillofac Surg 2008;66:2356–63.

[78] Jacobsen C, Zemann W, Obwegeser JA, Gratz KW, Metzler P. The phosphorous necrosis of the jaws and what can we learn from the past: a comparison of "phossy" and "bisphossy" jaw. Oral Maxillofac Surg 2014;18:31–7.

[79] Cardis E, Hatch M. The Chernobyl accident—an epidemiological perspective. Clin Oncol (R Coll Radiol) 2011;23:251–60.

[80] Lemon SM, Sparling PF, Hamburg MA, Relman DA, Choffnes ER, Mack A. Vector-Borne Diseases: Understanding the Environmental, Human Health, and Ecological Connections, Workshop Summary. Institute of Medicine (US) Forum on Microbial Threats, Washington, DC: National Academies Press; 2008.

[81] Aszterbaum M, Epstein J, Oro A, Douglas V, LeBoit PE, Scott MP, et al. Ultraviolet and ionizing radiation enhance the growth of BCCs and trichoblastomas in patched heterozygous knockout mice. Nat Med 1999;5:1285–91.

[82] Epstein EH. Basal cell carcinomas: attack of the hedgehog. Nat Rev Cancer 2008;8:743–54.

[83] Ling G, Ahmadian A, Persson A, Unden AB, Afink G, Williams C, et al. PATCHED and p53 gene alterations in sporadic and hereditary basal cell cancer. Oncogene 2001;20:7770–8.

[84] Chaudhary SC, Tang X, Arumugam A, Li C, Srivastava RK, Weng Z, et al. Shh and p50/Bcl3 signaling crosstalk drives pathogenesis of BCCs in Gorlin syndrome. Oncotarget 2015;6(34):36789–814.

[85] Long F. When the gut talks to bone. Cell 2008;135:795–6.

[86] Zhang W, Drake MT. Potential role for therapies targeting DKK1, LRP5, and serotonin in the treatment of osteoporosis. Curr Osteoporos Rep 2012;10:93–100.

[87] Paisan-Ruiz C, Jain S, Evans EW, Gilks WP, Sim n J, van der Brug M, et al. Cloning of the gene containing mutations that cause PARK8-linked Parkinson's disease. Neuron 2004;44:595–600.

[88] Taymans J-M, Greggio E. LRRK2 kinase inhibition as a therapeutic strategy for Parkinson's disease, where do we stand? Curr Neuropharmacol 2016;14:214–25.

[89] Myers VC. Practical chemical analysis of blood. St. Louis, MO: C.V. Mosby Company; 1921.

[90] Goldstein JL, Brown MS. Cholesterol: a century of research. HHMI Bulletin 2012;16:1–4. September 20.

[91] Tobert JA. Lovastatin and beyond: the history of the HMG-CoA reductase inhibitors. Nat Rev Drug Discov 2003;2:517–26.

[92] Biggerstaff KD, Wooten JS. Understanding lipoproteins as transporters of cholesterol and other lipids. Adv Physiol Educ 2004;28:105–6.

[93] Ebihara K, Kusakabe T, Hirata M, Masuzaki H, Miyanaga F, Kobayashi N, et al. Efficacy and safety of leptin-replacement therapy and possible mechanisms of leptin actions in patients with generalized lipodystrophy. J Clin Endocrinol Metab 2007;92:532–41.

[94] Jazet IM, Jonker JT, Wijngaarden MA, Lamb H, Smelt AH. Therapy resistant diabetes mellitus and lipodystrophy: leptin therapy leads to improvement. Ned Tijdschr Geneeskd 2013;157:A5482.

[95] Huang Y, Paxton WA, Wolinsky SM, Neumann AU, Zhang L, He T, et al. The role of a mutant CCR5 allele in HIV-1 transmission and disease progression. Nat Med 1996;2:1240–3.

[96] Smallpox demise linked to spread of HIV infection. BBC News; May 17, 2010.

[97] Arevalo-Herrera M, Castellanos A, Yazdani SS, Shakri AR, Chitnis CE, Dominik R, et al. Immunogenicity and protective efficacy of recombinant vaccine based on the receptor-binding domain of the Plasmodium vivax Duffy binding protein in Aotus monkeys. Am J Trop Med Hyg 2005;73:25–31.

[98] Miller LH, Mason SJ, Clyde DF, McGinniss MH. The resistance factor to Plasmodium vivax in blacks. The Duffy-blood-group genotype, FyFy. N Engl J Med 1976;295:302–4.

[99] Hill AVS. Evolution, revolution and heresy in the genetics of infectious disease susceptibility. Philos Trans R Soc Lond Ser B Biol Sci 2012;367:840–9.

[100] Kitamura H, Okudela K. Bronchioloalveolar neoplasia. Int J Clin Exp Pathol 2011;4:97–9.

[101] Pitteloud N, Quinton R, Pearce S, Raivio T, Acierno J, Dwyer A, et al. Digenic mutations account for variable phenotypes in idiopathic hypogonadotropic hypogonadism. J Clin Invest 2007;117:457–63.

[102] Smulders YM, Eussen BHJ, Verhoef S, Wouters CH. Large deletion causing the TSC2-PKD1 contiguous gene syndrome without infantile polycystic disease. J Med Genet 2003;40:e17.

[103] Ikegawa S. A short history of the genome-wide association study: where we were and where we are going. Genomics Inform 2012;10:220–5.

[104] Platt A, Vilhjalmsson BJ, Nordborg M. Conditions under which genome-wide association studies will be positively misleading. Genetics 2010;186:1045–52.

[105] Beekman M, Blanch H, Perola M, Hervonen A, Bezrukov V, Sikora E, et al. Genome-wide linkage analysis for human longevity: genetics of healthy aging study. Aging Cell 2013;12:184–93.

[106] Couzin-Frankel J. Major heart disease genes prove elusive. Science 2010;328:1220–1.

[107] Cantor RM, Lange K, Sinsheimer JS. Prioritizing GWAS results: a review of statistical methods and recommendations for their application. Am J Hum Genet 2010;86(1):6–22.

[108] Ford ES, Giles WH, Dietz WH. Prevalence of the metabolic syndrome among US adults: findings from the Third National Health and Nutrition Examination Survey. JAMA 2002;287:356–9.

[109] Bierig JR. Actions for damages against medical examiners and the defense of sovereign immunity. Clin Lab Med 1998;18:139–50.

[110] Anderson LM, Bhalchandra A, Diwan BA, Nicola T, Fear NT, Roman E. Critical windows of exposure for children's health: cancer in human epidemiological studies and neoplasms in experimental animal models. Environ Health Perspect 2000;108(Suppl. 3):573–94.

[111] Altman LK. For 3 Nobel winners, a molecular mystery solved. The New York Times; October 7, 2013.

CHAPTER

6

Precision Organisms

SECTION 6.1 MODERN TAXONOMY OF INFECTIOUS DISEASES

Life is a concept.
Patrick Forterre [1]

Nobody goes there anymore. It's too crowded.
Yogi Berra

In a nutshell, about 300 infectious pathogens account for more than 95% of the diseases caused by living organisms. About 150 viruses and five types of prions account for the vast majority of infections due to nonliving organisms. There are at least 1400 species of organisms that are known to produce disease in humans, and most of these are rare occurrences appearing as case reports describing one or several individuals, sometimes occurring in an isolated geographic region. Increasingly, newly discovered pathogens are otherwise-harmless organisms that cause disease under some special set of circumstances. [Glossary Exotic diseases]

Precision Medicine and the Reinvention of Human Disease
https://doi.org/10.1016/B978-0-12-814393-3.00006-8

181

According to World Health Organization, in 1996, about 33% of human deaths were attributable to infections [2]. About a dozen organisms, give or take, account for the bulk of those deaths. Here are some of the frightening highlights:

- Each year, about 4 million children die from lung infections, and about 3 million children die from infectious diarrheal diseases [2]. Rotaviruses are one of many causes of diarrheal disease (Group III Viruses). In 2004, rotaviruses were responsible for about half a million deaths, mostly in developing countries [3].
- About 2 billion people have been infected with Mycobacterium tuberculosis. Tuberculosis kills about 3 million people each year [2].
- Malaria infects 500 million people. About 2 million people die each year from malaria [2].
- Worldwide, about 350 million people are chronic carriers of Hepatitis B, and about 100 million people are chronic carriers of Hepatitis C. In aggregate, about one-quarter (25 million) of these chronic carriers will eventually die from ensuing liver diseases [2].

Infectious organisms can kill individuals through mechanisms other than through the direct pathologic effects of growth, invasion, and inflammation. Infectious organisms have been implicated in vascular disease. The organisms implicated in coronary artery disease and stroke include Chlamydia pneumoniae and Cytomegalovirus [4]. In addition, infections caused by a wide variety of pathogenic organisms can result in cancer. About 7.2 million deaths occur each year from cancer, worldwide. About one-fifth of these cancer deaths are caused by infectious organisms [5]. Hepatitis B alone accounts for about 700,000 cancer deaths each year, from hepatocellular carcinoma [6]. Organisms contributing to cancer deaths include bacteria (Helicobacter pylori), animal parasites (schistosomes and liver flukes), and viruses (Herpesviruses, Papillomaviruses, Hepadnaviruses, Flaviviruses, Retroviruses, Polyomaviruses). Though fungal and plant organisms do not seem to cause cancer through human infection, they produce a multitude of biologically active secondary metabolites (i.e., synthesized molecules that are not directly involved in the growth of the organism), some of which are potent carcinogens. For example, aflatoxin, produced by Aspergillus flavus, is possibly the most powerful carcinogen ever studied [7,8]. [Glossary Invasion]

In summary, infectious diseases are the number one killer of humans worldwide, and they contribute to vascular disease and cancer, the two leading causes of death in the most developed countries. Despite the large toll of human lives taken by pathogenic organisms, most of the life forms on this planet have not been implicated in human disease. If we look no further than our own bodies, we see that 90% of the living cells that compose the human body are either bacteria, fungi, or single-cell eukaryotes. The human intestines alone are home to about 40,000 species of bacteria [9]. For the sake of discussion, let us accept that there are 50 million species of organisms on earth (a gross underestimate by some accounts). There have been about 1400 pathogenic species reported in the medical literature. This means that if you should stumble randomly upon a member of one of the species of life on earth, the probability that it is an infectious pathogen is only about 0.000028.

Given the many millions of living species on our planet, how can we comprehend the natural world in which we live? We do this with Taxonomy, the science of classifying the elements of a knowledge domain, and assigning names to the classes and the elements. In the case of terrestrial life forms, taxonomy involves assigning a name and a class to every species of life. The creation of the modern taxonomy of living organisms is one of the greatest achievements of science. The taxonomy that we use today was developed over two millennia and absorbed the lifetime efforts of dozens of generations of dedicated biologists. We use the taxonomy in full knowledge that it is a work-in-progress that will continue for as long as our planet continues to sustain life. [Glossary Taxon]

From the viewpoint of medical science, the entire set of organisms that are known to be human pathogens fits neatly into the preexisting taxonomy of living organisms. There is no need to reinvent a classification for the approximately 1400 species of organisms that are known to cause disease in humans. Conveniently, each species of infectious organism in humans can be assigned to one of about 40 classes within the taxonomy. Methods for identifying organisms within classes, and the general biological properties of organisms within classes are, for the most part, understood. Our taxonomy-based knowledge greatly simplifies the process of diagnosing, preventing, and treating infectious diseases. We can thank the precision of the taxonomy of living organisms for much of what we have come to recognize as Precision Microbiology.

Biologists presume that that there are about 50 million living species of organisms, and an untold number of extinct ancestral organisms. Most biologists would agree that the following generalizations describe earthly life, as we know it:

1. All living organisms on earth contain DNA, a highly stable nucleic acid. DNA is transcribed into a less stable, single-stranded molecule called RNA, and RNA is translated into proteins. All living organisms replicate their DNA and produce more organisms of the same genotype. [Glossary Nonliving organism]

2. All living organisms on earth can be divided into two broad classes, the prokaryotes (organisms with a simple string of DNA and without a membrane-delimited nucleus), and eukaryotes (organisms with a membrane-delimited nucleus) [10].

3. The prokaryotes preceded the emergence of the eukaryotes, and the first eukaryotes were built from the union of two or more prokaryotes [11].

4. Every eukaryotic organism that lives today is a descendant of the root ancestral eukaryote [11].

5. Every organism belongs to a species that has a set of features that characterize every member of the species and that distinguish the members of the species from organisms belonging to any other species.

6. The term species describes a biological entity, and is not an arbitrary abstraction invented to help differentiate the parts of a continuous spectrum of organisms that differ from one another on a scale of minor genomic differences.

Of course, it is difficult to garner unanimous agreement by scientists, and every fundamental principle of taxonomy has been challenged at one time or another. For those who would include viruses and prions among the living organisms, statements 1 and 2 are debatable. The validity of statements 3 and 4 has also been questioned. Some scientists have postulated that prokaryotes descended from eukaryotes, shucking off organelles in favor of a more simpler bacterial lifestyle. Others suggest that prokaryotes and eukaryotes arose simultaneously. In this case, any genetic or metabolic homologies between eukaryotes and prokaryotes results from a laterally shared gene pool.

Statements 5 and 6 have a long and disputatious history. It has been argued that nature produces individuals, not species; the concept of species being a mere figment of the human imagination, created for the convenience of taxonomists who need to group similar organisms.

Species is the bottom-most class of the taxonomy of living organisms. The term always refers to the plurality of members and this is the reason that only the plural form is used (i.e., species, never specie). Because the species class contains the individual objects of the classification, it is the only class which is not abstract. Every species of organism contains individuals that share a common ancestral relationship to one another. If we use the modern definition of species as an evolving gene pool, we see that the species can be thought of as a biological life form, with substance (a population of propagating genes) and a function (evolving to produce new species) [12–14]. **Put simply, species speciate; individuals merely procreate. Hence, the species class is an identifiable biological entity with its own unique functions**. Nontaxonomists tend to focus on the lives of individual things and have difficulty contemplating the life of a species. Taxonomists focus on the relationship among classes and recognize that a species fits the criteria of a class and of a biological entity.

Taxonomists are constantly engaged in an intellectual battle fought over the principles of biological classification. They all know that the stakes are high. When unrelated organisms are mixed together in the same class, and when related organisms are separated into unrelated classes, the value of the classification is lost, perhaps forever. To understand why this is true, you need to understand that the properties shared by members of classes of organisms allow scientists to form and test general hypotheses that may apply to all the members of a class and their descendant subclasses. Without an accurate classification of living organisms, it would be impossible to draw any general conclusions based on observations of individual organisms (Fig. 6.1).

The biological properties of infectious organisms are inherited from their ancestral classes. For example, the class of organisms known as Apicomplexa contains the organisms responsible for malaria, babesiosis, cryptosporidiosis, cyclosporan gastroenteritis, isosporiasis, sarcocystosis, and toxoplasmosis. When you learn the class properties of the apicomplexans, you gain a basic understanding of the biological features that characterize every infectious organism within Class Apicomplexa. Hence, the moment you learn an organism's proper class, you gain information that you might use to detect, diagnose, prevent, and treat the infections produced by the organism.

If you are a student of microbiology, or a healthcare professional, you need to be familiar with hundreds of infections organisms. There are many resources, web-based and paper-based, that describe all of these pathogens in great detail, but how can you be expected to integrate volumes of information when you are confronted by a sick patient? It is not humanly possible. A much better strategy starts with learning the basic biology of the 40 classes of organisms that account for all of the infectious diseases that occur in humans.

Efforts to sequence the genomes of prokaryotic, eukaryotic, and viral species, thereby comparing the genomes of different classes of organisms, have revitalized the field of evolutionary taxonomy (phylogenetics). The analysis of normal and abnormal homologous genes in related classes of organisms has inspired new disease treatments targeted against specific molecules and pathways characteristic of species or classes or organisms. **Students who do not understand the principles of modern taxonomy have little chance of perceiving the connections between medicine, genetics, pharmacology, or pathology, to say nothing of clinical microbiology**.

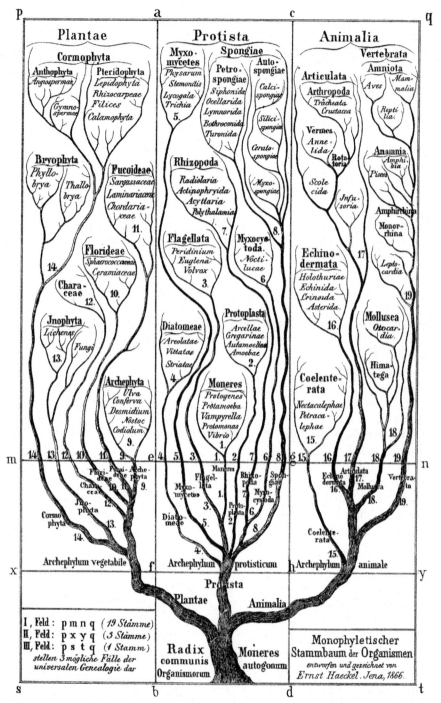

FIG. 6.1 The classification of all living organisms, circa 1866. This classification was drawn by Ernst Haeckel, a contemporary of Charles Darwin, more than 150 years ago. It predates the discovery of genes, and the major fossil discoveries of the early 20th centuries (e.g.,Burgess shale, 1909), but it remains a fairly good representation of taxonomy. Every organism can be assigned to one, and only one, of the primary classes (Plants, Protista or one-celled animals, and Animalia, or multicellular animals with organs), and every class is related by evolutionary lineage. *Reproduced from Wikipedia, from a drawing by Ernst Haeckel, 1866.*

If we confine our attention to the subset of taxonomy classes that contain pathogenic organisms, we see that the entire field can be reduced to about 40 classes [8]:

Bacteria
    Proteobacteria
        Alpha Proteobacteria
        Beta Proteobacteria
        Gamma Proteobacteria
        Epsilon Proteobacteria
    Spirochaetes
    Bacteroidetes
    Fusobacteria
    Firmicutes
        Bacilli
        Clostridia
        Mollicutes
    Chlamydiae
    Actinobacteria
Eukaryota (organisms that have nucleated cells)
    Bikonta (2-flagella)
        Excavata
            Metamonada
            Discoba
            Euglenozoa
            Percolozoa
        Archaeplastida, from which Kingdom Plantae derives
        Chromalveolata
            Alveolata
            Apicomplexa
            Ciliophora (ciliates)
            Heterokontophyta
    Unikonta (1-flagellum)
        Amoebozoa
        Opisthokonta
            Choanozoa
            Animalia
            Fungi

In addition to the classes of infectious living organisms, there are seven additional classes of nonliving organisms:

Viruses
    Group I, double-stranded DNA
    Group II, single-stranded DNA
    Group III, double-stranded RNA
    Group IV, positive sense single-stranded RNA

Group V, negative sense single-stranded RNA ssRNA
Group VI, single-stranded RNA with a reverse transcriptase
Group VII, double-stranded DNA with a reverse transcriptase

Prions

In the early days of Precision Medicine, it was expected that comparisons between whole-genome sequences, on many different organisms, would resolve internecine battles over the structure of the tree of life. Such expectations were overly optimistic, due, in no small part, to an analytic phenomenon now known as "nonphylogenetic signal" [15]. When gene sequence data is analyzed, and two organisms share the same sequence in a stretch of DNA, it can be very tempting to infer that the two organisms belong to the same class (i.e., that they inherited the identical sequence from a common ancestor). This inference is not necessarily correct. Because DNA mutations arise stochastically over time (i.e., at random locations in the gene and at random times), two organisms having different ancestors may achieve the same sequence in a chosen stretch of DNA. When mathematical phylogeneticists began modeling inferences drawn from analyses of genomic data, they assumed that most class assignment errors would occur when the branches between sister taxa were long (i.e., when a long time elapsed between evolutionary divergences, allowing for many random substitutions in base pairs). They called this phenomenon, wherein nonsister taxa were assigned the same ancient ancestor class, "long branch attraction." In practice, errors of this type can occur whether the branches are long, or short, or in between. Over the years, the accepted usage of the term "long branch attraction" has been extended to just about any error in phylogenetic grouping due to gene similarities acquired through any mechanism other than inheritance from a shared ancestor. This would include random mutational and adaptive convergence [16]. The moral here is that powerful data-intensive analytic techniques are sometimes more confusing than they are clarifying [8]. [Glossary Nonphylogenetic property, Long branch attraction, Taxa, Nonphylogenetic signal]

A good classification always requires persistent, continuous testing. Hence, much of the value of the newest molecular and computational approaches to taxonomy has one of the following applications [8].

- To confirm candidate classes originally determined by nongenetic analysis (e.g., morphology, biological markers). You would expect key sequences among members of a class to be similar.
- To indicate classification errors. Sequence dissimilarities would indicate that the taxonomist must seriously consider reassigning classes and species.
- To provide informative biological markers that are not found by morphologic examination, thus permitting more accurate assignment of species.
- To act as a phylogenetic chronometer to determine when subclasses may have first appeared.
- To help explain the biological significance of morphologic markers whose biological significance is not apparent

As just one example of the value of taxonomy, let's consider a recent manuscript reporting the efficacy of proteosome inhibitors in the treatment of three common diseases that are, together, responsible for a good portion of the morbidity and mortality of infections diseases,

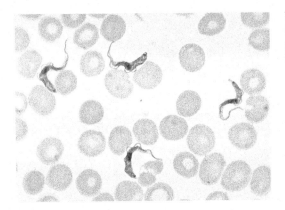

FIG. 6.2 Trypanosomes, observed as dark wavy flakes, in blood smear from patient with African trypanosomiasis. *Reproduced from US Centers for Disease Control and Prevention, public domain image.*

worldwide [17]. These three are Chagas disease, sleeping sickness, and leishmaniasis. Trypanosoma cruzi is the cause of Chagas disease, also known as American trypanosomiasis. Chagas disease affects about eight million people [18]. Trypanosoma brucei is the cause of African trypanosomiasis (sleeping sickness). It has been reported that Trypanosoma brucei accounts for about 50,000 deaths each year. Leishmania species cause leishmaniasis, a disease that infects about 12 million people worldwide. Each year, about 60,000 people die from the visceral form of the disease. How did researchers suspect that these three organisms would be susceptible to the same drug? Our taxonomy of living organisms holds the answer. All three organisms descend from Class Trypanosomatida (Fig. 6.2).

Trypanosoma cruzi, the root cause organism of Chagas disease

Order	Trypanosomatida
Genus	Trypanosoma
Species	*T. cruzi*

Trypanosoma brucei, the root cause organism of sleeping sickness

Order	Trypanosomatida
Genus	Trypanosoma
Species	*T. brucei*

Leishmania donovani, the root cause organism of leishmaniasis

Order	Trypanosomatida
Genus	Leishmania
Species	*L. donovani*

Notice that *L. donovani* has a different parent class (i.e., Leishmania) than *T. cruzi* and *T brucei* (i.e., Trypanosoma). Nonetheless, all three organisms have the same grandparent class (Trypanosomatida), and all three organisms inherit the class properties associated with Trypanosomatida. [Glossary Parent class]

Without a taxonomy, we would have no rational method for finding relationships among organisms. Hence, we would have no rational methods for finding treatments that might be effective against related organisms. The refinement of the taxonomy of living organisms is one of the ongoing achievements of Precision Medicine. Because infectious diseases produce much more morbidity and mortality than other causes of disease, nowhere has Precision Medicine had a greater potential value than the precise diagnosis and improved treatment of infectious organisms.

SECTION 6.2 OUR GENOME IS A BOOK TITLED "THE HISTORY OF HUMAN INFECTIONS"

> The cell is basically an historical document, and gaining the capacity to read it (by the sequencing of genes) cannot but drastically alter the way we look at all of biology.
> *Carl Woese [19]*

> We are just "a volume of diseases bound together."
> *John Donne (1572–1631)*

The Taino Indians were the indigenous people of the island of Hispaniola, today recognized as the island containing the nations of the Dominican Republic and Haiti. When Columbus first landed on Hispaniola, in 1492, hundreds of thousands of Taino lived on the island. The Taino population was soon thereafter decimated by plagues of the flu (1493) and smallpox (1518), and various other diseases introduced by European colonialists. These infections included hepatitis, measles, tuberculosis, diphtheria, cholera, and typhus. By 1550, there were only about 500 Tainos in Hispaniola [20].

Why did the Tainos die in large number, while the Europeans, who brought these disease to the new world, managed to survive? The pat answer to this question is that the Taino were new to these infections and were thus immunologically unprepared to launch an effective biological defense. Hence, many of the Taino died from infections that produced relatively minor illness in Europeans. Does this answer really make much sense? Every individual, whether Taino or European, is immunologically naive to an organism prior to their first infectious encounter. If the Taino died because they had never before been infected by organisms of European origin, then we would expect Europeans to die, with equal frequency, when they are exposed to indigenous organisms, for the first time.

The historical tragedy of the Taino of Hispaniola is mentioned here to draw attention to a theme that has run throughout this book. Diseases develop through a sequence of steps, occurring over time, and it is silly to try to explain diseases in terms of any single condition. Infectious diseases are no exception to the rule, and we can expect that multiple conditions account for the invasion and growth of infectious organisms; and that multiple conditions, in addition to adaptive immunity, will account for an individual's response to an infection. [Glossary Adaptive immunity]

In the context of Precision Medicine, infections draw our attention because they have played an important role in the evolution of the eukaryotic genome. In this section, we will explore the following assertions:

- The majority of the human genome consists of relic DNA derived from ancient invasive organisms.
- Some of the key steps in the development of vertebrate animals, and mammals in particular, have come from DNA acquired from infectious organisms.
- A good portion of the genes in humans (perhaps 10%) are involved in responses to infectious organisms.
- Most of the cells in the human (at least 90%) consist of infectious organisms and commensals that have adapted to life within human hosts. [Glossary Commensal]
- Normal defenses can block every infectious disease. Hence, every infectious disease results from a failure of our normal defenses, immunologic and otherwise.
- Cellular defects that have no direct connection to immunity may increase susceptibility to infectious organisms.
- By dissecting the biological steps involved in the pathogenesis of infectious disease, it is possible to develop new treatments, other than antibiotics, that will be effective against a range of related organisms.

Let's see if we can justify these assertions.

- **The majority of the human genome consists of relic DNA derived from ancient invasive organisms.**

Nearly half of the human genome is filled with sequences such as LINE and Alu, and DNA transposons, all derived from ancient retroviruses [21]. About 8% of our genome is derived from longer sequences with similarity to known infectious retroviruses, and these longer sequences can usually be recognized by their contained subsequences (e.g., gag, pol, and env genes) and long terminal repeats. The viral sequences in our genomes are the remnants of ancient retroviral infections, and the occasional nonretroviral infection, that were branded into DNA, and subsequently amplified [21–23]. Because much of the endogenous retroviral load in the human genome is due to amplification, and subsequent mutation, it is hard to determine the number of retroviral species that established their niche in the human gene pool, but studies of these viral remains would suggest that we contain species from several dozen families of retroviruses, with an undetermined number of contributions from individual family members [24]. Based on comparisons of the viruses present in different species of primates, it would appear that the most recent acquisition of an endogenous retrovirus occurred in humans between 100,000 and 1 million years ago [25]. Most of the retroviral sequences in our genomes are inactivated due to an accumulation of degenerative mutations collected over the eons, indicating that there has been little or no selective pressure to conserve retroviruses in their pristine sequence. [Glossary Transposon]

- **Some of the key steps in the development of vertebrate animals, and mammals in particular, have come from DNA acquired from infectious organisms.**

The human genome has preserved its viral ballast, at some cost. At every cell division, energy is expended to replicate the genome, and the larger the genome, the more energy must be expended. Why do we spend a large portion of the energy required to replicate our genome, on inactive sequences, of viral origin? Why doesn't our genome simply eject the extra DNA, a biological process that is commonplace in the evolution of obligate intracellular parasitic organisms? [Glossary Facultative intracellular organism, Obligate intracellular organism]

Natural selection will preserve useful genes, even when those genes are derived from other organisms. Current evolutionary theory holds that the first eukaryotes (i.e., cells with a nucleus) were formed by a sequence of two fusions of prokaryotes in which one prokaryote became the nucleus and another became the mitochondria, and the third became the flagellated bag in which the nucleus and mitochondria floated. It makes for a messy story, but based on similarities between the eukaryotic nucleus and the genome of archaean cells, and based on observation of the organization of DNA, RNA, and ribosomes in archaeans, it has been hypothesized that the eukaryotic nucleus was derived from an archaean organism [26]. Conversely, similarities between mitochondria and eubacteria of Class Rickettsia suggest that the eukaryotic mitochondrium was derived from an ancestor of a modern rickettsia. Furthermore, evidence suggests that all existing eukaryotic organisms descended from ancestors that contained mitochondria. Mitochondria are found in eukaryotic organisms from every known class of eukaryotes. Even the so-called amitochondriate classes (i.e., organisms without mitochondria) contain vestigial forms of mitochondria (i.e., hydrogenosomes and mitosomes) [27–30]. In short, the root eukaryote owed its existence to cellular abductions.

Why do organisms need to steal genes from other organisms? The answer is simple. Evolution works through the selection of naturally occurring variants that arise in the gene pool, providing us with new genes that have subtle differences from old genes. Evolution is not a very efficient way to achieve metabolic breakthroughs that involve two or more independently evolved pathways that work together to perform a new function. If two pathways are required to achieve one metabolic process, then each pathway must evolve without the benefit of selective pressure for the complete pathway (which requires two intact pathways to yield a survival benefit). Achieving a complex, combined pathway through natural selection is possible, but it is highly improbable. When such pathways are achieved in one species of organism, they tend to take many millions of years to evolve. There's no guarantee that the feat will be repeated by other organisms any time soon. In this case, the mechanism through which the pathway will be attained is most likely going to be through genetic acquisition of a complete pathway, from an endowed organism, not through natural selection of preexisting gene variants.

This in fact was the history of terrestrial oxygenic photosynthesis, a metabolic pathway that required the independent evolution of two different pathways [11]. Cyanobacteria achieved oxygenic photosynthesis about 2.5 billion years ago. Subsequently, the cyanobacteria refined the process, and no organism other than cyanobacteria can be credited with oxygenic photosynthesis (though other organisms use photosynthetic processes that do not produce oxygen). All oxygenic photosynthesis in eukaryotes is accomplished with the use of chloroplasts, a symbiotic organelle formed from a captured cyanobacteria. An ancient member of Class Archaeplastida found that by engulfing a cyanobacteria, it too could photosynthesize. This indentured relationship between Archaeplastida and cyanobacteria became permanent, and every descendant of Class Archaeplastida, which includes all the green plants, have benefited from their ancestor's theft. It is generally believed that the acquisition of a cyanobacteria as a self-replicating organelle, occurred only once in earth's history. Chloroplast-containing organisms other than those within Class Archaeplastida must have seized chloroplasts (not cyanobacteria) from green algae or other members of Class Archaeplastida. How do we know that this is true? By counting the membranes that cover chloroplasts. Chloroplasts in the Archaeplastida are lined by two layers, corresponding to the inner and outer membranes of the original, indentured cyanobacteria. The chloroplasts of non-Archaeplastida eukaryotes have three or four membrane layers, suggesting that a member of Archaeplastida was engulfed, and the membranes of the chloroplast, and of the Arhaeplastida containing the chloroplast, were entrapped permanently in the host cell. [Glossary Cyanobacteria]

Infections pose a special problem for the host genome. How can natural selection, which works very gradually, cope with new infections, which kill quickly? In the case of infection, the acquisition of a gene may lead to a better, quicker defensive strategy than the evolution toward an altered set of genes that provide a slight survival advantage, over time.

New genes that fight infection are likely to have been acquired from infectious organisms. When a new gene appears rapidly, it is likely to have an exogenous source, and what source would be more available than the genes from an invading organism? As it happens, there are numerous examples of functional genes that contain inserts derived from retroviruses that have taken residence in the human genome. Among these are the oncogenes, to be discussed at some length in a later chapter [31–33].

Two additional evolutionary leaps, benefitting the ancestral classes of humans, include the attainment of adaptive immunity and the development of the mammalian placenta. Let's take a moment to see how these innovations came about. [Glossary Oncogene]

Adaptive immunity evolved at about the same time that jawed vertebrates first appeared on earth. The crucial gene responsible for the great leap to adaptive immunity, the recombination activating gene (RAG), was stolen from a retrovirus. To understand the pivotal evolutionary role of RAG, we need to review a bit of high school biology. The adaptive immune system responds to the specific chemical properties of foreign antigens, such as those that appear on viruses and other infectious agents. Adaptive immunity is a system wherein somatic T cells and B cells are produced, each with a unique and characteristic immunoglobulin (in the case of B cells) or T-cell receptor (in the case of T cells). Through a complex presentation and selection system, a foreign antigen elicits the replication of a B cell whose unique immunoglobulin molecule (i.e., so-called antibodies) matches the antigen. Secretion of matching antibodies leads to the production of antigen-antibody complexes that may deactivate and clear circulating antibodies, or may lead to the destruction of the organism that carries the antigen (e.g., virus or bacteria).

To produce the many unique B and T cells, each with a uniquely rearranged segment of DNA that encodes specific immunoglobulins or T-cell receptors, recombination and hypermutation must take place within a specific gene region. This process yields on the order of a billion unique somatic genes, and requires the participation of recombination activating genes (RAGs). The acquisition of a recombination activating gene is presumed to be the key evolutionary event that led to the development of the adaptive immune system present in all jawed vertebrates (gnathostomes). Before the appearance of the jawed vertebrates, this sort of recombination was genetically unavailable to animals. Our genes simply were not equal to the task. Retroviruses, however, are specialists at cutting, moving, and mutating DNA. Is it any wonder that the startling evolutionary leap to adaptive immunity was acquired from retrotransposons? Thus, we owe our most important defense against infections to genetic material retrieved from the vast trove of retrovirally derived DNA carried in our genome [33]. As one might expect, inherited mutations in RAG genes are the root causes of several immune deficiency syndromes [34,35].

Many millions of years later, vertebrates acquired another gene that did much to enable the evolution of all mammals. Members of Class Mammalia are distinguished by the development of the placenta, an organ that grows within the uterine cavity (i.e., the endometrium). After birth, the placenta must detach from the uterus. You can imagine the delicate balancing act between attaching firmly to the wall of the uterus and detaching cleanly from the wall of the uterus. During placental development, large, flat cells called cytotrophoblasts form the interface between placenta and uterus. To create the thin membrane that borders the lining of the uterus and that borders the blood received from the uterus in the spaces between the placental villi, the cytotrophoblasts must somehow fuse into a syncytium (i.e., multinucleate collections of cells that have fused together by dissolving their individual cytoplasmic membranes). [Glossary Craniata]

There is one task at which all animals excel: maintaining a clear separation between one cell and another. In point of fact, the most distinctive difference between animal cells and all other cells of eukaryotic origin happens to be the presence of cell junctions, whose purpose is to bind cells to one another without fusing cells. This being the case, you can see that the normal direction of animal evolution would preclude the appearance of a gene intended to form a huge syncytium of placental cells. Whereas animal cells are failures at fusion, viruses are champions. One of the most often-deployed methods by which viruses invade cells is through fusion at the cytoplasmic membrane. It happens that retroviral envelope genes, preserved in the human genome, do a very good job at fusing membranes. Animals captured a retroviral fusogenic envelope gene and inserted it into one of the first syncytin molecules involved the development of the placenta. Apparently, this acquisition worked out so well for mammals that later-evolving mammalian classes made their own retrovirus gene acquisitions to obtain additional syncytins, thus refining the placenta for their own subclasses [23,36].

- **A good portion of the genes in humans (perhaps 10%) are involved in responses to infectious organisms.**

It has been estimated that over 1000 human genes are involved in inflammation pathways [37]. Several studies have shown that following an inflammatory challenge or challenged by the introduction of a pathogen, more than a hundred genes are activated [38–40]. The activated genes include some of the same genes that have been associated with autoimmune diseases, suggesting that these disease-associated genes are conserved because they have a beneficial role, protecting us from invading pathogens [39]. The genetic profile of genes activated by inflammation is very similar from human to human, but quite dissimilar from the profile of genes activated by inflammation in the mouse [41]. This would suggest that species develop their own genome-wide responses to agents that cause inflammation (e.g., invading organisms).

- **Most of the cells residing in human bodies are nonhuman.**

There are about 10 times as many nonhuman cells living in our bodies as there are human cells [40]. The human intestines alone contain 40,000 different species of bacteria [9]. These 40,000 species contain about 9 million different genes. Compare that with the paltry 23,000 genes in the human genome, and we quickly see that we homo sapiens contribute very little to the genetic diversity of the human body's ecosystem. [Glossary Primary host, Intermediate host, Secondary host]

- **Normal defenses can block every infectious disease. Hence, every infectious disease results from a failure of our normal defenses, immunologic and otherwise.**

For any given infectious agent, no matter how virulent they may seem, there are always individuals who can resist infection. Moreover, as a generalization, the majority of individuals who are infected with a pathogenic microorganism will never develop any clinically significant disease [42].

As one example, Naegleria fowleri is often found in warm freshwater. Swimmers in contaminated waters may develop an infection that spreads from the nasal sinuses to the central nervous system, to produce an encephalitis that is fatal in 97% of cases [43]. Despite the hazard posed by Naegleria, health authorities do not generally test freshwater sources to determine the presence of the organism. Do not expect to find warning signs posted at swimming holes announcing that the water is contaminated by an organism that produces a disease that has a nearly 100% fatality rate. It is simply assumed that anyone who spends any time around freshwater will eventually be exposed to Naegleria. As it happens, although many thousands of individuals are exposed each year to Naegleria in the United States, only a few cases of Naegleria encephalitis occur in this country. In fact, since Naegleria was recognized as a cause of encephalitis, in 1965, fewer than 150 cases have been reported [44]. Most of the reported cases have occurred in children and adolescents and are associated with recreational water activities [45,46]. The children who develop Naeglerian encephalitis, though exhibiting no signs of immune deficiency, are nonetheless susceptible to Naegleria. What makes these children different from all the other children and adults who were exposed to the same organisms?

Neisseria meningitidis, a cause of bacterial meningitis, can be cultured from nasal swabs sampled from the general population. If N. meningitidis were a primary pathogen, then why doesn't it cause disease in the vast majority of infected individuals. If N. meningitidis were an opportunistic infection, then why does it typically cause disease in healthy college-age individuals (not immunocompromised individuals)? If this organism is neither a primary pathogen nor an opportunistic pathogen, then what kind of pathogen is it? More importantly, why is N. meningitidis a potentially fatal pathogen in some individuals and a harmless commensal in others [47]? [Glossary Opportunistic infection]

Organisms that were formerly thought to be purely pathogenic are now known to frequently live quietly within infected humans, without causing symptoms of disease. For example, parasites such as the agents that cause Chagas disease, leishmaniases, and toxoplasmosis are commonly found living in apparently normal individuals. Viruses, including the agents that cause herpes simplex infections and infections by hepatitis viruses B and C, can be found in healthy individuals. Mycobacterium tuberculosis can infect an individual, produce a limited pathologic reaction in the lung, and remain in the body in a quiescent state for the life of the individual. In fact, it has been estimated that about one out of three individuals, worldwide, is infected with Mycobacterium tuberculosis, and will never suffer any consequences. Luckily, asymptomatic carriers of tuberculosis, in whom the there is no active pulmonary disease, are noninfective. Staphylococcus aureus, a bacterial pathogen that is known to produce abscesses, invade through tissues, and release toxins, is also known to circulate in the blood, without causing symptoms, in a sizeable portion of the human population [40].

We now know that potentially virulent organisms are normally tamed within our bodies. Hence, the root cause of every clinical infection results from a deficiency in the defenses of particular subpopulations of individuals.

- **Cellular defects that have no direct connection to immunity may increase susceptibility to infectious organisms.**

If we want to understand why certain individuals are susceptible to infections and other individuals are not, we must understand that immune deficiencies cannot account for all infections. Infectious diseases, just like any other disease, develop in steps, and it stands to reason that there must be many different pathways through which those steps can be enhanced or blocked. Theory aside, what is the actual evidence that susceptibility to infectious diseases arise through deficiencies unrelated to the immune system?

- Time and again, we encounter serious infections from organisms thought to be nonpathogenic, occurring in immunocompetent individuals [48–51].
- Not everyone with an immune deficit will succumb to an infectious disease, implying that these individuals are protected by resistance mechanisms other than immunity.
- We know of various genetic conditions that increase our susceptibility to infectious diseases, and some of these genetic flaws have nothing to do with the adaptive (i.e., antibody-forming) immune systems. For example, children with sickle cell disease or congenital asplenia will have a heightened susceptibility to invasive pneumococcal diseases [52]. Otherwise-normal children with IRAK4 or NEMO gene mutations will also have a high risk of invasive pneumococcal disease [52]. IRAK4 or NEMO genes code for proteins involved in the phagocytosis of bacteria by splenic macrophages. Likewise, in mice, natural resistance to infection is influenced by the Bcg gene, which affects the early phagocytosis and destruction of intracellular organisms by macrophages [53]. As a final example, both humans and zebrafish that have mutations that reduce the synthesis of a proinflammatory leukotriene have heightened susceptibility to Mycobacterium tuberculosis [54]. It is easy to find examples of nonimmunologic mechanisms for susceptibility to infections [55,56].

- **By dissecting the biological steps involved in the pathogenesis of infectious disease, it is possible to develop new treatments, other than antibiotics, that will be effective against a range of related organisms.**

Nature, by interfering with the different steps in the development of infectious diseases, has a variety of protective mechanisms against organisms. For example, to defend against malaria, nature has preserved various mutations that render red cells unsuitable hosts for malarial guests. For example, individuals with hemoglobin variants HbS (sickle cell trait), HbC, and HbE increase the likelihood that an infected red cell will lyse. Likewise, but for obscure reasons, regulatory defects in hemoglobin synthesis, as seen in thalassemia, may also confer some protection against malaria. Also, variations in a structural protein of erythrocytes, SLC4A1, causing ovalocytosis; and polymorphisms of the glucose-6-phosphate dehydrogenase gene [57] both seem to protect against malaria.

We see individuals resistant to malaria due to absence of the Duffy protein required for Plasmodium vivax to bind and enter erythrocytes [58]. Knowing this, the Duffy-binding protein in the malaria parasite is now being studied as a potential drug or vaccine target as a new strategy against malaria [58]. More generally, drugs known as entry inhibitors are being developed based on knowledge that the attachment and entry of organisms may depend upon specific cooperative pathways, in host and invader cells, that can be targeted by drugs.

We know that there are many steps in the infection process that could be blocked by small changes in proteins that are unrelated to the immune process. For example, for an infectious agent to invade and flourish in an organism, it must gain entry into the tissues of the body, evading physical and chemical defenses along its way. It must find a place in which it can receive nourishment appropriate to its species and avoid any toxins that may be produced by its host. It must be able to grow as a collection of organisms, and this typically means that the host must permit some degree of invasion through its own tissues. These are just a few of the nonimmunological hurdles that invasive organisms must jump over, if they are to infect an organism. Every step in the pathogenesis of infectious disease provides another therapeutic opportunity. As we learn more about the pathways of development of infectious diseases that have become increasingly resistant to antibiotics, we will come to rely on Precision Medicine to prevent, diagnose, and treat infections.

Returning to the question posed at the beginning of this section, we can understand that the Taino were doomed from the moment that Columbus set foot on Hispaniola. Their problem was not that they had never encountered the pathogens carried by the Europeans. Their problem was that their ancestors had never encountered those pathogens. Hepatitis, measles, tuberculosis, diphtheria, cholera, and typhus had not written their chapters in the genome titled "The History of Taino Infections."

SECTION 6.3 INFLAMMATORY DISEASES: COLLATERAL DAMAGE IN THE WAR ON HUMAN INFECTION

> Nothing in biology makes sense except in the light of evolution
> *Theodosius Dobzhansky*

In the prior section, we remarked upon the large number of genes that are recruited in response to infections, with estimates ranging from the hundreds to in excess of 1000 [37–40]. Regardless of the precise number of genes involved, we have ample reason to believe that coordinated inflammatory responses are complex and involve multiple pathways. Because inflammation must begin quickly and must eventually resolve completely, we can assume that there are fine controls that initiate, limit, and terminate the pathways. Because multiple inflammatory pathways may be called into action at one time, we can expect to find multiple intersection points among the different pathways. Perhaps one pathway's initiator will serve as another pathway's inhibitor. The opportunities for speculation are endless.

All complex systems have one thing in common; they are all subject to catastrophic failure. Every part of the system provides an opportunity for system-wide error, and there is no foolproof way to guard against such problems. If you build a complex system to find and fix errors as they occur, you can expect to find errors occurring in the error-correction system. If you build redundant systems to take over in the event of a malfunction, then you run the risk of the problems in the redundant system spreading to the primary system [59,60].

The biological systems in place that protect us from invasive infections must eventually break down and produce diseases of their own internal systems. In the past several decades, we have come to divide the immune system diseases into two broad categories, based on our current, somewhat limited, understanding of human immune response mechanisms. These would be the autoimmune diseases of the adaptive immune system and the autoinflammatory diseases of the innate immune system.

As previously discussed, adaptive immunity is the system wherein somatic T cells and B cells are produced, each with a unique and characteristic immunoglobulin (in the case of B cells) or T-cell receptor (in the case of T cells). In addition, a specialized method of processing immunoglobulin heavy chain mRNA transcript accounts for the high levels of secretion of immunoglobulin proteins by plasma cells [61]. As one might expect, inherited mutations in the process through which antibody molecules are manufactured will lead to immune deficiency syndromes [34,35].

The adaptive immune system is designed to produce antibodies that can bind specific foreign (i.e., nonself) antigens. Antibody-antigen reactions occurring on the surface of an infectious organism may elicit an inflammatory response capable of killing foreign organisms. Though adaptive immunity plays an important role in protecting us from infection, errors in the adaptive immune system can lead to pathologic conditions when a response is launched against "self" antigens. As a group, such conditions are called autoimmune diseases. A list of some of the autoimmune diseases would include: multiple sclerosis, rheumatoid arthritis, systemic lupus erythematosus, myasthenia gravis, primary biliary cirrhosis, scleroderma, various types of glomerulonephritis, and relapsing polychondritis [62,63]. An acquired autoimmune disease may mimic a diseases of the innate immune system, by targeting a key gene in any of the various pathways involved [64]. [Glossary Autoantibody disease versus autoimmune disease, Innate immunity]

Rare monogenic disorders of the adaptive immune system can produce a wide array of clinical phenotypes. For example, a primary defect in the adaptive immune system can produce a disease characterized by widespread lymphadenopathy. ALPS (Autoimmune Lymphoproliferative syndrome) is a rare, inherited condition that is characterized by lymphocytosis and any of various types of autoimmune diseases, including autoimmune-mediated cytopenias of blood cells: hemolytic anemia, neutropenia, and thrombocytopenia. The term autoimmune lymphoproliferative syndrome covers a group of related disorders all caused by mutations of FAS, FASLG, CASPASE 8, CASPASE 10, or several RAS genes. These genes play a role in apoptosis, a normal pathway that induces cell death. Loss-of-function mutations in the genes that cause ALPS result in the persistence of lymphocytes that have outlived their usefulness. The persistent lymphocytes lead to the accumulation of lymphoid cells in circulation and in lymph nodes. Lymphocytes are the primary cells involved in the adaptive immune pathway, and a large elevation in the number of dysfunctional lymphocytes is thought to be the underlying mechanism by which inappropriate autoimmune responses against other types of blood cells occur in ALPS.

Another example of a rare genetic disorder of the adaptive immune system is autoimmune polyendocrinopathy-candidiasis-ectodermal dystrophy. This monogenic disease caused by mutations in AIRE (Autoimmune Regulator gene). The AIRE gene has a role in the development of normal immune tolerance, the process whereby the body determines the proteins that are "self" and thus privileged not to elicit an immune response [65]. AIRE permits thymic cells to broaden its repertoire of proteins to include a wide range of molecules that would ordinarily be confined to specific organs (e.g., cardiac-specific proteins, kidney-specific proteins). The expression of diverse proteins, within the thymus, at a particular stage of fetal development, somehow prepares the immune system to quell an adaptive immune reaction to these proteins, later in life. Dysfunction of the AIRE gene leads to an inappropriate adaptive immunity response against multiple tissues.

It should be remembered that a pathway may intersect with many other pathways. For example, the apoptosis pathway, partially disabled in ALPS, is known to interact with the innate immune system. This is accomplished via interplay of Apoptosis-associated speck-like protein with NLRP3 and pyrin of the cytokine pathway, an inflammation effector pathway of the innate immune system [66]. We should never be surprised when we see examples of diseases involving both the adaptive and innate immune systems.

If the adaptive immune system produces a bewildering array of clinical phenotypes, it is easily outdone by the innate immune system. The innate immune system is an ancient and somewhat nonspecific immune and inflammatory response system found in plants, fungi, insects, and most multicellular organisms [67]. Innate immunity uses at least six different systems to initiate inflammatory responses: Interleukin 1-beta (IL-1beta) activation (i.e., the inflammasome), Nuclear Factor kappa-light-chain-enhancer of activated B cells (NF-kappaB) activation, protein misfolding disorders, complement regulatory diseases, disturbances in cytokine signaling, and macrophage activation syndromes. [Glossary Enhancer, Inflammasome]

Here is a partial list of disorders that are generally credited to aberrations of the innate immune system, and categorized by component pathway [66]:

- IL-1-beta activation disorders: The inflammasomopathies
  - Familial cold autoinflammatory syndrome
  - Muckle-Wells syndrome
  - Neonatal-onset multisystem inflammatory disease/chronic neurologic cutaneous and articular syndrome
  - Familial Mediterranean fever
  - PAPA (pyogenic arthritis, pyoderma gangrenosum, and acne)
  - Chronic recurrent multifocal osteomyelitis/synovitis acne pustulosis hyperostosis osteitis
  - Majeed syndrome
  - Hyperimmunoglobinemia D with periodic fever syndrome
  - Recurrent hydatidiform mole [Glossary Hydatidiform mole]
  - Deficiency of the interleukin-1 receptor antagonist
  - Gout

- – Fibrosing disorders
- – Type 2 diabetes mellitus
- – Schnitzler syndrome

- – NF-B activation disorders
  - – Crohn disease
  - – Blau syndrome
  - – Familial cold autoinflammatory syndrome-2 (Guadaloupe periodic fever)

- – Protein folding disorders of the innate immune system
  - – TRAPS (the Tumor necrosis factor Receptor-Associated Periodic Syndrome)
  - – Spondyloarthropathies

- – Complement disorders
  - – Atypical hemolytic uremic syndrome
  - – Age-related macular degeneration

- – Cytokine signaling disorders
  - – Cherubism

- – Macrophage activation disorders
  - – Familial hemophagocytic lymphohistiocytosis
  - – Chediak-Higashi syndrome
  - – Griscelli syndrome
  - – X-linked lymphoproliferative syndrome
  - – Hermansky-Pudlak syndrome
  - – Secondary hemophagocytic lymphohistiocytosis
  - – Atherosclerosis

A cursory examination of this list tells us that acquired and genetic disorders of the innate immune system account for a stunningly diverse range of clinical diseases, attributed to a large collection of genes associated with at least six different crossreacting cellular pathways. Who would have imagined, 20 years ago, that recurrent hydatidiform mole, gout, Crohn disease, hemophagocytic lymphohistiocytosis, and atherosclerosis would ever appear together on a list of immune disorders?

Are there other immune systems, in addition to the adaptive and innate systems, whose disruptions can contribute to the development of human diseases? Because so much of the human genome is devoted to protecting us from infection, we can suspect that what we now have is only a vague and incomplete picture of immune systems. Recently, a third branch of immunity, named the intrinsic immune system, has been discovered. The intrinsic immune system is a cell-based (i.e., not humoral) antiviral system that is always "on" (i.e., not activated by the presence of its target) [68]. Intrinsic immunity has been studied for its role in controlling retrovirus infections (e.g., HIV infection). Intrinsic immunity is not strictly devoted to retroviruses, but its role in blocking other classes of virus is not well understood. At present, there are no specific human diseases that are categorized as disorders of the intrinsic immune system. [Glossary Intrinsic immunity]

Together, these immunologic systems produce inflammation through a large and growing number of pathways [66], and these different pathways may be activated by or coordinated with nonimmunologic pathways in response to pathogenic intracellular conditions including mitochondrial stresses, apoptosis, and proteosome activation [69,70]. The complexity of how these pathways operate and interact with one another is intellectually overwhelming. Moreover, we may be looking at the tip of a deep-dwelling iceberg, with many additional systems eventually coming to the surface. If acquired disorders of the immune system can mimic hundreds of different diseases, and if genetic disorders of the immune system can yield unpredictable clinical phenotypes, then how can we apply our knowledge of Precision Medicine to the treatment of the inflammatory diseases? Perhaps the following list of generalizations and observations may help:

- If one pathway dominates the clinical phenotype, then a drug that targets the dominant pathway is likely to yield the most clinical benefit.

Let's look at an example where an ancient cure for a common disease has been resurrected as a highly effective treatment for a monogenic disease of the innate immune system. Throughout human history, gout has plagued man. Untreated, gout is a painful, incapacitating, and mutilating disease. Luckily, there is a treatment, and this treatment has been known for several thousand years, at minimum. The Egyptian Ebers Papyrus, written about 1500 BC described the use of the autumn crocus (*Colchicum autumnale*) for the treatment of swollen joints, and the botanical source of colchicine was described again by the Greek Dioscorides in his magnum opus, Materia Medica, published circa AD 60. Even today, there is no better treatment for an acute gout attack than colchicine.

Familial Mediterranean fever is characterized clinically by recurrent fevers and painful serositis (i.e., inflammation of surfaces lined by a thin serosa, which includes the pleural lining of the lungs and chest cavity, the peritoneal lining of the abdomen and visceral surfaces, and the thin lining of the joint spaces). Unlike gout, familial Mediterranean fever is not triggered by the precipitation of uric acid crystals.

Colchicine was mentioned in the medical literature as a treatment for familial Mediterranean fever in 1972 [71]. It has since become the first-line drug in its treatment. Not only does colchicine prevent attacks, but it also blocks the development of secondary amyloidosis, one of the most pernicious consequences of recurring bouts of familial Mediterranean fever.

Why would a drug that is effective against gout, a disease caused by uric acid deposits in joints, also be effective against familial Mediterranean fever, a rare hereditary disease characterized by inflammation of serosal surfaces, that is not associated in any way with hyperuricemia and uric acid deposits in joints? The answer is simple. The urate crystals that are deposited in the joints of individuals affected with gout can activate inflammasomes, which happens to be the same component of the innate immune system that is activated in Familial Mediterranean fever [72]. The convergence of both diseases to the same inflammatory pathway provides a rationale for the use of colchicine in both diseases [73].

As a taxonomic oddity, please note that the disease familial Mediterranean fever should not be confused with the disease known as Mediterranean fever, an older term for brucellosis; nor should it be confused with Mediterranean anemia, an older term for thalassemia.

- If there is evidence that several pathways contribute to the clinical phenotype of the disease, then treatment with a combination of drugs that cover the known involved pathways may be of benefit to the patient.

As a rule of thumb, drugs that inhibit the function of T and B lymphocytes are likely to be effective against disorders of the adaptive immune system. Drugs that target myeloid cells, particularly monocytes, macrophages, and dendritic cells, are likely to be effective against disorders of the innate immune system. A combination of drugs (T and B lymphocyte inhibitors and myeloid inhibitors) is sometimes effective against disorders that involve both major arms of the human immune system [66].

- Inflammatory diseases are nearly always permanent and intransitive.

Once you develop rheumatoid arthritis, or autoimmune thyroiditis, multiple sclerosis, or gout, you're likely to keep the diagnosis for the duration of your life. If you're lucky, there will be periods of long remissions, but the possibility of a fresh attack will never disappear. Just as the immune systems "remember" the remote occurrence of an invasive organism, the disorders of the immune systems seem to remember how to produce the same set of symptoms, again and again, throughout life. Hence, if you have an episode of multiple sclerosis in March, you needn't expect it to transform into an attack of Crohn disease in May. Learning the "brake" mechanisms of immune pathways may one day provide useful therapeutic targets. [Glossary Intransitive property]

- Our best chance at finding clinically effective targets against specific inflammatory pathways will come from studying the rare monogenic inflammatory diseases that occur in children.

On an intuitive basis alone, it seems reasonable to infer that monogenic diseases are easier to understand and treat than diseases that involve multiple genes plus an indeterminate number of acquired attributes. Logically, the complex diseases develop under the same biological rules as the monogenic diseases, using the same available pathways, only more of them. Our best chance of understanding the individual pathways that help drive the common inflammatory diseases is to study disorders causes by gene mutations in single proteins that can be causally related to the function of a single pathway. There is every reason to expect that drugs effective against an immune pathway affected in a rare monogenic inflammatory disease will be of benefit in the treatment of a common disease driven by the same pathway [66].

SECTION 6.4 REVISING KOCH'S POSTULATES IN THE ERA OF PRECISION DIAGNOSTICS

> But though the professed aim of all scientific work is to unravel the secrets of nature, it has another effect, not less valuable, on the mind of the worker. It leaves him in possession of methods which nothing but scientific work could have led him to invent, and it places him in a position from which many regions of nature, besides that which he has been studying, appear under a new aspect.
> *James Clerk Maxwell, in essay "Molecules," 1873*

Robert Koch's postulates, published in 1890, are a set of criteria that establish whether a particular organism is the cause of a particular diseases. Today, Koch's postulates are taught in high school and college classrooms, as a demonstration of the rigor and legitimacy of clinical microbiology. To review, the four postulates of Koch are:

1. The microorganism must be found in the diseased animal, and not found in healthy animals.
2. The microorganism must be extracted and isolated from the diseased animal and subsequently grown in culture
3. The microorganism must cause disease when introduced to a healthy experimental animal
4. The microorganism must be extracted from the diseased experimental animal and demonstrated to be the same microorganism that was originally isolated from the first diseased animal.

Let's go over these four postulates once more, this time explaining how they ignore or contradict what we now know about infectious diseases.

1. The microorganism must be found in the diseased animal, and not found in healthy animals.

As previously discussed, lots of pathogenic organisms are found in healthy animals, producing disease in only a tiny fraction of the individuals who are infected, and some of these were discussed previously in this chapter. Let's look at one example of a bacteria that has not been previously discussed in much detail, but which has special relevance in this section because it infects and causes disease in humans and in animals. Bartonella species can live in blood without causing disease, producing an asymptomatic bacteremia in the wide assortment of animals that they may infect. Hence, we can no longer assume that blood samples from healthy animals are sterile. The mechanism of Bartonella transmission from animal to animal is not fully understood, but arthropod vectors (ticks, fleas, and lice) are suspected, as well as scratches and bites from infected animals (e.g., cats, rats) [74]. [Glossary Vector]

There are now about 8 species of Bartonella that are known or suspected to be human pathogens. Until just a few decades ago, only two of these species were known. Today, species of bartonella, which are ubiquitous among mammals, are known or suspected to cause a variety of phenotypically dissimilar diseases [74]:

– *Bartonella bacilliformis* → Carrion disease
– *Bartonella quintana* → Bacillary angiomatosis, trench fever, endocarditis
– *Bartonella henselae* → Bacillary angiomatosis, cat scratch disease, peliosis hepatis *B. henselae*
– *Bartonella clarridgeiae* → Cat scratch dise4ase [56]
– *Bartonella elizabethae* → Endocarditis
– *Bartonella vinsonii* subsp. berkhoffii → Endocarditis
– *Bartonella vinsonii* subsp. arupensis → Fever and a valvulopathy
– *Bartonella grahamii* → uveitis

The precise diagnosis of Bartonella species in human blood and lesions has provided us with the infectious organism associated with a number of diseases, but this new knowledge has not shed much light on why Bartonella can circulate in the blood without causing any reaction, for indefinite periods of time, or why any given Bartonella species may be associated with any of several diverse clinical manifestations. Furthermore, Koch's third postulate fails miserably for genus Bartonella; injecting any of these Bartonella species into experimental animals will more than likely produce no symptoms.

2. The microorganism must be extracted and isolated from the diseased animal and grown in culture.

Many pathogens do not grow in nutrient medium culture. This applies generally to common Mollicute bacteria, including Erysipelothrix, Mycoplasma, and Ureoplasma. This would also apply to viruses, none of which grow in cell-free media. Paradoxically, some of the organisms known to produce bacteremias in human blood grow very poorly in blood cultures, and this would include the aforementioned Bartonella species and the HACEK organisms [8,74]. The HACEK organisms are a group of proteobacteria, found in otherwise healthy individuals, that are known to cause some cases of endocarditis, especially in children, and which do not grow well in culture. The term HACEK is created from the initials of the organisms of the group: Haemophilus, particularly *Haemophilus parainfluenzae*; *Aggregatibacter*, including *Aggregatibacter actinomycetemcomitans* and *Aggregatibacter aphrophilus*; *Cardiobacterium hominis*; *Eikenella corrodens*; and *Kingella*, particularly *Kingella kingae*. [Glossary HACEK]

3. The microorganism must cause disease when introduced to a healthy experimental animal.

Again, some of the worst microorganisms will not produce disease in healthy animals. To confuse matters further, we now have examples of nonliving agents that will produce transmissible disease in healthy animals (prions).

This third postulate of Koch presumes that each occurrence of an infectious disease has a particular pathogen that is "the cause" of the disease. We must return here to our often-repeated theme that diseases do not have "a cause," and infectious diseases are no exception to the rule that pathogenesis is a multistep process. We have already seen that myocardial infarction results from a multitude of conditions that occur through time. In some cases, the last event is infectious, wherein a focal bacterial endocarditis precipitates a thrombus that blocks a narrowed coronary artery. It would be folly to believe that the sequence of events that lead to a myocardial infarction can be precipitated simply by injecting an organism into an animal. Later in this chapter, we will see two examples of rare infections for which several conditions must prevail before a disease emerges [75,76].

4. The microorganism must be extracted from the infected experimental animal and demonstrated to be the same microorganism that was originally isolated from the original diseased animal.

Many infections, considered the underlying cause of a disease, are absent from the lesions that ultimately develop. For example, Group A streptococcus infection is considered to be the underlying cause of rheumatic fever. The infection is long gone prior to the appearance of the valvular and endocardial lesions of rheumatic fever. As another example, several species of human papillomavirus are considered to be the underlying cause of nearly all cases of squamous carcinoma of the uterine cervix. Morphologic cytopathic effects are visible in the earliest precancers that precede the development of invasive carcinoma. The cancers, which may occur years following the early papillomavirus infections, will seldom contain recoverable virus.

Let's look at an example of an infectious disease that violates every one of Koch's postulates. Whipple disease, previously a disease of unknown etiology, is characterized by organ infiltration with foamy macrophages (i.e., specialized reticuloendothelial cells that "eat" bacteria and debris). The organ most often compromised in Whipple disease is the small intestine, where infiltration of infected macrophages in the lamina propria (i.e., a strip of loose connective tissue subjacent to the epithelial lining of the small intestine) causes malabsorption. Whipple disease is rare. It occurs most often in farmers and gardeners who work with soil.

Whipple disease was first described in 1907 [77], but its cause was unknown until 1992, when researchers isolated and amplified, from Whipple disease tissues, a 16s ribosomal RNA sequence that could only have a bacterial origin [78]. Based on molecular features of the ribosomal RNA molecule, the researchers assigned it to Class Cellulomonadacea, and named the species *Tropheryma whipplei*, after the man who first described the disease, George Hoyt Whipple.

Particularly noteworthy, in the case of Whipple disease, is that Koch's postulates never came close to being satisfied. For the experimentalist, the most important of the Koch's postulates require the extraction of the organism from a lesion (i.e., from diseased, infected tissue), the isolation and culture of the organism in the laboratory, and the consistent reproduction of the lesion in an animal injected with the organism. In the case of Whipple disease, none of these criteria were satisfied. The consistent identification in Whipple disease tissue of a particular molecule, characteristic of a particular species of bacteria, was deemed sufficient to establish the infectious origin of the disease.

In the general scheme of events, bacteria in the human body are eaten by macrophages, wherein they are degraded. In the case of *T. whipplei*, only a small population of susceptible individuals lack the ability to destroy *T. whipplei* organisms. In susceptible individuals, the organisms multiply within macrophages. When organisms are released from dying macrophages, additional macrophages arrive to feed, but this only results in the local accumulation of macrophages bloated by bacteria. Whipple disease is a good example of a disease caused by an organism but dependent on a genetic predisposition, expressed as a defect in innate immunity; specifically, a reduction of macrophages expressing CD11b (also known as macrophage-1 antigen) [79].

Whipple disease cannot be consistently reproduced in humans or any other animals, because it can only infect and grow in a small portion of the human population.

As we learn more and more about the complexity of disease causation, formerly useful paradigms, such as Koch's postulates, seem burdensome and useless. When we encounter rare diseases of infectious cause, we might expect to find that the pathogenesis of disease (i.e., the biological steps that lead to a clinical phenotype) may require several independent causal events to occur in sequence. In the case of Whipple disease, the infected individual must be exposed to a soil organism, limiting the disease to farmers and gardeners. The organism, residing in the soil, must be ingested, perhaps by the inhalation of dust. The organism must evade degradation by gut macrophages, limiting disease to individuals with a specific type of defect in cell-mediated immunity, and the individual must have disease that is sufficiently active to produce clinical symptoms.

Side-stepping Koch's postulates is de rigueur in Precision Medicine. The United States has experienced a recent increase in cases of acute flaccid myelitis, a rare disease of children [80]. Diagnosis is based on a metagenomic analysis (i.e., culture-independent sequence searches conducted on an assemblage of microbial gene sequences in a biologic sample) of DNA obtained from nasopharyngeal swabs. The organism that is present in most of the examined cases is enterovirus-D68, and this virus is the presumed causal organism of acute flaccid myelitis, until proven otherwise.

Precision Medicine changes the vocabulary of infection. Familiar terms such as primary pathogen, opportunistic infection, and immunocompetent patient need to be re-examined in light of what we have come to know. Even a fundamental concept, such as "the organism causing the disease," should probably be abandoned in light of the multistep pathogenesis of all diseases. Koch, in his own time, understood the practical limitations of his postulates. Maybe it's time to rewrite Koch's postulates to accommodate the kinds of experimental and diagnostic methods available to us through the practice of Precision Medicine [81].

SECTION 6.5 DISEASES-IN-WAITING

That which can be asserted without evidence, can be dismissed without evidence.
Christopher Hitchens

In Section 7.1, "The Principles of Classification," we will see that a good classification is complete when every member of the classification has a place in a class, every class has at least one member, and every member within a class has a defined relationship to every other member within the same class. Consequently, we avoid undefined classes with names such as "miscellaneous" or place-holding classes, named "not otherwise specified," filled with unrelated objects waiting for their proper class assignments. Adhering to this last provision may be very difficult. When a classification is being constructed, it is common to have some objects whose properties are a mystery, or objects that simply cannot be easily related to other objects. Taxonomists often have no choice but to put all their leftover objects into a miscellaneous class, until such time as additional information is obtained. The Latin term incertae sedis, meaning "of uncertain placement," puts a veneer of classical authority on the practice, but it never ends well. In the classification of living organisms, 19th-century taxonomists did not know quite what to do with the many different one-celled eukaryotes they were collecting. As a stopgap measure, they invented the Kingdom Protozoa, the class of all one-celled animals, the parent class of all multicellular organisms. Kingdom protozoa was a pseudoclass, consisting of all manner of organisms that were not closely related to one another, and which contained organisms that should have been assigned to classes in the plant kingdom or to the parent class of animals and fungi. Many decades passed before taxonomists caught up with the blunder, and reassigned individuals in class protozoa to proper classes of their own. As a result, the promiscuous blending of objects in Class Protozoa wreaked havoc on all their descending classes. It has taken taxonomists more than a century to defeat the Kingdom of the Protozoans and liberate its denizens.

The misclassification of fungi as a class of plants has been hard to rectify. We now know that fungi are much more closely related to animals than to plants, but current-day classifications persist in arranging their fungi with their flowers [82]. Most importantly, opportunities to find treatments that might have been effective against closely related eukaryotic classes of infectious organisms were missed because the relationships among classes were hopelessly blended. In retrospect, it would probably have been wiser to exclude objects from the classification when their proper assignments could not be determined with certainty. [Glossary Blended class]

If we're going to build a new classification of diseases, based on advances in the field of Precision Medicine, then what shall we do with diseases whose pathogenesis is unknown, despite our best efforts? Here is a partial list of diseases, some being common but most being rare, that are mysteries of modern medicine.

- Acrocyanosis
- Aphthous ulcers
- Balanitis xerotica obliterans
- Behcet disease
- Benign fasciculation syndrome
- Brainerd diarrhea
- Cardiac syndrome X
- Chronic fatigue syndrome
- Chronic prostatitis/chronic pelvic pain syndrome
- Cluster headache
- Complex regional pain syndrome
- Copenhagen disease
- Cronkhite-Canada syndrome
- Cyclic vomiting syndrome
- Dancing mania
- Danubian endemic familial nephropathy
- Eosinophilic granulomatosis with polyangiitis (Churg-Strauss syndrome)
- Electromagnetic hypersensitivity
- Encephalitis lethargica
- Exploding head syndrome
- Fibromyalgia
- Fields' disease
- Functional colonic disease
- Giant cell (temporal) arteritis
- Gluten-sensitive idiopathic neuropathies
- Gorham vanishing bone disease
- Granuloma annulare
- Granulomatosis with polyangiitis (Wegener syndrome)
- Gulf War syndrome
- Hallermann-Streiff syndrome
- Heavy legs
- Henoch-Schonlein purpura
- Interstitial cystitis
- Irritable bowel syndrome
- Kashin-Beck disease
- Kawasaki disease
- Lichen sclerosus
- Lytico-Bodig disease

- Microscopic polyangiitis
- Morgellons disease
- Mortimer disease
- Myofascial pain syndrome
- New daily persistent headache
- Nodding disease
- Picardy sweat
- Pigmented villonodular synovitis
- Pityriasis rosea
- Polyarteritis nodosa
- Posterior cortical atrophy
- Prurigo nodularis
- SAPHO syndrome
- Sarcoidosis
- Sick building syndrome
- Sjogren syndrome
- Spontaneous cerebrospinal fluid leak
- Stiff person syndrome
- Sudden unexpected death syndrome
- Sweating sickness
- Synovial osteochondromatosis
- Takayasu arteritis
- Torticollis
- Trichodynia
- Trigger finger
- Tropical sprue

We do not know the root causes, or the steps of development, or the fundamental biological properties of these diseases. In most cases, we can successfully diagnose these diseases based on their characteristic symptoms. In some cases, treating the symptoms of these diseases is sufficient to bring a remission or a cure (e.g., Takayasu arteritis). In other cases, the diseases are self-limited and the symptoms resolve without treatment (e.g., pityriasis rosea).

Given everything we have learned about the pathogenesis of diseases, is there anything that we can say now that will help us to use Precision Medicine to understand and classify these strange diseases? Most certainly, yes. If the diseases occur primarily in children, and if the disease runs in families, then we can say that, in all likelihood, a strong genetic influence is at work. If the disease causes a fever and signs of inflammation, and responds to antiinflammatory medication, then in all likelihood the complex and mysterious inflammasome is involved. If the disease arises as an epidemic, then an infection or a newly introduced environmental toxin is likely to blame. Most importantly, if all of the medical research at our disposal is brought to bear on a disease, and no root cause is found, then it's a very safe bet that multiple conditions and events converge to produce the disease, and that a single cause will never be assigned. Our attention should be focused on finding the factors that contribute to the development of the disease.

In point of fact, if we look at former diseases-in-waiting, we find that most are diseases whose causes are amalgamations of genetic, infectious, toxic, nutritional, and physical conditions. Let's consider Whipple disease, discussed in the prior section of this chapter. The disease is only observed in tillers of the soil (i.e., an occupational disease), who ingest the *T. whipplei* organism (i.e., an infectious disease), and who also happen to have a rare immune defect (i.e., a genetic disease). The multiplicity of events and conditions contributing to the development of Whipple disease confused early generations of medical researchers and earned it a prominent spot on the list of diseases-in-waiting. Using modern laboratory techniques and the knowledge that diseases are sequential, multievent processes, the mystery of Whipple disease was solved, 85 years after the first report of a human infection.

Celiac disease, a former disease-in-waiting, remains shrouded in biological ambiguity. Regardless, medical researchers believe that they know enough about this disease to drop it from the list. Celiac disease is triggered by the ingestion of gluten, a component of wheat (i.e., an environmental disease), and occurs in individuals who inherit Human Leucocytic Antigens DQ2 and DQ8 (i.e., a genetic disease) [83]. Gluten peptides are resistant to complete proteolytic digestion and enter the small intestinal lamina propria (i.e., the layer just beneath the epithelial cells lining the gut) where they elicit a strong, local immune reaction (i.e., a disease of immunity). Recent literature suggests that the inflammatory response to gluten is primed by reovirus infection (i.e., a microbial infection) [84]. Despite the complex etiology of the disease, symptoms of the disease can be ameliorated by removing gluten from the diet.

Another disease that seems to follow a pathogenesis similar to that of celiac disease is reactive arthritis, formerly known as Reiter syndrome. This inflammatory condition affects the joints, eyes, urethra, and skin. Symptoms from these different tissues may occur asynchronously, and the disease may occur as a succession of remissions and relapses. As in celiac disease, there seems to be a genetic component to the syndrome, with about 75% of affected individuals having the Human Leucocytic Antigens B27 marker. Human Leucocytic Antigen B27 is a major histocompatibility locus that has been associated with several other inflammatory conditions, including ankylosing spondylitis and acute anterior uveitis [85,86]. As in celiac disease, Reiter syndrome seems to have an infectious component, with most new cases following sexually transmitted infection by Chlamydia trachomatis or Ureaplasma urealyticum. Disease can also arise after gastrointestinal infection with shigella, salmonella, yersinia, or campylobacter bacteria.

Nodding disease, which may soon be removed from the list of diseases-in-waiting, is a frightening condition, first documented in the 1960s, that occurs almost exclusively in young children and adolescents living in certain regions of South Sudan, Tanzania, and Uganda. The disease stunts normal growth of the brain and produces seizures. During the seizures, the neck muscles do not support the weight of the head, resulting in a characteristic nod, emphasized in the name of the disease.

It was noticed that nodding disease occurs in areas where river blindness is endemic. River blindness is the second most common cause of infectious blindness worldwide and occurs in individuals infected by the filarial nematode Oncocerca volvulus [87]. The nematode migrates to the eyes, where a peculiar secondary infection takes control of the pathogenic process. Wolbachia pipientis happens to be an endosymbiont that infects most members of the filarial Class Onchocercidae [88]. It is the Wolobachia pipientis living within *Onchocerca volvulus* that causes the local inflammatory reaction that leads to blindness.

A recent paper found that patients with nodding disease have antibodies to *O. volvulus* proteins that crossreact with leiomodin-1, a protein expressed in areas of the brain affected by the disease [89]. If this early research is confirmed, then nodding disease will be seen as an infectious disease that elicits an antibody response that subsequently elicits a neurologic disorder. If so, nodding disease should be preventable by the avoidance or early treatment of *O. volvulus* infections. Hopefully, another disease with a complex etiology will be removed from the list of diseases-in waiting.

Keshan disease was a disease of unknown etiology that has been tentatively removed from the list of diseases-in-waiting. Endemic to the Keshan region of northeastern China, this disease, first reported in 1935, produces a cardiomyopathy, mostly in boys under 15 years old and women of childbearing age. This disease is often fatal, and thousands of deaths were reported in its peak incidence years (1960–70). Knowing that the region with the highest incidence of disease corresponded to a region with selenium deficiency, Chinese authorities treated spring crops with sodium selenite. It worked. The incidence of Keshan disease dropped in the areas where the crops were sprayed [90]. In 1981, a report came out indicating that Keshan disease patients had high levels of antibodies against Coxsackie virus, a virus known to produce cardiomyopathy [90,91]. Current thinking would suggest that Keshan disease occurs in individuals whose hearts are weakened by selenium-deficient individuals, and who subsequently become infected with a virulent and cardiotoxic strain of Coxsackie virus [75].

Big bone disease, also known as Kashin-Beck disease, or as osteoarthritis deformans endemica, is a mysterious disease that has been occurring for at least 150 years in Asia, with highest incidences in southwest China and Tibet. It strikes children, usually between the ages of 5 and 15, and is characterized by joint pain, and reduced joint mobility. The joints become enlarged, and pathologic examination shows death of cartilage at the growth plates of bone, and on articular surfaces.

Mysteries are easiest to solve when investigators can limit their inquiries to a few prime suspects. In the case of big bone disease, investigators found potential causes of disease everywhere they looked: selenium deficiency, contaminants in drinking water, mycotoxins from fungal infections of stored grains, iodine deficiency, and an inherited defect of the peroxisome proliferator-activated receptor gamma coactivator 1 beta gene. A causal role from any and all of these factors, all of which may produce chondrocyte toxicity, can be imagined. [Glossary Peroxisome disorder]

How does an investigator close a case where there are many different suspects, all lacking an alibi to establish their innocence? In the case of big bone disease, the Chinese authorities took an all-out approach by improving the level of hygiene, by providing a nutritious and varied diet, by supplementing the diet with selenium, by providing iodine-rich foods and clean water, and by improving housing conditions. These measures seem to be working [76]. Having nothing but a roster of suspect factors, and without ever solving the who-done-it, the incidence of new cases of big bone disease is reported to be rapidly declining in those areas that have been given a boost in living conditions [76].

In summary, the diseases-in-waiting seem to fit a common pattern characterized by:

- Complex chain of causal events
- Infection often involved somewhere in the process

- Tend to occur in rather specific populations, often based on age, geographic location, or occupation
- Unraveling their pathogenesis requires advanced diagnostic methodologies
- Hard to absolutely prove (there could be more to the story or the story could be wrong)

SECTION 6.6 PRECISION TAXONOMY

Bacteria will no longer be conceptualized mainly in terms of their morphologies and biochemistries; their relationships to other bacteria will be central to the concept as well.
Carl R. Woese [19]

Because all of biology is connected, one can often make a breakthrough with an organism that exaggerates a particular phenomenon, and later explore the generality.
Thomas R. Cech

Diagnosis of infectious disease isn't easy; the chief problem being that patients with early signs of infection will often present with nonspecific symptoms that could accompany the common cold, or the so-called intestinal flu, or as any other common condition producing generalized malaise and mild fever. American healthcare workers will not soon forget the first US case of Ebola. Thomas Duncan first arrived at the Emergency Room of the Texas Health Presbyterian Hospital, on the evening of September 25, 2014, complaining of fever, abdominal pain, dizziness, and nausea. After a few hours in the emergency room, Mr. Duncan was discharged with the diagnosis of sinusitis and a prescription for antibiotics. Mr. Duncan returned to the same emergency room two days later, much sicker. It turns out that Mr. Duncan had arrived in the United States just days previously, after having resided in Liberia, Africa. This time around, the correct diagnosis of Ebola virus infection was rendered. On October 8, Mr. Duncan died from Ebola virus hemorrhagic fever. Before his death, two healthcare workers from the hospital were infected, the first persons to contract Ebola virus infection while on US soil. Both were diagnosed in early stages of the disease, and both survived.

Let's examine some of the reasons why diagnosing an infectious disease can be very difficult, for even the most astute physicians:

- **Huge variety of potential clinical presentations for a single organism.**

As mentioned, the clinical presentation of an infectious disease is often nonspecific and may closely mimic other infectious and noninfectious conditions, particularly in the early stages of the disease. Many infections produce mild, self-limited disease and are not worth investigating clinically.

Infectious diseases may closely mimic one another, leading the unwary physician to mistakenly apply a common diagnosis to an uncommon infection. For example, Neorickettsia sennetsu causes a rare disease that closely mimics infectious mononucleosis, a common disease caused by the Epstein Barr virus. As another example, patients with HIV/AIDS are susceptible to two different skin conditions that closely resemble one another: bacillary angiomatosis and Kaposi sarcoma. Bacillary angiomatosis is an exaggerated overgrowth of small vessels of the skin, produced by infection with species of Bartonella (i.e., *Baronella quintana* and *Bartonella henhenselae*). Kaposi sarcoma is a cancer of vascular origin (i.e., a type of angiosarcoma) that is caused by Herpesvirus-8. Both bacillary angiomatosis and Kaposi sarcoma look very similar by gross examination and by microscopic examination with standard histological stains (i.e., Hematoxylin and eosin stains). Both bacillary angiomatosis and Kaposi sarcoma occur in AIDS patients, but their respective prognoses and treatments are very different. The correct diagnosis requires an astute pathologist who understands and anticipates the rare and the common causes of vascular proliferative lesions in immune-compromised patients. [Glossary Hematoxylin and eosin]

Just as several different infections may have a similar clinical phenotype, we can see that a single infection may manifest itself clinically in many different ways. One infection, many clinical phenotypes. Consider the progressively worsening options that describe the different clinical manifestations of fungal growth:

1. The fungus may grow in the external environment, usually in soil, water, or on plants, never interacting in any way with humans.
2. The fungus may emit spores and asexual reproductive forms into the air. In warm and tropical locations, fungal elements are the predominant particulate matter found in air samples. Humans are exposed constantly to a wide variety of fungi just by breathing (spores and conidia), by ingestion (fungi grow on the plants we eat), and by direct skin contact with fungal colonies in soil and airborne organisms. Airborne fungi may trigger an allergic response in sensitized individuals.
3. After exposure, fungi may transiently colonize a mucosal surface, such as the oral cavity, the nose, the gastrointestinal tract, the respiratory tract, or the skin. An acute allergic response may occur at these locations in sensitized individuals. After a time, the colony fails to thrive due to an inhospitable environment (e.g., insufficient nutrition, poor ionic milieu, effective host immune response).
4. After exposure, fungi permanently colonize the mucosal surface with no clinical effect. Candida species commonly colonize the mouth and the vagina. Aspergillus species may permanently colonize the respiratory surfaces (e.g., bronchi). It is not unusual for fungal colonies to persist as commensals (organisms that live within us, without causing disease).
5. Colonies persist, but the host reacts with an acute or chronic immune response. Chronic allergic aspergillosis of the bronchi is a good example. The patient may have a chronic cough. Microscopic examination of bronchial mucosa may reveal some inflammation, the presence of eosinophils, and the occasional hypha. Sometimes the host response is granulomatous, producing small nodules lining the bronchi, containing histiocytes and lymphocytes. A truce between the fungal colony and the host response is sometimes attained, in which the fungus colonies never leave, the inflammation never regresses, but the fungus does not invade into the underlying mucosa.
6. Fungi invade through the mucosa into the submucosa and underlying tissue. These locally invasive infections can manifest as a fungal ball, consisting of inflammatory cells admixed with fibrovascular tissue, necrotic cells, and fungal elements.

7. Fungal elements invade into lymphatics, traveling with the lymph fluid, and producing regional invasive fungal disease along the route of lymphatic drainage. The prototypical example of this process is found in infections with Sporothrix schenckii, which typically gains entrance to the skin, from the soil, through abrasions. Infection yields multiple skin papules, emanating from the point of primary infection (usually the hand or the foot), and following the route of lymphatic drainage.
8. Fungal elements invade into blood vessels.
9. Fungal elements become a blood constituent (i.e., fungemia) and disseminate throughout the body.
10. Fungal elements spread throughout the body to produce invasive fungal infections in multiple organs.

The aforementioned manifestations of fungal infection represent progressive steps in the growth and spread of disease. In the case of fungi, the development of disease can be stopped and can reside at virtually any stage of disease development. Most fungal diseases do not occur in immune-competent individuals. Of the hundreds of fungal infections that can occur in humans, only a dozen or so produce disease in apparently healthy persons. As a generality, the more immune-competent the individual, the less likely that a fungal infection will progress from one step to the next.

– Precision Medicine is broadening our concept of what it means to be a pathogenic organism

In 1950, the US navy conducted an ill-advised experiment on the unsuspecting citizens of San Francisco [92]. Large hoses sprayed out a fog of *Serratia marcescens* and *Bacillus globigii*, to determine whether this kind of dispersal mechanism might be an effective way of exposing a large population to a biological warfare agent. *Serratia marcescens* and *Bacillus globigii* were used because these organisms were considered to be completely harmless. From the viewpoint of the navy, this experiment was a success in that the bacteria were distributed widely over the Bay area, delivering a small dose of organisms to the target population.

The US navy declared a victory for itself in its undeclared war on San Francisco. The generals did not suspect that there would be any collateral damage. Unexpectedly, a small epidemic of Serratia marcescens infections were reported among the exposed population. Eleven individuals required hospitalization, and one individual died. No cases of Serratia marcescens infections had been previously reported in the hospital where the death occurred, and no clusters of Serratia marcescens infections occurred in the years subsequent to the navy's experiment. It seems that Serratia marcescens, though harmless to most individuals, was pathogenic to a tiny subpopulation of the population. Presumably, genetic susceptibility accounted for the shift from harmless organism to deadly pathogen, in at least one hapless victim. At the time, no civilians understood why this miniepidemic had hit San Francisco. It was not until 1976, when the navy experiment was declassified that the truth came to light.

What does it take to be a pathogen? Basically, any organism that can grow in human blood, or in human tissues, or on human endothelial or serosal surfaces, or in any internal sources of fluid (i.e., joint fluid, pleural fluid, urine) can be a pathogen. Even organisms that don't grow well in human blood and tissues can be pathogenic in a select group of individuals.

The proteobacteria Eikenella corrodens is a normal inhabitant of the mouth that is harmless under most, but not all, conditions. When the organism is mechanically forced into the blood stream (e.g., by accidentally biting through the oral mucosa while eating), it can produce a cellulitis or a bacteremia with endocarditis. It is included with the HACEK group of endocarditis-producing organisms. Eikenella corrodens can also produce disease in diabetics and immunocompromised individuals, apparently without inadvertent biting. Genus Prevotella contains oral inhabitants that can produce plaque, halitosis, and periodontal disease. Prevotella dentalis, like Eikenella corrodens, produces so-called bite infections, wherein oral bacteria are inoculated, by a bite or abrasion, into adjacent tissues, producing abscesses, wound infections, or bacteremia. Provotella dentalis bacteremia can lead to disseminated infections.

We now encounter instances wherein once-obscure organisms have risen to the level of common pathogens. Blastocystis hominis was a eukaryotic organism seen as an incidental finding, of no known significance, in stool examinations. For a long time, the proper taxonomic classification of this organism was undetermined, and it has been variously referred to as a yeast, a fungus, an ameba, a flagellated protozoa, or a sporozoan [93]. Today, Blastocystis is considered a genus belonging to the heterokonts, and is the only heterokont known to produce a human infection. Infection follows ingestion of the cyst, through the fecal-oral route. Most infections do not result in any clinical symptoms, but sometimes, a syndrome mimicking irritable bowel syndrome may occur. Among individuals who have microscopic stool examinations, for any reason, up to 25% of specimens contain Blastocystis [94]. Because Blastocystis in found in the stools of healthy individuals, the finding of the organism in the stool of a symptomatic patient does not necessarily establish a causal relationship. Treatment with metronidazole, an antibiotic effective against eukaryotes and prokaryotes, has its advocates [95,96], but can we do better? Blastocystis is the only heterokont known to cause disease in humans, and we know almost nothing about the heterokonts that would help us design a drug that would be effective against Bastocystis. Our experience with Blastocystis reminds us that as Precision Medicine allows us to accurately classify pathogens, we will need to find new, class-specific antibiotics. Let's look at another example wherein a taxonomic change requires us to develop a new approach to treatment.

For a long time, brain infections due to *Naegleria fowleri* were lumped with the amoebic encephalitides, and Naegleria was classified as an Acanthameoba, under class Ameoebozoa. We now know that Naegleria is a member of Class Percolozoa, and that the encephalitis caused by *Naegleria fowleri* is a percolozoan encephalitis. Why is this significant? Naegleria happens to be the only pathogenic species in Class Percolozoa, and we know almost nothing about the Percolozoan pathways that might render Naegleria sensitive to antibiotics. At present, Naegleria encephalitis is treated as though it were one of the amoebic encephalitides, with amphotericin B. With or without amphotericin B treatment, nearly all cases of percolozoan encephalitis are fatal [97]. Clearly, we need to learn a lot more about the biological pathways of members of Class Percolozoa, so that we can design a class-based strategy to prevent and treat Percolozoan encephalitis. Most importantly, we need to stop pretending that Naegleria is a genus in Class Amoebozoa, simply because it looks like an ameba.

While the list of common infections is growing slowly, the list of rare infectious diseases is exploding. Improvements in the taxonomic designations of infectious organisms, the availability of highly advanced reference laboratories capable of accurately identifying infectious organisms, increases in the number of immune-compromised patients susceptible to infections by organisms that are not otherwise pathogenic, and the ease with which infections can be transported from place to place throughout the modern world, have all contributed to the increase in newly encountered rare infectious diseases.

A source of new, rare infectious is invasive instruments and catheters, particularly those that dwell inside the body for prolonged periods, such as: bladder catheters, ventilator tubes and pulmonary assistive devices, shunts, venous and arterial lines, and indwelling drains and tubes. These devices provide a path of entry for a wide variety of organisms that would otherwise be halted at normal anatomic barriers. Of the different organisms that invade via indwelling devices, most are bacteria. Fungal disease has occurred in adults who receive intravenous parenteral nutrition, the fungi growing in the lipid-rich alimentation fluids [98]. The bacterial organisms that invade via indwelling devices include species of Pseudomonadales, Bacillales, Bacteroidetes, Fusobacteria, and Legionallales. Despite their taxonomic diversity, all these organisms seem to share an ability to secrete biofilms over surfaces and to glide through the biofilms they create. Biofilms are invisible, slimy coatings, composed of polysaccharides and cellular debris that provide sanctuary from the antibacterial sprays and solutions used in hospitals. Bacterial species that can glide through a biofilm can track a catheter into the body. For example, *Staphylococcus epidermidis* is a commensal organism that lives on human skin. Some of the organisms now known to cause catheter-associated hospital infections were previously obscure (e.g., Leclercia adecarboxylata [99]). The list of such organisms is constantly growing.

In the past, the rational basis for splitting a group of organisms into differently named species required, at the very least, heritable functional or morphologic differences among the members of the group. Gene sequencing has changed the rules for assigning new species. For example, various organisms with subtle differences from *Bacteroides fragilis* have been elevated to the level of species based on DNA homology studies. These include *Bacteroides distasonis*, *Bacteroides ovatus*, *Bacteroides thetaiotaomicron*, and *Bacteroides vulgatus* [8,100].

There is a growing list of infections known to be resistant to most types of antibiotic treatments. For the most part, these are not rare diseases; they are common diseases that happen to be resistant to antibiotics. Examples are resistant strains of *Staphylococcus aureus* and *Acinetobacter baumannii*, and *Klebsiella pneumoniae*. New techniques for subtyping strains, based on antibiotic resistance or susceptibilities, are being developed and will probably replace older agar growth tests [101]. [Glossary Serotype]

Most of the newly recognized pathogens are fungi. Approximately 54 fungi account for the vast majority of fungal infections, but the total number of fungi that are pathogenic in humans is much higher. It is estimated that there are about 20 new fungal diseases reported each year [102]. With advanced typing techniques, it is now possible to identify new species of fungi. For example, 34 new species of Aspergillus have been isolated from clinical specimens *Aspergillus fumigatus*, a common cause of severe pulmonary infections in immune-compromised patients [102]. We can now identify the specific fungal species responsible for infections that would formerly have been impossible to diagnose accurately [103]. If the number of diseases caused by other types of organisms (i.e., bacteria, protists, animals, viruses, and prions) remains steady, then it will not be long before the number of different fungal diseases exceeds the number of different diseases produced by all other organisms, combined.

- **Expanding number of previously unrecognized species and pathogenic subtypes of species**

Genus Plasmodium is responsible for human and animal malaria. About 300–500 million people are infected with malaria, worldwide. About 2 million people die each year from malaria [2,104]. There are several hundred species of Plasmodium that infect animals, but only a half dozen species are known to infect humans [104]. Newly emerging species, causing human disease, may arise from animal reservoirs. For example, *Plasmodium knowlesi*, a known cause of malaria in macaque monkeys, has emerged as a cause of human malaria in Southeast Asia, where it has grown in incidence to the point that it currently accounts for about two-thirds of malarial cases in this region. Malaria is commonly diagnosed with an antigen test developed against the common forms of human plasmodia. Patients with *P. knowlesi* may have a negative reaction to the standard Plasmodium antigen test [105]. If this were to occur, a *P. knowlesi* infection may go undiagnosed, and the patient might not be provided with needed antimalarial medication. Careful examination of blood will usually indicate the presence of parasites in cases of *P. knowlesi* malaria, and a specific diagnosis can be confirmed with advanced molecular tests. Here is an example of a rare infection, emerging as an endemic infection, whose diagnosis can be missed with testing methods designed for the common forms of disease [106].

Technical advances in the past decade have greatly improved our ability to diagnose species and subtypes (i.e., serotypes or serovars) [107,108]. At the point, two of the few remaining impediments to progress is the lack of reference genome sequences for every known or suspected pathogen, and their propensity to quickly alter their genotypes. The problem of species mutability is particularly prevalent among the RNA viruses (e.g., influenza virus, Newcastle disease virus, foot-and-mouth disease virus). Sometimes, precision diagnosis comes down to knowing enough about the characteristic genetic features of classes of organisms (i.e., not just the sequence) to correctly match a patient's sample to the correct class of organism. Put another way, no matter how precise the molecular test, the results mean nothing unless we have a comprehensive and sensible taxonomy that we can use to match a sequence to a known organism or to a class of related organisms. At that point, we can make a diagnosis and find a treatment.

A striking case-in-point was reported in 2014, when DNA was extracted from the spinal fluid from a child with meningitis of undetermined cause [109]. After two days of sequencing and computer searches through multiple DNA databases, a match was found with Leptospira. The patient was started on penicillin and recovered soon thereafter. This case is a shining example of Precision Medicine coming to the rescue of a gravely ill child.

It should be noted that when a clinician suspects that the cause of a child's meningitis is leptospirosis, diagnosis from CSF can be accomplished quickly using somewhat older technology (e.g., PCR) [110]. Leptospira is difficult to grow from spinal fluid. It has been observed that in children with meningitis, and despite no growth of bacteria from their cultured spinal fluid, Leptospira will account for more than a third of cases [110]. In retrospect, an astute clinician may have reached the tentative diagnosis of leptospirosis without the need for Precision Medicine tools.

We should be prepared to accept that there will always be circumstances wherein a precision diagnosis must give way to common sense:

- Some diagnoses can only be established by highly specialized laboratories. Some of these laboratories were created to find the cause of epidemics, not of isolated illnesses. Under normal conditions, empiric treatments may be a practical alternative to precision diagnoses.
- Sometimes, it is faster and more effective to deduce a diagnosis than to resort to sequence analyses
- Sometimes, precision diagnosis can be overly sensitive, detecting sequences of contaminants or of organisms that are present in such low numbers that they could not have caused the disease.
- Sometimes precise diagnoses are mistaken. Aside from sample contamination, which is a persistent problem whenever tiny quantities of diagnostic material are analyzed, we must be prepared to encounter instances when DNA sequences, thought to be characteristic of a species, are found in other organisms [111,112].
- Sometimes precise diagnoses will be irreproducible by other laboratories examining samples of the same specimen. The difficulties in verifying and reproducing the results obtained through precision measurements is a matter of deep concern to those who regulate new diagnostic tests [113–127].

- **Taxonomic instability**

Our knowledge of pathogenic organisms comes to us through taxonomy. If we create a false taxonomy, then we cannot effectively diagnose and treat infectious diseases. When we make corrections in the classification of living organisms, we must be prepared to rapidly adjust the way we practice medicine.

Let's look at a few examples where taxonomy plays a crucial role.

Class Fungi has recently undergone profound changes [106]. For example, consider the arduous journey of Allescheria boydii. Individuals infected with this fungal organism were said to suffer from the disease known as allescheriasis. When the organism's name was changed to Petriellidium boydii, the disease name was changed to petriellidosis. When the fungal name was changed, once more, to *Pseudallescheria boydii*, the disease name was changed to pseudallescheriosis [102]. Changes in the standard names of a fungus, appearing in the International Code of Botanical Nomenclature, should trigger concurrent changes in the standard nomenclatures of medicine, such as the World Health Organization's International Classification of Disease, and the National Library of Medicine's Medical Subject Headings, and a variety of specialized disease nomenclatures. Some of these nomenclatures update infrequently. When disease nomenclatures lag behind official fungal taxonomy, errors in coding and reporting infectious fungal diseases will ensue. [Glossary Dictionary, Nomenclature, Thesaurus]

Until recently, Pneumocystis was presumed to be a type of protozoa. Early papers concocted a detailed protozoan life cycle for Pneumocystis, complete with morphologically distinct developmental stages, that included cyst, trophozoite, sporozoite, and intracystic bodies [128]. Owing to molecular analyses, we now recognize that Pneumocystis is a fungus within Class Taphrinomycotina. Though Pneumocystis cannot be cultured, we have learned a great deal about the life-cycle of Pneumocystis by studying a sister organism, *Schizosaccharomyces pombe*, in Class Taphrinomycotina. *S. pombe* can be cultured. By observing *S. pombe*, microbiologists can infer that the yeast form of Pneumocystis creates an enclosed cyst, which eventually ruptures, releasing spores. These different forms of Pneumocystis comprise the various morphologic forms of the fungus upon which histologic diagnosis of *Pneumocystis jirovecii* (formerly *Pneumocystis carinii*) is rendered [106].

Until the past decade, members of Class Microsporidia were considered to be protozoa. With molecular techniques, the members of Class Microsporidia have been shown to contain ribosomal RNA sequences typical of fungi [129,130]. Aside from their phylogenetic relationship to fungi, these organisms are strikingly dissimilar, in morphology and lifestyle, from other fungi, being obligate intracellular parasites that have adapted themselves to parasitic lives in a wide range of eukaryotic organisms. Unlike virtually all other members of Class Fungi, the members of Class Microsporidia lack mitochondria [30], lack a hyphal form, and do not produce multicellular tissue structures. With all these nonfungal properties, taxonomists never entertained the notion that the microsporidia were fungi. Twentieth-century taxonomists overlooked an important clue, the microsporidia synthesize chitin, a structural feature found only in opisthokonts, such as fungi. A wide variety of animals are reservoirs for the various species of Microsporidia: mammals, birds, insects. The spores are passed in the stools, and infect humans through direct contact, water contamination, or through respiration of airborne spores. Preliminary evidence suggests that microsporidial infections are common in humans [48].

Neorickettsia, despite its name, is not a type of Rickettsia (i.e., not a member of Class Rickettsiaceae). Neorickettsia is a member of Class Anaplasmataceae; hence, the disease it produces is an ehrlichiosis, not a rickettsiosis. Therefore, we would expect Neorickettsia to share the biological attributes of its class, and we would hope that it would respond to antiehrlichial medications.

Here is a sampling of recent name changes, in species or genus:

- *Aggregatibacter actinomycetemcomitans*, formerly *Actinobacillus actinomycetemcomitans*
- *Anaplasma phagocytophilum*, formerly assigned two different species names: *Ehrlichia phagocytophilium* and *Ehrlichia equi* [131].
- *Aonchotheca philippinensis*, formerly *Capillaria philippinensis*
- *Arcanobacterium haemolyticum*, formerly *Corynebacterium haemolyticum*
- *Arcanobacterium pyogenes*, formerly *Actinomyces pyogenes*
- *Bartonella quintana*, formerly *Rochalimaea quintana*
- *Brachyspira pilosicoli*, formerly *Serpulina pilosicoli*
- *Burkholderia mallei*, formerly *Pseudomonas mallei*
- *Cladophialophora bantiana*, formerly *Xylohypha bantiana*
- *Cystoisospora belli*, formerly *Isospora belli*
- *Elizabethkingia meningoseptica*, formerly *Chryseobacterium meningosepticum*
- *Encephalitozoon intestinalis*, formerly *Septata intestinalis*
- *Fluoribacter bozemanae*, formerly *Legionella bozemanae*
- *Gardnerella vaginalis*, formerly *Corynebacterium vaginalis*, formerly *Haemophilus vaginalis*
- *Helicobacter pylori*, formerly *Campylobacter pylori*
- *Klebsiella granulomatis*, formerly *Calymmatobacterium granulomatis*, formerly *Donovania granulomatis*
- *Malassezia furfur*, formerly *Pityrosporum ovale*
- *Micromonas micros*, formerly *Peptostreptococcus micros* formerly *Parvimonas micros*

- *Mycolcadus corymbifera*, formerly *Absidia corymbifera*
- *Neorickettsia sennetsu*, formerly *Ehrlichia sennetsu*
- *Norovirus*, formerly *Norwalk virus* (epidemic gastroenteritis)
- *Pneumocystis jirovecii*, formerly *Pneumocystis carinii*
- *Rhodococcus equi*, formerly *Corynebacterium equi*, formerly *Bacillus hoagii*, formerly *Corynebacterium purulentus*, formerly *Mycobacterium equi*, formerly *Mycobacterium restrictum*, formerly *Nocardia restricta*, and formerly *Proactinomyces restrictus*.
- *Rotavirus* formerly known as gastrointeritis virus type B.
- *Sarcocystis suihominis*, formerly *Isospora hominis*
- *Stenotrophomonas maltophilia*, formerly *Pseudomonas maltophilia*
- *Volutella cinerescens*, formerly *Psilonia cinerescens*

If we are to practice Precision Medicine, we must be prepared to deal with a perplexing list of precision organisms.

Glossary

Adaptive immunity Immunity in which the response adapts to the specific chemical properties of foreign antigens. Adaptive immunity is a system wherein somatic T cells and B cells are produced, each with a unique and characteristic immunoglobulin (in the case of B cells) or T-cell receptor (in the case of T cells). Through a complex presentation and selection system, a foreign antigen elicits the replication of a B cell that produces an antibody whose unique immunoglobulin attachment site matches the antigen. Antigen-antibody complexes may deactivate and clear circulating antibodies, or may lead to the destruction of the organism that carries the antigen (e.g., virus or bacteria). The process of producing unique proteins requires that recombination and hypermutation take place within a specific gene region. Recombinations yield on the order of about a billion unique somatic genes, starting with one germinal genome. This process requires the participation of recombination activating genes (RAGs). The acquisition of an immunologically active recombination activating gene is presumed to be the key evolutionary event that led to the development of the adaptive immune system, present in all jawed vertebrates (gnathostomes). In addition, a specialized method of processing immunoglobulin heavy-chain mRNA transcript accounts for the high levels of secretion of immunoglobulin proteins by plasma cells [61]. As one might expect, inherited mutations in RAG genes cause immune deficiency syndromes [34,35].

Autoantibody disease versus autoimmune disease The two terms are often used interchangeably, but they probably represent two pathogenetically distinct conditions. Autoantibody diseases occur when the adaptive immune system synthesizes antibodies against some normal body constituent. In most cases, as far as anyone can tell, individuals with the common autoantibody diseases have normal functioning immune systems. For some unspecified reason (e.g., an antigen in an infectious organism elicits antibodies that happen to crossreact with a normal cellular protein), a pathological antibody is produced, occasionally having clinical consequences. In autoimmune diseases, there is a primary dysfunction of the immune system, often producing an array of clinical sequelae, including the synthesis of one or more antibodies that react against self-antigens [132].

Blended class Also known as class noise. Blended class refers to inaccuracies (e.g., misleading results) introduced in the analysis of data due to errors in class assignments (e.g., inaccurate diagnosis). If you are testing the effectiveness of an antibiotic on a class of people with bacterial pneumonia, the accuracy of your results will be forfeit when your study population includes subjects with viral pneumonia, or smoking-related lung damage. Errors induced by blending classes are often overlooked by data analysts who incorrectly assume that the experiment was designed to ensure that each data group is composed of a uniform and representative population. A common source of class blending occurs when the classification upon which the experiment is designed is itself blended. For example, imagine that you are a cancer researcher and you want to perform a study of patients with malignant fibrous histiocytomas (MFH), comparing the clinical course of these patients with the clinical course of patients who have other types of tumors. Let's imagine that the class of tumors known as MFH does not actually exist; that it is a grab-bag term erroneously assigned to a variety of other tumors that happened to look similar to one another. This being the case, it would be impossible to produce any valid results based on a study of patients diagnosed as MFH. The results would be a biased and irreproducible cacophony of data collected across different, and undetermined, classes of tumors. Believe it or not, this specific example, of the blended MFH class of tumors, is selected from the real-life annals of tumor biology [133–135]. The literature is rife with research of dubious quality, based on poorly designed classifications and blended classes. One caveat, efforts to reduce class blending can be counterproductive if undertaken with excess zeal. For example, in an effort to reduce class blending, a researcher may choose groups of subjects who are uniform with respect to every known observable property. For example, suppose you want to actually compare apples with oranges. To avoid class blending, you might want to make very sure that your apples do not included any cumquats, or persimmons. You should be certain that your oranges do not include any limes or grapefruits. Imagine that you go even further, choosing only apples and oranges of one variety (e.g., Macintosh apples and Navel oranges), size (e.g., 10 cm), and origin (e.g., California). How will your comparisons apply to the varieties of apples and oranges that you have excluded from your study? You may actually reach conclusions that are invalid and irreproducible for more generalized populations within each class. In this case, you have succeeded in eliminating class blending, at the expense of losing representative populations of the classes.

Commensal A symbiotic relationship between two organisms in which one of the organisms benefits and the other is unaffected, under normal conditions. A commensal may become an opportunistic pathogen when the host provides a physiologic opportunity for disease, such as malnutrition, advanced age, immunodeficiency, overgrowth of the organism (e.g., after antibiotic usage), or some mechanical portal that introduces the organism to a part of the body that is particularly susceptible to the pathologic expression of the organism, such as an indwelling catheter, or an intravenous line. In addition, a commensal relationship between bacteria and an animal parasite may produce a pathogenic relationship in the parasite's host. For example, The bacterium Wolbachia pipientis happens to be an endosymbiont that infects most members of the filarial Class Onchocercidae [88]. Onchocerca volvulus is a parasitic filarial nematode in humans. The filaria migrate to the eyes, causing river blindness, the second most common infectious cause of blindness worldwide [87]. Wolbachia pipientis lives within Onchocerca volvulus, and it is the Wolbachia organism that is responsible for the inflammatory reaction that leads to blindness. Hence, Wolbachia pipientis is a commensal in Onchocerca volvulus and a pathogen in humans, simultaneously. Treatment for river blindness may involve a vermicide, to kill Onchocerca voluvulus larvae, plus an antibiotic, to kill Wolbachia pipientis.

Craniata Craniata is the class of animals that have a cranium (skull) encasing a brain. Class Crianata is sometimes used in place of Class Vertebrata from which it is distinguished by the inclusion of several species that have skulls but lack vertebrae. Animals with a cranium have a neural crest. Before the appearance of organisms of class Craniata, there was no neural crest or the neural crest was primitive and incapable of producing all of the cell types and derivative tissues found in organisms of class Craniata. With the appearance of the neural crest came all of the diseases that derive from neural crest (i.e., the neurocristopathies). Conversely, noncraniate organisms do not develop the neurocristopathies.

Cyanobacteria The most influential organisms on earth, cyanobacteria, were the first and only organism to master the biochemical intricacies of photosynthesis (more than 3 billion years ago). Photosynthesis involves a photochemical reaction that takes carbon dioxide and water, and releases oxygen. All photosynthesizing life forms are either cyanobacteria, or they are eukaryotic cells (e.g., algae, plants) that have acquired chloroplasts (an organelle created in the distant past by endosymbiosis between a eukaryote and a cyanobacteria). Before the emergence of oxygen-producing cyanobacteria, the earth's atmosphere had very little oxygen.

Dictionary A word list, typically alphabetically arranged, for which each word is annotated with its definition.

Enhancer A sequence of DNA that can enhance a promoter's interaction with RNA polymerase. An enhancer need not be located adjacent to the promoter, but the enhancer and the promoter must be on the same chromosome.

Exotic diseases For many, the word "exotic" brings to mind all things strange and exciting. For clinical microbiologists, "exotic" refers to local infectious diseases that arise in a distant geographic location. In the United States, numerous exotic diseases have been introduced in the past few decades due, primarily, to two influences: global warming and global travel. These include Zika, Ebola, Dengue, Chikungunya, SARS, West Nile fever, Yellow fever, Mayaro fever, Monkeypox, CJD/BSE (Creutzfeldt-Jakob disease/Bovine spongiform encephalitis), HIV/AIDS, Lassa fever, Malaria, Leishmaniasis, Chagas disease, Cyclospora, and Cholera [104]. We can expect more exotic diseases to follow. As the temperature of the planet rises, the geographic range for tropical vectors expands. Many of these organisms arrive by jet. Airplanes provide quick transport to infectious organisms. Can it be a coincidence that the synonym for "airline" is "carrier"? Aside from causing disease in humans, exotic infections may ravage animals and plants. The much-dreaded New World screw-worm (*Cochliomyia hominivorax*), whose maggots eat the living flesh of the animals they infect, has recently returned to the United States. The medfly, or Mediterranean fruit fly (*Ceratitis capitata*) is a recurring threat to crops.

Facultative intracellular organism An organism that is capable of living, and reproducing inside or outside of cells. The term may apply to any class of organism, but most of the facultative intracellular organisms are bacteria. Example genera include: Brucella, Francisella, Histoplasma, Listeria, Legionella, Mycobacterium, Neisseria, and Yersinia.

HACEK A group of proteobacteria that may be found in otherwise healthy individuals, that are known to cause some cases of endocarditis, especially in children, and which do not grow well from cultured blood (due primarily to their slow growth rates). The term HACEK is created from the initials of the organisms of the group: Haemophilus, particularly *Haemophilus parainfluenzae*; Aggregatibacter, including *Aggregatibacter actinomycetemcomitans* and *Aggregatibacter aphrophilus*; *Cardiobacterium hominis*; *Eikenella corrodens*; and *Kingella*, particularly *Kingella kingae*.

Hematoxylin and eosin Better known by its abbreviation, H&E, the common stain employed in histology laboratories. With H&E staining, the nuclei of cells are blue, and the cytoplasm is pink. Without staining, most animal cells are colorless, and cellular organelles are virtually invisible. The development of histologic staining techniques in the 19th century constituted one of the most important advances in medical science.

Hydatidiform mole Also called gestational mole. A hydatidiform mole is a malformed conceptus that consists of edematous placental villi and a variable amount of malformed, nonviable embryonic tissue. There are two types of hydatidiform mole: complete mole and partial mole. Hydatidiform moles are associated with a risk of developing choriocarcinoma.

Inflammasome A protein complex expressed by white blood cells that activates inflammatory cytokines which, in turn, attract inflammatory cells. Examples of inflammasome proteins are caspase 1 and 5, PYCARD, and NALP. The inflammasome is part of the innate immune system.

Innate immunity An ancient and somewhat nonspecific immune and inflammatory response system found in plants, fungi, insects [67], and most multicellular organisms. This system recruits immune cells to sites of infection, using cytokines (chemical mediators). Innate immunity includes the complement system, which acts to clear dead cells. It also includes the macrophage system, also called the reticuloendothelial system, which engulfs and removes foreign materials. Crohn disease is the first of the common, genetically complex diseases that were shown to be associated with a germline polymorphism of a gene known to be a component of the innate immune system; specifically, the NF-kappa-B pathway [136,137]. Drugs that inhibit TNF (tumor necrosis factor), a participant in the cytokine pathway recruited by the innate immune system, are active against Crohn disease [73]. Examples of rare genetic disorders of the innate immune system include: Familial Mediterranean fever; TNF receptor-associated periodic syndrome; Hyperimmunoglobulin D syndrome; Familial cold autoinflammatory syndrome; Muckle-Wells syndrome; Neonatal-onset multisystem inflammatory disease, also known as chronic infantile neurologic, cutaneous, and arthritis syndrome; Pyogenic arthritis, pyoderma gangrenosum, and acne; Blau syndrome; Early-onset sarcoidosis, and Majeed syndrome [66,138].

Intermediate host Same as secondary host. A eukaryotic organism that contains a parasitic eukaryotic organism for a period of time during which the parasite matures in its life cycle, but in which maturation does not continue to the adult or sexual phase. Maturation to the adult or sexual phase only occurs in the primary, or definitive host. A parasitic eukaryotic organism may have more than one intermediate host. The survival advantages offered to the parasite by the intermediate host stage may include the following: to provide conditions in which the particular stages of the parasite can develop, that are not available within the primary host; to disseminate the parasite (e.g., via water or air) to distant sites; to protect the immature forms from being eaten by the adult forms; to protect the parasite from harsh conditions that prevail in the primary host; to protect the parasite from external environmental conditions that prevail when the parasite leaves the primary host.

Intransitive property One of the criteria for a classification is that every object (sometimes referred to as member or as instance) belongs to exactly one class. From this criteria comes the intransitive property of classifications, namely, an object cannot change its class. Otherwise, an object would belong to more than one class at different times. It is easy to apply the intransitive rule under most circumstances. A cat cannot become a dog and a horse cannot become a sheep. What do we do when a caterpillar becomes a butterfly? In this case, we must recognize that caterpillar and butterfly represent phases in the development of one particular instance of a species, and do not belong to separate classes.

Intrinsic immunity A cell-based (i.e., not humoral) antiviral system that is always "on" (i.e., not activated by the presence of its target, as is seen in the two other immune mechanisms available to many animals: adaptive immunity and innate immunity) [68]. Intrinsic immunity is a newly discovered immune response system, and there is much we need to learn about this type of immunity. Intrinsic immunity has been studied for its role in controlling retrovirus infections (e.g., HIV infection). It is known that intrinsic immunity is not restricted to retroviruses, but its role in blocking infection by other classes of virus is something of a mystery.

Invasion In the field of cancer, invasion occurs when tumor cells move into and through normal tissues. All tumors that can metastasize can also invade, and, for this reason, it is inferred that invasion is involved in the process of metastasis. For metastasis to occur, tumor cells invade through the walls of lymphatic and blood vessels, thus gaining access to the general circulation; likewise, tumor cells invade through vessels at the site of distant seeding. The opposite assertion is not true; tumors that invade do not necessarily metastasize. Examples of nonmetastasizing invasive tumors include basal cell carcinoma of skin, and most tumors arising within the brain.

Long branch attraction When gene sequence data is analyzed, and two organisms share the same sequence in a stretch of DNA, it can be very tempting to infer that the two organisms belong to the same class (i.e., that they inherited the identical sequence from a common ancestor). This inference is not necessarily correct. Because DNA mutations arise stochastically over time, two species with different ancestors may achieve the same sequence in a chosen stretch of DNA. There may be an identifiable ancestor with the same DNA sequence for one of the two organisms, but not for the other. When mathematical phylogeneticists began modeling inferences for gene data sets, they assumed that most of class assignment errors based on DNA sequence similarity would occur when the branches between sister taxa were long (i.e., when a long time elapsed between evolutionary divergences, allowing for many random substitutions in base pairs). They called this phenomenon, wherein nonsister taxa were assigned the same ancient ancestor class, "long branch attraction." In practice, errors of this type can occur whether the branches are long, or short, or in between. Over the years, the accepted usage of the term "long branch attraction" has been extended to just about any error in phylogenetic grouping due to gene similarities acquired through any mechanism other than inheritance from a shared ancestor. This would include random mutational and adaptive convergence [16].

Nomenclature A nomenclatures is a listing of terms that cover all of the concepts in a knowledge domain. A nomenclature is different from a dictionary for three reasons: (1) the nomenclature terms are not annotated with definitions, (2) nomenclature terms may be multiword, and (3) the terms in the nomenclature are limited to the scope of the selected knowledge domain. In addition, most nomenclatures group synonyms under a group code. For example, a food nomenclature might collect submarine, hoagie, po' boy, grinder, hero, and torpedo under an alphanumeric code such as "F63958." Nomenclatures simplify textual documents by uniting synonymous terms under a common code. Documents that have been coded with the same nomenclature can be integrated with other documents that have been similarly coded, and queries conducted over such documents will yield the same results, regardless of which term is entered (i.e., a search for either hoagie, or po' boy will retrieve the same information, if both terms have been annotated with the synonym code, "F63948"). Optimally, the canonical concepts listed in the nomenclature are organized into a hierarchical classification [139,140].

Nonliving organism Herein, viruses and prions are referred to as nonliving organisms. Viruses lack key features that distinguish life from nonlife. They depend entirely on host cells for replication; they do not partake in metabolism and do not yield energy; they cannot adjust to changes in their environment (i.e., no homeostasis), nor can they respond to stimuli. Most scientists consider viruses to be mobile genetic elements that can travel between cells (much as transposons are considered mobile genetic elements that travel within a cell). All viruses have a mechanism that permits them to infect cells and to use the host cell machinery to replicate. At minimum, viruses consist of a small RNA or DNA genome, encased by a protective protein coat, called a capsid. Class Mimiviridae, discovered in 1992, occupies a niche that seems to span the biological gulf separating living organisms from viruses. Members of Class Mimiviridae are complex, larger than some bacteria, with enormous genomes (by viral standards), exceeding a million base pairs and encoding upwards of 1000 proteins. The large size and complexity of Class Mimiviridae exemplifies the advantage of a double-stranded DNA genome. Class Megaviridae is a recently reported (October, 2011) class of viruses, related to Class Mimiviridae, but even larger [141]. Biologically, the life of a mimivirus is not very different from that of obligate intracellular bacteria (e.g., Rickettsia). The discovery of Class Mimiviridae inspires biologists to reconsider the "nonliving" status relegated to viruses and compels taxonomists to examine the placement of viruses within the phylogenetic development of prokaryotic and eukaryotic organisms.

Nonphylogenetic property Properties that do not hold true for a class, hence, cannot be used by taxonomists to build a class structure. For example, we do not classify animals by height or weight because animals of greatly different heights and weights may occupy the same biological class. Similarly, animals within a class may have widely ranging geographic habitats; hence, we cannot classify animals by locality. Case in point: penguins can be found virtually anywhere in the southern hemisphere, including hot and cold climates. Hence, we cannot classify penguins as animals that live in Antarctica or that prefer a cold climate. Scientists commonly encounter properties, once thought to be class-specific, that prove to be uninformative, for classification purposes. For many decades, all bacteria were assumed to be small, much smaller than animal cells. However, the bacterium Epulopiscium fishelsoni grows to about 600 μm by 80 μm, much larger than the typical animal epithelial cell (about 35 μm in diameter) [142]. *Thiomargarita namibiensis*, an ocean-dwelling bacterium, can reach a size of 0.75 mm, visible to the unaided eye. What do these admittedly obscure facts teach us about the art of classification? Superficial properties, such as size, seldom inform us how to classify objects. The ontologist much think very deeply to find the essential defining features of classes.

Nonphylogenetic signal DNA sequences that cannot yield any useful conclusions related to the evolutionary pathways. Because DNA mutations arise stochastically over time (i.e., at random locations in the gene, and at random times), two organisms having different ancestors may, by chance alone, achieve the same sequence in a chosen stretch of DNA.

Obligate intracellular organism An obligate intracellular organism cannot survive for very long outside its host. Obligate intracellular organisms live off cellular products produced by the host cell. This being the case, it would be redundant for such organisms to maintain all of the complex cellular machinger that a free-living organism must synthesize and maintain. Consequently, obligate intracellular organisms adapt simplified cellular anatomy, often dispensing with much of the genome, much of the cytoplasm, and most of the organelles that were present in their ancestral classes, prior to their transition to intracellular (i.e., parasitic) life.

Oncogene Normal genes or parts of genes that, when altered to a more active form, or are overexpressed, contribute toward a neoplastic phenotype in a particular range of cell types. The normal form of the oncogene is called the proto-oncogene. The altered, more active form of the gene, is called the activated oncogene. Activation usually involves mutation, or amplification (i.e., an increase in gene copy number), translocation, or fusion with an actively transcribed gene, or some sequence of events that increase the expression of the gene product. Some retroviruses contain oncogenes and can cause tumors by inserting into the host genome.

Opportunistic infection Opportunistic infections are diseases that do not typically occur in healthy individuals, but which can occur in individuals who have a physiologic status favoring the growth of the organisms (e.g., diabetes, malnutrition, immune deficiency). Having one disease may increase susceptibility to specific types of endogenous or ubiquitous organisms that would not otherwise pose risk. For example, diabetics are more likely to contract systemic fungal diseases than are nondiabetic individuals. Most of the infectious diseases occurring in the setting of AIDS arise from the population of organisms that live within most humans, without causing disease under normal circumstances (i.e., commensals). Such organisms include *Pneumocystis jirovecii*, *Toxoplasma gondii*, *Cryptococcus neoformans*, and *Cytomegalovirus*, among many others. The concept of an opportunistic organism is, at best, a gray area of medicine, as virtually all of the organisms that arise in immune-compromised patients will, occasionally, cause disease in seemingly immune-competent patients (e.g., *Cryptococcus neoformans*). Moreover, the so-called primary infectious organisms, that produce disease in normal individuals, will tend to produce a more virulent version of the disease in immunosuppressed individuals (e.g., *Coccidioides immitis*). Recent observations would suggest that many, if not most, of the seemingly immunocompetent individuals who contract opportunistic infections have identifiable genetic abnormalities that account, specifically, for their heightened susceptibilities [8,42,47,52,106].

Parent class The immediate ancestor, or the next-higher class (i.e., the direct superclass) of a class. For example, in the classification of living organisms, Class Vertebrata is the parent class of Class Gnathostomata. Class Gnathostomata is the parent class of Class Teleostomi, and so on.

Peroxisome disorder Eukaryotic organisms contain small organelles that are involved in the catabolism of very long-chain fatty acids. In humans, peroxisomes are also involved in the synthesis of various phospholipids essential to the brain. Hence, inherited peroxisomal disorders are neurologic disorders that are accompanied by developmental and organ (e.g., liver) dysfunctions. Examples of peroxisome disorders include Zellweger syndrome, rhizomelic chondrodysplasia punctata, neonatal adrenoleukodystrophy, and infantile Refsum disease [143].

Primary host Same as final host or definitive host. In the life cycle of infection by parasitic organisms, the primary host is the animal that is infected by the mature or reproductive stage of the parasite. In most cases, the mature stage of the parasite is the stage in which eggs, larvae, or cysts are produced.

Secondary host Synonymous with intermediate host.

Serotype Subtypes of a species of bacteria or virus that are distinguished from one another by their surface antigens. Same as serovar.

Taxa Plural of taxon.

Taxon A taxon is a class. The common usage of "taxon" is somewhat inconsistent, as it sometimes refers to the class name, and at other times refers to the instances (i.e., members) of the class. In this book, the term "taxon" is abandoned in favor of "class," the plesionym used by computer scientists. Hence, the term "class" is used herein in the same manner that it is used in modern object-oriented programming languages.

Thesaurus A vocabulary that groups together synonymous terms. A thesaurus is very similar to a nomenclature. There are two minor differences. Nomenclatures include multiword terms, whereas a thesaurus is typically composed of one-word terms. In addition, nomenclatures are typically restricted to a well-defined topic or knowledge domain (e.g., names of stars, infectious diseases, etc.).

Transposon Also called transposable element, and informally known as jumping gene. The name "transposable element" would seem to imply that a fragment of the genome (i.e., the transposable element) physically moves from one point in the genome to another. This is not the case. What actually happens (in the case of Class II transposons) is that a copy of the DNA sequence of the transposon is inserted elsewhere in the genome, resulting in the sequence now occupying two different locations in the genome. In the case of Class II transposons, the DNA sequence of the transposon is translated into RNA, then reverse-transcribed as DNA, and reinserted at another location; likewise resulting in two of the same sequence in two locations in the genome [144]. You can see how transposable elements might bloat the genome with repeated elements. Transposons are the ancient remnants of retroviruses and other horizontally transferred genes that insinuated their way into the eukaryotic genome. Because transposon DNA is not necessary for cell survival, the sequences of transposons are not conserved, and mutations occurring over time yield degenerate sequences that no longer function as retroviruses. As luck would have it, not all mutations to transposable elements are without benefit to the host cell. A transposon is credited with the acquisition of adaptive immunity in animals. The RAG1 gene was acquired as a transposon. This gene enabled the DNA that encodes a segment of the immunoglobulin molecule to rearrange, thus producing a vast array of protein variants [33]. A role for transposons in the altered expression of genes in cancer cells has been suggested [145].

Vector An organism that moves a disease-causing organism from one host to another. Diseases spread by vectors include: malaria, leishmaniasis, African trypanosomiasis, yellow fever, dengue fever, West Nile encephalitis, chikungunya. Arthropods are the most common vectors of human diseases, and all of the arboviruses have arthropod vectors. There are about 100 arboviruses known to produce human disease [104]. One vector can carry more than one type of infectious organism. For example, a single species of Anopheles mosquito can transmit *Dirofilaria immitis*, O'nyong'nyong fever virus, *Wuchereria bancrofti*, and *Brugia malayi*. Obversely, one disease organism can be spread by more than one vector. For example, orbiviruses are spread by mosquitoes, midges, gnats, sandflies, and ticks [8].

References

[1] Forterre P. The two ages of the RNA world, and the transition to the DNA world: a story of viruses and cells. Biochimie 2005;87:793–803.

[2] The state of world health. Chapter 1 in World Health Report 1996. World Health Organization; 1996. Available from: http://www.who.int/whr/1996/en/index.html.

[3] Weekly epidemiological record. World Health Organization 2007;32:285–296.

[4] Muhlestein JB, Anderson JL. Chronic infection and coronary artery disease. Cardiol Clin 2003;21:333–62.

[5] zur Hausen H. Infections causing human cancer. Hoboken: John Wiley and Sons; 2006.

[6] DNA Transforming Viruses. MicrobiologyBytes October 19, 2004.

[7] Wales JH, Sinnhuber RO, Hendricks JD, Nixon JE, Eisele TA. Aflatoxin B1 induction of hepatocellular carcinoma in the embryos of rainbow trout (Salmo gairdneri). J Natl Cancer Inst 1978;60:1133–9.

[8] Berman JJ. Taxonomic guide to infectious diseases: understanding the biologic classes of pathogenic organisms. Waltham: Academic Press; 2012.

[9] Frank DN, Pace NR. Gastrointestinal microbiology enters the metagenomics era. Curr Opin Gastroenterol 2008;24:4–10.

[10] Mayr E. Two empires or three? PNAS 1998;95:9720–3.

[11] Lane N. Life ascending: the ten great inventions of evolution. London: Profile Books; 2009.

[12] DeQueiroz K. Ernst Mayr and the modern concept of species. PNAS 2005;102(Suppl. 1):6600–7.

[13] DeQueiroz K. Species concepts and species delimitation. Syst Biol 2007;56:879–86.

[14] Mayden RL. Consilience and a hierarchy of species concepts: advances toward closure on the species puzzle. J Nematol 1999;31:95–116.

[15] Philippe H, Brinkmann H, Lavrov DV, Littlewood DT, Manuel M, Worheide G, et al. Resolving difficult phylogenetic questions: why more sequences are not enough. PLoS Biol 2011;9:e1000602.

[16] Bergsten J. A review of long-branch attraction. Cladistics 2005;21:163–93.

[17] Khare S, Nagle AS, Biggart A, Lai YH, Liang F, Davis LC, et al. Proteasome inhibition for treatment of leishmaniasis, Chagas disease and sleeping sickness. Nature 2016;537:229–33.

[18] Rassi Jr A, Rassi A, Marin-Neto JA. Chagas disease. Lancet 2010;375:1388–402.

[19] Woese CR. Bacterial evolution. Microbiol Rev 1987;51:221–71.

[20] Mann CC. 1493: Uncovering the New World Columbus Created. New York: Knopf; 2011.

[21] Griffiths DJ. Endogenous retroviruses in the human genome sequence. Genome Biol 2001;2. reviews10171–reviews10175 .

[22] Horie M, Honda T, Suzuki Y, Kobayashi Y, Daito T, Oshida T, et al. Endogenous non-retroviral RNA virus elements in mammalian genomes. Nature 2010;463:84–7.

[23] Patel MR, Emerman M, Malik HS. Paleovirology: ghosts and gifts of viruses past. Curr Opin Virol 2011; 1(4):304–9.

[24] Emerman M, Malik HS. Paleovirology: modern consequences of ancient viruses. PLoS Biol 2010;8:e1000301.

[25] Bannert N, Kurth R. The evolutionary dynamics of human endogenous retroviral families. Annu Rev Genomics Hum Genet 2006;7:149–73.

[26] Brocks JJ, Logan GA, Buick R, Summons RE. Archaean molecular fossils and the early rise of eukaryotes. Science 1999;285:1033–6.

[27] Stechmann A, Hamblin K, Perez-Brocal V, Gaston D, Richmond GS, van der Giezen M, et al. Organelles in Blastocystis that blur the distinction between mitochondria and hydrogenosomes. Curr Biol 2008;18:580–5.

[28] Tovar J, Leon-Avila G, Sanchez LB, Sutak R, Tachezy J, van der Giezen M, et al. Mitochondrial remnant organelles of Giardia function in iron-sulphur protein maturation. Nature 2003;426:172–6.

[29] Tovar J, Fischer A, Clark CG. The mitosome, a novel organelle related to mitochondria in the amitochondrial parasite Entamoeba histolytica. Mol Microbiol 1999;32:1013–21.

[30] Burri L, Williams B, Bursac D, Lithgow T, Keeling P. Microsporidian mitosomes retain elements of the general mitochondrial targeting system. PNAS 2006;103:15916–20.

[31] Kaneko-ishino T, Ishino F. Mammalian-specific genomic functions: newly acquired traits generated by genomic imprinting and LTR retrotransposon-derived genes in mammals. Proc Jpn Acad Ser B Phys Biol Sci 2015;91:511–38.

[32] Santangelo AM, de Souza FSJ, Franchini LF, Bumaschny VF, Low MJ, Rubinstein M. Ancient exaptation of a core-sine retroposon into a highly conserved mammalian neuronal enhancer of the proopiomelanocortin gene. PLoS Genet 2007;3:e166.

[33] Kapitonov VV, Jurka J. RAG1 core and V(D)J recombination signal sequences were derived from Transib transposons. PLoS Biol 2005;3:e181.

[34] Zhang J, Quintal L, Atkinson A, Williams B, Grunebaum E, Roifman CM. Novel RAG1 mutation in a case of severe combined immunodeficiency. Pediatrics 2005;116:445–9.

[35] de Villartay JP, Lim A, Al-Mousa H, Dupont S, D chanet-Merville J, Coumau-Gatbois E, et al. A novel immunodeficiency associated with hypomorphic RAG1 mutations and CMV infection. J Clin Invest 2005;115:3291–9.

[36] Cornelis G, Vernochet C, Carradec Q, Souquere S, Mulot B, Catzeflis F, et al. Retroviral envelope gene captures and syncytin exaptation for placentation in marsupials. Proc Natl Acad Sci U S A 2015;112:e487–496.

[37] Zheng SL, Liu W, Wiklund F, Dimitrov L, Balter K, Sun J, et al. A comprehensive association study for genes in inflammation pathway provides support for their roles in prostate cancer risk in the CAPS study. Prostate 2006;66:1556–64.

[38] Natoli G, Ghisletti S, Barozzi I. The genomic landscapes of inflammation. Genes Dev 2011;25:101–6.

[39] Fumagalli M, Sironi M, Pozzoli U, Ferrer-Admetlla A, Pattini L, Nielsen R. Signatures of environmental genetic adaptation pinpoint pathogens as the main selective pressure through human evolution. PLoS Genet 2011;7: e1002355.

[40] Banuls A, Thomas F, Renaud F. Of parasites and men. Infect Genet Evol 2013;20:61–70.

[41] Seok J, Warren HS, Cuenca AG, Mindrinos MN, Baker HV, Xu W, et al. Genomic responses in mouse models poorly mimic human inflammatory diseases. Proc Natl Acad Sci U S A 2013;110:3507–12.

[42] Casanova J-L. Human genetic basis of interindividual variability in the course of infection. Proc Natl Acad Sci U S A 2015;112:e7118–7127.

[43] Centers for Disease Control and Prevention. Naegleria fowleri—primary amebic meningoencephalitis—amebic encephalitis; April 12, 2016. http://www.cdc.gov/parasites/naegleria/general.html [Accessed 18 April 2017].

[44] Budge PJ, Lazensky B, Van Zile KW, Elliott KE, Dooyema CA, Visvesvara GS, et al. Primary amebic meningo-encephalitis in Florida: a case report and epidemiological review of Florida cases. J Environ Health 2013;75:26–31.

[45] Grace E, Asbill S, Virga K. Naegleria fowleri: pathogenesis, diagnosis, and treatment options. Antimicrob Agents Chemother 2015;59:6677–81.

[46] Hebbar S, Bairy I, Bhaskaranand N, Upadhyaya S, Sarma MS, Shetty AK. Fatal case of Naegleria fowleri meningo-encephalitis in an infant: case report. Ann Trop Paediatr 2005;25:223–6.

[47] Casanova J. Severe infectious diseases of childhood as monogenic inborn errors of immunity. Proc Natl Acad Sci 2015;112:e7128–7137.

[48] Sak B, Kvac M, Kucerova Z, Kvetonova D, Sakova K. Latent microsporidial infection in immunocompetent individuals: a longitudinal study. PLoS Negl Trop Dis 2011;5:e1162.

[49] Tehmeena W, Hussain W, Zargar HR, Sheikh AR, Iqbal S. Primary cutaneous mucormycosis in an immunocompetent host. Mycopathologia 2007;164:197–9.

[50] Jiang Y, Huang A, Fang Q. Disseminated nocardiosis caused by Nocardia otitidiscaviarum in an immunocompetent host: a case report and literature review. Exp Ther Med 2016;12:3339–46.

[51] Permi HS, Sunil KY, Karnaker VK, Kishan PHL, Teerthanath S, Bhandary SK. A rare case of fungal maxillary sinusitis due to Paecilomyces lilacinus in an immunocompetent host, presenting as a subcutaneous swelling. J Lab Physicians 2011;3:46–8.

[52] Ku CL, Picard C, Erdos M, Jeurissen A, Bustamante J, Puel A, et al. IRAK4 and NEMO mutations in otherwise healthy children with recurrent invasive pneumococcal disease. J Med Genet 2007;44:16–23.

[53] Vidal SM, Malo D, Vogan K, Skamene E, Gros P. Natural resistance to infection with intracellular parasites: isolation of a candidate for Bcg. Cell 1993;73:469–85.

[54] Tobin DM, Vary JC Jr, Ray JP, Walsh GS, Dunstan SJ, Bang ND, et al. The lta4h locus modulates susceptibility to mycobacterial infection in zebrafish and humans. Cell 2010;140:717-730.

[55] Warren HS, Fitting C, Hoff E, Adib-Conquy M, Beasley-Topliffe L, Tesini B, et al. Resilience to bacterial infection: difference between species could be due to proteins in serum. J Infect Dis 2010;201:223–32.

[56] Khor CC, Vannberg FO, Chapman SJ, Guo H, Wong SH, Walley AJ, et al. CISH and susceptibility to infectious diseases. N Engl J Med 2010;362:2092–101.

[57] Kwiatkowski DP. How malaria has affected the human genome and what human genetics can teach us about malaria. Am J Hum Genet 2005;77:171–92.

[58] Hill AVS. Evolution, revolution and heresy in the genetics of infectious disease susceptibility. Philos Trans R Soc Lond Ser B Biol Sci 2012;367:840–9.

[59] Leveson NG. System safety engineering: back to the future. Self-published ebook. Available from: http://sunnyday.mit.edu/book2.pdf; 2002.

[60] Leveson NG. Engineering a safer world. systems thinking applied to safety. Self-published book. Available from: http://sunnyday.mit.edu/safer-world.pdf; 2009.

[61] Borghesi L, Milcarek C. From B cell to plasma cell: regulation of V(D)J recombination and antibody secretion. Immunol Res 2006;36:27–32.

[62] Jacobson DL, Gange SJ, Rose NR, Graham NM. Epidemiology and estimated population burden of selected autoimmune diseases in the United States. Clin Immunol Immunopathol 1997;84:223–43.

[63] Pietropaolo M, Barinas-Mitchell E, Kuller LH. The heterogeneity of diabetes: unraveling a dispute: is systemic inflammation related to islet autoimmunity? Diabetes 2007;56:1189–97.

[64] Kleopa KA. Autoimmune channelopathies of the nervous system. Curr Neuropharmacol 2011;9:458–67.

[65] Anderson M, Su M. AIRE and T cell development. Curr Opin Immunol 2011;23:198–206.

[66] Masters SL, Simon A, Aksentijevich I, Kastner DL. Horror autoinflammaticus: the molecular pathophysiology of autoinflammatory disease. Annu Rev Immunol 2009;27:621–68.

[67] Vilmos P, Kurucz E. Insect immunity: evolutionary roots of the mammalian innate immune system. Immunol Lett 1998;62:59–66.

[68] Yan N, Chen ZJ. Intrinsic antiviral immunity. Nat Immunol 2012;13:214–22.

[69] Lupfer CR, Kanneganti T. The role of inflammasome modulation in virulence. Virulence 2012;3:262–70.

[70] Latz E, Xiao TS, Stutz A. Activation and regulation of the inflammasomes. Nat Rev Immunol 2013;13:10.

[71] Goldfinger SE. Colchicine for familial Mediterranean fever. N Engl J Med 1972;287:1302.

[72] Martinon F, Petrilli V, Mayor A, Tardivel A, Tschopp J. Gout-associated uric acid crystals activate the NALP3 inflammasome. Nature 2006;440:237–41.

[73] McGonagle D, McDermott MF. A proposed classification of the immunological diseases. PLoS Med 2006;3:e297.

[74] Jacomo V, Kelly PJ, Raoult D. Natural History of Bartonella Infections (an Exception to Koch's Postulate). Clin Diagn Lab Immunol 2002;9:8–18.

[75] Ren L-Q, Li X-J, Li G-S, Zhao Z-T, Sun B, Sun F. Coxsackievirus B3 infection and its mutation in Keshan disease. World J Gastroenterol 2004;10:3299–302.

[76] Wang SS. Big bone disease fades in China. The Wall Street Journal; August 13, 2011.

[77] Whipple GH. A hitherto undescribed disease characterized anatomically by deposits of fat and fatty acids in the intestinal and mesenteric lymphatic tissues. Bull Johns Hopkins Hosp 1907;18:382–93.

[78] Relman DA, Schmidt TM, MacDermott RP, Falkow S. Identification of the uncultured bacillus of Whipple's disease. N Engl J Med 1992;327:293–301.

[79] Marth T, Roux M, von Herbay A, Meuer SC, Feurle GE. Persistent reduction of complement receptor 3 alpha-chain expressing mononuclear blood cells and transient inhibitory serum factors in Whipple's disease. Clin Immunol Immunopathol 1994;72:217–26.

[80] Iverson SA, Ostdiek S, Prasai S, Engelthaler DM, Kretschmer M, Fowle N, et al. Notes from the Field: Cluster of Acute Flaccid Myelitis in Five Pediatric Patients—Maricopa County, Arizona, 2016. MMWR Morb Mortal Wkly Rep 2017;66:758–60.

[81] Inglis TJ. Principia aetiologica: taking causality beyond Koch's postulates. J Med Microbiol 2007;56:1419–22.

[82] Suggested Upper Merged Ontology (SUMO). The Ontology Portal. Available from: http://www. ontologyportal.org [Accessed 14 August 2012].

[83] Gayathri D, Rashmi BS. Development of celiac disease: pathogenesis and strategies to control: a molecular approach. J Nutr Food Sci 2014;4:310.

[84] Bouziat R, Hinterleitner R, Brown JJ, Stencel-Baerenwald JE, Ikizler M, Mayassi T, et al. Reovirus infection triggers inflammatory responses to dietary antigens and development of celiac disease. Science 2017;356:44–50.

[85] Heiligenhaus A, Kasper M, Grajewski R. hla-b27 positive acute anterior uveitis: a translational perspective. Klin Monatsbl Augenheilkd 2017;234:652–6.

[86] Chen B, Li J, He C, et al. Role of HLA-B27 in the pathogenesis of ankylosing spondylitis. Mol Med Rep 2017;15:1943–51.

[87] Resnikoff S, Pascolini D, Etyaale D, Kocur I, Pararajasegaram R, Pokharel GP, et al. Global data on visual impairment in the year 2002. Bull World Health Organ 2004;82:844–51.

[88] Slatko BE, Taylor MJ, Foster JM. The Wolbachia endosymbiont as an anti-filarial nematode target. Symbiosis 2010;51:55–65.

[89] Johnson TP, Tyagi R, Lee PR, Lee MH, Johnson KR, Kowalak J, et al. Nodding syndrome may be an autoimmune reaction to the parasitic worm Onchocerca volvulus. Sci Transl Med 2017;9(377).

[90] Liu Y, Chiba M, Inaba Y, Kondo M. Keshan disease—a review from the aspect of history and etiology. Nihon Eiseigaku Zasshi 2001;56:641–8.

[91] Badorff C, Lee GH, Knowlton KU. Enteroviral cardiomyopathy: bad news for the dystrophin-glycoprotein complex. Herz 2000;25:227–32.

[92] Loria K. One of the largest human experiments in history was conducted on unsuspecting residents of San Francisco. Business Insider; July 9, 2015.

[93] Silberman JD, Sogin ML, Leipe DD, Clark CG. Human parasite finds taxonomic home. Nature 1996;380:398.

[94] Amin OM. Seasonal prevalence of intestinal parasites in the United States during 2000. Am J Trop Med Hyg 2002;66:799–803.

[95] Sekas G, Hutson WR. Misrepresentation of academic accomplishments by applicants for gastroenterology fellowships. Ann Intern Med 1995;123:38–41.

[96] Samuelson J. Why metronidazole is active against both bacteria and parasites. Antimicrob Agents Chemother 1999;3:1533–41.

[97] Garrison FH. History of medicine. Philadelphia: WB Saunders; 1921.

[98] Inamadar AC, Palit A. The genus Malassezia and human disease. Indian J Dermatol Venereol Leprol 2003;69:265–70.

[99] de Mauri A, Chiarinotti D, Andreoni S, Molinari GL, Conti N, De Leo M. Leclercia Adecarboxylata and catheter-related bacteremia: review of the literature and outcome of catheters and patients. J Med Microbiol 2013;62:1620–3.

[100] Baron EJ, Allen SD. Should clinical laboratories adopt new taxonomic changes? If so, when? Clin Infect Dis 1993;16:S449–450.

[101] Committee on A Framework for Developing a New Taxonomy of Disease, Board on Life Sciences, Division on Earth and Life Studies, National Research Council of the National Academies. Toward precision medicine: building a knowledge network for biomedical research and a new taxonomy of disease. Washington, DC: The National Academies Press; 2011.

[102] Guarro J, Gene J, Stchigel AM. Developments in fungal taxonomy. Clin Microbiol Rev 1999;12:454–500.

[103] Pounder JI, Simmon KE, Barton CA, Hohmann SL, Brandt ME, Petti CA. Discovering potential pathogens among fungi identified as nonsporulating molds. J Clin Microbiol 2007;45:568–71.

[104] Lemon SM, Sparling PF, Hamburg MA, Relman DA, Choffnes ER, Mack A. Vector-borne diseases: understanding the environmental, human health, and ecological connections, workshop summary. Institute of Medicine (US) Forum on Microbial Threats, Washington, DC: National Academies Press (US); 2008.

[105] Fan L, Lee SY, Koay E, Harkensee C. Plasmodium knowlesi infection: a diagnostic challenge. BMJ Case Rep 2013;2013.

[106] Berman JJ. Rare diseases and orphan drugs: keys to understanding and treating common diseases. Cambridge, MA: Academic Press; 2014.

[107] Caboche S, Audebert C, David Hot D. High-throughput sequencing, a versatile weapon to support genome-based diagnosis in infectious diseases: applications to clinical bacteriology. Pathogens 2014;3:258–79.

[108] Zoll J, Snelders E, Verweij PE, Melchers WJ. Next-generation sequencing in the mycology lab. Curr Fungal Infect Rep 2016;10:37–42.

[109] Zimmer C. In a first, test of DNA finds root of illness. The New York Times; June 4, 2014.

[110] Romero EC, Billerbeck AEC, Lando VS, Camargo ED, Souza CC, Yasuda PH. Detection of Leptospira DNA in patients with Aseptic Meningitis by PCR. J Clin Microbiol 1998;36:1453–5.

[111] Sainani K. Error: what biomedical computing can learn from its mistakes. Biomed Comput Rev; Fall 2011, p. 12–19.

[112] Sainani K. Meet the skeptics: why some doubt biomedical models, and what it takes to win them over. Biomed Comput Rev; June 5, 2012.

[113] Unreliable research: Trouble at the lab. The Economist; October 19, 2013.

[114] Kolata G. Cancer fight: unclear tests for new drug. The New York Times; April 19, 2010.

[115] Baker M. Reproducibility crisis: Blame it on the antibodies. Nature 2015;521:274–6.

[116] Ioannidis JP. Is molecular profiling ready for use in clinical decision making? Oncologist 2007;12:301–11.

[117] Ioannidis JP. Why most published research findings are false. PLoS Med 2005;2:e124.

[118] Ioannidis JP. Some main problems eroding the credibility and relevance of randomized trials. Bull NYU Hosp Jt Dis 2008;66:135–9.

[119] Ioannidis JP. Microarrays and molecular research: noise discovery? Lancet 2005;365:454–5.

[120] Ioannidis JP, Panagiotou OA. Comparison of effect sizes associated with biomarkers reported in highly cited individual articles and in subsequent meta-analyses. JAMA 2011;305:2200–10.

[121] Ioannidis JP. Excess significance bias in the literature on brain volume abnormalities. Arch Gen Psychiatry 2011;68:773–80.

[122] Pocock SJ, Collier TJ, Dandreo KJ, deStavola BL, Goldman MB, Kalish LA, et al. Issues in the reporting of epidemiological studies: a survey of recent practice. BMJ 2004;329:883.

[123] Misconduct in science: an array of errors. The Economist; September 10, 2011.

[124] Begley S. In cancer science, many 'discoveries' don't hold up. Reuters; March 28, 2012.

[125] Abu-Asab MS, Chaouchi M, Alesci S, Galli S, Laassri M, Cheema AK, et al. Biomarkers in the age of omics: time for a systems biology approach. OMICS 2011;15:105–12.

[126] Moyer VA, On behalf of the U.S. Preventive Services Task Force. Screening for prostate cancer: U.S. Preventive Services Task Force recommendation statement. Ann Intern Med 2012;157:120–34.

[127] How science goes wrong. The Economist; October 19, 2013.

[128] Walker J, Conner G, Ho J, Hunt C, Pickering L. Giemsa staining for cysts and trophozoites of Pneumocystis carinii. J Clin Pathol 1989;42:432–4.

[129] Fischer WM, Palmer JD. Evidence from small-subunit ribosomal RNA sequences for a fungal origin of Microsporidia. Mol Phylogenet Evol 2005;36:606–22.

[130] Keeling PJ, Luker MA, Palmer JD. Evidence from beta-tubulin phylogeny that microsporidia evolved from within the fungi. Mol Biol Evol 2000;17:23–31.

[131] Malik A, Jameel MN, Sohail S, Mir S. Human granulocytic anaplasmosis affecting the myocardium. J Gen Intern Med 2005;20:958.

[132] Lleo A, Invernizzi P, Gao B, Podda M, Gershwin ME. Definition of human autoimmunity—autoantibodies versus autoimmune disease. Autoimmun Rev 2010;9:A259–266.

[133] Al-Agha OM, Igbokwe AA. Malignant fibrous histiocytoma: between the past and the present. Arch Pathol Lab Med 2008;132:1030–5.

[134] Nakayama R, Nemoto T, Takahashi H, Ohta T, Kawai A, Seki K, et al. Gene expression analysis of soft tissue sarcomas: characterization and reclassification of malignant fibrous histiocytoma. Mod Pathol 2007;20:749–59.

[135] Daugaard S. Current soft-tissue sarcoma classifications. Eur J Cancer 2004;40:543–8.

[136] Hugot JP, Chamaillard M, Zouali H, Lesage S, Lesage S, Cezard JP, et al. Association of NOD2 leucine-rich repeat variants with susceptibility to Crohn's disease. Nature 2001;411:599–603.

[137] Ogura Y, Bonen DK, Inohara N, Nicolae DL, Chen FF, Ramos R, et al. A frameshift mutation in NOD2 associated with susceptibility to Crohn's disease. Nature 2001;411:603–6.

[138] Glaser RL, Goldbach-Mansky R. The spectrum of monogenic autoinflammatory syndromes: understanding disease mechanisms and use of targeted therapies. Curr Allergy Asthma Rep 2008;8:288–98.

[139] Berman JJ. Tumor classification: molecular analysis meets Aristotle. BMC Cancer 2004;4:10.

[140] Berman JJ. Tumor taxonomy for the developmental lineage classification of neoplasms. BMC Cancer 2004;4:88.

[141] Arslan D, Legendre M, Seltzer V, Abergel C, Claverie J. Distant Mimivirus relative with a larger genome highlights the fundamental features of Megaviridae. PNAS 2011;108:17486–91.

[142] Angert ER, Clements KD, Pace NR. The largest bacterium. Nature 1993;362:239–41.

[143] Weller S, Cajigas I, Morrell J, Obie C, Steel G, Gould SJ, et al. Alternative splicing suggests extended function of PEX26 in peroxisome biogenesis. Am J Hum Genet 2005;76(6):987–1007.

[144] Holmes I. Transcendent elements: whole-genome transposon screens and open evolutionary questions. Genome Res 2002;12:1152–5.

[145] Lerat E, Semon M. Influence of the transposable element neighborhood on human gene expression in normal and tumor tissues. Gene 2007;396:303–11.

Reinventing Diagnosis

SECTION 7.1 THE PRINCIPLES OF CLASSIFICATION

Taxonomy is the oldest profession practiced by people with their clothes on.
Quentin Wheeler referring to the belief that Adam was given the task of naming all the creatures.

A classification is a way of grouping related objects into classes that follow the following rules [1–3]:

1. Each class of related objects can be described by a set of defining properties that apply to every member of the class and that establish the class relationships.
2. Every class must have a parent class; with the exception of the top class, sometimes referred to as the root class. The defining properties of the parent class apply to the child class. The child class must have at least one property that pertains to the members of its own class but not to the parent class. [Glossary Child class]
3. Any class may have one or more child classes of its own.
4. Every object (sometimes referred to as class member or as a class instance) belongs to exactly one class.

Technically, that's all there is to a classification. [Glossary Clade, Cladistics, Monophyletic class, Apomorphy, Multiclass classification, Multiclass inheritance, Unclassifiable objects]

With these four rules, there come a host of interesting and useful features.

– Completeness

Completeness is a conceptual by-product of our definition of a classification. A classification is always complete because every member of the classification has a place in a class, every class has at least one member, and every member within a class has a defined relationship to every other member within the same class.

– Sparseness of attributes

You don't need to know everything about every instance to start building a classification based on relationships. The classification of living organisms was intact, and more or less equivalent to today's classification, decades prior to the discovery of most of the major breakthroughs in evolution, genetics, and molecular biology. When new information came to light that called into question some of the suppositions upon which relationships were based, taxonomists were ready and able to modify the classification, as needed, without discarding their earlier work.

– Information retrieval

Classifications can function as the master index to the domain of included objects, supporting search and retrieval methods, and facilitating data analysis and data mining projects.

Because every class has only one parent class, it is easy to construct the full ancestry of every member of a classification. For example, if you have an instance of spider (for example, "inky-dinky spider"), you need only determine the binomial name of the species (i.e., *Tegenaria domestica*), to determine the name of its parent class (i.e., its genus, Tegenaria). You can look up the parent class of Tegenaria (i.e., Agelenidae) to determine the grandfather class. By iteratively determining the parent class of each ancestor, you can reconstruct the complete lineage of "inky dinky spider," namely: Tegenaria domestica, Tegenaria, Agelenidae, Araneomorphae, Araneae, Arichnida, Chelicerata, Arthropoda, Panarthropoda, Protostomia, Coelomata, Bilateria, Eumetazoa, Metazoa, Fungi/Metazoa group, Eukaryota, Cellular Organism (root class). [Glossary Metazoa]

– Classifications are interdisciplinary

Much, if not all, of the perceived complexity of the biological sciences derives from the growing interconnections of once-separate disciplines: cell biology, ecology, evolution, climatology, molecular biology, pharmacology, genetics, computer sciences, paleontology, pathology, statistics, and so on. Because classifications are built by finding the fundamental relationships among members, whatever they may be, we can expect that the process of building a classification will lead us into a diverse set of scientific realms. For example, if we subclassify a particular disease based on a genetic sequence in the genome, we'll need to familiarize ourselves with the fundamental rules of genetics and of bioinformatics. If we subclassify diseases based on the three-dimensional shape of proteins, then we may need to draw knowledge from the fields of X-ray crystallography and electron microscopy. When we classify based on developmental errors, we'll need to have a very deep understanding of embryology. The sciences follow the classification, wherever it may lead. [Glossary Bioinformatics]

– Classifications drive down the complexity of its included objects

You can begin to see how a classification can drive down the complexity of its contained objects. We have already seen, in the prior chapter, how classifications help clinical microbiologists. With over 1400 infectious diseases that physicians are expected to diagnose, it is important to have a way of grouping organisms into a manageable collection of classes. As it happens, every known disease-causing organism has been assigned to one of 40 well-defined classes of organisms, and each class fits within a simple ancestral lineage. This means that every known pathogenic organism inherits certain properties from its ancestral classes and shares these properties with the other members of its own class. When you learn the class properties, along with some basic information about the infectious members of the classes, you gain a comprehensive understanding of relationships and properties of every organism.

– Competence

Competence refers to the ability to make inferences based on knowledge of class properties and of the relationships among the classes. For example, you can infer that every member of a class will inherit all of the class properties and class methods available to the parent class. If it is known that a particular pathway is a class property, then we can infer that a drug that blocks the pathway in members of the class will also block the pathway in members of the descendant classes. [Glossary Rank]

For the modern scientist, the classification of living organisms is the inference engine around which all biological science is unified. In the case of infectious diseases, when scientists find a trait that informs us that what we thought was a single species is actually two species, it permits us to develop treatments optimized for each species, and to develop new methods to monitor and control the spread of both organisms. When we correctly group organisms within a common class, we can test and develop new drugs that are effective against all of the organisms within the class, particularly if those organisms are characterized by a molecule, pathway, or trait that is specifically targeted by a drug [4].

– Good classifications must be tested.

Until verified, any inference drawn from a classification is tentative. If an inference is demonstrated to be false, then we must revisit the classification and determine the reason for the error. Sometimes, we may find that the classification is valid, but that we made certain assumptions about the properties of classes that are untrue. At other times, we learn that our classification is imperfect and must be revised. All classifications must be continuously and endlessly tested. Otherwise, the classification is simply a pseudoscientific assertion.

Classifications, as described in this section, seem almost too good to be true. It happens that it is very difficult to create a self-consistent classification, and classifications have their logical pitfalls, often due, in one way or another, to paradoxes of self-reference. [Glossary Paradoxes of classification]

Of late, the eminence of classifications has been challenged by a relatively new invention in the field of taxonomy: the ontology. Ontologies are classifications that have abandoned the one class one parent rule (i.e., an ontology class is permitted to have more than one parent class). The relative strengths and weakness of ontologies, as compared with classifications, have been thoroughly examined in several of my previously published works [5–7].

SECTION 7.2 SUPERCLASSES

The ignoramus is a leaf who doesn't know he is part of a tree.
Michael Crichton

As a general rule, the first attempt at designing a classification will be a failure. The same generalization holds true for the second, third, fourth, and fifth attempts. The reason for this is simple. To build a classification, you must know the set of defining features that applies to every member of a class, and its descending subclass lineage, and which is absent from every member of every class that is not in the descending lineage of the class. Unfortunately, there is simply no way of knowing what these defining sets of features happen to be, until the classification has been completed. That is to say, you need to have completed the classification before you can begin to build the classification. Hence, it is impossible to build a classification without doing a lot of guessing and then correcting your guesses through multiple iterations of the class-creation process. The process of creation using the thing that you are creating to complete the creation is known as bootstrapping.

Bootstrapping is an often-encountered term in computer science. It derives from the idiomatic expression, "pulling yourself up by your own bootstraps," which conveys the mundane impossibility of the process. When you "boot" (short for bootstrap) your computer, the computer must use an operating system, that has not yet been activated, to activate itself. Somehow, the job gets done.

The difficulty involved in creating a good classification, in any knowledge domain, is attested by these four observations:

1. There are no examples of new classifications that are considered to be definitive and final.
2. For any medical discipline, there are likely to be several available classifications that cover much of the same ground, indicating that no single classification seems to meet every user's expectations.
3. All classifications that have been adopted by user communities have gone through multiple revisions, indicating dissatisfaction with each iteration.
4. The greatest biological classification ever devised by mankind is the classification of all living earthly organisms. This classification has gone through endless revisions extending over 2000 years. There is no reason to expect that the revision process will ever cease.

The medical field contains many different classifications of disease [8–16]. If you have a penchant for finding fault in the labors of scientists, then you will enjoy the time spent examining any existing classification. If you look hard enough, you will find fundamental design flaws in every classification you encounter [7]. Even the most carefully designed classifications are prone to logical paradoxes guaranteed to rankle the most earnest of taxonomists.

Why are we so inept at designing classification? Classifications are almost always created with a specific goal in mind. This is a fundamental flaw in the way that we approach classifications. The purpose of a classification is to represent reality, not to serve a particular interest. If we design a classification to meet a particular goal, we insert all the biases that come from goal-oriented thinking. For example, if we want to design a classification of automobiles that maximizes our ability to find and retrieved color-matched autos, we are likely to classify cars by their colors, putting fire engines in the same class as red corvettes. Such a classification may serve a short-sighted purpose, but it doesn't tell us much about what it means to be a motorized vehicle.

If we do not see the need to conform to the strict rules of classification, we tend to produce mere listings of things, grouped together by a by region (e.g., Tumors of the head and neck), or symptoms (e.g., Fever syndromes), or age (e.g., Geriatric diseases). Hence, most classifications are little better than collections items represented in a standard nomenclature.

Let's take a moment to inspect the higher order of classes in the International Classification of Disease.

Here are 10 of the 28 major classes of disease that are in draft form, awaiting inclusion in the upcoming release of ICD version 11, scheduled for 2018 [17].

- Certain infectious or parasitic diseases
- Neoplasms
- Diseases of the blood or blood-forming organs
- Diseases of the immune system
- Endocrine, nutritional, or metabolic diseases
- Mental, behavioral, or neurodevelopmental disorders
- Sleep-wake disorders
- Diseases of the nervous system
- Diseases of the visual system
- Diseases of the skin
- Diseases of the circulatory system
- Diseases of the musculoskeletal system or connective tissue

How do we fill these ICD-11 classes of disease? Does acute leukemia fall into class "Neoplasms," or should it go into "Diseases of the blood or blood-forming organs"? Is Alzheimer disease one of the "Mental, behavioral, or neurodevelopmental disorders" or is it one of the "Diseases of the nervous system"? Why would we want to include adrenal insufficiency, an endocrine disease, and scurvy, a nutritional deficiency, in the same class of "Endocrine, nutritional, or metabolic diseases"? What do we do with infectious diseases (e.g., Streptococcal infections) that would seem to transition to two other classes when rheumatic fever develops (i.e., Diseases of the immune system, or Diseases of the circulatory system, or Diseases of the musculoskeletal system or connective tissue)? There is no single way, by application of logic, to assign diseases to the high-level classes of ICD-11. No matter. The creators of ICD-11 have assigned every disease to some location in the classification, and those individuals who receive the proper training can successfully code diseases according to the prescribed listings under each class.

The World Health Organization has provided the following definition of ICD-11 [17]:

> ICD is the foundation for the identification of health trends and statistics globally, and the international standard for reporting diseases and health conditions. It is the diagnostic classification standard for all clinical and research purposes. ICD defines the universe of diseases, disorders, injuries and other related health conditions, listed in a comprehensive, hierarchical fashion that allows for:
> - Easy storage, retrieval, and analysis of health information for evidence-based decision making;
> - Sharing and comparing health information between hospitals, regions, settings, and countries; and
> - Data comparisons in the same location across different time periods.

Nowhere in the definition does it state that the ICD has an internal logical construct. Here are some of the shortcomings of ICD-11, based on the minimal criteria for a logical classification, as stipulated earlier in this chapter:

1. Assigns biologically unrelated diseases to the same class based solely on anatomic location.
2. Assigns diseases that are pathogenetically related into biologically unrelated classes.
3. Provides no set of class-defining features that adequately separate the members of a class, and its descendants, from the other classes. Instead, the ICD-11 employs exception lists added to each class that exclude diseases that meet class criteria but which must, nevertheless, be assigned to some other class.
4. Has no competence (i.e., cannot be used to draw inferences and create new hypotheses based on methods derived from the class properties).
5. Cannot be proven either right or wrong. Because no inferences can be drawn from a standardized listing of diseases, with no logical structure, there is no way to test that the listing is either correct or incorrect. It is what it is.

We should not criticize ICD-11 harshly; it may very well be the best disease classification in existence. We must remember that creating a not-so-good classification is a necessary step toward creating a good classification.

Let's take a moment to discuss whether we can suggest an alternate set of top-level classes that serve the need of scientists and clinicians in the new era of Precision Medicine. Consider the following:

1. Class Neoplasms—Neoplasms are growths of "new" cells, meaning that the cells in a neoplasm are demonstrably different from any known normal cell population, including the normal cells from which the neoplasm arose.
2. Class Degenerations—Diseases in which specific populations of cells degenerate, often with the death of individual cells. This would include most of the so-called diseases due to the aging process, which affect primarily postmitotic cells (i.e., cells that have lost the ability to divide) and would include many of the neurodegenerative disorders that affect adults (e.g., Alzheimer disease).
3. Class Malformations—All of the congenital dysmorphisms such as heart defects and skeletal defects. Included herein would be undergrowths and overgrowths of cell populations that appear normal and function normally, but which have been assembled as an tissue or organ that lacks normal anatomic structure (e.g., hamartomas)

4. Class Dysregulations—All the diseases whose phenotype is driven by a defect in a metabolic pathway, or a cellular organelle and whose clinical phenotype is driven largely by the consequences therefrom. This class would include all of the inborn diseases of metabolism, the immunologic disorder, the diseases of pathways that establish and maintain homeostasis (e.g., the coagulopathies and the hemophilias), the autoinflammatory diseases, and so on.
5. Class Infections—This would be subset of the classification of living organisms containing the known human pathogens. This means that Class Infections subsumes the classification of living organisms, in its entirety, and without alteration.

Let's stop here and ask ourselves whether these superclasses conform to the general principles of classification. Here is what we need to know:

– **Do these five classes include every disease that occurs in man?**

Hopefully, yes. Diseases due to exogenous toxins and nonchemical agents (e.g., radiation, heat) are not provided with their own class. Many of the toxic diseases target specific pathways and organelles and closely phenocopy metabolic diseases. We want to assign every toxic disease to the same class of disease that it phenocopies. Hence, we do not have a Class Toxin. Similarly, we do not have a class for the genetic diseases. We want to assign each genetic disease to its phenotypic category (e.g., Class Dysregulations, Class Malformations, or Class Neoplasms, as the case may be).

– **Does each of these five classes provide a set of defining features that apply to every member of the class and to every member of every subclass in its descendant lineage?**

Maybe. We haven't really looked at any of the subclasses of our five root classes of disease. Let's look at Class Neoplasms and see if we can produce a set of sensible subclasses. Current theory would suggest that every cancer derives from a particular type of cell, and that every cell in the body arises from a sequences of developmental steps, from an original totipotent cell. Basically, the story of cell lineage development is equivalent to the story of development of the blastula, embryo, and fetus. Hence, if we design the subclassification of neoplasms to recapitulate the cells that arise during human development, we should, if theory holds, include every type of tumor, and every tumor will relate to every other tumor in its developmental class. Furthermore, each tumor within a developmental class will exhibit class properties associated with its developmental lineage (Fig. 7.1).

Here is how the major subclasses of neoplasms, based on our understanding of embryonic development, might be listed:

1. Tumors of endoderm/ectoderm [Glossary Endoderm]
2. Tumors of mesoderm
3. Tumors of neuroectoderm [Glossary Neuroectoderm]
4. Tumors of neural crest
5. Tumors of germ cell (includes teratomatous neoplasms)
6. Tumors of trophectoderm (cells of extraembryonic origin) [Glossary Trophectoderm]

Let's look at each of these six classes of neoplasm to see how they were created.

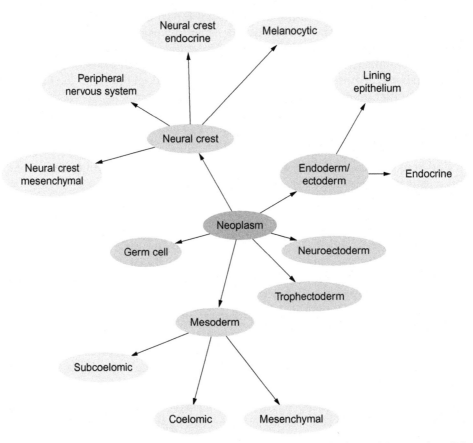

FIG. 7.1   The six major classes of neoplasms and their major subclasses can be depicted in a simple radial graph. Every type of tumor can be assigned to one, and only one, of these classes. Every member of every class of tumors is related to one another, by virtue of their embryologic origin. *From Jules J. Berman.*

In humans, gastrulation occurs after implantation on about day 16 and creates the two outer germ layers (ectoderm and endoderm) as well as the mesoderm and trophectoderm. The neuroectoderm and neural crest develop a bit later. The human body can be envisioned as a topological donut. It is covered by lining cells, with the donut hole lined by endoderm and the donut outer surface lined by ectoderm. The donut pastry would be the mesoderm. There is no anatomic border that separates Endoderm from Ectoderm, and they can both be perceived as the cells that line the outside of the body. After birth, the endoderm and ectoderm derivatives are directly exposed to exogenous chemicals delivered through the air or through the diet. Both endoderm and ectoderm produce the same basic types of cells (squamous cells, mucosal lining cells, and glandular cells). There does not seem to be any benefit in separating the tumors that derive from either of these classes.

The class of Endodermal/Ectodermal neoplasms can be subclassified as follows:

– Primitive
– Endoderm/ectoderm surface

- Endoderm/ectoderm endocrine
- Endoderm/ectoderm parenchymal
- Endoderm/ectoderm odontogenic

The class of Endoderm/Ectoderm tumors contains most (but not all) of the neoplasms that are morphologically epithelial. We will learn more about epithelial cells in Section 7.3. For now, it suffices to note that not all epithelial tumors are of endoderm/ectoderm origin. Some epithelial tumors derive from mesoderm (for example, renal cell carcinoma, adrenal cortical tumors, and ovarian carcinoma), or neural crest (for example, melanoma, medullary carcinoma of thyroid). A basic assumption in the design of the Developmental Classification is that epithelial tumors in different classes have class-specific phenotypic properties unrelated to their epithelial morphology. [Glossary Medullary thyroid carcinoma]

The mesoderm is a germ layer present in all animals descending from about the level of Coelomata. Mesoderm forms during gastrulation when some of the cells migrating inward to form the endoderm form an additional layer between the endoderm and the ectoderm. This inner layer gives rise to the internal body spaces (cell-lined coelomic cavities) and to a variety of structures that develop from the coelomic folds (i.e., subcoelomic derivatives), and to the connective tissues of the body.

The class of Mesodermal neoplasms can be subclassed as follows:

- Primitive
- Mesenchyme
- Connective_tissue
- Muscle
- Fibrous_tissue
- Vascular
- Adipose_tissue
- Bone_cartilage
- Heme_lymphoid
- Coelomic
- Coelomic_ductal
- Coelomic_cavities
- Coelomic_gonadal
- Sub_coelomic
- Sub_coelomic_gonadal
- Sub_coelomic_endocrine
- Sub_coelomic_ nephric

The neuroectoderm develops from the ectoderm and produces the central nervous system. Tumors of class Neuroectoderm account for most of the so-called central nervous system tumors. The class of Neuroectodermal neoplasms can be subclassed as follows:

- Primitive
- Neural_tube
- Neural_tube_parenchyma
- Neural_tube_lining

The neural crest derives from a specialized compartment of cells lying in the mesoderm between the ectoderm and the neural tube. The neural crest gives rise to the peripheral nervous system, to the connective tissue of the head, including a specialized type of flat bone composing the skull, to several endocrine glands, and to the connective tissue component of the teeth [18]. [Glossary Neurocristopathy, Dermal bone, Enchondral bone]

The class of Neural Crest neoplasms can be subclassed as follows:

- Primitive
- Peripheral nervous system
- Neural crest endocrine
- Neural crest melanocytic
- Neural crest odontogenic
- Neural crest mesenchymal

Germ cells are produced during gastrulation as specialized cells derived from endoderm. They give rise to differentiated gametes, the ova and the spermatocytes. Early-stage germ cells are called "primordial" and are multipotent. [Glossary Gamete]

Totipotent neoplasms of germ cell origin (teratomas and embryonal carcinomas and related tumors) can arise by one of two different mechanisms: malignant transformation of a primordial germ cell or through a transformative process occurring in neoplastic differentiated germ cells (dysgerminoma cells or seminoma cells). [Glossary Germ cell line]

The class of Germ cell neoplasms can be subclassed as follows:

- Differentiated
- Primordial (totipotent)
- Tumors of mixed differentiated germ cell and primordial germ cell

In humans, at about the third day of gestation, the morula divides into two parts: the embryoblast from which the embryo develops, and the trophoblast from which the nonembryonic parts, including the placenta, develop. The germ layer containing the tissues developing from the trophoblast is the trophectoderm. Tumors of the Trophectoderm class are somatic neoplasms that contain differentiated cells somewhat misleadingly named trophoblasts. These cells include cytotrophoblasts and syncytiotrophoblasts. Tumors of class Trophectoderm occur during or soon after gestation.

Some germ cell tumors produce subpopulations of cells that include trophoblasts, and these cells can be the dominant cell in a germ cell tumor. Though composed of trophoblasts, these germ-cell-derived tumors occur in a different patient population , behave differently than, and have very different genetic and epigenetic features from tumors of class Trophectoderm. Trophoblastic tumors of class Trophectoderm and trophoblastic tumors of class Germ cell are often referred to as gestational and nongestational trophoblastic neoplasms, respectively.

The class of Trophoectoderm neoplasms can be subclassed as follows:

- Molar
- Trophoblastic

These six classes account for all possible types of neoplasms and support a logical subclassification that conforms to the defining rules of classification [19–22]. [Glossary Extraembryonic cells and tissues, Gestational trophoblastic disease, Complete mole, Invasive mole, Partial mole]

- **Are these general classes of disease separable from one another, for every disease instance?**

This "class separability" criterion is probably the toughest to deal with, especially because we have already determined that diseases develop in steps, and that the different steps may be assigned to different class entities. For example a disease may seem to begin as an infection, but the infection may have had a conditional dependence on a preexisting metabolic disorder, and the expression of the disease may have a conditional dependence on an immunologic disorder. How do we choose the step in pathogenesis that determines a disease's class assignment? At this point, we must make a decision. Let's ignore every step in pathogenesis except for one: the pathway that seems to drive the clinical phenotype of the disease. By doing so, we match the subclass of a disease with the convergent pathway thought to account for the clinical phenotype of the disease. Thus all diseases that converge to a pathway are assigned the same class, and drugs that target the class-specific pathway will have a chance of being effective against every disease in the class and its descendant subclasses.

Is this really the best way to classify diseases? What if we're wrong? Well, if history is a guide, we can be quite certain that we are wrong. The question we must ask ourselves is: "Does this classification provide us with the opportunity to determine whether the classification is biologically valid? Yes, it does. If we are correct, then the classification will guide us to design clinical trials for classes of biologically related diseases that are likely to respond to drugs that target their converged pathway. If we are wrong, we'll need to adjust our thinking. This is how science works.

SECTION 7.3 CLASSIFICATIONS CANNOT BE BASED ON SIMILARITIES

> Individuals do not belong in the same taxon because they are similar, but they are similar because they belong to the same taxon.
> *George Gaylord Simpson [1]*

Aristotle, a Greek philosopher who lived circa BCE 384–322, amused his contemporaries by classifying dolphins as a type of mammal, not as a type of fish. It seemed obvious to nearly everyone, at the time, that dolphins were much more similar to fish than to mammals. Dolphins looked like fish, they lived in the ocean like fish, they lived with other fish, they swam like fish, and could be hooked or netted along with the fish. If it looks like a fish, and acts like a fish, then it must be a fish. So thought Aristotle's many detractors (Fig. 7.2).

Aristotle reasoned otherwise. For Aristotle, classifications were built on relationships among animals, not similarities. Aristotle found that one group of animals, the mammals, nourished their developing embryos with a placenta. At birth, the offspring are delivered into the world as formed, but small versions of the adult animals (i.e., not as eggs or as larvae), and

FIG. 7.2 Bottlenose dolphin. A dolphin is not a fish. *Reproduced from U.S. National Aeronautics and Space Administration.*

the newborn animals feed from milk excreted by specialized glandular organs (mammae). Aristotle knew that these birthing features uniquely characterized one group of animals and distinguished this group from all the other groups of animals. He also knew that dolphins had all these features, fish did not. He correctly reasoned that dolphins must be a type of mammal, not a type of fish. For nearly 2000 years, Aristotle's classification was ridiculed by biologists. Belatedly, we now know that Aristotle was right all along.

Likewise, we must resist the urge to assign a terrier to the same class as a house cat, just because both animals have many phenotypic features in common (e.g., similar size and weight, presence of a furry tail, four legs, tendency to snuggle in a lap). A terrier is dissimilar to a wolf, and a house cat is dissimilar to a lion, but the terrier and the wolf are directly related to one another, as are the house cat and the lion. For the purposes of creating a classification, relationships are all that are important. Similarities, when they occur, arise as a consequence of relationships; not the other way around.

Aristotle, and legions of taxonomists (i.e., experts in classification) that followed him, understood that taxonomy is all about finding the relationships among species, not their similarities. But isn't a similarity a type of relationship? Actually, no. To better understand the difference, consider the following. When you look up at the clouds, and you begin to see the shape of a lion. The cloud has a tail, like a lion's tail, and a fluffy head, like a lion's mane. With a little imagination, the mouth of the lion seems to roar down from the sky. You have succeeded in finding similarities between the cloud and a lion. When you look at a cloud and you imagine a tea kettle producing a head of steam, and you recognize that the physical forces that create a cloud from the ocean's water vapor and the physical forces that produce steam from the water in a heated kettle are the same, then you have found a relationship. Finding relationships is really what science is all about; it's how we make sense of reality. Finding similarities is an esthetic joy, but it is not science.

The first crude classifications of living organisms were similarity-based, producing classes such as flying animals (e.g., birds, bats, bumblebees) or swimming animals (e.g., fish, cephalopods, lampreys), or walking animals (e.g., man, bears, penguins). This approach cannot take into account the dissimilarities within a single entity during various stages of its life. For example, butterflies fly, but caterpillars do not; yet they are the same organism and hence both would belong to the class of flying animals. This approach did not take into account the disparate ways by which different animals achieve a similar property. For example, flying squirrels, birds, and "helicopter seeds" of maple trees all fly through the air, but they all achieve flight through different methods. These early classifications did not really add to our understanding of organisms and had value only as identification schemes. [Glossary Classification system versus identification system, Indexes versus classifications, Diagnosis versus Classification, Properties versus classes]

Modern classifications are all based on grouping organisms by their relationships to one another [1,2,23–25]. Nonetheless, it is exceedingly easy to fall back on similarities when you're creating a classification, for two reasons:

1. It happens to be very easy to find similarities, and it is human nature to follow the path of least resistance.
2. Sometimes, despite your best efforts, you cannot perceive the fundamental defining relationships among organisms, and you may feel compelled to rely on similarities; hoping that the observed similarities are the result of some as yet unexplained relationship.
3. Some investigators do not appreciate the conceptual difference between similarities and relationships.
4. Some investigators believe that the purpose of a classification is to standardize nomenclature, and that it doesn't make any difference how the classification is designed, so long as everyone uses the same grouping and naming conventions. Hence, objects in the classification can be grouped by similarity, or by alphabetical order, or by size, or by any arbitrary measure, so long as everyone follows the same procedures.

Let's look at a few of the consequences of classifying objects by anything other than relationships. Class fungi got off to a very bad start when classical taxonomists mistook these organisms for plants. Seeing that fungi grew in the soil and formed structures with a stem and a colorful top (i.e., mushrooms), it seemed logical to group the fungi with the chrysanthemums and other flowering plants. To this day, academic mycologists are employed by Botany Departments, and fungal taxonomy is subsumed under the International Code of Botanical Nomenclature (ICBN) [26]. We now know that fungi descended from a flagellated organism. Class Fungi was eventually reassigned to Class Opisthokonta (unikonts with a posterior flagellum), making Class Fungi a sister class to Class Animalia. A misunderstanding, based on an incorrect assumption related to the absence of a defining feature (in this case a flagellum) led to one of the most regrettable errors in the classification of living organisms.

Class Fungi is a Eukaryotic descendant of Class Unikonta (i.e., the class of eukaryotes with one flagellum). More specifically, Class Fungi, like Class Ameobozoa and Class Animalia, is a unikont descendant whose flagellum was positioned posteriorly (Class Opisthokonta). As a subclass of Class Opisthokonta, the fungi are much more closely related to animals than to the plants that they superficially resemble. Humans and fungi, like all opisthokonts, have a posterior flagellum, though it has been lost in all but a few of our cellular relics. Among the fungi, the only subclass with a flagellum is Class Chytrid, considered to be the most primitive fungal class [27]. Chytrids, a rare aquatic fungus (most fungi grow in soil), are currently ravaging amphibian populations. The chytrid *Batrachochytrium dendrobatidis* is capable of infecting thousands of different amphibian species and threatens many of these species with extinction.

Nonaquatic fungi (i.e., all classes of fungi other than the chytrids) lack flagella, presumably lost when these fungi adjusted to life in soil, and no longer needed a flagellum to propel themselves through water. The only human cells that have kept the flagellum is the spermatocyte, recognizable by its unique, waggling tail.

Aside from the ancestral single posterior flagellum, that establishes a close relationship between fungi and animals, there is also the presence of chitin. Chitin is a long-chain polymer built from units of N-acetylglucosamine and found in the cell walls of every fungus. It is analogous to cellulose, which is built from units of glucose. Importantly, chitin is never found in plants, and cellulose is never found in fungi. Aside from its presence in fungi, chitin is found in some member of Class Animalia (particularly arthropods). Chitin is the primary constituent of the exoskeleton of insects. The important structural role of chitin in fungi and animals should have been a clue to the close relationship between these two classes. It happens that chitin was not discovered until 1930. Well before that time, Class Fungi had been incorrectly assigned to the plant kingdom. Lastly, fungi and animals are heterotrophic, acquiring energy by metabolizing organic compounds obtained from the environment. Plants, unlike animals and fungi, are phototropic autotrophs, producing organic compounds from light, water, and carbon dioxide. Classifying the fungi as a type of plant was a big mistake, and demonstrates the perils of matching organisms by superficial similarities.

In the field of tumor biology, all cancers are divided into two broad classes based on similar morphology: epithelial tumors and sarcomas. The epithelial tumors are composed of round or polygonal cells, that line the surfaces of the gastrointestinal tract (i.e., mucosal lining cells) or the skin (i.e., epidermis); but also include the epithelium of the kidney, liver, uterus, salivary glands, and other tissues that have an epithelial lining or glandular structure. The sarcomas are composed of long, spindle-shaped cells. Sarcomas generally arise from so-called mesenchymal cells, the cells that provide the firm structure upon which the epithelium sits. Tumors arising from fibrous tissue, bone, cartilage, and muscle comprise most of the sarcomas.

As a consequence of classifying tumors by superficial morphologic similarities, pathologists have produced a general classification that makes no biological sense. For example, how would we explain the occurrence of tumors that are composed of both epithelial and sarcomatous components, as we see not uncommonly in uterine tumors (e.g., carcinosarcomas of uterus) and kidney tumors [28,29]?

The kidney is an example of an epithelial organ that derives from mesoderm; the same embryologic layer that gives rise to sarcomas. The tubules of the kidney derive from mesodermal cells. The mesodermal cells of the developing kidneys condense around the (metanephric) ureteric bud and acquire an epithelial morphology. These epithelial cells form convoluted tubes that merge into the ureteric bud. Tumors of the adult kidney usually have a purely epithelial morphology. Despite their epithelial morphology, renal tumors share biological properties with the sarcomas. In a recent paper that compared the gene expression profile of renal cell carcinomas (RCCs) with the gene expression profiles of other tumors, they found, "a RCC-specific set of oncogenesis-related genes was identified and surprisingly shared by sarcomas." [30] The finding that surprised the authors was that the gene expression profile of RCCs was not similar to the gene expression profile of epithelial tumors. They did not expect that RCCs would cluster with sarcomas. But we know that an epithelial morphology is not a biological class and does not confer a developmental relationship to any particular germ layer. Renal cell carcinomas are mesodermal tumors, just as all sarcomas are mesodermal tumors. The shared expression profile of RCCs and sarcomas illustrates that the basic structure and pathways of a cell are inherited through its mesodermal developmental lineage. Consequently, it should come as no surprise that Pazopanib, an effective drug in the treatment of some sarcomas, has also been shown to be effective against some cases of renal cell carcinoma [31].

Though most renal tumors have a purely epithelial morphology, some have a sarcomatous morphology, and others have a mixed epithelial-sarcoma morphology. The mixed tumors include primary renal synovial sarcomas, low-grade myxoid renal epithelial neoplasms with distal nephron differentiation, epithelioid angiomyolipoma, mixed epithelial and stromal tumor of kidney, and of course, nephroblastomas (Wilms tumors). These tumors violate the pseudodichotomy of epithelial cancer and sarcoma, because they all derive from mesoderm, an embryonic tissue capable of epithelial or connective tissue differentiation. This being the case, why do pathologists persist in classifying neoplasms as either epithelial or as sarcomatous, when we know these classes reflect morphologic similarities, not biological relationships? [Glossary Anlagen]

Tumors of the uterus provide additional examples wherein the dichotomous classification of neoplasms (i.e., epithelial versus sarcomatous) falls apart. The uterus, like the kidney, is derived entirely from mesoderm. The uterus is formed from a duct that forms within the mesoderm adjacent to the coelomic cavity (the paramesonephric duct). This paramesonephric duct gives rise to all of the uterus, including the endometrial epithelium and the underlying specialized stroma, and all of the fibromuscular tissue composing the uterine wall. Consequently, tumors of endometrial epithelial cells and endometrial stromal cells share the same lineage in the developmental classification (i.e., subcoelomic ductal).

Because pathologists have been "stuck" dividing tumors into carcinomas (i.e., epithelial tumors) or sarcomas (i.e., spindle-shaped tumors), the histogenesis of mixed epithelial/spindle tumors in the uterus has puzzled generations of morphologists. The explanation for the dual nature of some uterine cancers comes quite simply, once you understand that morphology is a similarity and not a relationship. The embryologic mesoderm, from which the uterus develops, gives rise to both epithelial cells (i.e., the endometrial mucosa in the case of the uterus) and to spindle cells (i.e., the fibromuscular wall in the case of the uterus). Hence, tumors that share the same cellular origin (i.e., embryonic mesoderm) can have a morphologic that is sarcomatous (e.g., leiomyosarcoma of uterus), or epithelial (e.g., uterine carcinoma), or mixed (carcinosarcoma of uterus). We now know that epithelial and nonepithelial tumors of the uterus, despite their dissimilar morphologies, are biologically related. Thus we should not be surprised to learn that tamoxifen, a uterine carcinogen, can produce tumors of epithelial or sarcomatous, or mixed tumors [32]. This suggests that the target cell of tamoxifen is a uterine mesodermal cell that is capable of developing into either an epithelial or stromal uterine tumor.

Classifying neoplasms based on similarity has created a pseudodichotomy responsible for considerable ambiguity and confusion in tumor pathology. Classical morphologists, long-considered luddites by modern medical scientists, are certainly no worse than some of the most advanced pioneers in Precision Medicine. The so-called classifier algorithms are commonly employed by bioinformaticians to group data objects by their similarities. The so-called recommender algorithms that put individuals into predictable groups, based on the similarities of their preferences, might also be considered types of classifier algorithms. In addition, machine learning algorithms are sometimes referred to as classifiers, when they are intended to match similar objects based on some learned object attributes. In all of such cases, the classifier algorithms group together similar items, but do not create a classification composed of related classes and subclasses. At the most, classifier algorithms provide data scientists with clues, from which a tentative classification can be constructed and tested. [Glossary Predictive analytics, Nongeneralizable predictor, Cluster analysis, Recommender algorithms, Data object, Classifier, Predictor, Data scientist]

SECTION 7.4 THE HORRIBLE CONSEQUENCES OF CLASS BLENDING

There's a big difference between knowing the name of something and knowing something.
Richard Feynman

Class blending refers to a mistake in proper classification, in which members are assigned to the wrong classes, or in which a class is created whose members are unrelated. These kinds of mistakes often arise when taxonomists are unaware of the differences among the members assigned to a class, or when taxonomists create an untenable class. For example, if you were to make a Mouse class, and you included Mickey Mouse as one of the instances of the class, you would be blending a cartoon with an animal, and this would be a mistake. If you were to create a Flying Animal class, you would be blending birds and houseflies and flying squirrels, none of which are biologically related. [Glossary Class noise]

After reading the preceding paragraph, you might be thinking that class blending is the kind of careless mistake that you will be smart enough to avoid. Prepared, as you are, with a deep understanding of the logic of biological classification, you can certainly skip past this overly cautious section of the book. Please don't. Class blending is a pervasive and costly sin that is committed by virtually every biological scientist at some point in his or her career. One error can easily set your search back a decade, if you're not mentally focused on this often subtle issue.

When you read old texts, written before we knew anything about micro-organisms, it's clear that the cause of epidemics in those days was unknown. We recognize today that one of the plague bacteria is Yersinia pestis. But, in fact, we do not know with certainty the specific causes of any of the major plagues in ancient Greece and medieval Europe. Typhus may have been involved. Measles and smallpox are likely causes of past plagues. Malarial outbreaks should not be overlooked.

Now suppose you are magically ported to Southern Italy, in the year 1640, when people are dying in great number, of the plague, and you are a doctor trying to cope with the situation. You're not a microbiologist, but you know something about designing clinical trials, and one of the local cognoscenti has just given you an herb that he insists is a cure for the plague. "Take this drug today, and your fever will be gone by the next morning," he tells you. As it happens, the herb is an extract of bark from the Cinchona tree, recently imported from Brazil. It is a sure-fire cure for malaria, a disease endemic to the region. But you don't know any of this. Before you start treating your patients, you'll want to conduct a clinical trial.

At this time, physicians knew nothing about the pathogenesis of malaria. Current thinking was that it was a disease caused by breathing in insalubrious swamp vapors; hence, the word roots "mal" meaning bad, and "aria" meaning air. You have just been handed a substance derived from the Cinchona tree, but you do not trust the herbalist. Insisting on a rational approach to the practice of medicine, you design a clinical trial, using 100 patients, all of whom have the same symptoms (delirium and fever) and all of whom carry the diagnosis of malaria. You administer the cinchona powder, also known as quinine, to all the patients. A few improve, but most don't. You place no significance on the results, recalling that the symptoms of malaria wax and wane, with the fever subsiding on its own every few days. It is not uncommon for malaria victims to recover, without any treatment. Everything considered, you call the trial a wash-out. You decide not to administer quinine to your patients.

What happened? We know that quinine arrived as a miracle cure for malaria. It should have been effective in a population of 100 patients. The problem with this hypothetical clinical trial is that the patients under study were assembled based on their mutual symptoms: fever and delirium. These same symptoms could have been accounted for by any of hundreds of other diseases that were prevalent in England at the time. The criteria employed at the time to render a diagnosis of malaria was imprecise, and the trial population was diluted with nonmalarial patients who were guaranteed to be nonresponders. Consequently, the trial failed, and you missed a golden opportunity to treat your malaria patients with quinine, a new, highly effective, miracle drug.

It isn't hard to imagine present-day dilemmas not unlike our fictitious quinine trial. If you are testing the effectiveness of an antibiotic on a class of people with bacterial pneumonia, the accuracy of your results will be jeopardized if your study population includes subjects with viral pneumonia, or smoking-related lung damage. The consequences of class blending are forever with us. In regions where malaria is endemic, it is commonplace to initiate antimalarial treatment for any individual with fever, without direct evidence that the patient has malaria. For the most part, this practice prevails wherever resources and expertise are scarce. As a result, it is very difficult to conduct rational trials for appropriate targeted therapies [33].

In this chapter, we have looked at a few examples of how improper classification might nullify the results of clinical trials. In practice, though, is this really much of a problem? Let's look at one subtle example of class blending that negatively impacted progress in the field of cancer research, for several decades. In the waning years of the 20th century, there was general agreement that the war on cancer had failed to discover drugs that were effective against advanced cases of any of the common cancers of humans (e.g., lung, colon, breast, prostate). The US cancer death rate was rising despite the best efforts of the US National Cancer Institute. A new approach to cancer therapy seemed warranted, and there was a growing consensus for a divide-and-conquer strategy in which treatments would be developed for biologically distinct subclasses of cancers. The idea seemed reasonable, but how would cancer researchers subclassify cancers? In the 1980s and 1990s, knowledge of genes and pathways was rudimentary, and clinical trial designers settled on a somewhat blunt classifier: clinical stage.

Some background is needed regarding the meaning of cancer stage. When cancers are diagnosed, a determination is made regarding the tumor's size, extent of local invasion, whether tumor deposits can be found in regional or distant lymph nodes, and whether the cancer has metastasized to distant organs. As an example, a stage III lung cancer is one that has spread to lymph nodes. Stage III lung cancers are further divided into Stage IIIA tumors, which have spread to lymph nodes confined to the same side of the body as the primary cancer; and Stage IIIB tumors where the tumor is of any size and has spread to distant lymph nodes and invaded chest structures other than the lungs, such as the heart or esophagus. Because staging requires an accurate, well-documented, assessment of the extent of spread of the tumor at the time of diagnosis, the staging process necessitates the professional services of radiologists, pathologists, oncologists, surgeons, and nurses. Furthermore, the information upon which the staging was determined would need to be reviewed by a set of experts, to verify the accuracy of the original reports. The process of cancer staging required a lot of work, but the end product was the best available method for dividing cancer patients into clinically defined subsets. [Glossary Staging]

In retrospect, a very strong argument can be made that stage-stratified clinical trials conducted in the last few decades of the 20th century, were a failure, generally. Results tended to show little or no benefit for candidate drugs in stage-stratified classes. One of the prominent reasons for these failures was class blending. With the benefit of hindsight, it is easy to see that a clinical stage is not a biological class. If we look at Stage III tumors, we know that some of the patients assigned to this class may have had progressed rapidly through Stages I and II, exhibiting rapid growth and early invasiveness. Other patients may have had an indolent growth history, requiring years or even decades to qualify as a Stage III tumor. The observation that these biologically diverse tumors had attained the same clinical stage (i.e., similar size and similar status regarding metastases) at a certain point of time does not put the tumors into a biologically related class.

As discussed previously, a valid biological class is intransitive. This means that the members of a class do not move from one class into another. The progression of a tumor from Stage I to Stage II to Stage III to Stage IV should have told the trial designers, from the very start, that a clinical stage cannot serve as the basis of a biological class.

We run against the problem of blended classes all the time. For example, consider the example of Alzheimer disease. Because Alzheimer disease is so very common, with widely varying clinical courses, and with no identified genetic markers that apply to everyone with the disease, it is likely that a diagnosis of Alzheimer disease covers a multitude of clinically similar but biologically distinctive disorders. The suspected blending of multiple diseases into one diagnostic entity may be the reason why clinical trials of Alzheimer drugs have not yielded any breakthroughs. Similar confusion holds for the common lung disorder COPD (Chronic Obstructive Pulmonary Disease) [34]. Because we persist in defining diseases by their clinical phenotype, rather than by pathogenesis, class blending may taint just about every common noninfectious disease occurring in humans. [Glossary Blended class, COPD]

Today, thanks to advances in Precision Medicine, we are beginning to design clinical trials in which diseases can be subtyped based on pathway biomarkers. Hence, clinical trials may now be designed around biologically defined subclasses that are likely to respond to drugs that target their class-defining pathways.

It should be noted that it is almost impossible to know when class blending is not an issue. That is to say that it is difficult to know when you are dealing with a class that does not require further subclassification. The consequences of discovering unsuspected subtypes of a class account for a well-known statistical anomaly known as Simpson's paradox. The paradox is based on the observation that findings that apply to each of two data sets may be reversed when the two data sets are combined.

One of the most famous examples of Simpson's paradox was demonstrated in the 1973 Berkeley gender bias study [35]. A preliminary review of admissions data indicated that women had a lower admissions rate than men. Specifically, the admission rate for men was 44% (of 8442 male applicants). The admission rate for women was 35% (of 4321 female applicants). A nearly 10% difference is highly significant, but what does it mean? Was the admissions office guilty of gender bias? A closer look at admissions department-by-department showed a very different story. Women were being admitted at higher rates than men, in almost every department. The department-by-department data seemed incompatible with the combined data. The explanation was simple. Women tended to apply to the most popular and oversubscribed departments, such as English and History, that had a high rate of admission denials. Men tended to apply to departments that the women of 1973 avoided, such as mathematics, engineering, and physics. Men tended not to apply to the high-occupancy departments that women preferred. Though women had an equal footing with men in departmental admissions, the high rate of women applying to the high-rejection departments, accounted for an overall lower acceptance rate for women at Berkeley. Simpson's paradox demonstrates that data is not necessarily additive. It also shows us that data is not transitive; you cannot make inferences based on subset comparisons. For example in randomized drug trials, you cannot assume that if drug A tests better than drug B, and drug B tests better than drug C, then drug A will test better than drug C [36]. When drugs are tested, even in well-designed trials, the test populations are drawn from a general population sampled for the trial. When you compare results from different trials, you can never be sure whether the different sets of subjects are comparable. Each set may contain individuals whose responses to a third drug are unpredictable. Transitive inferences (i.e., if A is better than B, and B is better than C, then A is better than C) are unreliable.

SECTION 7.5 WHAT IS PRECISION DIAGNOSIS?

Diagnosis is treatment
Old axiom of medicine, sometimes attributed to Wayne Babcock [37]

Many patients with rare diseases today have difficulty in finding providers with the expertise and resources to diagnose and treat their conditions.
Committee on Accelerating Rare Diseases Research and Orphan Product Development, Institute of Medicine of the National Academies (United States), 2010 [38]

Physicians like to say that diagnosis is treatment. This simple assertion indicates that there is a known treatment available for every possible diagnosis. The treatment may not be effective, and the diagnosis may be a mistake; nonetheless, treatment can begin when a diagnosis is rendered. It should surprise no one that diagnosis is the cornerstone of medicine.

What happens when a disease is given two diagnoses? In 1993, Reggie Lewis was the 27-year-old captain of the Boston Celtics basketball team. Mr. Lewis enjoyed good health until the moment when he collapsed during a basketball game. Mr. Lewis' collapse attracted the attention of cardiologists across the nation. A medical team assembled by the New England

Baptist Hospital opined that Mr. Lewis had focal cardiomyopathy, a life-threatening condition that would require Mr. Lewis to retire from basketball, immediately. A second team of experts, assembled at the Brigham and Women's Hospital, disagreed. They rendered a diagnosis of vasovagal fainting, a benign condition. A third team of experts, from St. John's Hospital in Santa Monica, California, was noncommittal. The Santa Monica team suggested that Mr. Lewis play basketball, but with a heart monitor attached to his body. With three discordant diagnoses, Mr. Lewis decided to take his chances, continuing his athletic career. Soon thereafter, Lewis died, quite suddenly, from cardiomyopathy, while playing basketball [39]. Reggie Lewis' tragic story comes as no great surprise to healthcare workers. Practical-minded physicians who seek an expert diagnosis will solicit a consultation from no more than one authority. Asking for three opinions is almost guaranteed to cause confusion.

Individuals with uncommon diseases have great difficulty finding physicians with the necessary expertise to render a correct diagnosis [38]. Surprisingly, it has been claimed that 20% of patients with any kind of serious condition are initially misdiagnosed [40]. As we saw in Chapter 4, diseases tend to converge to a limited number of possible clinical phenotypes. When diagnoses are rendered by cataloging clinical symptoms, we can expect that mistakes will be made. In particular, rare diseases are easily misdiagnosed when they mimic a common disease. Common diseases are easily misdiagnosed when they have uncommon clinical presentations.

What should we realistically expect of medical diagnoses in this new era of Precision Medicine? Because Precision Medicine provides insight into the pathogenesis of each disease, including the various stages of disease development, and the key pathways that drive the clinical phenotype, we can begin to provide the types of diagnostic guidance that clinicians and patients have always hoped for. When we review the various new diagnostic activities at our disposal, we will see that they recapitulate the steps of disease pathogenesis: the conditions that place an individual at risk of developing disease, the earliest steps in pathogenesis, the development of precursor lesions, response pathways, and disease progression, and markers of disease persistence.

Beyond rendering a simple diagnosis (i.e., assigning the name of a disease to a patient's condition), precision diagnosis will aid in the following areas:

– **Risk prediction and screening tests**

For many of the public, Precision Medicine extends a promise that our genes will predict our futures. This promise is premature, at best. Biological processes are way too complex for the kinds of accurate predictions that the lay public had been led to expect. Nonetheless, we now know a great deal more about the sequential steps that precede the development of diseases. When we determine that an individual has progressed through one or more of these steps, we can say something about the likelihood that other steps will follow, and we can take some steps to intervene in the process. Hence, in the era of Precision Medicine, risk prediction and screening tests will consist of determining whether an individual is following a pathogenetic path, and, if so, where that path seems to be leading.

– **Early disease detection, before clinical symptoms develop**

With few, if any, exceptions, it is easier to treat a disease in its early stages, when the patient is apparently healthy, than it is to treat an advanced stage disease, when the patient is debilitated. An example of early detection would include finding an immunoglobulin spike in an electrophoresis blood test. Normal blood contains many different molecular species that separate individually, by size and electric charge (i.e., on blood protein electrophoresis). When there is a sharp spike in the immunoglobulin range, this indicates that one species of immunoglobulin molecule appears in blood in high concentration. A spike is produced by a clonal expansion of an immunoglobulin-producing cell (i.e., a plasma cell). Multiple myeloma is a cancer composed of neoplastic plasma cells. In the presence of advanced symptoms of multiple myeloma (e.g., characteristic bone lesions, elevated Calcium levels), an immunoglobulin spike is almost always associated with malignancy. In the absence of clinical findings, a monoclonal spike might indicate a very early form of disease. As previously discussed in Section 2.2, Monoclonal Gammopathy of Undetermined Significance (MGUS) is a proliferative lesion of plasma cells, occurring in otherwise asymptomatic patients that sometimes progresses to multiple myeloma. Virtually every case of multiple myeloma is preceded by MGUS [41]. An immunoglobulin spike, found in an asymptomatic individual, is an example of a laboratory observation that detects multiple myeloma in an early stage of development (i.e., MGUS). Because most cases of MGUS do not progress to multiple myeloma within the lifetime of the individual (i.e., patients typically die of some other cause before the MGUS progresses into multiple myeloma), a strategy of watchful waiting, with bone lesion surveillance, may be appropriate [42] (Fig. 7.3).

Patients are coming to their doctors in the very early stages of disease, before the full constellation of diagnostic symptoms occurs. The benefits of Precision Medicine should include diagnosis of disease in preclinical stages. Screening for patients in the earliest steps of disease development is a topic that will be discussed in more depth in Section 9.4.

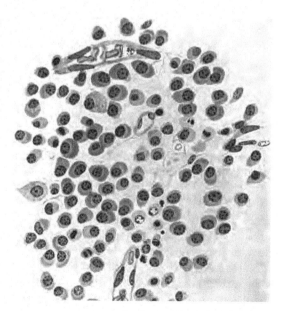

FIG. 7.3 A thin histopathologic section of multiple myeloma, featuring a rather uniform collection of neoplastic cells that closely resemble normal plasma cells. The nuclei are round and eccentric (i.e., seemingly pushed against the cytoplasmic membrane). The cytoplasm has a uniform dark color, indicating a high protein concentration, with the exception of a light area touching the nucleus, the site of intense synthesis of immunoglobulins and other proteins. *Reproduced from MacCallum WG. A text-book of pathology. 2nd ed. Philadelphia, London: WB Saunders Company; 1921.*

– **Prediction of response to treatment**

For clinicians and their patients, diagnosis serves no useful purpose if it does not lead to effective treatment. For many treatments, including virtually all of the newer generation of treatments targeted to a specific protein or pathway, not all individuals will respond to treatment. In the era of Precision Medicine, diagnosis should include some indication of the likelihood of a satisfactory response for the different treatment options that are available. Modern clinical trials are designed to find the subpopulations, often based on genetic biomarkers, that will have the best responses to a trial drug (discussed further in Section 9.6).

– **Diagnosing subtypes**

Much of medical diagnosis involves separating the biologically distinctive subtypes of disease from groups of diseases aggregated by clinical phenotype. For example, there is a type of lung cancer that occurs primarily in young individuals, along the midline axis, and has a characteristic mutation in the NUT gene [43]. These tumors, currently called NUT midline carcinomas, are highly aggressive and have no effective cure, at the moment [44]. When an effective treatment is found, it is likely to be a very different therapy than is currently employed against common lung cancers that are not characterized by the NUT gene mutation.

Similarly, a rare type of invasive ductal breast cancer occurs mostly in adolescent women and is characterized by a specific ETV6-NTRK3 fusion gene [45,46]. This rare breast cancer, known as secretory breast carcinoma owing to the prominence of mucin-producing tumor cells, is typically negative for hormone receptors and for human epidermal growth (HER)-2/neu. In a commonly occurring ductal carcinoma of breast, negativity for these hormones would suggest that the tumor is aggressive and difficult to treat. Secretory carcinoma of breast, despite its hormone negativity, is a generally slow-growing cancer with a good prognosis, and it is important to distinguish this subtype from other breast cancers [47].

Here is one last example from the neoplastic diseases. Myelodysplastic syndrome is a preleukemic condition characterized by anemia and dyserythropoiesis. The preponderance of cases occurs in elderly individuals. Myelodysplasia may also occur in children who have inherited a predisposition to losing chromosome 7 in somatic blood-forming cells [48,49]. Hence, monosomy 7 in myelodysplastic cells serves as a cytogenetic marker that distinguishes commonly occurring myelodysplasia from a biological subtype of the disease that occurs in children. [Glossary Dyserythropoiesis]

Can we say that every common disease can be divided into biologically distinct subtypes? Of course, we cannot be certain until we have succeeded in finding subtypes for every common disease, but we can make a fairly good argument, based on basic principles. Every disease, including common diseases, develops from a sequence of events, over time. Isn't it likely that a disease that occurs commonly would have many ways of developing, and that many different sequences of events, with many different time schedules, will produce a common convergent phenotype? Hence, we might expect that common diseases develop from multiple pathogenetic processes. Conversely, in the case of extremely rare diseases, we might expect that only one, or perhaps several, pathogenetic processes account for every occurrence of the disease. Put simply, common diseases are common because there are many subtypes of the disease, and rare diseases are rare because there are very few subtypes of the disease.

– Staging

Staging has importance for most types of diseases. Physicians need to know whether they are dealing with a localized disease, or whether the disease has spread to distant organs. Among the common diseases, staging has its greatest importance in cancer. When a cancer is confined to its site of origin, then surgical removal of the cancer is curative. This is true even if the tumor is highly malignant, locally invasive, and with a predisposition for distant metastasis. If the tumor is removed before it has metastasized, then the tumor is cured. Contrariwise, if a tumor has metastasized, then complete excision of the tumor at its primary site is noncurative. Even if the tumor is generally an indolent neoplasm, with a low likelihood of distant metastasis, it may eventually kill the patient if it bucked the odds and metastasized prior to being excised at its site of origin. For these reasons, physicians try to stage cancers, to determine whether and how far the tumor may have traveled from its origin. [Glossary Metastasis]

When metastases are very small, it may be difficult or impossible to observe them, using currently available scanning techniques (e.g., bone scans, computed tomography). As a surrogate technique, oncologists have been trying to find a battery of molecular markers, found in DNA extracted from a sample of the primary tumor (i.e., the tumor at its site of origin), that can predict the tumor stage [50,51].

– Surveillance for minimal residual disease and recurrence.

The issue of finding residual disease and recurrent disease is most relevant to the infectious diseases and to cancer. For the infectious diseases, residual and recurrent disease often involves measuring titers of infectious organisms (e.g., viruses, bacteria, fungi) in blood samples. For the most part, searches for residual infectious organisms or response-to-infection markers are most useful for infectious diseases that have chronic, subclinical, or latent phases. For example IRF5 is an interferon regulatory factor that influences susceptibility to systemic lupus erythematosus, an autoimmune disease. IRF7 is a related factor, and both IRF5 and IRF7 participate in systemic responses to infection. These markers have been used to detect inflammatory diseases, including recurrent systemic lupus erythematosus [52] and latent Epstein-Barr virus infections [53].

For the cancers, minimal residual disease and recurrence are monitored for altered genes and proteins that characterize the primary tumor (e.g., alpha fetoprotein blood levels in recurrent liver cancer, high levels of prostate specific antigen in recurrent prostate cancers, human chorionic gonadotrophin in recurrent choriocarcinoma and germ cell tumors, carcinoembryonic antigen in recurrent colon cancers). Because the rare cancers tend to have specific monogenic markers (e.g., bcr/abl fusion gene in chronic myelogenous leukemia, CD117 gene mutations in gastrointestinal stromal tumors, myc translocation in Burkitt lymphoma), the most promising tests for minimal disease and for recurrent disease will come from the rare cancers [54].

– Biomarkers

The term "biomarker" encompasses all tests related to disease pathogenesis, including the ancillary studies described earlier in this chapter (e.g., risk prediction, early detection, prognosis, response-to-therapy prediction, staging, and surveillance for minimal disease or for recurrences). Technically, the term "biomarker" might apply to diagnostic tests. As it is commonly used, however, the term "biomarker" excludes diagnostic tests, and refers to tests for abnormal findings associated with some feature-of-interest, other than diagnosis. For example, measuring glucose is a biomarker for diabetes, because uncontrolled diabetics have high glucose levels. The glucose assay is not, by itself, diagnostic of diabetes because controlled diabetics will have normal glucose levels, and nondiabetics will have high glucose levels from time to time.

Though there was a great deal of time and money invested in biomarker development in the last quarter of the 20th century, very few candidate biomarkers were shown to have much value, and there was a general sense that the pipeline for new biomarkers had simply dried up [55–58]. In the first decade of the new millennium, the biomarker industry turned to large, data-intensive methodologies (e.g., genomics, proteomics, metabolomics, and clinical informatics). Still, progress remained slow [59]. We are finding that biomarkers found using advanced analytic techniques applied to complex biomedical data are seldom validated when the study is repeated in another laboratory with the same methodology, or when examined with a different methodology [60,61]. An article published in 2010 asserted that despite enormous efforts, only a few predictive markers have proven useful to guide breast cancer therapy (e.g., Her2/neu [62]). In most instances, molecular profiling has not been shown to have more clinical value than standard histologic methods (i.e., looking at tissues under a microscope) [63]. Not only have there been a paucity of new, validated biomarkers, but the availability of large data sets has served to discredit some of the biomarkers that were previously held in high esteem [64,65]. [Glossary Data resource, Predictive test]

Where did the field of biomarker research go wrong? We thought that progress was limited by the quality and quantity of available data resources. The problem may actually lie much deeper. It seems that we do not know as much as we need to know about biological systems. Perhaps we are trying too hard to understand diseases in all their complexity, when we should be satisfied with a step-by-step approach, understanding the relatively simple sequence of biological events that eventually lead to the emergence of complex and chaotic diseases.

One of the most important goals of Precision Medicine is to dissect the steps that lead to the development of disease. In doing so, we have an excellent chance of finding biomarkers that precede the development of disease and that tell us a great deal about how cells will respond to treatments directed toward the individual steps of disease development. It is important to understand that the individual steps that lead to the development of disease are not unique for each disease. For example, step 5 in the development of disease X may be equivalent to step 3 of disease Y and step 7 of disease Z. Hence, as we learn more and more about the precise steps in pathogenesis, we can expect our biomarkers to show disease nonspecificity. This might be a good thing, if all diseases that share a biomarker will respond to the same drug.

Glossary

Anlagen Embryologic precursors for fetal organs and tissues.

Apomorphy A trait found in the parent class and all of the classes in its descendant lineage.

Bioinformatics The science of the curation and analysis of biological data. The field of bioinformatics focused on genomic data for several decades. Presently, the field has expanded its purview into epigenomics, proteomics, metabolomics, and so on. Not to be confused with biomedical informatics.

Blended class Also known as class noise. Blended class refers to inaccuracies (e.g., misleading results) introduced in the analysis of data due to errors in class assignments (e.g., inaccurate diagnosis). If you are testing the effectiveness of an antibiotic on a class of people with bacterial pneumonia, the accuracy of your results will be forfeit when your study population includes subjects with viral pneumonia, or smoking-related lung damage. Errors induced by blending classes are often overlooked by data analysts who incorrectly assume that the experiment was designed to ensure that each data group is composed of a uniform and representative population. A common source of class blending occurs when the classification upon which the experiment is designed is itself blended. For example, imagine that you are a cancer researcher and you want to perform a study of patients with malignant fibrous histiocytomas (MFH), comparing the clinical course of these patients with the clinical course of patients who have other types of tumors. Let's imagine that the class of tumors known as MFH does not actually exist; that it is a grab-bag term erroneously assigned to a variety of other tumors that happened to look similar to one another. This being the case, it would be impossible to produce any valid results based on a study of patients diagnosed as MFH. The results would be a biased and irreproducible cacophony of data collected across different, and undetermined, classes of tumors. This specific example, of the blended MFH class of tumors, is selected from the real-life annals of tumor biology [66–68]. The literature is rife with research of dubious quality, based on poorly designed classifications and blended classes. One caveat, efforts to reduce class blending, can be counterproductive if undertaken with excess zeal. For example, in an effort to reduce class blending, a researcher may choose groups of subjects who are uniform with respect to every known observable property. For example, suppose you want to actually compare apples with oranges. To avoid class blending, you might want to make very sure that your apples do not included any cumquats or persimmons. You should be certain that your oranges do not include any limes or grapefruits. Imagine that you go even further, choosing only apples and oranges of one variety (e.g., Macintosh apples and Navel oranges), size (e.g., 10 cm), and origin (e.g., California). How will your comparisons apply to the varieties of apples and oranges that you have excluded from your study? You may actually reach conclusions that are invalid and irreproducible for more generalized populations within each class. In this case, you have succeeded in eliminating class blending, at the expense of losing representative populations of the classes.

COPD An abbreviation for chronic obstructive pulmonary disease. COPD covers a range of lung disorders characterized by airway damage. COPD is a common sequelae of chronic cigarette abuse.

Child class The direct or first-generation subclass of a class. Sometimes referred to as the daughter class or, less precisely, as the subclass.

Clade A clade consists of a class and all of its descendant subclasses.

Cladistics The assignment of classes and subclasses within a classification by strict order of lineage (i.e., through clades). Classifications, as they are defined in this book, are cladistic.

Class noise Equivalent to the blending of classes.

Classification system versus identification system It is important to distinguish a classification system from an identification system. An identification system matches an individual organism with its assigned object name (or species name, in the case of the classification of living organisms). Identification is based on finding several features that, taken together, can help determine the name of an organism. For example, if you have a list of characteristic features: large, hairy, strong, African, jungle-dwelling, knuckle-walking; you might correctly identify the organisms as a gorilla. These identifiers are different from the phylogenetic features that were used to classify gorillas within the hierarchy of organisms (Animalia: Chordata: Mammalia: Primates: Hominidae: Homininae: Gorillini: Gorilla). Specifically, you can identify an animal as a gorilla without knowing that a gorilla is a type of mammal. You can classify a gorilla as a member of Class Gorillini without knowing that a gorilla happens to be large. One of the most common mistakes in taxonomy is to confuse an identification system with a classification system. The former simply provides a handy way to associate an object with a name; the latter is a system of relationships among objects.

Classifier As used herein, refers to algorithms that assign a class (from an existing classification) to an object whose class is unknown [69]. One example of a popular classifier algorithm is the k-nearest neighbor algorithm. From a collection of data objects whose class is known, the algorithm computes the distances from the object of unknown class to the objects of known class. This involves a distance measurement from the feature set of the objects of unknown class to every object of known class (the test set). The distance measure uses the set of attributes that are associated with each object. After the distances are computed, the k-classed objects with the smallest distance to the object of unknown class are collected. The most common class in the nearest k-classed objects is assigned to the object of unknown class. If the chosen value of k is 1, then the object of unknown class is assigned the class of its closest classed object (i.e., the nearest neighbor).

Cluster analysis Clustering algorithms provide a way of taking a large set of data objects that seem to have no relationship to one another, and to produce a visually simple collection of clusters wherein each cluster member is similar to every other member of the same cluster. The algorithmic methods for clustering are simple. One of the most popular clustering algorithms is the k-means algorithm, which assigns any number of data objects to one of k clusters [69]. The number k of clusters is provided by the user. The algorithm is easy to describe and to understand, but the computational task of completing the algorithm can be difficult when the number of dimensions in the object (i.e., the number of attributes associated with the object) is large. There are some serious drawbacks to the algorithm: (1) The final set of clusters will sometimes depend on the initial choice of k data objects. This means that multiple runs of the algorithm may produce different outcomes; (2) The algorithms are not guaranteed to succeed. Sometimes, the algorithm does not converge to a final, stable set of clusters; (3) When the dimensionality is very high, the distances between data objects (i.e., the square root of the sum of squares of the measured differences between corresponding attributes of two objects) can be ridiculously large and of no practical meaning. Computations may bog down, cease altogether, or produce meaningless results. In this case, the only recourse may require eliminating some of the attributes (i.e., reducing dimensionality of the data objects); (4) The clustering algorithm may succeed, producing a set of clusters of similar objects, but the clusters may have no practical value. They may miss important relationships among the objects, or they might group together objects whose similarities are totally noninformative. The biggest drawback associated with cluster analyses is that Precision Medicine researchers may make the mistake of believing that that the groupings produced by the method constitute a valid biological classification. This is not the case because biological entities (genes, proteins, cells, organs, organisms) may share many properties and still be fundamentally different. For example, two genes may have the same length and share some subsequences, but both genes may have no homology with one another (i.e., no shared ancestry) and may have no common or similar expressed products. Another set of genes may be structurally dissimilar but may belong to the same family. The groupings produced by cluster analysis should never be equated with a classification. At best, cluster analysis produces groups that can be used to start piecing together a biological classification.

Complete mole A mass of fluid-filled extraembryonic (i.e., placental) tissue formed in the uterus around a nonviable embryo. Typically, when the complete mole is evacuated from the uterus and examined, there is little or no embryonic tissue remaining. Complete moles can sometimes give rise to invasive moles or choriocarcinoma. Complete moles occur after an anucleate ovum is fertilized by two sperm. The cells of a complete mole are diploid with both sets of chromosomes having a paternal origin.

Data object A data object is whatever is being described by the data. For example, if the data is "6 feet tall," then the data object is the person or thing to which "6 feet tall" applies. Minimally, a data object is a metadata/data pair, assigned to a unique identifier. In practice, the most common data objects are simple data records, corresponding to a row in a spreadsheet or a line in a flat-file. Data objects in object-oriented programming languages typically encapsulate several items of data, including an object name, an object unique identifier, multiple data/metadata pairs, and the name of the object's class.

Data resource A collection of data made available for data retrieval. The data can be distributed over servers located anywhere on earth or in space. The resource can be static (i.e., having a fixed set of data), or in flux. Plesionyms for data resource are: data warehouse, data repository, data archive, data store.

Data scientist Anyone who practices data science and who has some expertise in a field subsumed by data science (i.e., informatics, statistics, data analysis, programming, and computer science).

Dermal bone Bone that arises by calcification of a preshaped mesenchymal matrix. The bones of the skull, and most of the bones of the head, are dermal bones [70,71]. Dermal bone formation is synonymous with intramembranous bone formation. Dermal bones are embryologically derived from the neural crest, whereas enchondral bones are derived from mesenchyme.

Diagnosis versus Classification Diagnosis is the process by which a disease is assigned a name (i.e., a taxonomic term) that fits into a class of diseases, within a disease classification. For example, a pathologist may look at a stained section of a tumor under the microscope and declare that the tumor is a squamous cell carcinoma of the skin. Doing so is a diagnostic exercise. The taxon (i.e., the named disease) fits into the class of lesions known as neoplasms. The class of neoplasms resides in a general classification of diseases. Classification is different from diagnosis, the former referring to the process of building the class structure into which the taxonomy (i.e., the list of names of diagnosed diseases) must fit. You'll occasionally hear sentences such as "The pathologist classified this lesion as a squamous cell carcinoma of skin." This is an inaccurate use of terminology. Strictly speaking, pathologists diagnose lesions; they do not classify them.

Dyserythropoiesis A dysfunctional form of blood cell formation in which there is excessive cell death of precursor and differentiated blood cells, often leading to pancytopenia. The death of precursor blood cells forces hematopoietically active tissues (i.e., blood forming tissues such as bone marrow) to produce more and more precursor cells, compensating for high cell death rates. This leads to the expansion of hematopoietic tissue, sometimes resulting in blood cell formation in sites other than the bone marrow, such as spleen, lymph nodes, and liver.

Ineffective hematopoiesis is a near-synonym for dyserythropoiesis. HEMPAS (Hereditary Erythroblastic Multinuclearity with Positive Acidified-Serum test), also known as congenital dyserythropoietic anemia type II (CDAN2), is an inherited dyserythropoiesis caused by a mutation in the SEC23B gene.

Enchondral bone Bone that forms through ossification of a growing zone of cartilage at each end of the bone. Long bones (for example, the femur) are enchondral bones. There are two major types of bone, based on their method of growth, and on their embryologic origin: enchondral and dermal. Enchondral bones are of mesenchymal origin. Dermal bones are of neural crest origin.

Endoderm There are three embryonic layers that eventually produce the fully developed animal: endoderm, mesoderm, and ectoderm. The endoderm forms a tube extending from the embryonic mouth to the embryonic anus. The mucosa of the gastrointestinal tract, the glandular cells of the liver and pancreas, and the lining cells of the respiratory system all derive from the endoderm.

Extraembryonic cells and tissues These are the cells that arise in the early embryo but which are not destined to be retained in the embryo as it develops. The extraembryonic tissues include the placenta, the umbilical cord, the yolk sac, and the amniotic sac.

Gamete A fully differentiated germ cell (i.e., an egg in the female or a sperm cell in the male).

Germ cell line The germ cell line is a specialized lineage of cells that appears early in embryogenesis. The germ cell line produces gametes (ova in females and sperm in males). In addition, the earliest cells of the lineage have the ability to "erase" their epigenome, yielding an uncommitted, hence totitpotent, cell that can differentiate towards any lineage. Tumors that arise from the germ cell line are the tumors of the ova and sperm cell precursors (dysgerminomas and seminomas) and the tumors that arise from totipotent cells (for example, teratomas and embryonal carcinomas). "Germ cell line" needs to be distinguished from "Germline," the lineage that includes all cells derived from the original zygote.

Gestational trophoblastic disease Refers to neoplasms and malformations arising from cells of the trophectoderm (i.e., the extraembryonic tissue of the conceptus that gives rise to the placenta). The most studied gestational trophoblastic diseases are: hydatidiform mole (complete and partial types), invasive mole, choriocarcinoma, placental site trophoblastic tumor, and epithelioid trophoblastic tumor.

Indexes versus classifications Indexes and classifications both help us to expand and simplify our perception of a subject or a knowledge domain. The key difference between the two concepts is that indexes are method of searching and retrieving data objects, whereas classifications are a method of describing the relationships among data objects.

Invasive mole Previously called chorioadenoma destruens. Occurs when the growing placental villi of a hydatidiform mole invades into the myometrium (i.e., wall of the uterus). The presence of invading molar villi, and the occasional co-occurrence with morphologically similar noninvasive molar tissue, helps to distinguish an invasive mole from a choriocarcinoma.

Medullary thyroid carcinoma A tumor of the thyroid arising from specialized C cells that produce calcitonin, a hormone involved in calcium homeostasis.

Metastasis Tumor growth at locations that are noncontiguous with the primary growth site of the tumor. In most cases, a primary tumor (e.g., lung cancer, colon cancer, breast cancer) can be successfully removed surgically. Hence, deaths from cancer are almost always the result of metastatic, not primary, disease (e.g., multiple tumor masses in lungs, brain, lymph nodes, liver, bone, and other sites).

Metazoa Class Metazoa is equivalent to Class Animalia. It contains two subclasses: Class Parazoa and Class Eumetazoa. Class Eumetazoans contain all the animals that develop from a blastula. Class Parazoa contain two small subclasses: Class Porifera (the sponges) and Class Placozoa. Class Placozoa contains a single species, Trichoplax adhaerens. Sponges and Trichoplax adhaerens are exceedingly simple animals, consisting of a layer of jelly-like mesoderm sandwiched between simple epithelium. Neither sponges nor Trichoplax adhaerens have specialized organs.

Monophyletic class A class of organisms that includes a parent organism and all its descendants, while excluding any organisms that did not descend from the parent. If a subclass of a parent class omits any of the descendants of the parent class, then the parent class is said to be paraphyletic. If a subclass of a parent class includes organisms that did not descend from the parent, then the parent class is polyphyletic. A class can be paraphyletic and polyphyletic, if it excludes organisms that were descendants of the parent and if it includes organisms that did not descend from the parent. The goal of cladistics is to create a hierarchical classification that consists exclusively of monophyletic classes (i.e., no paraphyly, no polyphyly).

Multiclass classification A misnomer imported from the field of machine translation and indicating the assignment of an instance to more than one class. Classifications, as defined in this book, impose one-class classification (i.e., an instance can be assigned to one and only one class). It is tempting to think that a ball should be included in class "toy" and in class "spheroids," but multiclass assignments create unnecessary classes of inscrutable provenance, and taxonomies of enormous size, consisting largely of replicate items.

Multiclass inheritance In ontologies, multiclass inheritance occurs when a child class has more than one parent class. For example, a member of Class House may have two different parent classes: Class Shelter and Class Property. Multiclass inheritance is generally permitted in ontologies but is forbidden in classifications, which restrict inheritance to a single parent class (i.e., each class can have at most one parent class, though it may have multiple child classes). When an object-oriented program language permits multiparental inheritance (e.g., Perl and Python programming languages), data objects may have many different ancestral classes spread horizontally and vertically through the class libraries. There are many drawbacks to multiclass inheritance in object-oriented programming languages, and these have been discussed at some length in the computer science literature [6]. Medical taxonomists should understand that when multiclass inheritance is permitted, a class may be an ancestor of a child class that is an ancestor of its parent class (e.g., a single class might be a grandfather and a grandson to the same class). An instance of a class might be an instance of two classes, at once. The combinatorics and the recursive options can become computationally difficult or impossible. Those who use taxonomies that permit multiclass inheritance will readily acknowledge that they have created a system that is complex. Ontology experts justify the use of multiclass inheritance on the observation that such ontologies provide accurate models of nature and that faithful models of reality cannot be created with simple, uniparental classification. Taxonomists who rely on simple, uniparental classifications base their model on epistemological grounds, on the nature of objects. They hold that an object can have only one nature, and can belong to only one defining class, and can be derived from exactly one parent class. Taxonomists who insist upon uniparental class inheritance believe that assigning more than one parental class to an object indicates that you have failed to grasp the essential nature of the object [5,6,72].

Neurocristopathy A disease of neural crest cells. Examples include MEN2 (multiple endocrine neoplasm syndrome type 2), aganglionic diseases of the GI tract, and neurofibromatosis.

Neuroectoderm The embryologic layer that gives rise to the central nervous system.

Nongeneralizable predictor Sometimes data analysis can yield results that are true, but nongeneralizable (i.e., irrelevant to everything outside the set of data under study). The most useful scientific findings are generalizable (e.g., the laws of physics operate on the planet Jupiter or the star Alpha Centauri much as they do on earth). Many of the most popular analytic methods are not generalizable because they produce predictions that only apply to highly restricted sets of data; or the predictions are not explainable by any underlying theory that relates input data with the calculated predictions. Data analysis is incomplete until a comprehensible, generalizable, and testable theory for the predictive method is developed.

Paradoxes of classification The rules for constructing classifications seem obvious and simplistic. Surprisingly, the task of building a logical and self-consistent classification is extremely difficult. Most classifications are rife with logical inconsistencies and paradoxes. Let's look at a few examples. In 1975, NIH's Building 10 (the Clinical Center), located in Bethesda, Maryland, was touted as the largest all-brick building in the world, providing a home to over 7 million bricks. Soon thereafter, an ambitious construction project was undertaken to greatly expand the size of Building 10. When the work was finished, building 10 was no longer the largest all-brick building in the world. What happened? The builders used material other than brick, and Building 10 lost its place in the class of all-brick buildings. This poses something of a paradox; objects in a classification are not permitted to move about from one class to another. An object assigned to a class must stay in its class (i.e., the nontransitive property of classifications). Apparent paradoxes that plague any formal conceptualization of classifications are not difficult to find. Let's look at a few more examples. Consider the geometric class of ellipses: planar objects in which the sum of the distances to two focal points is constant. Class Circle is a child of Class Ellipse, for which the two focal points of instance members occupy the same position, in the center, producing a radius of constant size. Imagine that Class Ellipse is provided with a class method called "stretch," in which the foci are moved further apart, thus producing flatter objects. When the parent class' "stretch" method is applied to members of Class Circle, the circle stops being a circle and becomes an ordinary ellipse. Hence the inherited "stretch" method forces members of Class Circle to transition out of their assigned class, violating the intransitivity rule. Let's look at the "Bag" class of objects. A "Bag" is a collection of objects, and Class Bag is included in most object-oriented programming languages. A "Set" is also a collection of objects (i.e., a subclass of Bag), with the special feature that duplicate instances are not permitted. For example, if Kansas is a member of the set of US States, then you cannot add a second state named "Kansas" to the set. If Class Bag were to have an "increment" method, that added "1" to the total count of objects in the bag, whenever an object is added to Class Bag, then the "increment" method would be inherited by all of the subclasses of Class Bag, including Class Set. But Class Set cannot increase in size when duplicate items are added. Hence, inheritance creates a paradox in Class Set. Here's another example. The Suggested Upper Merged Ontology (SUMO) in an ontology designed to contain classes for general types of objects that might be included in other, more specific knowledge domains. SUMO, as one might expect from an ontology, allows multiple class inheritance. For example, in SUMO, the class of humans is assigned to two different parent classes: Class Hominid and Class CognitiveAgent. "HumanCorpse," another SUMO class, is defined in SUMO as "A dead thing which was formerly a Human." Human corpse is a subclass of Class OrganicObject, not of Class Human. This means that a human, once it ceases to live, transits to a class that is not directly related to the class of humans. Basically, a member of Class Human, in the SUMO ontology, will change its class and its ancestral lineage, at different moments. One last dalliance. Consider these two classes from the SUMO ontology, both of which happen to be subclasses of Class Substance: Subclass NaturalSubstance Subclass SyntheticSubstance It would seem that these two subclasses are mutually exclusive. However, diamonds occur naturally, and diamonds can be synthesized. Hence, diamond belongs to Subclass NaturalSubstance and to Subclass SyntheticSubstance. The ontology creates two mutually exclusive classes that contain some of the same objects, thus creating a paradox [5].

Partial mole There are two types of hydatidiform mole: complete mole, and partial mole. A partial mole is characterized by edematous and nonedematous placental villi and a variable amount of malformed embryonic tissue. A partial mole, like a complete mole, can develop into an invasive mole or a choriocarcinoma, but the incidence of conversion is much smaller (about 20% for complete mole and about 3% for partial mole). Nearly all partial moles are diandric (two sets of paternal chromosomes) and triploid [73]. The use of the word "mole" in this term should not be confused with the use of the word "mole" as a synonym for nevus (a benign melanocytic lesion of skin).

Predictive analytics Predictive analytics is concerned with guessing, using mathematical algorithms, how an individual, group, or data object will behave, based on past outcomes or based on the observed behaviors of similar individuals or groups. Predictive analytics includes three types of algorithms: recommenders, classifiers, and clustering [74].

Predictive test A test that estimates a patient's response to a particular treatment. The terms "predictive test" and "prognostic test" should not be confused with one another.

Predictor In medical practice, a predictor indicates the likelihood of a particular clinical response to a particular choice of treatment. In other words, the term "predictor," as it is currently used, is a shortened version of the more complete term, "response predictor." The concept of a predictive test should be distinguished from the concept of a screening test. A screening test is performed to divide members of a population into two groups: a group that is likely to have the disease and another group that is unlikely to have the disease. The determination of the presence or absence of disease in individuals is accomplished with a diagnostic test (i.e., not with a predictive test and not with a "screening test).

Properties versus classes When creating classifications, the most common mistake is to assign class status to a property. When a property is inappropriately assigned as a class, then the entire classification is ruined. Hence, it is important to be very clear on the difference between these two concepts, and to understand why it is human nature to confuse one with the other. A class is a holder of related objects (e.g., items, records, categorized things). A property is a feature or trait that can be assigned to an item. When inclusion in a class requires items to have a specific property, we often name the class by its defining property. For example Class Rodentia, which includes rats, mice, squirrels, and gophers, are all gnawing mammals. The word rodent derives from the Latin roots rodentem, rodens, from rodere, "to gnaw." Although all rodents gnaw, we know that gnawing is not unique to rodents. Rabbits (Class Lagormorpha) also gnaw. Objects from many different classes may have some of the same properties. Here's another example. Normal human anatomy includes two legs. This being the case, is "leg" a subclass of "human." The answer is no. A leg is not a type of human. Having a leg is just one of many properties associated with normal human anatomy. You would be surprised how many people can be tricked into thinking that a leg, which is itself an object, should be assigned as a subclass of the organisms to which it is attached. Some of this confusion comes from the way that we think about object relationships. We say "He is hungry," using a term of equality, "is" to describe the relationship between "He" and "hungry." Technically, the sentence, "He is hungry" asserts that "He" and "hungry" are equivalent objects. We never bother to say "He has hunger," but other languages are more fastidious. A German might say "Ich habe Hunger," indicating that he has hunger, and avoiding any inference that he and hunger are equivalent terms. It may seem like a trivial point, but creating classes based on properties is always wrong and always disastrous.

Rank Synonymous with Taxonomic order. In hierarchical biological nomenclatures, classes are given ranks. In early versions of the classification of living organisms, it was sufficient to divide the classification into a neat handful of divisions: Kingdom, Phylum, class, Order, Family, Genus, Species. Today, the list of divisions has nearly quadrupled. For example, Phylum has been split into the following divisions: Superphylum, Phylum, Subphylum, Infraphylum, and Microphylum. The other divisions are likewise split. The subdivisions often have a legitimate scientific purpose. Nonetheless, current taxonomic order is simply too detailed for readers to memorize. Is this growing nomenclature for ranking ancestral classes really necessary? Not at all. Taxonomic complexity can be easily averted by dropping named ranks and simply referring to every class as "Class." Modern specifications for class hierarchies encapsulate each class with the name of its superclass. When every object yields its class and superclass, it is possible to trace any object's class lineage. For example, in the classification of living organisms, if you know the name of the parent for each class (i.e., its superclass), you can write a simple software program that generates the complete ancestral lineage for every class and species within the classification, without resorting to a specialized nomenclature [75]. Furthermore, the complex taxonomic ranking system for living organisms does not carry over to the ranking systems that might be used for other scientific domains (e.g., classification of diseases, classification of genes, etc.) and creates an impediment for software developers who wish to write programs that traverse the hierarchy of multiple classifications, in search of relationships among data objects. Hence, the venerable ranking nomenclature, which has served generations of biologists, may need to be eliminated for the current era, wherein computationally driven research prevails.

Recommender algorithms When a data object is very similar to another data object, the two objects are likely to behave similarly. Recommender techniques typically measure the distance between one data object (e.g., a potential customer), and other data items (e.g., customers who have bought a particular product or who have indicated a product preference). The data objects that are closest to one another will tend to have the same preferences and can serve as recommenders. Distances between data objects are measured with feature-by-feature numeric comparisons.

Staging The process of determining the extent of disease at the time of diagnosis. Usually applied to cancers.

Trophectoderm The trophectoderm is formed in the blastocyst stage and consists of everything that is not part of the inner cell mass. The trophectoderm gives rise to the placenta and the amniotic membranes. Since these tissues are not part of the developed animal, they are referred to as extraembryonic tissue. Gestational trophoblastic neoplasia (e.g., tumors that arise in the pregnant mother's uterus, such as gestational choriocarcinoma), all come from the trophectoderm.

Unclassifiable objects Classifications create an hierarchical collection of classes, and taxonomies assign each and every named object to its correct class. This means that a classification is not permitted to contain unclassified objects, a condition that puts fussy taxonomists in an untenable position. Suppose you have an object, and you simply do not know enough about the object to confidently assign it to a class. Or, suppose you have an object that seems to fit more than one class, and you can't decide which class is the correct class. What do you do? Historically, scientists have resorted to creating a "miscellaneous" class into which otherwise unclassifiable objects are given a temporary home, until more suitable accommodations can be provided. Historically, the promiscuous application of "miscellaneous" classes has proven to be a huge impediment to the advancement of science. In the case of the classification of living organisms, the class of protozoans stands as a case in point. Ernst Haeckel, a leading biological taxonomist in his time, created the Kingdom Protista (i.e., protozoans), in 1866, to accommodate a wide variety of simple organisms with superficial commonalities. Haeckel himself understood that the protists were a blended class that included unrelated organisms, but he believed that further study would resolve the confusion. In a sense, he was right, but the process took much longer than he had anticipated, occupying generations of taxonomists over the following 150 years. Today, Kingdom Protista no longer exists. Its members have been reassigned to positions among the animals, plants, and fungi. Nonetheless, textbooks of microbiology still describe the protozoans, just as though this name continued to occupy a legitimate place among terrestrial organisms. In the meantime, therapeutic opportunities for eradicating so-called protozoal infections, using class-targeted agents, have no doubt been missed [4]. You might think that the creation of a class of living organisms, with no established scientific relation to the real world, was a rare and ancient event in the annals of biology, having little or no chance of being repeated. Not so. A special pseudoclass of fungi, deuteromycetes (spelled with a lowercase "d," signifying its questionable validity as a true biologic class), has been created to hold fungi of indeterminate speciation. At present, there are several thousand such fungi, sitting in a taxonomic limbo, waiting to be placed into a definitive taxonomic class [4,26].

References

[1] Simpson GG. Principles of animal taxonomy. New York: Columbia University Press; 1961.
[2] Mayr E. The growth of biological thought: diversity, evolution and inheritance. Cambridge: Belknap Press; 1982.

[3] Smith B, Ceusters W, Klagges B, Kohler J, Kumar A, Lomax J, et al. Relations in biomedical ontologies. Genome Biol 2005;6:R46. Available from: http://genomebiology.com/2005/6/5/R46.

[4] Berman JJ. Taxonomic guide to infectious diseases: understanding the biologic classes of pathogenic organisms. Waltham: Academic Press; 2012.

[5] Berman JJ. Data simplification: taming information with open source tools. Waltham, MA: Morgan Kaufmann; 2016.

[6] Berman JJ. Principles of big data: preparing, sharing, and analyzing complex information. Waltham, MA: Morgan Kaufmann; 2013.

[7] Berman JJ. Biomedical informatics. Sudbury, MA: Jones and Bartlett; 2007.

[8] Fritz A, Percy C, Jack A, Shanmugaratnam K, Sobin L, Parkin DM, et al. International Classification of Diseases for Oncology (ICD-O). 3rd ed. Lyons: World Health Organization; 2001.

[9] International Classification of Diseases, Tenth Revision, Clinical Modification (ICD-10-CM). Centers for Disease Control and Prevention. https://www.cdc.gov/nchs/icd/icd10cm.htm [Accessed 15 May 2017].

[10] Unified Medical Language System (UMLS). U.S. National Library of Medicine. Available from: http://www.nlm.nih.gov/research/umls/umlsmain.html [Accessed 15 May 2017].

[11] Medical Subject Headings. U.S. National Library of Medicine. Available from: https://www.nlm.nih.gov/mesh/filelist.html [Accessed 29 July 2015].

[12] Lee D, de Keizer N, Lau F, Cornet R. Literature review of SNOMED CT use. JAMIA 2014;21:e11–9.

[13] Jaffe ES. The 2008 WHO classification of lymphomas: implications for clinical practice and translational research. Hematology Am Soc Hematol Educ Program 2009;523–31.

[14] Kleihues P, Burger PC, Scheithauer BW. The new WHO classification of brain tumours. Brain Pathol 1993;3:255–68.

[15] Berman JJ. A tool for sharing annotated research data: the "category 0" UMLS (unified medical language system) vocabularies. BMC Med Inform Decis Mak 2003;3:6.

[16] SNOMED CT FAQs, National Library of Medicine, National Institutes of Health. Available from: http://www.nlm.nih.gov/research/umls/Snomed/snomed_faq.html [Accessed 5 July 2017].

[17] Classifications. World Health Organization. http://www.who.int/classifications/icd/en/ [Accessed 4 July 2017].

[18] Bolande RP. Neurocristopathy: its growth and development in 20 years. Pediatr Pathol Lab Med 1997;17:1–25.

[19] Berman JJ. Modern classification of neoplasms: reconciling differences between morphologic and molecular approaches. BMC Cancer 2005;5:100.

[20] Berman JJ. Tumor taxonomy for the developmental lineage classification of neoplasms. BMC Cancer 2004;4:88.

[21] Berman JJ. developmental lineage classification and taxonomy of neoplasms. Available from: http://www.julesberman.info/neoclxml.gz.

[22] Berman JJ. Neoplasms: principles of development and diversity. Sudbury: Jones and Bartlett; 2009.

[23] Simpson GG. The principles of classification and a classification of mammals. Bull Am Mus Nat Hist 1945;85. New York.

[24] Mayr E. Two empires or three? PNAS 1998;95:9720–3.

[25] Woese CR. Default taxonomy: Ernst Mayr's view of the microbial world. PNAS 1998;95(19):11043–6.

[26] Guarro J, Gene J, Stchigel AM. Developments in fungal taxonomy. Clin Microbiol Rev 1999;12:454–500.

[27] Baldauf SL. An overview of the phylogeny and diversity of eukaryotes. J Syst Evol 2008;46:263–73.

[28] Mohanty SK, Parwani AV. Mixed epithelial and stromal tumors of the kidney: an overview. Arch Pathol Lab Med 2009;133:1483–6.

[29] Nayak A, Iyer VK, Agarwala S. The cytomorphologic spectrum of Wilms tumour on fine needle aspiration: a single institutional experience of 110 cases. Cytopathology 2011;22:50–9.

[30] Wang E, Lichtenfels R, Bukur J, Ngalame Y, Panelli MC, Seliger B, et al. Ontogeny and oncogenesis balance the transcriptional profile of renal cell cancer. Cancer Res 2004;64:7279–87.

[31] Frampton JE. Pazopanib: a review in advanced renal cell carcinoma. Target Oncol 2017;12:543–54.

[32] Hubalek M, Ramoni A, Mueller-Holzner E, Marth C. Malignant mixed mesodermal tumor after tamoxifen therapy for breast cancer. Gynecol Oncol 2004;95:264–6.

[33] Committee on A Framework for Developing a New Taxonomy of Disease, Board on Life Sciences, Division on Earth and Life Studies, National Research Council of the National Academies. Toward Precision Medicine: Building a Knowledge Network for Biomedical Research and a New Taxonomy of Disease. Washington, DC: The National Academies Press; 2011.

[34] Rennard SI, Vestbo J. The many "small COPDs", COPD should be an orphan disease. Chest 2008;134:623–7.

[35] Bickel PJ, Hammel EA, O'Connell JW. Sex bias in graduate admissions: data from Berkeley. Science 1975;187:398–404.

[36] Baker SG, Kramer BS. The transitive fallacy for randomized trials: if A bests B and B bests C in separate trials, is A better than C? BMC Med Res Methodol 2002;2:13.

[37] Babcock WW. Bacteriology: its practical value to the general practitioner. In: Shattock SG, editor. An Atlas of the Bacteria Pathogenic in Man. New York: EB Treat and Company; 1899.

[38] Field MJ, Boat T. Rare diseases and orphan products: accelerating research and development. Institute of Medicine (US) Committee on Accelerating Rare Diseases Research and Orphan Product Development, Washington, DC: The National Academics Press; 2010. Available from: http://www.ncbi.nlm.nih.gov/books/NBK56189/.

[39] Altman LK. After a highly publicized death, second-guessing second opinions NY Times; August 3, 1993.

[40] Bernstein L. 20 percent of patients with serious conditions are first misdiagnosed, study says. Washington Post; April 4, 2017.

[41] Landgren O, Kyle RA, Pfeiffer RM. Monoclonal gammopathy of undetermined significance (MGUS) consistently precedes multiple myeloma: a prospective study. Blood 2009;113:5412–7.

[42] Hillengass J, Weber MA, Kilk K, Listl K, Wagner-Gund B, Hillengass M, et al. Prognostic significance of whole-body MRI in patients with monoclonal gammopathy of undetermined significance. Leukemia 2014;28:174–8.

[43] French CA, Kutok JL, Faquin WC, Toretsky JA, Antonescu CR, Griffin CA, et al. Midline carcinoma of children and young adults with NUT rearrangement. J Clin Oncol 2004;22:4135–9.

[44] French CA. NUT midline carcinoma. Cancer Genet Cytogenet 2010;203:16–20.

[45] Tognon C, Knezevich SR, Huntsman D, Roskelley CD, Melnyk N, Mathers JA, et al. Expression of the ETV6-NTRK3 gene fusion as a primary event in human secretory breast carcinoma. Cancer Cell 2002;2:367–76.

[46] Makretsov N, He M, Hayes M, Chia S, Horsman DE, Sorensen PH, et al. A fluorescence in situ hybridization study of ETV6-NTRK3 fusion gene in secretory breast carcinoma. Genes Chromosom Cancer 2004;40:152–7.

[47] Lee SG, Jung SP, Lee HY, Kim S, Kim HY, Kim I, et al. Secretory breast carcinoma: a report of three cases and a review of the literature. Oncol Lett 2014;8:683–6.

[48] Lizcova L, Zemanova Z, Malinova E, Jarosova M, Mejstrikova E, Smisek P, et al. A novel recurrent chromosomal aberration involving chromosome 7 in childhood myelodysplastic syndrome. Cancer Genet Cytogenet 2010;201:52–6.

[49] Shannon KM, Turhan AG, Chang SS, Bowcock AM, Rogers PC, Carroll WL, et al. Familial bone marrow monosomy 7. Evidence that the predisposing locus is not on the long arm of chromosome 7. J Clin Invest 1989;84:984–9.

[50] Gokmen-Polar Y, Cook RW, Goswami CP, Wilkinson J, Maetzold D, Stone JF, et al. A gene signature to determine metastatic behavior in thymomas. PLoS One 2013;8:e66047.

[51] Fang ZQ, Zang WD, Chen R, Ye BW, Wang XW, Yi SH, et al. Gene expression profile and enrichment pathways in different stages of bladder cancer. Genet Mol Res 2013;12:1479–89.

[52] Sweeney SE. Hematopoietic stem cell transplant for systemic lupus erythematosus: Interferon regulatory factor 7 activation correlates with the IFN signature and recurrent disease. Lupus 2011;20:975–80.

[53] Zhang L, Pagano JS. IRF-7, a new interferon regulatory factor associated with Epstein-Barr virus latency. Mol Cell Biol 1997;17:5748–57.

[54] Waterhouse M, Bertz H, Finke J. Fast and simple approach for the simultaneous detection of hematopoietic chimerism, NPM1, and FLT3-ITD mutations after allogeneic stem cell transplantation. Ann Hematol 2014;93:293–8.

[55] Innovation or Stagnation: Challenge and Opportunity on the Critical Path to New Medical Products. U.S. Department of Health and Human Services, Food and Drug Administration; 2004.

[56] Wurtman RJ, Bettiker RL. The slowing of treatment discovery, 1965-1995. Nat Med 1996;2:5–6.

[57] Saul S. Prone to error: earliest steps to find cancer. NY Times; July 19, 2010.

[58] Benowitz S. Biomarker boom slowed by validation concerns. J Natl Cancer Inst 2004;96:1356–7.

[59] Ioannidis JP. Microarrays and molecular research: noise discovery? Lancet 2005;365:454–5.

[60] Begley S. In cancer science, many 'discoveries' don't hold up. Reuters; March 28, 2012.

[61] Abu-Asab MS, Chaouchi M, Alesci S, Galli S, Laassri M, Cheema AK, et al. Biomarkers in the age of omics: time for a systems biology approach. OMICS 2011;15:105–12.

[62] Swain SM, Baselga J, Kim SB, Ro J, Semiglazov V, Campone M, et al. Pertuzumab, trastuzumab, and docetaxel in HER2-positive metastatic breast cancer. N Engl J Med 2015;372:724–34.

[63] Weigelt B, Reis-Filho JS. Molecular profiling currently offers no more than tumour morphology and basic immunohistochemistry. Breast Cancer Res 2010;12:S5.

[64] Moyer VA, On behalf of the U.S. Preventive Services Task Force. Screening for prostate cancer: U.S. Preventive Services Task Force recommendation statement. Ann Intern Med 2012;157:120–34.

[65] Ioannidis JP, Panagiotou OA. Comparison of effect sizes associated with biomarkers reported in highly cited individual articles and in subsequent meta-analyses. JAMA 2011;305:2200–10.

[66] Al-Agha OM, Igbokwe AA. Malignant fibrous histiocytoma: between the past and the present. Arch Pathol Lab Med 2008;132:1030–5.

[67] Nakayama R, Nemoto T, Takahashi H, Ohta T, Kawai A, Seki K, et al. Gene expression analysis of soft tissue sarcomas: characterization and reclassification of malignant fibrous histiocytoma. Mod Pathol 2007;20:749–59.

[68] Daugaard S. Current soft-tissue sarcoma classifications. Eur J Cancer 2004;40:543–8.

[69] Wu X, Kumar V, Quinlan JR, Ghosh J, Yang Q, Motoda H, et al. Top 10 algorithms in data mining. Knowl Inf Syst 2008;14:1–37.

[70] Jiang X, Iseki S, Maxson RE, Sucov HM, Morriss-Kay GM. Tissue origins and interactions in the mammalian skull vault. Dev Biol 2002;241:106–16.

[71] Kuratani S. Craniofacial development and the evolution of the vertebrates: the old problems on a new background. Zool Sci 2005;22:1–19.

[72] Berman JJ. Repurposing legacy data: innovative case studies. Waltham, MA: Morgan Kaufmann; 2015.

[73] Banet N, DeScipio C, Murphy KM, Beierl K, Adams E, Vang R, et al. Characteristics of hydatidiform moles: analysis of a prospective series with p57 immunohistochemistry and molecular genotyping. Mod Pathol 2014;27:238–542.

[74] Owen S, Anil R, Dunning T, Friedman E. Mahout in action. Shelter Island, NY: Manning Publications Co.; 2012.

[75] Berman JJ. Methods in medical informatics: fundamentals of healthcare programming in Perl, Python, and Ruby. Boca Raton, FL: Chapman and Hall; 2010.

SECTION 8.1 WHAT ARE THE MINIMAL NECESSARY PROPERTIES OF GOOD DATA?

In God we trust, all others bring data.
William Edwards Deming (1900–93)

Most of the data that has been collected and stored has no scientific value, because it is not good data. Everyone knows the "garbage in garbage out" adage of data analysts. Well, just imagine a world where 98% of everything is garbage. That's about the shape of things today [1–4]. This may seem like an outrageous claim, particularly when you consider how much of the world's activities are data-driven. If you speak with scientists who collect and analyze data, and that would include just about every scientist you are likely to encounter, you will hear them tell you that their data is just fine, and perfectly suitable for their own scientific studies. The point that must be made is that the value of scientific data cannot be judged by the scientists who collected and analyzed the data. The true value of data must be assessed by the scientists who verify, validate, and reanalyze the data that was collected by other scientists. If the original data cannot be obtained and analyzed by the scientific community, now and in the future, then the original assertions cannot be confirmed, and the data cannot be usefully extended, merged with other data sets, and repurposed. [Glossary Data versus datum]

For data to be useful to the scientific community, it must have a set of properties, and, unfortunately, these properties are seldom taught or utilized. Here are the universal properties of good data that has lasting scientific value.

- Data that has been annotated with metadata
- Data that establishes uniqueness or identity
- Time-stamped data that accrues over time [Glossary Time, Time-stamp]
- Data that resides within a data object
- Data that has membership in a defined class
- Introspective data—data that explains itself
- Immutable data

Let us take a moment to examine each of these data features:

- **Data that has been annotated with metadata**

Metadata is data that explains data. For example, if a data spreadsheet lists an individual's weight as "180," you would need to know whether the number represents pounds or kilograms, or some other unit of weight. If that information were not present, the data would be, quite literally, meaningless. Fortunately, we have a formal way of providing descriptive data about data, and this is known as XML (eXtended Markup Language). [Glossary Data annotation, Annotation, Data sharing, Reanalysis]

The importance of XML to data scientists cannot be overstated. As a data-organizing technology, it is as important as the invention of written language (circa 3000 BC) or the appearance of mass-printed books (circa AD 1450). Markup allows us to convey any message as XML (a pathology report, a radiology image, a genome database, a workflow process, a software program, or an email). XML markup, also known as XML tags, are alphanumeric descriptors enclosed by angle brackets. Each tag is repeated at the beginning and end of the data element, with the end-tag recognized by its slash character. [Glossary Semantics]

The following are examples of XML markup [5].

```
<name_of_patient>John Public</name_of_patient>
<age_of_patient>25 years</age_of_patient>
<gender_of_patient>Male</gender_of_ patient>
<birthdate_of_patient>January 1,1954</birthdate_of_patient>
```

When the data element "25 years" is flanked by <age_of_patient> tags, we can be sure that it is not referring to an anniversary event, the length of a mortgage, or a prison sentence. XML tags can appear in narrative text. For example:

```
<pathological_diagnosis>Adenocarcinoma of colon</pathological_diagnosis>
Extends to the <anatomic_site>muscularis propria</anatomic_site>.
```

– Data that establishes uniqueness or identity

The most useful data establishes the identity of objects. In many cases, objects have their own, natural identifiers that come very close to establishing uniqueness. Examples include fingerprints, iris patterns, and the sequence of nucleotides in an organism's genetic material. [Glossary Identifier, Data repurposing]

With the exception of identical twins, parthenogenetic offspring, and clones, every organism on earth has a unique sequence of DNA-forming nucleotides that distinguish its genetic material (i.e., its genome) from the genome of every other organism. If we were to have a record of the complete sequence of nucleotides in an individual's genome, we could distinguish that individual from every other organism on earth. This would require a lot of digital storage for every organism. In the case of humans, the genome is 3 billion nucleotides in length. As luck would have it, because there is enormous variation in genome sequence, from individual to individual, the identity of human individuals can be established by sampling just 13 short segments of DNA.

CODIS (Combined DNA Index System) collects the unique nucleotide sequences of 13 specific segments of DNA, for every individual included in the database [6]. Using CODIS, DNA sampled at a crime scene can be matched against DNA samples contained in the database. Hence, the identity of individuals whose DNA is found at a crime scene can often be established. In the absence of a match, it is sometimes possible to link crime scene samples to close relatives (paternal or maternal) included in the database.

CODIS serves an example of database with narrow scope (i.e., names of people and associated DNA sequences) and broad societal value. The basic design of the CODIS database can be extended to any organism. For example, a database of DNA samples collected from individual trees in a geographic location can establish the source of seeds or pollen grains sticking to an article of clothing, and this information might lead to the location where a criminal event transpired. A population database containing full genome DNA sequences could be used to determine the presence or absence of disease-causing genes in individuals or to predict the response of an individual to a particular drug [7–10].

Returning to the issue of object identification, we need not depend on each data object having its own naturally occurring identifier. This can be accomplished by generating and assigning unique identifiers to our data objects [4,11–13].

The UUID (Universally Unique IDentifier) is an example of one type of algorithm that creates collision-free identifiers that can be generated on command, at the moment when new objects are created (i.e., during the run-time of a software application). Linux systems have a built-in UUID utility. [Glossary Universally unique identifier]

Here is an example of an identifier generated by the "uuidgen.exe" utility:

```
312e60c9-3d00-4e3f-a013-0d6cb1c9a9fe
```

When we use the same utility again, we get another string, that we can use as an identifier for some other data object:

```
822df73c-8e54-45b5-9632-e2676d178664
```

In theory, identifier systems are incredibly easy to implement. Here is exactly how it is done:

1. Generate a unique character sequence, such as UUID, or a long random number.
2. Assign the unique character sequence (i.e., identifier) to each new object, at the moment that the object is created. In the case of a hospital, a patient identifier is created at the moment he or she is registered into the hospital information system. In the case of a bank, a customer identifier is created at the moment that he or she is provided with an account number. In the case of an object-oriented programming language, such as Ruby, an object identifier is generated the moment when the "new" method is sent to a class object, instructing the class object to create a class instance. [Glossary Object-oriented programming language]
3. Preserve the identifier number and bind it to the object. In practical terms, this means that whenever the data object accrues new data, the new data is assigned to the identifier number. In the case of a hospital system, this would mean that all of the lab tests, billable clinical transactions, pharmacy orders, and so on, are linked to the patient's unique identifier number, as a service provided by the hospital information system. In the case of a banking system, this would mean that all of the customer's deposits and withdrawals and balances are attached to the customer's unique account number.

Identifiers are data simplifiers, when implemented properly. The allow us to collect all of the data associated with a unique object, while ensuring that we exclude any data that should be associated with some other object.

— Time-stamped data that accrues over time

We need above all to know about changes; no one wants or needs to be reminded 16 hours a day that his shoes are on.
David Hubel

When a data set contains data records that collect over time, it becomes possible to measure how the attributes of data records may change as the data accumulates. Signals analysts use the term time series to refer to attribute measurements that change over time. The shape of the time series can be periodic (i.e., repeating over specific intervals), linear, nonlinear, Gaussian, or multimodal (i.e., having multiple peaks and troughs). A large part of data science is devoted to finding trends in data, determining simple functions that model the variation of data over time, or predicting how data will change in the future. All these analytic activities require data that is annotated with the time that a measurement is made, or the time that a record is prepared, or the time that an event has occurred. [Glossary Data science]

You may be shocked to learn that many, if not most, web pages lack a time-stamp to signify the date and time when the page's textual content was created. This oversight applies to news reports, announcements from organizations and governments, and even scientific papers; all being instances for which a time-stamp would seem to be an absolute necessity. When a scientist publishes an undated manuscript, how would anyone know if the results are novel? If a news article describes an undated event, how would anyone know whether the report is current? For the purposes of data analysis, undated documents and data records are useless.

Whereas undated documents have very little value, all transactions, statements, documents and data points that are annotated with reliable time-stamps will always have some value, particularly if the information continues to collect over time. Today, anyone with a computer can easily time-stamp their data, with the date and the time, accurate to within a second. It happens that this paragraph was composed using a text editor that inserts a time-stamp into the text whenever and wherever the F5 and F6 keys are pushed in tandem, just so: "(date Tuesday, December 5, 2017, 11:19 and 35 seconds, AM)." The programmer who wrote the editing software understood the value of documenting time. Every operating system and every programming language has access to the time, and can easily annotate any data point with the time that it was created. Time data can be formatted in any of dozens of ways, all of which can be instantly converted to an international standard [14].

It's human nature to value newly collected data and to dismiss old data as being outdated or irrelevant. Nothing could be further from the truth. New data, in the absence of old data, has little value. All biological phenomena develop over time, and the observations made at any given moment in time are always influenced by events that transpired at earlier times. Whenever we speak of "new" data, alternately known as prospectively acquired data, we must think in terms that relate the new data to the "old" data that preceded it. Old data can be used to analyze trends over time and to predict data values into the future. Essentially, old data provides the opportunity to see the past, the present, and the future. The dependence of new data on old data can be approached computationally. The autocorrelation function is a method for producing a type of measurement indicating the dependence of data elements on prior data elements. Long-range dependence occurs when a value is dependent on many prior values. Long-range dependence is determined when the serial correlation (i.e., the autocorrelation over multiple data elements) is high when the number of sequential elements is large [15]. These are nifty tools for data analysis, but they cannot be employed if the data is not time-tamped [2]. [Glossary Correlation distance]

- **Data that is held in a data object**

A data object is whatever is being described by the data. For example, if the data is "6 feet tall," then the data object is the person or thing to which "6 feet tall" applies. Minimally, a data object is a metadata/data pair, assigned to a unique identifier (i.e., together forming a so-called data triple). In practice, the most common data objects are simple data records, corresponding to a row in a spreadsheet or a line in a flat file. Data objects in object-oriented programming languages typically encapsulate several items of data, including an object name, an object unique identifier, multiple data/metadata pairs, the name of the object's class, and the name of the object's parent class. [Glossary Triple, Identifier, Metadata]

Anyone who has ever used a spreadsheet can understand that a data record (i.e., in this case, one horizontal line in a spreadsheet) is a data object. Today, data objects are used for all types of information. For example, when you send an email, your client software automatically creates a data object that holds the contents of your message, descriptive information about the message, a message identifier, and a time stamp.

Here is a sample email header, obtained by selecting the email client's long or detailed version of the message. The actual message contents would normally follow, but are omitted here for brevity.

```
MIME-Version: 1.0
Received: by 10.36.165.75 with HTTP; Tue, 2 May 2017 14:46:47 -0700 (PDT)
Date: Tue, 2 May 2017 17:46:47 -0400
Delivered-To: you@gmail.com
Message-ID: <CALVNVe-kk7fqYJ82MfsV6a4kFKW4v57c4y9BLpOUYf1cBHq9pQ@mail.gmail.com>
Subject: tiny fasts
From: Anybody <me@gmail.com>
To: Anybody Else <you@gmail.com>
Content-Type: multipart/alternative; boundary=94eb2c07ab4c054062054e917a03
```

Notice that each line of the header consists of a colon ":" flanked to the left by metadata (e.g., Subject, From, To) and on the right by the described data. There is a line for a time-stamp and a line for an identifier assigned by the email client.

```
Date: Tue, 2 May 2017 17:46:47 -0400
Message-ID: <CALVNVe-kk7fqYJ82MfsV6a4kFKW4v57c4y9BLpOUYf1cBHq9pQ@mail.gmail.com>
```

Whenever you take a photograph with your cellphone's camera, it automatically generates a data object and inserts it into the header of the image, a text entry that is embedded in the image file, and which is not seen unless it is extracted by a software application. Every image contains a wealth of useful information that most people never see.

Here is a sample header of an image file, denver.jpg

```
Image: myphoto.jpg
Format: JPEG (Joint Photographic Experts Group JFIF format)
Mime type: image/jpeg
Class: DirectClass
Geometry: 640x480+0+0
Resolution: 72x72
Rendering intent: Perceptual
Gamma: 0.454545
Compression: JPEG
Quality: 96
Properties:
Date:create: 2017-05-28T07:26:02-04:00
Date:modify: 2017-05-28T07:26:02-04:00
Exif:DateTime: 2017:05:25 19:14:29
Exif:DateTimeDigitized: 2017:05:25 19:14:29
Exif:DateTimeOriginal: 2017:05:25 19:14:29
Signature: 6c31fce75fd7dc2d5e11a65daa2f53f4512f7b212797e82aa64be73898010f66
Filesize: 134KB
Number pixels: 307K
Elapsed time: 0:01.068
```

Here a flanked ":" on each line separates the data (on the right) from its metadata (on the left). Once more, we find the all-important time-stamp and identifier.

```
Date:create: 2017-05-28T07:26:02-04:00
Signature: 6c31fce75fd7dc2d5e11a65daa2f53f4512f7b212797e82aa64be73898010f66
```

– Data that has membership in a defined class

In Chapter 7, we discussed classifications and ontologies and explained the importance of assigning instances (e.g., diseases, genes, pathways) to classes wherein every instance shares a set of features typical of the class. The importance of classifications to biologists is easy to understand. The importance of classifications to data analysts is a bit less obvious.

As discussed in Section 7.1, all good classifications have a feature that is known as competence; the ability to draw inferences about data objects, and their relationships to other data objects, based on class definitions. The class definition contains the name of the class, its parent class, the features that qualify instances as members of the class, and the list of properties that are not class specific, and their range (i.e., the list of classes to which the property applies). We cannot go into the specifics here, but there are formal ways of documenting the definitions of related classes, in data structures known as schemas (e.g., RDF Schema). An elegant joining of object-oriented programming and biological classifications enables data scientists to interrogate data sets in which data objects have been assigned membership to classes defined in schemas [2,16].

– Introspective data (data that explains itself)

Introspection is a term borrowed from object-oriented programming. It refers to the ability of data (e.g., data records, documents, and all types of data objects) to describe itself when interrogated. Introspection gives data users the opportunity to see relationships among the individual data records that are distributed in different data sets, and is one of the most useful features of data objects, when implemented properly. [Glossary Introspection]

Introspection is built into object-oriented programming languages. To illustrate, let us see how Ruby, a popular object-oriented programming language, implements introspection [16].

In Ruby, we can create a new object, "x," and assign it a string, such as "hello world."

```
x = "hello world"
```

Because the data object, "x," contains a string, Ruby knows that x belongs to the String class of objects. If we send the "class" method to the object, "x," Ruby will return a message indicating that "x" belongs to class String.

```
x.class        yields String
```

In Ruby, every object is automatically given an identifier (i.e., character string that is unique for the object). If we send the object the method "object_id," Ruby will tell us its assigned identifier.

```
x.object_id      yields 22502910
```

Ruby tells us that the unique object identifier assigned to the object "x" is 22502910.

In Ruby, should we need to learn the contents of "x," we can send the "inspect" method to the object. Should we need to know the methods that are available to the object, we can send the "methods" method to the object. All modern object-oriented languages support syntactic equivalents of these basic introspective tools.

The point of this short diversion from medicine is to demonstrate that modern programming languages allow the programmer to interrogate data, and learn everything there is to know about the information contained in data objects. Information about data objects, acquired during the execution of a program, can be used to modify a program's instructions, during run-time, a useful feature known as "reflection." Detailed information about every piece of data in a data set (e.g., the identifier associated with the data object, the class of objects to which the data object belongs, the data that the data object was created, the metadata and the data values that are associated with the data object) permit data scientists to integrate, relate, and repurpose individual data objects from one data set with data objects from other data sets, stored on many different servers, at many different locations.

Alas, most of the data available to data analysts lack introspection. In this age of Precision Medicine, the data that we have collected seldom rises to the level where it can usefully tell us what we need to know. Hence, data analysts must be prepared to expend a great deal of their time and energy trying to understand the content and organization of precision data [4]. [Glossary Abandonware, Dark data, Legacy data, Universal and perpetual]

– Immutable data

Immutability is the principle that data is permanent and can never be modified. At first thought, it would seem that immutability is a ridiculous and impossible constraint. In the real world, mistakes are made, and information changes. Surely, you can delete data when you know it's wrong. Not so. [Glossary Immutability]

Immutability is one of those issues, like identifiers and introspection, that seem trivial, until something goes terribly wrong. Then, in the midst of the problem, you suddenly realize that your entire information system was designed incorrectly, and there really is nothing you can do to cope.

Here is an example of an immutability problem. You are a pathologist working in a university hospital that has just installed a new, $600 million information system. On Tuesday, you released a report on a surgical biopsy, indicating that it contained cancer. On Friday morning, you showed the same biopsy to your colleagues, who agreed with one another that the biopsy was not malignant, and that your diagnosis was simply wrong. Now, you must rectify the error. In a panic, you return to the computer, and access the prior report, changing the wording of the diagnosis to indicate that the biopsy is benign. You can do this, because pathologists are granted "edit" access for pathology reports. Now, everything seems to have been set right. The report has been corrected, and all is well.

Unknown to you, the patient's doctor read the incorrect report on Wednesday, the day after it was issued, and two days before the correct report replaced the incorrect report. Major surgery was scheduled for the following Wednesday (5 days after the corrected report was issued). Most of the patient's liver was removed. No cancer was found in the excised liver. Eventually, the surgeon and patient learned that the original report had been altered. The patient sued the surgeon, the pathologist, and the hospital.

You, the pathologist, argued in court that the final report in the computer is correct, and that the surgeon should have read the final report, not the precorrected early report. The patient's lawyer had access to a medical chart in which paper versions of the diagnosis had been kept. The lawyer produced, for the edification of the jury, two reports that had been released by the pathologist (i.e., you) on two separate dates: one positive for cancer, the other benign. The hospital, conceding that they had no credible defense, settled out of court for a very large quantity of money. Meanwhile, back in the hospital, a fastidious intern is deleting an erroneous diagnosis, and substituting his improved rendition.

One of the most important features of any data resource (e.g., data collected in hospital information systems and research laboratories) is immutability. The rule is simple. Data is immortal and cannot change. You can add data to the system, but you can never alter data and you can never erase data. Immutability is counterintuitive to most people, including most data analysts. If a patient has a glucose level of 100 on Monday, and the same patient has a glucose level of 115 on Tuesday, then it would seem obvious that his glucose level changed between Monday and Tuesday. Not so. To the end of time, Monday's glucose level will always be 100, and Tuesday's glucose level does not alter Monday's data. By annotating Monday's data with a time and date, and Tuesday's data with another time and date, you permit data to change, without deleting data.

Time-stamping is a component of data objects. Events (e.g., a part purchased, a report issued, a file opened) have no meaning unless you know when they occurred. Time-stamps must be unique and immutable. A single event cannot occur at two different times, but modifications to the event can occur at many different times and can be appended without changing existing data. In the case of the retracted pathology report, the pathologist should have preserved and time-stamped the original (incorrect report), and issued a time-stamped addendum to the report, indicating a change in diagnosis. The pathologist should have contacted the patient's physicians and notified them that a change had taken place, and each of these notifications should have been recorded and time-stamped. In a well-maintained hospital information system, a data analyst would have been able to follow all of these transactions, as a documented sequence of time-stamped events.

When you are permitted to change preexisting data, all of your collected data becomes tainted. None of the analyses performed on the data in the database can be verified, because the data that was originally analyzed no longer exists. It has become something else, that you cannot fully understand. Whenever you change data, you put the data analyst in the impossible position of deciding which data to believe, the old data or the new data.

SECTION 8.2 DATA IDENTIFICATION AND DATA DEIDENTIFICATION

> I always wanted to be somebody, but now I realize I should have been more specific.
> *Lily Tomlin*

In the prior section, we discussed identifiers. Measurements, annotations, properties, and classes of information have no meaning unless they are attached to an identifier that distinguishes one data object from all other data objects, and that link together all of the information that has been or will be associated with the identified data object.

Knowing this, we are ready to discuss identifier systems. To understand the difference between an identifier and an identifier system, it's best to imagine the difference between having a $10 bill in your pocket and having a $10 credit in your bank account. The bank account assigns a credit of $10 to your identifier. Fundamentally, a $10 bill is just a piece of paper. A bank account is just an identified entry in a database. Their value depends on the behavior of society (i.e., the social operating system in which they exist).

Every electronic medical record system is built upon an identifier system. Every patient is assigned an identifier number, and the database attaches transactional data (e.g., clinic visits, biopsy results, radiology reports, pharmacy orders) to the correctly identified patients. The purpose of this section is to explain why it is that electronic medical record systems (EMRs) with good identifier systems and transactional time-stamping protocols are essential for the advancement of Precision Medicine. EMRs that lack good identifier systems and transactional time-stamping protocols are always disruptive and counterproductive.

Here is what goes wrong when a patient identifier system, in a hospital, clinic, or research lab, is poorly implemented.

- You search for and find a patient's record. Unknown to you, the patient has five records in the system, and you have only retrieved a small fraction of the data you need.
- You search for and find a patient's record. Unknown to you, the record contains data on several additional patients, all of whom happen to have the same given name and surname.
- You search for and find a patient's record. The record is empty. Unknown to you, your patient's data has been inadvertently entered into another patient's record.
- You search for a patient's record. You cannot find the record. Unknown to you, you searched under the patient's name, and the patient's actual record was recorded under a different spelling of the same name.
- You search for a patient's record. You cannot find the record. Someone has inadvertently removed the identifier from the record.
- You search for a patient's record. You cannot find the record. All preexisting records, and their identifiers, were expunged when your institution deployed a new $800 million hospital information system. Whoops.

These eventualities may seem farfetched, but they are all quite common. Such mistakes occur when designers of information systems devote their energies to service functions such as ease-of-use, integration of services, inventory management, and so on. In the rush to provide versatile systems, that provide the kinds of services demanded by busy hospital staff, issues of patient identifiers can be forgotten. Nonetheless, every good EMR is, at heart, an identifier system. The object identifiers are unique alphanumeric strings permanently assigned to patients. The identifier system is the set of protocols ensuring that the identifiers are linked to the proper patients.

The properties of a good identifier system, as listed in Principles of Big Data: Preparing, Sharing, and Analyzing Complex Information [4], are as follows:

1. Completeness. Every unique object in the big data resource must be assigned an identifier.
2. Uniqueness. Each identifier is a unique sequence.

3. Exclusivity. Each identifier is assigned to a unique object, and to no other object.

4. Authenticity. The objects that receive identification must be verified as the objects that they are intended to be. For example, if a young man walks into a bank and claims to be Richie Rich, then the bank must ensure that he is, in fact, who he says he is.

5. Aggregation. The data set must have a mechanism to aggregate all of the data that is properly associated with the identifier (i.e., to bundle all of the data that belongs to the uniquely identified objected). In the case of a bank, this might mean collecting all of the transactions associated with an account holder. In a hospital, this might mean collecting all of the data associated with a patient's identifier: clinic visit reports, medication transactions, surgical procedures, laboratory results. If the identifier system performs properly, aggregation methods will always collect all of the data associated with an object, and will never collect any data that is associated with a different object.

6. Permanence. The identifiers and the associated data must be permanent. In the case of a hospital system, when the patient returns to the hospital after 30 years of absence, the record system must be able to access his identifier and aggregate his data. When a patient dies, the patient's identifier must not perish.

7. Reconciliation. There should be a mechanism whereby the data associated with a unique, identified object in one data set can be merged with the data held in another resource, for the same unique object. This process, which requires comparison, authentication, and merging, is known as reconciliation. Reconciliation is closely related to health record portability. When a patient visits a hospital, it may be necessary to transfer her electronic medical record from another hospital. Both hospitals need a way of confirming the identity of the patient and combining the records. [Glossary Authentication, Reconciliation]

8. Immutability. In addition to being permanent (i.e., never destroyed or lost), the identifier must never change [17]. In the event that two data sets are merged, or that legacy data is merged into a new resource, or that individual data objects from two different data sets are merged, a single data object will be assigned two identifiers, one from each of the merging systems. In this case, the identifiers must be preserved as they are, without modification. The merged data object must be provided with annotative information specifying the origin of each identifier (i.e., clarifying which identifier came from which data set).

9. Security. The identifier system is vulnerable to malicious attack. An EMR can be irreversibly corrupted if the identifiers are modified.

10. Documentation and Quality Assurance. A system should be in place to find and correct errors in the patient identifier system. Protocols must be written for establishing the identifier system, for assigning identifiers, for protecting the system, and for monitoring the system. Every problem and every corrective action taken must be documented and reviewed. Review procedures should determine whether the errors were corrected effectively, and measures should be taken to continually improve the identifier system. All procedures, all actions taken, and all modifications of the system should be thoroughly documented. This is a big job.

11. **Centrality.** The patient identifier is the central key to which every transaction for the patient is attached.
12. **Autonomy.** An identifier system has a life of its own, independent of the data contained in the data set. The identifier system can persist, documenting and organizing existing and future data objects even if all of the data in the data set were to suddenly vanish (i.e., when all of the data contained in all of the data object are deleted).

The term "identified data" is a concept central to modern data science and must be distinguished from "data that concerns an identified individual," a concept that has legal and ethical importance. All good data must be identified. If the data isn't identified, then there is no way of aggregating data that pertains to an identifier, and there is no way of distinguishing one data assertion from another (e.g., one observation on ten samples versus ten observations on one sample) [18]. **Data that is identified (i.e., assigned a permanent unique identifying sequence) is fundamentally different from data that is linked to an identified individual (i.e., associated with the name of a person). Unfortunately, in the privacy realm, "data that is linked to an identified individual," is shortened to "identified data," and this indulgence has caused no end of confusion. It is absolutely crucial to understand and accept that the identity of data is not equivalent to the identity of the individual to whom the data applies. In particular, we can remove the links to the identity of individuals without removing data identifiers. This subtle point accounts for much of the gratuitous rancor in the field of data privacy.**

Some find it difficult to accept, but all good deidentified data, just like all good data in general, must be permanently linked to an identifier. To illustrate, consider this example, discussed in Data Simplification: Taming Information With Open Source Tools [2]. Imagine, for a moment, that you are a data analyst who is tasked with analyzing cancer genes. You find a large public database consisting of DNA sequences obtained from human cancer specimens. The tissues have been stripped of all identifiers to protect the privacy of the individuals from whom the tissue samples were taken. All of this data is available for download. As the gigabytes stream into your computer, you think you have arrived in heaven. Before too long, you have completed your analysis on tissues from dozens of lung cancers. You draw a conclusion that most lung cancers express a particular genetic variation, and you suggest in your paper that this variation is a new diagnostic marker. You begin the process of seeking patent protection for your discovery. You believe that you are on a fast track leading to fame and fortune. At lunch, in the University cafeteria, one of your colleagues poses the following question, "If all the tissues in the public data set were deidentified, and you studied 36 samples, how would you know whether your 36 samples came from 36 different tumors in 36 patients, or whether they represented 36 samples taken from one tumor in one patient?" A moment of sheer panic follows. If all the samples came from a single patient, then your research is only relevant to one tumor. In that case, you would expect a variation in the genome of one tumor sample to show up in every sample. Your finding would have no particular relevance to lung tumors, in general. Frantically, you contact the registrar at the tissue resource from which you had obtained your data. He informs you that because the tissues are deidentified, for the protection of patients, he cannot resolve your dilemma. You happen to know the director of the tissue resource, and you explain your problem to her. She indicates that she cannot answer your question, but she happens to know that all of the lung cancer specimens were contributed by a single laboratory. She puts you in touch with the principal investigator at the lab. He remembers that his lab contributed tissues, and that all their tissues were samples of a single large tumor. Your greatest fears are confirmed. Your findings have no general relevance, and no scientific value. [Glossary Privacy versus confidentiality, Deidentification]

In this hypothetical dramatization, the specimens were stripped of all identifiers. Because there were no identifying sequences to establish the uniqueness of specimens, you, the researcher, could not know that every sample you examined came from the same specimen. Had each cancer specimen been assigned a unique identifier, you would have seen that the samples all belonged to one data object.

There are actually simple methods for deidentifying data objects. For example, the original identifier could be supplemented with a deidentifying identifier (i.e., another unique alphanumeric sequence), and the data could be distributed publicly with the "deidentifying identifier" replacing the original identifier. If there were a desire to irreversibly deidentify the data, then the data manager could delete the file that links the original identifier to the "deidentifying identifier." The deidentified data will still have its own unique identifier, but the researcher who holds the public data will never be able to link the data back to its original identifier.

Needless to say, it is impossible to deidentify or to reidentify a record that has never been properly identified. If a record has not been identified, then the record may have arisen from an individual with another identity than the identity of the person thought to be associated with the record, or from a duplicate record from one patient. Hence, when a record is not identified, attempts to deidentify the record (i.e., stripping the record of identifying elements and providing a new unique alphanumeric that will be associated with the deidentified record) serve no purpose because we cannot say that the record is unique.

The field of data deidentification is a difficult but essential component of Precision Medicine. Much of the advancement in Precision Medicine will come from analyzing very large databases of biomedical data, looking for adverse effects to medications, exceptional responders, outlier data, distinguishable biological subgroups of individuals with diseases, outcome data on treated patients, and so on. All of this work will need to be done on data that is properly identified and deidentified (i.e., given a new "deidentification identifier") and stripped of information that can establish a link to any individuals.

In this short section, it is impossible to describe all of the available and effective techniques for medical data deidentification, but a rich literature is available for study [3,19–24]. For now, you should familiarize yourself with a few terms that cause some confusion in the field.

Anonymization is a process whereby all the links between an individual and the individual's data record are irreversibly removed. The difference between anonymization and deidentification is that anonymization is irreversible. Because anonymization is irreversible, the opportunities for verifying the quality of data are limited. For example, if someone suspects that samples have been switched in a data set, thus putting the results of the study into doubt, an anonymized set of data would afford no opportunity to resolve the problem by reidentifying the original samples. The process by which deidentification can be reversed is known a reidentification. In common parlance, the term reidentification is used to describe criminal or mischievous attempts to discover the identity of individuals whose private information has been deidentified. In the parlance of professionals who work in the field of data privacy, the term "reidentification" has a different meaning. Reidentification is a legally sanctioned process whereby a petitioner requests an Institutional Review Board to re-establish the link between a deidentified specimen and its original identifier sequence. Reidentification may be scientifically and ethically justifiable if there is some question as to the validity of the original specimen (i.e., could there have been a sample mix-up?) or if exigent circumstances require that a human subject be informed of test results on his or her deidentified sample. It is the job of the Institutional Review Board to weigh the value of reidentification against the possible harm of violating an individual's privacy.

The subject of data identification and deidentification cannot be closed without mention of the National Patient Identifier. Readers from outside the United States are probably wondering why the United States agonizes over the problem of patient identification. In many other countries, individuals are given a unique national identifier, and all medical data associated with the individual is kept in a central data repository under the aegis of the government's health service. A single, permanent identifier is used by a patient throughout life, in every encounter with a hospital, clinic, or private physician. As a resource for researchers, the national patient identifier ensures the completeness of data sets and eliminates many of the problems associated with poorly implemented local identifier systems. [Glossary National Patient Identifier]

In the United States, there has been fierce resistance to the idea of national patient identifiers. The call for a national patient identification system is raised from time to time. The benefits to patients and to society are many. Regardless, US citizens are reluctant to have an identifying number that is associated with a federally controlled electronic record of their private medical information. In part, this distrust results from the lack of any national insurance system in the United States. Most health insurance in the United States is private, and private insurers have wide discretion over the fees and services provided to enrollees. There is a fear that if there were a national patient identifier with centralized electronic medical records, insurers would withhold reimbursements or raise premiums or otherwise endanger the health of patients. Because the cost of US medical care is the highest in the world, medical bills for uninsured patients can quickly mount, impoverishing individuals and families [25]. Realistically, no data is safe. Medical records can be stolen, and governments can demand access to medical records, when necessary [26]. [Glossary Encryption]

Life has its compromises. Everyone wants their privacy and we all get angry when we hear that our confidential information has been stolen. Data breaches today may involve hundreds of millions of confidential records. The majority of Americans have had social security numbers, credit card information, and private identifiers (e.g., birth dates, city of birth, names of relatives) misappropriated or stolen. It's natural to object to anything that might jeopardize our privacy. Nonetheless, we must ask ourselves the following: "Is it rational to forfeit the very real opportunity of developing new safe and effective treatments for serious diseases, for the very small likelihood that someone will crack your deidentified research record and somehow leverage this information to your disadvantage?" [Glossary Social Security Number]

Suppose everyone in the United States were given a choice: you can be included in a national patient identifier system, or you can opt out. Most likely, there would be many millions of citizens who would opt out of the offer, seeing no particular advantage in having a national patient identifier, and sensing some potential harm. Now, suppose you were told that if you chose to opt out, you would not be permitted to use any of the therapeutic or preventive benefits that come from studies performed with data collected from the national patient identifier system. These lost benefits would include safe and effective drugs, warnings of emerging epidemics, information on side effects associated with your medications, biomarker tests for preventable illnesses, and so on. Those who made no effort to help the system would be barred from any of the benefits that the system provided. Would you reconsider your refusal to cooperate, if you knew the consequences? Of course, this is a fanciful scenario, but it makes a point.

SECTION 8.3 WHAT DO WE DO WITH NONQUANTITATIVE, DESCRIPTIVE DATA?

> Not everything that counts can be counted, and not everything that can be counted counts.
> **William Bruce Cameron**

Wouldn't it be grand if life was fundamentally quantitative? Don't get your hopes up. Data analysis books typically ignore the topic of nonquantitative data, but any serious work in the field of Precision Medicine must deal with the fact that most medical data is textual and nonquantitative: descriptions from the radiologists, diagnostic comments from the pathologists, operating room reports, nursing plans, discharge summaries, and lab notes. Furthermore, the quantitative data in medicine has very little value unless it is annotated with lots and lots of text. For example, if you're given a PSA value, you'll need access to the units of measurement, and the laboratory protocol employed to measure the value, and the instrument in which the protocol was deployed, and the name of the laboratory where the test was done, the name of the technician who performed the test, and on and on. You may not need all this descriptive data, in all circumstances, but when you start to merge data collected from different facilities, you'll find that data has no meaning without textual description.

In this section, we will review two of the simplest computational methods whereby scientists can draw useful information from descriptive data: autocoding and indexing. Before getting into the mechanics of the process, though, let's look at one example of data that is purely descriptive, to see how it relates to Precision Medicine.

Anatomic pathologists are the doctors who examine tissues under a microscope and render diagnoses based on the morphology of cells. All such data is descriptive and nonquantitative. For nearly two centuries, the field of anatomic pathology has sailed along smoothly with its microscopes and glass slides and descriptive diagnoses. Lately, though, the seas have been rough, and the purely morphologic approach to pathology has lost much of its glory. Here are some of the drawbacks to traditional morphologic examination of tissues. [Glossary Anatomic pathologist]

- The results of tissue examination are nonquantitative and cannot be usefully inserted into databases without standardizing the pathology reports, a process that has never been achieved to anyone's satisfaction. For example, autopsy reports are generated at great expense, but these reports are rarely inserted into databases that can be queried and analyzed. Hence, the studies that come from autopsy services are often case reports of an anecdotal nature or they are studies based on a limited number of cases chosen to meet some qualifying criteria [27–30].

- Morphology cannot always help us distinguish the clinical subtypes of disease. One of the chief complaints leveled at pathologists is that their diagnoses are nonpredictive. Two individuals with the same lesion, as assessed on morphologic grounds, may respond differently to treatment. The presumption is that morphologic features cannot distinguish biologically distinct subtypes of disease [31–33]. Much of the impetus behind Precision Medicine is based on the premise that nonmorphologic approaches (e.g., gene profiles, metabolic profiles, proteomic profiles, and biochemical markers) will provide diagnoses with improved clinical relevance.
- The accuracy of morphologic assessments is highly dependent on sampling. Pathologists do not examine every cell of every lesion that is diagnosed. Pathologic examination is always a sampling process, in which thin cross-sections of the specimen are examined under the microscope. If the cross-section lacks diagnostic cells, the pathologist cannot reach a correct diagnosis [34]. In theory, sensitive quantitative measurements of diagnostic biomarkers, using whole tissue homogenates, will yield a correct diagnosis in cases where histologic sampling errors might otherwise occur.
- Morphologic diagnoses are inconsistent. It is not uncommon for a pathologist to disagree over histologic diagnosis [35]. Some diagnostic entities have subtle findings, and ancillary evaluations such as cancer grade, depth of invasion, and clinical significance can be points of contention [36–40].
- Morphologic diagnoses are sometimes wrong. Every pathologist understands that diagnostic errors are inevitable. Quality assurance programs that find and review errors are generally considered to be the most realistic way of coping with the problem [41].

Despite its many drawbacks, no quantitative methods have been shown to be better than morphologic examination for diagnosing tumors and for separating tumors into clinically useful subtypes. The influence of the common light microscope has not dimmed in the molecular age [42,43]. What is the basis for the enduring popularity of histologic analysis? Imagine, for a moment, that you have made a life-long career studying human histology, and that you had never studied tissues from any other animal. One day, just by accident, a colleague shows you a photomicrograph of a single mouse liver cell. You take one brief glance, no longer than a single breath, and in that moment of time, your understanding of the natural world has changed forever. It takes you just a moment to see that the mouse liver cell is morphologically identical to the human liver cell. All the mouse organelles look like human organelles. The nucleus looks like a human nucleus: same size, same chromatin texture. This tells you that mouse cells have the same molecular organization, the same biochemical machinery, the same structures, in the same quantities, and the same cell-type functionality, as the human. You infer that the mouse almost certainly has nearly the same genes as the human, and that the mouse and the human must have a close phylogenetic relationship [44]. This has been a lot to absorb, and it's all done in an instant, but it illustrates some of the power of cellular examination.

Tissue examination captures the essential features of biological expression, but it does not necessarily provide us with any great insight into the mechanisms that produce the morphologic changes. When we look at cells under a microscope, we see clues, not answers. The clues are always nonquantitative, and not directly amenable to mathematical analysis.

Despite its vagaries, nonquantitative data is more important to the advancement of Precision Medicine than is quantitative data. Much of the captured quantitative data has no direct relevance to any disease processes. We cannot analyze measurements until we can relate those measurements to a hypothesis or biological process. Hence, much of the work of quantitative data analysis in the realm of Precision Medicine is expended trying to determine the meaning of nonquantitative descriptive information.

As an example of the role of morphology in Precision Medicine, let's look at a quintessentially morphologic group of features that pathologists love to examine: the inclusion body. Inclusion bodies are small intracellular objects that can be seen in some of the cells of pathologic lesions, and which are absent or seldom seen in normal cells. There are literally hundreds of morphologic types of inclusion bodies, and some of them are considered to be pathognomonic of particular diseases (i.e., present in every case of the disease, and absent from all other diseases and from normal tissues). Just to give you an idea of the variety of named inclusion bodies, here is a sampling of inclusion bodies every pathologist would know: ferruginous bodies (seen after asbestos exposure), Mallory bodies (seen in liver diseases), psammoma bodies (commonly seen in papillary thyroid cancer and meningiomas), Lewy bodies (seen in Lewy body dementia), Barr bodies (the inactivated x chromosome in the nuclei of females), Bunina bodies (seen in motor neuron diseases).

Every inclusion body tells a biological story, and every biological story provides us with a new opportunity to advance the field of Precision Medicine. Here is a list of general features of inclusion bodies that make them useful to disease researchers.

- Inclusion bodies are, on occasion, pathognomonic for one disease. In some cases, the disease is named for its characteristic inclusion (e.g., Lewy body dementia, ragged red fiber myopathy, distal myopathy with rimmed vacuoles, inclusion conjunctivitis).
- Most inclusion bodies are composed of an insoluble substance. The fact that the substance is not soluble tells us a great deal about the body. The location of a body within the cell (e.g., in a lysosome, in an autophagosome, in the endoplasmic reticulum) indicates how the cell processed the inclusion.
- Understanding the chemical or biological nature of the body nearly always tells us something about the disease in which the body is found.
- If a morphologically identical body occurs in diseases a, b, and c, and if you know the etiology of diseases b and c and you know nothing about the etiology of disease a, then you can infer that there must be some pathway, common to all three diseases, that accounts for the inclusion.
- When an animal model of a human disease contains the same inclusion body that is seen in its human equivalent, then it strongly suggests that the body is related to the pathogenesis of the disease. When animal models of the disease lack the body, it suggests that the body is either an inconsequential epiphenomenon, or that the animal model is not a faithful model of the human disease.

We know that inclusion bodies do not appear by magic. Efforts to explain the existence of bodies have led to fundamental advances in medicine (Fig. 8.1).

The easiest way to understand inclusion bodies is to imagine that the human cell is equivalent, in many fundamental ways, to a condominium apartment. If you're too lazy to take out the trash, it accumulates in the apartment. If there's one room that you refuse to clean, the garbage will stay in that one room, and will be composed of the items you keep in that room. If you have no trash cans in your apartment, garbage may accumulate where it shouldn't. If

FIG. 8.1 Cytomegalovirus infection of the lung. Near the center of the image is an infected pneumocyte with a highly enlarged nucleus. The bulk of the nucleus is occupied by dense inclusions, sometimes called Cowdry bodies, containing viral nucleocapsids. Surrounding the inclusion is a clear zone. Such nuclear inclusions, observed with all species of herpes viruses that infect humans, have long served as an important clue to the diagnosis and the pathogenesis of viral diseases. *From U.S. Centers for Disease Control and Prevention Public Health Image Library.*

there is a problem with your sewage (a blocked pipe, or no water), then the bathroom will be the source of very specific types of waste products. If your local garbage collector refuses to take more than a certain quota of garbage each week, and you exceed the quota, you can expect your garbage to accumulate. If you are creating garbage that is of a shape that makes it impossible to eject through your door, then you will have an accumulation of that specific type of garbage. If mice take refuge in your apartment, you'll find mouse droppings under the stove and under the refrigerator. The annoying responsibilities of apartment living are many.

Basically, examining inclusion bodies is not much different from inspecting a filthy apartment. Every process known to account for cytoplasmic inclusion bodies can be fully replicated within your own apartment or house, with a little imagination. Let's make a list.

- Overproduction of a normal cellular constituent at a rate that exceeds the rate at which it can be eliminated. (e.g., Gaucher cells seen in Gaucher disease, but occasionally observed in active macrophages of unaffected individuals [45])
- Material that simply cannot be broken down or extruded (e.g., ferruginous bodies of asbestosis)
- Cytopathic effects that produce an abnormal zone within the cell (e.g., koilocytotic changes within squamous cervical cells infected with human papillomavirus) (Fig. 8.2)

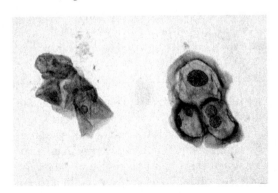

FIG. 8.2 Koilocytosis. The clump of flat epithelial cells on the left contains normal squamous cells of the type that line the uterine cervix. The clump of three cells on the right contains squamous epithelial cells demonstrating koilocytosis, a cytopathic effect produced by human papillomavirus infection. Notice that the nuclei are enlarged, appearing ~2–3 times as large as normal nuclei (on left). Surrounding each nucleus (right clump) is an abnormal zone of pale cytoplasm, typical of koilocytosis. Beyond the pale zone is a thinner zone of normal-appearing cytoplasm extending out to the cell membrane. *From Wikipedia, courtesy of Euthman, who contributed the photograph to the public domain.*

– Degenerate protein molecules that are malformed and indigestible (e.g., tauopathies and synucleinopathies [46])
– Accumulation of proteins and other molecules synthesized by invasive organisms (e.g., Cowdry bodies of Herpes simplex virus, varicella-zoster virus, and cytomegalovirus)
– Defects in the transport mechanisms (e.g., the vesicular transport disorders [47])
– Defects in lysosomes or in specific lysosomal enzymes that result in the intralysosomal accumulation of undigested products of normal metabolism (e.g., Hurler disease, Hunter disease)
– Remnants of defective cellular constituents (e.g., Cabot rings in red blood cells, Michaelis-Gutmann bodies of malakoplakia)
– Unphagocytosed organisms (e.g., Whipple disease, in which a reduction of macrophage-1 antigen results in the accumulation of Tropheryma whipplei organisms in macrophages [48])

Aside from the body itself, which can be analyzed for chemical composition, medical scientists can draw inferences of the body's role in disease development. This is accomplished by determining whether the body is cell-type specific or found in various other cell types; whether the body is associated with an inherited syndrome or acquired after exposure to a specific toxin; whether the body is pathognomonic for one disease or found in various diseases or in disease-free individuals; whether the body is reversible (i.e., disappears, possibly after treatment); and the stage of disease in which the body first appears.

For example, scientists have long wondered whether tau proteins, a hallmark of several neurodegenerative diseases, are causal factors, or just innocent bystanders. Frontotemporal dementia and parkinsonism linked to chromosome 17 (FTDP-17) is an inherited disease characterized by mutations in the gene coding for Tau. In this disease, a specific Tau inclusion is always found in the pathologic lesions and never in control subjects. Most importantly, the appearance of the tau inclusion always precedes the development of neural degeneration; hence, the inclusion does not occur as a consequence of neural degeneration. All these observations have led researchers to believe that the altered Tau protein plays a causal role in the pathogenesis of FTDP-17 [46].

The point here is that advances in medicine nearly always begin with observations of biological processes that occur in diseased tissues (e.g., the occurrence of inclusion bodies). Morphology tells the shrewd bioinformaticist what to look for and how to relate findings to disease processes. It is unrealistic to think that data analysts, with access to large collections of quantitative biomedical data, can contribute to the field of Precision Medicine, without the benefit of descriptive observations.

There is a relatively new field that spans the chasm between the medical scientists and computer scientists. This field is known as medical informatics, or sometimes, biomedical informatics. Much of this field is devoted to the task of transforming biomedical free text into a form that allows computers to quickly retrieve all of the information pertaining to a query. The way that this is achieved is with automatic coding (i.e., attaching terms found in medical free-text to a standard representation of the term that computers can find) and indexing (i.e., reorganizing the coded terms extracted from the text into forms that facilitate the retrieval)

Autocoding involves tagging terms with an identifier code that corresponds to a synonymous term listed in a standard nomenclature. For example, a medical nomenclature might contain the term renal cell carcinoma, a type of kidney cancer, attaching a unique identifier code for the term, such as "C9385000." There are about 50 recognized synonyms and near-synonyms for "renal cell carcinoma." A few of these equivalent terms are listed here to show that a single concept can be expressed many different ways: adenocarcinoma arising from kidney, adenocarcinoma involving kidney, cancer arising from kidney, carcinoma of kidney, grawitz tumor, grawitz tumor, hypernephroid tumor, hypernephroma, kidney adenocarcinoma, renal adenocarcinoma, and renal cell carcinoma. All of these terms could be assigned the same identifier code, "C9385000." In the case of "renal cell carcinoma," if all of the 50+ synonymous terms, appearing anywhere in a medical text, were tagged with the code "C938500," then a search engine could retrieve documents containing this code, regardless of which specific synonym was queried (e.g., a query on Grawitz tumor would retrieve documents containing the word "hypernephroid tumor"). The search engine would simply translate the query word, "Grawitz tumor" into its nomenclature code, "C938500" and would pull every record that had been tagged by the code.

The process of coding a text document involves finding all the terms that belong to a specific nomenclature, and tagging those terms with their corresponding code. A nomenclature is a specialized vocabulary, usually containing terms that comprehensively cover a well-defined domain of knowledge. For example, there may be a nomenclature of diseases, or celestial bodies, or makes and models of automobiles. Nomenclatures have many purposes: to enhance interoperability and integration, to allow synonymous terms to be aggregated and retrieved, to support comprehensive analyses of textual data, to express detail, to tag information in textual documents, and to drive down the complexity of documents. [Glossary Interoperability]

Traditionally, nomenclature coding, much like language translation, has been considered a specialized and highly detailed task that is best accomplished by human beings. Just as there are highly trained translators who will prepare foreign language versions of popular texts, there are highly trained coders, intimately familiar with specific nomenclatures, who create tagged versions of documents. Tagging documents with nomenclature codes is serious business. If the coding is flawed, the consequences can be dire. In 2009, the Department of Veterans Affairs sent out hundreds of letters to veterans with the devastating news that they had contracted Amyotrophic Lateral Sclerosis, also known as Lou Gehrig disease, a fatal degenerative neurologic condition. About 600 of the recipients did not, in fact, have the disease. The VA retracted these letters, attributing the confusion to a coding error [49]. Coding text is difficult. Human coders are inconsistent, idiosyncratic, and prone to error. Coding accuracy for humans seems to fall in the range of 85%–90% [50]. [Glossary Precision, Accuracy versus precision]

When dealing with text in gigabyte and greater quantities, human coding is simply out of the question. There is not enough time or money or talent to manually code the text. Computerized coding (i.e., autocoding) is the only practical solution. Autocoding is a specialized form of machine translation, the field of computer science wherein dealing with drawing meaning from narrative text, or translating narrative text from one language to another. Not surprisingly, autocoding algorithms have been adopted directly from the field of machine translation, particularly algorithms for natural language processing. A popular approach to autocoding involves using the natural rules of language to find words or phrases found in text and matching them to nomenclature terms. Ideally the correct text term is matched to its equivalent nomenclature term, regardless of the way that the term is expressed. For instance, the term "adenocarcinoma of lung" has much in common with alternate terms that have minor variations in word order, plurality, inclusion of articles, terms split by a word inserted for informational enrichment, and so on. Alternate forms would be "adenocarcinoma of the lung," "adenocarcinoma of the lungs," "lung adenocarcinoma," and "adenocarcinoma found in the lung." A natural language algorithm takes into account grammatic variants, allowable alternate term constructions, word roots, and syntax variation. Clever improvements on natural language methods might include string similarity scores, intended to find term equivalences in cases where grammatic methods come up short.

A limitation of the natural language approach to autocoding is encountered when synonymous terms lack etymologic commonality. Consider the term "renal cell carcinoma." Synonyms include terms that have no grammatic relationship with one another. For example, hypernephroma, and Grawitz tumor are synonyms for renal cell carcinoma. It is impossible to compute the equivalents among these terms through the implementation of natural language rules or word similarity algorithms. The only way to attain adequate synonymy is through the use of a comprehensive nomenclature that lists every synonym for every canonical term in the knowledge domain.

Speed is another drawback of natural language autocoders. The best natural language autocoders are pitifully slow. The reason for the slowness relates to their algorithms, which require the following steps, at a bare minimum: parsing text into sentences; parsing sentences into grammatic units; rearranging the units of the sentence into grammatically permissible combinations; expanding the combinations based on stem forms of words; allowing for singularities and pluralities of words, and matching the allowable variations against the terms listed in the nomenclature. A typical natural language autocoder parses text at about 1 kilobyte per second. This means that if an autocoder must parse and code a terabyte of textual material, it would require one thousand million seconds to execute, or about 30 years. Modern data repositories contain terabytes of data; thus, natural language autocoding software, like manual coding, is unsuitable for the task.

A faster alternative to natural language parsing is lexical parsing. This involves parsing text, word by word, looking for exact matches between runs of words and entries in a nomenclature. When a match occurs, the words in the text that matched the nomenclature term are assigned the nomenclature code that corresponds to the matched term [51,52]. For the truly impatient, on-the-fly coding is now feasible. Using this method, a text corpus can be queried for any term, and all the records containing the exact term, or any synonym for the term, are quickly collected, using a very efficient algorithm [53].

Textual data that has been autocoded can subsequently be indexed, a simple process that greatly expands the scientific utility of data. Thoughtfully designed indexes organize the conceptual content of free-text. Ultimately, an index gives us an opportunity to grow beyond the text, revealing relationships among the contained terms that could not have been otherwise found. Here are a few of the specific strengths of modern indexes [2,4].

- An index can be read, as a stand-alone document, to acquire a quick view of the book's contents [54].
- When you do a "find" search in a query box, your search may come up empty if there is nothing in the text that matches your query. This can be very frustrating if you know that the text covers the topic entered into query box. Indexes avoid the problem of fruitless searches. By browsing the index, you can often find the term you need, without foreknowledge of its exact wording within the text. When you find a term in the index, you may also find closely related terms, subindexed under your search term, or alphabetically indexed above or below your search term.
- Searches on computerized indexes are nearly instantaneous, because the index is precompiled. Even when the text is massive (e.g., Gigabytes, Terabytes), information retrieval via an index will be nearly instantaneous.
- Indexes can be tied to a classification or other specialized nomenclature. Doing so permits the analyst to know the relationships among different topics within the index, and within the text [55].
- Many indexes are crossindexed, providing a set of relationships among different terms, that a clever data analyst might find useful.
- Indexes can be merged. If the location entries for index terms are annotated with some identifier for the source text, then searches on a merged index will yield locators that point to specific locations from all of the sources.
- Indexes can be embedded directly in the text [56]. Whereas conventional indexes contain locators to the text, embedded indexes are built into the locations where the index term if found in the text, with each location listing other locations where the term can be found. These on-site lists of term locations can be hidden from the viewer with formatting instructions (e.g., pop-up link tags in the case of HTML). Programmers can reconstitute conventional indexes from location-embedded tags, as required.
- Indexes can be created to satisfy a particular goal; and the process of creating a made-to-order index can be repeated again and again. For example, if you have a massive or complex data resource devoted to ornithology, and you have an interest in the geographic location of species, you might want to create an index specifically keyed to localities, or you might want to add a locality subentry for every indexed bird name in your original index. Such indexes can be constructed as add-ons, when needed.
- Indexes can be updated. If terminologies change, there is nothing stopping you from rebuilding the index with an updated nomenclature, without modifying your source data. [Glossary Specification, Standard]
- Indexes are created after the database has been created. In some cases, the data manager does not envision the full potential of a data resource until after it is built. The index can be designed to encourage novel uses for the data resource.
- Indexes can occasionally substitute for the original text. A telephone book is an example of an index that serves its purpose without being attached to a related data source (e.g., caller logs, switching diagrams).

You'll notice that the majority of the listed properties of indexes were impossible to achieve before the advent of computers. Today, data scientists can prepare innovative and powerful indexes, from gigabytes of descriptive data, with great ease and speed [2,13].

There is a perception that Precision Medicine will somehow replace imprecise descriptive data with precise quantitative data. More often, Precision Medicine is about using precise, quantitative data to better understand imprecise descriptive data. Hence, the job of the data analyst in the era of Precision Medicine is not to abandon descriptive information, but to make descriptive data relevant.

SECTION 8.4 INCREDIBLY SIMPLE METHODS TO UNDERSTAND PRECISION MEDICINE DATA

Every simplifying principle in biology, no matter how basic, represents compelling ideas and is potentially applicable to other areas of thought.
Alain Berthoz and Giselle Weiss [57]

On two occasions I have been asked, 'If you put into the machine wrong figures, will the right answers come out?' I am not able rightly to apprehend the kind of confusion of ideas that could provoke such a question.
Charles Babbage (1791–1871)

Before you call in the statisticians and the deep data analysts, do some data review of your own. If you can't make sense of your own data, then chances are that your data analysts won't be able to help you, either. By far, the most important analysis tool is the human brain. A set of personal attributes that include critical thinking, an inquisitive mind, the patience to spend hundreds of hours reviewing data, is certain to come in handy.

Expertise in analytic algorithms is an overrated skill. Most data analysis projects require the ability to understand the data, and this can often be accomplished with simple data visualization tools. The application of rigorous mathematical and statistical algorithms typically comes at the end of the project, after the key relationships among data objects are discovered. It is important to remember that if your old data is verified, organized, annotated, and preserved, the analytic process can be repeated and improved. In most cases, the first choice of analytic method is not the best choice. No single analytic method is critical when the data analyst has the opportunity to repeat his work applying many different methods, all the while attaining a better understanding of the data and more meaningful computational results. [Glossary P-value, Overfitting, Type errors]

Here are a few very simple data analysis techniques that you can do without any expertise in statistics, using only a few free and widely available general software utilities.

- **Looking at the data (seeing what's there and what's not there)**

It is a commonly held misconception that the purpose of data analysis is to find answers to your questions. More often than not, the job of the data analyst is to understand what the data is trying to say. If you want to understand your data, you need to spend some time acquainting yourself with the contents. Toward this end, here are a few recommendations.

- Find a free ASCII editor. Popular word processors cannot open and read large data files, above about 100 MB in length. Free software is available that will quickly open files in the rage of 100 MB to 1 GB, allowing you to skim through the contents. Two of the more popular, freely available editors are Emacs and vi (also available under the name vim). Downloadable versions are available for Linux, Windows, and Macintosh systems.
- Read the "readme" file. In prior decades, large collections of data were often assembled as files within subdirectories, and these files could be downloaded in part or in toto, via ftp (file transfer protocol). Traditionally, a "readme" file would be included with the files, and the "readme" file would explain the purpose, contents, and organization of the data. In some cases, an index file might be available, providing a list of terms covered in the files, and their locations. The "readme" files are much like treasure maps. The data files contain great treasure, but you're unlikely to find anything of value unless you study the map.
- Assess the number of records included in the data files. If there are far fewer records than you had hoped for, you can save yourself a lot of wasted time and energy pursuing analyses that are insufficiently powered by the data.
- Determine how data objects are identified and classified. If you know the identifier for a data object, you can collect all of the information associated with the object, regardless of its location in the resource. If the data records are not properly identified, it is unlikely that the data resource will meet your needs. If the data objects are assigned membership in a competent classification, you can draw inferences from the data.
- Determine whether data objects are self-descriptive. If not the data resource may still be of great value, but you'll need to acquire expertise in the construction of the data, and you will probably need the assistance of software designed or customized for the data.
- Assess whether the data is complete and representative. You must be prepared to spend many hours reviewing individual records. It may sometimes help to run simple query scripts that scour the contents of the data resource looking for representative samples of all the kinds of data you would expect or need to find. You will be surprised to learn that many huge data resources omit essential forms of data. It is not at all odd to examine a surgical pathology database with hundreds of thousands of records that contains no skin biopsies and no hematology cases. In some centers, skin biopsies are handled by the dermatology department and are not received by surgical pathology. Likewise, a hospital may send all of its blood work and marrow biopsies to the hematology department, bypassing surgical pathology. Anyone in need of a complete repertoire of cases, from all anatomic sites, would need to somehow unite the surgical pathology data with data held by other departments, or would need to seek the resources of another hospital.

Only if you take the time to study raw data, can you spot systemic deficiencies in the data.

- **Counting data objects**

A half-century after the Korean War hostilities ended, the US Department of State downsized its long-standing count of US military war deaths to 36,616 down from an earlier figure of about 54,000. The drop of 17,000 deaths resulted from the exclusion of US military deaths that occurred during the Korean War, in countries outside Korea [58]. The old numbers reflected deaths during the Korean War; the newer number reflects deaths occurring due to the Korean War. Counting is a more difficult task than we might imagine.

All data analysis begins with counting. Systemic counting errors account for unreproducible or misleading results. Surprisingly, there is very little written about proper counting techniques. Presumably, the subject is considered too trivial for serious study. Here are a few examples, from the realm of medicine, where society may have benefited if counting were taken more seriously.

- Beachy Head is a cliff in England with a straight vertical drop and a beautiful seaview. It is a favorite jumping off point for suicides. The suicide rate at Beachy Head dropped as sharply as the cliff when the medical examiner made a small policy change. From a certain moment on, bodies found at the cliff bottom would be counted as suicides only if their postmortem toxicology screen was negative for alcohol. Intoxicated subjects were pronounced dead by virtue of accident (i.e., not suicide) [59]. The abrupt change in policy nullified all prior suicide-related data.
- Sudden Infant Death Syndrome (SIDS, also known as crib death) was formerly considered to be a disease of unknown etiology that caused infants to stop breathing, and die, often during sleep. Today, most SIDS deaths are presumed to be due to unintentional suffocation from bedclothes, often in an overheated environment, and aggravated by a prone (i.e., face down) sleeping position. Consequently, about half of infant deaths that would have been diagnosed as SIDS, in past decades, are now diagnosed as unintentional suffocations. This diagnostic switch has resulted in a trend characterized by increasing numbers of infant suffocations and a decreasing number of SIDS cases [60]. The new counts are, in part, artifactual, arising from changes in reporting criteria.
- The Human Genome Project is a massive bioinformatics project in which multiple laboratories helped to sequence the 3 billion base pair haploid human genome. The project began its work in 1990, a draft human genome was prepared in 2000, and a completed genome was finished in 2003, marking the start of the so-called postgenomics era. There are about 2 million species of proteins synthesized by human cells. If every protein had its own private gene containing its specific genetic code, then there would be about two million protein-coding genes contained in the human genome. As it turns out, this estimate is completely erroneous. Analysis of the human genome indicates that there are somewhere between 20,000 and 150,000 genes. Why are the current estimates so much lower than the number of proteins, and why is there such a large variation in the lower and upper estimates (20,000–150,000)? Once again, we see that counting (and recounting) is a serious endeavor, requiring data analysts to continually re-examine their assumptions.

Often, data analysts do not really know how or what to count until they have come to fully understand the data source. Unfortunately, we often cannot fully understand the data source until we have finished counting its data. Perceived this way, counting is a bootstrapping problem. In the case of proteins, a small number of genes can account for a much larger number of protein species, because proteins can be assembled from combinations of genes, and the final form of a unique protein can be modified by posttranslational events (e.g., folding variations, chemical modifications, sequence shortening, clustering by fragments). The methods used to count protein-coding genes vary [61]. One technique might look for sequences that mark the beginning and the end of a coding sequence; another method might look for segments containing base triplets that correspond to amino acid codons. The former method might count genes that code for elements other than proteins, and the latter might miss fragments whose triplet sequences do not match known protein sequences [62]. Improved counting methods are being developed to replace older methods, but a definitive number always eludes our grasp. [Glossary Codon]

After data is counted, accurately or not, you should plot the results. Plotting data is quick, easy, and surprisingly productive. Within minutes, the data analyst can assess long-term trends, short-term, and periodic trends, the general shape of data distributions, and general notions of the kinds of functions that might represent the data (e.g., linear, exponential, power series). Simply knowing that the data can be expressed as a graph is immeasurably reassuring to the data analyst.

For those with a bit of computer savvy, there are many excellent data visualization tools that are widely available. Matplotlib, a plotting library for the Python programming language, and Gnuplot, a graphing utility available for a variety of operating systems, are open source applications that can be downloaded, at no cost, and are available at www. sourceforge.net [2,13,16,63]. Every scientist should attain some rudimentary skills with a graphing utility.

Gnuplot is extremely easy to use, either as stand-alone scripts containing gnuplot commands, or from the system command line, or from the command line editor provided with the application software. Most types of plots can be created with a single gnuplot command line. Gnuplot can fit a mathematically expressed curve to a set of data using the nonlinear least-squares Marquardt-Levenberg algorithm [64,65]. Gnuplot can also provide a set of statistical descriptors (e.g., median, mean, standard deviation) for plotted sets of data. If you have some programming skills, you can transform and filter your data, before plotting.

After the plot is graphed, adept data analysts can sometimes eyeball the data distribution and guess the kind of function that might model the data. For example, a symmetric bell-shaped curve is probably a normal or Gaussian distribution. A curve with an early peak and a long, flat tail is often a power law distribution. Curves that are simple exponential or linear can also be assayed by visual inspection. Distributions that may be described by a Fourier series or a power series, or that can be separated into intervals and described by several different distributions, can also be assessed (Fig. 8.3). [Glossary Power law]

– Co-occurrences

One of the most ancient maxims in medicine, that has been taught for over 2000 years, is the heedful tip to beware the man with the glass eye and the enlarged liver. It is uncommon to find a person with a glass eye. It is also uncommon to find a person with an enlarged liver. When both are present, the cause is likely to be a primary melanoma of the eye that has necessitated extraction and replacement with a glass ball; with metastases to the liver (causing liver enlargement) [66].

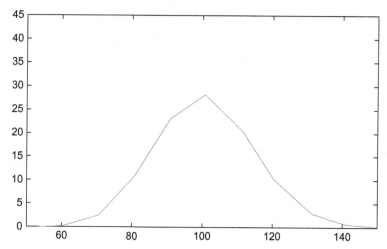

FIG. 8.3   A normal (bell-shaped and symmetric) curve. *From Jules J. Berman.*

Another example of the related co-occurrences of two rare conditions occurs when bronchiectasis (dilatation of the bronchus) and cutis laxa (loose skin) are observed in the same patient. Both conditions can be found to occur in Mounier-Kuhn syndrome, a inherited disease that may not express itself clinically until the affected patient reaches adulthood, at which time bronchiectasis may produce clinical symptoms (e.g., pneumonia) and cutis laxa may be noticed. The co-occurrence of both conditions might suggest that the underlying defect might involve a mutation in a protein whose deficiency leads to a reduction in the rigidity or tension of connective tissue or muscle. An awareness of this rare disease might also lead an astute clinician to look for an inherited cause of tracheobronchomegaly in young adults with unexplained recurrent bouts of pneumonia [67,68].

One last example: the co-occurrence of Horner syndrome and heterochromasia iridum. Horner syndrome is a constellation of symptoms that occur when the sympathetic trunk of the peripheral nervous system, involving the chest neck, and head, is damaged. Symptoms occur on the same side of the body as the trunk damage, and classic signs of disease include miosis (constricted pupil), partial ptosis (droopy eyelid), and decreased sweating. The syndrome may occur congenitally, often resulting from birth trauma, or can be acquired later in life (often from trauma or from a tumor encroaching on truncal nerves). Pigmentation of the iris does not occur in the absence of sympathetic innervation. Hence, differences in eye color (heterochromasia iridum), with less pigmentation in the eye affected by Horner syndrome, are a rare co-occurrence. Heterochromasia iridum is observed in congenital cases of Horner syndrome, but has also been reported in an adult [69].

Experience indicates that when two rare diseases or conditions occur together, we can almost always find a link, if we look hard enough [70]. This is particularly true when the co-occurrences are ordered (i.e., disease A nearly always precedes disease B). Finding co-occurrences is an extremely easy simple computational task.

– **Filtering data**

There is a commonly held belief that computers can process large amounts of complex data (nucleotide sequences, measurements, relational rules) and quickly come to a correct conclusion, at lightning speed. Thus, with the advent of supercomputers, and with the availability of high-quality molecular and biomedical data, new safe and effective treatments for diseases will be momentarily forthcoming. Of course, our experiences over the past few decades should lead us to understand that biomedical problems cannot be solved by computers. Life and disease are too complex for facile computational solutions.

What, then, is the primary role of computers in the realm of Precision Medicine? Computers help scientists in many ways, but one of the simplest, and most productive uses of computers is as a filtering agent that parses through enormous troves of data to produce an aggregate output that fulfills a set of criterion.

Here are just a few examples:

- Extract the names, and count the occurrences, of every organism encountered in a diagnostic microbiology laboratory
- Extract a list of genes that contain a particular subsequence
- Extract all palindromes from a gene sequence database
- Extract, from a surgical pathology database, all neoplasms of germ cell origin
- From a database of whole genome sequences from tumors, select all samples containing a specific mutation of BRAF
- From a patient's DNA sample, find sequences that match entries in a database of collected polymorphisms

Nothing is better than a computer at searching and retrieving data that has a specific feature of interest. Regardless of the programming language employed, the basic algorithm for all these activities is always the same:

1. Go to the database of interest.
2. Open the database for reading.
3. Parse through the entire database, object by object.
4. Within each data object, go to the location where the data of interest is contained (e.g., the sequence data, the diagnostic line, the outcome data).
5. Compare the contained data with what you're looking for.
6. If it's what you want, add the data to your output file and include the data object's identifier.
7. Continue through the entire data set for every data object in the collection.
8. Continue onto other databases, if desired.
9. When all the parsing if finished, save and close the output file.

The research scientist can look at the data file; refining the search if the output is too large; expanding the search if the output is too small; conducting new searches based on the findings of the original search.

Most of the basic search/compare/retrieve algorithms can be written in under a dozen lines of computer code. A resourceful scientist can make serious contributions to the field of Precision Medicine using one basic program that can be modified to meet any desired search criteria. Free, open source, prefabricated source code for such projects are readily available [2,13,16,63].

– Profiling Data

Data profiling involves creating a distillation of the most salient features of a data object that can be used for comparison with other objects. When a unique, identifying profile can be expressed as a character string, or a number, it is called a data signature. The algorithms for creating data profiles are many. Various profiling algorithms have been suggested for text [71], fingerprints, cancers genes [72], images, and web pages. Some of the attractions of profiling are:

1. A profile is much smaller than the object being profiled, making it easier to compare different data objects.
2. Profiles can be precomputed and encapsulated within the data object or archived with the data object's identifier. By precomputing and storing profiles, a data object can be quickly compared against many profiles (jb simplify_jb.txt).
3. The process of developing successful profiles always teaches you something about the class of data objects you are studying. When a profile works well, its underlying assumptions about the important attributes of the data object are most likely correct [2].

There are two general types of data: quantitative and categorical. Quantitative data refers to measurements. Categorical data tells you whether a particular feature is present or absent, and analyses of categorical data depend heavily on counting and binning. In the natural world, categorical data almost always conforms to a Zipf distributions. George Kingsley Zipf (1902–50) was an American linguist who demonstrated that, for most languages, a small number of words account for the majority of occurrences of all the words found in prose. Specifically, he found that the frequency of any word is inversely proportional to its placement in a list of words, ordered by their decreasing frequencies in text. The first word in the frequency list will occur about twice as often as the second word in the list, three times as often as the third word in the list, and so on. Many large data collections follow a Zipf distribution (e.g., income distribution in a population, energy consumption by country, and so on). Beyond word counting, Zipf distributions describe much of what we encounter in everyday life. For example, a small number of rich people account for the majority of wealth. Likewise, a small number of diseases account for the vast majority of human illnesses. A small number of children account for the majority of the behavioral problems encountered in a school. A small number of states hold the majority of the population of the United States. A small number of book titles, compared with the total number of publications, account for the majority of book sales [73,74]. Other terms whose meanings are close to that of Zipf distribution, and that you will encounter in the data science literature, are Pareto principle and Power law (Fig. 8.4). [Glossary Pareto's principle, Zipf distribution]

A typical cumulative Zipf distribution is characterized by a smooth curve with a quick rise, followed by a long flattened tail. By comparing plots, we can usually tell, at a glance, whether a data set behaves like a Zipf distribution, or like a Gaussian distribution.

A clever analyst will always produce a frequency distribution for categorical data. A glance at the output always reveals a great deal about the contents of the data.

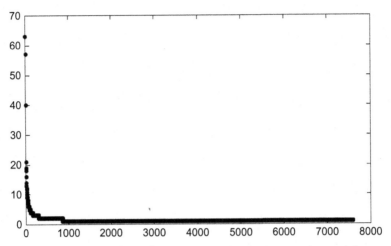

FIG. 8.4 A Zipf curve displaying the frequencies of work occurrences in a sample text. A few common words account for the bulk of word occurrences, as seen in the extreme left side of the graph. The curve drops quickly, to show a long tail of the many different words that occur infrequently in the text. In this example, about 8000 different words account for the long tail of the graph that hovers close to the abscissa as it moves toward the right side of the graph. Graphs with this shape are sometimes referred to as Zipf distributions. *From Jules J. Berman.*

Profiling does not always help. In 1999, the US National Cancer Institute announced a funding initiative intended to change the basis of tumor classification from morphological to molecular characteristics of tumors [75]. In response to the challenge, a number of techniques were developed and tested wherein tumors were profiled by their expressed genes (i.e., the genes that were transcribed into RNA). The thinking, at the time, reflected the hope that the biology of a tumor could be revealed by a quantitative analysis of the amounts and types of gene expression in the tumor. Despite some encouraging early work [76], the attempt to find expression patterns that were unique to specific diagnostic categories of tumors, or to specific stages of tumor development, or to specific types of tumor behavior, has not met with a high level of success [77–82].

– **Finding Subpopulations**

Much of Precision Medicine is based on finding subtypes of diseases. A disease subtype may be responsive to a new drug targeted against a pathway that is specific for the subtype. An easy way to find disease subtypes is to inspect graphed data for multiple peaks (i.e., so-called multimodal data distributions). Multimodality always tells us that the population is somehow nonhomogeneous. Hodgkin lymphoma is an example of a cancer with a bimodal age distribution. There is a peak in occurrences at a young age, and another peak of occurrences at a more advanced age. This two-peak phenomenon can be found whenever Hodgkin Lymphoma is studied in large populations [13] (Fig. 8.5).

In the case of Hodgkin lymphoma, lymphomas occurring in the young may share diagnostic features with the lymphomas occurring in the older population, but the occurrence of lymphomas in two separable populations may indicate that some important distinction may have

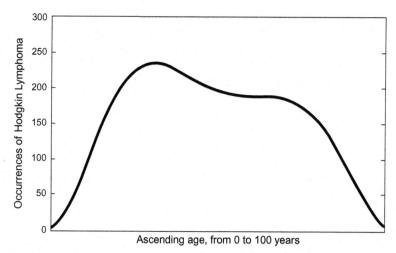

FIG. 8.5   The number of occurrences of Hodgkin Lymphoma in persons of different ages. There are two peaks in the graph. The first peak occurs in the early 20s. After the first peak, there is a trough, in the mid 40s, after which occurrences of cancer increase with age, toward a second peak. *From Jules J. Berman.*

been overlooked. Modern data resources, by providing large number of cases, make it easy to detect data incongruities, when they are present.

We see multimodality in some of the common diseases. There are two age peaks in diabetes. An early age peak corresponds to newly diagnosed cases of type 1 diabetes. The later age peak corresponds to newly diagnosed cases of type 2 diabetes. In this case, there is no disagreement that there are two biologically distinctive variants of diabetes, occurring with two different age peaks.

We see two age peaks in the development of neuroblastoma and for retinoblastoma, and these have been shown to correspond to an early age peak in young individuals with an inherited gene conferring cancer risk, and a second peak for adults whose disease is sporadic. As a general rule, inherited cancer syndromes produce cancers in children or young adults; are more likely to produce bilateral disease (e.g., both eyes, both adrenals); and account for the early peak in occurrences [83–89]. The sporadic tumors occur in an older age group and account for the majority of tumors. [Glossary Inherited retinoblastoma, Trilateral retinoblastoma]

Occasionally, we can determine the biological mechanism that accounts for a bimodal age distribution. For example, Kaposi sarcoma, caused by human herpesvirus-8, has two peaks in occurrence. The first peak, in young people, occurs in individuals with AIDS-related Kaposi sarcoma. The second peak occurs in older men, was a recognized disease entity prior to the AIDS epidemic (i.e., prior to 1980s), and is often referred to as "classic" Kaposi sarcoma. Classic Kaposi sarcoma is slow growing, arises on the skin, often on the leg, and does not metastasize. It tends to occur in individuals of Mediterranean descent.

In other diseases a two-peak age distribution is established, but we cannot, as yet, account for the differences. This would include ulcerative colitis, which has an early peak in the 15–25 year age group and another peak in individuals over the age of 50 [90]. Similarly, we know that there are young and old peaks in the ages of occurrence of myelodysplastic syndrome. In this case, we can associate a characteristic cytogenetic finding in many of the myelodysplatic disorders of childhood, but we have yet to establish the pathway that accounts for the two-peak distribution [91].

The 1918 flu epidemic, which is credited with killing 25–40 million individuals, worldwide, is an example of a disease whose peak lethality had three age peaks. Most flu epidemics cause deaths to two populations: the very young and the very old. Neither of these populations have the strength to withstand a disease that is generally debilitating and prone to causing pneumonia. The 1918 flu had a third peak occurring in deaths in young adults 20–40 years of age [92]. Theories abound purporting to explain the third peak in the 1918 flu, but at present, the mystery persists [92].

When the disease age distribution graph expresses two or more peaks, several possibilities should be considered:

- The two peaks result from two different diseases that mimic one another, clinically. Each disease occurs in a different age group. Data that erroneously combines the data on the two diseases produces a graph with two peaks.
- One disease is caused by either of two different environmental agents; one agent exerts its effect more slowly than the other agent. Two peaks in age distribution occur, corresponding to populations exposed to one or the other of the agents.
- One agent is responsible for causing disease in two age groups, but one subpopulation is exposed to a different concentration of disease-causing agent, or is exposed at a different age, than the general population of exposed individuals. As a result, two peaks occur in the age distribution.
- The disease can be caused by errors in either of two genes. One gene error produces disease in individuals at a very young age. The other gene error produces disease that becomes detectable in an older age group. As a result, two peaks occur in the age distribution.
- Two distinct subpopulations of individuals who have the same disease are subject to different sets of disease modifiers (e.g., susceptibility genes or environmental conditions) that alter the age at which the disease is expressed clinically. As a result, two peaks occur in the age distribution.
- The data is faulty, and the two peaks are artifactual.

- **Outliers and narrow norms**

One of the first and most important measurements for any collection of data is the range (i.e., the highest and the lowest observed values). The range provides two of the most important numbers in any set of data, even more important than determining the average or the standard deviation. There is always a compelling reason to learn where and why the data begin and end.

Here is an example. You are looking at human subject data that include weights of individuals. The minimum weight is a pound (the round-off weight of a viable but premature newborn infant). You find that the maximum weight in the data set is 300 pounds, exactly. You find that there are many individuals in the data set who have a measured weight of exactly 300 pounds, but no individuals with a weight exceeding 300 pounds. You also find that the number of individuals weighing 300 pounds is much greater than the number of individuals weighting 290 or 280 pounds. What does this tell you? Obviously, the people included in the data set have been weighed on a scale that tops off at 300 pounds. Most of the people whose weight was recorded as 300 will have a false weight measurement. Had we not looked for the maximum value in the data set, we would have assumed, incorrectly, that the weights were always accurate.

It would be useful to get some idea of how weights are distributed in the population exceeding 300 pounds. One way of estimating the error is to look at the number of people weighing 295, 290, 285 pounds, etc. By observing the trend, and knowing the total number of individuals whose weight is 300 pounds or higher, you can estimate the number of people falling into weight categories exceeding 300 pounds.

Most physiologic measurements fall into a narrow norm. We all walk around with a temperature very close to 98.6°F, give or take one or two degrees; we all breathe about 10–15 times a minute, when we are relaxed; most adults weigh between 100 and 250 pounds and our heights typically fall in a narrow range from just under 5 feet to about 6 feet 5 inches. Likewise, when we look at the chemicals and cells that circulate in our blood (e.g., neutrophils, red blood cells, albumin), their concentrations fall neatly into narrow ranges that apply to nearly every human. Because the normal range for each measurable property of human life is narrow, much of modern medicine is focused on investigating and correcting the causes of values that lie outside the normal range.

On occasion, the maxima or minima of a set of data will be an outlier (i.e., a data value that lies beyond anything you would expect to encounter, and nowhere near the next-highest or next-lowest value in the data set). The occurrence of outliers hinders the task of developing models, equations, or curves that closely fit all the available data. In some cases, outliers are simply mistakes that can be ignored by the data analyst. In other cases, the outlier may be the most important data in the data set. There is no simple method to know the importance of an outlier; it usually falls to the judgment of the data analyst.

In the field of Precision Medicine, clinical trial outliers have come to sudden prominence. Occasionally, a clinical trial will fail to show any benefit for the drug under study, when the control and test groups are compared. Nonetheless, among the test group, there may be found one or two exceptional responders, who show remarkable improvement [93,94]. These outliers are the topic of great excitement in the clinical trial community, and there is considerable hope that the proper analysis of outliers will yield new drug targets [95,96].

– Estimations

Sometimes, no matter how hard you try, you cannot produce an accurate count. One such situation arose during the Chicago heat wave of 1995. Municipalities must budget for supportive services such as municipal cooling stations, the free delivery of ice, increased staffing for emergency personnel, during heat waves. If the number of heat-related deaths is high, the governor may justifiably call a state of emergency. Hence, an accurate count of heat-wave-related deaths is vitally important.

During a heat wave, the number of deceased individuals with a heat-related cause of death seldom rises as much as anyone would expect [97]. The reason for this is that stresses produced by heat cause death by exacerbating preexisting nonheat-related conditions. A heat-caused death can be established if the deceased has a high body temperature measured shortly after death, but in many cases, the body is not discovered until long after the time of death.

How would you, lacking proof of heat-related deaths, estimate the magnitude of deaths caused by a heat wave? You might take the total number of deaths that occurred during the heat wave. Then you might review the records of deaths occurring in the same period, in the same geographic region, over a series of years in which a heat wave did not occur. You average that number, giving you the expected number of deaths in a normal (i.e., without heat wave) period. You subtract that number from the number of deaths that occurred during the heat wave, and that gives you an estimate of the number of people who died from heat-related mortality. This strategy was applied to find the number of heat-related deaths occurring in the 1995 Chicago heat wave [98]. [Glossary Cause of death error]

As a general rule, it is a good idea to estimate the solution of computationally difficult problems at the outset of your project. You may find that a reasonable solution to almost every complex problem can usually be estimated in just a few hours, or less. If you cannot find the data for a quick and dirty estimate, then you will probably never find the data needed to produce a precise determination.

When data analysts go straight to complex calculations, before producing a simple estimation, they may find themselves accepting wildly ridiculous calculations. For comparison purposes, there is nothing quite like a straight-forward estimate to pull an overly eager analyst back to reality. Often, the simple act of looking at a stripped-down version of the problem reveals a new approach that can drastically reduce computation time.

As the complexity and size of data increases, the value of simple arithmetic analyses (e.g., sums, proportions) increases. The curse of dimensionality makes it impossible to perform many of the most advanced analytic techniques on massive data sets. Contrariwise, it is always feasible, regardless of the size of a data set, to perform basic operations such as addition and subtraction, and multiplication, on enormous data sets. [Glossary Dimensionality, Curse of dimensionality]

– Random number generators and resampling statistics

By far, the most powerful and generally useful technique available to the new generation of medical researchers is repetitive random sampling, widely known by the more popular but less accurate term, "resampling." With resampling methods, applied to large or small data collections, the nonstatistician can simulate and solve virtually every computational problem that he or she is likely to encounter. These would include:

- General problems of probability
- Statistical tests
- Monte Carlo simulations
- Bayesian models
- Methods for determining whether there are multiple populations represented in a data set (i.e., the presence of a subpopulation in a mixture of cells or organisms, or DNA sequences).
- Determining the minimal sample size required to test a hypothesis (e.g., the minimum number of patients that must be enrolled in a clinical trial) [Glossary Power]

The good news is that these powerful techniques require only two free and ubiquitous ingredients. The bad news is that both of these ingredients lie somewhat outside the scope of this book. The first ingredient is a random number generator. The second ingredient is a computer programming language; almost any language will suffice.

Resampling methods are not new. The resampling methods that are commonly used today by data analysts have been around since the early 1980s [99–101]. The underlying algorithms for these methods are so very simple that they have certainly been in use, using simple casts of dice, for thousands of years. The following is an example of a very simple experiment, performed with a pair of dice that anyone can perform.

Let's say you want to know the likelihood of rolling the dice and coming up with two sixes. If you have an analytic mind, you may calculate that the odds of either die coming up a six is one-sixth, and since each die is independent of the other, the chances of two die coming up six is one-sixth times one-sixth or 1 out of 36. If you don't trust your calculation, and if you have the time, you can roll the dice 36,000 times and keep score of the results. You should find that double-six comes up about a thousand times.

Today, we do not need to roll the dice 36,000 times to solve our problem. We can simulate the procedure using a short program that employs a random number generator that chooses a number between 1 and 6, as many times as we like.

```
for (1..36000)
  {
  $winner1 = int(rand(6) + 1 );
  $winner2 = int(rand(6) + 1 );
  if ($winner1 == 6)
    {
    if ($winner2 == 6)
      {
      $count = $count + 1;
      }
    }
  }
print $count;
```

Five executions of this program produced the following results, instantly: 1014, 981, 1077, 986, and 963. These numbers are as close to 1000 as we can expect, from dumb luck.

The early 20th century saw the rise of mathematically rigorous statistical methods that enabled scientists to test hypotheses and draw conclusions from small or large collections of data. These tests, which required nothing more than pencil and paper to perform, dominated the field of analysis, and are not likely to be replaced anytime soon. Nonetheless, the advent of fast computers provides us with alternative methods of analysis that may lack the rigor of advanced statistics, but have the advantage of being easily comprehensible. Calculations that require millions of operations can be done essentially instantly and can be programmed with ease. Never before, in the history of the world, has it been possible to design and perform resampling exercises, requiring millions or billions of iterative operations, in a matter of seconds, on computers that are affordable to a vast number of individuals in developed or developing countries. The current literature abounds with resources for scientists with rudimentary programming skills, who might wish to employ resampling techniques [2,13].

Before closing this section, let us walk through two examples that demonstrate some of the benefits of resampling statistics.

Suppose you have two sample populations, each consisting of 100 data objects, with each data object containing one data value. The average data value in the first population is 90, and the average data value of the second population is 110. Hence, there is a difference of 20 in the average data value of the two populations. You want to determine whether these two populations are statistically equivalent to one another. Here is how you would answer this question, using resampling methodology. First, you would combine the two populations, producing 200 data objects. Then you would select, randomly, 100 objects from the aggregate population, yielding two new populations, each consisting of 100 data objects randomly mixed with objects from the two original populations. You would then compute the average data value of the first resampled population and the average data value of the second resampled population. Repeat this exercise 100,000 times, each time randomly selecting two new populations from the aggregate population. After you have collected data on 100,000 trials of resampled populations, ask yourself how often you saw differences in the average data values for the two resampled populations that equaled or exceeded 20 (the difference found in the original two sample populations). If it is rare to see differences of 20 or greater in the resampled populations, then it is likely that the two original populations were demonstrably different from one another. The reasoning behind our inference, in this example, is that the values observed in the two original arrays could not be explained by random selection from a combined population.

The power of a trial is the likelihood of detecting a difference in two populations, if the difference actually exists. The power is related to the sample size. At a sufficiently large sample size, you can be virtually certain that differences between the two populations will be observed, if the difference exists. How might we use resampling methods to determine the power of an experiment or clinical trial? Resampling permits the experimenter to conduct repeated trials, with different sample sizes, and under conditions that simulate the population differences that are expected. For example, an experimenter might expect that a certain drug produces a 15% difference in the measured outcomes in the treated population compared with the control population. By setting the conditions of the trials, and by performing repeated trials with increasing sizes of simulated populations, the data scientist can determine the minimum sampling size that consistently (e.g., in >95% of the trials), demonstrates that the treated population and the control population are separable. Hence, using a random number generator and a short program, the data scientist can determine the sampling size required to yield a power that is acceptable for a "real" trial.

SECTION 8.5 DATA REANALYSIS: MORE IMPORTANT THAN THE ORIGINAL DATA ANALYSIS

> A new thing is just an old thing that hasn't had an opportunity to disappoint you.
> *Anon*

A funny thing happened on the way to the "Precision Medicine" bandwagon. It seems that many of the fundamental studies in the field had yielded irreproducible results. We found that we could not depend on the data that we depended on. When we tried to understand why this was happening, we discovered that just about everything that could go wrong was indeed going wrong.

Consider these shocking headlines.

- "Unreliable research: Trouble at the lab" [102]. *The Economist*, in 2013, ran an article examining flawed biomedical research. The magazine article referred to an NIH official who indicated that "researchers would find it hard to reproduce at least three-quarters of all published biomedical findings, the public part of the process seems to have failed." The article described a study conducted at the pharmaceutical company Amgen, wherein 53 landmark studies were repeated. The Amgen scientists were successful at reproducing the results of only 6 of the 53 studies. Another group, at Bayer HealthCare, repeated 63 studies. The Bayer group succeeded in reproducing the results of only one-fourth of the original studies.
- "A decade of reversal: an analysis of 146 contradicted medical practices" [103]. The authors reviewed 363 journal articles, re-examining established standards of medical care. Among these articles were 146 manuscripts (40.2%) claiming that an existing standard of care had no clinical value.
- "Cancer fight: unclear tests for new drug" [104]. This *New York Times* article examined whether a common test performed on breast cancer tissue (Her2) was repeatable. It was shown that for patients who tested positive for Her2, a repeat test indicated that 20% of the original positive assays were actually negative (i.e., falsely positive on the initial test) [104].
- "Reproducibility crisis: Blame it on the antibodies" [105]. Biomarker developers are finding that they cannot rely on different batches of a reagent to react in a consistent manner, from test to test. Hence, laboratory analytic methods, developed using a controlled set of reagents, may not have any diagnostic value when applied by other laboratories, using different sets of the same analytes [105].
- "Why most published research findings are false" [106]. Modern scientists often search for small effect sizes, using a wide range of available analytic techniques, and a flexible interpretation of outcome results. The manuscript's author found that research conclusions are more likely to be false than true [106,107].
- "We found only one-third of published psychology research is reliable - now what?" [108]. The manuscript authors suggest that the results of first studies should be considered preliminary.

It is now abundantly clear that many scientific findings, particularly those findings based on analyses of large and complex data sets, are yielding irreproducible results [109]. Anyone who attempts to stay current in the sciences soon learns that almost anything published today might be retracted tomorrow. This appalling truth applies to some of the most respected and trusted laboratories in the world [110–117]. Those of us who have been involved in assessing the rate of progress in disease research are painfully aware of numerous reports indicating a general slowdown in medical advancement [10,42,78,118–122]. For the optimists, it is tempting to assume that the problems that we may be experiencing today are par for the course, and temporary. It is the nature of science to stall for a while and lurch forwards in sudden fits. Errors and retractions will always be with us so long as humans are involved in the scientific process. For the pessimists among us, there seems to be something going on that is really new and different, a game changer. This game changer is the "complexity barrier," a term credited to Boris Beizer, who used it to describe the impossibility of managing increasingly complex software applications [123]. The complexity barrier applies to every modern area of science and engineering, including Precision Medicine [2,124,125]

Some of the mistakes that lead to erroneous conclusions in published research are well known and include the following:

– Errors in sample selection, labeling, and measurement

Data errors and data documentation errors are common, and there are many examples, from the scientific literature, where such errors are documented [126–131]. The journal *Nature* published an interesting article, under the droll banner, "Agony for researchers as mix-up forces retraction of ecstasy study" [128]. It seems that scientists at the Johns Hopkins University School of Medicine had reported in the journal *Science* that the drug ecstasy, in small doses, damaged dopamine-producing brain cells in monkeys. This observation fits the authors' original hypothesis that ecstasy is a neurotoxin. As it turned out, the Johns Hopkins scientists were obliged to retract their original article when it was determined that the wrong drug had been injected, by mistake, during the experiment (i.e., no ecstasy; just agony) [128].

Huntington disease is associated with a repeated trinucleotide occurring in a specific chromosome region (i.e., the CAG repeat). In a review of over 1000 persons with Huntington disease, 30 were found to lack the diagnostic CAG repeat. 18 of these 30 "normal DNA" cases were accounted for by misdiagnosis, sample mix-up, or clerical error [132]. Likewise, anomalous and impossible results have been obtained from DNA sequence analyses of mitochondria. Laboratories were finding examples wherein a single individual was shown to have multiple ancestries, a biological impossibility. Sample mix-up and sample contamination (from other specimens) were demonstrated in these cases [127,133]. Setting aside sampling errors, data analysts must contend with the problem of insufficient sampling [129]. No amount of experimental precision can compensate for a statistically inadequate number of sample specimens [129].

– Outright fraud

We do not know the frequency of scientific fraud, but there is absolutely no reason to believe that fraud is rare [117,134–136]. When a scientist's career is on the line, the temptations to fabricate or fudge data can be overwhelming. The literature is rich with examples of fraud committed in some of the most respected laboratories on earth [111,136–146]. It is best to assume that every scientific publication is tentative, until other laboratories confirm the findings.

– Misinterpretation of the data

The most common source of scientific errors are postanalytic, arising from the interpretation of results [4,78,106,147–152]. Virtually every journal article contains, hidden in the introduction and discussion sections, some distortion of fact or misleading assertion. Scientists cannot be objective about their own work. As humans, we tend to interpret observations to reinforce our beliefs and prejudices and to advance our agendas.

Large, multiinstitutional studies involving many human subjects, many specimens, and large collections of data, analyzed by teams of statisticians and computer scientists, carry the veneer of respectability. Manuscript reviewers may be reluctant to reject a work submitted by a group of 100 scientists. Nonetheless, large studies are just as susceptible to errors of data interpretation as are studies performed by a single investigator, on a small set of data. Today, some of the largest experimental studies and clinical trials produce results with very small differences between the experimental group and the control group (e.g., an extension of cancer survival time of 2 weeks, a 1% difference in biomarker levels). When the stakes are high, as is always the case with expensive multiinstitutional studies, scientists will be inclined to exaggerate the benefits of a positive finding, no matter how insignificant the results may be.

One of the most common strategies whereby scientists distort their own results, to advance a self-serving conclusion, is message framing [153]. In message framing, scientists omit from discussion any pertinent findings that might diminish or discredit their own conclusions. The common practice of message framing is conducted on a subconscious, or at least a subrational, level. A scientist is not apt to read articles whose conclusions contradict his own hypotheses and will not cite disputatious works is his manuscripts. Furthermore, if a paradigm is held in high esteem by a majority of the scientists in a field, then works that contradict the paradigm are not likely to pass peer review. Hence, it is difficult for contrary articles to be published in scientific journals. In any case, the message delivered in a journal article is almost always framed in a manner that promotes the author's interpretation.

It must be noted that throughout human history, no scientist has ever gotten into any serious trouble for misinterpreting results. Scientific misconduct comes, as a rule, from the purposeful production of bad data, either through falsification, fabrication, or through the refusal to remove and retract data that is known to be false, plagiarized, or otherwise invalid. In the United States, allegations of research misconduct are investigated by The Office of Research Integrity. Funding agencies in other countries have similar watchdog institutions. The Office of Research Integrity makes its findings a matter of public record [154]. Of 150 cases investigated between 1993 and 1997, all but one case had an alleged component of data falsification, fabrication or plagiarism [155]. In 2007, of the 28 investigated cases, 100% involved allegations of falsification, fabrication, or both [156]. No cases of misconduct based on data misinterpretation were prosecuted. Perhaps the Office of Research Integrity understands that the self-serving interpretation of data is entrenched deep within the human psyche, and cannot be removed.

- **In a world where scientific research results are tentative, the process of data reanalysis assumes paramount importance. Here are the roles of data reanalysis in Precision Medicine [1].**

- Validation of conclusions

It is difficult to repeat a complex experiment or an expensive multiyear clinical trial. In many instances, the best we can hope for is to reanalyze the original study, to verify that the data was obtained properly and to validate that the conclusions fit the results

[82,149,157–160]. Scientists rankle at the idea that their data must be inspected, reanalyzed, and sometimes repeated, by other scientists, including competitors. Scientists should understand that data validation requires a great deal of effort, and that the scientists who devote themselves to this task are often interrupting their own careers because they believe that the results under review are of sufficient importance to justify their sacrifice. We should remember that the primary purpose of every validation effort is to legitimize the original work, not to discredit the work. It is better to have a genuine scientific advancement than to have a huge waste of everyone's time and money. [Glossary Primary data, Secondary data]

– Performing additional analyses

It is impossible to fully analyze a complex study, on the first attempt. There will always be some analytic opportunity that was overlooked [161].

– Updating results

Analysis is never really finished, but there comes a time when you need to stop and report what you've done so far. As new data arrives, the original data needs to be reanalyzed, with the newer data. In some cases, the newer data permits the data curator to fill in missing data points, to enter corrections in the original data, and to achieve a more accurate assessment of outlier data points in the original data set. It is a terrible waste to simply abandon an old project, when a reanalysis at some future time, would help tie loose ends and clarify unanswered questions [1]. [Glossary Curator]

– Extending the scope of the original study

Sometimes, data collected for one project can be usefully merged with data collected in other projects. Such projects may be previous, concurrent, or future works, just so long as they contain related data.

– Performing original research that was not conceived when the data was collected

Old data can sometimes be reanalyzed to answer questions that were not anticipated by the scientists who performed the original study. Getting new uses from old data is the most cost-effective means of conducting research, and should be encouraged [1]. [Glossary Data archeology]

SECTION 8.6 WHAT IS DATA SHARING, AND WHY DON'T WE DO MORE OF IT?

Science advances funeral by funeral.
Folk wisdom

Without data sharing, there can be very little progress in the field of Precision Medicine. The reasons for this are simple:

– Laboratory findings have limited value unless they are correlated with clinical information, and this requires access to full medical records.

- All findings, even those based on reliable clinical data, are tentative, and researchers must have access to information (e.g., side-effects, exceptional events, genetic or demographic response variations) that can only come from shared data on wider populations.
- Unless data is shared, scientists cannot build upon the work of others, and the field of Precision Medicine becomes a collection of research laboratories working in isolation from one another, leading to intellectual stagnation [162,163].
- Scientific conclusions have no credibility when the research community, oversight agencies, and the interested public cannot review the data upon which the findings were based.

Without data sharing, we don't have science. We just have people with their own agendas asking us to believe their conclusions. As we have previously discussed, in the complex realm of Precision Medicine, first analyses are often wrong. A seemingly infinite list of official position papers, urging clinicians and researchers to share their research data, has been published [164–169]. To be sure, there are technical obstacles to data sharing, but for every technical obstacle, there is a wealth of literature offering solutions [2,4,19,170–178].

In this section, we will be looking at all of the impediments to data sharing, but first, let's look at how we will be finding the genetic mutations that are thought to be the root cause of human diseases. For the sake of discussion, here is a grossly oversimplified, 3-step view of the kind of gene-based disease research currently conducted in Precision Medicine:

1. Sequence the genome of an individual affected by a monogenic disease whose underlying gene has not been identified.
2. Look for any variation in any gene in the genome by comparing the individual's sequence with the sequences found in a database of genome sequences collected from normal (i.e., unaffected individuals)
3. The candidate genes (i.e., the genes that may be the root cause of the disease) are those genes containing variants that are not present in the database of normal gene variants.

Step 2 tells us that we need to have detailed population data, on millions of gene variants, with which to correlate the findings [179–184]. Specifically, we need to know whether a variant is present in the normal population, with no clinical significance; or whether variants are associated with disease. The lives of patients are put at risk when we are deprived of timely and open access to data relating genetic findings to clinical phenotypes.

In 2008, a 2-year-old child had a severe seizure and died. In the prior year, the child had been tested, by a large reference laboratory, for mutations in the SCN1A gene. The child's doctors were concerned that the patient might have Dravet syndrome, a seizure disorder in which about 80% of patients have a mutation in the SCN1A gene. The laboratory discovered a mutation in the child's SCN1A gene, but remarked that the mutation was a variant of unknown significance. Their reference database of sequence variants did not provide them with the information that specifically linked the mutation to Dravet syndrome. Under this circumstance, the laboratory report could not rule out the possibility that the mutation might be a variant of normal, with no clinical significance. Some time later, the child died.

In a wrongful death lawsuit filed by the child's mother, the complaint was made that two published reports, appearing in 2006 and 2007, had linked the specific SCN1A gene mutation that was subsequently found in her child's DNA, with an epileptic encephalopathy [185]. According to the mother, the reporting laboratory should have known the significance of her child's mutation [185,186]. Regardless of the verdict rendered at this trial, the circumstances tell us something about the importance, in the practice of Precision Medicine, of having access to genetic data produced by other laboratories. In the era of Precision Medicine, testing laboratories need access to the most current data available, including the data generated by competing laboratories.

Despite the imperatives of data sharing, the field of medicine has been slow to adopt data-sharing policies. The obstacles to data sharing are legendary. The same problems that plagued the field in its early days have lingered, over the past three decades, to threaten the fledgling field of Precision Medicine [167,187]. Because the issue of data sharing is so important to every scientist living today, it is worth reviewing the impediments to its successful implementation.

Here is a listing of the commonly heard reasons for withholding data from the public, along with suggested remedies.

- **To protect scientists from "research parasites"**

A recent opinion expressed by two editors of the *New England Journal of Medicine*, in an essay entitled "Data Sharing," expressed concern that a new brand of researcher uses data generated by others, for his or her own ends. The editors indicated that some front-line researchers characterize such individuals as "research parasites" [188]. The essay suggested that researchers who want to use the data produced by others should do so by forming collaborative partnerships with the group that produced the original data [188].

The idea of collaboration through data sharing may have been a reasonable strategy 30 years ago, before the emergence of enormous datasets, built from the work of hundreds of data contributors. Today, well-designed data sets can be merged with other sources of data, and repurposed for studies that were never contemplated by the original data contributors [1]. Attempting to form collaborations with individual data owners, who may be only dimly aware of their own contribution to an aggregate database with hundreds of contributors, is no longer feasible.

A 2011 study has shown that researchers with high-quality data were, generally, willing to share their data [189]. Researchers who had weak data that might support various interpretations and contrasting conclusions were less willing to share their data. It is important to convince the scientists who create and hold data that the researchers who use their data, without asking permission and without forming collaborations, are not "research parasites"; they are the people who will validate good work, improve upon imperfect work, and create new work from otherwise abandoned data. The societal push toward data sharing should provide a strong impetus for scientists to improve the value of their data, so that they will have something worth sharing.

- **To avoid data misinterpretation**

Every scientist who releases data to the public must contend with the fear that a member of the public will misinterpret the data, reach an opposite conclusion, publish their false interpretation, and destroy the career of the trusting soul who was kind enough to provide the ammunition for his own execution. Teams of scientists developing a new drug or treatment protocol may fear that if their data is released to the public, their competitors may seize the opportunity to unjustly critique their work and thus jeopardize their project.

Examples of such injustices have been sought, but not found [167]. There is no evidence that would lead anyone to believe that a misinterpretation of data has ever overshadowed a correct interpretation of data. Scientists have endured the withering criticisms of their colleagues from time immemorial. As they say, it comes with the territory. Hiding data for the purpose of avoiding criticism is unprofessional.

– To limit access to a few selected professionals

Some researchers believe that data sharing must be a conditional process wherein investigators submit their data requests to a committee of scientists who decide whether the request is justified [190]. In some cases, the committee retains the right to review any results predicated on the shared data, with the intention of disallowing publication of results that they consider to be objectionable.

There are serious drawbacks to subjecting scientists to a committee approval process. The public needs unfettered access to the original data upon which published research results are based. Anything less makes it impossible to validate the conclusions drawn from the data, and invites all manner of scientific fraud. In the United States, this opinion is codified by law. The Data Quality Act of 2002 restrains government agencies from developing policies based on data that is unavailable for quality review by the public [191–194]. [Glossary Data Quality Act]

There is the risk that a nonvigilant public, overwhelmed by the complexity of Precision Medicine, will slide into complacency, and the scientific community will automatically accept the conclusions of unseen third parties, without inspecting the data upon which those conclusions were based. Here is an example. A clinician, seeking to determine the proper drug and dosage for a patient, based on the patient's genetic profile, may send an information request to a pharmacogenomic data corporation. The corporation keeps a database holding the genetic sequence of every individual in the country. It performs an analysis on its own data, and recommends a drug and a dosage based on the analysis. The doctor receives the recommendation, and writes a prescription for the patient. This scenario is not very different from current projections discussed in a workshop sponsored by the National Academy of Sciences [195]. The doctor neither sees nor interprets the data that determines her patient's treatment. Will this be the new standard of care in the era of Precision Medicine? [Glossary Pharmacogenomics]

– To sustain the traditional role of data protector

All healthcare workers are trained to preserve patient confidentiality, much like priests protect the confessional. It is understandable that hospital professionals are reluctant to share their data with the world-at-large.

Before confidential medical information is released, healthcare professionals must be convinced that data sharing can be accomplished without breaching patient confidentiality, and that the effort spent in the process will yield some medical benefit to the patients whose data is being appropriated.

– To await forthcoming universal data standards

Trying to merge data sets that are disorganized is impossible, as is merging data sets wherein equivalent types of data are discordantly annotated. Because hospitals and laboratories use a variety of different types of software to collect and organize their data, obstacles raised by data incompatibility have been a major impediment to data sharing. The knee-jerk solution to the problem has always been to create new data standards.

In the past few decades, the standards-making process has evolved into a major industry. There are standards for describing, organizing, and transmitting data. There are dozens of separate standards for many of the types of data that might be of interest to practitioners of Precision medicine, and all such standards are subject to multiple revisions. There are numerous ontologies designed for various scientific disciplines, permitting particular types of data to be assigned to classes. These ontologies undergo constant revision, as new relationships among classes are proposed. [Glossary Classification versus ontology]

The hunger for standards is insatiable. The calls for new standards never seem to end. All these standards-making activities have led to several negative consequences for the field of Precision Medicine.

- Because Precision Medicine is interdisciplinary, drawing data from various types of research laboratories, and from all sorts of clinical reports and ancillary testing realms, it is virtually impossible for any individual scientist to master all the data standards that might pertain to his or her research projects.
- Because the standards are constantly changing, legacy data sets that have been annotated or organized with older versions of standards, cannot be directly merged with new data.
- Because the standards are complex, project teams produce idiosyncratic implementations of the standards, yielding data sets that cannot be usefully merged with data from other sources, even when those other sources have chosen to organize their data with the same standards.

The drawbacks of data standards are many and have been described at great length in the informatics literature [3]. Suffice it to say that data standards are difficult and expensive to create, sustain, and implement, and that most new data standards are soon abandoned. The demise of a $17 billion interoperability project undertaken by the UK's National Health Service serves as a notorious example of the failure of data standards [196]. A report published by the NHS Information Authority cited fundamental flaws in the standard that set the language, structure, and data types required for integrating clinical data between systems [197]. Despite all the effort devoted to data standards, there is no widely adopted system for organizing and sharing the different types of data employed in the field of Precision Medicine. Perhaps the "standard" answer is not the correct answer. Specifications are a possible alternative to standards and should be considered an option for those who are open to suggestion in this matter. Specifications, unlike standards, provide general ways of describing any kind of data. Specifications can be adapted to accommodate formal classifications or ontologies created for any scientific discipline [2–4,13].

– To protect legal ownership

Who owns confidential medical data? Is it owned by the patient? Is it owned by the medical center? Is it owned by anyone? Ownership is a mercantile concept conferring the right to sell.

If someone owns a cow, that means that they have the right to sell the cow. If you own a house, even a mortgaged house, then you have the right to sell the house. In law, there does not seem to be anyone who has the right to sell medical records; hence, it is likely that nobody can claim ownership. Still, medical institutions have a fiduciary responsibility to maintain medical records for their patients, and this entitles both patients and healthcare providers to use the records, as needed. Patients have the right to ask hospitals to send their medical records to other medical centers or to themselves. Hospitals are expected to archive tissues, medical reports, and patient charts to serve the patient and society. In the United States, State health departments, the Centers for Disease Control and Prevention (CDC), and cancer registries all expect medical centers to deliver medical reports on request.

Without seeking ownership, researchers can request access to medical records. Institutional Review Boards or Privacy Boards, without owning the records, can provide medical records to researchers, if the research can be conducted without harming patients [20,21]. With few exceptions, the potential harms that may come to a patient, as the result of human subject research using medical records, are confined to loss of privacy and breach of confidentiality. Scientists adept at eliminating or minimizing such harms, through thorough data deidentification and data scrubbing, have a reasonably good chance at gaining access to patient data [23]. [Glossary Data scrubbing]

– To comply with rules issued from above

It is not uncommon for researchers to claim that they would love to share their data, but they are forbidden from doing so by the lawyers and administrators at their institutions. Two issues tend to dissuade administrators from data sharing. The first is legal liability. Institutions have a responsibility to avoid punitive tort claims, such as those that may arise if human subjects complain that their privacy has been violated when their confidential information is shared. From the viewpoint of the institution, the best remedy is to forbid scientists from sharing their data. Secondly, institutions want to protect their own intellectual property, and this would include patents, drug discoveries, manufacturing processes, and even data generated by their staff scientists. Institutions may sometimes equate data sharing with poor stewardship of intellectual property. [Glossary Intellectual property]

When an institution forbids data sharing, as a matter of policy, scientists should argue that data sharing serves the interests of medical institutions. Simply put, if Institution A does not share its data with Institution B, then Institution B will not share its data with Institution A. In addition, when Institution A publishes a scientific breakthrough, then Institution B will not find those claims credible, until their own researchers can review the primary data.

It is easy to forget that human subjects benefit when scientific projects lead to medical discoveries. Without data sharing, those benefits will come at a glacial pace, and at great expense. Institutional Review Boards should be prepared to oversee and assist data-sharing activities that are conducted in a safe and responsible manner. When the lawyers and administrators are taught that data sharing is a normal scientific activity, bringing negligible risk to individuals, then they might be swayed to lift sanctions. [Glossary Fair use]

– To avoid distributing flawed data

Scientists are reluctant to release data that that is full of errors. In particular, data curators may fear that if such data is released to the public, they will be inundated with complaints from angry data analysts, demanding that every error be corrected.

Aside from corrections, all data sets need constant updating, and there are proper and improper ways of revising data (discussed in Section 7.1). Dealing with change, in the form of revised systems of annotations, revised standards of data encapsulation, and revised data elements, is part of the job of the modern data curator. [Glossary Encapsulation]

Institutions cannot refuse to share their data simply because their data contains errors or is awaiting revisions. Flawed data is common, and it's a safe bet that every large data set contains errors [198]. The best solution is for institutions and scientific teams to hire professionals with the requisite skills to properly prepare and improve collections of data.

- **To protect against data hackers**

Properly deidentified, medical records may contain information that, when combined with data held in other databases, may uniquely identify patients [199]. As an obvious example, if a medical record contains an un-named patient's birth date, gender and zip-code, and a public database lists names of people in a zip-code, along with their birth dates and gender, it is a simple step to ascertain the identity of "deidentified" patients.

A specific instance, making national news headlines, may serve to clarify just how this may work [200]. A male child was fathered using anonymously donated sperm. When the boy was 15 years of age, he became curious to know the identify of his biological father. A private company had created a DNA Database from 45,000 DNA samples. The purpose of the database was to allow clients to discover kin by having their DNA compared with all the DNA samples in the database. The boy sent his DNA sample to the company, along with a fee. A comparison of the boy's Y chromosome DNA (inherited exclusively from the father) was compared with Y chromosome DNA in the database. The names of two men with close matches to the boy's Y chromosome were found.

The boy's mother had been provided (from the sperm bank) with the sperm donor's date of birth and birthplace. The boy used an online service to obtain the name of every man born in the sperm donor's place of birth on the sperm donor's date of birth. Among those names, one name matched one of the two Y-chromosome matches from the DNA database search. This name, according to newspaper reports, identified the child's father. [Glossary Y-chromosome]

In this case, the boy had access to his own uniquely identifying information (i.e., his DNA and specifically his Y chromosome DNA), and he was lucky to be provided with the date of birth and birthplace of his biological father. He was also extremely lucky that the biological father had registered his DNA in a database of 45,000 samples. And he was lucky that the DNA database revealed the names of its human subjects. The boy's success in identifying his father required a string of unlikely events, and a lax attitude toward subject privacy on the part of the personnel at the sperm bank and the personnel at the DNA database.

Regardless of theoretical security flaws, the criminal or malicious identification of human subjects included in deidentified research data sets is extremely rare. More commonly, confidential records (e.g., personnel records, credit records, fully identified medical records) are stolen wholesale, relieving thieves from the intellectually challenging task of finding obscure information that may link a deidentified record to the identity of its subject.

- **To preserve compartmentalization of data**

Most data created by modern laboratories has not been prepared in a manner that permits its meaningful use in other laboratories. In many cases, the data has been compartmentalized, so that the data is disbursed in different laboratories. It is par for the course that a no single individual has taken the responsibility of collecting and reviewing all of the data that has been used to support the published conclusions of a multiinstitutional project.

In the late 1990s, Dr. Wu Suk Hwang was a world-famous cloning researcher. The government of South Korea was so proud of Dr. Hwang that they issued a commemorative stamp to celebrate his laboratory's achievements. Dr. Hwang's status drastically changed when fabrications were discovered in a number of the manuscripts produced by his laboratory. Dr. Hwang had a habit of placing respected scientists as coauthors on his papers [201]. When the news broke, Hwang pointed a finger at several of his collaborators.

A remarkable aspect of Dr. Hwang's publications was his ability to deceive the coworkers in his own laboratory, and the coauthors located in laboratories around the world, for a very long time. Dr. Hwang used a technique known as compartmentalization; dividing his projects into tasks distributed to small groups of scientists who specialized in one step of a multistep research project. By so doing, his coworkers never had access to the entire set of research data. The data required to validate the final achievement of the research was not examined by his coworkers [201,202].

For several years, South Korean politicians defended the scientist, to the extent of questioning the patriotism of his critics. Over time, additional violations committed by Dr. Hwang were brought to light. In 2009, Hwang was sentenced in Seoul, S. Korea, to a 2-year suspended prison sentence for embezzlement and bioethical violations; but he was never found guilty of fabrication.

Large data projects are almost always compartmentalized. When you have dozens or even hundreds of individuals contributing to a project, compartmentalization occurs quite naturally. In fact, what would you do without compartmentalization? Wait for every scientist involved in the project to review and approve one another's data? Many scientific research projects, in the realm of precision medicine, may involve dozens or even hundreds of scientists. Without compartmentalization, nothing would ever get published. With compartmentalization, nothing would ever be validated. That lesson here is that at the end of every research project, all of the data that contributed to the results must be gathered together as an organized and well-annotated dataset for public review.

– **To guard research protocols**

In every scientific study, the measurements included in the data must be linked to the study protocols (e.g., laboratory procedures) that produced the data. In some cases, the protocols are not well documented. In other cases, the protocols are well documented, but the researchers may have failed to follow the recommended protocols, thus rendering the data irreproducible. Occasionally, the protocols are the intellectual property of an entity other than the persons who created the data. In this case, the persons producing and managing the data may be unable to distribute their data protocols to the public.

– **To conceal instances of missing data**

It is almost inevitable, when data sets are large and complex, that there will be some missing data points. In this case, data may be added "by imputation." This involves computing a statistical best bet on what the missing data element value might have been, and inserting the calculated number into the data set. A data manager may be reluctant to release to the public a database with "fudged" data.

It is perfectly legitimate to include imputed data points, on the condition that all the data is properly annotated, so that reviewers are aware of imputed values, and of the methods used to generate such values.

– To avoid bureaucratic hurdles

As previously discussed, institutions may resort to Kafkaesque measures to ensure that only qualified and trusted individuals gain access to research data. It should come as no surprise that formal requests for data may take 2 years or longer to review and approve [203]. The approval process is so cumbersome that it simply cannot be implemented without creating major inconveniences and delays, for everyone involved (i.e., data manager and data suppliant).

In the United States, federal agencies often seek to share data with one another. Such transactions require Memoranda of Understanding between agencies, and these memoranda can take months to negotiate and finalize [203]. In some cases, try as they might, data cannot be shared among federal agencies due to a lack of regulatory authorization that cannot be resolved in anyone's favor [203].

Hypervigilance, on the part of US Federal agencies, may stem from unfortunate incidents from the past, which cannot be easily forgotten. One such incident, which attracted international attention, occurred when the United States accidentally released details of hundreds of its nuclear sites and programs, including the exact locations of nuclear stockpiles [204].

Despite their reluctance to share some forms of data, US agencies have been remarkably generous with biomedical data, and the National Institutes of Health commonly attaches data-sharing requirements to grants, and other awards.

In the US, Federal regulations impose strict controls on sharing identified medical data. Those same regulations specify that deidentified human subject data is exempted from those controls and can be freely shared [20,21]. Data holders must learn the proper methods for deidentifying or anonymizing private and confidential medical data. Such data can be freely shared, without creating an onerous set of obstacles for scientists.

Whew! Where does this leave us? The points raised in this section of the book clearly indicate that data sharing is not easy. Nonetheless, scientific claims cannot be validated unless the data is made available to the public. The field of Precision Medicine cannot advance if scientists cannot build upon the data produced by their colleagues. Research institutions, both public and private, must find ways to share data responsibly. They might begin by hiring professionals who are steeped in the craft of data sharing.

Glossary

Abandonware Software that is abandoned (e.g., no longer updated, supported, distributed, or sold) after its economic value is depleted. In academic circles, the term is often applied to software that is developed under a research grant. When the grant expires, so does the software. A generous interpretation of the term abandonware might include all of the databases and digital information that have not been maintained in a manner that would allow its reuse or reanalysis. Arguably, virtually all of the software and information in the digital universe has been effectively abandoned and could be denoted as "abandonware."

Accuracy versus precision Accuracy measures how close your data comes to being correct. Precision relates to exactness and reproducibility of measurements reproducibility (i.e., whether repeated measurements of the same quantity produce the same result). Data can be accurate but imprecise. If you have a 10-pound object, and you report its weight as 7.2376 pounds, on every occasion when the object is weighed, then your precision is remarkable, but your accuracy is dismal.

Anatomic pathologist Anatomic pathologists are physicians who have been trained to examine and diagnose lesions by gross (i.e., naked eye) and microscopic appearances.

Annotation In the field of informatics, annotation is the attachment of additional data to a data record or to a data object. The most important annotation is always self-descriptive data (e.g., the name of the entity that owns the data, the date that the data was created, descriptions of how the data was obtained, a statement explaining whether the data can be used freely, or any restrictions that might apply, a description of how the data was obtained, a data identifier).

Authentication A process for determining if the data object that is received (e.g., document, file, image) is the data object that was intended to be received. Simple protocols are available for authenticating digital files and messages [2].

Cause of death error Cause of death data comes from death certificates [205]. Death certificate data have many deficiencies [206,207]. The most common error occurs when a mode of death (i.e., the way that an individual dies) is listed as the cause of death. For example, cardiac arrest is not a cause of death, though it appears incorrectly as the cause of death on many death certificates. An international survey has shown very little consistency in the way that death data are collected [208]. Most death certificates are completed without benefit of an autopsy (i.e., without using the most thorough and reliable medical procedure designed to establish the causes of death). In the absence of an autopsy, a death certificate expresses a clinician's reasonable judgment at the time of a patient's death.

Classification versus ontology A classification is a system in which every object in a knowledge domain is assigned to a class within a hierarchy of classes. The properties of superclasses are inherited by the subclasses. Every class has one immediate superclass (i.e., parent class), although a parent class may have more than one immediate subclass (i.e., child class). Objects do not change their class assignment in a classification, unless there was a mistake in the assignment. For example, a rabbit is always a rabbit and does not change into a tiger. Classifications can be thought of as the simplest and most restrictive type of ontology, and serve to reduce the complexity of a knowledge domain [209]. Classifications can be easily modeled in an object-oriented programming language and are nonchaotic (i.e., calculations performed on the members and classes of a classification should yield the same output, each time the calculation is performed). A classification should be distinguished from an ontology. In an ontology, a class may have more than one parent class and an object may be a member of more than one class. A classification can be considered a special type of ontology wherein each class is limited to a single parent class and each object has membership in one and only one class.

Codon A codon is a sequence of three nucleotides specifying an amino acid or a stop instruction. Synonym: nucleotide triplet. There are 64 possible triplets, and only about 20 naturally occurring proteogenic amino acids. Hence, there is considerable redundancy in the code.

Correlation distance The correlation distance provides a measure of similarity between two variables. Two similar variables will rise and fall together, and it is this coordinated variation in value that is measured by correlation distance scores [210,211].

Curator The word "curator" derives from the latin, "curatus," the same root for "curative," indicating that curators "take care of" things. A data curator collects, annotates, indexes, updates, archives, searches, retrieves, and distributes data. Curator is another of those somewhat arcane terms (e.g., indexer, data archivist, lexicographer) that are being rejuvenated in the new millennium. It seems that if we want to enjoy the benefits of a data-centric world, we will need the assistance of curators, trained in data organization.

Curse of dimensionality As the number of attributes for a data object increases, the multidimensional space becomes sparsely populated, and the distances between any two objects, even the two closest neighbors, becomes absurdly large. When you have thousands of dimensions (e.g., data values in a data record, cells in the rows of a spreadsheet), the space that holds the objects is so large that distances between data objects become difficult or impossible to compute, and most computational algorithms become useless.

Dark data Unstructured and ignored data, presumed to account for most of the data in the "infoverse." The term gets its name from "dark matter," which is the invisible stuff that accounts for most of the gravitational attraction in the physical universe.

Data Quality Act In the United States the data upon which public policy is based must have quality and must be available for review by the public. Simply put, public policy must be based on verifiable data. The Data Quality Act of 2002 requires the Office of Management and Budget to develop government-wide standards for data quality [191].

Data annotation The process of supplementing data objects with additional data, often providing descriptive information about the data (i.e., metadata, identifiers, time information, and other forms of information that enhances the utility of the data object).

Data archeology The process of recovering information held in abandoned or unpopular physical storage devices, or packaged in formats that are no longer widely recognized, and hence unsupported by most software applications. The definition encompasses truly ancient data, such as cuneiform inscriptions stored on clay tablets circa BCE 3300, and digital data stored on 5.25-inch floppy disks in Xyrite wordprocessor format, circa 1994.

Data repurposing Involves using old data in new ways that were not foreseen by the people who originally collected the data. Data repurposing comes in the following categories: (1) Using the existing data to ask and answer questions that were not contemplated by the people who designed and collected the data; (2) Combining existing data with additional data, of the same kind, to produce aggregate data that suits a new set of questions that could not have been answered with any one of the component data sources; (3) Reanalyzing data to validate assertions, theories, or conclusions drawn from the original studies; (4) Reanalyzing the original data set using alternate or improved methods to attain outcomes of greater precision or reliability than the outcomes produced in the original analysis; (5) Integrating heterogeneous data sets (i.e., data sets with seemingly unrelated types of information), for the purpose an answering questions or developing concepts that span diverse scientific disciplines; (6) Finding subsets in a population once thought to be homogeneous; (7) Seeking new relationships among data objects; (8) Creating, on-the-fly, novel data sets through data file linkages; (9) Creating new concepts or ways of thinking about old concepts, based on a re-examination of data; (10) Fine-tuning existing data models; and (11) Starting over and remodeling systems [1].

Data science A vague term encompassing all aspects of data collection, organization, archiving, distribution, and analysis. The term has been used to subsume the closely related fields of informatics, statistics, data analysis, programming, and computer science.

Data scrubbing A term that is very similar to data deidentification and is sometimes used improperly as a synonym for data deidentification. Data scrubbing refers to the removal, from data records, of information that is considered unwanted. This may include identifiers, private information, or any incriminating or otherwise objectionable language contained in data records, as well as any information deemed irrelevant to the purpose served by the record.

Data sharing Providing one's own data to another person or entity. This process may involve free or purchased data, and it may be done willingly, or under coercion, as in compliance with regulations, laws, or court orders.

Data versus datum The singular form of data is datum, but the word "datum" has virtually disappeared from the computer science literature. The word "data" has assumed both a singular and plural form. In its singular form, it is a collective noun that refers to a single aggregation of many data points. Hence, current usage would be "The data is enormous," rather than "These data are enormous."

Deidentification The process of removing all of the links in a data record that can connect the information in the record to an individual. This usually includes the record identifier, demographic information (e.g., place of birth), personal information (e.g., birthdate), biometrics (e.g., fingerprints), and so on. The process of deidentification will vary based on the type of records examined. Deidentifying protocols exist wherein deidentified records can be reidentified, when necessary.

Dimensionality The dimensionality of a data objects consists of the number of attributes that describe the object. Depending on the design and content of the data structure that contains the data object (i.e., database, array, list of records, object instance, etc.), the attributes will be called by different names, including field, variable, parameter, feature, or property. Data objects with high dimensionality create computational challenges, and data analysts typically reduce the dimensionality of data objects wherever possible.

Encapsulation The concept, from object oriented programming, that a data object contains its associated data. Encapsulation is tightly linked to the concept of introspection, the process of accessing the data encapsulated within a data object. Encapsulation, Inheritance, and Polymorphism are available features of all object-oriented languages.

Encryption A common definition of encryption involves an algorithm that takes some text or data and transforms it, bit-by-bit, into an output that cannot be interpreted (i.e., from which the contents of the source file cannot be determined). Encryption comes with the implied understanding that there exists some reverse transform that can be applied to the encrypted data, to reconstitute the original source.

Fair use Copyright and Patent are legal constructs designed to provide intellectual property holders with the uninfringed power to profit from their creative labors, while still permitting the public to have full access to the holders' properties. When Public use of copyrighted material does not limit its profitability to the copyright holder, then the "fair use" of the material is generally permitted, even when those uses exceed customary copyright limits. Most countries have some sort of "fair use" provisions for copyrighted material. In the United States,

Fair Use is described in the Copyright Act of 1976, Title 17, U.S. Code, section 107, titled, Limitations on exclusive rights: Fair use. Here is an excerpt of the Act: "Notwithstanding the provisions of sections 106 and 106A, the fair use of a copyrighted work, including such use by reproduction in copies or phonorecords or by any other means specified by that section, for purposes such as criticism, comment, news reporting, teaching (including multiple copies for classroom use), scholarship, or research, is not an infringement of copyright. In determining whether the use made of a work in any particular case is a fair use the factors to be considered shall include (1) the purpose and character of the use, including whether such use is of a commercial nature or is for nonprofit educational purposes; (2) the nature of the copyrighted work; (3) the amount and substantiality of the portion used in relation to the copyrighted work as a whole; and (4) the effect of the use upon the potential market for or value of the copyrighted work. The fact that a work is unpublished shall not itself bar a finding of fair use if such finding is made upon consideration of all the above factors" [212].

Identifier A string that is associated with a particular thing (e.g., person, document, transaction, data object), and not associated with any other thing [213]. Object identification usually involves permanently assigning a seemingly random sequence of numeric digits (0–9) and alphabet characters (a–z and A–Z) to a data object. A data object can be a specific piece of data (e.g., a data record), or an abstraction, such as a class of objects or a number or a string or a variable.

Immutability Permanent data that cannot be modified is said to be immutable. At first thought, it would seem that immutability is a ridiculous and impossible constraint. In the real world, mistakes are made, information changes, and the methods for describing information changes. This is all true, but the astute data manager knows how to accrue information into data objects without changing the existing data. In practice, immutability is maintained by time-stamping all data and storing annotated data values with any and all subsequent time-stamped modifications.

Inherited retinoblastoma Inherited retinoblastomas are often bilateral and often occur in children. Nonfamilial or "sporadic" retinoblastomas are almost always unilateral and tend to arise in adults. Children born with inherited retinoblastoma syndrome have a germline inactivation of a tumor suppressor (the RB gene). To develop cancer, they need to acquire one additional mutation inactivating the alternate allele. Because only one additional mutational event is required in the inherited syndrome, tumors occur much more frequently and much earlier than the retinoblastomas that arise without inheritance of the RB gene mutation. In the noninherited cases of retinoblastoma, two mutational events (one for each allele of the RB gene) must occur sometime during the life of the patient, and this usually takes time (accounting for the late onset) and occurs only rarely [83]. A similar process holds true for the tumors associated with neurofibromatosis type 1. Individuals with neurofibromatosis type 1 are born with a mutation of the gene that codes for neurofibrin. Tumors develop in individuals who acquire a second mutation, involving the second allele of neurofibrin, in somatic cells, after birth. Patients with neurofibromatosis type 1 may develop thousands of neurofibromas, indicating that allelic mutations of the gene that codes for neurofibromin occur commonly in somatic cells. It should be noted that although both examples (i.e., inherited retinoblastoma and inherited neurofibromas) seem to require biallelic mutation of a gene, we should not assume that these biallelic mutations are sufficient, by themselves, to produce tumors. Presumably, multiple steps, occurring over time, must also occur.

Intellectual property Data, software, algorithms, and applications that are created by an entity capable of ownership (e.g., humans, corporations, universities). The owner entity holds rights over the manner in which the intellectual property can be used and distributed. Protections for intellectual property may come in the form of copyrights, patents, and laws that apply to theft. Copyright applies to published information. Patents apply to novel processes and inventions. Certain types of intellectual property can only be protected by being secretive. For example, magic tricks cannot be copyrighted or patented; this is why magicians guard their intellectual property against theft. Intellectual property can be sold outright, or used under a legal agreement (e.g., license, contract, transfer agreement, royalty, usage fee, and so on). Intellectual property can also be shared freely, while retaining ownership (e.g., open source license, GNU license, FOSS license, Creative Commons license).

Interoperability It is desirable and often necessary to create software that operates with other software, regardless of differences in hardware, operating systems and programming language. Interoperability, though vital to the field of Precision Medicine, remains an elusive goal.

Introspection A method by which data objects can be interrogated to yield information about themselves (e.g., properties, values, and class membership). Through introspection, the relationships among the data objects can be examined. Introspective methods are built into object-oriented languages. The data provided by introspection can be applied, at run-time, to modify a script's operation, a technique known as reflection. Specifically, any properties, methods, and encapsulated data of a data object can be used in the script to modify the script's run-time behavior.

Legacy data Data collected by an information system that has been replaced by a newer system, and which cannot be immediately integrated into the newer system's database. For example, hospitals regularly replace their hospital information systems with new systems that promise greater efficiencies, expanded services, or improved inter-operability with other information systems. In many cases, the new system cannot readily integrate the data collected from the older system. The previously collected data becomes a legacy to the new system. In many cases, legacy data is simply "stored" for some arbitrary period of time, in case someone actually needs to retrieve any of the legacy data. After a decade or so, the hospital may find itself without any staff members who are capable of locating the storage site of the legacy data, or moving the data into a modern operating system, or interpreting the stored data, or retrieving appropriate data records, or producing a usable query output.

Metadata Data that describes data. For example in XML, a data description language, metadata flanks the included data quantity. <age>48 years</age>. In this example, <age> is the metadata and 48 years is the data.

National Patient Identifier Some countries employ a National Patient Identifier (NPI) system. In these cases, when a citizen receives treatment at any medical facility in the country, the transaction is recorded under the same permanent and unique identifier. Doing so enables the data collected on individuals, from multiple hospitals, to be merged. Hence, physicians can retrieve patient data that was collected anywhere in the nation. In countries with NPIs, data scientists have access to complete patient records and can perform healthcare studies that would be impossible to perform in countries that lack NPI systems. In the United States, where a system of NPIs has not been adopted, there is a perception that such a system would constitute an invasion of privacy.

Object-oriented programming language Although programming is a subject that cannot be covered in this book, it is worth noting that all of the general features of an object-oriented programming language are found in classifications, as described in Section 7.1, "The Principles of Classification." In particular, all objects are assigned a class; classes have parent classes, and the class-specific properties and behaviors of ancestral classes (i.e., the class methods) are inherited by all of the classes in its descendant lineage. Hence, data objects assigned to formal classifications can be seamlessly adopted to an object-oriented framework. This has been explored in the computer science literature [2,16].

Overfitting Overfitting occurs when a formula describes a set of data very closely, but does not lead to any sensible explanation for the behavior of the data, and does not predict the behavior of comparable data sets. In the case of overfitting, the formula is said to describe the noise of the system, rather than the characteristic behavior of the system. Overfitting occurs frequently with models that perform iterative approximations on training data, coming closer and closer to the training data set with each iteration. Neural networks are an example of a data modeling strategy that is prone to overfitting [4].

P-value The p-value is the probability of getting a set of results that are as extreme or more extreme than the set of results you observed, assuming that the null hypothesis is true (that there is no statistical difference between the results). The p-value has come under great criticism over the decades, with a growing consensus that the p-value is subject to misinterpretation or used in situations wherein it does not apply [214]. Repeated samplings of data from large data sets will produce small p-values that cannot be directly applied to determining statistical significance. It is best to think of the p-value as just another piece of information that tells you something about how sets of observations compare with one another, and not as a test of statistical significance.

Pareto's principle Also known as the 80/20 rule, Pareto's principle holds that a small number of items account for the vast majority of observations. For example, a small number of rich people account for the majority of wealth. Just two countries, India plus China, account for 37% of the world population. Within most countries, a small number of provinces or geographic areas contain the majority of the population of a country (e.g., East and West coastlines of the United States) A small number of books, compared with the total number of published books, account for the majority of book sales. Likewise, a small number of diseases account for the bulk of human morbidity and mortality. For example, two common types of cancer, basal cell carcinoma of skin and squamous cell carcinoma of skin, account for about 1 million new cases of cancer each year in the United States. This is approximately the sum total of for all other types of cancer combined. We see a similar phenomenon when we count causes of death. About 2.6 million people die each year in the United States [215]. The top two causes of death account for 1,171,652 deaths (596,339 deaths from heart disease and 575,313 deaths from cancer [216]), or about 45% of all United States deaths. All of the remaining deaths are accounted for by more than 7000 conditions. Sets of data that follow Pareto's principle are often said to follow a Zipf distribution, or a power law distribution. These types of distributions are not tractable by standard statistical descriptors because they do not produce a symmetric bell-shaped curve. Simple measurements such as average and standard deviation have virtually no practical meaning when applied to Zipf distributions. Furthermore, the Gaussian distribution does not apply, and none of the statistical inferences built upon an assumption of a Gaussian distribution will hold on data sets that observe Pareto's principle.

Pharmacogenomics Pharmacogenomics refers to pharmacologic studies wherein the entire genome is examined, and correlations are pursued among sets of genes. Drug response predictions based on gene expression profiles could be described with the term "pharmacogenomics." Tests on a single gene, or on several individual genes, intended to predict the response to a drug might be described with the term "pharmacogenetics." The central dictum of pharmacogenomics seems to be that every individual's genome is unique; hence, every disease occurring in an individual is unique; hence, every response to treatment is unique for each individual; hence, every occurrence of disease deserves to be treated with a medication designed for the unique individual. Underlying these hypotheses is the assumption that the key elements of an individual's disease are captured in the unique sequence of the individual's genome. This assumption short-changes the complexity of genetics. Biological systems have multiple dependencies, and the genome is one player, among many. Furthermore, the artifactual distinction between "etics" and "omics" creates a dichotomy where none exists. A gene belongs in a genome, and a genome contains genes; they are interrelated and codependent concepts. As it happens, the terms "pharmacogenetics" and "pharmacogenomics" are commonly used interchangeably.

Power In statistics, power describes the likelihood that a test will detect an effect, if the effect actually exists. In many cases, power reflects sample size. The larger the sample size, the more likely that an experiment will detect a true effect, thus correctly rejecting the null hypothesis.

Power law A mathematical formula wherein a particular value of some quantity varies as an inverse power of some other quantity [73,74]. The power law applies to many natural phenomena and describes the Zipf distribution or Pareto's principle. The power law is unrelated to the power of a statistical test.

Precision Precision is the degree of exactitude of a measurement and is verified by its reproducibility (i.e., whether repeated measurements of the same quantity produce the same result). Accuracy measures how close your data comes to being correct. Data can be accurate but imprecise or precise but inaccurate. If you have a 10-pound object, and you report its weight as 7.2376 pounds, every time you weigh the object, then your precision is remarkable, but your accuracy is dismal. What are the practical limits of precision measurements? Let us stretch our imaginations, for a moment, and pretend that we have just found an artifact left by an alien race that excelled in the science of measurement. As a sort of time capsule for the universe, their top scientists decided to collect the history of their civilization, encoded in binary. Their story looked something like "001011011101000..." extended to about 5 million places. Rather than print the sequence out on a piece of paper or a computer disc, these aliens simply converted the sequence to a decimal length (i.e., ".001011011101000...") and marked the length on a bar composed of a substance that would never change its size. To decode the bar, and recover the history of the alien race, one would simply need to have a highly precise measuring instrument that would yield the original binary sequence. Computational linguists could translate the sequence to text, and the recorded history of the alien race would be revealed! Of course, the whole concept is built on an impossible premise. Nothing can be measured accurately to 5 million places. We live in a universe with practical limits (i.e., the sizes of atomic particles, the speed of light, the Heisenberg uncertainty principle, the maximum mass of a star, the second law of thermodynamics, the unpredictability of highly complex systems, division by zero). There are many things that we simply cannot do, no matter how hard we try. The most precise measurement achieved by modern science has been in the realm of atomic clocks, where accuracy of 18 decimal places has been claimed [217]. Nonetheless, many scientific disasters are caused by our ignorance of our own limitations, and our persistent gullibility, leading us to believe that precision claimed is precision obtained.

Primary data The original set of data, collected to serve a particular purpose or to answer a particular set of questions, and usually intended for use by the same individuals who collected the data. Primary data is referred to as secondary data when it is used by someone other than the original person or persons who collected the data. Confusing, insofar as primary data and secondary data can both refer to the same data set.

Privacy versus confidentiality The concepts of confidentiality and of privacy are often confused, and it is useful to clarify their separate meanings. Confidentiality is the process of keeping a secret with which you have been entrusted. You break confidentiality if you reveal the secret to another person. You violate privacy when you use the secret to annoy the person whose confidential information was acquired. If you give a friend your unlisted telephone number in confidence, then your friend is expected to protect this confidentiality by never revealing the number to other persons. In addition, your friend may be expected to protect your privacy by resisting the temptation to call you in the middle of the night, to complain about a mutual acquaintance. In this case, the same information object (unlisted telephone number) is encumbered by separable confidentiality and privacy obligations.

Reanalysis Subjecting a study to a new analysis, using the same data and beginning with the same questions. First analyses should always be considered tentative until such time as they undergo reanalysis and validation. **One could argue that the most important purpose of analysis is to serve as the prelude to reanalysis. Although there have been instances when reanalysis has discredited published conclusions, it should be remembered that the goal of reanalysis is to confirm, strengthen, and extend prior knowledge.**

Reconciliation Usually refers to identifiers, and involves verifying an object that is assigned a particular identifier in one information system has been provided the same identifier in some other system. For example, if you were assigned identifier 967bc9e7-fea0-4b09-92e7-d9327c405d78 in a legacy record system, you should like to be assigned the same identifier in the new record system. If that were the case, your records in both systems could be combined. If you were assigned an identifier in one system that is different from your assigned identifier in another system, then the two identifiers must be reconciled to determine that they both refer to the same unique data object (i.e., yourself). Despite claims to the contrary, there is no possible way by which information systems with poor identifier systems can be sensibly reconciled. Consider this example. A hospital has two separate registry systems: one for dermatology cases and another for psychiatry cases. The hospital would like to merge records from the two services. Because of sloppy identifier and registration protocols, a single patient has been registered 10 times in the dermatology system, and 6 times in the psychiatry system, each time with different addresses, social security numbers, birthdates, and spellings of the name. A reconciliation algorithm is applied, and one of the identifiers from the dermatology service is matched positively against one of the records from the psychiatry service. Performance studies on the algorithm indicate that the merged records have a 99.8% chance of belonging to the same patient. So what? Though the two merged identifiers correctly point to the same patient, there are 14 (9 + 5) residual identifiers for the patient still unmatched. The patient's merged record will not contain his complete clinical history. Furthermore, in this hypothetical instance, analyses of patient population data will mistakenly attribute one patient's clinical findings to as many as 15 different patients, and the set of 15 records in the corrupted deidentified dataset may contain mixed-in information from an indeterminate number of additional patients! If the preceding analysis seems harsh, consider these words, from the Healthcare Information and Management Systems Society, "A local system with a poorly maintained or 'dirty' master person index (MPI) will only proliferate and contaminate all of the other systems to which it links [218]."

Secondary data Data collected by someone else. Much of the data analyses performed today are done on secondary data [219]. Because secondary data is, by definition, prepared by someone else, who cannot anticipate how you will use the data, it is important to provide secondary data that is introspective (i.e., self-explanatory).

Semantics The study of meaning (Greek root, semantikos, significant meaning). In the context of data science, semantics is the technique of creating meaningful assertions about data objects. A meaningful assertion, as used here, is a triple consisting of an identified data object, a data value, and a descriptor for the data value. In practical terms, semantics involves making assertions about data objects (i.e., making triples), combining assertions about data objects (i.e., merging triples), and assigning data objects to classes; hence relating triples to other triples. As a word of warning, few informaticians would define semantics in these terms, but most definitions for semantics are functionally equivalent to the definition offered here. Most language is unstructured and meaningless. Consider the assertion: Sam is tired. This is an adequately structured sentence with a subject verb and object. But what is the meaning of the sentence? There are a lot of people named Sam. Which Sam is being referred to in this sentence? What does it mean to say that Sam is tired? Is "tiredness" a constitutive property of Sam, or does it only apply to specific moments? If so, for what moment in time is the assertion, "Sam is tired" actually true? To a computer, meaning comes from assertions that have a specific, identified subject associated with some sensible piece of fully described data (metadata coupled with the data it describes). As you may suspect, virtually all data contained in databases does not qualify as "meaningful."

Social Security Number The common strategy, in the United States, of employing social security numbers as identifiers is often counterproductive, owing to entry error, mistaken memory, or the intention to deceive. Efforts to reduce errors by requiring individuals to produce their original social security cards put an unreasonable burden on honest individuals, who rarely carry their cards, and provide an advantage to dishonest individuals, who can easily forge social security cards. Institutions that compel patients to provide a social security number have dubious legal standing. The social security number was originally intended as a device for validating a person's standing in the social security system. More recently, the purpose of the social security number has been expanded to track taxable transactions (i.e., bank accounts, salaries). Other uses of the social security number are not protected by law. The Social Security Act (section 208 of Title 42 U.S. Code 408) prohibits most entities from compelling anyone to divulge his/her social security number. Legislation or judicial action may one day stop healthcare institutions from compelling patients to divulge their social security numbers as a condition for providing medical care. Prudent and forward-thinking institutions will limit their reliance on social security numbers as personal identifiers.

Specification A specification is a formal method for describing objects (physical objects such as nuts and bolts or symbolic objects, such as numbers, or concepts expressed as text). In general, specifications do not require specific items of information (i.e., they do not impose restrictions on the content that is included in or excluded from documents), and specifications do not impose any order of appearance of the data contained in the document (i.e., you can mix up and rearrange specified objects, if you like). Specifications are not generally certified by a standards organization. They are generally produced by special interest organizations, and the legitimacy of a specification depends on its popularity. Examples of specifications are RDF (Resource Description Framework) produced by the W3C (World Wide Web Consortium), and TCP/IP (Transfer Control Protocol/Internet Protocol), maintained by the Internet Engineering Task Force. The most widely implemented specifications are simple and easily implemented. The concept of "data specification" needs to be distinguished from the concept of "data standard." Data standards, in general, tell you what must be included in a conforming document, and, in most cases, dictates the format of the final document. In many instances, standards bar inclusion of any data that is not included in the standard (e.g., you should not include astronomical data in a clinical X-ray report). Specifications simply provide a formal way for describing the data that you choose to include in your document. XML and RDF, a semantic dialect of XML, are examples of specifications. They both tell you how data should be represented, but neither tell you what data to include, or how your document or data set should appear. Files that comply with a standard are rigidly organized and can be easily parsed and manipulated by software specifically designed to adhere to the standard. Files that comply with a specification are typically self-describing documents that contain within themselves all the information necessary for a human or a computer to derive meaning from the file contents. In theory, files that comply with a specification can be parsed and manipulated by generalized software designed to parse the markup language of the specification (e.g., XML, RDF) and to organize the data into data structures defined within the file.

Standard A standard is a set of rules for doing a particular task or expressing a particular kind of information. The purpose of standards is to ensure that all objects that meet the standard have certain physical or informational features in common, thus facilitating interchange, reproducibility, interoperability, and reducing costs of operation. In the case of standards for data and information, standards typically dictate what data is to be included, how that data should be expressed and arranged, and what data is to be excluded. Standards are developed by any of hundreds of standards developing agencies, but there are only a few international agencies that bestow approval of standards.

Time A large portion of data analysis is concerned, in one way or another, with the times that events occur or the times that observations are made, or the times that signals are sampled. Here are three examples that demonstrate why this is so: (1) most scientific and predictive assertions relate how variables change with respect to one another, over time; and (2) a single data object may have many different data values, over time, and only timing data will tell us how to distinguish one observation from another; (3) computer transactions are tracked in logs, and logs are composed of time-annotated descriptions of the transactions. Data objects often lose their significance if they are not associated with an accurate time measurement. Because accurate time data is easily captured by modern computers, time annotations should be attached to all archived measurements, transactions, and events.

Time-stamp Many data objects are temporal events and all temporal events must be given a time-stamp indicating the time that the event occurred, using a standard measurement for time. The time-stamp must be accurate, persistent, and immutable. The Unix epoch time (equivalent to the Posix epoch time) is available for most operating systems and consists of the number of seconds that have elapsed since January 1, 1970, midnight, Greenwich mean time. The Unix epoch time can easily be converted into any other standard representation of time. The duration of any event can be easily calculated by subtracting the beginning time from the ending time. Because the timing of events can be maliciously altered, scrupulous data managers may choose to employ a trusted timestamp protocol by which a timestamp can be verified.

Trilateral retinoblastoma The occurrence of hereditary bilateral retinoblastomas is sometimes followed by the occurrence of a pineoblastoma, and this is referred to as trilateral retinoblastoma. The pineal gland has an evolutionary anlage identical to that of the eye. The development of a pineal equivalent of a retinoblastoma, in the same individual with bilateral retinoblastomas, suggests that, in the case of these hereditary tumors, pathogenesis follows a sequence of steps that begins early in embryologic development [220].

Triple In computer semantics, a triple is an identified data object associated with a data element and the description of the data element. In theory, all data sets can be designed as collections of triples. When the data and metadata held in triples are organized into ontologies consisting of classes of objects and associated properties, the data set can provide introspection (the ability of a data object to be self-descriptive).

Type errors Statistical tests should not be confused with mathematical truths. Every statistician understands that conclusions drawn from statistical analyses are occasionally wrong. Statisticians, resigned to accept their own fallibilities, have classified their errors into five types: Type 1 error—Rejecting the null hypothesis when the null hypothesis is correct (i.e., seeing an effect when there was none). Type 2 error—Accepting the null hypotheses when the null hypothesis is false. (i.e., seeing no effect when there was one). Type 3 error—Rejecting the null hypothesis correctly, but for the wrong reason, leading to an erroneous interpretation of the data in favor of an incorrect affirmative statement. Type 4 error—Erroneous conclusion based on performing the wrong statistical test. Type 5 error—Erroneous conclusion based on bad data.

Universal and perpetual Wherein a set of data or methods can be understood and utilized by anyone, from any discipline, at any time. It's a tall order, but a worthy goal. Much of the data collected over the centuries of recorded history is of little value because it was never adequately described when it was recorded (e.g., unknown time of recording, unknown source, unfamiliar measurements, unwritten protocols). Efforts to resuscitate large collections of painstakingly collected data are often abandoned simply because there is no way of verifying, or even understanding, the original data [1]. Data scientists who want their data to serve for posterity should use simple specifications, and should include general document annotations such as the Dublin Core.

Universally unique identifier (UUID) A protocol for producing unique identifiers (i.e., a long sequence of seemingly random alphanumeric characters) that can be attached to data objects [11]. This protocol is very useful, and most modern programming languages have modules for generating UUIDs [2].

Y-chromosome The male sex chromosome. Genetically normal human males have one X chromosome and one Y chromosome. The Y chromosome contains genes inherited exclusively from the paternal side; hence, Y chromosome variations and abnormalities serve as clues to paternal lineage.

Zipf distribution George Kingsley Zipf (1902–50) was an American linguist who demonstrated that, for most languages, a small number of words account for the majority of occurrences of all the words found in prose. Specifically, he found that the frequency of any word is inversely proportional to its placement in a list of words, ordered by their decreasing frequencies in text. The first word in the frequency list will occur about twice as often as the second word in the list, three times as often as the third word in the list, and so on. Many data collections follow a Zipf distribution (e.g., income distribution in a population, energy consumption by country, and so on) [73,74]. Zipf distributions cannot be sensibly described by the standard statistical measures that apply to normal distributions. Zipf distributions are instances of Pareto's principle. The Zipf distribution is discussed in depth elsewhere.

References

[1] Berman JJ. Repurposing legacy data: innovative case studies. Waltham, MA: Morgan Kaufmann; 2015.

[2] Berman JJ. Data simplification: taming information with open source tools. Waltham, MA: Morgan Kaufmann; 2016.

[3] Berman JJ. Biomedical informatics. Sudbury, MA: Jones and Bartlett; 2007.

[4] Berman JJ. Principles of big data: preparing, sharing, and analyzing complex information. Waltham, MA: Morgan Kaufmann; 2013.

[5] Berman JJ, Bhatia K. Biomedical data integration: using xml to link clinical and research datasets. Expert Rev Mol Diagn 2005;5:329–36.

[6] Katsanis SH, Wagner JK. Characterization of the standard and recommended CODIS markers. J Forensic Sci 2013;58(Suppl 1):S169–72.

[7] Guessous I, Gwinn M, Khoury MJ. Genome-wide association studies in pharmacogenomics: untapped potential for translation. Genome Med 2009;1:46.

[8] McCarthy JJ, Hilfiker R. The use of single-nucleotide polymorphism maps in pharmacogenomics. Nat Biotechnol 2000;18:505–8.

[9] Nebert DW, Zhang G, Vesell ES. From human genetics and genomics to pharmacogenetics and pharmaco-genomics: past lessons, future directions. Drug Metab Rev 2008;40:187–224.

[10] Personalised medicines: hopes and realities. London: The Royal Society; 2005. Available from: https://royalsociety.org/~/media/Royal_Society_Content/policy/publications/2005/9631.pdf [Accessed 29 July 2017].

[11] Leach P, Mealling M, Salz R. A Universally Unique IDentifier (UUID) URN Namespace. Network Working Group, Request for Comment 4122, Standards Track. Available from: http://www.ietf.org/rfc/rfc4122.txt [Accessed 1 January 2015].

[12] Mealling M. RFC 3061. A URN Namespace of Object Identifiers. Network Working Group; 2001. Available from: https://www.ietf.org/rfc/rfc3061.txt [Accessed 1 January 2015].

[13] Berman JJ. Methods in medical informatics: fundamentals of healthcare programming in Perl, Python, and Ruby. Boca Raton: Chapman and Hall; 2010.

[14] Klyne G. Newman C. Date and Time on the Internet: Timestamps. Network Working Group Request for Comments RFC:3339, Available from: http://tools.ietf.org/html/rfc3339 [Accessed 15 September 2015].

[15] Downey AB. Think DSP: digital signal processing in Python. Version 0.9.8.Needham, MA: Green Tea Press; 2014.

[16] Berman JJ. Ruby programming for medicine and biology. Sudbury, MA: Jones and Bartlett; 2008.

[17] Joint NEMA/COCIR/JIRA Security and Privacy Committee (SPC). Identification and allocation of basic security rules in healthcare imaging systems; September, 2002. Available from: http://www.medicalimaging.org/wp-content/uploads/2011/02/Identification_and_Allocation_of_Basic_Security_Rules_In_Healthcare_Imaging_Systems-September_2002.pdf [Accessed 10 January 2013].

[18] Committee on A Framework for Developing a New Taxonomy of Disease, Board on Life Sciences, Division on Earth and Life Studies, National Research Council of the National Academies. Toward precision medicine: building a knowledge network for biomedical research and a new taxonomy of disease. Washington, DC: The National Academies Press; 2011.

[19] Berman JJ. De-Identification. U.S. Office of Civil Rights (HHS), Workshop on the HIPAA Privacy Rule's De-identification Standard, Washington, DC; March 8–9, 2010, Available from: http://hhshipaaprivacy.com/assets/4/resources/Panel1_Berman.pdf [Accessed 24 August 2012].

[20] Department of Health and Human Services. 45 CFR (Code of Federal Regulations), Parts 160 through 164. Standards for Privacy of Individually Identifiable Health Information (Final Rule). Federal Register, Vol. 65, No. 250, p. 82461–510; December 28, 2000.

[21] Department of Health and Human Services.45 CFR (Code of Federal Regulations), 46. Protection of Human Subjects (Common Rule). Federal Register, Vol. 56, p. 28003–32; June 18, 1991.

[22] Berman JJ. Threshold protocol for the exchange of confidential medical data. BMC Med Res Methodol 2002;2:12.

[23] Berman JJ. Confidentiality for medical data miners. Artif Intell Med 2002;26:25–36.

[24] Berman JJ, Moore GW, Hutchins GM. Maintaining patient confidentiality in the public domain internet autopsy database. Proc AMIA Annu Fall Symp 1996;328–32.

[25] Dalen JE. Only in America: bankruptcy due to health care costs. Am J Med 2009;122:699.

[26] Lewin T. Texas orders health clinics to turn over patient data. The New York Times; October 23, 2015.

[27] Hutchins GM, Berman JJ, Moore GW, Hanzlick R. Practice guidelines for autopsy pathology. Arch Pathol Lab Med 1999;123:1085–92.

[28] Hutchins GM, Berman JJ, Moore GW, Hanzlick RL, Collins K. Autopsy reporting. In: Collins KA, Hutchins GM, editors. Autopsy performance and reporting. 2nd ed. Northfield, IL: College of American Pathologists; 2003. p. 265–74.

[29] Berman JJ, Moore GW, Hutchins GM. Internet Autopsy Database. Hum Pathol 1997;28:393–4.

[30] Moore GW, Berman JJ, Hanzlick RL, Buchino JJ, Hutchins GM. A prototype international autopsy database: 1625 consecutive fetal and neonatal autopsy facesheets spanning twenty years. Arch Pathol Lab Med 1996;120:782–5.

[31] Ulbright T. Germ cell tumors of the gonads: a selective review emphasizing problems in differential diagnosis, newly appreciated, and controversial issues. Mod Pathol 2005;18:S61–79.

[32] Alizadeh AA, Eisen MB, Davis RE, Ma C, Lossos IS, Rosenwald A, et al. Distinct types of diffuse large B-cell lymphoma identified by gene expression profiling. Nature 2000;403:503–11.

[33] Rosenwald A, Wright G, Chan WC, Connors JM, Campo E, Fisher RI, et al. Lymphoma/leukemia molecular profiling project: The use of molecular profiling to predict survival after chemotherapy for diffuse large-B-cell lymphoma. N Engl J Med 2002;346:1937–47.

[34] Hearp ML, Locante AM, Ben-Rubin M, Dietrich R, David O. Validity of sampling error as a cause of noncorrelation. Cancer 2007;111:275–9.

[35] Baak JPA. Manual of quantitative pathology in cancer diagnosis and prognosis. Heidelberg: Springer Verlag; 1991. p. 14.

[36] Saul S. Prone to error: earliest steps to find cancer. New York Times; July 19, 2010.

[37] Hruban RH, Wilentz RE, Maitra A. Identification and analysis of precursors to invasive pancreatic cancer. Methods Mol Med 2005;103:1–13.

[38] Schnitt SJ. The diagnosis and management of pre-invasive breast disease: flat epithelial atypia—classification, pathologic features and clinical significance. Breast Cancer Res 2003;5:263–8.

[39] Tzen C, Huang Y, Fu Y. Is atypical follicular adenoma of the thyroid a preinvasive malignancy? Hum Pathol 2003;34:666–9.

[40] Van de Vijver MJ, Peterse H. The diagnosis and management of pre-invasive breast disease: pathological diagnosis—problems with existing classifications. Cancer Res 2003;5:269.

[41] Nakhleh RE, Nose V, Colasacco C, Fatheree LA, Lillemoe TJ, DC MC, et al. Interpretive diagnostic error reduction in surgical pathology and cytology: guideline from the College of American pathologists pathology and laboratory quality center and the association of directors of anatomic and surgical pathology. Arch Pathol Lab Med 2016;140:29–40.

[42] Weigelt B, Reis-Filho JS. Molecular profiling currently offers no more than tumour morphology and basic immunohistochemistry. Breast Cancer Res 2010;12:S5.

[43] Rosai J. The continuing role of morphology in the molecular age. Mod Pathol 2001;14:258–60.

[44] Why mouse matters. National Human Genome Institute. Available from: https://www.genome.gov/10001345 [Accessed 19 July 2017].

[45] Berman JJ, Iseri OA. Acquired Gaucher cells located in dermis near a malignant hidradenoma. Ultrastruct Pathol 1988;12:245–6.

[46] Delacourte A. Tauopathies: recent insights into old diseases. Folia Neuropathol 2005;43(4):244–57.

[47] Gissen P, Maher ER. Cargos and genes: insights into vesicular transport from inherited human disease. J Med Genet 2007;44:545–55.

[48] Marth T, Roux M, von Herbay A, Meuer SC, Feurle GE. Persistent reduction of complement receptor 3 alpha-chain expressing mononuclear blood cells and transient inhibitory serum factors in Whipple's disease. Clin Immunol Immunopathol 1994;72:217–26.

[49] Hayes A. VA to apologize for mistaken Lou Gehrig's disease notices. CNN; August 26, 2009. Available from: http://www.cnn.com/2009/POLITICS/08/26/veterans.letters.disease [Accessed 4 September 2012].

[50] Hall PA, Lemoine NR. Comparison of manual data coding errors in 2 hospitals. J Clin Pathol 1986;39:622–6.

[51] Berman JJ. Doublet method for very fast autocoding. BMC Med Inform Decis Mak 2004;4:16.

[52] Berman JJ. Resources for comparing the speed and performance of medical autocoders. BMC Med Inform Decis Mak 2004;4:8.

[53] Berman JJ. Nomenclature-based data retrieval without prior annotation: facilitating biomedical data integration with fast doublet matching. In Silico Biol 2005;5:0029.

[54] Mallon T. The best part of every book comes last. The New York Times; March 10, 1991.

[55] Shah NH, Jonquet C, Chiang AP, Butte AJ, Chen R, Musen MA. Ontology-driven indexing of public datasets for translational bioinformatics. BMC Bioinformatics 2009;10:S1.

[56] Lamb J. Embedded indexing. Indexer 2005;24:206–9.

[57] Berthoz A, Weiss G. Simplexity: simplifying principles for a complex world. London: Editions Odile Jacob Book, Yale University Press; 2012.

[58] Rigler T. DOD discloses new figures on Korean War dead. Army News Service; May 30, 2000.

[59] Gordon R. Great medical disasters. New York: Dorset Press; 1986. p. 155–60.

[60] Centers for disease Control and Prevention, editor. Vital signs: unintentional injury deaths among persons aged 0-19 Years; United States, 2000-2009. MMWR Morb Mortal Wkly Rep 2012;61:1–7.

[61] Pennisi E. Gene counters struggle to get the right answer. Science 2003;301:1040–1.

[62] How many genes are in the human genome? Human genome project information. Available from: http://www.ornl.gov/sci/techresources/Human_Genome/faq/genenumber.shtml [Accessed 10 June 2012].

[63] Berman JJ. Perl programming for medicine and biology. Sudbury, MA: Jones and Bartlett; 2007.

[64] Levenberg K. A method for the solution of certain non-linear problems in least squares. Q Appl Math 1944;2:164–8.

[65] Marquardt DW. An algorithm for the least-squares estimation of nonlinear parameters. SIAM J Appl Math 1963;11:431–41.

[66] Vassallo E, Azzopardi C, Pullicino R, Grech R. Beware the person with the glass eye and the large liver. BMJ Case Rep May 21, 2014.

[67] Azzopardi C, Attard J, Vassallo E, Grech R. Mounier-Kuhn syndrome: more than just a cough. BMJ Case Rep Sep 21, 2014.

[68] Cook DP, Adam RJ, Abou Alaiwa MH, Eberlein M, Klesney-Tait JA, Parekh KR, et al. Mounier-Kuhn syndrome: a case of tracheal smooth muscle remodeling. Clin Case Rep 2016;5:93–6.

[69] Byrne P, Clough C. Hypochromia iridis in acquired Horner's syndrome. J Neurol Neurosurg Psychiatry 1992;55:413.

[70] Fikes BJ. The patient from the future, here today. The San Diego Union-Tribune; March 5, 2014.

[71] Grivell L. Mining the bibliome: searching for a needle in a haystack? EMBO Rep 2002;3:200–3.

[72] Pusztai L, Mazouni C, Anderson K, Wu Y, Symmans WF. Molecular classification of breast cancer: limitations and potential. Oncologist 2006;11:868–77.

[73] Clauset A, Shalizi CR, Newman MEJ. Power-law distributions in empirical data. SIAM Rev 2009;51:661–703.

[74] Newman MEJ. Power laws, Pareto distributions and Zipf's law. Contemp Phys 2005;46:323–51.

[75] Director's challenge: toward a molecular classification of tumors Available from: http://grants.nih.gov/grants/guide/rfa-files/RFA-CA-98-027.html [Accessed 20 July 2017].

[76] Ramaswamy S, Tamayo P, Rifkin R, Mukherjee S, Yeang C, Angelo M, et al. Multiclass cancer diagnosis using tumor gene expression signatures. Proc Natl Acad Sci U S A 2001;98:15149–15154.

[77] Venet D, Dumont JE, Detours V. Most random gene expression signatures are significantly associated with breast cancer outcome. PLoS Comput Biol 2011;7:e1002240.

[78] Ioannidis JP. Microarrays and molecular research: noise discovery? Lancet 2005;365:454–5.

[79] Irizarry RA, Warren D, Spencer F, Kim IF, Biswal S, Frank BC, et al. Multiple-laboratory comparison of microarray platforms. Nat Methods 2005;2:345–50.

[80] Larkin JE, Frank BC, Gavras H, Sultana R, Quackenbush J. Independence and reproducibility across microarray platforms. Nat Methods 2005;2:337–44.

[81] Michiels S, Koscielny S, Hill C. Prediction of cancer outcome with microarrays: a multiple random validation strategy. Lancet 2005;365:488–92.

[82] Misconduct in science: an array of errors. The Economist; September 10, 2011.

[83] Knudson Jr AG, Hethcote HW, Brown BW. Mutation and childhood cancer: a probabilistic model for the incidence of retinoblastoma. Proc Natl Acad Sci U S A 1975;72:5116–20.

[84] Knudson AG. Mutation and cancer: statistical study of retinoblastoma. Proc Natl Acad Sci U S A 1971;68:820–3.

[85] French CA. NUT midline carcinoma. Cancer Genet Cytogenet 2010;203:16–20.

[86] Lee SG, Jung SP, Lee HY, Kim S, Kim HY, Kim I, et al. Secretory breast carcinoma: a report of three cases and a review of the literature. Oncol Lett 2014;8:683–6.

[87] Makretsov N, He M, Hayes M, Chia S, Horsman DE, Sorensen PH, et al. A fluorescence in situ hybridization study of ETV6-NTRK3 fusion gene in secretory breast carcinoma. Genes Chromosom Cancer 2004; 40:152–7.

[88] Blanquet V, Turleau C, Gross-Morand MS, Senamaud-Beaufort C, Doz F, et al. Spectrum of germline mutations in the RB1 gene: a study of 232 patients with hereditary and nonhereditary retinoblastoma. Hum Mol Genet 1995;4:383–8.

[89] Bessho F. Effects of mass screening on age-specific incidence of neuroblastoma. Int J Cancer 1996;67:520–2.

[90] Takahashi H, Matsui T, Hisabe T, Hirai F, Takatsu N, Tsurumi K, et al. Second peak in the distribution of age at onset of ulcerative colitis in relation to smoking cessation. J Gastroenterol Hepatol 2014;29:1603–8.

[91] Lizcova L, Zemanova Z, Malinova E, Jarosova M, Mejstrikova E, Smisek P, et al. A novel recurrent chromosomal aberration involving chromosome 7 in childhood myelodysplastic syndrome. Cancer Genet Cytogenet 2010;201:52–6.

[92] Taubenberger JK, Morens DM. 1918 influenza: the mother of all pandemics. Emerg Infect Dis 2006;12:15–22.

[93] Subbiah IM, Subbiah V. Exceptional responders: in search of the science behind the miracle cancer cures. Future Oncol 2015;11:1–4.

[94] Exceptional responders initiative: questions and answers. National Cancer Institute Press Office; September 24, 2014, updated: March 23, 2015. Available from: https://www.cancer.gov/news-events/press-releases/2014/ExceptionalRespondersQandA [Accessed 5 January 2017].

[95] Zhu Z, Ihle NT, Rejto PA, Zarrinkar PP. Outlier analysis of functional genomic profiles enriches for oncology targets and enables precision medicine. BMC Genomics 2016;17:455.

[96] Abushakra S, Porsteinsson A, Vellas B, et al. Clinical benefits of tramiprosate in Alzheimer's disease are associated with higher number of APOE4 alleles: the APOE4 gene-dose effect. J Prev Alzheimers Dis 2016;3:219–28.

[97] Perez-Pena R. New York's tally of heat deaths draws scrutiny. The New York Times; August 18, 2006.

[98] Chiang S. Heat waves, the "other" natural disaster: perspectives on an often ignored epidemic. Global Pulse. American Medical Student Association; 2006.

[99] Diaconis P, Efron B. Computer-intensive methods in statistics. Sci Am 1983;116–130.

[100] Simon JL. Resampling: the new statistics. 2nd ed; Available from: http://www.resample.com/intro-text-online/.

[101] Efron B, Tibshirani RJ. An introduction to the bootstrap. Boca Raton, FL: CRC Press; 1998.

[102] Unreliable research: trouble at the lab. The Economist; October 19, 2013.

[103] Prasad V, Vandross A, Toomey C, Cheung M, Rho J, Quinn S, et al. A decade of reversal: an analysis of 146 contradicted medical practices. Mayo Clin Proc 2013;88:790–8.

[104] Kolata G. Cancer fight: unclear tests for new drug. The New York Times; April 19, 2010.

[105] Baker M. Reproducibility crisis: blame it on the antibodies. Nature 2015;521:274–6.

[106] Ioannidis JP. Why most published research findings are false. PLoS Med 2005;2:e124.

[107] Labos C. It ain't necessarily so: why much of the medical literature is wrong. Medscape News and Perspectives; September 09, 2014.

[108] Gilbert E, Strohminger N. We found only one-third of published psychology research is reliable—now what? The Conversation; August 27, 2015. Available from: http://theconversation.com/we-found-only-one-third-of-published-psychology-research-is-reliable-now-what-46596 [Accessed 27 August 2015].

[109] Naik G. Scientists' elusive goal: reproducing study results. Wall Street Journal; December 2, 2011.

[110] Zimmer C. A sharp rise in retractions prompts calls for reform. The New York Times; April 16, 2012.

[111] Altman LK. Falsified data found in gene studies. The New York Times; October 30, 1996.

[112] Weaver D, Albanese C, Costantini F, Baltimore D. Retraction: altered repertoire of endogenous immunoglobulin gene expression in transgenic mice containing a rearranged mu heavy chain gene. Cell 1991;65:536 [inclusive].

[113] Chang K. Nobel winner in physiology retracts two papers. The New York Times; September 23, 2010.

[114] Fourth paper retracted at Potti's request. The Chronicle; March 3, 2011.

[115] Whoriskey P. Doubts about Johns Hopkins research have gone unanswered, scientist says. The Washington Post; March 11, 2013.

[116] Lin YY, Kiihl S, Suhail Y, Liu SY, Chou YH, Kuang Z, et al. Retraction: functional dissection of lysine deacetylases reveals that HDAC1 and p300 regulate AMPK. Nature 2013;482:251–5. retracted November.

[117] Shafer SL. Letter: to our readers. Anesthesia and Analgesia; February 20, 2009.

[118] Innovation or stagnation: challenge and opportunity on the critical path to new medical products. U.S. Department of Health and Human Services, Food and Drug Administration; 2004.

[119] Hurley D. Why are so few blockbuster drugs invented today? The New York Times; November 13, 2014.

[120] Angell M. The truth about the drug companies. The New York Review of Books Vol. 51; July 15, 2004.

[121] Quality of Health Care in America Committee, editor. Crossing the quality chasm: a new health system for the 21st Century. Washington, DC: Institute of Medicine; 2001.

[122] Wurtman RJ, Bettiker RL. The slowing of treatment discovery, 1965-1995. Nat Med 1996;2:5–6.

[123] Beizer B. Software testing techniques. 2nd ed. Hoboken, NJ: Van Nostrand Reinhold; 1990.

[124] Vlasic B. Toyota's slow awakening to a deadly problem. The New York Times; February 1, 2010.

[125] Lanier J. The complexity ceiling. In: Brockman J, editor. The next fifty years: science in the first half of the twenty-first century. New York: Vintage; 2002. p. 216–29.

[126] Sainani K. Error: What biomedical computing can learn from its mistakes. In: Biomedical Computation Review; 2011. p. 12–9. Fall.

[127] Bandelt H, Salas A. Contamination and sample mix-up can best explain some patterns of mtDNA instabilities in buccal cells and oral squamous cell carcinoma. BMC Cancer 2009;9:113.

[128] Knight J. Agony for researchers as mix-up forces retraction of ecstasy study. Nature 2003;425:109.

[129] Gerlinger M, Rowan AJ, Horswell S, Larkin J, Endesfelder D, Gronroos E, et al. Intratumor heterogeneity and branched evolution revealed by multiregion sequencing. N Engl J Med 2012;366:883–92.

[130] Kuderer NM, Burton KA, Blau S, Rose AL, Parker S, Lyman GH, et al. Comparison of 2 commercially available next-generation sequencing platforms in oncology. JAMA Oncol 2017;3:996–8.

[131] Satter RG. UK investigates 800,000 organ donor list errors. Associated Press; April 10, 2010.

[132] Andrew SE, Goldberg YP, Kremer B, Squitieri F, Theilmann J, Zeisler J, et al. Huntington disease without CAG expansion: phenocopies or errors in assignment? Am J Hum Genet 1994;54:852–63.

[133] Palanichamy MG, Zhang Y. Potential pitfalls in MitoChip detected tumor-specific somatic mutations: a call for caution when interpreting patient data. BMC Cancer 2010;10:597.

[134] Marshall E. How prevalent is fraud? That's a million dollar question. Science 2000;290:1662–3.

[135] Martin B. Scientific fraud and the power structure of science. Prometheus 1992;10:83–98.

[136] Berman JJ. Machiavelli's laboratory. Seattle, WA: Amazon Digital Services, Inc.; 2010.

[137] Findings of scientific misconduct. NIH Guide Vol. 26, No. 23; July 18, 1997 Available from: http://grants.nih.gov/grants/guide/notice-files/not97-151.html.

[138] Findings of scientific misconduct. Department of Health and Human Services. Notice NOT-OD-01-048; July 10, 2001 Available from: http://grants.nih.gov/grants/guide/notice-files/NOT-OD-01-048.html [Accessed 8 October 2009].

[139] Findings of scientific misconduct. NIH GUIDE, Vol. 26, No. 15; May 9, 1997. Available from: http://grants.nih.gov/grants/guide/notice-files/not97-097.html.

[140] Findings of scientific misconduct. NOT-OD-02-020; December 13, 2001. Available from: http://grants.nih.gov/grants/guide/notice-files/NOT-OD-02-020.html.

[141] Findings of scientific misconduct. NIH GUIDE, Vol. 24, No. 33; September 22, 1995. Available from: http://grants.nih.gov/grants/guide/notice-files/not95-208.html.

[142] Cyranoski D. Woo Suk Hwang convicted, but not of fraud. Cloning pioneer gets two years for embezzlement and bioethics breach. Nature 2009;461:1181.

[143] Fuyuno I, Cyranoski D. Doubts over biochemist's data expose holes in Japanese fraud laws. Nature 2006;439:514.

[144] Sontag D. In harm's way: research, fraud and the V.A.; abuses endangered veterans in cancer drug experiments. The New York Times; February 6, 2005.

[145] Oltermann P. 'Superstar doctor' fired from Swedish institute over research 'lies'. The Guardian; March 24, 2016. Available from: https://www.theguardian.com/science/2016/mar/23/superstar-doctor-fired-from-swedish-institute-over-research-lies-allegations-windpipe-surgery [Accessed 24 March 2016].

[146] Harris G. Diabetes drug maker hid test data, files indicate. The New York Times; July 12, 2010.

[147] Ioannidis JP. Is molecular profiling ready for use in clinical decision making? Oncologist 2007;12:301–11.

[148] Ioannidis JP. Some main problems eroding the credibility and relevance of randomized trials. Bull NYU Hosp Jt Dis 2008;66:135–9.

[149] Ioannidis JP, Panagiotou OA. Comparison of effect sizes associated with biomarkers reported in highly cited individual articles and in subsequent meta-analyses. JAMA 2011;305:2200–10.

[150] Ioannidis JP. Excess significance bias in the literature on brain volume abnormalities. Arch Gen Psychiatry 2011;68:773–80.

[151] Pocock SJ, Collier TJ, Dandreo KJ, deStavola BL, Goldman MB, Kalish LA, et al. Issues in the reporting of epidemiological studies: a survey of recent practice. BMJ 2004;329:883.

[152] McGauran N, Wieseler B, Kreis J, Schuler Y, Kolsch H, Kaiser T. Reporting bias in medical research—a narrative review. Trials 2010;11:37.

[153] Wilson JR. Rhetorical strategies used in the reporting of implantable defibrillator primary prevention trials. Am J Cardiol 2011;107:1806–11.

[154] Office of Research Integrity. Available from: http://ori.dhhs.gov.

[155] Scientific misconduct investigations 1993–1997. Office of Research Integrity, Office of Public Health and Science, Department of Health and Human Services; December, 1998.

[156] Office of research integrity annual report 2007; June 2008. Available from: http://orihhsgov/images/ddblock/ori_annual_report_2007pdf [Accessed 1 January 2015].

[157] Begley S. In cancer science, many 'discoveries' don't hold up. Reuters; March 28, 2012.

[158] Abu-Asab MS, Chaouchi M, Alesci S, Galli S, Laassri M, Cheema AK, et al. Biomarkers in the age of omics: time for a systems biology approach. OMICS 2011;15:105–12.

[159] Moyer VA, On behalf of the U.S. Preventive Services Task Force. Screening for prostate cancer: U.S. Preventive Services Task Force recommendation statement. Ann Intern Med 2012;157:120–34.

[160] How science goes wrong. The Economist; October 19, 2013.

[161] Kangaspeska S, Hultsch S, Edgren H, Nicorici D, Murumagi A, Kallioniemi O. Reanalysis of RNA-sequencing data reveals several additional fusion genes with multiple isoforms. PLoS One 2012;7:e48745.

[162] Markoff J. Troves of personal data, forbidden to researchers. The New York Times; May 21, 2012.

[163] Markoff J. A deluge of data shapes a new era in computing. The New York Times; December 15, 2009.

[164] Guidance for sharing of data and resources generated by the molecular libraries screening centers network (mlscn)—addendum to rfa rm-04-017. NIH notice not-rm-04-014; July 22, 2004. Available from: http://grants.nih.gov/grants/guide/notice-files/NOT-RM-04-014.html [Accessed 19 September 2012].

[165] Sharing publication-related data and materials: responsibilities of authorship in the life sciences. Washington, DC: The National Academies Press; 2003. Available from: http://www.nap.edu/openbook.php?isbn=0309088593 [Accessed 10 September 2012].

[166] NIH policy on data sharing; 2003. Available from: http://grants.nih.gov/grants/guide/notice-files/NOT-OD-03-032.html [Accessed 13 September 2015].

[167] Fienberg SE, Martin ME, Straf ML, Committee on National Statistics, Commission on Behavioral and Social Sciences and Education, National Research Council, editors. Sharing research data. Washington, DC: National Academy Press; 1985.

[168] Policy on enhancing public access to archived publications resulting from NIH-funded research. Notice Number: NOT-OD-05-022; 2005.

[169] Revised policy on enhancing public access to archived publications resulting from NIH-funded research. Notice Number: NOT-OD-08-033; Release date: January 11, 2008. Effective date: April 7, 2008. Available from: http://grantsnihgov/grants/guide/notice-files/not-od-08-033html [Accessed 28 December 2009].

[170] Berman JJ. A tool for sharing annotated research data: the "Category 0" UMLS (Unified Medical Language System) vocabularies. BMC Med Inform Decis Mak 2003;3:6.

[171] Berman JJ, Edgerton ME, Friedman B. The tissue microarray data exchange specification: a community-based, open source tool for sharing tissue microarray data. BMC Med Inform Decis Mak 2003;3:5.

[172] Berman JJ. Racing to share pathology data. Am J Clin Pathol 2004;121:169–71.

[173] de Bruijn J. Using ontologies: enabling knowledge sharing and reuse on the Semantic Web. Digital Enterprise Research Institute Technical Report DERI-2003-10-29; October 2003. Available from: http://www.deri.org/fileadmin/documents/DERI-TR-2003-10-29.pdf [Accessed 14 August 2012].

[174] Drake TA, Braun J, Marchevsky A, Kohane IS, Fletcher C, Chueh H, et al. A system for sharing routine surgical pathology specimens across institutions: the Shared Pathology Informatics Network (SPIN). Hum Pathol 2007;38:1212–25.

[175] Sweeney L. Guaranteeing anonymity when sharing medical data, the Datafly system. Proc AMIA Annu Fall Symp 1997;51–5.

[176] Sweeney L. Three computational systems for disclosing medical data in the year 1999. Stud Health Technol Inform 1998;52(Pt 2):1124–9.

[177] Malin B, Sweeney L. How (not) to protect genomic data privacy in a distributed network: using trail re-identification to evaluate and design anonymity protection systems. J Biomed Inform 2004;37:179–92.

[178] Neamatullah I, Douglass MM, Lehman LW, Reisner A, Villarroel M, Long WJ, et al. Automated de-identification of free-text medical records. BMC Med Inform Decis Mak 2008;8:32.

[179] Gilissen C, Hoischen A, Brunner HG, Veltman JA. Disease gene identification strategies for exome sequencing. Eur J Hum Genet 2012;20:490–7.

[180] Bodmer W, Bonilla C. Common and rare variants in multifactorial susceptibility to common diseases. Nat Genet 2008;40:695–701.

[181] Wallis Y, Payne S, McAnulty C, Bodmer D, Sistermans E, Robertson K, Moore D, Abbs D, Deans Z, Devereau A. Practice guidelines for the evaluation of pathogenicity and the reporting of sequence variants in clinical molecular genetics. Association for Clinical Genetic Science 2013. Available from: http://www.acgs.uk.com/media/774853/evaluation_and_reporting_of_sequence_variants_bpgs_june_2013_-_finalpdf.pdf [Accessed 26 May 2017].

[182] Pritchard JK. Are rare variants responsible for susceptibility to complex diseases? Am J Hum Genet 2001;69:124–37.

[183] Pennisi E. Breakthrough of the year: human genetic variation. Science 2007;318:1842–3.

[184] MacArthur DG, Manolio TA, Dimmock DP, Rehm HL, Shendure J, Abecasis GR, et al. Guidelines for investigating causality of sequence variants in human disease. Nature 2014;508:469–76.

[185] Ray T. Mother's negligence suit against Quest's Athena could broadly impact genetic testing labs. GenomeWeb; March 14, 2016.

[186] Ray T. Wrongful death suit awaits input from South Carolina supreme court. GenomeWeb; April 4, 2017.

[187] Clinical Cancer Genome Task Team of the Global Alliance for Genomics and Health, Lawler M, Haussler D, Siu LL, Haendel MA, JA MM, et al. Sharing clinical and genomic data on cancer—the need for global solutions. N Engl J Med 2017;376:2006–9.

[188] Longo DL, Drazen JM. Data sharing. N Engl J Med 2016;374:276–7.

[189] Wicherts JM, Bakker M, Molenaar D. Willingness to share research data is related to the strength of the evidence and the quality of reporting of statistical results. PLoS One 2011;6:e26828.

[190] Frellick M. Models for sharing trial data abound, but with little consensus; Auguat 3, 2016. www.medscape.com.

[191] Data Quality Act. 67 Fed. Reg. 8,452, February 22, 2002, addition to FY 2001 Consolidated Appropriations Act (Pub. L. No. 106-554. codified at 44 U.S.C. 3516).

[192] Tozzi JJ, Kelly Jr WG, Slaughter S. Correspondence: data quality act: response from the Center for Regulatory Effectiveness. Environ Health Perspect 2004;112:A18–19.

[193] Guidelines for ensuring and maximizing the quality, objectivity, utility, and integrity of information disseminated by federal agencies. Federal Register Vol. 67, No. 36; February 22, 2002.

[194] Sass JB, Devine Jr JP. The Center for Regulatory Effectiveness invokes the Data Quality Act to reject published studies on atrazine toxicity. Environ Health Perspect 2004;112:A18.

[195] Olson S, Beachy SH, Giammaria CF, Berger AC. Integrating large-scale genomic information into clinical practice: workshop summary. Washington, DC: The National Academies Press; 2012.

[196] Lohr S. Lessons from Britain's Health Information Technology Fiasco. The New York Times; September 27, 2011.

[197] Robinson D, Paul Frosdick P, Briscoe E. HL7 Version 3: an impact assessment. NHS Information Authority; March 23, 2001.

[198] Goldberg SI, Niemierko A, Turchin A. Analysis of data errors in clinical research databases. AMIA Annu Symp Proc 2008;2008:242–6.

[199] Behlen FM, Johnson SB. Multicenter patient records research: security policies and tools. J Am Med Inform Assoc 1999;6:435–43.

[200] Stein R. Found on the Web, with DNA: a boy's father. The Washington Post; Sunday, November 13, 2005.

[201] Hwang WS, Roh SI, Lee BC, Kang SK, Kwon DK, Kim S, et al. Patient-specific embryonic stem cells derived from human SCNT blastocysts. Science 2005;308:1777–83.

[202] Wade N. Clone scientist relied on peers and Korean pride. The New York Times; December 25, 2005.

[203] National Academies of Sciences, Engineering, and Medicine. Innovations in Federal Statistics: Combining Data Sources While Protecting Privacy. Washington, DC: The National Academies Press; 2017.

[204] Broad WJ. U.S. accidentally releases list of nuclear sites. The New York Times; June 3, 2009.

[205] Frey CM, McMillen MM, Cowan CD, Horm JW, Kessler LG. Representativeness of the surveillance, epidemiology, and end results program data: recent trends in cancer mortality rate. JNCI 1992;84:872.

[206] Ashworth TG. Inadequacy of death certification: proposal for change. J Clin Pathol 1991;44:265.

[207] Kircher T, Anderson RE. Cause of death: proper completion of the death certificate. JAMA 1987;258:349–52.

[208] Walter SD, Birnie SE. Mapping mortality and morbidity patterns: an international comparison. Int J Epidemiol 1991;20:678–89.

[209] Patil N, Berno AJ, Hinds DA, Barrett WA, Doshi JM, Hacker CR, et al. Blocks of limited haplotype diversity revealed by high-resolution scanning of human chromosome 21. Science 2001;294:1719–23.

[210] Reshef DN, Reshef YA, Finucane HK, Grossman SR, McVean G, Turnbaugh PJ, et al. Detecting novel associations in large data sets. Science 2011;334:1518–24.

[211] Szekely GJ, Rizzo ML. Brownian distance covariance. Ann Appl Stat 2009;3:1236–65.

[212] Copyright Act, Section 107, Limitations on exclusive rights: Fair use. Available from: http://www.copyright.gov/title17/92chap1.html [Accessed 18 May 2017].

[213] Paskin N. Identifier interoperability: a report on two recent ISO activities. D-Lib Magazine 2006;12:1–23.

[214] Cohen J. The Earth Is Round (p < .05). Am Psychol 1994;49:997–1003.

[215] The World Factbook. Washington, DC: Central Intelligence Agency; 2009.

[216] Hoyert DL, Heron MP, Murphy SL, Kung H-C. Final Data for 2003. Natl Vital Stat Rep 2006;54(13).

[217] Bloom BJ, Nicholson TL, Williams JR, Campbell SL, Bishof M, Zhang X, et al. An optical lattice clock with accuracy and stability at the 10-18 level. Nature 2014;506:71–5.

[218] Patient Identity Integrity. A White Paper by the HIMSS Patient Identity Integrity Work Group; December 2009. Available from: http://www.himss.org/content/files/PrivacySecurity/PIIWhitePaper.pdf [Accessed 19 September 2012].

[219] Smith AK, Ayanian JZ, Covinsky KE, Landon BE, McCarthy EP, Wee CC, et al. Conducting high-value secondary dataset analysis: an introductory guide and resources. J Gen Intern Med 2011;26:920–9.

[220] Kivela T. Trilateral retinoblastoma: a meta-analysis of hereditary retinoblastoma associated with primary ectopic intracranial retinoblastoma. J Clin Oncol 1999;17:1829–37.

SECTION 9.1 HYPERSURVEILLANCE

It's hard to make predictions, especially about the future.
Variously attributed to Niels Bohr and to Markus M. Ronner

One of the marks of a good model - it is sometimes smarter than you are.
Paul Krugman

Precision Medicine is a field that does not have a very long past. Faith in the field is based largely on hope for the future. Therefore, it's impossible to write a book on Precision Medicine without speculating on its future. At this point, we have several new technologies poised to disrupt even modest predictions. These technologies include gene editing [1–4], nanotechnology [5], tricorders (as featured on Star Trek) [6,7] virtual and augmented reality devices, and deep analytics. There is always the chance that long-awaited cures for common diseases such as cancer, Alzheimer disease, and antibiotic resistance infections will actually arrive, thus radically changing the practice of medicine. Barring any revolutionary developments, what might we expect, in the next decade, based on extrapolating forward from current trends in the field?

The first item on our list is the hypersurveillance model of Precision Medicine, which builds upon our growing capacity to monitor and record physiological data, and to use these collected data to improve our health. It's difficult to determine the moment in history when this trend began. Perhaps it started with the invention of the stethoscope. Rene-Theophile-Hyacinthe Laennec (1781–1826) is credited with inventing this device, which provided us with the opportunity to listen to the sounds generated within our bodies. Laennec's 1816 invention was soon followed by his 900-page *Traite de l'Aascultation Mediate* (1819). Laennec's meticulous observations brought us closer to a hypersurveillance model of medicine. A few decades later, in 1854, Karl Vierordt's 1854 sphygomograph was employed to routinely monitor the pulse of patients. Perhaps the first large monitoring project came in 1868 when Carl Wunderlich published *Das Verhalten der Eigenwarme in Krankheiten*, which collected body temperature data on ~25,000 patients [8]. Wunderlich associated peaks and fluctuations of body temperature with 32 different diseases. Not only did this work result in a large collection of patient data, it also sparked considerable debate over the best way of visualizing datasets. Competing suggestions for the representation of thermometric data (as it was called) included time interval (discontinuous) graphs and oscillating real-time (continuous) charts. Shortly after body temperature measurements became widely popular, sphygmomanometry (blood pressure recordings) was invented (1896). With bedside recordings of pulse, blood pressure, respirations, and temperature (the so-called vital signs), the foundations of modern medical data collection were laid.

At the same time that surveillance of vital signs became commonplace, a vast array of chemical assays of blood and body fluids were being developed. By the third decade of the twentieth century, physicians had at their disposal most of the common blood tests known to modern medicine (e.g., electrolytes, blood cells, lipids, glucose, nitrogenous compounds). What the early 20th century physicians lacked was any sensible way to interpret the test results. Learning how to make clinical sense of blood tests required examination of old data collected on many thousands of individuals, and it took considerable time and effort to interpret the aggregated results.

The results of blood tests, measured under a wide range of physiologic and pathologic circumstances, produced a stunning conclusion. It was shown that nearly every blood test conducted on healthy individuals fell into a very narrow range, with very little change between individuals. This was particularly true for electrolytes (e.g., Sodium and Calcium) and to a somewhat lesser extent for blood cells (e.g., white blood cells, red blood cells). Furthermore, for any individual, multiple recordings at different times of the day and on different days, tended to produce consistent results (e.g., Sodium concentration in the morning was equivalent to Sodium concentration in the evening). These findings were totally unexpected, at the time.

Analysis of the data also showed that significant deviations from the normal concentrations of any one of these blood chemicals is always an indicator of disease. Backed by data, but lacking any deep understanding of the physiologic role of blood components, physicians learned to associate deviations from the normal range with specific disease processes. The discovery of the "normal range" revolutionized the field of physiology. Thereafter, physiologists concentrated their efforts toward understanding how the body regulates its blood constituents. Their early studies led to nearly everything we now know about homeostatic control mechanisms, and the diseases thereof.

To this day, much of medicine consists of monitoring vital signs, blood chemistries, and hematologic cell indices (i.e., the so-called complete blood count), and seeking to remedy deviations from the normal. For example, if the blood pressure is high, make it normal. If the glucose is high, lower it. If the practice of preventive medicine is based on regular check-ups with system monitoring, in the form of blood tests, or EKGs (electrocardiograms), and other standard measurements, then might the health of individuals be improved if monitoring were done continuously, and abnormal values readjusted with the utmost diligence?

With the advent of inexpensive self-monitoring devices, we can see that it won't be long before anyone with a smartphone will be able to monitor a range of physiological and chemical signals that were formerly the provenance of medical practitioners. It is quite likely that blood glucose, lipids, EKGs, and brain activity will soon be available. Will these new capabilities herald a new age of self-hypersurveillance, or will this be another passing fad? At this moment, there is no evidence that hypersurveillance has much benefit for people who are healthy and who have normal values, and who are monitored at yearly medical examinations. Hypersurveillance requires a level of commitment that might be a bit too much for any but the most self-obsessed individuals. A thin line separates prudence from hypochondria.

For those individuals who suffer from illnesses that require blood monitoring, the new technologies brought to Precision Medicine may be life savers. It should be noted that close monitoring and strict control of glucose levels in diabetics, beyond standard compliance protocols, does not bring any added benefit, and may even be detrimental to health [9].

Perhaps the ultimate in hypersurveillance is genomic testing, which is coming to mean whole-genome sequencing of individuals. As a general rule, physicians are loathe to order tests that they cannot sensibly interpret. Individuals may have an abiding interest in learning their risks for diseases that could be prevented, delayed, or mitigated. In addition, an individual might be interested in knowing of any mutations that might pose a risk to an offspring or family members. At this point of time, a physician who orders such tests is likely to waste the patient's money (or the insurer's money) unless there is some specific mutation that needs to be screened (e.g., an oncogene mutation in a cancer patient, the presence of which would qualify the patient for treatment with a therapy of proven value). Otherwise, the likelihood of false-positive, false-negative, and inconclusive findings is, at present, large enough to discourage routine genomic testing. In the public's mind, Precision Medicine is virtually equivalent to genomic testing. For those who hold this view, the future of Precision Medicine will be determined by the success or failure of genomic tests.

SECTION 9.2 DO-IT-YOURSELF MEDICINE

Man needs more to be reminded than instructed.
Samuel Johnson

In a sense, we've reached a postinformation age. At this point, we've collected an awful lot of information, and we all have access to much more information than we can possibly analyze within our lifetimes. In fact, all the professional scientists and data analysts who are living today could not possibly exhaust the information available to them. If we want to get the most out of the data that currently resides within our grasps, we will need to call upon everyone's talents, including amateurs. Today, the baby boomer generation is amassing an army of well-trained scientists who are retiring into a world that provides them with unfettered access to limitless data. We can presume that the number of amateur scientists may possibly exceed the number of professional scientists.

Historically, some of the greatest advancements in science have come from amateurs. For example, Antonie van Leeuwenhoek (1632–1723), one of the earliest developers of the compound microscope, who is sometimes credited as the father of microbiology, was a janitor. Augustin-Jean Fresnel (1788–1827) was a civil engineer who found time to make significant and fundamental contributions to the theory of wave optics. Johann Jakob Balmer (1825–March 12, 1898), who earned his living as a teacher in a school for girls, formulated the mathematical equation describing the spectral emission lines of hydrogen. His work, published in 1885, led others, over the next four decades, to develop the new field of quantum mechanics. Of course, Albert Einstein was a patent clerk who found time, in 1905, to publish three papers that forever changed the landscape of science.

In the past few decades, a wealth of scientific resources has been made available to anyone who has access to the Internet. Many of the today's most successful amateurs are autodidacts with Internet connections [10–15]. In the field of Precision Medicine, some of the most impressive work has come from individuals affected by rare diseases who have used publicly available resources to research their own diseases.

Jill Viles is a middle-aged woman who, when she was a college undergraduate, correctly determined that she was suffering from Emery-Dreifuss muscular dystrophy. The diagnosis of this very rare form of muscular dystrophy was missed by her physicians. After her self-diagnosis was confirmed, she noticed that her father, who had never been told he had any muscular condition, had a distribution of his muscle mass that was suggestive of Emery-Dreifuss. Jill's suspicions initiated a clinical consultation indicating that her father indeed had a mild form of the same disorder, and that his heart had been affected. Her father received a needed pacemaker, and Jill's shrewd observations were credited with saving her father's life. Jill pursued her interest in her own condition and soon became one of the early beneficiaries of genome sequencing. A mutation of the lamin gene was apparently responsible for her particular variant of Emery-Dreifuss muscular dystrophy. Jill later realized that in addition to Emery-Dreifuss muscular dystrophy, she also exhibited phenotypic features of partial lipodystrophy, a disease characterized by a decrease in the fat around muscles. When the fat around muscles is decreased, the definition of the muscles (i.e., the surface outline of musculature) is enhanced. She reasoned, correctly, that the lamin gene, in her case, was responsible for both conditions (i.e., Emery-Dreifuss muscular dystrophy and partial lipodystrophy).

Jill's story does not end here. While looking at photographs of a Priscilla Lopes-Schlief, an Olympic athlete known for her hypertrophied muscles, Jill noticed something very peculiar. The athlete had a pattern of fat-deficient muscle definition on her shoulders, arms, hips and butt, that was identical to Jill's; the difference being that Priscilla's muscles were large, and Jill's muscles were small. Jill contacted the Olympian, and the discussions that followed eventually led to Priscilla's diagnosis of lipodystrophy due to a mutation on the lamin gene, different from Jill's. Lipodystrophy can produce a dangerous elevation in triglycerides, and

Priscilla's new diagnosis prompted a blood screen for elevated lipids. Priscilla had high levels of triglyceride, requiring prompt treatment. Once again, Jill had made a diagnosis that was missed by physicians, linked the diagnosis to a particular gene, and uncovered a treatable and overlooked secondary condition (i.e., hypertriglyceridemia). And it was all done without any formal medical training [16].

Jill Viles' story is not unique. Kim Goodsell, a patient with two rare diseases, Charcot-Marie-Tooth disease and arrhythmogenic right ventricular cardiomyopathy, searched the literature until she found a single gene that might account for both of her conditions. After much study, she determined for herself that it must be LMNA. Kim paid $3,000 for gene sequencing of her own DNA, and a rare point mutation on LMNA was found [17]. When a point mutation in a highly conserved gene is found in a patient and not found as a normal variant in the human population and is also not found as a normal variant in the animal homolog of the gene, it is reasonable to conclude that the mutation is a disease-causing mutation. In this case, because the LMNA gene had been predicted as a candidate gene capable of producing all of the symptoms observed in Kim Goodsell, it was concluded that the point mutation in LMNA was responsible for her dual afflictions. In Kim's case, as in Jill's case, a persistent patient can be credited with a significant advance in the genetics of human disease.

Should we be surprised to learn that a young doctor, with swollen lymph nodes, night sweats, and fevers, correctly diagnosed his own illness (a rare case of Castleman disease), and developed a treatment that seems to have worked quite well in his case (an mTOR inhibitor) [18]? We can expect this kind of thing to happen, more and more frequently, just one more of the many benefits of Precision Medicine.

SECTION 9.3 EUGENICS

I conclude that for a number of diseases the mutation rate increases with age and at a rate much faster than linear. This suggests that the greatest mutational health hazard in the human population at present is fertile old males.
James F. Crow [19] [Glossary Mutation rate]

The dream of every cell, to become two cells!
Francois Jacob

It is impossible to discuss the future of Precision Medicine, which depends so much on our knowledge of disease-causing genes, without touching on the subject of eugenics. Eugenics, which derives from the Greek roots "eu," good and "genos," race, generally refers to any efforts aimed at improving the human gene pool. As it is broadly used today, it would also include efforts to eliminate the genetic causes of disease, in individuals or in populations. The purpose of this section is to explain that eugenics, as a field is science, has limited value because we are pretty much clueless as to what constitutes "an improved gene pool." Advances in the field of Precision Medicine do not seem to be bringing us any closer to a solution. Furthermore, it seems as though we won't be eliminating the genetic causes of disease anytime soon, because the genes associated with the common diseases are normal variants, and are constantly re-entering the gene pool. Furthermore, many of the genes causing rare, fatal disease are de novo mutations, and we have no way to prevent these mutations from occurring. These assertions are somewhat counterintuitive, and we ought to review the supporting evidence. [Glossary De novo mutation disease]

Here are some of the reasons why eugenics will not play much of a role in the near future of Precision Medicine:

– No such thing as a superior being

We marvel at the success of animal breeders who seem capable of producing made-to-order animals. The results are deceptive. Breeders select for a single trait (e.g., size, speed, strength, muscle mass, milk production). All traits other than the trait under selection are unpredicted consequences of the process. When we look at any breed of animal, we are not looking at a superior race of the species; we are only looking at a kindred that have certain family traits, one of which was purposely selected by a breeder.

Suppose we wanted to breed a superior human being. How might we go about doing that? You would need to start with some idea of the traits that must be present in the superior person (e.g., strength, endurance, height, longevity, intelligence, attractiveness). The problem here is that we do not really know how to gauge the quality of any of these traits. A very tall person might be useful for fetching the cereal box from the top shelf of the cabinet, but a short person might be a better choice to stock the bottom shelf in the grocery store. A math wizard may have the kind of intelligence needed to calculate the best trajectory for a space ship traveling to Pluto, but a social worker might have the kind of intelligence needed to keep the space ship's crew from murdering one another on the way over.

Basically, we have no idea what, if anything, makes one person superior to another. Even if we could agree on what we wanted, we would have no way of preparing ourselves for the consequences. If we bred for creativity, then we might produce a population of self-absorbed individuals who had no interest in nurturing children. A race bred for fertility might overpopulate the planet. A race bred for size and strength might have dietary requirements so high that they outstripped food production.

Not convinced? Humans routinely employ a fairly brutal eugenics policy, without knowing it. It's called marriage. The males are on the lookout for the most superior woman, and the women are trying to find the most superior male. If you want to know whether eugenics works, then take a hard look at your own extended family. The unintended consequences of our best efforts at breeding are often disappointing.

– Breeds are susceptible to being nearly wiped out by a single disease

Ironically, a race of superior beings may be a race that is unfit to survive. The purebred dogs, particularly those selected for size and strength, have the shortest life expectancies, and carry the greatest burden of disease. While golden retrievers and Bernese mountain dogs have their charms, they also carry a set of genes that predispose them to very high rates of cancer, an unintended consequence of the breeding process [20]. Any veterinarian will tell you that the longest-lived, healthiest dogs are the small mutts (Fig. 9.1).

Suppose you breed a stronger human. Let's pretend that the new breed is so popular that within a few generations, everyone on the planet is effortlessly bench-pressing 500 pounds of

FIG. 9.1 The Irish wolfhound was bred for size and strength. The life expectancy of the Irish wolfhound is 7 years. Most mixed-breed dogs have a life-span twice as long. Their most frequent cause of death in the Irish wolfhound is bone cancer, an uncommon cause of death in most other breeds. *From Wikipedia, courtesy of National Library of Ireland on The Commons historical photograph taken February 21, 1917.*

steel. Genetic variations may have pleiotropic effects. In this case, let's imagine that the strong breed of humans came with an unintended feature: heightened susceptibility to an uncommonly virulent form of the common flu virus. Just when everything was looking swell, a flu epidemic comes, wiping out 90% of the earth's human population. Does this seem farfetched? There is an inherited immunodeficiency of cattle caused by a deficiency of leukocyte adhesion factor. Affected cattle are homozygous for a gene allele that codes for a substitution in a single amino acid in the protein product. Heterozygotes (i.e., cattle with an unpaired mutant allele) are common in the United States, with a carrier rate of about 10%. Every cattle with a mutant allele is a descendant from one prize bull, whose sperm was used to artificially inseminate cows in the 1950s and 1960s [21]. A disease that was essentially nonexistent in 1950 became a common scourge of the dairy industry within a half-century, all due to the founder effect amplified by modern animal husbandry. Eugenics is a tricky business. [Glossary Founder effect]

– It is difficult to eliminate polygenic traits from the human gene pool

A trait is a feature that we all have, but to a different extent, varying from individual to individual. Size, strength, and intelligence are examples of human traits. It has been accepted for nearly a century that traits are seldom determined by a single gene; they are always polygenic [22–24]. You would guess that something like intelligence, that has so many different forms, and that can scarcely be sensibly defined, could not be the product of a single gene. In point of fact, genome-wide association analyses have already identified dozens of genes that correlate with intelligence [25]. At least 180 gene variants are known to be associated with variations of normal height. These 180 variants may represent only a fraction of the total number of gene variants that influence the height of individuals, as they account for only about 10% of the spread [26].

The polygenic diseases have a non-Mendelian pattern of inheritance (i.e., neither autosomal dominant, autosomal recessive, or sex-linked). The reason for this is that each of the variant genes that contribute to the expression of a polygenic disease is inherited independently, from either parent. Hence, the set of genes that together account for the polygenic disease is not present, as a complete set, in either parent. Hence, inheritance of polygenic traits and polygenic diseases cannot be assigned to either parent. Hence, the inheritance pattern in non-Mendelian. [Glossary Autosomal dominance]

As we have previously noted, hypertension is polygenic, and we can presume that some portion of the many different genes that contribute to hypertension are normal variants of genes. Other common diseases, such as type 2 diabetes, are also polygenic [27].

The common diseases of humans can be thought of as traits that are expressed strongly in some individuals (the individuals who get sick) and weakly in other individuals (the ones that are not affected). For example, we all have glucose circulating in our blood; it's a trait of the human species. Some of us sustain glucose levels high enough to be categorized as diabetic. The lucky ones maintain glucose levels in the normal range. We might be able to produce a breed of humans that have a low incidence of diabetes, if we tried very hard. It wouldn't do us much good, though. Diabetes is a polygenic disease, and natural selection does not provide a way to eliminate a large collection of genes through breeding. This means that the set of genes that can produce type 2 diabetes will remain more or less intact in the gene pool of the diabetes-free, pure-bred population. Over time, conditions may favor the emergence of new gene variants that work in concert with the retained set of diabetes genes that may herald the return of diabetes, or the emergence of a new clinical form of diabetes, or that may produce a new disease entirely, that nobody could have predicted.

    – It is hard to improve the human gene pool by screening for disease gene carriers

Screening for heterozygotes who carry a recessive disease gene has been proven to be a very effective way of reducing the incidence of disease, with 90%–95% reduction of disease in the cases of Tay-Sachs disease and beta-thalassemia [28–30], and equally promising results for cystic fibrosis and Gaucher disease [31].

Screening programs are not always as successful as we might have hoped. In 1949, Linus Pauling and coworkers showed that sickle cell anemia is a disease produced by an inherited alteration in hemoglobin, producing a molecule that is separable from normal hemoglobin, by electrophoresis. Electrophoresis is still used to distinguish sickle hemoglobin from normal hemoglobin. In 1956, Vernon Ingram and J.A. Hunt sequenced the hemoglobin protein molecule (normal and sickle cell) and showed that the inherited alteration in sickle cell hemoglobin is due to a single amino acid substitution in the protein sequence.

Because the sickle cell gene mutation is highly specific, and because two identical alleles are required to produce the disease in an offspring (i.e., one allele from each parent), we know that sickle cell disease can only occur as an inherited disease. This means that no new cases of sickle cell would be expected to occur due to de novo mutations and that every new case of sickle cell disease has a genetic contribution from both parents. Because sickle cell hemoglobin can be detected by a simple blood test, carriers of the disease can be easily identified, and all new cases of sickle cell disease can be avoided. Healthcare workers back in the 1950s were elated to learn that advances in genetics had led to a nearly foolproof strategy to eliminate sickle cell disease from the human population. Back then, everyone expected to see a sharp and dramatic drop in the incidence of this disease over the next few decades.

If we fast forward to present-day United States, we find that sickle cell disease is the most common inherited disease in the African-American population. Furthermore, there has been no appreciable decrease in hospital admission rates, or in mortality, over the decades [32,33]. What went wrong? Healthcare workers must never forget that patients do not automatically comply with every order rendered by a physician. This is especially true if the doctor's orders intrude upon a basic human right, such as procreation. To prevent the occurrence of new cases of sickle cell disease, healthy married couples were being asked to refrain from having children, on the basis of a blood test indicating that their child would have a 25% chance of contracting the disease.

It should be kept in mind that screening for heterozygote carriers does not eliminate the gene from the gene pool. In addition, many genetic diseases are caused by de novo mutations for which screening of the parent serves no purpose. Furthermore, most birth defects that are associated with genetic aberrations are characterized by chromosomal anomalies (e.g., trisomies, deletions) and cannot be attributed to any particular gene. [Glossary Chromosomal disorder, Congenital anomaly, Contiguous gene deletion syndrome]

 – New gene-editing techniques may have negligible effect on the human gene pool

New methodologies, such as CRISPR (Clustered Regularly Interspaced Short Palindromic Repeats) gene editing, have been heralded as opportunities to cure and eventually eliminate genetic diseases [1,34]. At the current time, editing of human germline DNA (i.e., the DNA of human embryos) will not be funded by NIH and would most likely not meet approval by the FDA [35]. Using CRISPR to edit the germline of nonhuman animals is proceeding rapidly [2]. In the United States, the direct clinical uses of CRISPR will be focused on repairing somatic mutations. This type of procedure might involve taking unhealthy cells from a patient, editing the DNA to repair or eliminate the disease gene, growing the repaired cell in culture, and infusing the cells back into the patient. Such efforts, targeted against somatic cells, though nothing short of medical miracles, will have no positive effect on the human gene pool.

Patients who are cured of their diseases will carry the defective gene in their germ cells and may pass the gene to the next generation. Even if we were permitted to edit and repair inherited mutations in embryonic cells, a host of unintended consequences would emerge (e.g., introducing new mutations in the gene-editing process, inadvertently killing embryos, coping with the consequences of somatic mosaicism, and failing to detect and repair de novo mutations).

Because de novo mutations represent an important obstacle for those among us who have visions of improving the human gene pool, we should pause here a moment to discuss these mutations, and how the circumstances of their occurrence will influence the ways we think about genetic diseases. De novo mutations occur in the sperm cell that fertilizes the mother's ovum, or occur in the mother's ovum, or occur during the fertilization process when the sperm and ovum combine, or in the fertilized zygote, or in any postzygotic cell of the offspring (i.e., morula cell, blastula cell, embyronic cell, fetal cell, or cell of the developed organism). From the definition of a de novo mutation disease, we can draw numerous inferences and develop various testable hypotheses. Let's consider a few.

- De novo mutation diseases are not found in the parents or family members of the affected individuals.
- Deleterious De novo mutation diseases occurring in the earliest cells (e.g., fertilizing gametes, zygote) will usually cause symptoms in neonates and children.
- De novo mutations account for most of the spontaneous abortions occurring in humans [36].
- De novo mutations account for many of the most serious genetic diseases that occur in humans. As a general rule, the inherited conditions seldom cause early life fatality; elsewise, the root causal mutation would be eliminated from the gene pool by natural selection. Contrariwise, a de novo mutation can occur anywhere in the genome, with no limit to the amount of resulting damage.
- Nearly all genetic mosaicisms are caused by de novo mutations. The exceptions would be X-chromosome mosaicisms and revertant mosaicisms [37]
- The de novo mosaic diseases can be passed to offspring only if the germ cell line happens to carry the mutation.
- Somatic mutation diseases are a type of de novo mutation; hence, most cancers are de novo mutation diseases wherein the mutation occurs in a cell in the adult organism.
- By studying the de novo mutations, we can accurately determine the mutation rate in humans and the distribution of new mutations in the genome (e.g., coding versus noncoding regions). With genome-wide sequencing, we can actually count the new SNPs occurring in offspring that were not present in the parents. This comes out to about 60 de novo SNPs in the genome in each of us, with one to two new SNPs in coding sequences [38]. Likewise, using genome sequencing and looking for new SNPs in haplotypes identified by their parental origins (i.e., maternal or parental), we can determine whether newly occurring SNPs are preferentially associated with either parent. It turns out that most germline de novo mutations have a paternal origin and the older the father, the greater the de novo mutation burden [39].
- At this point of time, we know of no way of applying eugenic techniques, such as CRISPR, to reduce the reduce the incidence of de novo mutation diseases.

If all the technical, ethical, and economic problems raised by CRISPR technology were solved, we would still face the fact that disease-gene carriers, who would not be expected to receive the benefits of gene editing, will continue to procreate, thus passing their disease genes to the human gene pool. Furthermore, gene editing on monogenic disorders will have no effect on disease genes involved in polygenic disorders [40].

Historically, important technological advances in molecular biology, such as next-generation sequencing, polymerase chain reaction, gene microarrays, and gene-silencing techniques, have had their greatest impact on discovery, not on treatment. Before we can treat diseases, we must know the biological mechanisms that account for the development of the disease, and the clinical phenotype of the disease. If the past serves as an indicator of the future, the greatest value of CRISPR will be its ability to modify genes, under controlled laboratory conditions, permitting us to carefully observe the consequences [41]. [Glossary Microarray, Next-generation sequencing]

As for the future of eugenics, as a social movement, it suffices to say that the eugenics movement in the twentieth century was a horrible travesty of science. In this new era of Precision Medicine, in which genes can be written, revised, and erased, much like words on a piece of paper, it is imperative that we do not repeat the mistakes of our recent ancestors.

SECTION 9.4 PUBLIC HEALTH

Intellectuals solve problems; geniuses prevent them.
Albert Einstein (1879–1955)

In 1736 I lost one of my sons, a fine boy of four years old, by the small-pox, taken in the common way. I long regretted bitterly, and still regret that I had not given it to him by inoculation. This I mention for the sake of parents who omit that operation, on the supposition that they should never forgive themselves if a child died under it; my example showing that the regret may be the same either way, and that, therefore, the safer should be chosen.
Benjamin Franklin (1706–90)

Despite having the most advanced healthcare technology on the planet, life expectancy in the United States is not particularly high. Citizens from most of the European countries and the highly industrialized Asian countries enjoy longer life expectancies than the United States. According to the World Health Organization, the United States ranks 31st among nations, trailing behind Greece, Chile, and Costa Rica, and barely edging out Cuba [42]. Similar rankings are reported by the US Central Intelligence Agency [43]. These findings lead us to infer that access to advanced technologies, such as those offered by Precision Medicine, will not extend lifespan significantly.

Every healthcare professional knows that most of the deaths occurring in this country can be attributed to personal lifestyle choices: smoking, drinking, drug abuse, and over-eating. Lifestyle diseases account for the majority of deaths in the United States and in other western countries, these being: heart disease, diabetes, obesity, and cancer. Population-based trials that seek to improve the ways in which individuals live, by introducing a daily exercise routine, healthy diet, and cigarette abstinence, have yielded huge benefits, in terms of extending average lifespans [44]. At the front end of the human life cycle, it has been demonstrated that infant mortalities can be markedly reduced with simple measures, focusing on improved maternal education [45]. It has been credibly argued that clean water, clean air, clean housing, clean food, and clean living yield greater societal benefits than clean operating rooms [46,47]. If this be the case, should we be investing heavily in Precision Medicine, when simple, low-tech public health measures are likely to provide a greater return on investment, in terms of overall morbidity and mortality?

In a certain sense, public health is the opposite of personalized medicine. Whereas personalized medicine involves finding the best possible treatment for individuals, based on their uniqueness, public health involves finding ways of treating whole populations based on their collective sameness. Let's not dwell on these somewhat contrived philosophic points. Precision Medicine, as viewed in this book, is a new way of understanding human diseases. As such, Precision Medicine provides opportunities to advance both personalized medicine and public health.

Precision Medicine tells us that we should think of diseases as developmental process, with each step in the process representing an opportunity for intervention. Perhaps the most important function of Precision Medicine will be to give society the opportunity to institute public health measures aimed at blocking the pathogenesis of human diseases. Here are just a few examples:

- **Population screening for early stages of common diseases.**

The successful reduction in deaths from cervical cancer demonstrates the effectiveness of screening for early stages of disease. Cervical cancer is a type of squamous cell carcinoma that develops at the junction between the ectocervix (the squamous lined epithelium) and the endocervix (the glandular lined epithelium) in the os of the uterine cervix of women. Before the introduction of cervical precancer treatment, cervical carcinoma was one of the leading causes of cancer deaths in women worldwide. Today, in many countries that have not deployed precancer treatment, cervical cancer remains the leading cause of cancer deaths in women [48–50]. In the United States, a 70% drop in cervical cancer deaths followed the adoption of routine Pap smear screening [51–53]. No effort aimed at treating invasive cancers has provided an equivalent reduction in the number of cancer deaths. [Glossary Age-adjusted incidence, Pap smear]

Today, we know that cervical carcinogenesis begins with a localized infection by one of several strains of human papillomavirus, transmitted during sexual intercourse by an infected male partner. In the late 1940s (and really up until the early 1980s), the viral etiology of cervical cancer was unknown. We did know that squamous cells sampled from the uterine os had highly characteristic morphologic appearances that preceded the development of invasive cancer. Thanks largely to the persistence of Dr. Papanicolaou and his coworkers, a standard screening test, known as the Pap smear, was developed to detect cervical precancers. If precancerous changes were found in a smear, a gynecologist could remove a superficial portion of the affected epithelium, and this would, in the vast majority of cases, stop the cancer from ever developing.

Morphologic and epidemiologic observations on Pap smears provided clues that eventually led to the identification of several strains of human papillomavirus as the major causes of cervical cancer. Today, a vaccine protective against carcinogenic strains of human papilloma virus is available [54].

As discussed in Section 7.5, "What Is Precision Diagnosis?" new biomarkers are being developed for the early stages of disease, often preceding the development of any clinical symptoms. In general, diseases are easiest to treat in early stages, before they have had the chance to do any harm to organs. For example, precancers can often be effectively treated by excision, or, in some cases, by withdrawal of the agents that would otherwise lead to the progression of the precancer to the cancerous stage (e.g., cessation of hormonal replacement therapy to block breast cancer, cessation of smoking to block lung cancer, treatment of Helicobacter pylori infection to block MALToma). [Glossary MALToma]

We can hope that in the future advances in the field of Precision Medicine will identify the intermediate stages of development for common diseases. With this information, public health measures aimed at detecting and blocking diseases, in an early stage of development, will be deployed.

- **The aggressive prevention and treatment for the most common patterns of diseases that lead to death**

As discussed in Section 2.3, "Cause of Death," a well-composed death certificate contains a thoughtful sequence of medical conditions that develop over time, and that ultimately lead to the death of the patient. This data, if properly recorded and aggregated into a mortality database, should provide the most frequently occurring chains of events that account for human deaths. A public health effort aimed at breaking the early steps of these processes has the potential of extending the life expectancy of the population.

– Aggressive screening for carriers of infectious diseases

As discussed in Section 6.2, "Our Genome Is a Book Titled 'The History of Human Infections,'" organisms that were formerly thought to be purely pathogenic are now known to frequently live quietly within infected humans, without causing symptoms of disease, and this would include the organisms that cause Chagas disease, leishmaniases, toxoplasmosis, tuberculosis, viruses such as Herpes viruses and hepatitis viruses B and C, and bacterial organisms, some of which circulate in the blood without causing disease under normal circumstances.

Sensitive diagnostic techniques, including genome sequencing of DNA in blood, may provide us with the opportunity to perform population screening for organisms that are opportunistic pathogens, or that produce long-term damage to carriers, or that are transmissible from carriers.

– Finding targets for vaccines that confer effectiveness against more than one target organism.

Thanks in no small part to Precision Medicine, we are learning that organisms play a role in many diseases that were once thought to have no infectious component. In particular, it is now widely accepted that infections contribute to at least one-fifth of all cancers occurring in humans. Examples of cancer causing organisms are:

- Epstein-Barr virus (B-cell lymphomas, Burkitt lymphoma, nasopharyngeal cancer, Hodgkin disease and T-cell lymphomas)
- Hepatitis B virus (hepatocellular carcinoma)
- Human papillomavirus types 5, 8, 14, 17, 20, and 47 (skin cancer)
- Human papillomavirus types 16, 18, 31, 33, 35, 39, 45, 52, 56, 58 (cervical cancer, anogenital cancer)
- Human papillomavirus types 6 and 11 (verrucous carcinoma)
- Human papillomavirus types 16, 18, 33, 57, 73 (cancers of oral cavity, tongue, larynx, nasal cavity, and esophagus)
- Merkel cell polyomavirus (MCPyV) (Merkel cell carcinoma)
- HTLV-1 (adult T-cell leukemia)
- Human herpesvirus 8 (Kaposi sarcoma)
- Hepatitis C virus—hepatocellular carcinoma and low-grade lymphomas
- JC, BK, and SV40-like polyoma viruses (tumors of brain and pancreatic islet tumors, and mesotheliomas)
- Human endogenous retrovirus HERV-K (seminomas and germ cell tumors)
- Schistosomiasis and squamous cell carcinoma of bladder
- Opisthorchis viverrini and Clinorchis sinensis, flatworms (flukes), found in Southeast Asia, (cholangiocarcinoma)
- Helicobacter pylori and gastric MALToma (Mucosa-Associated Lympoid tissue lymphoma) [55]

Carcinogenic viruses profoundly influence the number of cancer deaths, worldwide. These include hepatitis B virus (associated with an increased incidence of hepatocellular carcinoma) and human papillomavirus (which causes cervical cancer). Liver cancer is the third leading cause of cancer deaths worldwide, accounting for 611,000 deaths in 2000 [50]. It is easy to understand that the importance of vaccine development for infections that contribute to chronic diseases and cancers cannot be overstated. As we learn more about the biological steps involved in the infection process, hope looms that vaccines and preventive drugs will be developed that target different types of organisms, based on shared properties of infection, invasion, immunologic resistance, persistence, or phylogeny, as discussed in Section 4.4, "Pathway-Directed Treatments for Convergent Diseases," [56–60]. [Glossary Phylogeny]

SECTION 9.5 THE DATA ANALYST OF TOMORROW

> At this very moment, there's an odds-on chance that someone in your organization is making a poor decision on the basis of information that was enormously expensive to collect.
> *Shvetank Shah, Andrew Horne, and Jaime Capella [61]*

> A futurist is never wrong today.
> *Unknown*

We have reached a point where we need not remind ourselves that huge amounts of data are being collected daily, and that this data is accumulating at a rate that outpaces our ability to analyze it all. A 2011 report from the McKinsey Global Institute suggested that there would be millions of jobs for individuals trained in analyzing large and complex data sets [62]. Workers in the field of data analysis have added a new term to their lexicon to describe the technology that will be employed when conducting queries on immense sets of data: deep analytics.

What will data analysis, in the field of Precision Medicine, look like? To begin with, it has been often remarked that in the future, every one of us will have our genomes sequenced. That's 3 billion nucleotides worth of data for each person. Add to that our electronic medical records, which can easily exceed a gigabyte of data per person. The expectation is that data analysts will take all that information and use it to predict the diseases that we are likely to develop over our lifetimes, and to suggest personalized lifestyle changes to change our fates. If you believe the hype, such activities will require new algorithms, supercomputers, and a new breed of healthcare worker endowed with a deep analytic skillset.

For the sake of discussion, consider the following alternate assessment of data analytics, and where it would lead in the next decade. Let's begin with the assertion that we are already living in a postinformatics era. We have technology for sequencing DNA cheaply and for collecting detailed medical information on large populations of individuals. We have lots of clever algorithms and statistical methods by which we can analyze large data sets. We have very fast supercomputers for processing all the data and producing a result. And we have a lot of bright people trained in deep analytics. What we're lacking are clear answers to the kinds of questions that have been raised through this book. They would include the following:

- What are the events and pathways that lead to the common diseases of humans?
- Where is our competent classification of human disease?
- How do we apply our successful experiences with rare monogenic diseases to the common polygenic diseases?
- How might we best prepare out data, so that we can merge, preserve, analyze, reanalyze, and repurpose our data resources?

Without the answers to these fundamental questions in the realm of Precision Medicine, the future role of data analysis, in the field of Precision Medicine, will not be very different from its somewhat limited current role. Who will solve our most pressing data-related puzzles? The following types of data scientists may be able to help.

- **Experts in data collection, annotation, curation, and simplification**

Most of the data relevant to the field of Precision Medicine has been collected in a complex and inchoate form that defies analysis. Data complexity seems to be the root cause of many of our most dramatic failures. It is common for large, academic medical centers to purchase information systems that cost in excess of $500 million. Despite these enormous investments, the majority of hospital information systems are considered failures that must be replaced [63–66]. As a general rule, data projects that are characterized by large size, high complexity, and novel technology, aggravate existing deficiencies in management, personnel, or process practices [67–71]. It seems that project failure rates are positively correlated with the size and cost of the projects [67]. The largest projects tend to be the most complex projects and the most difficult to manage.

Successfully implemented electronic health record systems have not been shown to improve patient outcomes [72,73]. Despite what you may hear about the wild successes of artificial intelligence, it would seem that clinical decision support systems, built into electronic health record systems, have not had much impact on physician practice [74]. These systems tend to be too complex for the hospital staff to master and are not well utilized [75].

Complex systems fail because they are inherently unpredictable, and because they exceed our comprehension. To be useful, complex data must first be simplified. There are established techniques whereby data can be properly collected, classified, curated, and shared. Some of these activities were discussed in Section 8.1, and all of these activities vastly simplify data resources. Regrettably, there are very few professionals who are trained to do the job, and that is why so much data is wasted [75–77]. Individuals who are willing to spend a considerable portion of their time preparing simplified data resources will be in an excellent position to advance the field of Precision Medicine. [Glossary Data merging, Data fusion, Data integration, Data cleaning, Data reduction, Data flattening, Data mining, Data modeling, Data munging, Data scraping, Data wrangling, Modeling algorithms]

- **Data readers**

You may be surprised to know that most collected data has never been read by anyone, and that includes the people who collected the data. It takes a certain type of mentality to pour over megabytes and gigabytes of data to get a feel for what's included in the data set, what's missing from the data set, what kinds of questions can be answered with the data, and, basically, what the data is trying to say. Every scientist has heard stories of professionals who collected data but never looked at the data that was collected [78], or who simply lost track of the data's whereabouts [76,79,80]. Every team of data analysts should include at least one individual who is assigned to familiarize himself with the data under study.

- **Generalist problem solvers and first-pass analysts**

Individuals who have a genuine interest in many different fields, a naturally inquisitive personality, and who have a talent for seeing relationships where others do not, are good to have around. Historically, academic training narrows the interests of students and professionals. Early in their college training, clueless undergraduates are expected to select their major field of study. As postdoctoral trainees, they narrow their interests even further. By the time they become tenured professors, their expertise is so limited that they cannot see how other fields relate to their own studies.

The world will always need people who devote their professional careers to a single subdiscipline, but the future will need fewer and fewer of these specialists [81]. Many of the most important advances in science have come from crossdisciplinary efforts. Regrettably, most journals are focused on a particular branch of a particular scientific discipline, and it can be very difficult to publish manuscripts that draw from methods and perspectives developed in multiple fields. Such manuscripts are typically rejected by editors, often without review, as falling outside the interests of the readership.

To derive the greatest value from Precision Medicine, we need to drop our make-believe boundaries between zoology and molecular biology, between morphology and gene, between medicine and computer science. We need to have general problem solvers who understand how to integrate and analyze data from sources whose content lies outside the professional comfort zones enclosing yesterday's scientists.

- **Professionals who can verify results and validate conclusions**

It's easy to confuse verification with validation, but they are two separate processes requiring different sets of technical skills. Verification is the process by which data is checked to determine whether the data was obtained properly (i.e., according to approved protocols), and that the data accurately measured what it was intended to measure, on the correct specimens. Data verification is not easy [82]. In one celebrated case, involving a microarray study, two statisticians devoted 2000 h to the job [83]. Two thousand hours is just about one full man-year of effort.

Validation is the process that checks whether the conclusions drawn from data analysis are correct [82]. Validation usually starts with repeating the same analysis of the same data, using the methods that were originally recommended. Obviously, if a different set of conclusions is drawn from the same data and methods, the original conclusions cannot be validated. Validation may involve applying a different set of analytic methods to the same data, to determine if the conclusions are consistent. It is always reassuring to know that conclusions are repeatable, with different analytic methods. In prior eras, experiments were validated by repeating the entire experiment, thus producing a new set of observations for analysis. Many of today's scientific experiments are far too complex and costly to repeat. In such cases, validation requires access to the complete collection of the original data, and to the detailed protocols under which the data were generated.

One of the most useful methods of data validation involves testing new hypotheses, based on the assumed validity of the original conclusions. For example, if you were to accept Darwin's analysis of barnacle data, leading to his theory of evolution, then you would expect to find a chronologic history of fossils in ascending layers of shale rock. This was the case; thus, paleontologists studying the Burgess shale reserves provided some degree of validation to Darwin's conclusions. Validation is not proof, but it comes close. The repeatability of conclusions, over time, with the same or different sets of data, and the demonstration of consistency with other, independent, observations, is all that we can hope for in this imperfect world.

Because much of Precision Medicine is based on the analysis of complex data sets, and because there are so many opportunities for error, all Precision Medicine studies will need to be verified and validated. This means that there will be a growing need for professionals skilled in these matters.

– Professionals who know how to share data

In Section 8.6, we discussed the necessity for data sharing, and we listed most of the currently prevailing excuses for withholding data. Professionals who can navigate the impedimenta, and bring their data to the public, will be the new heroes of the Precision Medicine era.

– Freelance data analysts

In the recent past, data analysts worked in universities, research institutions, and private corporations. Because data is now distributed and detached from the laboratory in which it was created, and because data analysts are often tasked with integrating many different sources of data, there is no particular need to tether a data analyst to any single location or any single employer. In the near future, it is likely that data analysts will function as knights-errant, using freely available information and software tools to render consultative reports. It is possible that the next generation of data analysts will receive a significant portion of their training outside the university classroom, through apprenticeships within the guild of free lancers.

SECTION 9.6 FAST, CHEAP, PRECISE CLINICAL TRIALS

Only theory can tell us what to measure and how to interpret it.
Albert Einstein

Medicine can only cure curable diseases, and then not always.
Chinese proverb

Clinical trials had their heyday in the late 1960s and early 1970s, when highly effective chemotherapeutic agents were found to be effective against a wide range of rare, childhood cancers [84]. The prospective randomized control trial, performed on children with cancer, was so very successful that it served as a required standard for drug trials, for the past half-century.

Today, large, randomized prospective clinical trials remain the standard for common diseases, such as cancer. The problem has been that almost none of the drugs tested on adults with cancer have brought the remarkable cure rates seen with the childhood tumors. Larger, longer, and increasingly expensive studies were conducted to demonstrate incremental improvements in chemotherapeutic regimens. The common cancers occurring in the adult population remain hard to cure.

Modern clinical trials are long and expensive. It takes about 10–15 years for an experimental drug to be developed [85]. Only 5 in 5000 compounds that have preclinical testing will enter clinical trials [85]. The cost of developing a drug and bringing it to market is about $1 billion [75]. [Glossary Preclinical trial]

Clinical trials can be very large. In the realm of cancer trials, the Prostate, Lung, Colorectal, and Ovarian Cancer Screening Trial (PLCO, NIH/NCI trial NO1 CN25512) serves as an example. The PLCO is a randomized controlled cancer trial. Between 1992, when the trial opened, and 2001, when enrollment ended, 155,000 participants were recruited [86]. The study ended in 2016. Clinical trials for cardiovascular disease, diabetes, or depression are designed to be even larger than cancer trials [87].

It can be difficult or impossible to enroll all the patients required for a clinical trial [88]. In an analysis of 500 planned cancer trials, 40% of trials failed to accrue the minimum necessary number of patients. Furthermore, trial populations often fail to include sufficient numbers of minorities (e.g., African-Americans, Hispanics, children), and overenroll white males, yielding results that may not be generally applicable to a diverse population of patients [89]. Of cancer trials that have passed through the early phases of clinical trial, three out of five drugs failed to achieve the necessary patient enrollment to move into the final (i.e., phase III) clinical trial [87]. Overall, about 95% of drugs that enter the clinical trial gauntlet will fail [90].

While our need for faster trials has grown, the historic trend has favored slower, more complex trials. A trial that may have taken a matter of weeks to design and initiate, back in the 1980s, may require several years of preliminary development, today [91]. It now takes about 10–15 years for an experimental drug to be developed and tested [85]. To pass a clinical trial, a drug must have proven efficacy. It need not be curative, only safe and effective. Of the 5% of drugs that pass clinical trials, some will have negligible or incremental benefits. After a drug has reached market, its value to the general population might be less than anyone had anticipated. Clinical trials, like any human endeavor, are subject to error [92–94]. Like any experiment, clinical trials need to be validated [75]. It may take years or decades to determine whether a treatment that demonstrated a small, but statistically significant effect in a clinical trial will have equivalent value in clinical practice.

Clinical trials are the best method ever developed to determine whether a drug is safe and effective for a particular purpose, in a particular target population. Nonetheless, clinical trials cannot provide the clinical guidance we need to develop the new medications that will be needed to conquer the common diseases. We simply do not have the money, time, and talent to perform all the anticipated clinical trials for the candidate drugs that are waiting their turn in the Precision Medicine pipeline.

Shouldn't we be asking ourselves whether we can improve clinical trials, to yield credible, reproducible results in less time, and for less money [90,95]? Here are a few predictions for innovations in clinical trials, all based on insights from the field of Precision Medicine.

– Rare disease trials

Let's back up a moment and look at trends in cancer deaths, by age, since 1950 [96].

Age Group	1950	1978	2005
0-4	11.1	4.6	2.2
5-14	6.7	4.1	2.5
15-24	8.6	6.1	4.1
25-34	20.4	14.2	9.1
35-44	63.6	50.7	32.8
45-54	174.2	179.6	118.3
55-64	391.3	428.9	329.7
65-74	710.0	803.4	748.8
75-84	1167.2	1204.1	1265.1
85 and over	1450.7	1535.3	1643.7
All Ages	195.4	204.4	184.0

Cancer death rates stratified by age, all races, males and females, included [96].
Rates are per 100,000 population and are age-adjusted to the 2000 US population.

As we expected, the pediatric age group has seen the largest drop in cancer death rate since 1950. Individuals over the age of 65, the age group with the largest cancer burden, actually experienced an increase in the cancer death rate, since 1950 [96]. Age groups above 65, for which cancer is much more common, have had an increase in the cancer death rates. We see that despite adopting uniform clinical trial strategies for all cancer trials in all ages, the trials in adults never enjoyed anything remotely akin to the phenomenal trial successes seen in pediatric trials. Furthermore, because cancer deaths among adults are about 500 times more numerous than cancer deaths among children, the advances in the treatment of childhood cancer have not translated into any measurable benefit to the population death rate.

Why have the dramatic advances in the treatment of childhood cancers not carried over to the adult population? The answer relates to the difference in biology between rare diseases and common diseases, as discussed earlier, in Section 5.1. Summarized, rare diseases tend to be monogenic. This means that the root cause of every instance of a rare disease is likely to involve the same pathways as every other instance of the same disease. Hence, a clinical trial for a rare disease is virtually guaranteed to have a homogeneous and unblended patient population, with every disease occurrence having the same key pathway driving its clinical phenotype. This means that a drug that fails for one patient is likely to fail for most patients and that a drug that is effective in one patient is likely to be effective in most patients. Consequently, clinical trials designed for rare diseases can be smaller than clinical trials designed for common diseases, which are often of heterogeneous cause and tainted by blended subpopulations (i.e., containing individuals with clinically similar but pathogenetically distinctive diseases that are unlikely to respond to treatment) [90]. A review of clinical trial sizes for orphan drugs indicates that the average trial involved 588 subjects, ranging from 152 up to 1281. The typical common disease clinical trial size exceeds 5000 human subjects [97].

Sometimes, the clinical trial size for a rare disease can be as small as one patient. In Australia, a baby was born with molybdenum cofactor deficiency type A, a rare disease that accounts for about 100 childhood deaths worldwide, each year. A plant biologist in Germany had a compound that, he thought, might cure the child. After obtaining all the necessary approvals to try the drug, which had been previously tested only in mice, the child was administered the compound. By all accounts, the baby was pulled from the brink of death, and, as of the last report, was doing well [98–100].

In the United States, Public Law 111-80, the Agriculture, Rural Development, Food and Drug Administration, and Related Agencies Appropriations Act of 2010 authorized the FDA to appoint a review group to recommend design improvements for preclinical and clinical trials aimed at preventing, diagnosing, and treating rare diseases [101]. Trials on orphan drugs commonly accrue human subjects from vulnerable populations (e.g., children, mentally impaired subjects, subjects with multiple life-threatening conditions). In such cases, human subjects may not be able to provide informed consent, and a parent or guardian will need to be consulted. Trialists must be sensitive to the special needs of their subjects and their families. Recruiting an independent clinical safety board or institutional review board, with no financial ties to the trialists or their sponsors, is a prudent measure [102]. The Food and Drug Administration is poised to provide guidance to organizations and corporations conducting clinical trials on orphan drugs [102]. It is not surprising to see that clinical trials for the rare diseases are proceeding at a furious pace and have recently yielded effective treatments for hundreds of conditions. [Glossary Informed Consent]

All this excitement over rare diseases seems encouraging, but how does it help the general population, suffering from common diseases? As we have seen previously (Section 5.4. "Treatments for Rare Diseases are Effective Against the Common Diseases"), when we find a new treatment for a rare disease, we are likely to find a way to apply the treatment to individuals who have a common disease.

– Pathway trials

Until quite recently, clinical trials have been focused on finding cures for individual diseases. We now know that diseases are expressed through metabolic pathways, and that the pathway that drives one disease may play an important role in the pathogenesis of other diseases. Clinical trials for drugs that target a particular pathway may have wide application for the treatment of many different diseases.

We have previously provided examples of treatments that were effective against clinically diverse diseases, based on having a convergent pathway in common (Section 4.4, "Pathway-Directed Treatments for Convergent Diseases"). Here are a few additional examples:

- GM-CSF (Granulocyte/Macrophage Colony Stimulating Factor) for neutropenia [103], and for pulmonary alveolar proteinosis [104,105].
- Imatinib for chronic myelogenous leukemia [106] and for gastrointestinal stromal tumor [107].
- Crizotinib (Anaplastic lymphoma kinase, ALK) inhibitor for pathway-sensitive non-small-cell lung carcinoma [108] and for neuroblastoma, and inflammatory myofibroblastic tumor [109–112]. [Glossary Inflammatory myofibroblastic tumor]
- CD20 inhibitors that block B cell maturation (rituximab, obinutuzumab, ibritumomab tiuxetan, tositumomab, and ofatumumab) as potential treatments for chronic lymphocytic leukemia, follicullar lymphoma, rheumatoid arthritis, myalgic encephalomyelitis, and systemic lupus erythematosus [113].

There are two significant drawbacks to pathway-directed treatments. The first is that we really do not know all that much about the individual pathways that drive the expression of disease. Understanding these pathways is certainly one of the most important goals of Precision Medicine, but there are thousands of diseases, and we've barely scratched the surface. Second, most drugs affect many different pathways. For the most part, we lack objective measurements that tell us how greatly any one of those pathways is blocked, activated, or modified by the introduction of a new drug [114]. When a drug has a particular action in vitro, we often infer that the drug will have a similar action, on the same pathway, in clinical practice. In many cases, though, we're just guessing when we say that a given drug's clinical activity is due to its effect on a particular pathway. Nonetheless, an intelligent guess based on in vitro observations that correspond with validated clinical outcomes may be sufficient to justify a clinical trial whose primary purpose is to test the effect of a drug on a particular pathway operative in multiple diseases.

- **Trials of drugs that block the steps of development of diseases**

In addition to finding drugs that target the key pathways contributing to a clinical phenotype, we can also look for drugs that block the events that precede the fully developed disease. For example, in July 2002, results from a large randomized controlled trial indicated that hormone replacement therapy (HRT), commonly prescribed for postmenopausal women, carried an increased risk of developing breast cancer. Moreover, the risk of developing breast cancer exceeded the benefits that came from HRT treatments [115]. Following this news, there was an immediate nationwide withdrawal of HRT in the at-risk group of women. Over the next 5 months, a dramatic 15% drop in the breast cancer rate was noticed. This drop was attributed to HRT withdrawal [116].

How could that be possible? It is commonly accepted that breast carcinogenesis takes about 15 years to develop, from the time that the individual is exposed to a carcinogen, until the time that the tumor is clinically detected. That being the case, then wouldn't you need to wait 15 years following withdrawal of the presumptive carcinogen, in this case HRTs, before you could expect to see a drop in the incidence of breast cancer? How is it even remotely possible that the cessation of HRT therapy in July will cause a drop in the number of cancers reported in December?

The answer is obvious once we stop looking at the cause of breast cancer and begin to examine the sequence of steps that lead to the development of breast cancer. We can infer that the step in the development of breast cancer that is affected by HRT must occur late in the sequence (i.e., about year 14 or 15 of the process). In this case, it would seem, an intervention occurring in a late, precancerous stage, was sufficient to bring about the observed quick drop in the cancer rate. A simple intervention was enough to save many lives.

There are occasions when you can intervene at a particular step in the development of a disease and seemingly switch off the disease at that moment. For example, cardiofaciocutaneous syndrome is a rare monogenic inherited disorder characterized by a set of distinctive congenital abnormalities involving the face, heart, and other organs. It is caused by mutations in any of several different genes, including BRAF. In a zebrafish model of cardiofaciocutaneous syndrome, fish embryos express the BRAF disease allele. Treatment of the affected embryos with inhibitors of the pathway affected by the BRAF mutation will restore normal development in these fish [117]. The inhibitor needs to be administered in a window of time when the BRAF mutation exerted its teratogenic effect. In this case, the pathogenesis of disease could be interrupted by an intervening event occurring at a crucial moment of time.

Most remarkably, the disease process can be switched off without repairing the root cause (i.e., the BRAF mutation) of the disease.

A primary goal of Precision Medicine involves determining the biochemical events in pathogenesis. In the future, we can hope to see a great number of clinical trials to determine the safety and efficacy of interventions that block pathogenesis.

– Exceptional responder trials

The large size of standard clinical trials is necessitated by the need to provide a representative sampling of the affected population. For example, if you want to test a drug that will be used for persons of all ages, genders, ethnicities, and races, then you would want to include a statistically appropriate number of all these groups in your treatment and control groups. You'll be looking for any statistically significant difference in response between the treated groups and the control groups. This makes for a very large clinical trial. But if you want to focus the trial on a small subset of affected individuals who have a particular biomarker, and who present with a clinically well-defined variation of the disease, then you can use many fewer human subjects. You'll be looking for a certain type of biological response that should occur in most of your carefully selected subjects. Hence, clinical trials designed for biologically defined disease subpopulations require fewer enrolled subjects than standard clinical trials.

In the past few years, so-called exceptional responders have attracted the attention of clinical trialists. Exceptional responders are individuals who respond well to treatments that have little or no effectiveness for the majority of subjects. Investigators are trying to determine what makes the exceptional responders different. The idea here is that a drug that has little value for the general population may be curative for patients whose disease is driven by a particular metabolic pathway. A specific mutation or other biomarker may identify a patient as an exceptional responder for an otherwise ineffective treatment [118,119].

The pharmaceutical company Genentech employed this strategy when it developed the breast cancer drug trastuzuab (trade name herceptin). Trastuzumab is a monocloncal antibody against the HER2 receptor. Preclinical evidence indicated that trastuzumab might be effective against breast cancers that had high levels of HER2. By limiting their study to individuals with HER2-positive breast cancers, the company achieved success, with a relatively small number of trial participants [90,120].

Determining the key biological properties that define the exceptional responders may help us to develop drugs that will be effective for individuals who were nonresponsive to other forms of treatment [121]. Increasingly, clinical trials are being designed with the flexibility to target subtypes of diseases, testing multiple candidate drugs against their most likely responders, in a single study [90,122].

– Outcome data and observational trials

The classic randomized controlled trial will probably remain the best way to determine whether a drug is safe and effective for the general population, but it has its limitations. Randomized clinical trials do not tell us much about optimal drug dosages for various subpopulations of individuals (e.g., based on race or age or gender), or the optimal length of time to stay on the drug, or anything at all about drug interactions. Most importantly, the randomized control trial does not establish validity. A randomized control trial is an experiment.

Like all experiments, they can be poorly designed, misinterpreted, invalid for under-represented patient subpopulations, unrepeatable, and falsified. The best validation of clinical trials comes from continuously monitoring patient outcomes in medical centers wherein many different types of patients can be observed (e.g., male, female, different nationalities, different ages, concurrent diseases, multiple medications) [123]. Outcome data is crucial for those trials that had a small effect size (e.g., a 2-week survival benefit for individuals who have a malignant tumor). You need to wonder whether the same benefit will be observed when the drug is used to treat a large and diverse population of outpatients. Outcome data analysis, in addition to validating randomized clinical trials, provides the easiest way of finding exceptional responders and of correlating outcomes with patient demographics, dosages, drug interactions, clinical history, and ancillary medical tests.

In the past, statisticians have been wary of giving much credence to retrospective data, including analyses of hospital based outcome data. There are just too many biases and opportunities to reach misleading conclusions. Today, there is a growing feeling that we just do not have the luxury of ignoring hospital-based outcome data. Abandoning these large, existing resources seems like a waste of good data.

Perhaps the greatest value of outcome data is its historical reach. Hospitals keep their records for many years, permitting long-term outcome review. Prospective studies must drag on, at great expense, before long-term outcome data is collected. It seems that no matter how hard we try, we cannot avoid the fact that we need a minimum of 5 years to produce five years of follow-up for a prospective clinical trial.

Today, statisticians are using retrospective data in novel ways to determine the factors that contribute to the development of disease, traditionally the exclusive domain of prospective studies [95,124–126]. The incentives to use retrospective data are high. Funding agencies and corporations should ask themselves, before financing any large research initiative, whether the study can be performed using existing data [127]. Of course, initiatives using existing data will never come to pass if researchers are denied access to the data, a topic covered in Section 8.6, "What Is Data Sharing, and Why Don't We Do More of It?" [Glossary Observational data]

– Bypassing trials when diseases converge

The goal of precision medicine is NOT to design new drugs to treat unique patients for unique, genetically defined diseases. To the contrary, the goal of Precision Medicine is to find generally effective treatments for all the patients who have any of the diseases that are likely to respond to a treatment.

Case in point. We now have a number of drugs that target CD20, a B-lymphocyte surface molecule that plays a role in B-cell differentiation. These drugs, all of which are monoclonal antibodies, include: rituximab, obinutuzumab, ibritumomab tiuxetan, and tositumomab. One or another of these drugs has been approved in the treatment of most types of B cell lymphomas and leukemias (e.g., chronic lymphocytic leukemia). B cells play a key role in a number of chronic inflammatory conditions. It should be no surprise that CD20 inhibitors, effective against leukemias and lymphomas, have been added to trials as treatments for systemic lupus erythematosus, myalgic encephalomyelitis, follicular lymphoma, rheumatoid arthritis, multiple sclerosis, non-Hodgkin lymphoma, and immune thrombocytopenia [113]. Most drug trials ultimately fail in trial, but the expectation is that an effective drug that targets a disease pathway will have some value in the treatment of other diseases that are driven by the same pathway [122]. [Glossary Non-Hodgkin lymphoma]

It is worth noting that with or without clinical trials, patients and their physicians are already employing a crude approach to treating convergent diseases. When the FDA approves a drug, the approval is restricted to one or several particular uses of the product. Specifically, the FDA considers for approval those uses that are demonstrated to be safe and effective in clinical trials. The approved uses of a drug are listed on the labels attached to prescriptions. All drug uses other than the uses approved by the FDA are considered "off-label" uses. [Glossary Off-label]

It is not unusual for a drug to be prescribed more often for off-label uses than for its FDA-approved use. For example, Botox (Botulinum toxin type A) was originally developed, tested, and approved, in 1989, for the treatment of strabismus and blepharspasm. After approval was awarded, botox was found to be extremely effective for rare spasmodic conditions, including spasmodic torticollis (i.e., wry neck). It was subsequently noticed that Botox injections could temporarily erase wrinkles. The off-label uses of botox have given birth to a growing cosmetic industry.

In many cases, off-label drug uses have not been shown, in clinical trials, to be either safe or effective. Not surprisingly, it is illegal for drug companies to market drugs for off-label uses. Physicians, unlike drug manufacturers, are not regulated by the FDA. In the United States, physicians can legally prescribe drugs for off-label uses, and they do. In a 2006 study, it was found that "about 21% of all estimated uses for commonly prescribed medications were off-label, and that 15% of all estimated uses lacked scientific evidence of therapeutic efficacy" [128]. A published trial using a small and statistically inadequate patient population, or a single case report where a doctor communicates a successful outcome, may be all that a desperate patient and his doctor need to prescribe a drug for an off-label use.

There are thousands of rare diseases, and there are likely to be an even greater number of subtypes of common diseases. It is simply not feasible to conduct clinical trials and obtain FDA approval for drugs that can be proven effective against even a small fraction of these conditions. Physicians whose patients have a disease for which no FDA-approved drug exists will likely search for off-label options. When they do so, they will want accurate information about the pathogenesis of diseases, and they will also want a classification that groups disease by drug target pathways [129].

SECTION 9.7 ANIMAL EXPERIMENTATION

The proper study of Mankind is Man.
Alexander Pope in "An Essay on Man," 1734.

What trap is this? Where were its teeth concealed?
Philip Larkin, from his poem "Myxomatosis"

Myxoma virus produces a fatal disease, myxomatosis, in rabbits. The disease is characterized by the rapid appearance of skin tumors (myxomas), followed by severe conjunctivitis, a plethora of systemic symptoms, and fulminant pneumonia. Death usually occurs two to fourteen days after infection. In 1952, a French virologist, hoping to reduce the rabbit population on his private estate, inoculated a few rabbits with Myxoma virus. The results were much more than he had bargained for. Within 2 years, 90% of the rabbit population of France had succumbed to myxomatosis.

European rabbits, introduced to Australia in the nineteenth century, became feral and multiplied. By 1950 the feral rabbit population in Australia had grown to about 3 billion, and foraging rabbits were interfering with crop yield. Seizing upon the Myxoma virus as a solution to rabbit overpopulation, Australians launched a Myxoma virus inoculation program. In <10 years, the Australian rabbit population was reduced by 95% [130]. Nearly 3 billion rabbits died, a number very close to the number of humans living on the planet in the mid-1950s. A committee of scientists and bureaucrats had made a decision to unleash a plague upon rabbits, with devastating effect. Without commenting on the moral implications of animal eradication efforts, it is worth noting that rabbits are not the only mammals that can be exterminated by a pathogenic virus. Humans should take heed.

Looking back, we see that scientists exercise enormous power over the welfare of animals [131]. Now that Precision Medicine has emerged as a new approach to disease research, shouldn't we be asking ourselves whether we should change the ways in which we conduct animal research? Once again, let's examine some of the precepts of Precision Medicine, this time trying to imagine how they will change the culture of animal experimentation.

- **Diseases develop through a sequence of steps, over time, involving alterations in multiple pathways.**

Pathogenesis always involves a multistep process that unfolds within a complex biological system known as a species. If we think of pathogenesis as a system response that develops over time, then we must abandon any expectation that pathogenesis will be equivalent between species. Animal models have limited value in the era of Precision Medicine, when we are searching for the precise pathways that eventually lead to a clinical phenotype.

Animal models remind us that a genetic defect does not "cause" a disease. Here is just one example. Zebrafish, an organism popular among developmental biologists, can be infected with mycobacteria. A gene in the zebrafish was shown to modulate its susceptibility to mycobacterial infection [132]. Naturally, there was hope that the orthologous gene in humans would be associated with human susceptibility to tuberculosis. Despite a large study involving 9115 subjects, no such association was found [133]. **The genetic root cause of a disease does not account for pathogenesis, which is an emergent property of the system in which the mutation is expressed.**

It's asking a lot to expect animals to replicate all the steps of disease development that occur in humans [134]. Mutations in the RB1 gene are the root genetic cause of retinoblastoma, a cancer arising in the human retina. Producing the equivalent mutation in the nematode leads to ectopic vulvae [135]. A retinoblastoma is not equivalent to an ectopic vulva. Similarly, in a transgenic mouse model of cystic fibrosis, the target protein (CFTR) for a successful drug in humans (VX-770), was unaffected by the drug (i.e., did not replicate the human drug response) [136].

Lesch-Nyhan disease is a rare syndrome caused by a deficiency of HGPRT (hypoxanthine-guanine phosphoribosyl transferase), an enzyme involved in purine metabolism. In humans, HGPRT deficiency results in high levels of uric acid, with resultant renal disease and gout. Various severe neurologic and psychologic symptoms accompany the syndrome in humans, including self-mutilation. Neurologic features tend to increase as the affected child ages.

The same HGPRT deficiency of humans can be produced in mice. Mice with HGPRT deficiency do not have disease. As far as anyone can tell, mice with HGPRT deficiency are totally normal [137]. How can this be? Once again, a gene does not cause a disease, all by itself. The mouse, evidently, employs pathways that compensate for the deficiency in HGPRT. Likewise, two mouse models for the most commonly mutated gene in human nephronophthisis, a serious inherited kidney disease, produce no clinical phenotype in mice [138].

A form of familial Parkinson disease is associated with an inherited mutation in the PARK2 gene, which encodes a protein known as parkin. A "parkin knockout" mouse has been developed as a model for familial Parkinson disease. However, the parkin knockout mice do not display the trembling, rigid movements and unsteady gait that characterize the human disease [139].

After reading the aforementioned examples, are we surprised to learn that STAT1 deficiency, which leads to immunodeficiency in humans, results in breast cancer in mice [140,141]?

Though a gene mutation may be the root cause of a human disease, its pathogenesis in a mouse may follow a totally different route. Put another way, the cellular events that lead to the clinical expression of disease will often diverge between species. [Glossary Synteny]

– Koch's postulates do not apply to Precision Medicine

Back in Section 6.4, "Revising Koch's Postulates in the Era of Precision Diagnostics," we saw how Koch's postulates have come to be generally ignored. But Koch's postulates are very much animal-centric, requiring consistent replication of the human disease in animals using organisms isolated from the human lesions. Most of the newly emerging diseases are capable of producing disease in only a small percentage of the humans who are infected. In many cases, the presumptive infectious agent cannot be isolated, let alone cultivated. These infections, for the most part, will have no animal models.

Perhaps it is time to save our resources by abandoning Koch's requirement that infectious diseases must be reproducible in animal models. [Glossary Koch's postulates]

– Precision Medicine initiatives are human genome-centric

We are currently collecting whole genome data on populations of humans, for correlation with clinical information, with the expectation of identifying disease genes and developing new approaches to the treatment of diseases in humans. This is where the money and scientific expertise are being directed, under the US Precision Medicine Initiative [89,119,122,142]. Scientists who are trained to generate, collect, organize, share, and analyze large data resources, on human populations, will be in the best position to advance the field of Precision Medicine.

– Precision Medicine treatments are focused on pathways.

Researchers are dissecting the key pathways that are shared by rare diseases, common phenocopy diseases, and by common complex diseases whose clinical phenotype is driven by one or more of the same pathways.

Pathways are involved not just as the targets of new drugs, but also in the system responses to treatments with new drugs. Consider the following incident that occurred in 2006. Eight paid healthy volunteers were assembled. These subjects would be the first humans to receive the test drug, under any conditions. In a single session, six of the volunteers were infused with TGN1412, and two volunteers were infused with a placebo. In about an hour, all six of the subjects treated with TGN1412 developed cytokine storm, a life-threatening condition in which an immune-response precipitates shock, and a wide range of extreme system-wide responses, including multiorgan failure. Prompt treatment saved all their lives. Two of the six had prolonged hospital courses. All six patients must now deal with long-term medical consequences of the event. Again, in 2016, in France, an early clinical trial for a new drug led to serious adverse effects in five subjects, including the death of one [143]. In both the 2006 trial and the 2016 trial, preclinical animal studies failed to predict human toxicity. Why not?

Aside from differences in targeted disease pathways, each species has its own methods for dealing with toxic insults. In many cases, the toxin causes less cellular damage than the "defense" mechanisms created to nullify the damage. In the case of the TGN1412 study, patients were ravaged by an exaggerated inflammation pathway reaction known as a cytokine storm [144,145].

As discussed in Section 6.2, "Our Genome Is a Book Titled 'The History of Human Infections,'" Inflammatory responses are species-specific, hence unpredictable in rodent systems. In a review of human clinical trials based on research data collected from mouse models, every one of 150 clinical trials testing inflammation blockers was a failure [146]. Mice and men have widely divergent reactions to the same treatments. For example, Gram-negative bacteria produce shock in animals via lipopolysaccharide, a molecule found in their cell walls. Mice have high resistance to the shock-inducing effect of lipopolysaccharide. The dose of lipopolysaccharide causing death in mice happens to be one million times the dose that causes fever in humans and about 1000–10,000 times more than the dose that causes shock in humans [147].

Historically, the drug development process employs rodent models to identify candidate drugs for clinical trials in humans, but few such mouse-inspired trials have shown success [148–151]. The National Academy of Sciences recently convened a workshop entitled, "Therapeutic development in the absence of predictive animal models of nervous system disorders [152]." Mouse models for common neurological disorders, such as Alzheimer disease and Parkinson disease, have been largely unsuccessful [152,153]. In fact, multiple mouse models for Parkinson disease have been developed, including the "parkin knockout mouse" and LRRK2 knockouts, but none has shown dopamine degeneration, motor dysfunction, or even the synuclein bodies that are characteristic of human Parkinson disease [139]. Likewise, mouse models of Alzheimer disease fail to develop the neurofibrillary tangles and neuronal losses that are hallmarks for the human disease. Even if refinements in the mouse model may produce mice with disease that have the same pathological changes that are observed in the human disease, the treatments developed for mice may not carry over to clinical trials in humans [150,154]. One of the repeated themes emerging from the National Academy of Sciences workshop is that animal models cannot predict how humans will respond to drugs that perturb the complex system of pathways involved in common human diseases [152]. The situation in the neurosciences is sufficiently discouraging that signs of a withdrawal from animal research by the pharmaceutical industry have been reported [155].

We shouldn't be surprised. As discussed previously, the human genome is a document telling the story of how our species, and our ancestors, have survived environmental challenges. Much of our genome is devoted to responding, in one way or another, to toxins and infections. The mysterious ways in which we respond to drugs were written into the human genome [147].

Where traditional animal models fail, biologists are finding success with single-cell eukaryotes and insects. Though we can expect disease phenotypes to diverge among species affected by orthologous genes, we might be able to study specific pathways that have been conserved through most of the history of eukaryotic evolution. For example, the 2013 Nobel Prize in Physiology or Chemistry was awarded for work on vesicular transport disorders. Some of the progress in this area came from studies of human inherited transport disorders [156]. However, the vesicular transport pathway was dissected by studying orthologous genes in yeast [157]. Another example of a useful ortholog is found in Drosophila. Drosophila contains homologs of the genes that cause tuberous sclerosis, a hamartoma-cancer syndrome in humans. The brain tubers (hamartomas of the neuroectoderm, also called phakomas), for which tuberous sclerosis takes its name, contain large, multinucleate neurons. Loss of function of the same genes in Drosophila produces enlarged cells with many times the normal amount of DNA [158]. The tuberous sclerosis orthodisease in Drosophila is being studied to help us understand cell growth control mechanisms in humans. [Glossary Orthodisease]

Is there any value in animal experimentation? Of course. Some animal models of human disease are very helpful. For example, mice inoculated with prions develop a disease that closely resembles the pathological hallmarks of human prion disease [153]. Cisd2, a candidate aging-associated gene in humans, causes premature aging and a shortened life span, in Cisd2-null mice [159]. Xeroderma pigmentosum, complementation group f, which causes photosensitivity and a heightened risk of early skin cancer in humans, can be simulated in mice with an XPF-dependent loss in telomeres. Ligneous conjunctivitis due to plasminogen deficiency in humans can be modeled by a similar conjunctivitis in mice lacking the plasminogen gene [160]. Rare rhabdoid tumors in humans are modeled by INI1-negative rhabdoid tumors in mice [161].

The use of animals is ingrained in the culture of science, and in the federal agencies that fund and regulate research [162]. If Precision Medicine is to have its expected impact, researchers will need to give serious thought to the limits of traditional animal research.

Glossary

Age-adjusted incidence An age-adjusted incidence is the crude incidence of disease occurrence within an age category (e.g., age 0–10 years, age 70–80 years), weighted against the proportion of persons in the age groups of a standard population. When we age-adjust incidence, we cancel out the changes in the incidence of disease occurrence, in different populations, that result from differences in the proportion of people in different age groups. For example, suppose you were comparing the incidence of childhood leukemia in two populations. If the first population has a large proportion of children, then it will likely have a higher occurrences of childhood leukemia in its population, compared with another population with a low proportion of children. To determine whether the first population has a true, increased rate of leukemia, we need to adjust for the differences in the proportion of young people in the two populations.

Autosomal dominance Refers to a pattern of inheritance in which a one allelic variant in an autosomal location (i.e., not on the X or Y chromosome) is sufficient to produce a trait or a disease. For the most part, diseases that have an autosomal pattern of inheritance will involve a gene variant that codes for an altered, pathogenic protein. Why is this? When a mutation results in the elimination of a protein product, or a reduction in the amount of the normal protein product produced by an allele, it can often be compensated by protein production by its paired allele. We see this commonly in recessive diseases that require both alleles to be affected by a mutation. Contrariwise, when a mutation results in an abnormal and pathogenic structural protein, then disease will usually result, even though one allele is producing a normal protein product. Hence, mutations that produce an altered protein product may be expected to have a dominant pattern of inheritance. There are numerous examples of autosomally dominant inherited disorders that are characterized by altered protein products: altered tau protein and autosomal dominant Frontotemporal dementia and parkinsonism linked to chromosome 17 (FTDP-17) [163]; altered FGFR3 protein and autosomal dominant achondroplasia; altered neurofibromin and autosomal dominant neurofibromatosis type 1; altered elastin gene and autosomal dominant cutis laxa; altered huntingtin and Huntington disease; altered hamartin and tuberin in autosomal dominant tuberous sclerosis. There are exceptions. For example, sickle cell anemia is caused by a mutation that alters hemoglobin. We would expect sickle cell disease to have an autosomal dominant pattern of inheritance, but it does not. Apparently, one mutant allele is not sufficient to produce a full-blown case of sickle cell disease. Severely affected individuals must have the characteristic sickle cell mutation in both alleles, and for this reason, sickle cell disease is recessive. It can be mentioned, however, that individuals with only one allele affected by the sickle cell mutation do not have normal red blood cells. Their red blood cells have a tendency to deform (i.e., to sickle) in conditions of hypoxia, just not to the extent necessary to precipitate the devastating clinical symptoms that comprise sickle cell anemia.

Chromosomal disorder Disorders associated with abnormalities in the physical structure of the chromosome. An example is found in fragile X syndrome. In this disease, a not uncommon cause of mental retardation, fragile sites are inherited as poorly condensed regions of the chromosome. Under experimental conditions, these regions break easily. Fragile sites have been associated with CCG repeats. Other examples of chromosomal disorders include Pelger-Huet anomaly and Roberts syndrome.

Congenital anomaly A structural deformity observed at birth. A clinically significant abnormality is present in about 3% of human births, indicating that in the aggregate, congenital abnormalities represent a common disease. About 60% of congenital anomalies are considered to be sporadic (i.e., they occur without any recognized genetic or environmental or physical cause). About 12%–25% of congenital anomalies are associated with genetic alterations, and the majority of these are chromosomal disorders. Hence, only a small percentage of congenital anomalies (perhaps considerably <5%) are associated with an identified single gene mutation that is suspected of being the root cause of the deformity. This tells us that Precision Medicine has told us very little about congenital anomalies, and that it would be impossible, at this time, to create a credible classification of congenital anomalies for a genetic classification of diseases.

Contiguous gene deletion syndrome Also called "Contig disease." A syndrome caused by abnormalities of two or more genes that are located next to each other on a chromosome. When the abnormality is a deletion, a contiguous gene syndrome is equivalent to a microdeletion syndrome.

Data cleaning Strictly speaking, should be data "cleansing," but the colloquial form is popular. Data cleaning is the process by which errors, spurious anomalies, and missing values are somehow handled. The options for data cleaning are: correcting the error, deleting the error, leaving the error unchanged, or imputing a different value [164]. Data cleaning is synonymous with data fixing or data correcting. Data cleaning should not be confused with data scrubbing.

Data flattening In the field of informatics, data flattening is a popular but ultimately counterproductive method of data organization and data reduction. Data flattening involves removing data annotations that are deemed unnecessary for the intended purposes of the data (e.g., timestamps, field designators, identifiers for individual data objects referenced within a document). Data flattening makes it difficult or impossible to verify data or to discover relationships among data objects.

Data fusion Data fusion is very closely related to data integration. The subtle difference between the two concepts lies in the end result. Data fusion creates a new set of data representing the combined data sources. Data integration is an on-the-fly usage of data pulled from different domains and, as such, does not yield a new data set.

Data integration The process of drawing data from different sources and knowledge domains in a manner that uses and preserves the identities of data objects and the relationships among the different data objects. The term "integration" should not be confused with a closely related term, "interoperability." An easy way to remember the difference is to note that integration applies to data; interoperability applies to software.

Data merging A nonspecific term that includes data fusion, data integration, and any methods that facilitate the accrual of data derived from multiple sources.

Data mining Alternate form, datamining. The term "data mining" is closely related to "data repurposing" and both endeavors employ many of the same techniques. Accordingly, the same data scientists engaged in data mining efforts are likely to be involved in data repurposing efforts. In data mining, the data, and the expected purpose of the data, are typically provided to the data miner, often in a form suited for analysis. In data repurposing projects, the data scientists are expected to find unintended purposes for the data.

Data modeling Refers to the intellectual process of finding a mathematical expression (often, an equation) or a symbolic expression that describes or summarizes a system or a collection of data. In many cases, mathematical models describe how different variables will change with one another. Data models always simplify the systems they describe, and many of the greatest milestones in the physical sciences have arisen from a bit of data modeling supplemented by scientific genius (e.g., Newton's laws of mechanics and optics, Kepler's laws of planetary orbits). In many cases, the modeler simply plots the data and looks for familiar shapes and patterns that suggest a particular type of data distribution (e.g., logarithmic, linear, normal, periodic, Power law, etc.). The modeler has numerous means of testing whether the data closely fits the model.

Data munging Refers to a multitude of tasks involved in preparing data for some intended purpose (e.g., data cleaning, data scrubbing, data transformation). Synonymous with data wrangling.

Data reduction When a very large data set is analyzed, it may be impractical or counterproductive to work with every element of the collected data. In such cases, the data analyst may choose to eliminate some of the data, or develop methods whereby the data is approximated. Some data scientists reserve the term "data reduction" for methods that reduce the dimensionality of multivariate data sets.

Data scraping Pulling together desired sections of a data set or text, using software.

Data wrangling Jargon referring to a multitude of tasks involved in preparing data for eventual analysis. Synonymous with data munging [165].

De novo mutation disease A genetic disease that is caused by a new mutation that occurs in the sperm cell that fertilizes the mother's ovum, or occurs in the mother's ovum, or occurs during the fertilization process when the sperm and ovum combine, or in the fertilized zygote, or in any postzygotic cell of the offspring (i.e., morula cell, blastula cell, embyronic cell, fetal cell, or cell of the developed organism).

Founder effect Occurs when a specific mutation enters the population through the successful procreational activities of a founder and his or her offspring, who carry the founder's mutation. When all of the patients with a specific disease have an identical mutation, the disease may have been propagated through the population by a founder effect. This is particularly true when the disease is confined to a separable subpopulation, as appears to be the case for Navaho neurohepatopathy, in which the studied patients, all members of the Navaho community, have the same missense mutation. Not all diseases characterized by a single gene mutation arise as the result of a founder effect. In the case of cystic fibrosis, a dominant founder effect can be observed within a genetically heterogeneous disease population. One allele of the cystic fibrosis gene accounts for 67% of cystic fibrosis cases in Europe. Hundreds of other alleles of the same gene account for the remaining 33% of cystic fibrosis cases [166].

Inflammatory myofibroblastic tumor A neoplasm composed of spindle cells and inflammatory cells, occurring most often in adolescents, and formerly believed to be a nonneoplastic condition. Recent work has identified a clonal rearrangement of the ALK (Anaplastic Lymphoma Kinase) gene, consistent with a neoplastic origin [112]. For mysterious reasons, this tumor may sometimes respond well to treatment with nonsteroidal antiinflammatory drugs [167].

Informed consent Subjects who are put at risk in an experimental study must first confirm consent. To this end, researchers must provide prospective human subjects with a consent form that informs the subject of the purpose and risks of the study, and discloses any information that might reasonably affect the participant's decision to participate, such as financial conflicts of interest among the researchers. The informed consent must be understandable to laymen, must be revocable (i.e., subjects can change their mind and withdraw from the study), must not contain exculpatory language (i.e., no waivers of responsibility for the researchers), must not promise any benefit for participation, and must not be coercive.

Koch's postulates Koch's postulates are a set of observations and experimental requirements proposed by Heinrich Hermann Robert Koch in the late 1800s, intended to prove that a particular organism causes a particular infectious disease. Koch's postulates require that the suspected causal organism be extracted from the infected lesion (i.e., from diseased, infected tissue); that the organism be cultured in a laboratory; and that the lesion be reproduced in animals after inoculation with the cultured organism. Over the ensuing century, some modifications to Koch's original postulates were necessary, to accommodate our expanding experience with infectious agents, and our increasing awareness of the limits of biological causality [168]. For example, in the case of Whipple disease, the bacterial cause was determined without benefit of isolation or culture. The consistent extraction from Whipple disease tissue of a particular molecule, characteristic of a particular species of bacteria, was deemed sufficient to establish the infectious origin of the disease.

MALToma Mucosa-Associated Lymphoid Tissue lymphoma. Most of the GI tract and the salivary glands are lined by aggregated collections of mucosal lymphocytes lacking the typical architecture of lymph nodes (e.g., without a capsule). Most of the cells are specialized B lymphocytes. Tumors that arise from these cells are called MALTomas. MALTomas may occur in the stomach after chronic infection with Helicobacter pylori.

Microarray Also known as gene chip, gene expression array, DNA microarray, or DNA chips. These consist of thousands of small samples of chosen DNA sequences arrayed onto a block of support material (usually, a glass slide). When the array is incubated with a mixture of DNA sequences prepared from cell samples, hybridization will occur between molecules on the array and single-stranded complementary (i.e., identically sequenced) molecules present in the cell sample. The greater the concentration of complementary molecules in the cell sample, the greater the number of fluorescently tagged hybridized molecules in the array. A specialized instrument prepares an image of the array and quantifies the fluorescence in each array spot. Spots with high fluorescence indicate relatively large quantities of DNA in the cell sample that matches the specific sequence of DNA in the array spot. The data comprising all the fluorescent intensity measurements for every spot in the array produces a gene profile characteristic of the cell sample.

Modeling algorithms Modeling involves explaining the behavior of a system, often with a formula, sometimes with descriptive language. The formula for the data describes the distribution of the data and often predicts how the different variables will change with one another. Consequently, modeling often provides reasonable hypotheses to explain how the data objects within a system will influence one another. Many of the great milestones in the physical sciences have arisen from a bit of data modeling supplemented by scientific genius (e.g., Newton's laws of mechanics and optics, Kepler's laws of planetary orbits, Quantum mechanics). The occasional ability to relate observation with causality endows modeling with greater versatility and greater scientific impact than the predictive techniques (e.g., recommenders, classifiers, and clustering methods). Unlike the methods of predictive analytics, which tend to rest on a few basic assumptions about measuring similarities among data objects, the methods of data modeling are selected from every field of mathematics and provide an intuitive approach to data analysis. In some cases, the modeler simply plots the data and looks for familiar shapes and patterns that suggest a particular type of function (e.g., logarithmic, linear, normal, Fourier series, Power law, etc.). The modeler has various means of testing whether the data closely fits the model.

Mutation rate Over the years, many estimates for the spontaneous mutation rates have appeared in the literature. In humans, point mutations (i.e., mutations that occur in a single nucleotide base within the genome) seem to occur with a frequency of about $1–3 \times 10^{-8}$ per base per cell per generation [169–171]. Cancer cells, which are generally characterized by genetic instability and multiple genetic abnormalities, seem to have high rates of spontaneous mutation, with estimates about a hundred-fold higher than mutation rates in normal cells (e.g., 210×10^{-8} mutations per base per cell per generation) [172]. When we extrapolate the mutation rate for the many cells that compose a human body, we might expect that trillions of mutations occur every few seconds [173]. Past estimates were somewhat speculative, and provided little information about the rate of repair of mutations. Furthermore, estimates were generally restricted to one specific type of genetic error (i.e., point mutations). With the advent of next-generation sequencing, it became possible to look for somatic mutations of all types, in the entire genome of cells, comparing the number of mutations found in different tissues of the same person, or in persons of different ages. These kinds of studies, which are only now beginning to enter the literature, will tell us a great deal about the mutational burden on humans. In a recent study wherein samples of chronically sun-exposed eyelid skin were examined for oncogene mutations, the researchers found that about a quarter of the skin cells contained activating mutations in oncogenes [174]. We shouldn't be surprised by these findings. It has been estimated that by the time we reach the age of 60 years, every nucleotide in our genome has been mutated in at least one cell of the body [175].

Next-generation sequencing Refers to a variety of new technologies that rapidly and cheaply sequence genomes. These techniques involve sequencing millions of fragments of the genome, many times, in parallel, and sorting them out by comparing the individual sequences against a reference human genome [176]. At present (i.e., 2017), an entire human genome can be sequenced in about a day.

Non-Hodgkin lymphoma Lymphoid neoplasms are divided into two categories: Hodgkin lymphoma and non-Hodgkin lymphoma. Non-Hodgkin lymphoma comprises every lymphoid neoplasm other than Hodgkin lymphoma. The diagnosis of Non-Hodgkin lymphoma, communicated to a patient, is always uninformative and needlessly confusing. "Non-Hodgkin lymphoma" may be the only example of a diagnosis that informs patients what their diagnosis is not (i.e., it's not Hodgkin lymphoma), declining to specify what their diagnosis happens to be.

Observational data Data obtained by measuring existing things or things that occurred without the help of the scientist. Observational data needs to be distinguished from experimental data. In general, experimental data can be described with a Gaussian curve, because the experimenter is trying to measure what happens when a controlled process is performed on every member of a uniform population. Such experiments typically produce Gaussian (i.e., bell-shaped or normal) curves for the control population and the test population. The statistical analysis of experiments reduces to the chore of deciding whether the resulting Gaussian curves are different from one another. In observational studies, data is collected on categories of things, and the resulting data sets often follow a Zipf distribution, wherein a few types of data objects account for the majority of observations For this reason, many of the assumptions that apply to experimental data (i.e., the utility of parametric statistical descriptors including average, standard deviation and p-values) will not necessarily apply to observational data sets.

Off-label Refers to the use of a drug to treat a condition other than the condition for which the drug was awarded FDA approval. The term "off-label" comes from the section of the pill-bottle label that describes the intended use or uses of the drug. Treatments other than those described on the drug's label are "off-label." The FDA does not regulate the practice of medicine. Hence, physicians may use good professional judgment to prescribe an off-label treatment for an FDA-approved drug. Prudent physicians will not prescribe off-label until such uses are supported by credible, repeated studies published in highly regarded medical journals. It is impossible to know, with any precision or confidence, the prevalence of off-label treatments in the rare diseases. Still, it is a commonly held that about 90% of all treatments for rare diseases are conducted without specific FDA approval. Medicare and private insurers, at present, tend to pay for off-label uses of drugs, particularly when these drugs are used to treat rare diseases.

Orthodisease Genetic diseases occurring in different species that involve mutations in orthologous genes.

Pap smear Shortened form of Papanicolaou smear. A specimen obtained by scraping or brushing the junction between the endocervix and the ectocervix, spreading the sampled cells onto a glass slide, and staining the cells with a special histologic reagent (the Papanicolaou stain), allowing the cytologist to see subtle alterations in the morphology of cells and, in particular, nuclei. A smear contains about 20,000 cells, and every cell must be inspected to rule out abnormalities diagnostic of dysplasia or cancer. In the last half of the twentieth century, the Pap smear cytologic evaluation led to a 70%–90% drop in the number of deaths from cervical cancer in countries that fully deployed the test.

Phylogeny A method of classifications based on ancestral lineage. The classification of terrestrial organisms is a phylogenetic classification.

Preclinical trial Investigations of drug activity prior to human studies. The term often applies to animal experiments that determine how candidate human drugs are metabolized in animals, and that measure various parameters of animal toxicity. One of the measures that come from animal trials is the "No Observable Adverse Effect Level," which is used to calculate a range of dosages that might be used in the earliest clinical trials.

Synteny An ordering of a group of genes along the chromosome that is equivalent among different species. Evaluation of synteny across species can be helpful when trying to either validate or discredit an animal model of human disease. For example, human oligodendrogliomas are often characterized by losses of chromosomes 1p, or 19q. Regions in mouse syntenic to 1p are found on murine chromosomes 3 and 4 and regions on mouse syntenic to 19q are found on murine chromosome 7. In an experimental mouse oligodendroglioma model, no losses were found in either of these syntenic chromosomal regions, indicating that the cytogenetic markers for human oligodendroglioma are absent from the mouse tumor; hence, the mouse oligodendroglioma presumably has a different pathogenesis than the human oligodendroglioma [177].

References

[1] Gersbach CA, Perez-Pinera P. Activating human genes with zinc finger proteins, transcription activator-like effectors and CRISPR/Cas9 for gene therapy and regenerative medicine. Expert Opin Ther Targets 2014;18:835–9.

[2] Lv Q, Yuan L, Deng J, Chen M, Wang Y, Zeng J, et al. Efficient generation of myostatin gene mutated rabbit by CRISPR/Cas9. Sci Rep 2016;6:25029.

[3] Gill S, June CH. Going viral: chimeric antigen receptor T-cell therapy for hematological malignancies. Immunol Rev 2015;263:68–89.

[4] Zhang C, Liu J, Zhong JF, Zhang X. Engineering CAR-T cells. Biomark Res 2017;5:22.

[5] Ramos AP, Cruz MAE, Tovani CB, Ciancaglini P. Biomedical applications of nanotechnology. Biophys Rev 2017;9:79–89.

[6] Zhang J, Rector J, Lin JQ, Young JH, Sans M, Katta N, et al. Nondestructive tissue analysis for ex vivo and in vivo cancer diagnosis using a handheld mass spectrometry system. Sci Transl Med 2017;9:e3968.

[7] Anderton K. The contest to build the first star trek tricorder has a winner. Forbes; April 22, 2017.

[8] Wunderlich CR. Das Verhalten der Eigenw rme in Krankheiten ("The behavior of the self-warmth in diseases"). Leipzig: O. Wigand; 1868.

[9] Chrysant SG, Chrysant GS. Current status of aggressive blood glucose and blood pressure control in diabetic hypertensive subjects. Am J Cardiol 2011;107:1856–61.

[10] Brekke D. Quiet passing of unlikely hero. Wired; January 22, 2000.

[11] Meyer R. A Long-lost spacecraft, now saved, faces its biggest test yet. The Atlantic; June 3, 2014.

[12] Chang K. A hobbyist challenges papers on growth of dinosaurs. The New York Times; December 16, 2013.

[13] Chang K. A spat over the search for killer asteroids. The New York Times; May 23, 2016.

[14] Chung E. Stardust citizen scientist finds first dust from outside solar system: dust collected by NASA spacecraft a decade ago finally identified and analyzed. CBC News; August 14, 2014.

[15] Mims FM. Amateur science—strong tradition, bright future. Science 1999;284:55–6.

[16] Epstein D. The DIY Scientist, the Olympian, and the Mutated Gene: How a woman whose muscles disappeared discovered she shared a disease with a muscle-bound Olympic medalist. ProPublica; January 15, 2016.

[17] Fikes BJ. The patient from the future, here today. The San Diego Union-Tribune; March 5, 2014.

[18] Thomas K. His Doctors were stumped. Then he took over The New York Times; February 4, 2017.

[19] Crow JF. The high spontaneous mutation rate: is it a healthrisk? Proc Natl Acad Sci U S A 1997;94:8380–6.

[20] Komazawa S, Sakai H, Itoh Y, Kawabe M, Murakami M, Mori T, et al. Canine tumor development and crude incidence of tumors by breed based on domestic dogs in Gifu prefecture. J Vet Med Sci 2016;78:1269–75.

[21] Kehrli ME, Ackermann MR, Shuster DE, van der Maaten MJ, Schmalstieg FC, Anderson DC, et al. Bovine leukocyte adhesion deficiency: beta(2) integrin deficiency in young Holstein cattle. Am J Pathol 1992;140:1489–92.

[22] Fisher RA. The correlation between relatives on the supposition of Mendelian inheritance. Trans R Soc Edinb 1918;52:399–433.

[23] Ward LD, Kellis M. Interpreting noncoding genetic variation in complex traits and human disease. Nat Biotechnol 2012;30:1095–106.

[24] Visscher PM, McEvoy B, Yang J. From Galton to GWAS: quantitative genetics of human height. Genet Res 2010;92:371–9.

[25] Sniekers S, Stringer S, Watanabe K, Jansen PR, Coleman JRI, Krapohl E, et al. Genome-wide association meta-analysis of 78,308 individuals identifies new loci and genes influencing human intelligence. Nat Genet 2017;49:1107–12.

[26] Zhang G, Karns R, Sun G, Indugula SR, Cheng H, Havas-Augustin D, et al. Finding missing heritability in less significant Loci and allelic heterogeneity: genetic variation in human height. PLoS One 2012;7:e51211.

[27] Billings LK, Florez JC. The genetics of type 2 diabetes: what have we learned from GWAS? Ann N Y Acad Sci 2010;1212:59–77.

[28] Mitchell JJ, Capua A, Clow C, Scriver CR. Twenty-year outcome analysis of genetic screening programs for Tay-Sachs and beta-thalassemia disease carriers in high schools. Am J Hum Genet 1996;59:793–8.

[29] Bell CJ, Dinwiddie DL, Miller NA, Hateley SL, Ganusova EE, Mudge J, et al. Carrier testing for severe childhood recessive diseases by next-generation sequencing. Sci Transl Med 2011;3:65ra4.

[30] Kaback MM. Population-based genetic screening for reproductive counseling: the Tay-Sachs disease model. Eur J Pediatr 2000;159:S192–5.

[31] Kronn D, Jansen V, Ostrer H. Carrier screening for cystic fibrosis, Gaucher disease, and Tay-Sachs disease in the Ashkenazi Jewish population: the first 1000 cases at New York University Medical Center, New York, NY. Arch Intern Med 1998;158:777–81.

[32] Okam MM, Shaykevich S, Ebert BL, Zaslavsky AM, Ayanian JZ. National trends in hospitalizations for sickle cell disease in the United States following the FDA approval of hydroxyurea, 1998-2008. Med Care 2014;52:612–8.

[33] Berman JJ. Methods in medical informatics: fundamentals of healthcare programming in Perl, Python, and Ruby. Boca Raton, FL: Chapman and Hall; 2010.

[34] Wang D, Gao G. State-of-the-art human gene therapy: part II. Gene therapy strategies and applications. Discov Med 2014;18:151–61.

[35] Collins F. Statement on NIH funding of research using gene-editing technologies in human embryos. https://www.nih.gov/about-nih/who-we-are/nih-director/statements/statement-nih-funding-research-using-gene-editing-technologies-human-embryos; April 28, 2015.

[36] Hardy K, Hardy PJ. 1st trimester miscarriage: four decades of study. Transl Pediatr 2015;4:189–200.

[37] Jonkman MF. Revertant mosaicism in human genetic disorders. Am J Med Genet 1999;85:361–4.

[38] Acuna-Hidalgo R, Veltman JA, Hoischen A. New insights into the generation and role of de novo mutations in health and disease. Genome Biol 2016;17:241.

[39] Kong A, Frigge ML, Masson G, Besenbacher S, Sulem P, Magnusson G, et al. Rate of de novo mutations and the importance of father's age to disease risk. Nature 2012;488:471–5.

[40] Rochman B. Five myths about gene editing. The Washington Post; August 25, 2017.

[41] Shah RR, Cholewa-Waclaw J, Davies FCJ, Paton KM, Chaligne R, Heard E, et al. Efficient and versatile CRISPR engineering of human neurons in culture to model neurological disorders. Wellcome Open Res 2016;1:13.

[42] World Health Statistics 2016: Monitoring health for the SDGs Annex B: tables of health statistics by country, WHO region and globally World Health Organization; 2016. Available from: http://www.who.int/gho/publications/world_health_statistics/2016/en/ [Accessed 26 May 2017].

[43] Central Intelligence Agency World Factbook. Rank-order life expectancy at birth. https://www.cia.gov/library/publications/the-world-factbook/rankorder/2102rank.html.

[44] Puska P. Successful prevention of non-communicable diseases: 25 year experiences with North Karelia Project in Finland. Public Health Med 2002;4:5–7.

[45] Bang AT, Bang RA, Reddy HM, Deshmukh MD, Baitule SB. Reduced incidence of neonatal morbidities: effect of home-based neonatal care in rural Gadchiroli, India. J Perinatol 2005;25(Suppl 1):S51–61.

[46] Le Fanu J. The rise and fall of modern medicine. London: Little Brown; 1999.

[47] McKeown T. The role of medicine: dream, mirage or nemesis? (The Rock Carlington Fellow, 1976). London: Nuffield Provincial Hospital Trust; 1976.

[48] Wabinga HR. Pattern of cancer in Mbarara, Uganda. East Afr Med J 2002;79:193–7.

[49] Nze-Nguema F, Sankaranarayanan R, Barthelemy M, et al. Cancer in Gabon, 1984-1993: a pathology registry-based relative frequency study. Bull Cancer 1996;83:693–6.

[50] Mathers CD, Shibuya K, Boschi-Pinto C, Lopez AD, Murray CJL. Global and regional estimates of cancer mortality and incidence by site: I. Application of regional cancer survival model to estimate cancer mortality distribution by site. BMC Cancer 2002;2:36.

[51] Palatianos GM, Cintron JR, Narula T, et al. Father of modern cytology. A 30-year commemorative. J Fla Med Assoc 1992;79:837–8.

[52] Bergstrom R, Sparen P, Adami HO. Trends in cancer of the cervix uteri in Sweden following cytological screening. Br J Cancer 1999;81:159–66.

[53] Anttila A, Pukkala E, Soderman B, et al. Effect of organised screening on cervical cancer incidence and mortality in Finland, 1963-1995: recent increase in cervical cancer incidence. Int J Cancer 1999;83:59–65.

[54] De Vincenzo R, Conte C, Ricci C, Scambia G, Capelli G. Long-term efficacy and safety of human papillomavirus vaccination. Int J Women's Health 2014;6:999–1010.

[55] Komoto M, Tominaga K, Nakata B, Takashima T, Inoue T, Hirakawa K. Complete regression of low-grade mucosa-associated lymphoid tissue (MALT) lymphoma in the gastric stump after eradication of Helicobacter pylori. J Exp Clin Cancer Res 2006;25:283–5.

[56] Smallpox demise linked to spread of HIV infection. BBC News; May 17, 2010.

[57] Huang Y, Paxton WA, Wolinsky SM, Neumann AU, Zhang L, He T, et al. The role of a mutant CCR5 allele in HIV-1 transmission and disease progression. Nat Med 1996;2:1240–3.

[58] Arevalo-Herrera M, Castellanos A, Yazdani SS, Shakri AR, Chitnis CE, Dominik R, et al. Immunogenicity and protective efficacy of recombinant vaccine based on the receptor-binding domain of the Plasmodium vivax Duffy binding protein in Aotus monkeys. Am J Trop Med Hyg 2005;73:25–31.

[59] Miller LH, Mason SJ, Clyde DF, McGinniss MH. The resistance factor to Plasmodium vivax in blacks. The Duffy-blood-group genotype, FyFy. N Engl J Med 1976;295:302–4.

[60] Hill AVS. Evolution, revolution and heresy in the genetics of infectious disease susceptibility. Philos Trans R Soc Lond Ser B Biol Sci 2012;367:840–9.

[61] Shah S, Horne A, Capella J. Good data won't guarantee good decisions. Harvard Business Review; April, 2012.

[62] Manyika J, Chui M, Brown B, Bughin J, Dobbs R, Roxburgh C, et al. Big data: the next frontier for innovation, competition, and productivity. McKinsey Global Institute; 2011. June.

[63] Lohr S. Google to end health records service after it fails to attract users. The New York Times; June 24, 2011.

[64] Schwartz E. Shopping for health software, some doctors get buyer's remorse. The Huffington Post Investigative Fund; January 29, 2010.

[65] Heeks R, Mundy D, Salazar A. Why health care information systems succeed or fail. Institute for Development Policy and Management, University of Manchester; June 1999 Available from: http://www.sed.manchester.ac.uk/idpm/research/publications/wp/igovernment/igov_wp09.htm [Accessed 12 July 2012].

[66] Littlejohns P, Wyatt JC, Garvican L. Evaluating computerised health information systems: hard lessons still to be learnt. Br Med J 2003;326:860–3.

[67] Kappelman LA, McKeeman R, Lixuan ZL. Early warning signs of IT project failure: the dominant dozen. Inf Syst Manag 2006;23:31–6.

[68] Brooks FP. No silver bullet: essence and accidents of software engineering. Computer 1987;20:10–9.

[69] Vlasic B. Toyota's slow awakening to a deadly problem. The New York Times; February 1, 2010.

[70] Lanier J. The complexity ceiling. In: Brockman J, editor. The next fifty years: science in the first half of the twenty-first century. New York: Vintage; 2002. p. 216–29.

[71] Basili VR, Perricone BT. Software errors and complexity: an empirical investigation. Commun ACM 1984;27:556–63.

[72] Linder JA, Ma J, Bates DW, Middleton B, Stafford RS. Electronic health record use and the quality of ambulatory care in the United States. Arch Intern Med 2007;167:1400–5.

[73] Patient Safety in American Hospitals. HealthGrades; July, 2004. Available from: http://www.healthgrades.com/media/english/pdf/hg_patient_safety_study_final.pdf [Accessed 9 September 2012].

[74] Gill JM, Mainous AG, Koopman RJ, Player MS, Everett CJ, Chen YX, et al. Impact of EHR-based clinical decision support on adherence to guidelines for patients on NSAIDs: a randomized controlled trial. Ann Fam Med 2011;9:22–30.

[75] Berman JJ. Principles of big data: preparing, sharing, and analyzing complex information. Waltham, MA: Morgan Kaufmann; 2013.

[76] Berman JJ. Repurposing legacy data: innovative case studies. Waltham, MA: Morgan Kaufmann; 2015.

[77] Berman JJ. Data simplification: taming information with open source tools. Waltham, MA: Morgan Kaufmann; 2016.

[78] Hartocollis A. Heart tests at hospital went unread. The New York Times; May 25, 2010.

[79] Broad WJ. U.S. accidentally releases list of nuclear sites. The New York Times; June 3, 2009.

[80] Recovering the Missing ALSEP Data. Solar System Exploration Research Virtual Institute. NASA. Available from: http://sservi.nasa.gov/articles/recovering-the-missing-alsep-data/ [Accessed 13 October 2014].

[81] Tetlock PE. Expert political judgment: how good is it? How can we know? Princeton: Princeton University Press; 2005.

[82] Committee on Mathematical Foundations of Verification, Validation, and Uncertainty Quantification; Board on Mathematical Sciences and Their Applications, Division on Engineering and Physical Sciences, National Research Council. Assessing the reliability of complex models: mathematical and statistical foundations of verification, validation, and uncertainty quantification. National Academy Press; 2012. Available from: http://www.nap.edu/catalog.php?record_id=13395.

[83] Misconduct in science: an array of errors. The Economist; September 10, 2011.

[84] Rossig C, Juergens H, Schrappe M, Moericke A, Henze G, von Stackelberg A, et al. Effective childhood cancer treatment: the impact of large scale clinical trials in Germany and Austria. Pediatr Blood Cancer 2013;60:1574–81.

[85] Orphan Drugs in Development for Rare Diseases; 2011 Report. America's Biopharmaceutical Research Companies. Available from: http://www.phrma.org/sites/default/files/pdf/rarediseases2011.pdf [Accessed 14 July 2013].

[86] Prostate, lung, colorectal & ovarian cancer screening trial (PLCO) Available from: http://prevention.cancer.gov/plco [Accessed 22 August 2013].

[87] English R, Lebovitz Y, Griffin R. Transforming Clinical Research in the United States: Challenges and Opportunities: Workshop Summary. Washington, DC: The National Academies Press; 2010.

[88] Kitterman DR, Cheng SK, Dilts DM, Orwoll ES. The prevalence and economic impact of low-enrolling clinical studies at an academic medical center. Acad Med 2011;86:1360–6.

[89] The Precision Medicine Initiative Cohort Program—Building a Research Foundation for 21st Century Medicine. Precision Medicine Initiative Working Group Report to the Advisory Committee to the Director, NIH; September 17, 2015.

[90] Leaf C. Do clinical trials work? The New York Times; July 13, 2013.

[91] Steensma DP, Kantarjian HM. Impact of cancer research bureaucracy on innovation, costs, and patient care. J Clin Oncol 2014;32:376–8.

[92] Bossuyt PM, Reitsma JB, Bruns DE, Gatsonis CA, Glasziou PP, Irwig LM, et al. The STARD statement for reporting studies of diagnostic accuracy: explanation and elaboration. Clin Chem 2003;49:7–18.

[93] Ioannidis JP. Why most published research findings are false. PLoS Med 2005;2:e124.

[94] Ioannidis JP. Some main problems eroding the credibility and relevance of randomized trials. Bull NYU Hosp Jt Dis 2008;66:135–9.

[95] West H, Camidge DR. Have mutation, will travel: utilizing online patient communities and new trial strategies to optimize clinical research in the era of molecularly diverse oncology. J Thorac Oncol 2012;7:482–4.

[96] Seer Cancer Statistics Review 1975-2005. Table I-2 56-Year trends in U.S. cancer death rates. Available from: http://seer.cancer.gov/csr/1975_2005/results_merged/topic_historical_mort_trends.pdf.

[97] Balasubramaniam T. USFDA Orphan Drug Approvals; 1999. Available from: http://www.cptech.org/ip/health/orphan/orphan1999.html [Accessed 3 March 2017].

[98] Donovan S. Dying baby cured in world first. ABC News 5; November 5, 2009.

[99] Schwahn BC, Van Spronsen FJ, Belaidi AA, Bowhay S, Christodoulou J, Derks TG, et al. Efficacy and safety of cyclic pyranopterin monophosphate substitution in severe molybdenum cofactor deficiency type A: a prospective cohort study. Lancet 2015;15:00124–5.

[100] Schwarz G, Santamaria-Araujo JA, Wolf S, Lee HJ, Adham IM, Grone HJ, et al. Rescue of lethal molybdenum cofactor deficiency by a biosynthetic precursor from Escherichia coli. Hum Mol Genet 2004;13:1249–55.

[101] Field MJ, Boat T, Institute of Medicine (US) Committee on Accelerating Rare Diseases Research and Orphan Product Development. Rare Diseases and Orphan Products: Accelerating Research and Development. Washington, DC: The National Academics Press; 2010. Available from: http://www.ncbi.nlm.nih.gov/books/NBK56189/.

[102] Wizemann T, Robinson S, Giffin R. Breakthrough Business Models: Drug Development for Rare and Neglected Diseases and Individualized Therapies Workshop Summary. Washington, DC: National Academy of Sciences; 2009.

[103] Mehta HM, Malandra M, Corey SJ. G-CSF and GM-CSF in neutropenia. J Immunol 2015;195:1341–9.

[104] Zsengeller ZK, Reed JA, Bachurski CJ, LeVine AM, Forry-Schaudies S, Hirsch R, et al. Adenovirus-mediated granulocyte- macrophage colony-stimulating factor improves lung pathology of pulmonary alveolar proteinosis in granulocyte-macrophage colony stimulating factor-deficient mice. Hum Gene Ther 1998;9:2101–9.

[105] Venkateshiah SB, Yan TD, Bonfield TL, Thomassen MJ, Meziane M, Czich C, et al. An open-label trial of granulocyte macrophage colony stimulating factor therapy for moderate symptomatic pulmonary alveolar proteinosis. Chest 2006;130:227–37.

[106] Bower H, Bjorkholm M, Dickman PW, Hoglund M, Lambert PC, Andersson TM. Life expectancy of patients with chronic myeloid leukemia approaches the life expectancy of the general population. J Clin Oncol 2016;34:2851–7.

[107] Berman J, O'Leary TJ. Gastrointestinal stromal tumor workshop. Hum Pathol 2001 Jun;32(6):578–82.

[108] Shaw AT, Yeap BY, Solomon BJ, Riely GJ, Gainor J, Engelman JA, et al. Effect of crizotinib on overall survival in patients with advanced non-small-cell lung cancer harbouring ALK gene rearrangement: a retrospective analysis. Lancet Oncol 2011;12:1004–12.

[109] Janoueix-Lerosey I, Schleiermacher G, Delattre O. Molecular pathogenesis of peripheral neuroblastic tumors. Oncogene 2010;29:1566–79.

[110] Mano H. ALKoma: a cancer subtype with a shared target. Cancer Discov 2012;2:495–502.

[111] Butrynski JE, D'Adamo DR, Hornick JL, Dal Cin P, Antonescu CR, Jhanwar SC, et al. Crizotinib in ALK-rearranged inflammatory myofibroblastic tumor. N Engl J Med 2010;363:1727–33.

[112] Bridge JA, Kanamori M, Ma Z, Pickering D, Hill DA, Lydiatt W, et al. Fusion of the ALK gene to the clathrin heavy chain gene, CLTC, in inflammatory myofibroblastic tumor. Am J Pathol 2001;159:411–5.

[113] Lim SH, Beers SA, French RR, Johnson PWM, Glennie MJ, Cragg MS. Anti-CD20 monoclonal antibodies: historical and future perspectives. Haematologica 2010;95:135–43.

[114] Carlson RH. Precision medicine is more than genomic sequencing. www.medscape.com; October 24, 2016. Available from: http://www.medscape.com/viewarticle/870723_print [Accessed 11 March 2017].

[115] Rossouw JE, Anderson GL, Prentice RL, LaCroix AZ, Kooperberg C, Stefanick ML, et al. Risks and benefits of estrogen plus progestin in healthy postmenopausal women: principal results from the Women's Health Initiative randomized controlled trial. JAMA 2002;288:321–33.

[116] Kolata G. Reversing trend, big drop is seen in breast cancer. New York Times; December 15, 2006.

[117] Anastasaki C, Estep AL, Marais R, Rauen KA, Patton EE. Kinase-activating and kinase-impaired cardio-facio-cutaneous syndrome alleles have activity during zebrafish development and are sensitive to small molecule inhibitors. Hum Mol Genet 2009;18:2543–54.

[118] Exceptional Responders Initiative: Questions and Answers. National Cancer Institute Press Office; September 24, 2014, updated: March 23, 2015. Available from: https://www.cancer.gov/news-events/press-releases/2014/ExceptionalRespondersQandA [Accessed 5 January 2017].

[119] Zhu Z, Ihle NT, Rejto PA, Zarrinkar PP. Outlier analysis of functional genomic profiles enriches for oncology targets and enables precision medicine. BMC Genomics 2016;17:455.

[120] Swain SM, Baselga J, Kim SB, Ro J, Semiglazov V, Campone M, et al. Pertuzumab, trastuzumab, and docetaxel in HER2-positive metastatic breast cancer. N Engl J Med 2015;372:724–34.

[121] Subbiah IM, Subbiah V. Exceptional responders: in search of the science behind the miracle cancer cures. Future Oncol 2015;11:1–4.

[122] Do K, O'Sullivan Coyne G, Chen AP. An overview of the NCI precision medicine trials-NCI MATCH and MPACT. Chin Clin Oncol 2015;4:31.

[123] Hernan MA. With great data comes great responsibility: publishing comparative effectiveness research in epidemiology. Epidemiology 2011;22:290–1.

[124] Cook TD, Shadish WR, Wong VC. Three conditions under which experiments and observational studies produce comparable causal estimates: New findings from within-study comparisons. J Policy Anal Manage 2008;27:724–50.

[125] Robins JM. The control of confounding by intermediate variables. Stat Med 1989;8:679–701.

[126] Robins JM. Correcting for non-compliance in randomized trials using structural nested mean models. Commun Stat Theory Methods 1994;23:2379–412.

[127] Bornstein D. The dawn of the evidence-based budget. The New York Times; May 30, 2012.

[128] Radley DC, Finkelstein SN, Stafford RS. Off-label prescribing among office-based physicians. Arch Intern Med 2006;166:1021–6.

[129] Le Tourneau C, Delord JP, Goncalves A, Gavoille C, Dubot C, Isambert N, et al. Molecularly targeted therapy based on tumour molecular profiling versus conventional therapy for advanced cancer (SHIVA): a multicentre, open-label, proof-of-concept, randomised, controlled phase 2 trial. Lancet Oncol 2015;16:1324–34.

[130] Spiesschaert B, McFadden G, Hermans K, Nauwynck H, Van de Walle GR. The current status and future directions of myxoma virus, a master in immune evasion. Vet Res 2011;42:76.

[131] Russell WMS, Burch RL. The principles of humane experimental technique. London: Methuen; 1959.

[132] Tobin DM, Vary Jr JC, Ray JP, Walsh GS, Dunstan SJ, Bang ND, et al. The lta4h locus modulates susceptibility to mycobacterial infection in zebrafish and humans. Cell 2010;140:717–30.

[133] Curtis J, Kopanitsa L, Stebbings E, Speirs A, Ignatyeva O, Balabanova Y, et al. Association analysis of the LTA4H gene polymorphisms and pulmonary tuberculosis in 9115 subjects. Tuberculosis (Edinb) 2011; 91:22–5.

[134] Wiesmeier M, Gautam S, Kirschnek S, Hacker G. Characterisation of neutropenia-associated neutrophil elastase mutations in a murine differentiation model in vitro and in vivo. PLoS One 2016;11:e0168055.

[135] McGary KL, Park TJ, Woods JO, Cha HJ, Wallingford JB, Marcotte EM. Systematic discovery of nonobvious human disease models through orthologous phenotypes. Proc Natl Acad Sci U S A 2010;107:6544–9.

[136] Van Goor F, Hadida S, Grootenhuis PD, Burton B, Cao D, Neuberger T, et al. Rescue of CF airway epithelial cell function in vitro by a CFTR potentiator, VX-770. Proc Natl Acad Sci U S A 2009;106:18825–30.

[137] Engle SJ, Womer DE, Davies PM, Boivin G, Sahota A, Simmonds HA, et al. HPRT-APRT-deficient mice are not a model for lesch-nyhan syndrome. Hum Mol Genet 1996;5:1607–10.

[138] Novarino G, Akizu N, Gleeson JG. Modeling human disease in humans: the ciliopathies. Cell 2011;147:70–9.

[139] The mouse model: less than perfect, still invaluable. Johns Hopkins Medicine; October, 2010. Available from: http://www.hopkinsmedicine.org/institute_basic_biomedical_sciences/news_events/articles_and_stories/model_organisms/201010_mouse_model.html [Accessed 29 September 2016].

[140] Chan SR, Vermi W, Luo J, Lucini L, Rickert C, Fowler AM, et al. STAT1-deficient mice spontaneously develop estrogen receptor alpha-positive luminal mammary carcinomas. Breast Cancer Res 2012;14:R16.

[141] Sharfe N, Nahum A, Newell A, Dadi H, Ngan B, Pereira SL, et al. Fatal combined immunodeficiency associated with heterozygous mutation in STAT1. J Allergy Clin Immunol 2014;133:807–17.

[142] Unique scientific opportunities for the precision medicine initiative: a workshop of the precision medicine initiative working group of the Advisory Committee to the NIH Director, April 28–29, Bethesda, MD; 2015.

[143] Blamont M. French drug trial disaster leaves one brain dead, five injured. Reuters; January 15, 2016.

[144] D'Elia RV, Harrison K, Oyston PC, Lukaszewski RA, Clark GC. Targeting the cytokine storm for therapeutic benefit. Clin Vaccine Immunol 2013;20:319–27.

[145] Lee DW, Gardner R, Porter DL, Louis CU, Ahmed N, Jensen M, et al. Current concepts in the diagnosis and management of cytokine release syndrome. Blood 2014;124:188–95.

[146] Seok J, Warren HS, Cuenca AG, Mindrinos MN, Baker HV, Xu W, et al. Genomic responses in mouse models poorly mimic human inflammatory diseases. Proc Natl Acad Sci U S A 2013;110:3507–12.

[147] Warren HS, Fitting C, Hoff E, Adib-Conquy M, Beasley-Topliffe L, Tesini B, et al. Resilience to bacterial infection: difference between species could be due to proteins in serum. J Infect Dis 2010;201:223–32.

[148] Pound P, Ebrahim S, Sandercock P, Bracken MB, Roberts I. Reviewing animal trials systematically (rats) group. Where is the evidence that animal research benefits humans? BMJ 2004;328:514–7.

[149] Hackam DG, Redelmeier DA. Translation of research evidence from animals to humans. JAMA 2006;296:1731–2.

[150] Van der Worp HB, Howells DW, Sena ES, Porritt MJ, Rewell S, O'Collins V, et al. Can animal models of disease reliably inform human studies? PLoS Med 2010;7:e1000245.

[151] Rice J. Animal models: not close enough. Nature 2012;484:S9.

[152] National Academies of Sciences, Engineering, and Medicine. Therapeutic development in the absence of predictive animal models of nervous system disorders: proceedings of a workshop. Washington, DC: The National Academies Press; 2017.

[153] Watts JC, Prusiner S. Mouse models for studying the formation and propagation of prions. J Biol Chem 2014;289:19841–9.

[154] Dawson TM, Ko HS, Dawson VL. Genetic Animal Models of Parkinson's Disease. Neuron 2010;66(5):646–61.

[155] Choi DW, Armitage R, Brady LS, Coetzee T, Fisher W, Hyman S, et al. Medicines for the mind: Policy-based "pull" incentives for creating breakthrough CNS drugs. Neuron 2014;84:554–63.

[156] Gissen P, Maher ER. Cargos and genes: insights into vesicular transport from inherited human disease. J Med Genet 2007;44:545–55.

[157] Novick P, Field C, Schekman R. Identification of 23 complementation groups required for post-translational events in the yeast secretory pathway. Cell 1980;21:205–15.

[158] Tuberous sclerosis complex in flies too? a fly homolog to TSC2, called gigas, plays a role in cell cycle regulation. No attributed author; July 27, 2000. Available from: http://www.ncbi.nlm.nih.gov/books/bv.fcgi?rid=coffeebrk.chapter.25.

[159] Chen YF, Kao CH, Chen YT, Wang CH, CY W, Tsai CY, et al. Cisd2 deficiency drives premature aging and causes mitochondria-mediated defects in mice. Genes Dev 2009;23:1183–94.

[160] Drew AF, Kaufman AH, Kombrinck KW, Danton MJ, Daugherty CC, Degen JL, et al. Ligneous conjunctivitis in plasminogen-deficient mice. Blood 1998;91:1616–24.

[161] Roberts CW, Galusha SA, McMenamin ME, Fletcher CD, Orkin SH. Haploinsufficiency of Snf5 (integrase interactor 1)predisposes to malignant rhabdoid tumors in mice. Proc Natl Acad Sci U S A 2000;97:13796–800.

[162] Leaf C. Why We're losing the war on cancer: and how to win it. Fortune Magazine; March 22, 2004.

[163] Wszolek ZK, Tsuboi Y, Ghetti B, Pickering-Brown S, Baba Y, Cheshire WP. Frontotemporal dementia and parkinsonism linked to chromosome 17 (FTDP-17). Orphanet J Rare Dis 2006;1:30.

[164] Van den Broeck J, Cunningham SA, Eeckels R, Herbst K. Data cleaning: detecting, diagnosing, and editing data abnormalities. PLoS Med 2005;2:e267.

[165] Lohr S. For big-data scientists, 'janitor work' is key hurdle to insights. The New York Times; August 17, 2014.

[166] Estivill X, Bancells C, Ramos C. Geographic distribution and regional origin of 272 cystic fibrosis mutations in European populations. Hum Mutat 1997;10:135–54.

[167] Su W, Ko A, O'Connell T, Applebaum H. Treatment of pseudotumors with nonsteroidal antiinflammatory drugs. J Pediatr Surg 2000;35:1635–7.

[168] Inglis TJ. Principia aetiologica: taking causality beyond Koch's postulates. J Med Microbiol 2007;56:1419–22.

[169] Nachman MW, Crowell SL. Estimate of the mutation rate per nucleotide in humans. Genetics 2000;156:297–304.

[170] Roach JC, Glusman G, Smit AF, Huff CD, Hubley R, Shannon PT, et al. Analysis of genetic inheritance in a family quartet by whole-genome sequencing. Science 2010;328:636–9.

[171] Oller AR, Rastogi P, Morgenthaler S, Thilly WG. A statistical model to estimate variance in long term low dose mutation assays: testing of the model in a human lymphoblastoid mutation assay. Mutat Res 1989;216:149–61.

[172] Bierig JR. Actions for damages against medical examiners and the defense of sovereign immunity. Clin Lab Med 1998;18:139–50.

[173] Nagel ZD, Chaim IA, Samson LD. Inter-individual variation in DNA repair capacity: a need for multi-pathway functional assays to promote translational DNA repair research. DNA Repair (Amst) 2014;19:199–213.

[174] Martincorena I, Roshan A, Gerstung M, et al. High burden and pervasive positive selection of somatic mutations in normal human skin. Science 2015;348:880–6.

[175] Lynch M. Rate, molecular spectrum, and consequences of human mutation. Proc Natl Acad Sci U S A 2010;107:961–8.

[176] Behjati S, Tarpey PS. What is next generation sequencing? Arch Dis Child Educ Pract Ed 2013;98:236–8.

[177] Dai C, Celestino JC, Okada Y, Louis DN, Fuller GN, Holland EC. PDGF autocrine stimulation dedifferentiates cultured astrocytes and induces oligodendrogliomas and oligoastrocytomas from neural progenitors and astrocytes in vivo. Genes Dev 2001;15:1913–25.

Index

Note: Page numbers followed by *f* indicate figures, *t* indicate tables, and *ge* indicate glossary terms.